THE
OXFORD ANTHOLOGY OF
ENGLISH
POETRY

JOHN WAIN's output has been considerable, encompassing fiction, poetry, plays and literary criticism. He was winner of the Whitbread Award in 1982 for his novel *Young Shoulders*, and Professor of Poetry at Oxford from 1973 to 1978.

THE
OXFORD ANTHOLOGY OF
ENGLISH
POETRY

Chosen and Edited by
JOHN WAIN

VOLUME I

Spenser to Crabbe

OXFORD
UNIVERSITY PRESS

OXFORD
UNIVERSITY PRESS

Great Clarendon Street, Oxford OX2 6DP

Oxford University Press is a department of the University of Oxford.
It furthers the University's objective of excellence in research, scholarship,
and education by publishing worldwide in

Oxford New York

Auckland Bangkok Buenos Aires Cape Town Chennai
Dar es Salaam Delhi Hong Kong Istanbul Karachi Kolkata
Kuala Lumpur Madrid Melbourne Mexico City Mumbai Nairobi
São Paulo Shanghai Taipei Tokyo Toronto

Oxford is a registered trade mark of Oxford University Press
in the UK and in certain other countries

Published in the United States
by Oxford University Press Inc., New York

First published 1986 in three volumes and entitled *The Oxford
Library of English Poetry*
First issued (in two volumes—*Volume I, Spenser to Crabbe*,
Volume II, Blake to Heaney—entitled *The Oxford Anthology of English Poetry*)
as an Oxford University Press paperback 1990
Reissued 2003

British Library Cataloguing in Publication Data

Data available

Library of Congress Cataloging in Publication Data
Oxford library of English poetry.
The Oxford anthology of English poetry/chosen and edited by John Wain.
p. cm. Includes index.
"First published 1986 in three volumes and entitled The Oxford
library of English poetry"—
Contents: v. 1. Spenser to Crabbe—v. 2. Blake to Heaney.
1. English poetry. I. Wain, John. II. Title. III. Title:
Oxford anthology of English poetry.
821.008—dc20 PR1175.097 1990 90-7635

ISBN 0-19-280421-9

1 3 5 7 9 10 8 6 4 2

Printed in Great Britain by
Clays Ltd., St Ives plc

The preparation of these volumes was made possible
by the unstinted and discerning help of

WILLIAM WAIN

CONTENTS

CONTENTS

CONTENTS

CONTENTS

CONTENTS

CONTENTS

CONTENTS

CONTENTS

CONTENTS

CONTENTS

CONTENTS

INTRODUCTION

THE object of this collection is to provide a representative sample of the main course of English poetry during the last four centuries—taking the word 'English' to refer to language more than to nationality, and remembering that many of the most famous poets bred in these islands have been Scottish, Welsh, or Irish. The aim has been, within these two ample volumes, to find room for the familiar masterpieces whose names are household words, and also for a liberal sprinkling of poems less famous but each able to contribute some unique pleasure and stimulus.

Anyone who enjoys reading poetry will, I hope, find in these volumes a good showcase of what English poetry, from the Renaissance to the recent, has to offer. In terms of the output of the Oxford University Press it is, therefore, an effort to fill the gap left by the gradual obsolescence of that seven-volume World's Classics collection, *English Verse*, edited by W. Peacock. Those chunky, sturdy little volumes in their dark blue binding were a pleasure to read and handle: offering in compact shelf space a great wealth of the most familiar poetry of our language, they have been familiar to me throughout my life (the first volume appeared when I was three years old), an ingrained part of my, and many other people's, experience of poetry.

So the suggestion was that instead of simply jettisoning that series, I should use it as a basis, discarding here and adding there as seemed to me best to make the new collection serve the needs of a different time. And of course, since the old series ended with Rupert Brooke, who died in 1915, I should be on my own in choosing from anything since that day.

Many changes naturally suggested themselves. Some concern individual poems and poets, but one—the largest single change, in fact, as far as the last hundred and fifty years are concerned—is that we no longer think of American poetry as virtually symbiotic with English. The two literary traditions have moved decisively apart, more and more so as this century has gone on. Already in the nineteen-twenties poets like Edgar Lee Masters, Carl Sandburg, and E. E. Cummings stood out very sharply against most of the poetry being written in England, and since 1945 the distance has widened until the two literatures are out of sight of each other. There are, indeed, English poets who acknowledge an influence from America (the 'Black Mountain School', for instance, has its offshoot here), but these are poets who have consciously made the journey, who see themselves as to that extent importers of Americana. It was not always so. Except in the case of Whitman, who set himself to write a poetry that expressed America and could have come from nowhere else, the poets of America tended to have their being within that symbiosis. Until the early years of this century, a poet who had a wide sale in one country generally had it in the other. Whitman himself, during his lifetime, was more highly valued in England than in America; he was something of a cult among English literary people during years when his reputation at home was growing very slowly. As for a poet like Long-fellow, whose literary canons were broadly speaking those of Tennyson, in my childhood he was quoted so often that it was years before I realized that he was not an English poet.

The separation of the two traditions was not clear-cut. The boundaries were blurred by the fact that the transition to the modern idiom in poetry was largely accomplished by two American poets living in England, T. S. Eliot and Ezra Pound, who in turn relied on a sensibility largely nourished by certain French poets of the later nineteenth century. But the Pound and Eliot of 1909 to, say, 1920 do not strike one as 'American poets' in the same way that Robert Lowell or Theodore Roethke or John Berryman are American, encased in an American tradition that is self-referential and can choose largely to ignore the outside world. On the contrary, Pound had publicly renounced America as 'a half-savage country, out of date' and his formative influence on other poets was exercised from London. Eliot, though to the end of his life he remained recognizably American in the New England intellectual and religious tradition, took British citizenship in 1927. Both of them, in their different ways, belonged to the tradition of the American expatriate, the tradition of Henry James, Whistler, and Logan Pearsall Smith.

Now, however, that particular game is up; an American poet, whether he comes here or stays at home, is an American poet, and every poem in this collection is by a poet who was or is a native, or at any rate a citizen, of 'Britain'. If I were simply making an anthology of the best poems I know, it would contain many American poems. I would not dream of leaving out either Walt Whitman or Emily Dickinson, the two great polar opposites of nineteenth-century American poetry and both, in totally contrasting ways, poets of sublime genius. But, playing by the rules that have come in since Peacock's day, I am confined to gathering native flora—not much of a 'confinement', when one thinks of its vast range and richness.

*   *   *

For the rest, I have been content to follow Peacock's practice in certain small or smallish matters of detail. He began modernization of spelling with Shakespeare; and, since none of the poetry in his collection is strictly speaking medieval, that meant, virtually, modernizing throughout. He also introduced the late-medieval ballads at a point later than most of the seventeenth-century work. My own instinct would have been to place them earlier, since the tradition must have been in full swing by the days of Dunbar and Henryson. But we are dealing here with an oral tradition, and few of these ballads, immortal poetry though some of them are, were written down until the collectors went out into the field in the later eighteenth century: so we may assume that the ballad tradition remained, for three hundred years, as unchanging as the society that nurtured it. Given that, it hardly matters where we make room for our selection.

Outside such marginal considerations, I hope nothing in this selection will strike anyone as needing lengthy justification. In any case there is never much point in attacking or defending a selection of poetry; it always speaks for itself. But it is perhaps worth making the point that not every poem in these crowded pages is one that I would unhesitatingly label 'major' or 'great'. Sometimes a poem recommended itself as interesting on other grounds. England has produced so many great poets that the temptation, even in such an ample selection as this, is to concentrate on the certified masterpieces. It is hoped that most of the Crown Jewels of our poetry are here; but to be interested in poetry at all is to be interested in minor poetry as well as major. Occasionally a poem is here because it hits off an attitude or opinion characteristic of its time. Now and then, by contrast, a minor poem might offer itself as a useful corrective to some dominant tendency. For example: so much eighteenth-century poetry expresses rampant flag-waving patriotism, so much of its war poetry is about the *glories* of war, that a quiet counter-statement like John Scott of Amwell's Ode XIII 'The Drum' seemed worth putting in. Again, to stay with the eighteenth century for a moment, William Cowper's *The Task* (1785), represented here by an extract from one section, 'The Winter Morning Walk', is a discursive, even rambling, poem much occupied with the theme of the interplay of man and nature, and consciously aligned with a tradition already established by such works as Mark Akenside's once very popular *Pleasures of the Imagination* (1744). Another few years, and Wordsworth will handle this theme more strongly, but he will do so within the same literary convention, that of the blank verse essay, and to be aware of Akenside and Cowper is to be ready for *The Prelude*.

Though well aware that some of the finest poets have been dramatists, and a few have written virtually nothing outside the field of verse plays, I have decided to follow the precedent of leaving out the dramatists, on the grounds that the problems of presenting even a sketch of such a huge area of literature, within the confines of an anthology, are simply insuperable. The obvious exception is that of Shakespeare, who cannot be left out of any anthology of English poetry without reducing it to absurdity. Peacock's method with Shakespeare was simply to slice out his favourite passages, or perhaps they were what he thought would be other people's favourite passages, and serve them up. I have done the same, though I thought it would be interesting not to look up his selection till I had made my own.

There are evident dangers in representing Shakespeare by extracts, but the compensating advantages of doing so are overwhelming. Of course he was a playwright to his finger-tips, and that side of his achievement has to be represented in other ways; either by staging the plays, or by reading them with an eye to dramatic effect. (It is a mistake to read a Shakespearean play without, as you do so, producing it in the theatre of your mind—thinking at every significant point what you would tell an actor or actress to *do*.)

Shakespeare was in fact such a superbly *practical* writer, as well as a great lyricist and visionary, that hardly anything in his work serves one purpose alone. As a rule he succeeds in (to use a metaphor I dislike, but still) killing at least two birds with one stone. To take a simple example, anyone making a selection of Shakespeare's gems would naturally include the speech of Jaques in *As You Like It*, II. vii, beginning 'All the world's a stage'. It is enjoyable simply as a passage of graceful verse, shot through with a tender, ironic melancholy. But of course it is, in dramatic terms, a perfect expression of Jaques's philosophy (which is not quite, I think, Shakespeare's own). Not only that. It is a piece of excellent stagecraft; it solves an awkward little problem of time and space. Orlando has gone forth into the world with his faithful old family servant, Adam, who protests that he is physically quite capable of standing up to their adventurous life ('Though I look old, yet I am strong and lusty'). The pathetic boast is unfounded; the old man sinks exhausted at the edge of the forest and is resigned to dying there. Orlando, sword in hand, goes off to find some nourishment anywhere and to command it by any means. In this extremity he bursts in on the exiled duke with his 'co-mates and brothers', and roughly demands a share of their food. Their civilized and generous response disarms and abashes him, and at their invitation he goes off to fetch the old man to the feast. Since Adam has specifically been shown as incapable of walking unaided, Shakespeare has no means of getting him on to the scene without allowing time for Orlando to go and come back. Jaques fills the gap with a speech so exquisite that we do not notice the wait. Shakespeare seems to have had the gift of writing beautiful poetry almost as a matter of course, but very seldom is it *merely* beautiful; it bears at the same time the stamp of a master playwright, and it is essential to remember this as we read these, or any, selections.

Poetic drama is not the only problem area confronting the maker of a verse anthology. He has also to decide what to do about the long poem. Obviously one gets more diversity, and crowds one's table of contents more impressively with names, by printing ten poems of twenty lines than one of two hundred. But I am more concerned with representing the mainstream of English poetry than with window-dressing. I have included—especially in those pages I have chosen for myself rather than inheriting largely from Peacock—some longish poems complete, and some very long poems in substantial extracts. This is deliberate, and an important part of the enterprise. It is a modern fad to think of poetry as primarily a vehicle for short utterances. Such a view is an injustice to the memory of Langland, Chaucer, Spenser, Milton, Dryden, Pope, Wordsworth, Byron, to go no further; not to speak of the memory of Homer, Virgil, Dante, Camões, Tasso, Hölderlin, Pushkin, and the author of the *Chanson de Roland*. Clearly, the long poem is not going to go away however much we pretend not to see it. It is *there*, and it needs space to develop its effects—space which, owing to the amplitude of these volumes, I have now and then been able to provide.

*   *   *

Finally, I see after all a compensating advantage in being 'limited' to the poetry of the British Isles. The last forty years has seen the growth of a kind of processed, mass-market 'modern' poetry, very much the same in every country, easy enough to translate, to handle, to package, to ship across frontiers. This poetry is always in free verse, usually no more than a matter of writing it as prose and printing it to look like verse; it departs entirely from the tradition and the forms that grew up naturally in that particular culture. The individual poems are like flowers that are cut and put in a vase of water; they have no roots and no soil clinging to them.

People who write this kind of verse sometimes describe themselves as 'internationalist', as if by some mystery of arithmetic a series of losses could in the end add up to a gain. Personally I do not believe there can ever be an international idiom in poetry, or indeed in writing of any kind. Literature is the most national of the arts. It uses not colours or sounds which are the unsophisticated gifts of nature, but language which is the creation of a people, a people living in a particular place with its own climate, history, customs, beliefs, assumptions. A good wine or a good beer are eloquent of the place they come from; an international drink would be either as flavourless as tap water, or some fizzy stuff out of a can.

W. H. Auden, clearly one of the most interesting poets to use English in the twentieth century, changed his nationality, shortly before the mid-point in his life, from British to American, and had to get used to living in a different linguistic *milieu*; if his verse were to reflect the way he heard the language being spoken around him, it had to make major adaptations. For some years he seemed to be trying to write a flavourless, mid-Atlantic dialect, the language of international conferences and Unesco documents. Hence the dullness of *New Year Letter* and (most of)

The Age of Anxiety. But he was too intelligent not to see, before long, that this would not do. While still in mid-career he came back to seeing poetry as the verbal expression of a national tradition, giving 'to airy nothing A local habitation and a name'; a position which he wisely formulated by saying that the true poet was 'like a valley cheese: local, but prized elsewhere'.

EDMUND SPENSER

1552-1599

The Ruines of Time

IT chaunced me on day beside the shore
Of siluer streaming *Thamesis* to bee,
Nigh where the goodly *Verlame* stood of yore,
Of which there now remaines no memorie,
Nor anie little moniment to see,
By which the trauailer, that fares that way,
This once was she, may warned be to say.

There on the other side, I did behold
A Woman sitting sorrowfullie wailing,
Rending her yeolow locks, like wyrie golde,
About her shoulders careleslie downe trailing,
And streames of teares from her faire eyes forth railing.
In her right hand a broken rod she held,
Which towards heauen shee seemd on high to weld.

Whether she were one of that Riuers Nymphes,
Which did the losse of some dere loue lament,
I doubt; or one of those three fatall Impes,
Which draw the dayes of men forth in extent;
Or th'auncient *Genius* of that Citie brent:
But seeing her so piteouslie perplexed,
I (to her calling) askt what her so vexed.

Ah what delight (quoth she) in earthlie thing,
Or comfort can I wretched creature haue?
Whose happines the heauens enuying,
From highest staire to lowest step me draue,
And haue in mine owne bowels made my graue,
That of all Nations now I am forlorne,
The worlds sad spectacle, and fortunes scorne.

Much was I mooued at her piteous plaint,
And felt my heart nigh riuen in my brest
With tender ruth to see her sore constraint,
That shedding teares awhile I still did rest,
And after did her name of her request.

Name haue I none (quoth she) nor anie being,
Bereft of both by Fates vniust decreeing.

I was that Citie, which the garland wore
Of *Britaines* pride, deliuered vnto me
By *Romane* Victors, which it wonne of yore;
Though nought at all but ruines now I bee,
And lye in mine owne ashes, as ye see:
Verlame I was; what bootes it that I was
Sith now I am but weedes and wastfull gras?

O vaine worlds glorie, and vnstedfast state
Of all that liues, on face of sinfull earth,
Which from their first vntill their vtmost date
Tast no one hower of happines or merth,
But like as at the ingate of their berth,
They crying creep out of their mothers woomb,
So wailing backe go to their wofull toomb.

Why then dooth flesh, a bubble glas of breath,
Hunt after honour and aduauncement vaine,
And reare a trophee for deuouring death,
With so great labour and long lasting paine,
As if his daies for euer should remaine?
Sith all that in this world is great or gaie,
Doth as a vapour vanish, and decaie.

Looke backe, who list, vnto the former ages,
And call to count, what is of them become:
Where be those learned wits and antique Sages,
Which of all wisedome knew the perfect somme:
Where those great warriors, which did ouercomme
The world with conquest of their might and maine,
And made one meare of th'earth and of their raine?

What nowe is of th'*Assyrian* Lyonesse,
Of whome no footing now on earth appeares?
What of the *Persian* Beares outragiousnesse,
Whose memorie is quite worne out with yeares?
Who of the *Grecian* Libbard now ought heares,
That ouerran the East with greedie powre,
And left his whelps their kingdomes to deuoure?

And where is that same great seuen headded beast,
That made all nations vassals of her pride,
To fall before her feete at her beheast,
And in the necke of all the world did ride?
Where doth she all that wondrous welth nowe hide?
With her own weight down pressed now shee lies,
And by her heaps her hugenesse testifies.

O *Rome* thy ruine I lament and rue,
And in thy fall my fatall ouerthrowe,
That whilom was, whilst heauens with equall vewe
Deignd to behold me, and their gifts bestowe,
The picture of thy pride in pompous shew:
And of the whole world as thou wast the Empresse,
So I of this small Northerne world was Princesse.

To tell the beawtie of my buildings fayre,
Adornd with purest golde, and precious stone:
To tell my riches, and endowments rare
That by my foes are now all spent and gone:
To tell my forces matchable to none,
Were but lost labour, that few would beleeue,
And with rehearsing would me more agreeue.

High towers, faire temples, goodly theaters,
Strong walls, rich porches, princelie pallaces,
Large streetes, braue houses, sacred sepulchers,
Sure gates, sweete gardens, stately galleries,
Wrought with faire pillours, and fine imageries,
All those (O pitie) now are turnd to dust,
And ouergrowen with blacke obliuions rust.

Theretoo for warlike power, and peoples store,
In *Britannie* was none to match with mee,
That manie often did abie full sore:
Ne *Troynouant*, though elder sister shee,
With my great forces might compared bee;
That stout *Pendragon* to his perill felt,
Who in a siege seauen yeres about me dwelt.

But long ere this *Bunduca* Britonnesse
Her mightie hoast against my bulwarkes brought,
Bunduca, that victorious conqueresse,
That lifting vp her braue heroick thought
Boue womens weaknes, with the *Romanes* fought,

Fought, and in field against them thrice preuailed:
Yet was she foyld, when as she me assailed.

And though at last by force I conquered were
Of hardie *Saxons*, and became their thrall;
Yet was I with much bloodshed bought full deere,
And prizde with slaughter of their Generall:
The moniment of whose sad funerall,
For wonder of the world, long in me lasted;
But now to nought through spoyle of time is wasted.

Wasted it is, as if it neuer were,
And all the rest that me so honord made,
And of the world admired eu'rie where,
Is turned to smoake, that doth to nothing fade;
And of that brightnes now appeares no shade,
But greislie shades, such as doo haunt in hell
With fearfull fiends, that in deep darkness dwell.

Where my high steeples whilom vsde to stand,
On which the lordly Faulcon wont to towre,
There now is but an heap of lyme and sand,
For the Shriche-owle to build her balefull bowre:
And where the Nightingale wont forth to powre
Her restles plaints, to comfort wakefull Louers,
There now haunt yelling Mewes and whining Plouers.

And where the christall *Thamis* wont to slide
In siluer channell, downe along the Lee,
About whose flowrie bankes on either side
A thousand Nymphes, with mirthfull iollitee
Were wont to play, from all annoyance free;
There now no riuers course is to be seene,
But moorish fennes, and marshes euer greene.

Seemes, that that gentle Riuer for great griefe
Of my mishaps, which oft I to him plained;
Or for to shunne the horrible mischiefe,
With which he saw my cruell foes me pained,
And his pure streames with guiltles blood oft stained,
From my vnhappie neighborhood farre fled,
And his sweete waters away with him led.

There also where the winged ships were seene
In liquid waues to cut their fomie waie,

4

And thousand Fishers numbred to haue been,
In that wide lake looking for plenteous praie
Of fish, which they with baits vsde to betraie,
Is now no lake, nor anie fishers store,
Nor euer ship shall saile there anie more.

They all are gone, and all with them is gone,
Ne ought to me remaines, but to lament
My long decay, which no man els doth mone,
And mourne my fall with dolefull dreriment.
Yet it is comfort in great languishment,
To be bemoned with compassion kinde,
And mitigates the anguish of the minde.

But me no man bewaileth, but in game,
Ne sheddeth teares from lamentable eie:
Nor anie liues that mentioneth my name
To be remembred of posteritie,
Saue One that maugre fortunes iniurie,
And times decay, and enuies cruell tort,
Hath writ my record in true-seeming sort.

Cambden the nourice of antiquitie,
And lanterne vnto late succeeding age,
To see the light of simple veritie,
Buried in ruines, through the great outrage
Of her owne people, led with warlike rage.
Cambden, though time all moniments obscure,
Yet thy iust labours euer shall endure.

But whie (vnhappie wight) doo I thus crie,
And grieue that my remembrance quite is raced
Out of the knowledge of posteritie,
And all my antique moniments defaced?
Sith I doo dailie see things highest placed,
So soone as fates their vitall thred haue shorne,
Forgotten quite as they were neuer borne.

It is not long, since these two eyes beheld
A mightie Prince, of most renowmed race,
Whom *England* high in count of honour held,
And greatest ones did sue to gaine his grace;
Of greatest ones he greatest in his place,
Sate in the bosome of his Soueraine,
And *Right and loyall* did his word maintaine.

I saw him die, I saw him die, as one
Of the meane people, and brought foorth on beare.
I saw him die, and no man left to mone
His dolefull fate, that late him loued deare.
Scarce anie left to close his eylids neare;
Scarce anie left vpon his lips to laie
The sacred sod, or *Requiem* to saie.

O trustlesse state of miserable men,
That builde your blis on hope of earthly thing,
And vainly thinke your selues halfe happie then,
When painted faces with smooth flattering
Doo fawne on you, and your wide praises sing,
And when the courting masker louteth lowe,
Him true in heart and trustie to you trow.

All is but fained, and with oaker dide,
That euerie shower will wash and wipe away,
All things doo change that vnder heauen abide,
And after death all friendship doth decaie.
Therefore what euer man bearst worldlie sway,
Liuing, on God, and on thy selfe relie;
For when thou diest, all shall with thee die.

He now is dead, and all is with him dead.
Saue what in heauens storehouse he vplaid:
His hope is faild, and come to passe his dread,
And euill men, now dead, his deeds vpbraid:
Spite bites the dead, that liuing neuer baid.
He now is gone, the whiles the Foxe is crept
Into the hole, the which the Badger swept.

He now is dead, and all his glorie gone,
And all his greatnes vapoured to nought,
That as a glasse vpon the water shone,
Which vanisht quite, so soone as it was sought.
His name is worne alreadie out of thought,
Ne anie Poet seekes him to reuiue;
Yet manie Poets honourd him aliue.

Ne doth his *Colin*, carelesse *Colin Cloute*,
Care now his idle bagpipe vp to raise,
Ne tell his sorrow to the listning rout
Of shepherd groomes, which wont his songs to praise:
Praise who so list, yet I will him dispraise,

Vntill he quite him of this guiltie blame:
Wake shepheards boy, at length awake for shame.

And who so els did goodnes by him gaine,
And who so els his bounteous minde did trie,
Whether he shepheard be, or shepheards swaine,
(For manie did, which doo it now denie)
Awake, and to his Song a part applie:
And I, the whilest you mourne for his decease,
Will with my mourning plaints your plaint increase.

*   *   *

Thus hauing ended all her piteous plaint,
With dolefull shrikes shee vanished away,
That I through inward sorrowe wexen faint,
And all astonished with deepe dismay,
For her departure, had no word to say:
But sate long time in sencelesse sad affright,
Looking still, if I might of her haue sight.

Which when I missed, hauing looked long,
My thought returned greeued home againe,
Renewing her complaint with passion strong,
For ruth of that same womans piteous paine;
Whose wordes recording in my troubled braine,
I felt such anguish wound my feeble heart,
That frosen horror ran through euerie part.

So inlie greeuing in my groning brest,
And deepelie muzing at her doubtfull speach,
Whose meaning much I labored foorth to wreste,
Being aboue my slender reasons reach;
At length by demonstration me to teach,
Before mine eies strange sights presented were,
Like tragicke Pageants seeming to appeare.

I

I saw an Image, all of massie gold,
Placed on high vpon an Altare faire,
That all, which did the same from farre beholde,
Might worship it, and fall on lowest staire.
Not that great Idoll might with this compaire,

7

To which th'*Assyrian* tyrant would haue made
The holie brethren, falslie to haue praid.

But th'Altare, on the which this Image staid,
Was (O great pitie) built of brickle clay,
That shortly the foundation decaid,
With showers of heauen and tempests worne away:
Then downe it fell, and low in ashes lay,
Scorned of euerie one, which by it went;
That I it seing, dearelie did lament.

2

Next vnto this a statelie Towre appeared,
Built all of richest stone, that might bee found,
And nigh vnto the Heauens in height vpreared,
But placed on a plot of sandie ground:
Not that great Towre, which is so much renownd
For tongues confusion in holie writ,
King *Ninus* worke, might be compar'd to it.

But O vaine labours of terrestriall wit,
That buildes so stronglie on so frayle a soyle,
As with each storme does fall away, and flit,
And giues the fruit of all your trauailes toyle,
To be the pray of Tyme, and Fortunes spoyle:
I saw this Towre fall sodainlie to dust,
That nigh with griefe thereof my heart was brust.

3

Then did I see a pleasant Paradize,
Full of sweete flowres and daintiest delights,
Such as on earth man could not more deuize,
With pleasures choyce to feed his cheerefull sprights;
Not that, which *Merlin* by his Magicke slights
Made for the gentle squire, to entertaine
His fayre *Belphœbe*, could this gardine staine.

But O short pleasure bought with lasting paine,
Why will hereafter anie flesh delight
In earthlie blis, and ioy in pleasures vaine,
Since that I sawe this gardine wasted quite,
That where it was scarce seemed anie sight?
That I, which once that beautie did beholde,
Could not from teares my melting eyes withholde.

4

Soone after this a Giaunt came in place,
Of wondrous power, and of exceeding stature,
That none durst vewe the horror of his face,
Yet was he milde of speach, and meeke of nature.
Not he, which in despight of his Creatour
With railing tearmes defied the Iewish hoast,
Might with this mightie one in hugenes boast.

For from the one he could to th'other coast,
Stretch his strong thighes, and th'Occæan ouerstride,
And reach his hand into his enemies hoast.
But see the end of pompe and fleshlie pride;
One of his feete vnwares from him did slide,
That downe hee fell into the deepe Abisse,
Where drownd with him is all his earthlie blisse.

5

Then did I see a Bridge, made all of golde,
Ouer the Sea from one to other side,
Withouten prop or pillour it t'vpholde,
But like the coulored Rainbowe arched wide:
Not that great Arche, which *Traian* edifide,
To be a wonder to all age ensuing,
Was matchable to this in equall vewing.

But (ah) what bootes it to see earthlie thing
In glorie, or in greatnes to excell,
Sith time doth greatest things to ruine bring?
This goodlie bridge, one foote not fastened well,
Gan faile, and all the rest downe shortlie fell,
Ne of so braue a building ought remained,
That griefe thereof my spirite greatly pained.

6

I saw two Beares, as white as anie milke,
Lying together in a mightie caue,
Of milde aspect, and haire as soft as silke,
That saluage nature seemed not to haue,
Nor after greedie spoyle of blood to craue:
Two fairer beasts might not elswhere be found,
Although the compast world were sought around.

But what can long abide aboue this ground
In state of blis, or stedfast happinesse?
The Caue, in which these Beares lay sleeping sound,
Was but earth, and with her owne weightinesse
Vpon them fell, and did vnwares oppresse,
That for great sorrow of their sudden fate,
Henceforth all worlds felicitie I hate.

¶Much was I troubled in my heauie spright,
At sight of these sad spectacles forepast,
That all my senses were bereaued quight,
And I in minde remained sore agast,
Distraught twixt feare and pitie; when at last
I heard a voyce, which loudly to me called,
That with the suddein shrill I was appalled.

Behold (said it) and by ensample see,
That all is vanitie and griefe of minde,
Ne other comfort in this world can be,
But hope of heauen, and heart to God inclinde;
For all the rest must needs be left behinde:
With that it bad me, to the other side
To cast mine eye, where other sights I spide.

1

¶Vpon that famous Riuers further shore,
There stood a snowie Swan of heauenly hiew,
And gentle kinde, as euer Fowle afore;
A fairer one in all the goodlie criew
Of white *Strimonian* brood might no man view:
There he most sweetly sung the prophecie
Of his owne death in dolefull Elegie.

At last, when all his mourning melodie
He ended had, that both the shores resounded,
Feeling the fit that him forewarnd to die,
With loftie flight aboue the earth he bounded,
And out of sight to highest heauen mounted:
Where now he is become an heauenly signe;
There now the ioy is his, here sorrow mine.

2

Whilest thus I looked, loe adowne the *Lee*,
I sawe an Harpe stroong all with siluer twyne,

And made of golde and costlie yuorie,
Swimming, that whilome seemed to haue been
The harpe, on which *Dan Orpheus* was seene
Wylde beasts and forrests after him to lead,
But was th'Harpe of *Philisides* now dead.

At length out of the Riuer it was reard
And borne aboue the cloudes to be diuin'd,
Whilst all the way most heauenly noyse was heard
Of the strings, stirred with the warbling wind,
That wrought both ioy and sorrow in my mind;
So now in heauen a signe it doth appeare,
The Harpe well knowne beside the Northern Beare.

3

Soone after this I saw on th'other side,
A curious Coffer made of *Heben* wood,
That in it did most precious treasure hide,
Exceeding all this baser worldes good:
Yet through the ouerflowing of the flood
It almost drowned was, and done to nought,
That sight thereof much grieu'd my pensiue thought.

At length when most in perill it was brought,
Two Angels downe descending with swift flight,
Out of the swelling streame it lightly caught,
And twixt their blessed armes it carried quight
Aboue the reach of anie liuing sight:
So now it is transform'd into that starre,
In which all heauenly treasures locked are.

4

Looking aside I saw a stately Bed,
Adorned all with costly cloth of gold,
That might for anie Princes couche be red,
And deckt with daintie flowres, as if it shold
Be for some bride, her ioyous night to hold:
Therein a goodly Virgine sleeping lay;
A fairer wight saw neuer summers day.

I heard a voyce that called farre away
And her awaking bad her quickly dight,
For lo her Bridegrome was in readie ray
To come to her, and seek her loues delight:
With that she started vp with cherefull sight,

When suddeinly both bed and all was gone,
And I in languor left there all alone.

5

Still as I gazed, I beheld where stood
A Knight all arm'd, vpon a winged steed,
The same that was bred of *Medusaes* blood,
On which *Dan Perseus* borne of heauenly seed,
The faire *Andromeda* from perill freed:
Full mortally this Knight ywounded was,
That streames of blood foorth flowed on the gras.

Yet was he deckt (small ioy to him alas)
With manie garlands for his victories,
And with rich spoyles, which late he did purchas
Through braue atcheiuements from his enemies;
Fainting at last through long infirmities,
He smote his steed, that straight to heaven him bore,
And left me here his losse for to deplore.

6

Lastly I saw an Arke of purest golde
Vpon a brazen pillour standing hie,
Which th'ashes seem'd of some great Prince to hold,
Enclosde therein for endles memorie
Of him, whom all the world did glorifie:
Seemed the heauens with the earth did disagree,
Whether should of those ashes keeper bee.

At last me seem'd wing footed *Mercurie*,
From heauen descending to appease their strife,
The Arke did beare with him aboue the skie,
And to those ashes gaue a second life,
To liue in heauen, where happines is rife:
At which the earth did grieue exceedingly,
And I for dole was almost like to die.

L'Envoy

Immortall spirite of *Philisides*,
Which now art made the heauens ornament,
That whilome wast the worlds chiefst riches,
Giue leaue to him that lou'de thee to lament
His losse, by lacke of thee to heauen hent,
And with last duties of this broken verse,
Broken with sighes, to decke thy sable Herse.

And ye faire Ladie th'honor of your daies,
And glorie of the world, your high thoughts scorne;
Vouchsafe this moniment of his last praise,
With some few siluer dropping teares t'adorne:
And as ye be of heauenlie off spring borne,
So vnto heauen let your high minde aspire,
And loath this drosse of sinfull worlds desire.

Epithalamion

YE learned sisters which haue oftentimes
Beene to me ayding, others to adorne:
Whom ye thought worthy of your gracefull rymes,
That euen the greatest did not greatly scorne
To heare theyr names sung in your simple layes,
But ioyed in theyr prayse.
And when ye list your owne mishaps to mourne,
Which death, or loue, or fortunes wreck did rayse,
Your string could soone to sadder tenor turne,
And teach the woods and waters to lament
Your dolefull dreriment.
Now lay those sorrowfull complaints aside,
And hauing all your heads with girland crownd,
Helpe me mine owne loues prayses to resound,
Ne let the same of any be enuide:
So Orpheus did for his owne bride,
So I vnto my selfe alone will sing,
The woods shall to me answer and my Eccho ring.

Early before the worlds light giuing lampe,
His golden beame vpon the hils doth spred,
Hauing disperst the nights vnchearefull dampe,
Doe ye awake, and with fresh lusty hed,
Go to the bowre of my beloued loue,
My truest turtle doue,
Bid her awake; for Hymen is awake,
And long since ready forth his maske to moue,
With his bright Tead that flames with many a flake,
And many a bachelor to waite on him,
In theyr fresh garments trim.

EPITHALAMION: dreriment] dreariness, grief, sorrow   lusty hed] lustiness, energy,
vigour   Tead] torch

Bid her awake therefore and soone her dight,
For lo the wished day is come at last,
That shall for al the paynes and sorrowes past,
Pay to her vsury of long delight:
And whylest she doth her dight,
Doe ye to her of ioy and solace sing,
That all the woods may answer and your eccho ring.

Bring with you all the Nymphes that you can heare
Both of the riuers and the forrests greene:
And of the sea that neighbours to her neare,
Al with gay girlands goodly wel beseene.
And let them also with them bring in hand,
Another gay girland
For my fayre loue of lillyes and of roses,
Bound trueloue wize with a blew silke riband.
And let them make great store of bridale poses,
And let them eeke bring store of other flowers
To deck the bridale bowers.
And let the ground whereas her foot shall tread,
For feare the stones her tender foot should wrong
Be strewed with fragrant flowers all along,
And diapred lyke the discolored mead.
Which done, doe at her chamber dore awayt,
For she will waken strayt,
The whiles doe ye this song vnto her sing,
The woods shall to you answer and your Eccho ring.

Ye Nymphes of Mulla which with carefull heed,
The siluer scaly trouts doe tend full well,
And greedy pikes which vse therein to feed,
(Those trouts and pikes all others doo excell)
And ye likewise which keepe the rushy lake,
Where none doo fishes take,
Bynd vp the locks the which hang scatterd light,
And in his waters which your mirror make,
Behold your faces as the christall bright,
That when you come whereas my loue doth lie,
No blemish she may spie.
And eke ye lightfoot mayds which keepe the deere,
That on the hoary mountayne vse to towre,
And the wylde wolues which seeke them to deuoure,

discolored] vari-
ously coloured   diapred] variegated (with flowers)   dight] to deck, adorn

With your steele darts doo chace from comming neer
Be also present heere,
To helpe to decke her and to help to sing,
That all the woods may answer and your eccho ring.

Wake, now my loue, awake; for it is time,
The Rosy Morne long since left Tithones bed,
All ready to her siluer coche to clyme,
And Phœbus gins to shew his glorious hed.
Hark how the cheerefull birds do chaunt theyr laies
And carroll of loues praise.
The merry Larke hir mattins sings aloft,
The thrush replyes, the Mauis descant playes,
The Ouzell shrills, the Ruddock warbles soft,
So goodly all agree with sweet consent,
To this dayes merriment.
Ah my deere loue why doe ye sleepe thus long,
When meeter were that ye should now awake,
T'awayt the comming of your ioyous make,
And hearken to the birds louelearned song,
The deawy leaues among.
For they of ioy and pleasance to you sing,
That all the woods them answer and theyr eccho ring.

My loue is now awake out of her dreame,
And her fayre eyes like stars that dimmed were
With darksome cloud, now shew theyr goodly beams
More bright then Hesperus his head doth rere.
Come now ye damzels, daughters of delight,
Helpe quickly her to dight,
But first come ye fayre houres which were begot
In Ioues sweet paradice, of Day and Night,
Which doe the seasons of the yeare allot,
And al that euer in this world is fayre
Doe make and still repayre.
And ye three handmayds of the Cyprian Queene,
The which doe still adorne her beauties pride,
Helpe to addorne my beautifullest bride:
And as ye her array, still throw betweene
Some graces to be seene,
And as ye vse to Venus, to her sing,
The whiles the woods shal answer and your eccho ring.

make] companion, mate

Now is my loue all ready forth to come,
Let all the virgins therefore well awayt,
And ye fresh boyes that tend vpon her groome
Prepare your selues; for he is comming strayt.
Set all your things in seemely good aray
Fit for so ioyfull day,
The ioyfulst day that euer sunne did see.
Faire Sun, shew forth thy fauourable ray,
And let thy lifull heat not feruent be
For feare of burning her sunshyny face,
Her beauty to disgrace.
O fayrest Phœbus, father of the Muse,
If euer I did honour thee aright,
Or sing the thing, that mote thy mind delight,
Doe not thy seruants simple boone refuse,
But let this day, let this one day, be myne,
Let all the rest be thine.
Then I thy souerayne prayses loud wil sing,
That all the woods shal answer and theyr eccho ring.

Harke how the Minstrels gin to shrill aloud
Their merry Musick that resounds from far,
The pipe, the tabor, and the trembling Croud,
That well agree withouten breach or iar.
But most of all the Damzels doe delite,
When they their tymbrels smyte,
And thereunto doe daunce and carrol sweet,
That all the sences they doe rauish quite,
The whyles the boyes run vp and downe the street,
Crying aloud with strong confused noyce,
As if it were one voyce.
Hymen io Hymen, Hymen they do shout,
That euen to the heauens theyr shouting shrill
Doth reach, and all the firmament doth fill,
To which the people standing all about,
As in approuance doe thereto applaud
And loud aduaunce her laud,
And euermore they Hymen Hymen sing,
That al the woods them answer and theyr eccho ring.

Loe where she comes along with portly pace
Lyke Phœbe from her chamber of the East,

lifull] giving or bestowing life   Croud] fiddle or viol

Arysing forth to run her mighty race,
Clad all in white, that seemes a virgin best.
So well it her beseemes that ye would weene
Some angell she had beene.
Her long loose yellow locks lyke golden wyre,
Sprinckled with perle, and perling flowres a tweene,
Doe lyke a golden mantle her attyre,
And being crowned with a girland greene,
Seeme lyke some mayden Queene.
Her modest eyes abashed to behold
So many gazers, as on her do stare,
Vpon the lowly ground affixed are.
Ne dare lift vp her countenance too bold,
But blush to heare her prayses sung so loud,
So farre from being proud.
Nathlesse doe ye still loud her prayses sing.
That all the woods may answer and your eccho ring.

Tell me ye merchants daughters did ye see
So fayre a creature in your towne before,
So sweet, so louely, and so mild as she,
Adornd with beautyes grace and vertues store,
Her goodly eyes lyke Saphyres shining bright,
Her forehead yuory white,
Her cheekes lyke apples which the sun hath rudded,
Her lips lyke cherryes charming men to byte,
Her brest like to a bowle of creame vncrudded,
Her paps lyke lyllies budded,
Her snowie necke lyke to a marble towre,
And all her body like a pallace fayre,
Ascending vppe with many a stately stayre,
To honors seat and chastities sweet bowre.
Why stand ye still ye virgins in amaze,
Vpon her so to gaze,
Whiles ye forget your former lay to sing,
To which the woods did answer and your eccho ring.

But if ye saw that which no eyes can see,
The inward beauty of her liuely spright,
Garnisht with heauenly guifts of high degree,
Much more then would ye wonder at that sight,
And stand astonisht lyke to those which red
Medusaes mazeful hed.

vncrudded] uncurdled

There dwels sweet loue and constant chastity,
Vnspotted fayth and comely womanhood,
Regard of honour and mild modesty,
There vertue raynes as Queene in royal throne,
And giueth lawes alone.
The which the base affections doe obay,
And yeeld theyr seruices vnto her will,
Ne thought of thing vncomely euer may
Thereto approch to tempt her mind to ill.
Had ye once seene these her celestial threasures,
And vnreuealed pleasures,
Then would ye wonder and her prayses sing,
That al the woods should answer and your eccho ring.

Open the temple gates vnto my loue,
Open them wide that she may enter in,
And all the postes adorne as doth behoue,
And all the pillours deck with girlands trim,
For to recyue this Saynt with honour dew,
That commeth in to you.
With trembling steps and humble reuerence,
She commeth in, before th'almighties vew,
Of her ye virgins learne obedience,
When so ye come into those holy places,
To humble your proud faces:
Bring her vp to th'high altar, that she may
The sacred ceremonies there partake,
The which do endlesse matrimony make,
And let the roring Organs loudly play
The praises of the Lord in liuely notes,
The whiles with hollow throates
The Choristers the ioyous Antheme sing,
That al the woods may answere and their eccho ring.

Behold whiles she before the altar stands
Hearing the holy priest that to her speakes
And blesseth her with his two happy hands,
How the red roses flush vp in her cheekes,
And the pure snow with goodly vermill stayne,
Like crimsin dyde in grayne,
That euen th'Angels which continually,
About the sacred Altare doe remaine,
Forget their seruice and about her fly,

threasures] treasures

18

Ofte peeping in her face that seemes more fayre,
The more they on it stare.
But her sad eyes still fastened on the ground,
Are gouerned with goodly modesty,
That suffers not one looke to glaunce awry,
Which may let in a little thought vnsownd.
Why blush ye loue to giue to me your hand,
The pledge of all our band?
Sing ye sweet Angels, Alleluya sing,
That all the woods may answere and your eccho ring.

Now al is done; bring home the bride againe,
Bring home the triumph of our victory,
Bring home with you the glory of her gaine,
With ioyance bring her and with iollity.
Neuer had man more ioyfull day then this,
Whom heauen would heape with blis.
Make feast therefore now all this liue long day,
This day for euer to me holy is,
Poure out the wine without restraint or stay,
Poure not by cups, but by the belly full,
Poure out to all that wull,
And sprinkle all the postes and wals with wine,
That they may sweat, and drunken be withall.
Crowne ye God Bacchus with a coronall,
And Hymen also crowne with wreathes of vine,
And let the Graces daunce vnto the rest;
For they can doo it best:
The whiles the maydens doe theyr carroll sing,
To which the woods shal answer and theyr eccho ring.

Ring ye the bels, ye yong men of the towne,
And leaue your wonted labors for this day:
This day is holy; doe ye write it downe,
That ye for euer it remember may.
This day the sunne is in his chiefest hight,
With Barnaby the bright,
From whence declining daily by degrees,
He somewhat loseth of his heat and light,
When once the Crab behind his back he sees.
But for this time it ill ordained was,
To chose the longest day in all the yeare,

wull] will

And shortest night, when longest fitter weare:
Yet neuer day so long, but late would passe.
Ring ye the bels, to make it weare away,
And bonefiers make all day,
And daunce about them, and about them sing:
That all the woods may answer, and your eccho ring.

Ah when will this long weary day haue end,
And lende me leaue to come vnto my loue?
How slowly do the houres theyr numbers spend?
How slowly does sad Time his feathers moue?
Hast thee O fayrest Planet to thy home
Within the Westerne fome:
Thy tyred steedes long since haue need of rest.
Long though it be, at last I see it gloome,
And the bright euening star with golden creast
Appeare out of the East.
Fayre childe of beauty, glorious lampe of loue
That all the host of heauen in rankes doost lead,
And guydest louers through the nightes dread,
How chearefully thou lookest from aboue,
And seemst to laugh atweene thy twinkling light
As ioying in the sight
Of these glad many which for ioy doe sing,
That all the woods them answer and their echo ring.

Now ceasse ye damsels your delights forepast;
Enough is it, that all the day was youres:
Now day is doen, and night is nighing fast:
Now bring the Bryde into the brydall boures.
Now night is come, now soone her disaray,
And in her bed her lay;
Lay her in lillies and in violets,
And silken courteins ouer her display,
And odourd sheetes, and Arras couerlets.
Behold how goodly my faire loue does ly
In proud humility;
Like vnto Maia, when as Ioue her tooke,
In Tempe, lying on the flowry gras,
Twixt sleepe and wake, after she weary was,
With bathing in the Acidalian brooke.
Now it is night, ye damsels may be gon,
And leaue my loue alone,

bonefiers] bonfires   gloome] to gloom, become dusk

And leaue likewise your former lay to sing:
The woods no more shal answere, nor your echo ring.

Now welcome night, thou night so long expected,
That long daies labour doest at last defray,
And all my cares, which cruell loue collected,
Hast sumd in one, and cancelled for aye:
Spread thy broad wing ouer my loue and me,
That no man may vs see,
And in thy sable mantle vs enwrap,
From feare of perrill and foule horror free.
Let no false treason seeke vs to entrap,
Nor any dread disquiet once annoy
The safety of our ioy:
But let the night be calme and quietsome,
Without tempestuous storms or sad afray:
Lyke as when Ioue with fayre Alcmena lay,
When he begot the great Tirynthian groome:
Or lyke as when he with thy selfe did lie,
And begot Maiesty.
And let the mayds and yongmen cease to sing:
Ne let the woods them answer, nor theyr eccho ring.

Let no lamenting cryes, nor dolefull teares,
Be heard all night within nor yet without:
Ne let false whispers, breeding hidden feares,
Breake gentle sleepe with misconceiued dout.
Let no deluding dreames, nor dreadful sights
Make sudden sad affrights;
Ne let housefyres, nor lightnings helpelesse harmes,
Ne let the Pouke, nor other euill sprights,
Ne let mischiuous witches with theyr charmes,
Ne let hob Goblins, names whose sence we see not,
Fray vs with things that be not.
Let not the shriech Oule, nor the Storke be heard:
Nor the night Rauen that still deadly yels,
Nor damned ghosts cald vp with mighty spels,
Nor griesly vultures make vs once affeard:
Ne let th'unpleasant Quyre of Frogs still croking
Make vs to wish theyr choking.
Let none of these theyr drery accents sing;
Ne let the woods them answer, nor theyr eccho ring.

Pouke] Puck

But let stil Silence trew night watches keepe,
That sacred peace may in assurance rayne,
And tymely sleep, when it is tyme to sleepe,
May poure his limbs forth on your pleasant playne,
The whiles an hundred little winged loues,
Like diuers fethered doues,
Shall fly and flutter round about your bed,
And in the secret darke, that none reproues,
Their prety stealthes shal worke, and snares shal spread
To filch away sweet snatches of delight,
Conceal'd through couert night.
Ye sonnes of Venus, play your sports at will,
For greedy pleasure, carelesse of your toyes,
Thinks more vpon her paradise of ioyes,
Then what ye do, albe it good or ill.
All night therefore attend your merry play,
For it will soone be day:
Now none doth hinder you, that say or sing,
Ne will the woods now answer, nor your Eccho ring.

Who is the same, which at my window peepes?
Or whose is that faire face, that shines so bright,
Is it not Cinthia, she that neuer sleepes,
But walkes about high heauen al the night?
O fayrest goddesse, do thou not enuy
My loue with me to spy:
For thou likewise didst loue, though now vnthought,
And for a fleece of woll, which priuily,
The Latmian shephard once vnto thee brought,
His pleasures with thee wrought.
Therefore to vs be fauorable now;
And sith of wemens labours thou hast charge,
And generation goodly dost enlarge,
Encline thy will t'effect our wishfull vow,
And the chast wombe informe with timely seed,
That may our comfort breed:
Till which we cease our hopefull hap to sing,
Ne let the woods vs answere, nor our Eccho ring.

And thou great Iuno, which with awful might
The lawes of wedlock still dost patronize,
And the religion of the faith first plight
With sacred rites hast taught to solemnize:

sith] since

22

And eeke for comfort often called art
Of women in their smart,
Eternally bind thou this louely band,
And all thy blessings vnto vs impart.
And thou glad Genius, in whose gentle hand,
The bridale bowre and geniall bed remaine,
Without blemish or staine,
And the sweet pleasures of theyr loues delight
With secret ayde doest succour and supply,
Till they bring forth the fruitfull progeny,
Send vs the timely fruit of this same night.
And thou fayre Hebe, and thou Hymen free,
Grant that it may so be.
Til which we cease your further prayse to sing,
Ne any woods shal answer, nor your Eccho ring.

And ye high heauens, the temple of the gods,
In which a thousand torches flaming bright
Doe burne, that to vs wretched earthly clods,
In dreadfull darknesse lend desired light;
And all ye powers which in the same remayne,
More then we men can fayne,
Poure out your blessing on vs plentiously,
And happy influence vpon vs raine,
That we may raise a large posterity,
Which from the earth, which they may long possesse,
With lasting happinesse,
Vp to your haughty pallaces may mount,
And for the guerdon of theyr glorious merit
May heauenly tabernacles there inherit,
Of blessed Saints for to increase the count.
So let vs rest, sweet loue, in hope of this,
And cease till then our tymely ioyes to sing,
The woods no more vs answer, nor our eccho ring.

Song made in lieu of many ornaments,
With which my loue should duly haue bene dect,
Which cutting off through hasty accidents,
Ye would not stay your dew time to expect,
But promist both to recompens,
Be vnto her a goodly ornament,
And for short time an endlesse moniment.

Prothalamion

CALME was the day, and through the trembling ayre,
Sweete breathing *Zephyrus* did softly play
A gentle spirit, that lightly did delay
Hot *Titans* beames, which then did glyster fayre:
When I whom sullein care,
Through discontent of my long fruitlesse stay
In Princes Court, and expectation vayne
Of idle hopes, which still doe fly away,
Like empty shaddowes, did aflict my brayne,
Walkt forth to ease my payne
Along the shoare of siluer streaming *Themmes*,
Whose rutty Bancke, the which his Riuer hemmes,
Was paynted all with variable flowers,
And all the meades adornd with daintie gemmes,
Fit to decke maydens bowres,
And crowne their Paramours,
Against the Brydale day, which is not long:
    Sweete *Themmes* runne softly, till I end my Song.

There, in a Meadow, by the Riuers side,
A Flocke of *Nymphes* I chaunced to espy,
All louely Daughters of the Flood thereby,
With goodly greenish locks all lose vntyde,
As each had bene a Bryde,
And each one had a little wicker basket,
Made of fine twigs entrayled curiously,
In which they gathered flowers to fill their flasket:
And with fine Fingers, cropt full feateously
The tender stalkes on hye.
Of euery sort, which in that Meadow grew,
They gathered some; the Violet pallid blew,
The little Dazie, that at euening closes,
The virgin Lillie, and the Primrose trew,
With store of vermeil Roses,
To decke their Bridegromes posies,
Against the Brydale day, which was not long:
    Sweete *Themmes* runne softly, till I end my Song.

With that, I saw two Swannes of goodly hewe,
Come softly swimming downe along the Lee;

glyster] to glitter, shine   rutty] full of ruts   entrayled] entwined, interlaced
flasket] a long shallow basket   feateously] dexterously   vermeil] vermilion

Two fairer Birds I yet did neuer see:
The snow which doth the top of *Pindus* strew,
Did neuer whiter shew,
Nor *Ioue* himselfe when he a Swan would be
For loue of *Leda*, whiter did appeare:
Yet *Leda* was they say as white as he,
Yet not so white as these, nor nothing neare;
So purely white they were,
That euen the gentle streame, the which them bare,
Seem'd foule to them, and bad his billowes spare
To wet their silken feathers, least they might
Soyle their fayre plumes with water not so fayre
And marre their beauties bright,
That shone as heauens light,
Against their Brydale day, which was not long:
   Sweete *Themmes* runne softly, till I end my Song.

Eftsoones the *Nymphes*, which now had Flowers their fill,
Ran all in haste, to see that siluer brood,
As they came floating on the Christal Flood.
Whom when they sawe, they stood amazed still,
Their wondring eyes to fill,
Them seem'd they neuer saw a sight so fayre,
Of Fowles so louely, that they sure did deeme
Them heauenly borne, or to be that same payre
Which through the Skie draw *Venus* siluer Teeme,
For sure they did not seeme
To be begot of any earthly Seede,
But rather Angels or of Angels breede:
Yet were they bred of *Somers-heat* they say,
In sweetest Season, when each Flower and weede
The earth did fresh aray,
So fresh they seem'd as day,
Euen as their Brydale day, which was not long:
   Sweete *Themmes* runne softly, till I end my Song.

Then forth they all out of their baskets drew,
Great store of Flowers, the honour of the field,
That to the sense did fragrant odours yeild,
All which vpon those goodly Birds they threw,
And all the Waues did strew,
That like old *Peneus* Waters they did seeme,
When downe along by pleasant *Tempes* shore

least] lest

25

Scattred with Flowres, through *Thessaly* they streeme,
That they appeare through Lillies plenteous store,
Like a Brydes Chamber flore:
Two of those *Nymphes*, meane while, two Garlands bound,
Of freshest Flowres which in that Mead they found,
The which presenting all in trim Array,
Their snowie Foreheads therewithall they crownd,
Whil'st one did sing this Lay,
Prepar'd against that Day,
Against their Brydale day, which was not long:
    Sweete *Themmes* runne softly, till I end my Song.

Ye gentle Birdes, the worlds faire ornament,
And heauens glorie, whom this happie hower
Doth leade vnto your louers blisfull bower,
Ioy may you haue and gentle hearts content
Of your loues couplement:
And let faire *Venus*, that is Queene of loue,
With her heart-quelling Sonne vpon you smile,
Whose smile they say, hath vertue to remoue
All Loues dislike, and friendships faultie guile
For euer to assoile.
Let endlesse Peace your steadfast hearts accord,
And blessed Plentie wait vpon your bord,
And let your bed with pleasures chast abound,
That fruitfull issue may to you afford,
Which may your foes confound,
And make your ioyes redound,
Vpon your Brydale day, which is not long:
    Sweete *Themmes* run softlie, till I end my Song.

So ended she; and all the rest around
To her redoubled that her vndersong,
Which said, their bridale daye should not be long.
And gentle Eccho from the neighbour ground,
Their accents did resound.
So forth those ioyous Birdes did passe along,
Adowne the Lee, that to them murmurde low,
As he would speake, but that he lackt a tong
Yeat did by signes his glad affection show,
Making his streame run slow.

assoile] to absolve, free, release

And all the foule which in his flood did dwell
Gan flock about these twaine, that did excell
The rest, so far, as *Cynthia* doth shend
The lesser starres. So they enranged well,
Did on those two attend,
And their best seruice lend,
Against their wedding day, which was not long:
   Sweete *Themmes* run softly, till I end my Song.

At length they all to mery *London* came,
To mery London, my most kyndly Nurse,
That to me gaue this Lifes first natiue sourse:
Though from another place I take my name,
An house of auncient fame.
There when they came, whereas those bricky towres,
The which on *Themmes* brode aged backe doe ryde,
Where now the studious Lawyers haue their bowers,
There whylome wont the Templer Knights to byde,
Till they decayd through pride:
Next whereunto there standes a stately place,
Where oft I gayned giftes and goodly grace
Of that great Lord, which therein wont to dwell,
Whose want too well now feeles my freendles case:
But Ah here fits not well
Olde woes but ioyes to tell
Against the Brydale daye, which is not long:
   Sweete *Themmes* runne softly, till I end my Song.

Yet therein now doth lodge a noble Peer,
Great *Englands* glory and the Worlds wide wonder,
Whose dreadfull name, late through all *Spaine* did thunder,
And *Hercules* two pillors standing neere,
Did make to quake and feare:
Faire branch of Honor, flower of Cheualrie,
That fillest *England* with thy triumphs fame,
Ioy haue thou of thy noble victorie,
And endlesse happinesse of thine owne name
That promiseth the same:
That through thy prowesse and victorious armes,
Thy country may be freed from forraine harmes:
And great *Elisaes* glorious name may ring
Through al the world, fil'd with thy wide Alarmes,

shend] to surpass

Which some braue muse may sing
To ages following,
Vpon the Brydale day, which is not long:
 Sweete *Themmes* runne softly, till I end my Song.

From those high Towers, this noble Lord issuing,
Like Radiant *Hesper* when his golden hayre
In th'*Ocean* billowes he hath Bathed fayre,
Descended to the Riuers open vewing,
With a great traine ensuing.
Aboue the rest were goodly to bee seene
Two gentle Knights of louely face and feature
Beseeming well the bower of anie Queen,
With gifts of wit and ornaments of nature,
Fit for so goodly stature:
That like the twins of *Ioue* they seem'd in sight,
Which decke the Bauldricke of the Heauens bright.
They two forth pacing to the Riuers side,
Receiued those two faire Brides, their Loues delight,
Which at th'appointed tyde,
Each one did make his Bryde,
Against their Brydale day, which is not long:
 Sweete *Themmes* runne softly, till I end my Song.

from *The Faerie Queene*

Wнo trauels by the wearie wandring way,
 To come vnto his wished home in haste,
 And meetes a flood, that doth his passage stay,
 Is not great grace to helpe him ouer past,
 Or free his feet, that in the myre sticke fast?
 Most enuious man, that grieues at neighbours good,
 And fond, that ioyest in the woe thou hast.
 Why wilt not let him passe, that long hath stood
Vpon the banke, yet wilt thy selfe not passe the flood?

He there does now enioy eternall rest
 And happie ease, which thou doest want and craue,
 And further from it daily wanderest:
 What if some litle paine the passage haue,
 That makes fraile flesh to feare the bitter waue?

Bauldricke] belt, girdle

FROM THE FAERIE QUEENE: fond] foolish

Is not short paine well borne, that brings long ease,
And layes the soule to sleepe in quiet graue?
Sleepe after toyle, port after stormie seas,
Ease after warre, death after life does greatly please.

The knight much wondred at his suddeine wit,
And said, The terme of life is limited,
Ne may a man prolong, nor shorten it;
The souldier may not moue from watchfull sted,
Nor leaue his stand, vntill his Captaine bed.
Who life did limit by almightie doome,
(Quoth he) knowes best the termes established;
And he, that points the Centonell his roome,
Doth license him depart at sound of morning droome.

The Pageant of the Seasons and the Months

So, forth issew'd the Seasons of the yeare;
First, lusty *Spring*, all dight in leaues of flowres
That freshly budded and new bloosmes did beare
(In which a thousand birds had built their bowres
That sweetly sung, to call forth Paramours):
And in his hand a iauelin he did beare,
And on his head (as fit for warlike stoures)
A guilt engrauen morion he did weare;
That as some did him loue, so others did him feare.

Then came the iolly *Sommer*, being dight
In a thin silken cassock coloured greene,
That was vnlyned all, to be more light:
And on his head a girlond well beseene
He wore, from which as he had chauffed been
The sweat did drop; and in his hand he bore
A boawe and shaftes, as he in forrest greene
Had hunted late the Libbard or the Bore,
And now would bathe his limbes, with labor heated sore.

Then came the *Autumne* all in yellow clad,
As though he ioyed in his plentious store,

sted] place, situation   bed] to order, command   Centonell] sentinel   roome]
place, position   droome] drum

THE PAGEANT OF THE SEASONS AND THE MONTHS: dight] decked, adorned   stoures]
tumults, conflicts   morion] a kind of helmet, without beaver or visor, worn by
soldiers in the 16th and 17th c.   chauffed] rubbed   Libbard] leopard   Bore] boar

Laden with fruits that made him laugh, full glad
That he had banisht hunger, which to-fore
Had by the belly oft him pinched sore.
Vpon his head a wreath that was enrold
With eares of corne, of euery sort he bore:
And in his hand a sickle he did holde,
To reape the ripened fruits the which the earth had yold.

Lastly, came *Winter* cloathed all in frize,
Chattering his teeth for cold that did him chill,
Whil'st on his hoary beard his breath did freese;
And the dull drops that from his purpled bill
As from a limbeck did adown distill.
In his right hand a tipped staffe he held,
With which his feeble steps he stayed still:
For, he was faint with cold, and weak with eld;
That scarse his loosed limbes he hable was to weld.

These, marching softly, thus in order went,
And after them, the Monthes all riding came;
First, sturdy *March* with brows full sternly bent,
And armed strongly, rode vpon a Ram,
The same which ouer *Hellespontus* swam:
Yet in his hand a spade he also hent,
And in a bag all sorts of seeds ysame,
Which on the earth he strowed as he went,
And fild her womb with fruitfull hope of nourishment.

Next came fresh *Aprill* full of lustyhed,
And wanton as a Kid whose horne new buds:
Vpon a Bull he rode, the same which led
Europa floting through th'*Argolick* fluds:
His hornes were gilden all with golden studs
And garnished with garlonds goodly dight
Of all the fairest flowres and freshest buds
Which th'earth brings forth, and wet he seem'd in sight
With waues, through which he waded for his loues delight.

Then came faire *May*, the fayrest mayd on ground,
Deckt all with dainties of her seasons pryde,

yold] yielded   frize] frieze, coarse woollen cloth   limbeck] alembic, retort
eld] age   hable] able, powerful   weld] govern, control   hent] took, seized
ysame] together   lustyhed] lustiness, energy, vigour   floting] floating   fluds]
floods

And throwing flowres out of her lap around:
Vpon two brethrens shoulders she did ride,
The twinnes of *Leda*; which on eyther side
Supported her like to their soueraine Queene.
Lord! how all creatures laught, when her they spide,
And leapt and daunc't as they had rauisht beene!
And *Cupid* selfe about her fluttred all in greene.

And after her, came iolly *Iune*, arrayd
All in greene leaues, as he a Player were;
Yet in his time, he wrought as well as playd,
That by his plough-yrons mote right well appeare:
Vpon a Crab he rode, that him did beare
With crooked crawling steps an vncouth pase,
And backward yode, as Bargemen wont to fare
Bending their force contrary to their face,
Like that vngracious crew which faines demurest grace.

Then came hot *Iuly* boyling like to fire,
That all his garments he had cast away:
Vpon a Lyon raging yet with ire
He boldly rode and made him to obay:
It was the beast that whylome did forray
The Nemæan forrest, till th'*Amphytrionide*
Him slew, and with his hide did him array;
Behinde his back a sithe, and by his side
Vnder his belt he bore a sickle circling wide.

The sixt was *August*, being rich arrayd
In garment all of gold downe to the ground
Yet rode he not, but led a louely Mayd
Forth by the lilly hand, the which was cround
With eares of corne, and full her hand was found;
That was the righteous Virgin, which of old
Liv'd here on earth, and plenty made abound;
But, after Wrong was lov'd and Iustice solde,
She left th'vnrighteous world and was to heauen extold.

Next him, *September* marched eeke on foote;
Yet was he heauy laden with the spoyle
Of haruests riches, which he made his boot,
And him enricht with bounty of the soyle:

plough-yrons] coulter and share of a plough   mote] might   pase] pace
yode] went

In his one hand, as fit for haruests toyle,
He held a knife-hook; and in th'other hand
A paire of waights, with which he did assoyle
Both more and lesse, where it in doubt did stand,
And equall gaue to each as Iustice duly scann'd.

Then came *October* full of merry glee:
For, yet his noule was totty of the must,
Which he was treading in the wine-fats see,
And of the ioyous oyle, whose gentle gust
Made him so frollick and so full of lust.
Vpon a dreadfull Scorpion he did ride,
The same which by *Dianaes* doom vniust
Slew great *Orion*: and ecke by his side
He had his ploughing share, and coulter ready tyde.

Next was *Nouember*, he full grosse and fat,
As fed with lard, and that right well might seeme;
For, he had been a fatting hogs of late,
That yet his browes with sweat, did reek and steem,
And yet the season was full sharp and breem;
In planting eeke he took no small delight:
Whereon he rode, not easie was to deeme;
For it a dreadfull *Centaure* was in sight,
The seed of *Saturne*, and faire *Nais*, *Chiron* hight.

And after him, came next the chill *December*:
Yet he through merry feasting which he made,
And great bonfires, did not the cold remember;
His Sauiours birth his mind so much did glad:
Vpon a shaggy-bearded Goat he rode,
The same wherewith *Dan Ioue* in tender yeares,
They say, was nourish by th'*Idæan* mayd;
And in his hand a broad deepe boawle he beares;
Of which, he freely drinks an health to all his peeres.

Then came old *Ianuary*, wrapped well
In many weeds to keep the cold away;
Yet did he quake and quiuer like to quell,
And blowe his nayles to warme them if he may:

assoyle] to absolve, free, release   noule] head   totty] unsteady, dizzy
must] new wine   wine-fats] vats of wine   breem] cold, chill, rough, harsh
deeme] to think, consider

For, they were numbd with holding all the day
An hatchet keene, with which he felled wood,
And from the trees did lop the needlesse spray:
Vpon an huge great Earth-pot steane he stood;
From whose wide mouth, there flowed forth the Romane floud.

And lastly, came cold *February*, sitting
In an old wagon, for he could not ride;
Drawne of two fishes for the season fitting,
Which through the flood before did softly slyde
And swim away: yet had he by his side
His plough and harnesse fit to till the ground,
And tooles to prune the trees, before the pride
Of hasting Prime did make them burgein round:
So past the twelue Months forth, and their dew places found.

SIR WALTER RALEIGH

1552–1618

As you came from the Holy Land

As you came from the holy land of Walsinghame
Mett you not wth my true loue by the way as you came
How shall I know your trew loue
That haue mett many one
As I went to the holy lande
That haue come that haue gone
She is neyther whyte nor browne
Butt as the heauens fayre
There is none hathe a powre so diuine
In the earth or the ayre
Such an one did I meet good S^r
Suche an Angelyke face
Who lyke a queene lyke a nymph did appere
By her gate by her grace:
She hath lefte me here all alone
All allone as vnknowne

steane] stone

AS YOU CAME FROM THE HOLY LAND: powre] form   gate] gait

Who somtymes did me lead wth her selfe
And me loude as her owne:—
Whats the cause that she leaues you alone
And a new waye doth take:
Who loued you once as her owne
And her ioye did you make:
I haue loude her all my youth
Butt no ould as you see
Loue lykes not the fallyng frute
From the wythered tree:
Know that loue is a careless chylld
And forgett promysse paste:
He is blynd, he is deaff when he lyste
And in faythe neuer faste:
His desyre is a dureless contente
And a trustless ioye
He is won wth a world of despayre
And is Lost with a Joye:
Of women kynde suche indeed is the loue
Or the word Loue abused
Vnder wch many chyldysh desyres
And conceytes are excusde:
But Loue is a durable fyre
In the mynde euer burnynge:
Neuer sycke neuer ould neuer dead
From itt selfe neuer turnynge:

Verses made by Sir Walter Raleigh the Night before he was Beheaded

GIUE mee my Escallope shell of Quiett
My staffe of faith to walke vppon
My scripp of Joy Immortall dyett
My Bottle of Saluation
My Gowne of Glorye, hopes true gage
And thus I take my pilgrimage

loude] loved   loued] loved   no ould] now old   chylld] child
forgett promysse paste] forgets promise past   lyste] list   abused] abusèd
excusde] excusèd   but Loue] but [true] love

VERSES MADE BY SIR WALTER RALEIGH THE NIGHT BEFORE HE WAS BEHEADED: Escallope]
scallop   Quiett] quiet

Blood must bee my Bodyes Balmer
No other Balme will there be giuen
Whilst my Soule like Quitte Palmer
Trauills towards the land of heauen
Ouer the Siluer Mountaines
Whear Springes the Nectar fountaines
    And here Ile kiss
    the boule of bliss
    Drinck my eternall fill
    on euery Milky Hill
    My Soule will bee adry before
    But after ytt shall thirst no more

And In that bliss-full day
More peacefull Pillgrimms I shall see
That haue shooke of their gownes of Clay
And goe apparreld fresh-like mee
    Ile take them first
    to slacke thire thirst
    And then to tast of Nectars Suckettes
    Att these Clere Wells
    Whear Sweetnes dwells
    Drawne vpp by Sainctes in heauenly buckettes

And when our Bottles & All wee
Are fild wth Immortallite
Then those holye pathes well trauill
Strewd wth Rubies thicke as grauill
From thence to Heauens Bliss-full hall
Wheare noe Corrupted Lawyers brawle
    Noe Conscience Moulten Into gould
    Noe forge accuser bought or sould
    Noe cause defer'd, noe vayne spent Journye
    For there Christ is the Kinge's Attournye
    Who pleades for All, wthout degrees
    And hee hath Angells but noe fees

When the Grande twelue million Jurye
of our sines wth dreadfull furye
Gainst our soules blacke verdictes giue
Christ pleades his death, and then wee liue

ytt] it   shooke of] cast off   trauill] travel   grauill] gravel   forge
accuser] forged accuser

bee thou my speaker, taintles pleader
Vnblotted Lawyer true proceder
Thou wone'st Saluation euen by Almes
Not wth a bribed Lawyers palmes
And this is my eternall plea
To hym that made heauen Earth & Sea

Seeing my selfe must dye soe soone
And wante a head to dyne next noon
Just att the stroake when my vaynes start & spread
Sett on my Soule an Euerlasting head
     Then am I readye like a Palmer fitt
     To tredd those blest pathes wch before I writt

JOHN LYLY

1553-1606

Pan's Song

PAN's Syrinx was a girle indeed,
Though now shee's turn'd into a reed,
From that deare Reed Pan's pipe does come,
A Pipe that strikes Apollo dumbe;
Nor Flute, nor Lute, nor Gitterne can
So chant it, as the pipe of Pan;
Cross-gartrd swains, and Dairie girls,
With faces smug and round as Pearles,
When Pan's shrill pipe begins to play,
With dancing weare out night and day:
The bag-pipes drone his Hum laes by,
When Pan sounds vp his minstrelsie.
His minstrelsie! O Base! This Quill
Which at my mouth with winde I fill,
Puts me in minde, though Her I misse,
That still my Syrinx lips I kisse.

Cupid and Campaspe

CVPID and my Campaspe playd
At Cardes for kisses, Cupid payd;

He stakes his Quiuer, Bow, and arrows,
His Mothers doues, and teeme of sparrows;
Looses them too; then, downe he throwes
The corrall of his lippe, the rose
Growing on's cheek (but none knows how),
With these, the cristall of his Brow,
And then the dimple of his chinne:
All these did my Campaspe winne.
At last, hee set her both his eyes;
Shee won, and Cupid blind did rise.
    O Loue! has shee done this to Thee?
    What shall (Alas!) become of mee?

SIR PHILIP SIDNEY

1554-1585

Sonnets from 'Astrophel and Stella'

I

LOUING in truth, and faine in verse my loue to show,
  That she (deare she) might take some pleasure of my paine:
  Pleasure might cause her reade, reading might make her know,
  Knowledge might pitie win, and pitie grace obtaine,

I sought fit words to paint the blackest face of woe,
  Studying inuentions fine, her wits to entertaine:
  Oft turning others leaues, to see if thence would flow
  Some fresh and fruitfull showers vpon my sunne-burn'd braine.

But words came halting forth, wanting Inuention's stay,
  Invention Natures child, fled step-dame Studies blowes,
  And others feete still seem'd but strangers in my way.

Thus, great with child to speake, and helplesse in my throwes,
  Biting my trewand pen, beating my selfe for spite.
  Foole, said my Muse to me, looke in thy heart and write.

cristall] crystal, fairness

SONNETS FROM 'ASTROPHEL AND STELLA': trewand] truant

2

THE curious wits, seeing dull pensiuenesse
    Bewray it selfe in my long setled eyes,
    Whence those same fumes of melancholy rise,
    With idle paines, and missing ayme, do guesse.

Some that know how my spring I did addresse,
    Deeme that my Muse some fruit of knowledge plies:
    Others, because the Prince my seruice tries,
    Thinke that I thinke state errours to redresse.

But harder Iudges iudge ambitions rage,
    Scourge of it selfe, still climing slipprie place,
    Holds my young braine captiu'd in golden cage.

O fooles, or ouer-wise, alas the race
    Of all my thoughts hath neither stop nor start,
    But only *Stellas* eyes, and *Stellas* heart.

3

WITH how sad steps, ô Moone, thou climb'st the skies,
    How silently, and with how wanne a face,
    What may it be, that euen in heaunly place
    That busie archer his sharpe arrowes tries?

Sure if that long with *Loue* acquainted eyes
    Can iudge of *Loue*, thou feel'st a Louers case;
    I reade it in thy lookes, thy languisht grace,
    To me that feele the like, thy state descries.

Then ev'n of fellowship, ô Moone, tell me,
    Is constant *Loue* deem'd there but want of wit?
    Are Beauties there as proud as here they be?

Do they above *loue* to be lou'd, and yet
    Those Louers scorne whom that *Loue* doth possesse?
    Do they call *Vertue* there vngratefulnesse.

4

YOU that do search for euerie purling spring,
    Which from the ribs of old Parnassus flowes,
    And euerie floure not sweet perhaps, which growes
    Neare thereabouts, into your Poesie wring.

You that do Dictionaries methode bring
   Into your rimes, running in ratling rowes:
   You that poore *Petrarchs* long deceased woes,
With new-borne sighes and denisend wit do sing.

You take wrong waies those far-fet helpes be such,
   As do bewray a want of inward tuch:
   And sure at length stolne goods do come to light.

But if (both for your loue and skill) your name
   You seeke to nurse at fullest breasts of Fame,
   Stella behold, and then begin to endite.

5

O HAPPIE Tems, that didst my *Stella* beare,
   I saw thy selfe with many a smiling line
   Vpon thy cheereful face, ioyes livery weare:
While those faire planets on thy streames did shine.

The bote for ioy could not to daunce forbeare,
   While wanton winds with beauties so deuine
   Ravisht, staid not, till in her golden haire
They did themselves (ô sweetest prison) twine.

And faine those Æols youth there would their stay
   Have made, but, forst by Nature still to flie,
   First did with puffing kisse those lockes display:

She so discheveld, blusht: from window I
   With sight thereof cride out; ô faire disgrace,
   Let honor selfe to thee graunt highest place.

6

COME sleepe, ô sleepe, the certaine knot of peace,
   The baiting place of wit, the balme of woe,
   The poore mans wealth, the prisoners release,
Th'indifferent Iudge betweene the high and low;

With shield of proofe shield me from out the prease
   Of those fierce darts, dispaire at me doth throw:
   O make in me those ciuill warres to cease;
I will good tribute pay if thou do so.

far-fet] far-fetched   Tems] Thames   deuine] divine   prease] press

Take thou of me smooth pillowes, sweetest bed,
    A chamber deafe to noise, and blind to light:
    A rosie garland, and a wearie hed:

And if these things, as being thine in right,
    Move not thy heavy grace, thou shalt in me,
    Livelier than else-where *Stellas* image see.

7

O IOY, too high for my low stile to show:
    O blisse, fit for a nobler state then me:
    Enuie, put out thine eyes, least thou do see
    What oceans of delight in me do flow.

My friend, that oft saw through all maskes my wo,
    Come, come, and let me powre my selfe on thee;
    Gone is the winter of my miserie,
    My spring appeares, ô see what here doth grow.

For *Stella* hath with words where faith doth shine,
    Of her high heart giu'n me the monarchie:
    I, I, ô I may say, that she is mine.

And though she giue but thus conditionly
    This realme of blisse, while vertuous course I take,
    No kings be crown'd, but they some couenants make.

8

Stella since thou so right a Princesse art
    Of all the powers which life bestowes on me,
    That ere by them ought vndertaken be,
    They first resort vnto that soueraigne part;

Sweete for a while giue respite to my hart,
    Which pants as though it still should leape to thee;
    And on my thoughts giue thy Lieftenancy
    To this great cause, which needs both vse and art.

And as a Queene, who from her presence sends
    Whom she imploies, dismisse from thee my wit,
    Till it haue wrought what thy owne will attends.

hed] head   enuie] envy   least] lest   powre] pour

On seruants shame oft Maisters blame doth sit;
O let not fooles in me thy workes reproue
And scorning say, see what it is to loue.

Songs from 'Astrophel and Stella'

FIRST SONG

DOUBT you to whom my Muse these notes entendeth
Which now my breast ore charg'd to Musicke lendeth;
To you, to you, all song of praise is due,
Only in you my song begins and endeth.

Who hath the eyes which marrie state with pleasure,
Who keepes the key of Natures chiefest treasure:
To you, to you, all song of praise is due,
Only for you the heau'n forgate all measure.

Who has lips, where wit in fairenesse raigneth,
Who womankind at once both deckes and stayneth:
To you, to you, all song of praise is due,
Onely by you *Cupid* his crowne maintaineth.

Who hath the feet, whose step of sweetnesse planteth,
Who else for whom *Fame* worthy trumpets wanteth:
To you, to you, all song of praise is due,
Onely to you her Scepter *Venus* granteth.

Who hath the breast, whose milke doth passions nourish,
Whose grace is such, that when it chides doth cherish,
To you, to you, all song of praise is due,
Onelie through you the tree of life doth flourish.

Who hath the hand which without stroke subdueth,
Who long dead beautie with increase reneweth:
To you, to you, all song of praise is due,
Onely at you all enuie hopelesse rueth.

Who hath the haire which loosest fastest tieth,
Who makes a man liue then glad when he dieth:
To you, to you, all song of praise is due:
Only of you the flatterer neuer lieth.

SONGS FROM 'ASTROPHEL AND STELLA': stayneth] to stain here means to take out colour

Who hath the voyce, which soule from sences sunders,
Whose force but yours the bolts of beautie thunders:
To you, to you, all song of praise is due:
Only with you not miracles are wonders.

Doubt you to whom my Muse these notes entendeth,
Which now my breast orecharg'd to Musicke lendeth:
To you, to you, all song of praise is due:
Only in you my song begins and endeth.

ELEVENTH SONG

WHO is it that this darke night,
Vnderneath my window playneth?
It is one who from the sight,
Being (ah) exild, disdayneth
Euery other vulgar light.

Why alas, and are you he?
Be not yet those fancies changed?
Deere when you find change in me,
Though from me you be estranged,
Let my chaunge to ruine be.

Well in absence this will dy,
Leaue to see, and leaue to wonder:
Absence sure will helpe, if I
Can learne, how my selfe to sunder
From what in my hart doth ly.

But time will these thoughts remoue:
Time doth worke what no man knoweth,
Time doth as the subject proue,
With time still the affection groweth
In the faithfull Turtle doue.

What if you new beauties see,
Will not they stir new affection?
I will thinke th[e]y pictures be,
(Image like of Saints perfection)
Poorely counterfeting thee.

But your reasons purest light,
Bids you leaue such minds to nourish?

Deere, do reason no such spite,
Neuer doth thy beauty florish
More, then in my reasons sight.

But the wrongs loue beares, will make
Loue at length leaue vndertaking;
No the more fooles it do shake,
In a ground of so forme making,
Deeper still they driue the stake.

Peace, I thinke that some giue eare:
Come no more, least I get anger.
Blisse, I will my blisse forbeare,
Fearing (sweete) you to endanger,
But my soule shall harbour thee.

Well, be gone, be gone, I say,
Lest that *Argus* eyes perceiue you,
O vniust fortunes sway,
Which can make me thus to leaue you,
And from lowts to run away.

Splendidis Longum Valedico Nugis

LEAUE me ô Loue, which reachest but to dust,
And thou my mind aspire to higher things:
Grow rich in that which neuer taketh rust:
What euer fades, but fading pleasure brings.

Draw in thy beames, and humble all thy might
To that sweet yoke, where lasting freedomes be:
Which breakes the clowdes and opens forth the light,
That doth both shine and giue vs sight to see.

O take fast hold, let that light be thy guide
In this small course which birth drawes out to death,
And thinke how euill becommeth him to slide,
Who seeketh heau'n, and comes of heau'nly breath.
    Then farewell world, thy vttermost I see,
    Eternall Loue maintaine thy life in me.

- SPLENDIDIS LONGUM VALEDICO NUGIS: euill] evil

The Bargain

MY true loue hath my hart, and I haue his,
By iust exchange, one for another giu'ne.
I hold his deare, and myne he cannot misse:
There neuer was a better bargaine driu'ne.

His hart in me, keepes me and him in one,
My hart in him, his thoughts and senses guides:
He loues my hart, for once it was his owne:
I cherish his because in me it bides.

His hart his wound receiued from my sight:
My hart was wounded, with his wounded hart,
For as from me, on him his hurt did light,
So still me thought in me his hurt did smart:
    Both equall hurt, in this change sought our blisse:
    My true loue hath my hart and I haue his.

Dirge

RING out your belles, let mourning shewes be spread;
  For loue is dead:
    All Loue is dead, infected
    With plague of deepe disdaine:
    Worth as nought worth reiected,
    And Faith faire scorne doth gaine.
      From so vngrateful fancie,
      From such a femall franzie,
      From them that vse men thus,
      Good Lord deliver vs.

Weepe neighbours, weepe, do you not heare it said,
  That Loue is dead:
    His death-bed peacocks follie,
    His winding sheete is shame,
    His will false-seeming holie,
    His sole exectour blame.
      From so vngrateful fancie,
      From such a femall franzie,

giu'ne] given   driu'ne] driven
DIRGE: femall franzie] female frenzy   holie] wholly

From them that vse men thus,
Good Lord deliver vs.

Let Dirge be sung, and Trentals rightly read,
  For Loue is dead:
    Sir wrong his tombe ordaineth:
    My mistresse Marble-heart,
    Which Epitaph containeth,
    Her eyes were once his dart.
      From so vngrateful fancie,
      From such a femall franzie,
      From them that vse men thus,
      Good Lord deliver vs.

Alas, I lie: rage hath this errour bred,
  Loue is not dead.
    Loue is not dead, but sleepeth
    In her vnmatched mind:
    Where she his counsell keepeth,
    Till due desert she find.
      Therefore, from so vile fancie
      To call such wit a franzie,
      Who loue can temper thus,
      Good Lord deliver vs.

Philomela

THE Nightingale as soone as Aprill bringeth
Vnto her rested sense a perfect waking,
While late bare earth, proud of new clothing springeth,
Sings out her woes, a thorne her song-booke making;
  And mournfully bewailing,
  Her throate in tunes expresseth
  What griefe her breast oppresseth,
  For Thereus force on her chaste will prevailing.

  O *Philomela* faire, ô take some gladnesse,
  That here is iuster cause of plaintful sadnesse:
  Thine earth now springs, mine fadeth,
  Thy thorne without, my thorne my heart inuadeth.

DIRGE: Trentals] (? sets of) thirty masses for the dead

45

Alas she hath no other cause of anguish
But *Thereus* loue, on her by strong hand wrokne,
Wherein she suffring all her spirits languish,
Full womanlike complaines her will was brokne.
    But I who dayly crauing,
    Cannot haue to content me,
    Haue more cause to lament me,
    Since wanting is more woe then too much hauing.

        O *Philomela* faire, ô take some gladnesse,
        That here is iuster cause of plaintfull sadnesse;
        Thine earth now springs, mine fadeth,
        Thy thorne without, my thorne my heart inuadeth.

The Highway

HIGHWAY since you my chief *Pernassus* be,
And that my Muse to some eares not vnsweet,
Tempers her words to trampling horses feet
More oft then to a chamber melodie.

Now blessed you, beare onward blessed me
To her, where I my heart safeleft shall meet,
My Muse and I must you of dutie greet
With thankes and wishes, wishing thankfully.

Be you still faire, honourd by publike heed,
By no encrochment wrongd, nor time forgot:
Nor blam'd for bloud, nor sham'd for sinfull deed.

And that you know, I enuy you no lot
    Of highest wish, I wish you so much blisse,
    Hundreds of yeares you *Stellas* feet may kisse.

Epithalamium

LET mother earth now decke her selfe in flowers,
To see her ofspring seeke a good increase,
Where justest love doth vanquish *Cupids* powers
And ware of thoughts is swallow'd up in peace
    Which neuer may decrease

EPITHALAMIUM: ware] war

46

But like the turtells faire
Live one in two, a well united paire,
Which that no chaunce may staine,
O *Himen* long their coupled joyes maintaine.

O heav'n awake shewe forth thy stately face,
Let not these slumbring clowds thy beawties hide,
But with thy cheereful presence helpe to grace
The honest Bridegroome, and the bashfull Bride,
    Whose loves may ever bide,
    Like to the Elme and Vyne,
    With mutuall embracements them to twyne:
    In which delightfull paine,
    O *Himen* long their coupled joyes maintaine.

Yee Muses all which chaste affects allow,
And have to *Thyrsis* shewd your secret skill,
To this chaste love your sacred favours bow,
And so to him and her your giftes distill,
    That they all vice may kill:
    And like to lillies pure
    May please all eyes, and spotlesse may endure.
    Where that all blisse may raigne,
    O *Himen* long their coupled joyes maintaine.

Yee Nymphes which in the waters empire have,
Since *Thyrsis* musick oft doth yeeld you praise,
Graunt to the thing which we for *Thyrsis* crave.
Let one time (but long first) close up their daies,
    One grave their bodies seaze:
    And like two rivers sweete,
    When they though divers do together meete:
    One streame both streames containe,
    O *Himen* long their coupled joyes maintaine.

Pan, father *Pan*, the god of silly sheepe,
Whose care is cause that they in number growe,
Have much more care of them that them do keepe,
Since from these good the others good doth flowe,
    And make their issue showe
    In number like the hearde
    Of yonglings, which thy selfe with love hast rearde.

divers] diverse   silly] simple

Or like the drops of raine.
O *Himen* long their coupled joyes maintaine.

Vertue (if not a God) yet Gods chiefe parte,
Be thou the knot of this their open vowe,
That still he be her head, she be his harte,
He leane to her, she unto him do bow:
　　Each other still allow:
　　Like Oke and Mistletoe.
　　Her strength from him, his praise from her do growe.
　　In which most lovely traine,
　　O *Himen* long their coupled joyes maintaine.

But thou foule *Cupid* syre to lawlesse lust,
Be thou farre hence with thy empoyson'd darte,
Which though of glittring golde, shall heere take rust
Where simple love, which chastnesse doth imparte,
　　Avoydes thy hurtfull arte,
　　Not needing charming skill,
　　Such mindes with sweet affections for to fill,
　　Which being pure and plaine,
　　O *Himen* long their coupled joyes maintaine.

All churlish wordes, shrewd answeres, crabbed lookes,
All privatenes, selfe-seeking, inward spite,
All waywardnes, which nothing kindly brookes,
All strife for toyes, and clayming masters right:
　　Be hence aye put to flight,
　　All sturring husbands hate
　　Gainst neighbors good for womanish debate
　　Be fled as things most vaine,
　　O *Himen* long their coupled joyes maintaine.

All peacock pride, and fruites of peacocks pride
Longing to be with losse of substance gay
With retchlesnes what may thy house betide,
So that you may on hyer slippers stay
　　For ever hence awaye:
　　Yet let not sluttery,
　　The sinke of filth, be counted huswifery:
　　But keeping holesome meane,
　　O *Himen* long their coupled joyes maintaine.

retchlesnes] recklessness

But above all away vile jealousie,
The evill of evils just cause to be unjust,
(How can he love suspecting treacherie?
How can she love where love cannot win trust?)
  Goe snake hide thee in dust,
  Ne dare once shew thy face,
  Where open hartes do holde so constant place,
  That they thy sting restraine,
  O *Himen* long their coupled joyes maintaine.

The earth is deckt with flowers, the heav'ns displaid,
Muses graunt guiftes, Nymphes long and joyned life,
Pan store of babes, vertue their thoughts well staid,
Cupids lust gone, and gone is bitter strife,
  Happy man, happy wife.
  No pride shall them oppresse,
  Nor yet shall yeeld to loathsome sluttishnes,
  And jealousie is slaine:
  For *Himen* will their coupled joyes maintaine.

FULKE GREVILLE, LORD BROOKE

1554–1628

Chorus of Priests

OH wearisome Condition of Humanity!
Borne vnder one Law, to another bound:
Vainely begot, and yet forbidden vanity,
Created sicke, commanded to be sound:
What meaneth Nature by these diuerse Lawes?
Passion and Reason, selfe-diuision cause:
Is it the marke, or Maiesty of Power,
To make offences that it may forgiue?
Nature herselfe, doth her owne selfe defloure,
To hate those errors she her-selfe doth giue.
For how should man thinke that, he may not doe
If Nature did not faile, and punish too?
Tyrant to others, to her selfe vniust,
Onely commands things difficult and hard.

ne] nor

CHORUS OF PRIESTS: defloure] deflower

49

Forbids vs all things, which it knowes is lust,
Makes easie paines, vnpossible reward.
If Nature did not take delight in blood,
She would haue made more easie waies to good,
We that are bound by vowes, and by Promotion,
With pompe of holy Sacrifice and rites,
To teach beleefe in good and still deuotion,
To preach of Heauens wonders, and delights:
Yet when each of vs, in his owne heart lookes,
He finds the God there, farre vnlike his Bookes.

THOMAS LODGE
?1556-1625

Rosalynde's Description

Like to the cleere in highest spheare
Where all imperiall glorie shines,
Of selfe same colour is her haire
Whether vnfolded or in twines:
  Heigh ho, faire *Rosalynde*!
Her eyes are Saphires set in snow,
Refining heauen by euerie winke;
The Gods doo feare when as they glow,
And I doo tremble when I thinke.
  Heigh ho, would she were mine.

Her cheekes are like the blushing clowde
That beautefies *Auroraes* face,
Or like the siluer crimson shrowde
That *Phœbus* smiling lookes doth grace.
  Heigh ho, faire *Rosalynde*.
Her lippes are like two budded roses
Whom rankes of lillies neighbour nie,
Within which bounds she balme incloses,
Apt to intice a Deitie:
  Heigh ho, would she were mine.

Her necke like to a stately towre,
Where Loue himselfe imprisoned lies,

To watch for glaunces euerie howre,
From her deuine and sacred eyes,
    Heigh ho, fair *Rosalynde*.
Her pappes are centers of delight,
Her breasts are orbes of heauenlie frame,
Where Nature moldes the deaw of light
To feede perfection with the same:
    Heigh ho, would she were mine.

With orient pearle, with rubie red,
With marble white, with saphire blew,
Her bodie euerie way is fed;
Yet soft in touch, and sweete in view:
    Heigh ho, faire *Rosalynde*.
Nature her selfe her shape admires,
The Gods are wounded in her sight,
And Loue forsakes his heauenly fires,
And at her eyes his brand doth light:
    Heigh ho, would she were mine.

Then muse not Nymphes though I bemoane
The absence of faire *Rosalynde*:
Since for her faire there is fairer none,
Nor for her vertues so deuine.
    Heigh ho faire *Rosalynde*:
  Heigh ho my heart, would God that she were mine.

Rosalynde's Madrigal

LOUE in my bosome like a Bee
    doth sucke his sweete:
Now with his wings he playes with me,
    now with his feete.
  Within mine eies he makes his neast,
  His bed amidst my tender breast,
  My kisses are his daily feast;
  And yet he robs me of my rest.
    Ah wanton, will ye?

ROSALYNDE'S DESCRIPTION: euerie howre] every hour   moldes the deaw] moulds the dew   deuine] divine

And if I sleepe, then pearcheth he
    with prettie flight,
And makes his pillow of my knee
    the liuelong night.
  Strike I my lute, he tunes the string;
  He musicke playes if so I sing,
  He lends me euerie louelie thing,
  Yet cruell he my heart doth sting.
      Whist wanton, still ye.

Else I with roses euerie day
    will whip you hence;
And binde you when you long to play,
    for your offence.
  Ile shut mine eyes to keepe you in,
  Ile make you fast it for your sinne,
  Ile count your power not worth a pinne;
  Ahlas what hereby shall I winne
      If he gainsay me?

What if I beate the wanton boy
    with manie a rod?
He will repay me with annoy,
    because a God.
  Then sit thou safely on my knee,
  Then let thy bowre my bosome be:
  Lurke in mine eyes I like of thee;
  Oh *Cupid* so thou pitie me.
      Spare not but play thee.

Pluck the Fruit and Taste the Pleasure

PLUCKE the fruite and tast the pleasure
  Youthfull Lordings of delight,
Whil'st occasion giues you seasure,
  Feede your fancies and your sight:
    After death when you are gone,
    Joy and pleasure is there none.

Here on earth nothing is stable,
  Fortunes chaunges well are knowne,

PLUCK THE FRUIT AND TASTE THE PLEASURE: seasure] seizure

THOMAS LODGE

Whil'st as youth doth then enable,
  Let your seedes of ioy be sowne:
    After death when you are gone,
    Ioy and pleasure is there none.

Feast it freely with your Louers,
  Blyth and wanton sweetes doo fade,
Whilst that louely *Cupid* houers
  Round about this louely shade:
    Sport it freely one to one,
    After death is pleasure none.

Now the pleasant spring allureth,
  And both place and time inuites:
But alas, what heart endureth
  To disclaime his sweete delightes?
    After death when we are gone,
    Joy and pleasure is there none.

Robert, Second Duke of Normandy, 1591

GEORGE PEELE

?1558-1597

A Farewell to Arms

(*To Queen Elizabeth*)

His golden locks time hath to siluer turn'd,
O time too swift, O swiftnes neuer ceasing,
His youth gainst time & age hath euer spurnd,
But spurnd in vaine, youth waneth by encreasing:
  Beautie, strength, youth are flowers but fading seene,
  Duty, Faith, Loue, are roots and euer greene.

His helmet now shall make a hiue for bees,
And louers sonets turne to holy psalmes:
A man at armes must now serue on his knees,
And feed on prayers which are ages almes,
  But though from court to cotage he departe
  His saint is sure of his vnspotted hart.
And when he saddest sits in homely Cell,
Hele teach his swaines this Caroll for a songe,
Blest be the harts that wish my soueraigne well,

53

ROBERT GREENE

1560–1592

Sephestia's Song to her Child

WEEPE not my wanton, smile vpon my knee,
When thou art olde ther's griefe inough for thee.
    Mothers wagge, pretie boy,
    Fathers sorrow, fathers ioy.
    When thy father first did see
    Such a boy by him and mee,
    He was glad, I was woe,
    Fortune changde made him so,
    When he left his pretie boy,
    Last his sorrowe, first his ioy.
Weepe not my wanton, smile vpon my knee:
When thou art olde ther's griefe inough for thee.
    Streaming teares that neuer stint,
    Like pearle drops from a flint
    Fell by course from his eyes,
    That one anothers place supplies:
    Thus he grieud in euerie part,
    Teares of bloud fell from his hart,
    When he left his pretie boy,
    Fathers sorrow, fathers ioy.
Weepe not my wanton, smile vpon my knee:
When thou art olde ther's griefe inough for thee.

GEORGE CHAPMAN

1560–1634

from *Ovid's Banquet of Sence*

7

In a loose robe of Tynsell foorth she came,
Nothing but it betwixt her nakednes
And enuious light. The downward-burning flame,
Of her rich hayre did threaten new accesse,

SEPHESTIA'S SONG TO HER CHILD: changde] changèd

54

Of ventrous *Phaeton* to scorch the fields:
And thus to bathing came our Poets Goddesse,
   Her handmaides bearing all things pleasure yeelds
To such a seruice; Odors most delighted,
And purest linnen which her lookes had whited.

8

Then cast she off her robe, and stood vpright,
As lightning breakes out of a laboring cloude;
Or as the Morning heauen casts off the Night,
Or as that heauen cast off it selfe, and showde
   Heauens vpper light, to which the brightest day
Is but a black and melancholy shroude:
   Or as when *Venus* striu'd for soueraine sway
Of charmfull beautie, in yong Troyes desire,
So stood *Corynna* vanishing her tire.

9

A soft enflowered banck embrac'd the founte;
Of *Chloris* ensignes, an abstracted field;
Where grew Melanthy, great in Bees account,
Amareus, that precious Balme dooth yeeld,
   Enameld Pansies, vs'd at Nuptials still,
Dianas arrow, *Cupid's* crimson shielde,
   Ope-morne, night-shade, and *Venus* nauill,
Solemne Violets, hanging head as shamed,
And verdant Calaminth, for odor famed.

10

Sacred Nepenthe, purgatiue of care,
And soueraine Rumex that doth rancor kill,
Sya, and Hyacinth, that Furies weare,
White and red Iessamines, Merry, Melliphill:
   Fayre Crowne-imperiall, Emperor of Flowers,
Immortall Amaranth, white Aphrodill,
   And cup-like Twillpants, stroude in *Bacchus* Bowres,
These cling about this Natures naked Iem,
To taste her sweetes, as Bees doe swarme on them.

11

And now shee vsde the Founte, where *Niobe*,
Toomb'd in her selfe, pourde her lost soule in teares,
Vpon the bosome of this Romaine *Phoebe*;
Who, bathd and Odord, her bright lyms she rears,

And drying her on that disparent grounde;
Her Lute she takes t'enamoure heuenly eares,
    And try if with her voyces vitall sounde,
She could warme life through those cold statues spread,
And cheere the Dame that wept when she was dead.

12

And thus she sung, all naked as she sat,
Laying the happy Lute vpon her thigh,
Not thinking any neere to wonder at
The blisse of her sweet brests diuinitie.

The Song of Corynna

T'is better to contemne then loue,
And to be fayre then wise;
For soules are rulde by eyes:
And Ioues Bird, ceaz'd by Cypris Doue,
It is our grace and sport to see,
Our beauties sorcerie,
That makes (like destinie)
Men followe vs the more wee flee;
That sets wise Glosses on the foole,
And turns her cheekes to bookes,
Where wisdome sees in lookes
Derision, laughing at his schoole,
    Who (louing) proues, prophanenes, holy;
    Nature, our fate, our wisdome, folly.

ROBERT SOUTHWELL

1561-1595

The Burning Babe

As I in hoarie Winters night stood shiuering in the snow,
Surpris'd I was with sudden heat, which made my heart to glow;
And lifting vp a fearefull eye, to view what fire was neere,
A pretie Babe all burning bright did in the ayre appeare;

FROM OVID'S BANQUET OF SENCE: grounde] rounde

ROBERT SOUTHWELL

Who, scorched with excessiue heate, such floods of teares did shed,
As though his floods should quench his flames, which with his teares
   were bred:
'Alas!' quoth He, 'but newly born in fiery heats I fry,
Yet none approch to warme their hearts, or feele my fire but I;
My faultlesse brest the furnace is, the fuell wounding thornes:
Loue is the fire, and sighes the smoake, the ashes shames and scornes;
The fuell Iustice layeth on, and mercie blowes the coales,
The mettall in this Furnace wrought, are men's defiled soules:
For which, as now on fire I am to worke them to their good,
So will I melt into a bath, to wash them in my blood.'
With this he vanisht out of sight, and swiftly shrunke away,
And straight I called vnto mind, that it was Christmasse day.

Saint Peters Complaint

FRANCIS BACON
1561–1626

Life

THE world's a bubble, and the life of man
          lesse then a span,
In his conception wretched, from the wombe
          so to the tombe:
Curst from the cradle, and brought vp to yeares,
          with cares and feares.
Who then to fraile mortality shall trust,
But limmes the water, or but writes in dust.

Yet since with sorrow here we liue opprest:
          what life is best?
Courts are but only superficiall scholes
          to dandle fooles.
The rurall parts are turn'd into a den
          of sauage men.
And wher's a city from all vice so free,
But may be term'd the worst of all the three?

scorched] scorchèd   defiled] defilèd   called] callèd

LIFE: limmes] paints   the three] i.e. the Court, the Country, and the City

57

Domesticke cares afflict the husbands bed,
                              or paines his head:
Those that liue single take it for a curse,
                              or doe things worse.
Some would have children, those that have them, mone,
                              or wish them gone.
What is it then to haue or haue no wife,
But single thraldome, or a double strife?

Our owne affections still at home to please,
                              is a disease,
To crosse the sea to any foreine soyle,
                              perills and toyle.
Warres with their noyse affright vs: when they cease,
                              W'are worse in peace.
What then remaines? but that we still should cry,
Not to be borne, or, being borne, to dye.

Florilegium Epigrammatum Graecorum

SAMUEL DANIEL

1562-1619

Care-Charmer Sleep

CARE-CHARMER Sleep, sonne of the sable night,
    Brother to death, in silent darknes borne:
    Relieue my languish, and restore the light,
    With darke forgetting of my cares returne.
And let the day be time enough to mourne
    The shipwrack of my ill aduentied youth:
    Let waking eues suffise to waile their scorne,
    Without the torment of the nights vntruth.
Cease dreames, th' Images of day desires,
    To modell forth the passions of the morrow:
    Neuer let rising Sunne approue you liers,
    To adde more griefe to aggrauate my sorrow.

mone] moan

CARE-CHARMER SLEEP: restore the light] i.e. of unconsciousness   ill aduentied]
ill-adventured

Still let me sleep, imbracing clouds in vaine,
And neuer wake to feele the daies disdaine.

Ulysses and the Syren

Syren. COME worthy Greeke, *Vlisses* come
        Possesse these shores with me:
        The windes and Seas are troublesome,
        And heere we may be free.
          Here may we sit, and view their toile
        That trauaile in the deepe,
        And ioy the day in mirth the while,
        And spend the night in sleepe.

Vlis. Faire Nimph, if fame, or honor were
        To be attaynd with ease
        Then would I come, and rest with thee,
        And leaue such toyles as these.
          But here it dwels, and here must I
        With danger seeke it forth,
        To spend the time luxuriously
        Becomes not men of worth.

Syr. *Vlisses*, O be not deceiu'd
        With that vnreall name:
        This honour is a thing conceiu'd,
        And rests on others fame.
          Begotten onely to molest
        Our peace, and to beguile
        (The best thing of our life) our rest,
        And giue vs vp to toile.

Vlis. Delicious Nimph, suppose there were
        Nor honour, nor report,
        Yet manlines would scorne to weare
        The time in idle sport.
          For toyle doth giue a better touch,
        To make vs feele our ioy;
        And ease findes tediousness as much
        As labour yeelds annoy.

Syr. Then pleasure likewise seemes the shore,
        Whereto tends all your toyle,

SAMUEL DANIEL

Which you forgo to make it more,
And perish oft the while.
    Who may disporte them diuersly
Finde neuer tedious day,
And ease may haue varietie,
As well as action may.

Vlis.   But natures of the noblest frame
These toyles, and dangers please,
And they take comfort in the same,
As much as you in ease.
    And with the thought of actions past
Are recreated still;
When pleasure leaues a touch at last,
To shew that it was ill.

Syr.   That doth opinion onely cause,
That's out of custome bred,
Which makes vs many other lawes
Then euer Nature did.
    No widdowes waile for our delights,
Our sportes are without bloud,
The world we see by warlike wights
Receiues more hurt then good.

Vlis.   But yet the state of things require
These motions of vnrest,
And these great Spirits of high desire
Seeme borne to turne them best.
    To purge the mischiefes that increase,
And all good order mar:
For oft we see a wicked peace
To be well chang'd for war.

Syr.   Well, well *Vlisses* then I see,
I shall not haue thee heere,
And therefore I will come to thee,
And take my fortunes there.
    I must be wonne that cannot win,
Yet lost were I not wonne:
For beauty hath created bin,
T' vndoo, or be vndonne.

MICHAEL DRAYTON
1563-1631

Agincourt

FAIRE stood the Wind for *France*,
When we our Sayles aduance,
Nor now to proue our chance,
  Longer will tarry;
But putting to the Mayne,
At *Kaux*, the Mouth of *Sene*,
With all his Martiall Trayne,
  Landed King HARRY.

And taking many a Fort,
Furnish'd in Warlike sort,
Marcheth tow'rds *Agincourt*,
  In happy howre;
Skirmishing day by day,
With those that stop'd his way,
Where the *French* Gen'rall lay,
  With all his Power.

Which in his Hight of Pride,
King HENRY to deride,
His Ransome to prouide
  To the King sending.
Which he neglects the while,
As from a Nation vile,
Yet with an angry smile,
  Their fall portending.

And turning to his Men,
Quoth our braue HENRY then,
Though they to one be ten,
  Be not amazed.
Yet haue we well begunne,
Battles so brauely wonne,
Haue euer to the Sonne,
  By Fame beene raysed.

amazed] amazèd

61

And, for my Selfe (quoth he),
This my full rest shall be,
England ne'r mourne for Me,
    Nor more esteeme me.
Victor I will remaine,
Or on this Earth lie slaine,
Neuer shall Shee sustaine,
    Losse to redeeme me.

Poiters and *Cressy* tell,
When most their Pride did swell,
Vnder our Swords they fell,
    No lesse our skill is,
Than when our Grandsire Great,
Clayming the Regall Seate,
By many a Warlike feate,
    Lop'd the *French* Lillies.

The Duke of *Yorke* so dread,
The eager Vaward led;
With the maine, HENRY sped,
    Among'st his Hench-men.
EXCESTER had the Rere,
A Brauer man not there,
O Lord, how hot they were,
    On the false *French-men*!

They now to fight are gone,
Armour on Armour shone,
Drumme now to Drumme did grone,
    To heare, was wonder;
That with the cryes they make,
The very Earth did shake,
Trumpet to Trumpet spake,
    Thunder to Thunder.

Well it thine Age became,
O Noble ERPINGHAM,
Which didst the Signall ayme,
    To our hid Forces;
When from a Medow by,
Like a Storme suddenly
The *English* Archery
    Stuck the *French* Horses,

EXCESTER] Exeter

62

With *Spanish* Ewgh so strong,
Arrowes a Cloth-yard long,
That like to Serpents stung,
    Piercing the Weather;
None from his fellow starts,
But playing Manly parts,
And like true *English* hearts,
    Stuck close together.

When downe their Bowes they threw,
And forth their Bilbowes drew,
And on the French they flew,
    Not one was tardie;
Armes were from shoulders sent,
Scalpes to the Teeth were rent,
Downe the *French* Pesants went,
    Our Men were hardie.

This while our Noble King,
His broad Sword brandishing,
Downe the *French* Hoast did ding,
    As to o'r-whelme it;
And many a deepe Wound lent,
His Armes with Bloud besprent,
And many a cruell Dent
    Bruised his Helmet.

GLOSTER, that Duke so good,
Next of the Royall Blood,
For famous *England* stood,
    With his braue Brother;
CLARENCE, in Steele so bright,
Though but a Maiden Knight,
Yet in that furious Fight,
    Scarce such another.

WARWICK in Bloud did wade,
OXFORD the Foe inuade,
And cruell slaughter made,
    Still as they ran vp;
SVFFOLKE his Axe did ply,
BEAVMONT and WILLOVGHBY
Bare them right doughtily,
    FERRERS and FANHOPE.

Ewgh] yew   Bilbowes] swords from Bilboa   Bruised] bruisèd

Vpon Saint CRISPIN'S day
Fought was this Noble Fray,
Which Fame did not delay,
    To *England* to carry;
O, when shall *English* Men
With such Acts fill a Pen,
Or *England* breed againe,
    Such a King HARRY?

CHRISTOPHER MARLOWE

1564-1593

from *Hero and Leander*

O NONE but gods have power their love to hide,
Affection by the count'nance is descried.
The light of hidden fire itself discovers,
And love that is concealed betrays poor lovers.
His secret flame apparently was seen,
Leander's father knew where he had been,
And for the same mildly rebuked his son,
Thinking to quench the sparkles new begun.
But love resisted once grows passionate,
And nothing more than counsel lovers hate.
For as a hot proud horse highly disdains
To have his head controlled, but breaks the reins,
Spits forth the ringled bit, and with his hooves
Checks the submissive ground: so he that loves,
The more he is restrained, the worse he fares.
What is it now, but mad Leander dares?
'O Hero, Hero!' thus he cried full oft,
And then he got him to a rock aloft,
Where having spied her tower, long stared he on't,
And prayed the narrow toiling Hellespont
To part in twain, that he might come and go,
But still the rising billows answered 'No.'
With that he stripped him to the ivory skin,
And crying, 'Love, I come,' leapt lively in.
Whereat the sapphire-visaged god grew proud,
And made his capering Triton sound aloud,

Imagining that Ganymede, displeased,
Had left the heavens; therefore on him he seized.
Leander strived, the waves about him wound,
And pulled him to the bottom, where the ground
Was strewed with pearl, and in low coral groves
Sweet singing mermaids sported with their loves
On heaps of heavy gold, and took great pleasure
To spurn in careless sort the shipwrack treasure.
For here the stately azure palace stood
Where kingly Neptune and his train abode.
The lusty god embraced him, called him love,
And swore he never should return to Jove.
But when he knew it was not Ganymede,
For under water he was almost dead,
He heaved him up, and looking on his face,
Beat down the bold waves with his triple mace,
Which mounted up, intending to have kissed him,
And fell in drops like tears because they missed him.
Leander being up, began to swim,
And, looking back, saw Neptune follow him;
Whereat aghast, the poor soul 'gan to cry,
'O let me visit Hero ere I die.'
The god put Helle's bracelet on his arm,
And swore the sea should never do him harm.
He clapped his plump cheeks, with his tresses played,
And smiling wantonly, his love bewrayed.
He watched his arms, and as they opened wide
At every stroke, betwixt them would he slide
And steal a kiss, and then run out and dance,
And as he turned, cast many a lustful glance,
And threw him gaudy toys to please his eye,
And dive into the water, and there pry
Upon his breast, his thighs, and every limb,
And up again, and close beside him swim,
And talk of love. Leander made reply,
'You are deceived, I am no woman, I.'
Thereat smiled Neptune, and then told a tale,
How that a shepherd, sitting in a vale,
Played with a boy so fair and kind,
As for his love both earth and heaven pined;
That of the cooling river durst not drink,
Lest water-nymphs should pull him from the brink;
And when he sported in the fragrant lawns,
Goat-footed satyrs and up-staring fauns

Would steal him thence. Ere half this tale was done,
'Aye me,' Leander cried, 'th' enamoured sun,
That now should shine on Thetis' glassy bower,
Descends upon my radiant Hero's tower.
O that these tardy arms of mine were wings!'
And as he spake, upon the waves he springs.
Neptune was angry that he gave no ear,
And in his heart revenging malice bare:
He flung at him his mace, but as it went,
He called it in, for love made him repent.
The mace returning back, his own hand hit,
As meaning to be venged for darting it.
When this fresh bleeding wound Leander viewed,
His colour went and came, as if he rued
The grief which Neptune felt. In gentle breasts
Relenting thoughts, remorse and pity rests.
And who have hard hearts and obdurate minds,
But vicious, harebrained, and illit'rate hinds?
The god, seeing him with pity to be movèd,
Thereon concluded that he was belovèd.
(Love is too full of faith, too credulous,
With folly and false hope deluding us.)
Wherefore Leander's fancy to surprise,
To the rich Ocean for gifts he flies.
'Tis wisdom to give much, a gift prevails
When deep persuading oratory fails.

Elegia V

Corinnae concubitus

IN summer's heat, and mid-time of the day,
To rest my limbs upon a bed I lay;
One window shut, the other open stood,
Which gave such light as twinkles in a wood,
Like twilight glimpse at setting of the sun,
Or night being past, and yet not day begun.
Such light to shamefast maidens must be shown,
Where they may sport and seem to be unknown.
Then came Corinna in a long loose gown,
Her white neck hid with tresses hanging down,
Resembling fair Semiramis going to bed,
Or Lais of a thousand wooers sped.

I snatched her gown; being thin, the harm was small,
Yet strived she to be covered therewithal,
And striving thus as one that would be cast,
Betrayed herself, and yielded at the last.
Stark naked as she stood before mine eye,
Not one wen in her body could I spy.
What arms and shoulders did I touch and see,
How apt her breasts were to be pressed by me!
How smooth a belly under her waist saw I,
How large a leg, and what a lusty thigh!
To leave the rest, all liked me passing well;
I clinged her naked body, down she fell.
Judge you the rest: being tired she bade me kiss;
Jove send me more such afternoons as this.

The Passionate Shepherd to his Love

COME liue with mee and be my loue,
And we will all the pleasures proue,
That hills and valleys, dales and fields,
And all the craggy mountain yeeldes.

There we will sit vpon the Rocks,
And see the sheepheards feede theyr flocks
By shallow riuers, to whose falls
Melodious byrds sing Madrigalls.

And I will make thee beds of Roses,
And a thousand fragrant poesies,
A cap of flowers, and a kirtle,
Imbroydered all with leaues of Mirtle.

A gowne made of the finest wooll,
Which from our pretty Lambes we pull,
Fayre lined slippers for the cold,
With buckles of the purest gold.

A belt of straw and Iuie buds,
With Corall clasps and Amber studs,
And if these pleasures may thee moue,
Come liue with mee, and be my lóue.

THE PASSIONATE SHEPHERD TO HIS LOVE: Fayre lined] fair-linèd   Iuie] ivy

The sheepheard swains shall daunce and sing
For thy delight each May-morning.
If these delights thy minde may moue,
Then liue with mee, and be my loue.

WILLIAM SHAKESPEARE

1564–1616

from *3 Henry VI*

K. Henry. The owl shriek'd at thy birth, an evil sign;
The night-crow cried, aboding luckless time;
Dogs howl'd, and hideous tempest shook down trees!
The raven rook'd her on the chimney's top,
And chattering pies in dismal discords sung.
Thy mother felt more than a mother's pain,
And yet brought forth less than a mother's hope;
To wit an indigest deformed lump,
Not like the fruit of such a goodly tree.
Teeth hadst thou in thy head when thou wast born,
To signify thou cam'st to bite the world:
And, if the rest be true which I have heard,
Thou cam'st—
    Gloucester. I'll hear no more: die, prophet, in thy speech:

                                                 [*Stabs him.*

For this, amongst the rest, was I ordain'd.
    K. Hen. Ay, and for much more slaughter after this.
O, God forgive my sins, and pardon thee!   [*Dies.*
    Glo. What! will the aspiring blood of Lancaster
Sink in the ground? I thought it would have mounted.
See how my sword weeps for the poor king's death!
O! may such purple tears be always shed
From those that wish the downfall of our house.
If any spark of life be yet remaining,
Down, down to hell; and say I sent thee thither,   [*Stabs him again.*
I, that have neither pity, love, nor fear.
Indeed, 'tis true, that Henry told me of;
For I have often heard my mother say
I came into the world with my legs forward.
Had I not reason, think ye, to make haste,
And seek their ruin that usurp'd our right?

The midwife wonder'd, and the women cried
'O! Jesus bless us, he is born with teeth.'
And so I was; which plainly signified
That I should snarl and bite and play the dog.
Then, since the heavens have shap'd my body so,
Let hell make crook'd my mind to answer it.
I have no brother, I am like no brother;
And this word 'love,' which greybeards call divine,
Be resident in men like one another
And not in me: I am myself alone.   (v. vi. 44–83)

from *1 Henry VI*

Bedford. Hung be the heavens with black, yield day to night!
Comets, importing change of times and states,
Brandish your crystal tresses in the sky,
And with them scourge the bad revolting stars,
That have consented unto Henry's death!
King Henry the Fifth, too famous to live long!
England ne'er lost a king of so much worth.
   Gloucester. England ne'er had a king until his time.
Virtue he had, deserving to command:
His brandish'd sword did blind men with his beams;
His arms spread wider than a dragon's wings;
His sparkling eyes, replete with wrathful fire,
More dazzled and drove back his enemies
Than mid–day sun fierce bent against their faces.
What should I say? his deeds exceed all speech:
He ne'er lift up his hand but conquered.
   Exeter. We mourn in black: why mourn we not in blood?
Henry is dead and never shall revive.
Upon a wooden coffin we attend,
And death's dishonourable victory
We with our stately presence glorify,
Like captives bound to a triumphant car.   (I. i. 1–22)

from *Richard III*

Brakenbury. Why looks your Grace so heavily today?
   Clarence. O, I have pass'd a miserable night,
So full of ugly sights, of ghastly dreams,

That, as I am a Christian faithful man,
I would not spend another such a night,
Though 'twere to buy a world of happy days,
So full of dismal terror was the time.

    Brak. What was your dream, my lord? I pray you, tell me.
    Clar. Methought that I had broken from the Tower,
And was embark'd to cross to Burgundy;
And in my company my brother Gloucester,
Who from my cabin tempted me to walk
Upon the hatches: hence we look'd toward England,
And cited up a thousand heavy times,
During the wars of York and Lancaster,
That had befall'n us. As we pac'd along
Upon the giddy footing of the hatches,
Methought that Gloucester stumbled; and, in falling,
Struck me, that thought to stay him, overboard,
Into the tumbling billows of the main.
Lord, Lord! methought what pain it was to drown:
What dreadful noise of water in mine ears!
What sights of ugly death within mine eyes!
Methought I saw a thousand fearful wracks;
A thousand men that fishes gnaw'd upon;
Wedges of gold, great anchors, heaps of pearl,
Inestimable stones, unvalu'd jewels,
All scatter'd in the bottom of the sea.
Some lay in dead men's skulls; and in those holes
Where eyes did once inhabit, there were crept,
As 'twere in scorn of eyes, reflecting gems,
That woo'd the slimy bottom of the deep,
And mock'd the dead bones that lay scatter'd by.

    Brak. Had you such leisure in the time of death
To gaze upon those secrets of the deep?
    Clar. Methought I had; and often did I strive
To yield the ghost; but still the envious flood
Stopt in my soul, and would not let it forth
To find the empty, vast, and wandering air;
But smother'd it within my panting bulk,
Which almost burst to belch it in the sea.

    Brak. Awak'd you not with this sore agony?
    Clar. No, no, my dream was lengthen'd after life;
O! then began the tempest to my soul.
I pass'd, methought, the melancholy flood,
With that grim ferryman which poets write of,
Unto the kingdom of perpetual night.

The first that there did greet my stranger soul,
Was my great father-in-law, renowned Warwick;
Who cried aloud, 'What scourge for perjury
Can this dark monarchy afford false Clarence?'
And so he vanish'd: then came wandering by
A shadow like an angel, with bright hair
Dabbled in blood; and he shriek'd out aloud,
'Clarence is come,—false, fleeting, perjur'd Clarence,
That stabb'd me in the field by Tewksbury;—
Seize on him! Furies, take him unto torment.'
With that, methought, a legion of foul fiends
Environ'd me, and howled in mine ears
Such hideous cries, that, with the very noise
I trembling wak'd, and, for a season after
Could not believe but that I was in hell,
Such terrible impression made my dream.   (I. iv. 1-63)

from *Romeo and Juliet*

Romeo. [*To* JULIET.] If I profane with my unworthiest hand
    This holy shrine, the gentle sin is this;
My lips, two blushing pilgrims, ready stand
    To smooth that rough touch with a tender kiss.
Juliet. Good pilgrim, you do wrong your hand too much,
    Which mannerly devotion shows in this;
For saints have hands that pilgrims' hands do touch,
    And palm to palm is holy palmers' kiss.
Rom. Have not saints lips, and holy palmers too?
    Jul. Ay, pilgrim, lips that they must use in prayer.
Rom. O! then, dear saint, let lips do what hands do;
    They pray, grant thou, lest faith turn to despair.
    Jul. Saints do not move, though grant for prayers' sake.
    Rom. Then move not, while my prayers' effect I take.
Thus from my lips, by thine, my sin is purg'd.   [*Kissing her*.
    Jul. Then have my lips the sin that they have took.
Rom. Sin from my lips? O trespass sweetly urg'd!
    Give me my sin again.   (I. v. 91-108)

    Rom. But, soft! what light through yonder window breaks?
It is the east, and Juliet is the sun!
Arise, fair sun, and kill the envious moon,
Who is already sick and pale with grief,

That thou her maid art far more fair than she:
Be not her maid, since she is envious;
Her vestal livery is but sick and green,
And none but fools do wear it; cast it off.
It is my lady; O! it is my love:
O! that she knew she were.
She speaks, yet she says nothing: what of that?
Her eye discourses; I will answer it.
I am too bold, 'tis not to me she speaks:
Two of the fairest stars in all the heaven,
Having some business, do entreat her eyes
To twinkle in their spheres till they return.
What if her eyes were there, they in her head?
The brightness of her cheek would shame those stars
As daylight doth a lamp; her eyes in heaven
Would through the airy region stream so bright
That birds would sing and think it were not night.
See! how she leans her cheek upon her hand:
O! that I were a glove upon that hand,
That I might touch that cheek.

    Jul.   Ay me!

    Rom.   She speaks:
O! speak again, bright angel; for thou art
As glorious to this night, being o'er my head,
As is a winged messenger of heaven
Unto the white-upturned wond'ring eyes
Of mortals, that fall back to gaze on him
When he bestrides the lazy-pacing clouds,
And sails upon the bosom of the air.

    Jul. O Romeo, Romeo! wherefore art thou Romeo?
Deny thy father, and refuse thy name;
Or, if thou wilt not, be but sworn my love,
And I'll no longer be a Capulet.

    Rom. [*Aside.*] Shall I hear more, or shall I speak at this?

    Jul. 'Tis but thy name that is my enemy;
Thou art thyself though, not a Montague.
What's Montague? it is nor hand, nor foot,
Nor arm, nor face, nor any other part
Belonging to a man. O! be some other name:
What's in a name? that which we call a rose
By any other name would smell as sweet;
So Romeo would, were he not Romeo call'd,
Retain that dear perfection which he owes
Without that title. Romeo, doff thy name;

And for that name, which is no part of thee,
Take all myself.   (II. ii. 2-49)

   Rom.   O my love! my wife!
Death, that hath suck'd the honey of thy breath,
Hath had no power yet upon thy beauty:
Thou art not conquer'd; beauty's ensign yet
Is crimson in thy lips and in thy cheeks,
And death's pale flag is not advanced there.
Tybalt, liest thou there in thy bloody sheet?
O! what more favour can I do to thee,
Than with that hand that cut thy youth in twain
To sunder his that was thine enemy?
Forgive me, cousin! Ah! dear Juliet,
Why art thou yet so fair? Shall I believe
That unsubstantial Death is amorous,
And that the lean abhorred monster keeps
Thee here in dark to be his paramour?
For fear of that I still will stay with thee,
And never from this palace of dim night
Depart again: here, here will I remain
With worms that are thy chambermaids; O! here
Will I set up my everlasting rest,
And shake the yoke of inauspicious stars
From this world-wearied flesh. Eyes, look your last!
Arms, take your last embrace! and, lips, O you
The doors of breath, seal with a righteous kiss
A dateless bargain to engrossing death!
Come, bitter conduct, come, unsavoury guide!
Thou desperate pilot, now at once run on
The dashing rocks thy sea-sick weary bark!
Here's to my love! [*Drinks.*] O true apothecary!
Thy drugs are quick. Thus with a kiss I die.   (V. iii. 91-120)

from *Richard II*

   K. Richard. [*To the Combatants.*] Draw near,
And list what with our council we have done.
For that our kingdom's earth should not be soil'd
With that dear blood which it hath fostered;
And for our eyes do hate the dire aspect
Of civil wounds plough'd up with neighbours' swords;
And for we think the eagle-winged pride

Of sky-aspiring and ambitious thoughts,
With rival-hating envy, set on you
To wake our peace, which in our country's cradle
Draws the sweet infant breath of gentle sleep;
Which so rous'd up with boist'rous untun'd drums,
With harsh-resounding trumpets' dreadful bray,
And grating shock of wrathful iron arms,
Might from our quiet confines fright fair peace
And make us wade even in our kindred's blood:
Therefore, we banish you our territories:
You, cousin Hereford, upon pain of life,
Till twice five summers have enrich'd our fields,
Shall not regreet our fair dominions,
But tread the stranger paths of banishment.
    Bolingbroke. Your will be done: this must my comfort be,
That sun that warms you here shall shine on me;
And those his golden beams to you here lent
Shall point on me and gild my banishment.
    K. Rich. Norfolk, for thee remains a heavier doom,
Which I with some unwillingness pronounce:
The sly slow hours shall not determinate
The dateless limit of thy dear exile;
The hopeless word of 'never to return'
Breathe I against thee, upon pain of life.
    Mowbray. A heavy sentence, my most sovereign liege,
And all unlook'd for from your highness' mouth:
A dearer merit, not so deep a maim
As to be cast forth in the common air,
Have I deserved at your highness' hands.
The language I have learn'd these forty years,
My native English, now I must forego;
And now my tongue's use is to me no more
Than an unstringed viol or a harp,
Or like a cunning instrument cas'd up,
Or, being open, put into his hands
That knows no touch to tune the harmony:
Within my mouth you have engaol'd my tongue,
Doubly portcullis'd with my teeth and lips;
And dull, unfeeling, barren ignorance
Is made my gaoler to attend on me.
I am too old to fawn upon a nurse,
Too far in years to be a pupil now:
What is thy sentence then but speechless death,
Which robs my tongue from breathing native breath?

K. Rich. It boots thee not to be compassionate:
After our sentence plaining comes too late. (I. iii. 123–75)

Aumerle. Where is the duke my father with his power?
K. Rich. No matter where. Of comfort no man speak:
Let's talk of graves, of worms, and epitaphs;
Make dust our paper, and with rainy eyes
Write sorrow on the bosom of the earth;
Let's choose executors and talk of wills:
And yet not so—for what can we bequeath
Save our deposed bodies to the ground?
Our lands, our lives, and all are Bolingbroke's,
And nothing can we call our own but death,
And that small model of the barren earth
Which serves as paste and cover to our bones.
For God's sake, let us sit upon the ground
And tell sad stories of the death of kings:
How some have been depos'd, some slain in war,
Some haunted by the ghosts they have depos'd,
Some poison'd by their wives, some sleeping kill'd;
All murder'd: for within the hollow crown
That rounds the mortal temples of a king
Keeps Death his court, and there the antick sits,
Scoffing his state and grinning at his pomp;
Allowing him a breath, a little scene,
To monarchize, be fear'd, and kill with looks,
Infusing him with self and vain conceit
As if this flesh which walls about our life
Were brass impregnable; and humour'd thus
Comes at the last, and with a little pin
Bores through his castle wall, and farewell king!
Cover your heads, and mock not flesh and blood
With solemn reverence: throw away respect,
Tradition, form, and ceremonious duty,
For you have but mistook me all this while:
I live with bread like you, feel want,
Taste grief, need friends: subjected thus,
How can you say to me I am a king? (III. ii. 143–77)

K. Rich. I have been studying how I may compare
This prison where I live unto the world:
And for because the world is populous,
And here is not a creature but myself,
I cannot do it; yet I'll hammer it out.

My brain I'll prove the female to my soul;
My soul the father: and these two beget
A generation of still-breeding thoughts,
And these same thoughts people this little world
In humours like the people of this world.
For no thought is contented. The better sort,
As thoughts of things divine, are intermix'd
With scruples, and do set the word itself
Against the word:
As thus, 'Come, little ones;' and then again,
'It is as hard to come as for a camel
To thread the postern of a needle's eye.'
Thoughts tending to ambition, they do plot
Unlikely wonders; how these vain weak nails
May tear a passage through the flinty ribs
Of this hard world, my ragged prison walls;
And, for they cannot, die in their own pride.
Thoughts tending to content flatter themselves
That they are not the first of fortune's slaves,
Nor shall not be the last; like silly beggars
Who sitting in the stocks refuge their shame,
That many have and others must sit there:
And in this thought they find a kind of ease,
Bearing their own misfortune on the back
Of such as have before endur'd the like.
Thus play I in one person many people,
And none contented: sometimes am I king;
Then treason makes me wish myself a beggar,
And so I am: then crushing penury
Persuades me I was better when a king;
Then am I king'd again; and by and by
Think that I am unking'd by Bolingbroke,
And straight am nothing: but whate'er I be,
Nor I nor any man that but man is
With nothing shall be pleas'd, till he be eas'd
With being nothing. Music do I hear?   [*Music.*
Ha, ha! keep time. How sour sweet music is
When time is broke and no proportion kept!
So is it in the music of men's lives.
And here have I the daintiness of ear
To check time broke in a disorder'd string;
But for the concord of my state and time
Had not an ear to hear my true time broke.
I wasted time, and now doth time waste me;

For now hath time made me his numbering clock:
My thoughts are minutes, and with sighs they jar
Their watches on unto mine eyes, the outward watch,
Whereto my finger, like a dial's point,
Is pointing still, in cleansing them from tears.
Now sir, the sound that tells what hour it is
Are clamorous groans, that strike upon my heart
Which is the bell: so sighs and tears and groans
Show minutes, times, and hours; but my time
Runs posting on in Bolingbroke's proud joy,
While I stand fooling here, his Jack o' the clock.
This music mads me: let it sound no more;
For though it have holp madmen to their wits,
In me it seems it will make wise men mad.
Yet blessing on his heart that gives it me!
For 'tis a sign of love, and love to Richard
Is a strange brooch in this all-hating world.   (v. v. 1-66)

from *King John*

   Arthur. Must you with hot irons burn out both mine eyes?
   Hubert. Young boy, I must.
   Arth.   And will you?
   Hub.   And I will.
   Arth. Have you the heart? When your head did but ache,
I knit my handkercher about your brows,—
The best I had, a princess wrought it me,—
And I did never ask it you again;
And with my hand at midnight held your head,
And like the watchful minutes to the hour,
Still and anon cheer'd up the heavy time,
Saying, 'What lack you?' and, 'Where lies your grief?'
Or, 'What good love may I perform for you?'
Many a poor man's son would have lain still,
And ne'er have spoke a loving word to you;
But you at your sick-service had a prince.
Nay, you may think my love was crafty love,
And call it cunning: do an if you will.
If heaven be pleas'd that you must use me ill,
Why then you must. Will you put out mine eyes?
These eyes that never did nor never shall
So much as frown on you?

Hub.   I have sworn to do it;
And with hot irons must I burn them out.
    Arth. Ah! none but in this iron age would do it!
The iron of itself, though heat red-hot,
Approaching near these eyes, would drink my tears
And quench this fiery indignation
Even in the matter of mine innocence;
Nay, after that, consume away in rust,
But for containing fire to harm mine eye.
Are you more stubborn-hard than hammer'd iron?
An if an angel should have come to me
And told me Hubert should put out mine eyes,
I would not have believ'd him; no tongue but Hubert's.
    Hub. [*Stamps.*] Come forth.

                    Re-enter Attendants, *with cord, irons, &c.*

Do as I bid you do.
    Arth. O! save me, Hubert, save me! my eyes are out
Even with the fierce looks of these bloody men.
    Hub. Give me the iron, I say, and bind him here.
    Arth. Alas! what need you be so boisterous-rough?
I will not struggle; I will stand stone-still.
For heaven's sake, Hubert, let me not be bound!
Nay, hear me, Hubert: drive these men away,
And I will sit as quiet as a lamb;
I will not stir, nor wince, nor speak a word,
Nor look upon the iron angerly.
Thrust but these men away, and I'll forgive you,
Whatever torment you do put me to.
    Hub. Go, stand within: let me alone with him.
    First Attend. I am best pleas'd to be from such a deed.

                                                  [*Exeunt* Attendants.

    Arth. Alas! I then have chid away my friend:
He hath a stern look, but a gentle heart.
Let him come back, that his compassion may
Give life to yours.
    Hub.   Come, boy, prepare yourself.
    Arth. Is there no remedy?
    Hub.   None, but to lose your eyes.
    Arth. O heaven! that there were but a mote in yours,
A grain, a dust, a gnat, a wandering hair,
Any annoyance in that precious sense;
Then feeling what small things are boisterous there,
Your vile intent must needs seem horrible.
    Hub. Is this your promise? go to, hold your tongue.
    Arth. Hubert, the utterance of a brace of tongues

Must needs want pleading for a pair of eyes:
Let me not hold my tongue; let me not, Hubert:
Or Hubert, if you will, cut out my tongue,
So I may keep mine eyes: O! spare mine eyes,
Though to no use but still to look on you:
Lo! by my troth, the instrument is cold
And would not harm me.
   Hub.   I can heat it, boy.
   Arth. No, in good sooth; the fire is dead with grief,
Being create for comfort, to be us'd
In undeserv'd extremes: see else yourself;
There is no malice in this burning coal;
The breath of heaven hath blown his spirit out
And strew'd repentant ashes on his head.
   Hub. But with my breath I can revive it, boy.
   Arth. An if you do you will but make it blush
And glow with shame of your proceedings, Hubert:
Nay, it perchance will sparkle in your eyes;
And like a dog that is compell'd to fight,
Snatch at his master that doth tarre him on.
All things that you should use to do me wrong
Deny their office: only you do lack
That mercy which fierce fire and iron extends,
Creatures of note for mercy-lacking uses.
   Hub. Well, see to live; I will not touch thine eyes
For all the treasure that thine uncle owes:
Yet am I sworn and I did purpose, boy,
With this same very iron to burn them out.
   Arth. O! now you look like Hubert, all this while
You were disguised.
   Hub.   Peace! no more. Adieu.
Your uncle must not know but you are dead;
I'll fill these dogged spies with false reports:
And, pretty child, sleep doubtless and secure,
That Hubert for the wealth of all the world
Will not offend thee.   (IV. i. 39–132)

   Bastard. This England never did, nor never shall,
Lie at the proud foot of a conqueror,
But when it first did help to wound itself.
Now these her princes are come home again,
Come the three corners of the world in arms,
And we shall shock them. Nought shall make us rue,
If England to itself do rest but true.   (v. vii. 112–18)

from *The Merchant of Venice*

Enter ANTONIO, SALARINO, *and* SALANIO.

Antonio. In sooth, I know not why I am so sad:
It wearies me; you say it wearies you;
But how I caught it, found it, or came by it,
What stuff 'tis made of, whereof it is born,
I am to learn;
And such a want-wit sadness makes of me,
That I have much ado to know myself.
Salarino. Your mind is tossing on the ocean;
There, where your argosies with portly sail,—
Like signiors and rich burghers on the flood,
Or, as it were, the pageants of the sea,—
Do overpeer the petty traffickers,
That curtsy to them, do them reverence,
As they fly by them with their woven wings.
Salanio. Believe me, sir, had I such venture forth,
The better part of my affections would
Be with my hopes abroad. I should be still
Plucking the grass to know where sits the wind;
Peering in maps for ports, and piers, and roads;
And every object that might make me fear
Misfortune to my ventures, out of doubt
Would make me sad.
Salar.　　　　My wind, cooling my broth,
Would blow me to an ague, when I thought
What harm a wind too great might do at sea.
I should not see the sandy hour-glass run
But I should think of shallows and of flats.
And see my wealthy Andrew dock'd in sand
Vailing her high-top lower than her ribs
To kiss her burial. Should I go to church
And see the holy edifice of stone,
And not bethink me straight of dangerous rocks,
Which touching but my gentle vessel's side
Would scatter all her spices on the stream,
Enrobe the roaring waters with my silks;
And, in a word, but even now worth this,
And now worth nothing? Shall I have the thought
To think on this, and shall I lack the thought
That such a thing bechanc'd would make me sad?
But tell not me: I know Antonio
Is sad to think upon his merchandise.

Ant. Believe me, no: I thank my fortune for it.
My ventures are not in one bottom trusted,
Nor to one place; nor is my whole estate
Upon the fortune of this present year:
Therefore, my merchandise makes me not sad.
  Salar. Why, then you are in love.
  Ant.   Fie, fie!
  Salar. Not in love neither? Then let's say you are sad,
Because you are not merry: and 'twere as easy
For you to laugh and leap, and say you are merry,
Because you are not sad. Now, by two-headed Janus,
Nature hath fram'd strange fellows in her time:
Some that will evermore peep through their eyes
And laugh like parrots at a bag-piper,
And other of such vinegar aspect
That they'll not show their teeth in way of smile,
Though Nestor swear the jest be laughable.   (I. i. 1–56)

> Flourish of Cornets. Enter PORTIA, with the
> PRINCE OF MOROCCO, and their Trains.

  Portia. Go, draw aside the curtain, and discover
The several caskets to this noble prince.
Now make your choice.
  Morocco. The first, of gold, which this inscription bears:
Who chooseth me shall gain what many men desire.
The second, silver, which this promise carries:
Who chooseth me shall get as much as he deserves.
This third, dull lead, with warning all as blunt:
Who chooseth me must give and hazard all he hath.
How shall I know if I do choose the right?
  Por. The one of them contains my picture, prince:
If you choose that, then I am yours withal.
  Mor. Some god direct my judgment! Let me see:
I will survey the inscriptions back again:
What says this leaden casket?
Who chooseth me must give and hazard all he hath.
Must give: For what? for lead? hazard for lead?
This casket threatens. Men that hazard all
Do it in hope of fair advantages:
A golden mind stoops not to shows of dross;
I'll then nor give nor hazard aught for lead.
What says the silver with her virgin hue?
Who chooseth me shall get as much as he deserves.
As much as he deserves! Pause there, Morocco,

And weigh thy value with an even hand.
If thou be'st rated by thy estimation,
Thou dost deserve enough; and yet enough
May not extend so far as to the lady:
And yet to be afeard of my deserving
Were but a weak disabling of myself.
As much as I deserve! Why, that's the lady:
I do in birth deserve her, and in fortunes,
In graces, and in qualities of breeding;
But more than these, in love I do deserve.
What if I stray'd no further, but chose here?
Let's see once more this saying grav'd in gold:
Who chooseth me shall gain what many men desire.
Why, that's the lady: all the world desires her;
From the four corners of the earth they come,
To kiss this shrine, this mortal-breathing saint:
The Hyrcanian deserts and the vasty wilds
Of wide Arabia are as throughfares now
For princes to come view fair Portia:
The watery kingdom, whose ambitious head
Spits in the face of heaven, is no bar
To stop the foreign spirits, but they come,
As o'er a brook, to see fair Portia.
One of these three contains her heavenly picture.
Is't like that lead contains her? 'Twere damnation
To think so base a thought: it were too gross
To rib her cerecloth in the obscure grave.
Or shall I think in silver she's immur'd,
Being ten times undervalu'd to tried gold?
O sinful thought! Never so rich a gem
Was set in worse than gold. They have in England
A coin that bears the figure of an angel
Stamped in gold, but that's insculp'd upon;
But here an angel in a golden bed
Lies all within. Deliver me the key:
Here do I choose, and thrive I as I may!
   Por. There, take it, prince; and if my form lie there,
Then I am yours.   *[He unlocks the golden casket.*
   Mor.   O hell! what have we here?
A carrion Death, within whose empty eye
There is a written scroll. I'll read the writing.

         All that glisters is not gold;
         Often have you heard that told:

Many a man his life hath sold
But my outside to behold:
Gilded tombs do worms infold.
Had you been as wise as bold,
Young in limbs, in judgment old,
Your answer had not been inscroll'd:
Fare you well; your suit is cold.

Cold, indeed; and labour lost:
  Then, farewell, heat, and welcome, frost!
Portia, adieu. I have too griev'd a heart
To take a tedious leave: thus losers part.   (ii. vii. 1–77)

  Lorenzo. How sweet the moonlight sleeps upon this bank!
Here will we sit, and let the sounds of music
Creep in our ears: soft stillness and the night
Become the touches of sweet harmony.
Sit, Jessica: look, how the floor of heaven
Is thick inlaid with patines of bright gold:
There's not the smallest orb which thou behold'st
But in his motion like an angel sings,
Still quiring to the young-eyed cherubins;
Such harmony is in immortal souls;
But, whilst this muddy vesture of decay
Doth grossly close it in, we cannot hear it.

Enter Musicians.

Come, ho! and wake Diana with a hymn:
With sweetest touches pierce your mistress' ear,
And draw her home with music.   [*Music.*
  Jessica. I am never merry when I hear sweet music.
  Lor. The reason is, your spirits are attentive:
For do but note a wild and wanton herd,
Or race of youthful and unhandled colts,
Fetching mad bounds, bellowing and neighing loud,
Which is the hot condition of their blood;
If they but hear perchance a trumpet sound,
Or any air of music touch their ears,
You shall perceive them make a mutual stand,
Their savage eyes turn'd to a modest gaze
By the sweet power of music: therefore the poet
Did feign that Orpheus drew trees, stones, and floods;
Since nought so stockish, hard, and full of rage,
But music for the time doth change his nature.
The man that hath no music in himself,
Nor is not mov'd with concord of sweet sounds,

83

Is fit for treasons, stratagems, and spoils;
The motions of his spirit are dull as night,
And his affections dark as Erebus:
Let no such man be trusted. Mark the music.   (v. i. 54–88)

from *1 Henry IV*

ACT 1

SCENE I.—*London. The Palace.*

Enter KING HENRY, WESTMORELAND, *and Others.*

   K. Henry. So shaken as we are, so wan with care,
Find we a time for frighted peace to pant,
And breathe short-winded accents of new broils
To be commenc'd in stronds afar remote.
No more the thirsty entrance of this soil
Shall daub her lips with her own children's blood;
No more shall trenching war channel her fields,
Nor bruise her flowerets with the armed hoofs
Of hostile paces: those opposed eyes,
Which, like the meteors of a troubled heaven,
All of one nature, of one substance bred,
Did lately meet in the intestine shock
And furious close of civil butchery,
Shall now, in mutual well-beseeming ranks,
March all one way, and be no more oppos'd
Against acquaintance, kindred, and allies:
The edge of war, like an ill-sheathed knife,
No more shall cut his master. Therefore, friends,
As far as to the sepulchre of Christ,—
Whose soldier now, under whose blessed cross
We are impressed and engag'd to fight,—
Forthwith a power of English shall we levy,
Whose arms were moulded in their mother's womb
To chase these pagans in those holy fields
Over whose acres walk'd those blessed feet,
Which fourteen hundred years ago were nail'd
For our advantage on the bitter cross.   (I. i. 1–27)

   Vernon.   I have learn'd,
The king himself in person is set forth,
Or hitherwards intended speedily,
With strong and mighty preparation.

Hotspur. He shall be welcome too. Where is his son,
The nimble-footed madcap Prince of Wales,
And his comrades, that daff'd the world aside,
And bid it pass?
    Ver.   All furnish'd, all in arms,
All plum'd like estridges that wing the wind,
Baited like eagles having lately bath'd,
Glittering in golden coats, like images,
As full of spirit as the month of May,
And gorgeous as the sun at midsummer,
Wanton as youthful goats, wild as young bulls.
I saw young Harry, with his beaver on,
His cushes on his thighs, gallantly arm'd,
Rise from the ground like feather'd Mercury,
And vaulted with such ease into his seat,
As if an angel dropp'd down from the clouds,
To turn and wind a fiery Pegasus
And witch the world with noble horsemanship.
    Hot. No more, no more: worse than the sun in March
This praise doth nourish agues. Let them come;
They come like sacrifices in their trim,
And to the fire-ey'd maid of smoky war
All hot and bleeding will we offer them:
The mailed Mars shall on his altar sit
Up to the ears in blood. I am on fire
To hear this rich reprisal is so nigh
And yet not ours. Come, let me taste my horse,
Who is to bear me like a thunderbolt
Against the bosom of the Prince of Wales: (IV. i. 90-121)

    Hot. O, Harry! thou hast robb'd me of my youth.
I better brook the loss of brittle life
Than those proud titles thou hast won of me;
They wound my thoughts worse than thy sword my flesh:
But thought's the slave of life, and life time's fool;
And time, that takes survey of all the world,
Must have a stop. O! I could prophesy,
But that the earthy and cold hand of death
Lies on my tongue. No, Percy, thou art dust,
And food for—   [*Dies.*
    Prince. For worms, brave Percy. Fare thee well, great heart!
Ill-weav'd ambition, how much art thou shrunk!
When that this body did contain a spirit,
A kingdom for it was too small a bound;

But now, two paces of the vilest earth
Is room enough: this earth, that bears thee dead,
Bears not alive so stout a gentleman.
If thou wert sensible of courtesy,
I should not make so dear a show of zeal:
But let my favours hide thy mangled face,
And, even in thy behalf, I'll thank myself
For doing these fair rites of tenderness.
Adieu, and take thy praise with thee to heaven!
Thy ignomy sleep with thee in the grave,
But not remember'd in thy epitaph!   [*He spies* FALSTAFF *on the ground.*
What! old acquaintance! could not all this flesh
Keep in a little life? Poor Jack, farewell!
I could have better spar'd a better man.
O! I should have a heavy miss of thee
If I were much in love with vanity.
Death hath not struck so fat a deer to-day,
Though many dearer, in this bloody fray.
Embowell'd will I see thee by and by:
Till then in blood by noble Percy lie.   [*Exit.*
    Falstaff. [*Rising.*] Embowelled! if thou embowel me to-day, I'll give
you leave to powder me and eat me too, to-morrow.

(v. iv. 77–113)

from 2 *Henry IV*

K. Henry. But wherefore did he take away the crown?

Re-enter the PRINCE.

Lo, where he comes. Come hither to me, Harry.
Depart the chamber, leave us here alone.

[*Exeunt* WARWICK, *and the rest.*

    Prince. I never thought to hear you speak again.
    K. Hen. Thy wish was father, Harry, to that thought:
I stay too long by thee, I weary thee.
Dost thou so hunger for my empty chair
That thou wilt needs invest thee with mine honours
Before thy hour be ripe? O foolish youth!
Thou seek'st the greatness that will overwhelm thee.
Stay but a little; for my cloud of dignity
Is held from falling with so weak a wind
That it will quickly drop: my day is dim.

Thou hast stol'n that which after some few hours
Were thine without offence; and at my death
Thou hast seal'd up my expectation:
Thy life did manifest thou lov'dst me not,
And thou wilt have me die assur'd of it.
Thou hid'st a thousand daggers in thy thoughts,
Which thou hast whetted on thy stony heart,
To stab at half an hour of my life.
What! canst thou not forbear me half an hour?
Then get thee gone and dig my grave thyself,
And bid the merry bells ring to thine ear
That thou art crowned, not that I am dead.
Let all the tears that should bedew my hearse
Be drops of balm to sanctify thy head:
Only compound me with forgotten dust;
Give that which gave thee life unto the worms.
Pluck down my officers, break my decrees;
For now a time is come to mock at form.
Harry the Fifth is crown'd! Up, vanity!
Down, royal state! all you sage counsellors, hence!
And to the English court assemble now,
From every region, apes of idleness!
Now, neighbour confines, purge you of your scum:
Have you a ruffian that will swear, drink, dance,
Revel the night, rob, murder, and commit
The oldest sins the newest kind of ways?
Be happy, he will trouble you no more;
England shall double gild his treble guilt.
England shall give him office, honour, might;
For the fifth Harry from curb'd licence plucks
The muzzle of restraint, and the wild dog
Shall flesh his tooth in every innocent. (IV. v. 87–131)

K. Henry V. This new and gorgeous garment, majesty,
Sits not so easy on me as you think.
Brothers, you mix your sadness with some fear:
This is the English, not the Turkish court;
Not Amurath an Amurath succeeds,
But Harry Harry. Yet be sad, good brothers,
For, to speak truth, it very well becomes you:
Sorrow so royally in you appears
That I will deeply put the fashion on
And wear it in my heart. Why then, be sad;
But entertain no more of it, good brothers,

Than a joint burden laid upon us all.
For me, by heaven, I bid you be assur'd,
I'll be your father and your brother too;
Let me but bear your love, I'll bear your cares:
Yet weep that Harry's dead, and so will I;
But Harry lives that shall convert those tears
By number into hours of happiness.   (v. i. 44–61)

from *Much Ado About Nothing*

Balthazar. O! good my lord, tax not so bad a voice
To slander music any more than once.
Don Pedro. It is the witness still of excellency,
To put a strange face on his own perfection.
I pray thee, sing, and let me woo no more.
Balth.   Because you talk of wooing, I will sing;
Since many a wooer doth commence his suit
To her he thinks not worthy; yet he woos;
Yet will he swear he loves.
D. Pedro.   Nay, pray thee, come;
Or if thou wilt hold longer argument,
Do it in notes.
Balth.   Note this before my notes;
There's not a note of mine that's worth the noting.
D. Pedro. Why these are very crotchets that he speaks;
Notes, notes, forsooth, and nothing!   [*Music.*
Benedick. Now, divine air! now is his soul ravished! Is it not strange
that sheeps' guts should hale souls out of men's bodies? Well, a horn for
my money, when all's done.

BALTHAZAR *sings.*

Sigh no more, ladies, sigh no more,
  Men were deceivers ever;
One foot in sea, and one on shore,
  To one thing constant never.
    Then sigh not so,
    But let them go,
  And be you blithe and bonny,
Converting all your sounds of woe
  Into Hey nonny, nonny.

Sing no more ditties, sing no mo
  Of dumps so dull and heavy;
The fraud of men was ever so,
  Since summer first was leavy.

> Then sigh not so,
> But let them go,
> And be you blithe and bonny,
> Converting all your sounds of woe
> Into Hey nonny, nonny.

(II. iii. 47–82)

SCENE III.—*A Church-yard before a sepulchre. Night.*

Enter DON PEDRO, CLAUDIO, *and* Attendants,
with music and tapers.

Claudio. Is this the monument of Leonato?
A Lord. It is, my lord.
Claud. [*Reads from a scroll.*]

> Done to death by slanderous tongues
> Was the Hero that here lies:
> Death, in guerdon of her wrongs,
> Gives her fame which never dies.
> So the life that died with shame
> Lives in death with glorious fame.

Hang thou there upon the tomb,
Praising her when I am dumb.
Now, music, sound, and sing your solemn hymn.

SONG

> Pardon, goddess of the night,
> Those that slew thy virgin knight;
> For the which, with songs of woe,
> Round about her tomb they go.
> Midnight, assist our moan;
> Help us to sigh and groan,
> Heavily, heavily:
> Graves, yawn and yield your dead,
> Till death be uttered,
> Heavily, heavily.

Claud. Now, unto thy bones good night!
Yearly will I do this rite.
D. Pedro. Good morrow, masters: put your torches out.
The wolves have prey'd; and look, the gentle day,
Before the wheels of Phœbus, round about
Dapples the drowsy east with spots of grey.
Thanks to you all, and leave us: fare you well.
Claud. Good morrow, masters: each his several way.
D. Pedro. Come, let us hence, and put on other weeds;
And then to Leonato's we will go.
Claud. And Hymen now with luckier issue speed's,
Than this for whom we render'd up this woe!

[*Exeunt.*

SCENE IV.—*A Room in* LEONATO'S *House.*

Enter LEONATO, ANTONIO, BENEDICK, BEATRICE, MARGARET, URSULA, FRIAR FRANCIS, *and* HERO.

Friar. Did I not tell you she was innocent?

Leonato. So are the prince and Claudio, who accus'd her
Upon the error that you heard debated:
But Margaret was in some fault for this,
Although against her will, as it appears
In the true course of all the question.

Antonio. Well, I am glad that all things sort so well.

Benedick. And so am I, being else by faith enforc'd
To call young Claudio to a reckoning for it.

Leon. Well, daughter, and you gentlewomen all,
Withdraw into a chamber by yourselves,
And when I send for you, come hither mask'd:
The prince and Claudio promis'd by this hour
To visit me.   [*Exeunt ladies.*
                You know your office, brother;
You must be father to your brother's daughter,
And give her to young Claudio.

Ant. Which I will do with confirm'd countenance.

Bene. Friar, I must entreat your pains, I think.

Friar. To do what, signior?

Bene. To bind me, or undo me; one of them.
Signior Leonato, truth it is, good signior,
Your niece regards me with an eye of favour.

Leon. That eye my daughter lent her: 'tis most true.

Bene. And I do with an eye of love requite her.

Leon. The sight whereof I think, you had from me,
From Claudio, and the prince. But what's your will?

Bene. Your answer, sir, is enigmatical:
But, for my will, my will is your good will
May stand with ours, this day to be conjoin'd
In the state of honourable marriage:
In which, good friar, I shall desire your help.

Leon. My heart is with your liking.

Friar.   And my help.
Here come the prince and Claudio.

Enter DON PEDRO *and* CLAUDIO, *with* Attendants.

D. Pedro. Good morrow to this fair assembly.

Leon. Good morrow, prince; good morrow, Claudio:
We here attend you. Are you yet determin'd
To-day to marry with my brother's daughter?

Claud. I'll hold my mind, were she an Ethiop.

Leon. Call her forth, brother: here's the friar ready.   [*Exit* ANTONIO.

D. Pedro. Good morrow, Benedick. Why, what's the matter,
That you have such a February face,
So full of frost, of storm and cloudiness?

Claud. I think he thinks upon the savage bull.
Tush! fear not, man, we'll tip thy horns with gold,
And all Europa shall rejoice at thee,
As once Europa did at lusty Jove,
When he would play the noble beast in love.

Bene. Bull Jove, sir, had an amiable low:
And some such strange bull leap'd your father's cow,
And got a calf in that same noble feat,
Much like to you, for you have just his bleat.

Claud. For this I owe you: here come other reckonings.

Re-enter ANTONIO, *with the ladies masked.*

Which is the lady I must seize upon?

Ant. This same is she, and I do give you her.

Claud. Why, then she's mine. Sweet, let me see your face.

Leon. No, that you shall not, till you take her hand
Before this friar, and swear to marry her.

Claud. Give me your hand: before this holy friar,
I am your husband, if you like of me.

Hero. And when I liv'd, I was your other wife: [*Unmasking.*
And when you lov'd, you were my other husband.

Claud. Another Hero!

Hero.   Nothing certainer:
One Hero died defil'd, but I do live,
And surely as I live, I am a maid.

D. Pedro. The former Hero! Hero that is dead!

Leon. She died, my lord, but whiles her slander liv'd.

Friar. All this amazement can I qualify:
When after that the holy rites are ended,
I'll tell you largely of fair Hero's death:
Meantime, let wonder seem familiar,
And to the chapel let us presently.

Bene. Soft and fair, friar. Which is Beatrice?

Beatrice. [*Unmasking.*] I answer to that name. What is your will?

Bene. Do not you love me?

Beat.   Why, no; no more than reason.

Bene. Why, then, your uncle and the prince and Claudio
Have been deceived; for they swore you did.

Beat. Do not you love me?

Bene. Troth, no; no more than reason.

Beat. Why, then, my cousin, Margaret, and Ursula,
Are much deceiv'd; for they did swear you did.

Bene. They swore that you were almost sick for me.

Beat. They swore that you were well-nigh dead for me.

Bene. 'Tis no such matter. Then, you do not love me?

Beat. No, truly, but in friendly recompense.

Leon. Come, cousin, I am sure you love the gentleman.

Claud. And I'll be sworn upon 't that he loves her;
For here's a paper written in his hand,
A halting sonnet of his own pure brain,
Fashion'd to Beatrice.

Hero. And here's another,
Writ in my cousin's hand, stolen from her pocket,
Containing her affection unto Benedick.

Bene. A miracle! here's our own hands against our hearts. Come, I will have thee; but, by this light, I take thee for pity.

Beat. I would not deny you; but, by this good day, I yield upon great persuasion, and partly to save your life, for I was told you were in a consumption.

Bene. Peace! I will stop your mouth. [*Kisses her.*

D. Pedro. How dost thou, Benedick, the married man?

Bene. I'll tell thee what, prince; a college of witcrackers cannot flout me out of my humour. Dost thou think I care for a satire or an epigram? No; if a man will be beaten with brains, a' shall wear nothing handsome about him. In brief, since I do purpose to marry, I will think nothing to any purpose that the world can say against it; and therefore never flout at me for what I have said against it, for man is a giddy thing, and this is my conclusion. For thy part, Claudio, I did think to have beaten thee; but, in that thou art like to be my kinsman, live unbruised, and love my cousin.

Claud. I had well hoped thou wouldst have denied Beatrice, that I might have cudgelled thee out of thy single life, to make thee a double-dealer; which, out of question, thou wilt be, if my cousin do not look exceeding narrowly to thee.

Bene. Come, come, we are friends. Let's have a dance ere we are married, that we may lighten our own hearts and our wives' heels.

Leon. We'll have dancing afterward.

Bene. First, of my word; therefore play, music! Prince, thou art sad; get thee a wife, get thee a wife: there is no staff more reverend than one tipped with horn.

Enter a Messenger.

Mes. My lord, your brother John is ta'en in flight,
And brought with armed men back to Messina.

Bene. Think not on him till to-morrow: I'll devise thee brave punishments for him. Strike up, pipers!   [*Dance. Exeunt.*

(v. iii–iv)

from *Henry V*

Chorus. O! for a Muse of fire, that would ascend
The brightest heaven of invention;
A kingdom for a stage, princes to act
And monarchs to behold the swelling scene.
Then should the war-like Harry, like himself,
Assume the port of Mars; and at his heels,
Leash'd in like hounds, should famine, sword, and fire
Crouch for employment. But pardon, gentles all,
The flat unraised spirits that hath dar'd
On this unworthy scaffold to bring forth
So great an object: can this cockpit hold
The vasty fields of France? or may we cram
Within this wooden O the very casques
That did affright the air at Agincourt?
O, pardon! since a crooked figure may
Attest in little place a million;
And let us, ciphers to this great accompt,
On your imaginary forces work.   (I. i. Prologue)

Canterbury. The king is full of grace and fair regard.
Ely. And a true lover of the holy church.
Cant. The courses of his youth promis'd it not.
The breath no sooner left his father's body
But that his wildness, mortified in him,
Seem'd to die too; yea, at that very moment,
Consideration like an angel came,
And whipp'd the offending Adam out of him,
Leaving his body as a paradise,
To envelop and contain celestial spirits.   (I. i. 22–31)

Cant. Therefore doth heaven divide
The state of man in divers functions,
Setting endeavour in continual motion;
To which is fixed, as an aim or butt,
Obedience: for so work the honey-bees,
Creatures that by a rule in nature teach
The act of order to a peopled kingdom.

They have a king and officers of sorts;
Where some, like magistrates correct at home,
Others, like merchants, venture trade abroad,
Others, like soldiers, armed in their stings,
Make boot upon the summer's velvet buds;
Which pillage they with merry march bring home
To the tent-royal of their emperor:
Who, busied in his majesty, surveys
The singing masons building roofs of gold,
The civil citizens kneading up the honey,
The poor mechanic porters crowding in
Their heavy burdens at his narrow gate,
The sad-ey'd justice, with his surly hum,
Delivering o'er to executors pale
The lazy yawning drone. I this infer,
That many things, having full reference
To one consent, may work contrariously;
As many arrows, loosed several ways,
Fly to one mark; as many ways meet in one town;
As many fresh streams meet in one salt sea;
As many lines close in the dial's centre;
So may a thousand actions, once afoot,
End in one purpose, and be all well borne
Without defeat.   (I. ii. 183–213)

    Chor. Thus with imagin'd wing our swift scene flies
In motion of no less celerity
Than that of thought. Suppose that you have seen
The well-appointed king at Hampton pier
Embark his royalty; and his brave fleet
With silken streamers the young Phœbus fanning:
Play with your fancies, and in them behold
Upon the hempen tackle ship-boys climbing;
Hear the shrill whistle which doth order give
To sounds confus'd; behold the threaden sails,
Borne with the invisible and creeping wind,
Draw the huge bottoms through the furrow'd sea,
Breasting the lofty surge. O! do but think
You stand upon the rivage and behold
A city on the inconstant billows dancing;
For so appears this fleet majestical,
Holding due course to Harfleur. Follow, follow!
Grapple your minds to sternage of this navy,
And leave your England, as dead midnight still,

Guarded with grandsires, babies, and old women,
Either past or not arriv'd to pitch and puissance:
For who is he, whose chin is but enrich'd
With one appearing hair, that will not follow
Those cull'd and choice-drawn cavaliers to France?
Work, work your thoughts, and therein see a siege;
Behold the ordenance on their carriages.
With fatal mouths gaping on girded Harfleur.
Suppose the ambassador from the French comes back;
Tells Harry that the king doth offer him
Katharine his daughter; and with her, to dowry,
Some petty and unprofitable dukedoms:
The offer likes not: and the nimble gunner
With linstock now the devilish cannon touches.

[Alarum; and chambers go off.

And down goes all before them. Still be kind,
And eke out our performance with your mind. [Exit.

(III. Prologue)

K. Henry. Once more unto the breach, dear friends, once more;
Or close the wall up with our English dead!
In peace there's nothing so becomes a man
As modest stillness and humility:
But when the blast of war blows in our ears,
Then imitate the action of the tiger;
Stiffen the sinews, summon up the blood,
Disguise fair nature with hard-favour'd rage;
Then lend the eye a terrible aspect;
Let it pry through the portage of the head
Like the brass cannon; let the brow o'erwhelm it
As fearfully as doth a galled rock
O'erhang and jutty his confounded base,
Swill'd with the wild and wasteful ocean.
Now set the teeth and stretch the nostril wide,
Hold hard the breath, and bend up every spirit
To his full height! On, on, you noblest English!
Whose blood is fet from fathers of war-proof;
Fathers that, like so many Alexanders,
Have in these parts from morn til even fought,
And sheath'd their swords for lack of argument.
Dishonour not your mothers; now attest
That those whom you call'd fathers did beget you.
Be copy now to men of grosser blood.
And teach them how to war. And you, good yeomen,

Whose limbs were made in England, show us here
The mettle of your pasture; let us swear
That you are worth your breeding; which I doubt not;
For there is none of you so mean and base
That hath not noble lustre in your eyes.
I see you stand like greyhounds in the slips,
Straining upon the start. The game's afoot:
Follow your spirit; and, upon this charge
Cry 'God for Harry! England and Saint George!'   (III. i. 1–34)

 Chor. Now entertain conjecture of a time
When creeping murmur and the poring dark
Fills the wide vessel of the universe.
From camp to camp, through the foul womb of night,
The hum of either army stilly sounds,
That the fix'd sentinels almost receive
The secret whispers of each other's watch:
Fire answers fire, and through their paly flames
Each battle sees the other's umber'd face:
Steed threatens steed, in high and boastful neighs
Piercing the night's dull ear; and from the tents
The armourers, accomplishing the knights,
With busy hammers closing rivets up,
Give dreadful note of preparation.
The country cocks do crow, the clocks do toll,
And the third hour of drowsy morning name.
Proud of their numbers, and secure in soul,
The confident and over-lusty French
Do the low-rated English play at dice;
And chide the cripple tardy-gaited night
Who, like a foul and ugly witch, doth limp
So tediously away. The poor condemned English,
Like sacrifices, by their watchful fires
Sit patiently, and inly ruminate
The morning's danger, and their gesture sad
Investing lank-lean cheeks and war-worn coats
Presenteth them unto the gazing moon
So many horrid ghosts. O! now, who will behold
The royal captain of this ruin'd band
Walking from watch to watch, from tent to tent,
Let him cry 'Praise and glory on his head!'
For forth he goes and visits all his host,
Bids them good morrow with a modest smile,
And calls them brothers, friends, and countrymen.

WILLIAM SHAKESPEARE

Upon his royal face there is no note
How dread an army hath enrounded him;
Nor doth he dedicate one jot of colour
Unto the weary and all-watched night:
But freshly looks and overbears attaint
With cheerful semblance and sweet majesty;
That every wretch, pining and pale before,
Beholding him, plucks comfort from his looks.
A largess universal, like the sun
His liberal eye doth give to every one,
Thawing cold fear. Then mean and gentle all,
Behold, as may unworthiness define,
A little touch of Harry in the night.   (IV. Prologue, 1-47)

    Westmoreland. O! that we now had here
But one ten thousand of those men in England
That do no work to-day.
    K. Henry.   What's he that wishes so?
My cousin Westmoreland? No, my fair cousin:
If we are mark'd to die, we are enow
To do our country loss; and if to live,
The fewer men, the greater share of honour.
God's will! I pray thee, wish not one man more.
By Jove, I am not covetous for gold,
Nor care I who doth feed upon my cost;
It yearns me not if men my garments wear;
Such outward things dwell not in my desires:
But if it be a sin to covet honour,
I am the most offending soul alive.
No, faith, my coz, wish not a man from England:
God's peace! I would not lose so great an honour
As one man more, methinks, would share from me,
For the best hope I have. O! do not wish one more:
Rather proclaim it, Westmoreland, through my host,
That he which hath no stomach to this fight,
Let him depart; his passport shall be made,
And crowns for convoy put into his purse:
We would not die in that man's company
That fears his fellowship to die with us.
This day is call'd the feast of Crispian:
He that outlives this day, and comes safe home,
Will stand a tip-toe when this day is nam'd,
And rouse him at the name of Crispian.
He that shall live this day, and see old age,

97

WILLIAM SHAKESPEARE

Will yearly on the vigil feast his neighbours,
And say, 'To-morrow is Saint Crispian:'
Then will he strip his sleeve and show his scars,
And say, 'These wounds I had on Crispin's day.'
Old men forget: yet all shall be forgot,
But he'll remember with advantages
What feats he did that day. Then shall our names,
Familiar in his mouth as household words,
Harry the king, Bedford and Exeter,
Warwick and Talbot, Salisbury and Gloucester,
Be in their flowing cups freshly remember'd.
This story shall the good man teach his son;
And Crispin Crispian shall ne'er go by,
From this day to the ending of the world,
But we in it shall be remembered;
We few, we happy few, we band of brothers;
For he to-day that sheds his blood with me
Shall be my brother; be he ne'er so vile
This day shall gentle his condition:
And gentlemen in England now a-bed
Shall think themselves accurs'd they were not here,
And hold their manhoods cheap whiles any speaks
That fought with us upon Saint Crispin's day. (IV. iii. 16-67)

from *Julius Caesar*

Casca. Who ever knew the heavens menace so?
Cassius. Those that have known the earth so full of faults.
For my part, I have walk'd about the streets,
Submitting me unto the perilous night,
And, thus unbraced, Casca, as you see,
Have bar'd my bosom to the thunder-stone;
And, when the cross blue lightning seem'd to open
The breast of heaven, I did present myself
Even in the aim and very flash of it.
Casca. But wherefore did you so much tempt the heavens?
It is the part of men to fear and tremble
When the most mighty gods by tokens send
Such dreadful heralds to astonish us.
Cas. You are dull, Casca, and those sparks of life
That should be in a Roman you do want,
Or else you use not. You look pale, and gaze,
And put on fear, and cast yourself in wonder,

98

To see the strange impatience of the heavens;
But if you would consider the true cause
Why all these fires, why all these gliding ghosts,
Why birds and beasts, from quality and kind;
Why old men, fools, and children calculate;
Why all these things change from their ordinance,
Their natures, and pre-formed faculties,
To monstrous quality, why, you shall find
That heaven hath infus'd them with these spirits
To make them instruments of fear and warning
Unto some monstrous state.
Now could I, Casca, name to thee a man
Most like this dreadful night,
That thunders, lightens, opens graves, and roars
As doth the lion in the Capitol,
A man no mightier than thyself or me
In personal action, yet prodigious grown
And fearful as these strange eruptions are.
   Casca. 'Tis Cæsar that you mean; is it not, Cassius?
   Cas. Let it be who it is: for Romans now
Have thews and limbs like to their ancestors;
But, woe the while! our fathers' minds are dead,
And we are govern'd with our mothers' spirits;
Our yoke and sufferance show us womanish.
   Casca. Indeed, they say the senators to-morrow
Mean to establish Cæsar as a king;
And he shall wear his crown by sea and land,
In every place, save here in Italy.
   Cas. I know where I will wear this dagger then;
Cassius from bondage will deliver Cassius: (I. iii. 44–90)

   Brutus. Since Cassius first did whet me against Cæsar,
I have not slept.
Between the acting of a dreadful thing
And the first motion, all the interim is
Like a phantasma, or a hideous dream:
The genius and the mortal instruments
Are then in council; and the state of man,
Like to a little kingdom, suffers then
The nature of an insurrection.   (II. i. 61–9)

   Antonius. O mighty Cæsar! dost thou lie so low?
Are all thy conquests, glories, triumphs, spoils,
Shrunk to this little measure? Fare thee well.

I know not, gentlemen, what you intend,
Who else must be let blood, who else is rank:
If I myself, there is no hour so fit
As Cæsar's death's hour, nor no instrument
Of half that worth as those your swords, made rich
With the most noble blood of all this world.
I do beseech ye, if ye bear me hard,
Now, whilst your purpled hands do reek and smoke,
Fulfil your pleasure. Live a thousand years,
I shall not find myself so apt to die:
No place will please me so, no mean of death,
As here by Cæsar, and by you cut off,
The choice and master spirits of this age.

(III. i. 148-63)

Ant. O! pardon me, thou bleeding piece of earth,
That I am meek and gentle with these butchers;
Thou art the ruins of the noblest man
That ever lived in the tide of times.
Woe to the hand that shed this costly blood!
Over thy wounds now do I prophesy,
Which like dumb mouths do ope their ruby lips,
To beg the voice and utterance of my tongue,
A curse shall light upon the limbs of men;
Domestic fury and fierce civil strife
Shall cumber all the parts of Italy;
Blood and destruction shall be so in use,
And dreadful objects so familiar,
That mothers shall but smile when they behold
Their infants quarter'd with the hands of war;
All pity chok'd with custom of fell deeds:
And Cæsar's spirit, ranging for revenge,
With Ate by his side come hot from hell,
Shall in these confines with a monarch's voice
Cry 'Havoc!' and let slip the dogs of war;
That this foul deed shall smell above the earth
With carrion men, groaning for burial.

(III. i. 254-75)

Ant. Friends, Romans, countrymen, lend me your ears;
I come to bury Cæsar, not to praise him.
The evil that men do lives after them,
The good is oft interred with their bones;
So let it be with Cæsar. The noble Brutus
Hath told you Cæsar was ambitious;
If it were so, it was a grievous fault,

And grievously hath Cæsar answer'd it.
Here, under leave of Brutus and the rest,—
For Brutus is an honourable man;
So are they all, all honourable men,—
Come I to speak in Cæsar's funeral.
He was my friend, faithful and just to me:
But Brutus says he was ambitious;
And Brutus is an honourable man.
He hath brought many captives home to Rome,
Whose ransoms did the general coffers fill:
Did this in Cæsar seem ambitious?
When that the poor have cried, Cæsar hath wept;
Ambition should be made of sterner stuff:
Yet Brutus says he was ambitious;
And Brutus is an honourable man.
You all did see that on the Lupercal
I thrice presented him a kingly crown,
Which he did thrice refuse: was this ambition?
Yet Brutus says he was ambitious;
And, sure, he is an honourable man.
I speak not to disprove what Brutus spoke,
But here I am to speak what I do know.
You all did love him once, not without cause:
What cause withholds you then to mourn for him?
O judgment! thou art fled to brutish beasts,
And men have lost their reason. Bear with me;
My heart is in the coffin there with Cæsar,
And I must pause till it come back to me.   (III. ii. 79-113)

    Ant. If you have tears, prepare to shed them now.
You all do know this mantle: I remember
The first time ever Cæsar put it on;
'Twas on a summer's evening, in his tent,
That day he overcame the Nervii.
Look! in this place ran Cassius' dagger through:
See what a rent the envious Casca made:
Through this the well-beloved Brutus stabb'd;
And, as he pluck'd his cursed steel away,
Mark how the blood of Cæsar follow'd it,
As rushing out of doors, to be resolv'd
If Brutus so unkindly knock'd or no;
For Brutus, as you know, was Cæsar's angel:
Judge, O you gods! how dearly Cæsar lov'd him.
This was the most unkindest cut of all:

For when the noble Cæsar saw him stab,
Ingratitude, more strong than traitors' arms,
Quite vanquish'd him: then burst his mighty heart;
And, in his mantle muffling up his face,
Even at the base of Pompey's statua,
Which all the while ran blood, great Cæsar fell.
O! what a fall was there, my countrymen;
Then I, and you, and all of us fell down.
Whilst bloody treason flourish'd over us.
O! now you weep, and I perceive you feel
The dint of pity; these are gracious drops.
Kind souls, what! weep you when you but behold
Our Cæsar's vesture wounded? Look you here,
Here is himself, marr'd, as you see, with traitors.   (III. ii. 174-202)

   Messala. How died my master, Strato?
   Strato. I held the sword, and he did run on it.
   Mes. Octavius, then take him to follow thee,
That did the latest service to my master.
   Ant. This was the noblest Roman of them all;
All the conspirators save only he
Did that they did in envy of great Cæsar;
He only, in a general honest thought
And common good to all, made one of them.
His life was gentle, and the elements
So mix'd in him that Nature might stand up
And say to all the world, 'This was a man!'   (v. v. 64-75)

from *As You Like It*

   Duke Senior. Now, my co-mates and brothers in exile,
Hath not old custom made this life more sweet
Than that of painted pomp? Are not these woods
More free from peril than the envious court?
Here feel we but the penalty of Adam,
The seasons' difference; as, the icy fang
And churlish chiding of the winter's wind,
Which, when it bites and blows upon my body,
Even till I shrink with cold, I smile and say
'This is no flattery: these are counsellors
That feelingly persuade me what I am.'
Sweet are the uses of adversity,

Which like the toad, ugly and venomous,
Wears yet a precious jewel in his head;
And this our life exempt from public haunt,
Finds tongues in trees, books in the running brooks,
Sermons in stones, and good in every thing.
I would not change it.   (II. i. 1–18)

   Duke S. What would you have? Your gentleness shall force
More than your force move us to gentleness.
   Orlando. I almost die for food; and let me have it.
   Duke S. Sit down and feed, and welcome to our table.
   Orl. Speak you so gently? Pardon me, I pray you:
I thought that all things had been savage here,
And therefore put I on the countenance
Of stern commandment. But whate'er you are
That in this desert inaccessible,
Under the shade of melancholy boughs,
Lose and neglect the creeping hours of time;
If ever you have look'd on better days,
If ever been where bells have knoll'd to church,
If ever sat at any good man's feast,
If ever from your eyelids wip'd a tear,
And know what 'tis to pity, and be pitied,
Let gentleness my strong enforcement be:
In the which hope I blush, and hide my sword.
   Duke S. True is it that we have seen better days,
And have with holy bell been knoll'd to church,
And sat at good men's feasts, and wip'd our eyes
Of drops that sacred pity hath engender'd;
And therefore sit you down in gentleness
And take upon command what help we have
That to your wanting may be minister'd.
   Orl. Then but forbear your food a little while,
Whiles, like a doe, I go to find my fawn
And give it food. There is an old poor man,
Who after me hath many a weary step
Limp'd in pure love: till he be first suffic'd,
Oppress'd with two weak evils, age and hunger,
I will not touch a bit.
   Duke S.   Go find him out,
And we will nothing waste till you return.
   Orl. I thank ye; and be bless'd for your good comfort!   [*Exit.*
   Duke S. Thou seest we are not all alone unhappy:
This wide and universal theatre

Presents more woful pageants than the scene
Wherein we play in.
Jaques.   All the world's a stage,
And all the men and women merely players:
They have their exits and their entrances;
And one man in his time plays many parts,
His acts being seven ages. At first the infant,
Mewling and puking in the nurse's arms.
And then the whining school-boy, with his satchel,
And shining morning face, creeping like snail
Unwillingly to school. And then the lover,
Sighing like furnace, with a woful ballad
Made to his mistress' eyebrow. Then a soldier,
Full of strange oaths, and bearded like the pard,
Jealous in honour, sudden and quick in quarrel,
Seeking the bubble reputation
Even in the cannon's mouth. And then the justice,
In fair round belly with good capon lin'd,
With eyes severe, and beard of formal cut,
Full of wise saws and modern instances;
And so he plays his part. The sixth age shifts
Into the lean and slipper'd pantaloon,
With spectacles on nose and pouch on side,
His youthful hose well sav'd, a world too wide
For his shrunk shank; and his big manly voice,
Turning again toward childish treble, pipes
And whistles in his sound. Last scene of all,
That ends this strange eventful history,
Is second childishness and mere oblivion,
Sans teeth, sans eyes, sans taste, sans everything.

Re-enter ORLANDO, *with* ADAM.

Duke S. Welcome. Set down your venerable burden,
And let him feed.
Orl.   I thank you most for him.   (II. vii. 102–68)

SONG

Amiens. Blow, blow, thou winter wind,
            Thou art not so unkind
              As man's ingratitude;
            Thy tooth is not so keen,
            Because thou art not seen,
              Although thy breath be rude.
Heigh-ho! sing, heigh-ho! unto the green holly:
Most friendship is feigning, most loving mere folly.
        Then heigh-ho! the holly!
        This life is most jolly.

Freeze, freeze, thou bitter sky,
That dost not bite so nigh
     As benefits forgot:
Though thou the waters warp,
Thy sting is not so sharp
     As friend remember's not.
Heigh-ho! sing, heigh-ho! unto the green holly:
Most friendship is feigning, most loving mere folly.
     Then heigh-ho! the holly!
     This life is most jolly.

                              (II. vii. 174-93)

SONG

It was a lover and his lass,
   With a hey, and a ho, and a hey nonino,
That o'er the green corn-field did pass,
   In the spring time, the only pretty ring time,
When birds do sing, hey ding a ding, ding;
Sweet lovers love the spring.

Between the acres of the rye,
   With a hey, and a ho, and a hey nonino,
These pretty country folks would lie,
   In the spring time, &c.

This carol they began that hour,
   With a hey, and a ho, and a hey nonino,
How that a life was but a flower
   In the spring time, &c.

And therefore take the present time,
   With a hey, and a ho, and a hey nonino;
For love is crowned with the prime
   In the spring time, &c.   (v. iii. 18-35)

from *Twelfth Night*

Viola. I see you what you are: you are too proud;
But, if you were the devil, you are fair.
My lord and master loves you: O! such love
Could be but recompens'd, though you were crown'd
The nonpareil of beauty.
   Olivia.   How does he love me?
   Vio. With adorations, with fertile tears,
With groans that thunder love, with sighs of fire.
   Oli. Your lord does know my mind; I cannot love him;
Yet I suppose him virtuous, know him noble,

Of great estate, of fresh and stainless youth;
In voices well divulg'd, free, learn'd, and valiant;
And, in dimension and the shape of nature
A gracious person; but yet I cannot love him:
He might have took his answer long ago.

   Vio. If I did love you in my master's flame,
With such a suffering, such a deadly life,
In your denial I would find no sense;
I would not understand it.

      Oli.   Why, what would you?

   Vio. Make me a willow cabin at your gate,
And call upon my soul within the house;
Write loyal cantons of contemned love,
And sing them loud even in the dead of night,
Holla your name to the reverberate hills,
And make the babbling gossip of the air
Cry out, 'Olivia!' O! you should not rest
Between the elements of air and earth,
But you should pity me!

   Oli. You might do much. What is your parentage?

   Vio. Above my fortune, yet my state is well:
I am a gentleman.

      Oli.   Get you to your lord:
I cannot love him. Let him send no more,
Unless, perchance, you come to me again,
To tell me how he takes it. Fare you well:
I thank you for your pains: spend this for me.

   Vio. I am no fee'd post, lady; keep your purse:
My master, not myself, lacks recompense.
Love make his heart of flint that you shall love,
And let your fervour, like my master's, be
Plac'd in contempt! Farewell, fair cruelty.   [*Exit.*

   Oli. 'What is your parentage?'
'Above my fortunes, yet my state is well:
I am a gentleman.' I'll be sworn thou art:
Thy tongue, thy face, thy limbs, actions, and spirit,
Do give thee five-fold blazon. Not too fast: soft! soft!
Unless the master were the man. How now!
Even so quickly may one catch the plague?
Methinks I feel this youth's perfections
With an invisible and subtle stealth
To creep in at mine eyes. Well, let it be.   (I. v. 271-319)

Clown. O mistress mine! where are you roaming?
    O! stay and hear; your true love's coming,
       That can sing both high and low.
    Trip no further, pretty sweeting;
    Journeys end in lovers meeting,
       Every wise man's son doth know.

Sir Andrew. Excellent good, i' faith.
Sir Toby. Good, good.

Clo. What is love? 'tis not hereafter;
    Present mirth hath present laughter;
       What's to come is still unsure:
    In delay there lies no plenty;
    Then come kiss me, sweet and twenty,
       Youth's a stuff will not endure.

                     (II. iii. 38-55)

SONG

Clown. When that I was and a little tiny boy
    With hey, ho, the wind and the rain;
    A foolish thing was but a toy,
      For the rain it raineth every day.

    But when I came to man's estate,
    With hey, ho, the wind and the rain;
    'Gainst knaves and thieves men shut their gates,
      For the rain it raineth every day.

    But when I came, alas! to wive,
    With hey, ho, the wind and the rain;
    By swaggering could I never thrive,
      For the rain it raineth every day.

    But when I came unto my beds,
    With hey, ho, the wind and the rain;
    With toss-pots still had drunken heads,
      For the rain it raineth every day.

    A great while ago the world begun,
    With hey, ho, the wind and the rain;
    But that's all one, our play is done,
      And we'll strive to please you every day.

                     (V. i. 401-20)

from *Hamlet*

Horatio. A mote it is to trouble the mind's eye.
In the most high and palmy state of Rome,
A little ere the mightiest Julius fell,
The graves stood tenantless and the sheeted dead

Did squeak and gibber in the Roman streets;
As stars with trains of fire and dews of blood,
Disasters in the sun; and the moist star
Upon whose influence Neptune's empire stands
Was sick almost to doomsday with eclipse;
And even the like precurse of fierce events,
As harbingers preceding still the fates
And prologue to the omen coming on,
Have heaven and earth together demonstrated
Unto our climatures and countrymen.
But, soft! behold! lo! where it comes again.

Re-enter Ghost.

I'll cross it, though it blast me. Stay, illusion!
If thou hast any sound, or use of voice,
Speak to me:
If there be any good thing to be done,
That may to thee do ease and grace to me,
Speak to me:
If thou art privy to thy country's fate,
Which happily foreknowing may avoid,
O! speak;
Or if thou hast uphoarded in thy life
Extorted treasure in the womb of earth,
For which, they say, you spirits oft walk in death,   [*Cock crows.*
Speak of it: stay, and speak! Stop it, Marcellus.
  Marcellus. Shall I strike at it with my partisan?
  Hor. Do, if it will not stand.
  Bernardo.   'Tis here!
  Hor.   'Tis here!   [*Exit* Ghost.
  Mar. 'Tis gone!
We do it wrong, being so majestical,
To offer it the show of violence;   (I. i. 112-44)

  Hamlet. O! that this too too solid flesh would melt,
Thaw and resolve itself into a dew;
Or that the Everlasting had not fix'd
His canon 'gainst self-slaughter! O God! O God!
How weary, stale, flat, and unprofitable
Seem to me all the uses of this world.
Fie on't! O fie! 'tis an unweeded garden,
That grows to seed; things rank and gross in nature
Possess it merely. That it should come to this!
But two months dead: nay, not so much, not two:
So excellent a king; that was, to this,

Hyperion to a satyr; so loving to my mother
That he might not beteem the winds of heaven
Visit her face too roughly. Heaven and earth!
Must I remember? why, she would hang on him,
As if increase of appetite had grown
By what it fed on; and yet, within a month,
Let me not think on't: Frailty, thy name is woman!
A little month; or ere those shoes were old
With which she follow'd my poor father's body,
Like Niobe, all tears; why she, even she,—
O God! a beast, that wants discourse of reason,
Would have mourn'd longer,—married with mine uncle,
My father's brother, but no more like my father
Than I to Hercules: within a month,
Ere yet the salt of most unrighteous tears
Had left the flushing in her galled eyes,
She married. O! most wicked speed, to post
With such dexterity to incestuous sheets.
It is not nor it cannot come to good;
But break, my heart, for I must hold my tongue!   (I. ii. 129-59)

Enter GHOST.

  Hor.   Look, my lord, it comes.
  Ham. Angels and ministers of grace defend us!
Be thou a spirit of health or goblin damn'd,
Bring with thee airs from heaven or blasts from hell,
Be thy intents wicked or charitable,
Thou com'st in such a questionable shape
That I will speak to thee: I'll call thee Hamlet,
King, father; royal Dane, O! answer me:
Let me not burst in ignorance; but tell
Why thy canoniz'd bones, hearsed in death,
Have burst their cerements; why the sepulchre,
Wherein we saw thee quietly inurn'd,
Hath op'd his ponderous and marble jaws,
To cast thee up again. What may this mean,
That thou, dead corse, again in complete steel
Revisit'st thus the glimpses of the moon,
Making night hideous; and we fools of nature
So horridly to shake our disposition
With thoughts beyond the reaches of our souls?
Say, why is this? wherefore? what should we do?
                              [*The Ghost beckons* HAMLET.

Hor. It beckons you to go away with it,
As if it some impartment did desire
To you alone.
    Mar.   Look, with what courteous action
It waves you to a more removed ground:
But do not go with it.
    Hor.   No, by no means.
    Ham. It will not speak; then, will I follow it.
    Hor. Do not, my lord.
    Ham.   Why, what should be the fear?
I do not set my life at a pin's fee;
And for my soul, what can it do to that,
Being a thing immortal as itself?
It waves me forth again; I'll follow it.
    Hor. What if it tempt you toward the flood, my lord,
Or to the dreadful summit of the cliff
That beetles o'er his base into the sea,
And there assume some other horrible form,
Which might deprive your sovereignty of reason
And draw you into madness? think of it;
The very place puts toys of desperation,
Without more motive, into every brain
That looks so many fathoms to the sea
And hears it roar beneath.
    Ham. It waves me still. Go on, I'll follow thee.
    Mar. You shall not go, my lord.
    Ham.   Hold off your hands!
    Hor. Be rul'd; you shall not go.
    Ham.   My fate cries out,
And makes each petty artery in this body
As hardy as the Nemean lion's nerve.   [Ghost *beckons.*
Still am I call'd. Unhand me, gentlemen,   [*Breaking from them.*
By heaven! I'll make a ghost of him that lets me:
I say, away! Go on, I'll follow thee.   [*Exeunt* Ghost *and* HAMLET.
    Hor. He waxes desperate with imagination.
    Mar. Let's follow; 'tis not fit thus to obey him.
    Hor. Have after. To what issue will this come?
    Mar. Something is rotten in the state of Denmark.
    Hor. Heaven will direct it.
    Mar.   Nay, let's follow him.   (I. iv. 38-91)

Ophelia. My lord, as I was sewing in my closet,
Lord Hamlet, with his doublet all unbrac'd;
No hat upon his head; his stockings foul'd,

Ungarter'd, and down–gyved to his ancle;
Pale as his shirt; his knees knocking each other;
And with a look so piteous in purport
As if he had been loosed out of hell
To speak of horrors, he comes before me.
   Polonius. Mad for thy love?
   Oph.   My lord, I do not know;
But truly I do fear it.
   Pol.   What said he?
   Oph. He took me by the wrist and held me hard,
Then goes he to the length of all his arm,
And, with his other hand thus o'er his brow,
He falls to such perusal of my face
As he would draw it. Long stay'd he so;
At last, a little shaking of mine arm,
And thrice his head thus waving up and down,
He rais'd a sigh so piteous and profound
That it did seem to shatter all his bulk
And end his being. That done, he lets me go,
And, with his head over his shoulder turn'd,
He seem'd to find his way without his eyes;
For out o' doors he went without their help,
And to the last bended their light on me.
   Pol. Come, go with me; I will go seek the king.
This is the very ecstasy of love,
Whose violent property fordoes itself
And leads the will to desperate undertakings
As oft as any passion under heaven
That does afflict our natures. I am sorry.
What! have you given him any hard words of late?
   Oph. No, my good lord: but, as you did command,
I did repel his letters and denied
His access to me.
   Pol.   That hath made him mad.
I am sorry that with better heed and judgment
I had not quoted him; I fear'd he did but trifle,
And meant to wrack thee; but, beshrew my jealousy!
By heaven, it is as proper to our age
To cast beyond ourselves in our opinions
As it is common for the younger sort
To lack discretion.   (II. i. 77–117)

   Ham. Ay, so, God be wi' ye! Now I am alone.
O! what a rogue and peasant slave am I:

Is it not monstrous that this player here,
But in a fiction, in a dream of passion,
Could force his soul so to his own conceit
That from her working all his visage wann'd,
Tears in his eyes, distraction in 's aspect,
A broken voice, and his whole function suiting
With forms to his conceit? and all for nothing!
For Hecuba!
What's Hecuba to him or he to Hecuba
That he should weep for her? What would he do
Had he the motive and the cue for passion
That I have? He would drown the stage with tears,
And cleave the general ear with horrid speech,
Make mad the guilty and appal the free,
Confound the ignorant, and amaze indeed
The very faculties of eyes and ears.
Yet I,
A dull and muddy-mettled rascal, peak,
Like John-a-dreams, unpregnant of my cause,
And can say nothing; no, not for a king,
Upon whose property and most dear life
A damn'd defeat was made. Am I a coward?
Who calls me villain? breaks my pate across?
Plucks off my beard and blows it in my face?
Tweaks me by the nose? gives me the lie i' the throat,
As deep as to the lungs? Who does me this?
Ha!
Swounds, I should take it, for it cannot be
But I am pigeon-liver'd, and lack gall
To make oppression bitter, or ere this
I should have fatted all the region kites
With this slave's offal. Bloody, bawdy villain!
Remorseless, treacherous, lecherous, kindless villain!
O! vengeance!
Why, what an ass am I! This is most brave
That I, the son of a dear father murder'd,
Prompted to my revenge by heaven and hell,
Must, like a whore, unpack my heart with words,
And fall a–cursing, like a very drab,
A scullion!
Fie upon't! foh! About, my brain! I have heard,
That guilty creatures sitting at a play
Have by the very cunning of the scene
Been struck so to the soul that presently

WILLIAM SHAKESPEARE

They have proclaim'd their malefactions;
For murder, though it have no tongue, will speak
With most miraculous organ. I'll have these players
Play something like the murder of my father
Before mine uncle; I'll observe his looks;
I'll tent him to the quick: if he but blench
I know my course. The spirit that I have seen
May be the devil: and the devil hath power
To assume a pleasing shape; yea, and perhaps
Out of my weakness and my melancholy—
As he is very potent with such spirits—
Abuses me to damn me. I'll have grounds
More relative than this: the play's the thing
Wherein I'll catch the conscience of the king.   (II. ii. 583-642)

　　Ham. To be, or not to be: that is the question:
Whether 'tis nobler in the mind to suffer
The slings and arrows of outrageous fortune,
Or to take arms against a sea of troubles,
And by opposing end them? To die: to sleep;
No more; and, by a sleep to say we end
The heart-ache and the thousand natural shocks
That flesh is heir to, 'tis a consummation
Devoutly to be wish'd. To die, to sleep;
To sleep: perchance to dream: ay, there's the rub;
For in that sleep of death what dreams may come
When we have shuffled off this mortal coil,
Must give us pause. There's the respect
That makes calamity of so long life;
For who would bear the whips and scorns of time,
The oppressor's wrong, the proud man's contumely,
The pangs of dispriz'd love, the law's delay,
The insolence of office, and the spurns
That patient merit of the unworthy takes,
When he himself might his quietus make
With a bare bodkin? who would fardels bear,
To grunt and sweat under a weary life,
But that the dread of something after death,
The undiscover'd country from whose bourn
No traveller returns, puzzles the will,
And makes us rather bear those ills we have
Than fly to others that we know not of?
Thus conscience does make cowards of us all;

And thus the native hue of resolution
Is sicklied o'er with the pale cast of thought,
And enterprises of great pith and moment
With this regard their currents turn awry,
And lose the name of action. Soft you now!
The fair Ophelia! Nymph, in thy orisons
Be all my sins remember'd.   (III. i. 56-90)

   King. O! my offence is rank, it smells to heaven;
It hath the primal eldest curse upon't;
A brother's murder! Pray can I not,
Though inclination be as sharp as will:
My stronger guilt defeats my strong intent;
And, like a man to double business bound,
I stand in pause where I shall first begin,
And both neglect. What if this cursed hand
Were thicker than itself with brother's blood,
Is there not rain enough in the sweet heavens
To wash it white as snow? Whereto serves mercy
But to confront the visage of offence?
And what's in prayer but this two-fold force,
To be forestalled, ere we come to fall,
Or pardon'd, being down? Then, I'll look up;
My fault is past. But, O! what form of prayer
Can serve my turn? 'Forgive me my foul murder'?
That cannot be; since I am still possess'd
Of those effects for which I did the murder,
My crown, mine own ambition, and my queen.
May one be pardon'd and retain the offence?
In the corrupted currents of this world
Offence's gilded hand may shove by justice,
And oft 'tis seen the wicked prize itself
Buys out the law; but 'tis not so above;
There is no shuffling, there the action lies
In his true nature, and we ourselves compell'd
Even to the teeth and forehead of our faults
To give in evidence. What then? what rests?
Try what repentance can: what can it not?
Yet what can it, when one can not repent?
O wretched state! O bosom black as death!
O limed soul, that struggling to be free
Art more engaged! Help, angels! make assay;
Bow, stubborn knees; and heart with strings of steel

Be soft as sinews of the new-born babe.
All may be well.   (III. iii. 36-72)

  Ham. Look here, upon this picture, and on this;
The counterfeit presentment of two brothers.
See, what a grace was seated on this brow;
Hyperion's curls, the front of Jove himself,
An eye like Mars, to threaten and command,
A station like the herald Mercury
New-lighted on a heaven-kissing hill,
A combination and a form indeed,
Where every god did seem to set his seal,
To give the world assurance of a man.
This was your husband: look you now, what follows.
Here is your husband; like a mildew'd ear,
Blasting his wholesome brother. Have you eyes?
Could you on this fair mountain leave to feed,
And batten on this moor? Ha! have you eyes?
You cannot call it love, for at your age
The hey-day in the blood is tame, it's humble,
And waits upon the judgment; and what judgment
Would step from this to this? Sense, sure, you have,
Else could you not have motion; but sure, that sense
Is apoplex'd; for madness would not err,
Nor sense to ecstasy was ne'er so thrall'd
But it reserv'd some quantity of choice,
To serve in such a difference. What devil was 't
That thus hath cozen'd you at hoodman-blind?
Eyes without feeling, feeling without sight,
Ears without hands or eyes, smelling sans all,
Or but a sickly part of one true sense
Could not so mope.
O shame! where is thy blush? Rebellious hell,
If thou canst mutine in a matron's bones,
To flaming youth let virtue be as wax,
And melt in her own fire.   (III. iv. 53-85)

  Queen. One woe doth tread upon another's heel,
So fast they follow: your sister's drown'd, Laertes.
  Laertes. Drown'd! O, where?
  Queen. There is a willow grows aslant a brook,
That shows his hoar leaves in the glassy stream;
There with fantastic garlands did she come,
Of crow-flowers, nettles, daisies, and long purples,

That liberal shepherds give a grosser name,
But our cold maids do dead men's fingers call them:
There, on the pendent boughs her coronet weeds
Clambering to hang, an envious sliver broke,
When down her weedy trophies and herself
Fell in the weeping brook. Her clothes spread wide,
And, mermaid-like, awhile they bore her up;
Which time she chanted snatches of old tunes,
As one incapable of her own distress,
Or like a creature native and indu'd
Unto that element; but long it could not be
Till that her garments, heavy with their drink,
Pull'd the poor wretch from her melodious lay
To muddy death.   (IV. vii. 164-84)

Hor. You will lose this wager, my lord.

Ham. I do not think so; since he went into France, I have been in continual practice; I shall win at the odds. But thou wouldst not think how ill all's here about my heart; but it is no matter.

Hor. Nay, good my lord,—

Ham. It is but foolery; but it is such a kind of gain-giving as would perhaps trouble a woman.

Hor. If your mind dislike any thing, obey it; I will forestal their repair hither, and say you are not fit.

Ham. Not a whit, we defy augury; there's a special providence in the fall of a sparrow. If it be now, 'tis not to come; if it be not to come, it will be now; if it be not now, yet it will come: the readiness is all. Since no man has aught of what he leaves, what is't to leave betimes? Let be.

(V. ii. 219-38)

from *Troilus and Cressida*

Troilus. Peace, you ungracious clamours! peace, rude sounds!
Fools on both sides! Helen must needs be fair,
When with your blood you daily paint her thus.
I cannot fight upon this argument;
It is too starv'd a subject for my sword.
But Pandarus,—O gods! how do you plague me.
I cannot come to Cressid but by Pandar;
And he's as tetchy to be woo'd to woo
As she is stubborn-chaste against all suit.
Tell me, Apollo, for thy Daphne's love,
What Cressid is, what Pandar, and what we?

Her bed is India; there she lies, a pearl:
Between our Ilium and where she resides
Let it be call'd the wild and wandering flood;
Ourself the merchant, and this sailing Pandar
Our doubtful hope, our convoy and our bark.   (I. i. 94–109)

   Tro. You are for dreams and slumbers, brother priest;
You fur your gloves with reason. Here are your reasons:
You know an enemy intends you harm;
You know a sword employ'd is perilous,
And reason flies the object of all harm:
Who marvels then, when Helenus beholds
A Grecian and his sword, if he do set
The very wings of reason to his heels,
And fly like chidden Mercury from Jove,
Or like a star disorb'd? Nay, if we talk of reason,
Let's shut our gates and sleep: manhood and honour
Should have hare-hearts, would they but fat their thoughts
With this cramm'd reason: reason and respect
Make livers pale, and lustihood deject.
   Hector. Brother, she is not worth what she doth cost
The holding.
   Tro.   What is aught but as 'tis valu'd?
   Hect. But value dwells not in particular will;
It holds his estimate and dignity
As well wherein 'tis precious of itself
As in the prizer. 'Tis mad idolatry
To make the service greater than the god;
And the will dotes that is inclinable
To what infectiously itself affects,
Without some image of the affected merit.
   Tro. I take to-day a wife, and my election
Is led on in the conduct of my will;
My will enkindled by mine eyes and ears,
Two traded pilots 'twixt the dangerous shores
Of will and judgment. How may I avoid,
Although my will distaste what it elected,
The wife I chose? there can be no evasion
To blench from this and to stand firm by honour.
We turn not back the silks upon the merchant
When we have soil'd them, nor the remainder viands
We do not throw in unrespective sink
Because we now are full. It was thought meet

Paris should do some vengeance on the Greeks:
Your breath of full consent bellied his sails;
The seas and winds—old wranglers—took a truce
And did him service: he touch'd the ports desir'd,
And for an old aunt whom the Greeks held captive
He brought a Grecian queen, whose youth and freshness
Wrinkles Apollo's, and makes stale the morning.
Why keep we her? the Grecians keep our aunt:
Is she worth keeping? why, she is a pearl,
Whose price hath launch'd above a thousand ships,
And turn'd crown'd kings to merchants.
If you'll avouch 'twas wisdom Paris went,—
As you must needs, for you all cried 'Go, go,'—
If you'll confess he brought home noble prize,—
As you must needs, for you all clapp'd your hands,
And cry'd 'Inestimable!'—why do you now
The issue of your proper wisdoms rate,
And do a deed that Fortune never did,
Beggar the estimation which you priz'd
Richer than sea and land? O! theft most base,
That we have stol'n what we do fear to keep!
But thieves unworthy of a thing so stol'n,
That in their country did them that disgrace
We fear to warrant in our native place.
    Cassandra. [*Within.*] Cry, Trojans, cry!
    Priam.   What noise? what shriek?
    Tro. 'Tis our mad sister, I do know her voice.
    Cas. [*Within.*] Cry, Trojans!
    Hect. It is Cassandra.

Enter CASSANDRA, *raving.*

    Cas. Cry, Trojans, cry! lend me ten thousand eyes,
And I will fill them with prophetic tears.
    Hect. Peace, sister, peace!
    Cas. Virgins and boys, mid-age and wrinkled eld,
Soft infancy, that nothing canst but cry,
Add to my clamours! let us pay betimes
A moiety of that mass of moan to come.
Cry, Trojans, cry! practise your eyes with tears!
Troy must not be, nor goodly Ilion stand;
Our firebrand brother, Paris, burns us all.
Cry, Trojans, cry! a Helen and a woe!
Cry, cry! Troy burns, or else let Helen go.   [*Exit.*
                                           (II. ii. 37-112)

Pandarus. Have you seen my cousin?
  Tro. No, Pandarus: I stalk about her door,
Like a strange soul upon the Stygian banks
Staying for waftage. O! be thou my Charon,
And give me swift transportance to those fields
Where I may wallow in the lily-beds
Propos'd for the deserver! O gentle Pandarus!
From Cupid's shoulder pluck his painted wings,
And fly with me to Cressid.
      Pan. Walk here i' the orchard. I'll bring her straight.   [*Exit.*
      Tro. I am giddy, expectation whirls me round.
The imaginary relish is so sweet
That it enchants my sense. What will it be
When that the watery palate tastes indeed
Love's thrice-repured nectar? death, I fear me,
Swounding destruction, or some joy too fine,
Too subtle-potent, tun'd too sharp in sweetness
For the capacity of my ruder powers:
I fear it much; and I do fear besides
That I shall lose distinction in my joys;
As doth a battle, when they charge on heaps
The enemy flying.   (III. ii. 7-28)

  Achilles. What! are my deeds forgot?
  Ulysses. Time hath, my lord, a wallet at his back,
Wherein he puts alms for oblivion,
A great-siz'd monster of ingratitudes:
Those scraps are good deeds past; which are devour'd
As fast as they are made, forgot as soon
As done: perseverance, dear my lord,
Keeps honour bright: to have done, is to hang
Quite out of fashion, like a rusty mail
In monumental mockery. Take the instant way;
For honour travels in a strait so narrow
Where one but goes abreast: keep, then, the path;
For emulation hath a thousand sons
That one by one pursue: if you give way,
Or hedge aside from the direct forthright,
Like to an enter'd tide they all rush by
And leave you hindmost;
Or, like a gallant horse fall'n in first rank,
Lie there for pavement to the abject rear,
O'errun and trampled on: then what they do in present,
Though less than yours in past, must o'ertop yours;

For time is like a fashionable host,
That slightly shakes his parting guest by the hand,
And with his arms outstretch'd, as he would fly,
Grasps in the comer: welcome ever smiles,
And farewell goes out sighing. O! let not virtue seek
Renumeration for the thing it was;
For beauty, wit,
High birth, vigour of bone, desert in service,
Love, friendship, charity, are subjects all
To envious and calumniating time.
One touch of nature makes the whole world kin,
That all with one consent praise new-born gawds,
Though they are made and moulded of things past,
And give to dust that is a little gilt
More laud than gilt o'er-dusted. (III. iii. 144–79)

    Cressida. And is it true that I must go from Troy?
    Tro. A hateful truth.
    Cres.   What! and from Troilus too?
    Tro. From Troy and Troilus.
    Cres.   Is it possible?
    Tro. And suddenly; where injury of chance
Puts back leave-taking, justles roughly by
All time of pause, rudely beguiles our lips
Of all rejoindure, forcibly prevents
Our lock'd embrasures, strangles our dear vows
Even in the birth of our own labouring breath.
We two, that with so many thousand sighs
Did buy each other, must poorly sell ourselves
With the rude brevity and discharge of one,
Injurious time now with a robber's haste
Crams his rich thievery up, he knows not how;
As many farewells as be stars in heaven,
With distinct breath and consign'd kisses to them,
He fumbles up into a loose adieu,
And scants us with a single famish'd kiss,
Distasted with the salt of broken tears.
    Æneas. [*Within.*] My lord, is the lady ready?
    Tro. Hark! you are call'd: some say the Genius so
Cries 'Come!' to him that instantly must die.
Bid them have patience; she shall come anon. (IV. iv. 30–52)

    Tro. This she? no, this is Diomed's Cressida.
If beauty have a soul, this is not she;

If souls guide vows, if vows be sanctimony,
If sanctimony be the gods' delight,
If there be rule in unity itself,
This is not she. O madness of discourse,
That cause sets up with and against itself;
Bi-fold authority! where reason can revolt
Without perdition, and loss assume all reason
Without revolt: this is, and is not, Cressid.
Within my soul there doth conduce a fight
Of this strange nature that a thing inseparate
Divides more wider than the sky and earth;
And yet the spacious breadth of this division
Admits no orifice for a point as subtle
As Ariachne's broken woof to enter.
Instance, O instance! strong as Pluto's gates;
Cressid is mine, tied with the bonds of heaven:
Instance, O instance! strong as heaven itself;
The bonds of heaven are slipp'd, dissolv'd, and loos'd;
And with another knot, five-finger-tied,
The fractions of her faith, orts of her love,
The fragments, scraps, the bits, and greasy reliques
Of her o'er-eaten faith, are bound to Diomed.   (v. ii. 134–57)

from *All's Well That Ends Well*

Parolles. O Lord, sir, let me live, or let me see my death!
First Soldier. That shall you, and take your leave of all your friends.
                                                    [*Unmuffling him.*

So, look about you: know you any here?
  Bertram. Good morrow, noble captain.
  Sec. Lord. God bless you, Captain Parolles.
  First Lord. God save you, noble captain.
  Sec. Lord. Captain, what greeting will you to my Lord Lafeu? I am
for France.
  First Lord. Good captain, will you give me a copy of the sonnet you
writ to Diana in behalf of the Count Rousillon? an I were not a very
coward I'd compel it of you; but fare you well.
                                    [*Exeunt* BERTRAM *and* Lords.
  First Sold. You are undone, captain; all but your scarf; that has a knot
on't yet.
  Par. Who cannot be crushed with a plot?
  First Sold. If you could find out a country where but women were

that had received so much shame, you might begin an impudent nation.
Fare ye well, sir; I am for France too: we shall speak of you there. [*Exit.*

 Par. Yet am I thankful: if my heart were great
'Twould burst at this. Captain I'll be no more;
But I will eat and drink, and sleep as soft
As captain shall: simply the thing I am
Shall make me live. Who knows himself a braggart,
Let him fear this; for it will come to pass
That every braggart shall be found an ass.
Rust, sword! cool, blushes! and Parolles, live
Safest in shame! being fool'd, by foolery thrive!
There's place and means for every man alive.
I'll after them.   [*Exit.*

                 (IV. iii. 348–75)

from Othello

 Othello. Her father lov'd me; oft invited me;
Still question'd me the story of my life
From year to year, the battles, sieges, fortunes
That I have pass'd.
I ran it through, even from my boyish days
To the very moment that he bade me tell it;
Wherein I spake of most disastrous chances,
Of moving accidents by flood and field,
Of hair-breadth 'scapes i' the imminent deadly breach,
Of being taken by the insolent foe
And sold to slavery, of my redemption thence
And portance in my travel's history;
Wherein of antres vast and desarts idle,
Rough quarries, rocks and hills whose heads touch heaven,
It was my hint to speak, such was the process;
And of the Cannibals that each other eat,
The Anthropophagi, and men whose heads
Do grow beneath their shoulders. This to hear
Would Desdemona seriously incline;
But still the house-affairs would draw her thence;
Which ever as she could with haste dispatch,
She'd come again, and with a greedy ear
Devour up my discourse. Which I observing,
Took once a pliant hour, and found good means
To draw from her a prayer of earnest heart
That I would all my pilgrimage dilate,

Whereof by parcels she had something heard,
But not intentively: I did consent;
And often did beguile her of her tears,
When I did speak of some distressful stroke
That my youth suffer'd. My story being done,
She gave me for my pains a world of sighs:
She swore, in faith, 'twas strange, 'twas passing strange;
'Twas pitiful, 'twas wondrous pitiful:
She wish'd she had not heard it, yet she wish'd
That heaven had made her such a man; she thank'd me,
And bade me, if I had a friend that lov'd her,
I should but teach him how to tell my story,
And that would woo her. Upon this hint I spake:
She lov'd me for the dangers I had pass'd,
And I lov'd her that she did pity them.
This only is the witchcraft I have us'd: (I. iii. 128–69)

   Oth. O my fair warrior!
   Desdemona.   **My dear Othello!**
   Oth. It gives me wonder great as my content
To see you here before me. O my soul's joy!
If after every tempest come such calms,
May the winds blow till they have waken'd death!
And let the labouring bark climb hills of seas
Olympus-high, and duck again as low
As hell's from heaven! If it were now to die,
'Twere now to be most happy, for I fear
My soul hath her content so absolute
That not another comfort like to this
Succeeds in unknown fate.
   Des.   The heavens forbid
But that our loves and comforts should increase
Even as our days do grow!
   Oth.   Amen to that, sweet powers!
I cannot speak enough of this content;
It stops me here; it is too much of joy:
And this, and this, the greatest discords be,   [*Kissing her*.
That e'er our hearts shall make!
   Iago. [*Aside*.] O! you are well tun'd now,
But I'll set down the pegs that make this music,
As honest as I am.   (II. i. 185–204)

   Iago. I will in Cassio's lodging lose this napkin,
And let him find it; trifles light as air

Are to the jealous confirmations strong
As proofs of holy writ; this may do something.
The Moor already changes with my poison:
Dangerous conceits are in their natures poisons,
Which at the first are scarce found to distaste,
But with a little act upon the blood,
Burn like the mines of sulphur. I did say so.
Look! where he comes!

Enter OTHELLO.

              Not poppy, nor mandragora,
Nor all the drowsy syrups of the world,
Shall ever medicine thee to that sweet sleep
Which thou ow'dst yesterday.
    Oth.   Ha! ha! false to me?
    Iago. Why, how now, general! no more of that.
    Oth. Avaunt! be gone! thou hast set me on the rack;
I swear 'tis better to be much abus'd
Than but to know't a little.
    Iago.   How now, my lord!
    Oth. What sense had I of her stol'n hours of lust?
I saw't not, thought it not, it harm'd not me;
I slept the next night well, was free and merry;
I found not Cassio's kisses on her lips;
He that is robb'd, not wanting what is stol'n,
Let him not know't and he's not robb'd at all.
    Iago. I am sorry to hear this.
    Oth. I had been happy, if the general camp,
Pioners and all, had tasted her sweet body,
So I had nothing known. O! now, for ever
Farewell the tranquil mind; farewell content!
Farewell the plumed troop and the big wars
That make ambition virtue! O, farewell!
Farewell the neighing steed, and the shrill trump,
The spirit-stirring drum, the ear-piercing fife,
The royal banner, and all quality,
Pride, pomp, and circumstance of glorious war!
And, O you mortal engines, whose rude throats
The immortal Jove's dread clamours counterfeit,
Farewell! Othello's occupation 's gone!   (III. iii. 322-58)

    Oth. Soft you; a word or two before you go.
I have done the state some service, and they know't;
No more of that. I pray you, in your letters,

When you shall these unlucky deeds relate,
Speak of me as I am; nothing extenuate,
Nor set down aught in malice: then, must you speak
Of one that lov'd not wisely but too well;
Of one not easily jealous, but, being wrought,
Perplex'd in the extreme; of one whose hand,
Like the base Indian, threw a pearl away
Richer than all his tribe; of one whose subdu'd eyes
Albeit unused to the melting mood,
Drop tears as fast as the Arabian trees
Their med'cinable gum. Set you down this;
And say besides, that in Aleppo once,
Where a malignant and a turban'd Turk
Beat a Venetian and traduc'd the state,
I took by the throat the circumcised dog,
And smote him thus.   (v. ii. 337–55)

from *King Lear*

Lear. I prithee, daughter, do not make me mad:
I will not trouble thee, my child; farewell.
We'll no more meet, no more see one another;
But yet thou art my flesh, my blood, my daughter;
Or rather a disease that 's in my flesh,
Which I must needs call mine: thou art a boil,
A plague-sore, an embossed carbuncle,
In my corrupted blood. But I'll not chide thee;
Let shame come when it will, I do not call it:
I do not bid the thunder-bearer shoot,
Nor tell tales of thee to high-judging Jove.
Mend when thou canst; be better at thy leisure:
I can be patient; I can stay with Regan,
I and my hundred knights.
    Regan.   Not altogether so:
I look'd not for you yet, nor am provided
For your fit welcome. Give ear, sir, to my sister;
For those that mingle reason with your passion
Must be content to think you old, and so—
But she knows what she does.
    Lear.   Is this well spoken?
    Reg. I dare avouch it, sir: what! fifty followers?
Is it not well? What should you need of more?
Yea, or so many, sith that both charge and danger

Speak 'gainst so great a number? How, in one house,
Should many people, under two commands,
Hold amity? 'Tis hard; almost impossible.

   Goneril. Why might not you, my lord, receive attendance
From those that she calls servants, or from mine?

   Reg. Why not, my lord? If then they chanc'd to slack you
We could control them. If you will come to me,—
For now I spy a danger,—I entreat you
To bring but five-and-twenty; to no more
Will I give place or notice.

   Lear. I gave you all—

   Reg.   And in good time you gave it.

   Lear. Made you my guardians, my depositaries,
But kept a reservation to be follow'd
With such a number. What! must I come to you
With five-and-twenty? Regan, said you so?

   Reg. And speak 't again, my lord; no more with me.

   Lear. Those wicked creatures yet do look well-favour'd,
When others are more wicked; not being the worst
Stands in some rank of praise. [*To* GONERIL.] I'll go with thee:
Thy fifty yet doth double five-and-twenty,
And thou art twice her love.

   Gon.   Hear me, my lord.
What need you five-and-twenty, ten, or five,
To follow in a house, where twice so many
Have a command to tend you?

   Reg.   What need one?

   Lear. O! reason not the need; our basest beggars
Are in the poorest thing superfluous:
Allow not nature more than nature needs,
Man's life is cheap as beast's. Thou art a lady;
If only to go warm were gorgeous,
Why, nature needs not what thou gorgeous wear'st,
Which scarcely keeps thee warm. But, for true need,—
You heavens, give me that patience, patience I need!
You see me here, you gods, a poor old man,
As full of grief as age; wretched in both!
If it be you that stir these daughters' hearts
Against their father, fool me not so much
To bear it tamely; touch me with noble anger,
And let not women's weapons, water-drops,
Stain my man's cheeks! No, you unnatural hags,
I will have such revenges on you both
That all the world shall—I will do such things.—

What they are yet I know not,—but they shall be
The terrors of the earth. You think I'll weep;
No, I'll not weep:
I have full cause of weeping, but this heart
Shall break into a hundred thousand flaws
Or ere I'll weep. O fool! I shall go mad.   (II. iv. 221–89)

Lear. Blow, winds, and crack your cheeks! rage! blow!
You cataracts and hurricanoes, spout
Till you have drench'd our steeples, drown'd the cocks!
You sulphurous and thought-executing fires,
Vaunt-couriers to oak-cleaving thunderbolts,
Singe my white head! And thou, all-shaking thunder,
Strike flat the thick rotundity o' the world!
Crack nature's moulds, all germens spill at once
That make ingrateful man!
Fool. O nuncle, court holy-water in a dry house is better than this
rain-water out o' door. Good nuncle, in, and ask thy daughters' blessing;
here's a night pities neither wise man nor fool.
Lear. Rumble thy bellyful! Spit, fire! spout, rain!
Nor rain, wind, thunder, fire, are my daughters:
I tax not you, you elements, with unkindness;
I never gave you kingdom, call'd you children,
You owe me no subscription: then, let fall
Your horrible pleasure; here I stand, your slave,
A poor, infirm, weak, and despis'd old man.
But yet I call you servile ministers,
That have with two pernicious daughters join'd
Your high-engender'd battles 'gainst a head
So old and white as this. O! O! 'tis foul.
Fool. He that has a house to put his head in has a good head-piece.

> The cod-piece that will house
> Before the head has any,
> The head and he shall louse;
> So beggars marry many.
> The man that makes his toe
> What he his heart should make,
> Shall of a corn cry woe,
> And turn his sleep to wake.

For there was never yet fair woman but she made mouths in a glass.
                                                        (III. ii. 1–36)

Kent. Here is the place, my lord; good my lord, enter:
The tyranny of the open night 's too rough
For nature to endure.   [*Storm still.*

Lear.   Let me alone.

Kent. Good my lord, enter here.

Lear.   Wilt break my heart?

Kent. I'd rather break mine own. Good my lord, enter.

Lear. Thou think'st 'tis much that this contentious storm
Invades us to the skin: so 'tis to thee;
But where the greater malady is fix'd,
The lesser is scarce felt. Thou'dst shun a bear;
But if thy flight lay toward the roaring sea,
Thou'dst meet the bear i' the mouth. When the mind's free
The body's delicate; the tempest in my mind
Doth from my senses take all feeling else
Save what beats there. Filial ingratitude!
Is it not as this mouth should tear this hand
For lifting food to 't? But I will punish home:
No, I will weep no more. In such a night
To shut me out! Pour on; I will endure.
In such a night as this! O Regan, Goneril!
Your old kind father, whose frank heart gave all,—
O! that way madness lies; let me shun that;
No more of that.

Kent.   Good my lord, enter here.

Lear. Prithee, go in thyself; seek thine own ease:
This tempest will not give me leave to ponder
On things would hurt me more. But I'll go in.
[*To the* Fool.] In, boy; go first. You houseless poverty,—
Nay, get thee in. I'll pray, and then I'll sleep.   [Fool *goes in.*
Poor naked wretches, wheresoe'er you are,
That bide the pelting of this pitiless storm,
How shall your houseless heads and unfed sides,
Your loop'd and window'd raggedness, defend you
From seasons such as these? O! I have ta'en
Too little care of this. Take physic, pomp;
Expose thyself to feel what wretches feel,
That thou mayst shake the superflux to them,
And show the heavens more just.   (III. iv. 1-36)

DOCTOR *draws the curtain and discovers* LEAR *asleep in bed.*

Cordelia. O my dear father! Restoration, hang
Thy medicine on my lips, and let this kiss
Repair those violent harms that my two sisters
Have in thy reverence made!

Kent.   Kind and dear princess!

Cor. Had you not been their father, these white flakes
Had challeng'd pity of them. Was this a face
To be expos'd against the warring winds?
To stand against the deep dread-bolted thunder?
In the most terrible and nimble stroke
Of quick cross lightning? to watch—poor perdu!—
With this thin helm? Mine enemy's dog,
Though he had bit me, should have stood that night
Against my fire. And wast thou fain, poor father,
To hovel thee with swine and rogues forlorn,
In short and musty straw? Alack, alack!
'Tis wonder that thy life and wits at once
Had not concluded all. He wakes; speak to him.
    Doc. Madam, do you; 'tis fittest.
    Cor. How does my royal lord? How fares your majesty?
    Lear. You do me wrong to take me out o' the grave;
Thou art a soul in bliss; but I am bound
Upon a wheel of fire, that mine own tears
Do scald like molten lead.
    Cor.   Sir, do you know me?
    Lear. You are a spirit, I know; when did you die?
    Cor. Still, still, far wide.
    Doc. He 's scarce awake; let him alone awhile.
    Lear. Where have I been? Where am I? Fair day-light?
I am mightily abus'd. I should even die with pity
To see another thus. I know not what to say.
I will not swear these are my hands: let 's see;
I feel this pin prick. Would I were assur'd
Of my condition!
    Cor.   O! look upon me, sir,
And hold your hands in benediction o'er me.
No, sir, you must not kneel.
    Lear.   Pray, do not mock me:
I am a very foolish fond old man,
Fourscore and upward, not an hour more or less;
And, to deal plainly,
I fear I am not in my perfect mind.
Methinks I should know you and know this man;
Yet I am doubtful: for I am mainly ignorant
What place this is, and all the skill I have
Remembers not these garments; nor I know not
Where I did lodge last night. Do not laugh at me;
For, as I am a man, I think this lady
To be my child Cordelia.   (IV. vii. 26–70)

Edgar. Come on, sir; here 's the place: stand still.
How fearful
And dizzy 'tis to cast one's eyes so low!
The crows and choughs that wing the midway air
Show scarce so gross as beetles; half way down
Hangs one that gathers samphire, dreadful trade!
Methinks he seems no bigger than his head.
The fishermen that walk upon the beach
Appear like mice, and yond tall anchoring bark
Diminish'd to her cock, her cock a buoy
Almost too small for sight. The murmuring surge,
That on the unnumber'd idle pebbles chafes,
Cannot be heard so high. I'll look no more,
Lest my brain turn, and the deficient sight
Topple down headlong.   (IV. vi. 11-25)

Enter LEAR, *with* CORDELIA *dead in his arms:*
EDGAR, Officer, *and Others.*

Lear. Howl, howl, howl, howl! O! you are men of stones:
Had I your tongues and eyes, I'd use them so
That heaven's vaults should crack. She 's gone for ever.
I know when one is dead, and when one lives;
She 's dead as earth. Lend me a looking-glass;
If that her breath will mist or stain the stone,
Why, then she lives.
  Kent.   Is this the promis'd end?
  Edg. Or image of that horror?
  Albany.   Fall and cease?
  Lear. This feather stirs; she lives! if it be so,
It is a chance which does redeem all sorrows
That ever I have felt.
  Kent. [*Kneeling.*]   O, my good master!
  Lear. Prithee, away.
  Edg.   'Tis noble Kent, your friend.
  Lear. A plague upon you, murderers, traitors all!
I might have sav'd her; now, she 's gone for ever!
Cordelia, Cordelia! stay a little. Ha!
What is 't thou sayst? Her voice was ever soft,
Gentle and low, an excellent thing in woman.
I kill'd the slave that was a hanging thee.   (V. iii. 259-76)

WILLIAM SHAKESPEARE

from *Macbeth*

Lady Macbeth. Glamis thou art, and Cawdor; and shalt be
What thou art promis'd. Yet do I fear thy nature;
It is too full o' the milk of human kindness
To catch the nearest way; thou wouldst be great,
Art not without ambition, but without
The illness should attend it; what thou wouldst highly,
That thou wouldst holily; wouldst not play false,
And yet wouldst wrongly win; thou'dst have, great Glamis,
That which cries, 'Thus thou must do, if thou have it';
And that which rather thou dost fear to do
Than wishest should be undone. Hie thee hither,
That I may pour my spirits in thine ear,
And chastise with the valour of my tongue
All that impedes thee from the golden round,
Which fate and metaphysical aid doth seem
To have thee crown'd withal.

                    Enter a Messenger.
                         What is your tidings?
Mess. The king comes here to-night.
    Lady M.   Thou 'rt mad to say it.
Is not thy master with him? who, were 't so,
Would have inform'd for preparation.
    Mess. So please you, it is true: our thane is coming;
One of my fellows had the speed of him,
Who, almost dead for breath, had scarcely more
Than would make up his message.
    Lady M.   Give him tending;
He brings great news.—[*Exit* Messenger.] The raven himself is hoarse
That croaks the fatal entrance of Duncan
Under my battlements. Come, you spirits
That tend on mortal thoughts! unsex me here,
And fill me from the crown to the toe top full
Of direst cruelty; make thick my blood,
Stop up the access and passage to remorse,
That no compunctious visitings of nature
Shake my fell purpose, nor keep peace between
The effect and it! Come to my woman's breasts,
And take my milk for gall, you murdering ministers,
Wherever in your sightless substances
You wait on nature's mischief! Come, thick night,
And pall thee in the dunnest smoke of hell,

That my keen knife see not the wound it makes,
Nor heaven peep through the blanket of the dark,
To cry, 'Hold, hold!'

               Enter MACBETH.

        Great Glamis! worthy Cawdor!
Greater than both, by the all-hail hereafter!
Thy letters have transported me beyond
This ignorant present, and I feel now
The future in the instant.
    Macb.   My dearest love,
Duncan comes here to-night.
    Lady M.   And when goes hence?
    Macb. To-morrow, as he purposes.
    Lady M.   O! never
Shall sun that morrow see.   (I. v. 16–62)

    Macb. If it were done when 'tis done, then 'twere well
It were done quickly; if the assassination
Could trammel up the consequence, and catch
With his surcease success; that but this blow
Might be the be-all and the end-all here.
But here, upon this bank and shoal of time,
We'd jump the life to come. But in these cases
We still have judgment here; that we but teach
Bloody instructions, which, being taught, return
To plague the inventor; this even-handed justice
Commends the ingredients of our poison'd chalice
To our own lips. He 's here in double trust:
First, as I am his kinsman and his subject,
Strong both against the deed; then, as his host,
Who should against his murderer shut the door,
Not bear the knife myself. Besides, this Duncan
Hath borne his faculties so meek, hath been
So clear in his great office, that his virtues
Will plead like angels trumpet-tongu'd against
The deep damnation of his taking-off;
And pity, like a naked new-born babe,
Striding the blast, or heaven's cherubin, hors'd
Upon the sightless couriers of the air,
Shall blow the horrid deed in every eye,
That tears shall drown the wind. I have no spur
To prick the sides of my intent, but only
Vaulting ambition, which o'er-leaps itself
And falls on the other. —   (I. vii. 1–28)

Macb.   Now o'er the one half-world
Nature seems dead, and wicked dreams abuse
The curtain'd sleep; witchcraft celebrates
Pale Hecate's offerings; and wither'd murder,
Alarum'd by his sentinel, the wolf,
Whose howl 's his watch, thus with his stealthy pace,
With Tarquin's ravishing strides, toward his design
Moves like a ghost. Thou sure and firm-set earth,
Hear not my steps, which way they walk, for fear
The very stones prate of my whereabout,
And take the present horror from the time,
Which now suits with it. Whiles I threat he lives:
Words to the heat of deeds too cold breath gives.   [*A bell rings.*
I go, and it is done; the bell invites me.
Hear it not, Duncan; for it is a knell
That summons thee to heaven or to hell.   (II. i. 49-64)

Macb. I have done the deed. Didst thou not hear a noise?
Lady M. I heard the owl scream and the crickets cry.
Did not you speak?
    Macb.   When?
    Lady M.   Now.
    Macb.   As I descended?
    Lady M. Ay.
    Macb. Hark!
Who lies i' the second chamber?
    Lady M.   Donalbain.
    Macb. [*Looking on his hands.*] This is a sorry sight.
    Lady M. A foolish thought to say a sorry sight.
    Macb. There 's one did laugh in 's sleep, and one cried 'Murder!'
That they did wake each other: I stood and heard them;
But they did say their prayers, and address'd them
Again to sleep.
    Lady M.   There are two lodg'd together.
    Macb. One cried 'God bless us!' and 'Amen' the other:
As they had seen me with these hangman's hands.
Listening their fear, I could not say 'Amen',
When they did say 'God bless us!'
    Lady M.   Consider it not so deeply.
    Macb. But wherefore could not I pronounce 'Amen'?
I had most need of blessing, and 'Amen'
Stuck in my throat.
    Lady M. These deeds must not be thought
After these ways; so, it will make us mad.

Macb. Methought I heard a voice cry 'Sleep no more!
Macbeth does murder sleep', the innocent sleep,
Sleep that knits up the ravell'd sleave of care,
The death of each day's life, sore labour's bath,
Balm of hurt minds, great nature's second course,
Chief nourisher in life's feast,—
    Lady M.   What do you mean?
    Macb. Still it cried, 'Sleep no more!' to all the house:
'Glamis hath murder'd sleep, and therefore Cawdor
Shall sleep no more, Macbeth shall sleep no more!'
    Lady M. Who was it that thus cried? Why, worthy thane,
You do unbend your noble strength to think
So brainsickly of things. Go get some water,
And wash this filthy witness from your hand.
Why did you bring these daggers from the place?
They must lie there: go carry them, and smear
The sleepy grooms with blood.
    Macb.   I'll go no more:
I am afraid to think what I have done;
Look on 't again I dare not.
    Lady M.   Infirm of purpose!
Give me the daggers. The sleeping and the dead
Are but as pictures; 'tis the eye of childhood
That fears a painted devil. If he do bleed,
I'll gild the faces of the grooms withal;
For it must seem their guilt.   *[Exit. Knocking within.*
    Macb.   Whence is that knocking?
How is 't with me, when every noise appals me?
What hands are here! Ha! they pluck out mine eyes.
Will all great Neptune's ocean wash this blood
Clean from my hand? No, this my hand will rather
The multitudinous seas incarnadine,
Making the green one red.   (II. ii. 16-64)

    Macb. We have scotch'd the snake, not kill'd it:
She'll close and be herself, whilst our poor malice
Remains in danger of her former tooth.
But let the frame of things disjoint, both the worlds suffer,
Ere we will eat our meal in fear, and sleep
In the affliction of these terrible dreams
That shake us nightly. Better be with the dead,
Whom we, to gain our peace, have sent to peace,
Than on the torture of the mind to lie
In restless ecstasy. Duncan is in his grave;

After life's fitful fever he sleeps well;
Treason has done his worst: nor steel, nor poison,
Malice domestic, foreign levy, nothing
Can touch him further.

   Lady M.   Come on;
Gentle my lord, sleek o'er your rugged looks;
Be bright and jovial among your guests to-night.

   Macb. So shall I, love; and so, I pray, be you.
Let your remembrance apply to Banquo;
Present him eminence, both with eye and tongue:
Unsafe the while, that we
Must lave our honours in these flattering streams,
And make our faces vizards to our hearts,
Disguising what they are.

   Lady M.   You must leave this.

   Macb. O! full of scorpions is my mind, dear wife;
Thou know'st that Banquo and his Fleance lives.

   Lady M. But in them nature's copy 's not eterne.

   Macb. There 's comfort yet; they are assailable;
Then be thou jocund. Ere the bat hath flown
His cloister'd flight, ere, to black Hecate's summons
The shard-borne beetle with his drowsy hums
Hath rung night's yawning peal, there shall be done
A deed of dreadful note.

   Lady M.   What 's to be done?

   Macb. Be innocent of the knowledge, dearest chuck,
Till thou applaud the deed. Come, seeling night,
Scarf up to the tender eye of pitiful day,
And with thy bloody and invisible hand
Cancel and tear to pieces that great bond
Which keeps me pale! Light thickens, and the crow
Makes wing to the rooky wood;
Good things of day begin to droop and drowse,
Whiles night's black agents to their preys do rouse.
Thou marvell'st at my words: but hold thee still;
Things bad begun make strong themselves by ill:
So, prithee, go with me.   (III. ii. 13-56)

   Macb.   Seyton!—I am sick at heart
When I behold—Seyton, I say!—This push
Will cheer me ever or disseat me now.
I have liv'd long enough: my way of life
Is fall'n into the sear, the yellow leaf:
And that which should accompany old age,

As honour, love, obedience, troops of friends,
I must not look to have; but, in their stead,
Curses, not loud but deep, mouth-honour, breath,
Which the poor heart would fain deny, and dare not.   (v. iii. 19-28)

Macb. Hang out our banners on the outward walls;
The cry is still, 'They come'; our castle's strength
Will laugh a siege to scorn; here let them lie
Till famine and the ague eat them up;
Were they not forc'd with those that should be ours,
We might have met them dareful, beard to beard,
And beat them backward home.   [*A cry of women within.*
                    What is that noise?
Seyton. It is the cry of women, my good lord.   [*Exit.*
Macb. I have almost forgot the taste of fears.
The time has been my senses would have cool'd
To hear a night-shriek, and my fell of hair
Would at a dismal treatise rouse and stir
As life were in 't. I have supp'd full with horrors;
Direness, familiar to my slaughterous thoughts,
Cannot once start me.

                    Re-enter SEYTON.
                    Wherefore was that cry?
Sey. The queen, my lord, is dead.
Macb. She should have died hereafter;
There would have been a time for such a word.
To-morrow, and to-morrow, and to-morrow,
Creeps in this petty pace from day to day,
To the last syllable of recorded time;
And all our yesterdays have lighted fools
The way to dusty death. Out, out, brief candle!
Life 's but a walking shadow, a poor player
That struts and frets his hour upon the stage,
And then is heard no more; it is a tale
Told by an idiot, full of sound and fury,
Signifying nothing.   (v. v. 1-28)

from *Antony and Cleopatra*

Agrippa. Thou hast a sister by the mother's side,
Admir'd Octavia; great Mark Antony
Is now a widower.

136

Cæsar.   Say not so, Agrippa:
If Cleopatra heard you, your reproof
Were well deserv'd of rashness.

Antony. I am not married, Cæsar; let me hear
Agrippa further speak.

Agr. To hold you in perpetual amity,
To make you brothers, and to knit your hearts
With an unslipping knot, take Antony
Octavia to his wife; whose beauty claims
No worse a husband than the best of men,
Whose virtue and whose general graces speak
That which none else can utter. By this marriage,
All little jealousies which now seem great,
And all great fears which now import their dangers,
Would then be nothing; truths would be but tales
Where now half tales be truths; her love to both
Would each to other and all loves to both
Draw after her. Pardon what I have spoke,
For 'tis a studied, not a present thought,
By duty ruminated.

Ant.   Will Cæsar speak?

Cæs. Not till he hears how Antony is touch'd
With what is spoke already.

Ant.   What power is in Agrippa,
If I would say, 'Agrippa, be it so,'
To make this good?

Cæs.   The power of Cæsar, and
His power unto Octavia.

Ant.   May I never
To this good purpose, that so fairly shows,
Dream of impediment! Let me have thy hand;
Further this act of grace, and from this hour
The heart of brothers govern in our loves
And sway our great designs!

Cæs.   There is my hand.
A sister I bequeath you, whom no brother
Did ever love so dearly; let her live
To join our kingdoms and our hearts, and never
Fly off our loves again!

Lepidus.   Happily, amen!

Ant. I did not think to draw my sword 'gainst Pompey,
For he hath laid strange courtesies and great
Of late upon me; I must thank him only,

Lest my remembrance suffer ill report;
At heel of that, defy him.

Lep.　　　　　　　　Time calls upon 's:
Of us must Pompey presently be sought,
Or else he seeks out us.

Ant.　　　　　　　　Where lies he?

Cæs. About the Mount Misenum.

Ant.　　　　　　　　　　What's his strength
By land?

Cæs. Great and increasing; but by sea
He is an absolute master.

Ant.　　　　　　So is the fame.
Would we had spoke together! Haste we for it;
Yet, ere we put ourselves in arms, dispatch we
The business we have talk'd of.　　　　　　(II. ii. 124-72)

Enobarbus. When she first met Mark Antony she pursed up his heart,
upon the river of Cydnus.

Agr. There she appeared indeed, or my reporter devised well for her.

Eno. I will tell you.
The barge she sat in, like a burnish'd throne,
Burn'd on the water; the poop was beaten gold,
Purple the sails, and so perfumed, that
The winds were love-sick with them, the oars were silver,
Which to the tune of flutes kept stroke, and made
The water which they beat to follow faster,
As amorous of their strokes. For her own person,
It beggar'd all description; she did lie
In her pavilion,—cloth-of-gold of tissue,—
O'er-picturing that Venus where we see
The fancy outwork nature; on each side her
Stood pretty-dimpled boys, like smiling Cupids,
With divers-colour'd fans, whose wind did seem
To glow the delicate cheeks which they did cool,
And what they undid did.

Agr.　　　　　　O! rare for Antony.

Eno. Her gentlewomen, like the Nereides,
So many mermaids, tended her i' the eyes,
And made their bends adornings; at the helm
A seeming mermaid steers; the silken tackle
Swell with the touches of those flower-soft hands,
That yarely frame the office. From the barge
A strange invisible perfume hits the sense
Of the adjacent wharfs. The city cast

Her people out upon her, and Antony,
Enthron'd i' the market-place, did sit alone,
Whistling to the air; which, but for vacancy,
Had gone to gaze on Cleopatra too
And made a gap in nature.   (II. ii. 194-226)

Enter a Soldier of CÆSAR'S.

Soldier.   Enobarbus, Antony
Hath after thee sent all thy treasure, with
His bounty overplus: the messenger
Came on my guard; and at thy tent is now
Unloading of his mules.
    Eno.   I give it you.
    Sold. Mock not, Enobarbus.
I tell you true: best you saf'd the bringer
Out of the host; I must attend mine office
Or would have done 't myself. Your emperor
Continues still a Jove.   [*Exit.*
    Eno. I am alone the villain of the earth,
And feel I am so most. O Antony!
Thou mine of bounty, how wouldst thou have paid
My better service, when my turpitude
Thou dost so crown with gold! This blows my heart:
If swift thought break it not, a swifter mean
Shall outstrike thought; but thought will do 't, I feel.
I fight against thee! No: I will go seek
Some ditch, wherein to die; the foul'st best fits
My latter part of life.   (IV. vi. 20-39)

    Eno.   O! bear me witness, night,—
    Third Sold. What man is this?
    Sec. Sold.   Stand close and list him.
    Eno. Be witness to me, O thou blessed moon,
When men revolted shall upon record
Bear hateful memory, poor Enobarbus did
Before thy face repent!
    First Sold.   Enobarbus!
    Third Sold.   Peace!
Hark further.
    Eno. O sovereign mistress of true melancholy,
The poisonous damp of night disponge upon me,
That life, a very rebel to my will,
May hang no longer on me; throw my heart

Against the flint and hardness of my fault,
Which, being dried with grief, will break to powder,
And finish all foul thoughts. O Antony!
Nobler than my revolt is infamous,
Forgive me in thine own particular;
But let the world rank me in register
A master-leaver and a fugitive.
O Antony! O Antony!   [*Dies.*

(IV. ix. 5–23)

Ant. Eros, thou yet behold'st me?
Eros.   Ay, noble lord.
Ant. Sometimes we see a cloud that's dragonish;
A vapour sometime like a bear or lion,
A tower'd citadel, a pendant rock,
A forked mountain, or blue promontory
With trees upon 't, that nod unto the world
And mock our eyes with air: thou hast seen these signs;
They are black vesper's pageants.
Eros.   Ay, my lord.
Ant. That which is now a horse, even with a thought
The rack dislimns, and makes it indistinct,
As water is in water.
Eros.   It does, my lord.
Ant. My good knave, Eros, now thy captain is
Even such a body.

(IV. xii. 1–13)

Enter, below, DIOMEDES.

Cleopatra.   How now! is he dead?
Diomedes. His death's upon him, but not dead.
Look out o' the other side your monument;
His guard have brought him thither.

Enter, below, ANTONY, *borne by the* Guard.

Cleo.   O sun!
Burn the great sphere thou mov'st in; darkling stand
The varying star o' the world. O Antony,
Antony, Antony! Help, Charmian, help, Iras, help;
Help, friends below! let's draw him hither.
Ant.   Peace!
Not Cæsar's valour hath o'erthrown Antony,
But Antony's hath triumph'd on itself.
Cleo. So it should be, that none but Antony
Should conquer Antony; but woe 'tis so!

Ant. I am dying, Egypt, dying; only
I here importune death awhile, until
Of many thousand kisses the poor last
I lay upon thy lips.
    Cleo.   I dare not, dear,—
Dear my lord, pardon,—I dare not,
Lest I be taken: not the imperious show
Of the full-fortun'd Cæsar ever shall
Be brooch'd with me; if knife, drugs, serpents, have
Edge, sting, or operation, I am safe:
Your wife Octavia, with her modest eyes
And still conclusion, shall acquire no honour
Demuring upon me. But come, come, Antony,—
Help me, my women,—we must draw thee up.
Assist, good friends.
    Ant.   O! quick, or I am gone.
    Cleo. Here 's sport indeed! How heavy weighs my lord!
Our strength is all gone into heaviness,
That makes the weight. Had I great Juno's power,
The strong-wing'd Mercury should fetch thee up,
And set thee by Jove's side. Yet come a little,
Wishers were ever fools. O! come, come, come;
                        [*They heave* ANTONY *aloft to* CLEOPATRA.
And welcome, welcome! die where thou hast liv'd;
Quicken with kissing; had my lips that power,
Thus would I wear them out.
    All.   A heavy sight!
    Ant. I am dying, Egypt, dying:
Give me some wine, and let me speak a little.
    Cleo. No, let me speak; and let me rail so high,
That the false housewife Fortune break her wheel,
Provok'd by my offence.   (IV. xiii. 6–45)

    Cleo.   Noblest of men, woo't die?
Hast thou no care of me? shall I abide
In this dull world, which in thy absence is
No better than a sty? O! see my women,   [ANTONY *dies.*
The crown o' the earth doth melt. My lord!
O! wither'd is the garland of the war,
The soldier's pole is fall'n; young boys and girls
Are level now with men; the odds is gone,
And there is nothing left remarkable
Beneath the visiting moon.   [*Swoons.*
    Charmian.   O, quietness, lady!

Iras. She is dead too, our sovereign.
    Char.   Lady!
    Iras.   Madam!
    Char. O madam, madam, madam!
    Iras.   Royal Egypt!
Empress!
    Char. Peace, peace, Iras!
    Cleo. No more, but e'en a woman, and commanded
By such poor passion as the maid that milks
And does the meanest chares. It were for me
To throw my sceptre at the injurious gods;
To tell them that this world did equal theirs
Till they had stol'n our jewel. All 's but naught;
Patience is sottish, and impatience does
Become a dog that 's mad; then is it sin
To rush into the secret house of death,
Ere death dare come to us? How do you, women?
What, what! good cheer! Why, how now, Charmian!
My noble girls! Ah, women, women, look!   (IV. xiii. 59-84)

Enter DOLABELLA

Dolabella. Most noble empress, you have heard of me?
    Cleo. I cannot tell.
    Dol.   Assuredly you know me.
    Cleo. No matter, sir, what I have heard or known.
You laugh when boys or women tell their dreams;
Is 't not your trick?
    Dol.   I understand not, madam.
    Cleo. I dream'd there was an Emperor Antony:
O! such another sleep, that I might see
But such another man.
    Dol.   If it might please ye,—
    Cleo. His face was as the heavens, and therein stuck
A sun and moon, which kept their course, and lighted
The little O, the earth.
    Dol.   Most sovereign creature,—
    Cleo. His legs bestrid the ocean; his rear'd arm
Crested the world; his voice was propertied
As all the tuned spheres, and that to friends;
But when he meant to quail and shake the orb,
He was as rattling thunder. For his bounty,
There was no winter in 't, an autumn 'twas
That grew the more by reaping; his delights
Were dolphin-like, they show'd his back above

The element they liv'd in; in his livery
Walk'd crowns and crownets, realms and islands were
As plates dropp'd from his pocket.
    Dol.   Cleopatra,—
    Cleo. Think you there was, or might be, such a man
As this I dream'd of ?
    Dol.   Gentle madam, no.
    Cleo. You lie, up to the hearing of the gods.
But, if there be, or ever were, one such,
It 's past the size of dreaming; nature wants stuff
To vie strange forms with fancy; yet to imagine
An Antony were nature's piece 'gainst fancy,
Condemning shadows quite.   (v. ii. 71–100)

    Cleo. Give me my robe, put on my crown; I have
Immortal longings in me; now no more
The juice of Egypt's grape shall moist this lip.
Yare, yare, good Iras; quick. Methinks I hear
Antony call; I see him rouse himself
To praise my noble act; I hear him mock
The luck of Cæsar, which the gods give men
To excuse their after wrath: husband, I come:
Now to that name my courage prove my title!
I am fire, and air; my other elements
I give to baser life. So; have you done?
Come then, and take the last warmth of my lips.
Farewell, kind Charmian; Iras, long farewell.
                    [*Kisses them.* IRAS *falls and dies.*
Have I the aspic in my lips? Dost fall?
If thou and nature can so gently part,
The stroke of death is as a lover's pinch,
Which hurts, and is desir'd. Dost thou lie still?
If thus thou vanishest, thou tell'st the world
It is not worth leave-taking.
    Char. Dissolve, thick cloud, and rain; that I may say,
The gods themselves do weep.
    Cleo.   This proves me base:
If she first meet the curled Antony,
He'll make demand of her, and spend that kiss
Which is my heaven to have. Come, thou mortal wretch,
              [*To the asp, which she applies to her breast.*
With thy sharp teeth this knot intrinsicate
Of life at once untie; poor venomous fool,
Be angry, and dispatch. O! couldst thou speak,

That I might hear thee call great Cæsar ass
Unpolicied.
  Char.   O eastern star!
  Cleo.   Peace, peace!
Dost thou not see my baby at my breast,
That sucks the nurse asleep?
  Char.   O, break! O, break!
  Cleo. As sweet as balm, as soft as air, as gentle,—
O Antony!—Nay, I will take thee too. [*Applying another asp to her arm.*
What should I stay—   [*Dies.*
  Char. In this vile world? So, fare thee well.
Now boast thee, death, in thy possession lies
A lass unparallel'd. Downy windows, close;
And golden Phœbus never be beheld
Of eyes again so royal! Your crown 's awry;
I'll mend it, and then play—   (v. ii. 282-321)

from *Coriolanus*

Enter a Gentlewoman.

Gentlewoman. Madam, the Lady Valeria is come to visit you.
Virgilia. Beseech you, give me leave to retire myself.
Volumnia. Indeed, you shall not.
Methinks I hear hither your husband's drum,
See him pluck Aufidius down by the hair,
As children from a bear, the Volsces shunning him:
Methinks I see him stamp thus, and call thus:
'Come on, you cowards! you were got in fear,
Though you were born in Rome.' His bloody brow
With his mail'd hand then wiping, forth he goes,
Like to a harvestman that 's task'd to mow
Or all or lose his hire.
  Vir. His bloody brow! O Jupiter! no blood.
  Vol. Away, you fool! it more becomes a man
Than gilt his trophy: the breasts of Hecuba,
When she did suckle Hector, look'd not lovelier
Than Hector's forehead when it spit forth blood
At Grecian swords, contemning. Tell Valeria
We are fit to bid her welcome.   (I. iii. 29-48)

  Vol. Why dost not speak?
Think'st thou it honourable for a noble man
Still to remember wrongs? Daughter, speak you:

He cares not for your weeping. Speak thou, boy:
Perhaps thy childishness will move him more
Than can our reasons. There is no man in the world
More bound to 's mother; yet here he lets me prate
Like one i' the stocks. Thou hast never in thy life
Show'd thy dear mother any courtesy;
When she—poor hen! fond of no second brood—
Has cluck'd thee to the wars, and safely home,
Loaden with honour. Say my request's unjust,
And spurn me back; but if it be not so,
Thou art not honest, and the gods will plague thee,
That thou restrain'st from me the duty which
To a mother's part belongs. He turns away:
Down, ladies; let us shame him with our knees.
To his surname Coriolanus 'longs more pride
Than pity to our prayers. Down: an end;
This is the last: so we will home to Rome,
And die among our neighbours. Nay, behold us.
This boy, that cannot tell what he would have,
But kneels and holds up hands for fellowship,
Does reason our petition with more strength
Than thou hast to deny 't. Come, let us go:
This fellow had a Volscian to his mother;
His wife is in Corioli, and his child
Like him by chance. Yet give us our dispatch:
I am hush'd until our city be a-fire,
And then I'll speak a little.
  Coriolanus. [*Holding* VOLUMNIA *by the hand, silent.*]
         O, mother, mother,
What have you done? Behold! the heavens do ope,
The gods look down, and this unnatural scene
They laugh at. O my mother! mother! O!
You have won a happy victory to Rome;
But, for your son, believe it, O! believe it,
Most dangerously you have with him prevail'd,
If not most mortal to him. But let it come.
Aufidius, though I cannot make true wars,
I'll frame convenient peace. Now, good Aufidius,
Were you in my stead, would you have heard
A mother less, or granted less, Aufidius?
  Aufidius. I was mov'd withal.   (v. iii. 153-94)

  Auf.   Read it not, noble lords;
But tell the traitor in the highest degree
He hath abus'd your powers.

Cor. Traitor! How now?
Auf.   Ay, traitor, Marcius.
Cor.   Marcius!
Auf. Ay, Marcius, Caius Marcius. Dost thou think
I'll grace thee with that robbery, thy stol'n name
Coriolanus in Corioli?
You lords and heads of the state, perfidiously
He has betray'd your business, and given up,
For certain drops of salt, your city Rome,
I say 'your city', to his wife and mother;
Breaking his oath and resolution like
A twist of rotten silk, never admitting
Counsel o' the war, but at his nurse's tears
He whin'd and roar'd away your victory,
That pages blush'd at him, and men of heart
Look'd wondering each at other.
    Cor.   Hear'st thou, Mars?
    Auf. Name not the god, thou boy of tears.
    Cor.   Ha!
    Auf. No more.
    Cor. Measureless liar, thou hast made my heart
Too great for what contains it. Boy! O slave!
Pardon me, lords, 'tis the first time that ever
I was forc'd to scold. Your judgments, my grave lords,
Must give this cur the lie: and his own notion—
Who wears my stripes impress'd upon him, that
Must bear my beating to his grave—shall join
To thrust the lie unto him.
    First Lord. Peace, both, and hear me speak.
    Cor. Cut me to pieces, Volsces; men and lads,
Stain all your edges on me. Boy! False hound!
If you have writ your annals true, 'tis there,
That, like an eagle in a dove-cote, I
Flutter'd your Volscians in Corioli:
Alone I did it. Boy!   (v. v. 84–117)

from *Timon of Athens*

Enter TIMON *from the Cave.*

    Timon. O blessed breeding sun! draw from the earth
Rotten humidity; below thy sister's orb
Infect the air! Twinn'd brothers of one womb,

Whose procreation, residence and birth,
Scarce is dividant, touch them with several fortunes;
The greater scorns the lesser: not nature,
To whom all sores lay siege, can bear great fortune,
But by contempt of nature.
Raise me this beggar, and deny't that lord;
The senator shall bear contempt hereditary,
The beggar native honour.
It is the pasture lards the rother's sides,
The want that makes him lean. Who dares, who dares,
In purity of manhood stand upright,
And say, 'This man's a flatterer?' if one be,
So are they all; for every grize of fortune
Is smooth'd by that below: the learned pate
Ducks to the golden fool: all is oblique;
There's nothing level in our cursed natures
But direct villany. Therefore, be abhorr'd
All feasts, societies, and throngs of men!
His semblable, yea, himself, Timon disdains:
Destruction fang mankind! Earth, yield me roots!   [*Digging.*
Who seeks for better of thee, sauce his palate
With thy most operant poison! What is here?
Gold! yellow, glittering, precious gold! No, gods,
I am no idle votarist. Roots, you clear heavens!
Thus much of this will make black white, foul fair,
Wrong right, base noble, old young, coward valiant.
Ha! you gods, why this? What this, you gods? Why, this
Will lug your priests and servants from your sides,
Pluck stout men's pillows from below their head:
This yellow slave
Will knit and break religions; bless the accurs'd;
Make the hoar leprosy ador'd; place thieves,
And give them title, knee, and approbation,
With senators on the bench; this is it
That makes the wappen'd widow wed again;
She, whom the spital-house and ulcerous sores
Would cast the gorge at, this embalms and spices
To the April day again. Come, damned earth,
Thou common whore of mankind, that putt'st odds
Amond the rout of nations, I will make thee
Do thy right nature.—[*March afar off.*] Ha! a drum? thou'rt quick,
But yet I'll bury thee: thou'lt go, strong thief,
When gouty keepers of thee cannot stand:
Nay, stay thou out for earnest.   [*Keeping some gold.*

Enter ALCIBIADES, *with drum and fife, in warlike manner;* PHRYNIA *and* TIMANDRA.

Alcibiades. What art thou there? speak.

Tim. A beast, as thou art. The canker gnaw thy heart,
For showing me again the eyes of man!

Alcib. What is thy name? Is man so hateful to thee,
That art thyself a man?

Tim. I am *Misanthropos*, and hate mankind.
For thy part, I do wish thou wert a dog,
That I might love thee something.   (IV. iii. 1–55)

Timon. Put up thy gold: go on,—here's gold,—go on;
Be as a planetary plague, when Jove
Will o'er some high-vic'd city hang his poison
In the sick air: let not thy sword skip one.
Pity not honour'd age for his white beard;
He is a usurer. Strike me the counterfeit matron;
It is her habit only that is honest,
Herself's a bawd. Let not the virgin's cheek
Make soft thy trenchant sword; for those milk-paps,
That through the window-bars bore at men's eyes,
Are not within the leaf of pity writ,
But set them down horrible traitors. Spare not the babe,
Whose dimpled smiles from fools exhaust their mercy;
Think it a bastard, whom the oracle
Hath doubtfully pronounc'd thy throat shall cut,
And mince it sans remorse. Swear against objects;
Put armour on thine ears and on thine eyes,
Whose proof nor yells of mothers, maids, nor babes,
Nor sight of priests in holy vestments bleeding,
Shall pierce a jot. There's gold to pay thy soldiers:
Make large confusion; and, thy fury spent,
Confounded be thyself! Speak not, be gone.

Alcibiades. Hast thou gold yet? I'll take the gold thou giv'st me,
Not all thy counsel.

Tim. Dost thou, or dost thou not, heaven's curse upon thee!

Phrynia.
Timandra. } Give us some gold, good Timon: hast thou more?

Tim. Enough to make a whore forswear her trade,
And to make whores a bawd. Hold up, you sluts,
Your aprons mountant: you are not oathable,
Although, I know, you'll swear, terribly swear
Into strong shudders and to heavenly agues
The immortal gods that hear you, spare your oaths,

I'll trust to your conditions: be whores still;
And he whose pious breath seeks to convert you,
Be strong in whore, allure him, burn him up;
Let your close fire predominate his smoke,
And be no turncoats: yet may your pains, six months,
Be quite contrary: and thatch your poor thin roofs
With burdens of the dead; some that were hang'd,
No matter; wear them, betray with them: whore still;
Paint till a horse may mire upon your face:
A pox of wrinkles!

    Phry. ⎫
    Timan. ⎭   Well, more gold. What then?

Believe't, that we'll do anything for gold.   (IV. iii. 108–51)

from *Pericles*

  Pericles. A terrible child-bed hast thou had, my dear;
No light, no fire: the unfriendly elements
Forgot thee utterly; nor have I time
To give thee hallow'd to thy grave, but straight
Must cast thee, scarcely coffin'd, in the ooze;
Where, for a monument upon thy bones,
And aye-remaining lamps, the belching whale
And humming water must o'erwhelm thy corpse,
Lying with simple shells!   (III. i. 57–65)

from *Cymbeline*

  Belarius. How found you him?
  Arviragus.   Stark, as you see:
Thus smiling, as some fly had tickled slumber,
Not as death's dart, being laugh'd at; his right cheek
Reposing on a cushion.
  Guiderius.   Where?
  Arv.   O' the floor,
His arms thus leagu'd; I thought he slept, and put
My clouted brogues from off my feet, whose rudeness
Answer'd my steps too loud.
  Gui.   Why, he but sleeps:
If he be gone, he'll make his grave a bed;
With female fairies will his tomb be haunted,
And worms will not come to thee.

Arv.   With fairest flowers
While summer lasts and I live here, Fidele,
I'll sweeten thy sad grave; thou shalt not lack
The flower that's like thy face, pale primrose, nor
The azur'd hare-bell, like thy veins, no, nor
The leaf of eglantine, whom not to slander,
Out-sweeten'd not thy breath: the ruddock would,
With charitable bill,—O bill! sore-shaming
Those rich-left heirs, that let their fathers lie
Without a monument,—bring thee all this;
Yea, and furr'd moss besides, when flowers are none,
To winter-ground thy corse.
Gui.   Prithee, have done,
And do not play in wench-like words with that
Which is so serious. Let us bury him,
And not protract with admiration what
Is now due debt. To the grave!   (IV. ii. 209–33)

Gui.   Fear no more the heat o' the sun,
              Nor the furious winter's rages:
         Thou thy worldly task hast done,
              Home art gone, and ta'en thy wages;
         Golden lads and girls all must,
              As chimney-sweepers, come to dust.

Arv.   Fear no more the frown o' the great,
              Thou art past the tyrant's stroke:
         Care no more to clothe and eat;
              To thee the reed is as the oak;
         The sceptre, learning, physic, must
              All follow this, and come to dust.

Gui.   Fear no more the lightning-flash,
Arv.   Nor the all-dreaded thunder-stone;
Gui.   Fear not slander, censure rash;
Arv.   Thou hast finish'd joy and moan:
Both. All lovers young, all lovers must
              Consign to thee, and come to dust.

Gui.   No exorciser harm thee!
Arv.   Nor no witchcraft charm thee!
Gui.   Ghost unlaid forbear thee!
Arv.   Nothing ill come near thee!
Both. Quiet consummation have:
              And renowned be thy grave!   (IV. ii. 258–81)

from *The Winter's Tale*

Hermione.　　　　　If you would seek us,
We are yours i' the garden: shall 's attend you there?
　Leontes.　To your own bents dispose you: you'll be found,
Be you beneath the sky.—[*Aside.*] I am angling now,
Though you perceive me not how I give line.
Go to, go to!
How she holds up the neb, the bill to him!
And arms her with the boldness of a wife
To her allowing husband!
　　　　　　　　[*Exeunt* POLIXENES, HERMIONE, *and* Attendants.
　　　　　　　　　Gone already!
Inch-thick, knee-deep, o'er head and ears a fork'd one!
Go play, boy, play; thy mother plays, and I
Play too, but so disgrac'd a part, whose issue
Will hiss me to my grave: contempt and clamour
Will be my knell. Go play, boy, play. There have been,
Or I am much deceiv'd, cuckolds ere now;
And many a man there is even at this present,
Now, while I speak this, holds his wife by the arm,
That little thinks she has been sluic'd in 's absence,
And his pond fish'd by his next neighbour, by
Sir Smile, his neighbour: nay, there 's comfort in 't,
Whiles other men have gates, and those gates open'd,
As mine, against their will. Should all despair
That have revolted wives the tenth of mankind
Would hang themselves. Physic for 't there is none;
It is a bawdy planet, that will strike
Where 'tis predominant; and 'tis powerful, think it,
From east, west, north, and south: be it concluded,
No barricado for a belly: know 't;
It will let in and out the enemy
With bag and baggage. Many a thousand on 's
Have the disease, and feel 't not. How now, boy!
　Mamillius.　I am like you, they say.
　Leon.　　　　　　　Why, that 's some comfort.
　　　　　　　　　　　　　　(I. ii. 177–208)

　Leon.　　　　　　　　I have said
She 's an adulteress; I have said with whom:
More, she 's a traitor, and Camillo is
A federary with her, and one that knows
What she should shame to know herself

But with her most vile principal, that she 's
A bed-swerver, even as bad as those
That vulgars give bold'st titles; ay, and privy
To this their late escape.

Her.   No, by my life,
Privy to none of this. How will this grieve you
When you shall come to clearer knowledge that
You thus have publish'd me! Gentle my lord,
You scarce can right me throughly then to say
You did mistake.

Leon.   No; if I mistake
In those foundations which I build upon,
The centre is not big enough to bear
A schoolboy's top. Away with her to prison!
He who shall speak for her is afar off guilty
But that he speaks.

Her.   There 's some ill planet reigns:
I must be patient till the heavens look
With an aspect more favourable. Good my lords,
I am not prone to weeping, as our sex
Commonly are; the want of which vain dew
Perchance shall dry your pities; but I have
That honourable grief lodg'd here which burns
Worse than tears drown. Beseech you all, my lords,
With thoughts so qualified as your charities
Shall best instruct you, measure me; and so
The king's will be perform'd!

Leon.   [*To the* Guards.] Shall I be heard?

Her. Who is 't that goes with me? Beseech your highness,
My women may be with me; for you see
My plight requires it. Do not weep, good fools;
There is no cause; when you shall know your mistress
Has deserv'd prison, then abound in tears
As I come out: this action I now go on
Is for my better grace.   (II. i. 86-121)

When daffodils begin to peer,
  With heigh! the doxy, over the dale,
Why, then comes in the sweet o' the year;
  For the red blood reigns in the winter's pale.

The white sheet bleaching on the hedge,
  With heigh! the sweet birds, O, how they sing!
Doth set my pugging tooth on edge;
  For a quart of ale is a dish for a king.

The lark, that tirra-lirra chants,
　　With, heigh! with, heigh! the thrush and the jay,
Are summer songs for me and my aunts,
　　While we lie tumbling in the hay.

(IV. ii. 1-12)

Perdita.　Give me those flowers there, Dorcas. Reverend sirs,
For you there 's rosemary and rue; these keep
Seeming and savour all the winter long:
Grace and remembrance be to you both,
And welcome to our shearing!
　Polixenes.　　　　　　　Shepherdess,—
A fair one are you,—well you fit our ages
With flowers of winter.
　Per.　　　　　　Sir, the year growing ancient,
Not yet on summer's death, nor on the birth
Of trembling winter, the fairest flowers o' the season
Are our carnations, and streak'd gillyvors,
Which some call nature's bastards: of that kind
Our rustic garden 's barren, and I care not
To get slips of them.
　Pol.　　　　　Wherefore, gentle maiden,
Do you neglect them?
　Per.　　　　　　For I have heard it said
There is an art which in their piedness shares
With great creating nature.
　Pol.　　　　　　　Say there be;
Yet nature is made better by no mean
But nature makes that mean: so, over that art,
Which you say adds to nature, is an art
That nature makes. You see, sweet maid, we marry
A gentler scion to the wildest stock,
And make conceive a bark of baser kind
By bud of nobler race: this is an art
Which does mend nature, change it rather, but
The art itself is nature.
　Per.　　　　　So it is.
　Pol.　Then make your garden rich in gillyvors,
And do not call them bastards.
　Per.　　　　　　　　I'll not put
The dibble in earth to set one slip of them;
No more than, were I painted, I would wish
This youth should say, 'twere well, and only therefore
Desire to breed by me. Here 's flowers for you;

Hot lavender, mints, savory, marjoram;
The marigold, that goes to bed wi' the sun,
And with him rises weeping: these are flowers
Of middle summer, and I think they are given
To men of middle age. You're very welcome.   (IV. iii. 73-108)

    Paulina.   As she liv'd peerless,
So her dead likeness, I do well believe,
Excels whatever yet you look'd upon
Or hand of man hath done; therefore I keep it
Lonely, apart. But here it is: prepare
To see the life as lively mock'd as ever
Still sleep mock'd death: behold! and say 'tis well.
    [PAULINA *draws back a curtain, and discovers* HERMIONE *as a statue.*
I like your silence: it the more shows off
Your wonder; but yet speak: first you, my liege.
Comes it not something near?
    Leon.   Her natural posture!
Chide me, dear stone, that I may say, indeed
Thou art Hermione; or rather, thou art she
In thy not chiding, for she was as tender
As infancy and grace. But yet, Paulina,
Hermione was not so much wrinkled; nothing
So aged as this seems.
    Pol.   O! not by much.
    Paul. So much the more our carver's excellence;
Which lets go by some sixteen years and makes her
As she liv'd now.
    Leon.   As now she might have done,
So much to my good comfort, as it is
Now piercing to my soul. O! thus she stood,
Even with such life of majesty,—warm life,
As now it coldly stands,—when first I woo'd her.
I am asham'd: does not the stone rebuke me
For being more stone than it? O, royal piece!
There 's magic in thy majesty, which has
My evils conjur'd to remembrance, and
From thy admiring daughter took the spirits,
Standing like stone with thee.
    Per.   And give me leave,
And do not say 'tis superstition, that
I kneel and then implore her blessing. Lady,
Dear queen, that ended when I but began,
Give me that hand of yours to kiss.

Paul.   O, patience!
The statue is but newly fix'd, the colour's
Not dry.
    Camillo. My lord, your sorrow was too sore laid on,
Which sixteen winters cannot blow away,
So many summers dry: scarce any joy
Did ever so long live; no sorrow
But kill'd itself much sooner.
    Pol.   Dear my brother,
Let him that was the cause of this have power
To take off so much grief from you as he
Will piece up in himself.
    Paul.   Indeed, my lord,
If I had thought the sight of my poor image
Would thus have wrought you,—for the stone is mine,—
I'd not have show'd it.
    Leon.   Do not draw the curtain.
    Paul. No longer shall you gaze on 't, lest your fancy
May think anon it moves.
    Leon.   Let be, let be!
Would I were dead, but that, methinks, already—
What was he that did make it? See, my lord,
Would you not deem it breath'd, and that those veins
Did verily bear blood?
    Pol.   Masterly done:
The very life seems warm upon her lip.
    Leon. The fixture of her eye has motion in 't,
As we are mock'd with art.
    Paul.   I'll draw the curtain;
My lord 's almost so far transported that
He'll think anon it lives.
    Leon.   O sweet Paulina!
Make me to think so twenty years together:
Not settled senses of the world can match
The pleasure of that madness.   (v. iii. 14-73)

from *The Tempest*

Prospero.   Hast thou, spirit,
Perform'd to point the tempest that I bade thee?
    Ariel. To every article.
I boarded the king's ship; now on the beak,
Now in the waist, the deck, in every cabin,

I flam'd amazement: sometime I'd divide
And burn in many places; on the topmast,
The yards, and boresprit, would I flame distinctly,
Then meet, and join: Jove's lightnings, the precursors
O' the dreadful thunder-claps, more momentary
And sight-outrunning were not: the fire and cracks
Of sulphurous roaring the most mighty Neptune
Seem to besiege and make his bold waves tremble,
Yea, his dread trident shake.
    Pro.   My brave spirit!
Who was so firm, so constant, that this coil
Would not infect his reason?
    Ari.   Not a soul
But felt a fever of the mad and play'd
Some tricks of desperation. All but mariners,
Plunged in the foaming brine and quit the vessel,
Then all a-fire with me: the king's son, Ferdinand,
With hair up-staring,—then like reeds, not hair,—
Was the first man that leap'd; cried, 'Hell is empty,
And all the devils are here.'   (I. ii. 193–215)

    Pro.   Dost thou forget
From what a torment I did free thee?
    Ari.   No.
    Pro. Thou dost; and think'st it much to tread the ooze
Of the salt deep,
To run upon the sharp wind of the north,
To do me business in the veins o' th' earth
When it is bak'd with frost.
    Ari.   I do not, sir.
    Pro. Thou liest, malignant thing! Hast thou forgot
The foul witch Sycorax, who with age and envy
Was grown into a hoop? hast thou forgot her?
    Ari. No, sir.
    Pro.   Thou hast. Where was she born? speak; tell me.
    Ari. Sir, in Argier.
    Pro.   O! was she so? I must,
Once in a month, recount what thou hast been,
Which thou forget'st. This damn'd witch, Sycorax,
For mischiefs manifold and sorceries terrible
To enter human hearing, from Argier,
Thou know'st, was banish'd: for one thing she did
They would not take her life. Is not this true?
    Ari. Ay, sir.

Pro. This blue-ey'd hag was hither brought with child
And here was left by the sailors. Thou, my slave,
As thou report'st thyself, wast then her servant:
And, for thou wast a spirit too delicate
To act her earthy and abhorr'd commands.
Refusing her grand hests, she did confine thee,
By help of her more potent ministers,
And in her most unmitigable rage,
Into a cloven pine; within which rift
Imprison'd, thou didst painfully remain
A dozen years; within which space she died
And left thee there, where thou didst vent thy groans
As fast as mill-wheels strike. Then was this island,—
Save for the son that she did litter here,
A freckled whelp hag-born,—not honour'd with
A human shape.
    Ari.   Yes; Caliban her son.
    Pro. Dull thing, I say so; he that Caliban,
Whom now I keep in service. Thou best know'st
What torment I did find thee in; thy groans
Did make wolves howl and penetrate the breasts
Of ever-angry bears: it was a torment
To lay upon the damn'd, which Sycorax
Could not again undo; it was mine art,
When I arriv'd and heard thee, that made gape
The pine, and let thee out.
    Ari.   I thank thee, master.
    Pro. If thou more murmur'st, I will rend an oak
And peg thee in his knotty entrails till
Thou hast howl'd away twelve winters.   (I. ii. 250–96)

    Caliban. Be not afeard: the isle is full of noises,
Sounds and sweet airs, that give delight, and hurt not.
Sometimes a thousand twangling instruments
Will hum about mine ears; and sometime voices,
That, if I then had wak'd after long sleep,
Will make me sleep again: and then, in dreaming,
The clouds methought would open and show riches
Ready to drop upon me; that, when I wak'd
I cried to dream again.   (III. ii. 147–55)

    Pro. Ye elves of hills, brooks, standing lakes, and groves;
And ye, that on the sands with printless foot
Do chase the ebbing Neptune and do fly him

When he comes back; you demi-puppets, that
By moonshine do the green sour ringlets make
Whereof the ewe not bites; and you, whose pastime
Is to make midnight mushrooms; that rejoice
To hear the solemn curfew; by whose aid,—
Weak masters though ye be—I have bedimm'd
The noontide sun, call'd forth the mutinous winds,
And 'twixt the green sea and the azur'd vault
Set roaring war: to the dread-rattling thunder
Have I given fire and rifted Jove's stout oak
With his own bolt: the strong-bas'd promontory
Have I made shake; and by the spurs pluck'd up
The pine and cedar: graves at my command
Have wak'd their sleepers, op'd, and let them forth
By my so potent art. But this rough magic
I here abjure; and, when I have requir'd
Some heavenly music,—which even now I do,—
To work mine end upon their senses that
This airy charm is for, I'll break my staff,
Bury it certain fathoms in the earth,
And, deeper than did ever plummet sound,
I'll drown my book.   (v. i. 33-57)

The Phoenix and the Turtle

LET the bird of loudest lay,
On the sole Arabian tree,
Herald sad and trumpet be,
To whose sound chaste wings obey.

But thou shrieking harbinger,
Foul precurrer of the fiend,
Augur of the fever's end,
To this troop come thou not near.

From this session interdict
Every fowl of tyrant wing,
Save the eagle, feather'd king:
Keep the obsequy so strict.

Let the priest in surplice white
That defunctive music can,
Be the death-divining swan,
Lest the requiem lack his right.

And thou treble-dated crow,
That thy sable gender mak'st
With the breath thou giv'st and tak'st,
'Mongst our mourners shalt thou go.

Here the anthem doth commence:
Love and constancy is dead;
Phœnix and the turtle fled
In a mutual flame from hence.

So they lov'd, as love in twain
Had the essence but in one;
Two distincts, division none:
Number there in love was slain.

Hearts remote, yet not asunder;
Distance, and no space was seen
'Twixt the turtle and his queen:
But in them it were a wonder.

So between them love did shine,
That the turtle saw his right
Flaming in the phœnix' sight;
Either was the other's mine.

Property was thus appall'd,
That the self was not the same;
Single nature's double name
Neither two nor one was call'd.

Reason, in itself confounded,
Saw division grow together;
To themselves yet either neither,
Simple were so well compounded,

That it cried, 'How true a twain
Seemeth this concordant one!
Love hath reason, reason none,
If what parts can so remain.'

Whereupon it made this threne
To the phœnix and the dove,
Co-supremes and stars of love,
As chorus to their tragic scene.

Threnos

Beauty, truth, and rarity
Grace in all simplicity,
Here enclos'd in cinders lie.

Death is now the phœnix' nest;
And the turtle's loyal breast
To eternity doth rest,

Leaving no posterity:
'Twas not their infirmity,
It was married chastity.

Truth may seem, but cannot be;
Beauty brag, but 'tis not she;
Truth and beauty buried be.

To this urn let those repair
That are either true or fair;
For these dead birds sigh a prayer.

Sonnets

XVIII

SHALL I compare thee to a summer's day?
Thou art more lovely and more temperate:
Rough winds do shake the darling buds of May,
And summer's lease hath all too short a date:
Sometime too hot the eye of heaven shines,
And often is his gold complexion dimm'd:
And every fair from fair sometime declines,
By chance, or nature's changing course untrimm'd;
But thy eternal summer shall not fade,
Nor lose possession of that fair thou ow'st,
Nor shall death brag thou wander'st in his shade,
When in eternal lines to time thou grow'st;
    So long as men can breathe, or eyes can see,
    So long lives this, and this gives life to thee.

XIX

DEVOURING Time, blunt thou the lion's paws,
And make the earth devour her own sweet brood;
Pluck the keen teeth from the fierce tiger's jaws,
And burn the long-liv'd phœnix in her blood;
Make glad and sorry seasons as thou fleets,
And do whate'er thou wilt, swift-footed Time,
To the wide world and all her fading sweets;
But I forbid thee one most heinous crime:
O! carve not with thy hours my love's fair brow,
Nor draw no lines there with thine antique pen;
Him in thy course untainted do allow
For beauty's pattern to succeeding men.
  Yet, do thy worst, old Time: despite thy wrong,
  My love shall in my verse ever live young.

XX

A WOMAN'S face with Nature's own hand painted
Hast thou, the master-mistress of my passion;
A woman's gentle heart, but not acquainted
With shifting change, as is false women's fashion;
An eye more bright than theirs, less false in rolling,
Gilding the object whereupon it gazeth;
A man in hue all hues in his controlling,
Which steals men's eyes and women's souls amazeth.
And for a woman wert thou first created;
Till Nature, as she wrought thee, fell a-doting,
And by addition me of thee defeated,
By adding one thing to my purpose nothing.
  But since she prick'd thee out for women's pleasure,
  Mine be thy love, and thy love's use their treasure.

XXV

LET those who are in favour with their stars
Of public honour and proud titles boast,
Whilst I, whom fortune of such triumph bars,
Unlook'd for joy in that I honour most.
Great princes' favourites their fair leaves spread
But as the marigold at the sun's eye,

WILLIAM SHAKESPEARE

And in themselves their pride lies buried,
For at a frown they in their glory die.
The painful warrior famoused for fight,
After a thousand victories once foil'd,
Is from the book of honour razed quite,
And all the rest forgot for which he toil'd:
    Then happy I, that love and am belov'd,
    Where I may not remove nor be remov'd.

XXIX

WHEN in disgrace with fortune and men's eyes
I all alone beweep my outcast state,
And trouble deaf heaven with my bootless cries,
And look upon myself, and curse my fate,
Wishing me like to one more rich in hope,
Featur'd like him, like him with friends possess'd,
Desiring this man's art, and that man's scope,
With what I most enjoy contented least;
Yet in these thoughts myself almost despising,
Haply I think on thee,—and then my state,
Like to the lark at break of day arising
From sullen earth, sings hymns at heaven's gate;
    For thy sweet love remember'd such wealth brings
    That then I scorn to change my state with kings.

XXX

WHEN to the sessions of sweet silent thought
I summon up remembrance of things past,
I sigh the lack of many a thing I sought,
And with old woes new wail my dear times' waste:
Then can I drown an eye, unus'd to flow,
For precious friends hid in death's dateless night,
And weep afresh love's long since cancell'd woe,
And moan the expense of many a vanish'd sight:
Then can I grieve at grievances foregone,
And heavily from woe to woe tell o'er
The sad account of fore-bemoaned moan,
Which I new pay as if not paid before.
    But if the while I think on thee, dear friend,
    All losses are restor'd and sorrows end.

XXXIII

FULL many a glorious morning have I seen
Flatter the mountain-tops with sovereign eye,
Kissing with golden face the meadows green,
Gilding pale streams with heavenly alchymy;
Anon permit the basest clouds to ride
With ugly rack on his celestial face,
And from the forlorn world his visage hide,
Stealing unseen to west with this disgrace:
Even so my sun one early morn did shine,
With all-triumphant splendour on my brow;
But, out! alack! he was but one hour mine,
The region cloud hath mask'd him from me now.
    Yet him for this my love no whit disdaineth;
    Suns of the world may stain when heaven's sun staineth.

XXXIV

WHY didst thou promise such a beauteous day,
And make me travel forth without my cloak,
To let base clouds o'ertake me in my way,
Hiding thy bravery in their rotten smoke?
'Tis not enough that through the cloud thou break,
To dry the rain on my storm-beaten face,
For no man well of such a salve can speak
That heals the wound and cures not the disgrace:
Nor can thy shame give physic to my grief;
Though thou repent, yet I have still the loss:
The offender's sorrow lends but weak relief
To him that bears the strong offence's cross.
    Ah! but those tears are pearl which thy love sheds,
    And they are rich and ransom all ill deeds.

XXXV

No more be griev'd at that which thou hast done:
Roses have thorns, and silver fountains mud;
Clouds and eclipses stain both moon and sun,
And loathsome canker lives in sweetest bud.
All men make faults, and even I in this,
Authorising thy trespass with compare,

Myself corrupting, salving thy amiss,
Excusing thy sins more than thy sins are;
For to thy sensual fault I bring in sense,—
Thy adverse party is thy advocate,—
And 'gainst myself a lawful plea commence:
Such civil war is in my love and hate,
    That I an accessary needs must be
    To that sweet thief which sourly robs from me.

XL

TAKE all my loves, my love, yea, take them all;
What hast thou then more than thou hadst before?
No love, my love, that thou mayst true love call;
All mine was thine before thou hadst this more
Then, if for my love thou my love receivest,
I cannot blame thee for my love thou usest;
But yet be blam'd, if thou thyself deceivest
By wilful taste of what thyself refusest.
I do forgive thy robbery, gentle thief,
Although thou steal thee all my poverty;
And yet, love knows it is a greater grief
To bear love's wrong than hate's known injury.
    Lascivious grace, in whom all ill well shows,
    Kill me with spites; yet we must not be foes.

XLI

THOSE pretty wrongs that liberty commits,
When I am sometimes absent from thy heart,
Thy beauty and thy years full well befits,
For still temptation follows where thou art.
Gentle thou art, and therefore to be won,
Beauteous thou art, therefore to be assail'd;
And when a woman woos, what woman's son
Will sourly leave her till she have prevail'd?
Ay me! but yet thou mightst my seat forbear,
And chide thy beauty and thy straying youth,
Who lead thee in their riot even there
Where thou art forc'd to break a twofold truth;—
    Hers, by thy beauty tempting her to thee,
    Thine, by thy beauty being false to me.

XLII

THAT thou hast her, it is not all my grief,
And yet it may be said I lov'd her dearly;
That she hath thee, is of my wailing chief,
A loss in love that touches me more nearly.
Loving offenders, thus I will excuse ye:
Thou dost love her, because thou know'st I love her;
And for my sake even so doth she abuse me,
Suffering my friend for my sake to approve her.
If I lose thee, my loss is my love's gain,
And losing her, my friend hath found that loss;
Both find each other, and I lose both twain,
And both for my sake lay on me this cross:
　　But here 's the joy; my friend and I are one;
　　Sweet flattery! then she loves but me alone.

XLIX

AGAINST that time, if ever that time come,
When I shall see thee frown on my defects,
When as thy love hath cast his utmost sum,
Call'd to that audit by advis'd respects;
Against that time when thou shalt strangely pass,
And scarcely greet me with that sun, thine eye,
When love, converted from the thing it was,
Shall reasons find of settled gravity;
Against that time do I ensconce me here
Within the knowledge of mine own desert,
And this my hand against myself uprear,
To guard the lawful reasons on thy part:
　　To leave poor me thou hast the strength of laws,
　　Since why to love I can allege no cause.

L

HOW heavy do I journey on the way,
When what I seek, my weary travel's end,
Doth teach that ease and that repose to say,
'Thus far the miles are measur'd from thy friend!'
The beast that bears me, tired with my woe,
Plods dully on, to bear that weight in me,

As if by some instinct the wretch did know
His rider lov'd not speed, being made from thee:
The bloody spur cannot provoke him on
That sometimes anger thrusts into his hide,
Which heavily he answers with a groan
More sharp to me than spurring to his side;
    For that same groan doth put this in my mind:
    My grief lies onward, and my joy behind.

LII

So am I as the rich, whose blessed key
Can bring him to his sweet up-locked treasure,
The which he will not every hour survey,
For blunting the fine point of seldom pleasure.
Therefore are feasts so solemn and so rare,
Since, seldom coming, in the long year set,
Like stones of worth they thinly placed are,
Or captain jewels in the carcanet.
So is the time that keeps you as my chest,
Or as the wardrobe which the robe doth hide,
To make some special instant special blest
By new unfolding his imprison'd pride.
    Blessed are you, whose worthiness gives scope,
    Being had, to triumph; being lack'd, to hope.

LIII

What is your substance, whereof are you made,
That millions of strange shadows on you tend?
Since every one hath, every one, one shade,
And you, but one, can every shadow lend.
Describe Adonis, and the counterfeit
Is poorly imitated after you;
On Helen's cheek all art of beauty set,
And you in Grecian tires are painted new:
Speak of the spring and foison of the year,
The one doth shadow of your beauty show,
The other as your bounty doth appear;
And you in every blessed shape we know.
    In all external grace you have some part,
    But you like none, none you, for constant heart.

LV

Not marble, nor the gilded monuments
Of princes, shall outlive this powerful rime;
But you shall shine more bright in these contents
Than unswept stone, besmear'd with sluttish time.
When wasteful war shall statues overturn,
And broils root out the work of masonry,
Nor Mars his sword nor war's quick fire shall burn
The living record of your memory.
'Gainst death and all-oblivious enmity
Shall you pace forth; your praise shall still find room
Even in the eyes of all posterity
That wear this world out to the ending doom.
    So, till the judgment that yourself arise,
    You live in this, and dwell in lovers' eyes.

LX

Like as the waves make towards the pebbled shore,
So do our minutes hasten to their end;
Each changing place with that which goes before,
In sequent toil all forwards do contend.
Nativity, once in the main of light,
Crawls to maturity, wherewith being crown'd,
Crooked eclipses 'gainst his glory fight,
And Time that gave doth now his gift confound.
Time doth transfix the flourish set on youth
And delves the parallels in beauty's brow,
Feeds on the rarities of nature's truth,
And nothing stands but for his scythe to mow:
    And yet to times in hope my verse shall stand,
    Praising thy worth, despite his cruel hand.

LXII

Sin of self-love possesseth all mine eye
And all my soul and all my every part;
And for this sin there is no remedy,
It is so grounded inward in my heart.
Methinks no face so gracious is as mine,
No shape so true, no truth of such account;

And for myself mine own worth do define,
As I all other in all worths surmount.
But when my glass shows me myself indeed,
Beated and chopp'd with tann'd antiquity,
Mine own self-love quite contrary I read;
Self so self-loving were iniquity.
   'Tis thee, myself,—that for myself I praise,
   Painting my age with beauty of thy days.

LXIV

WHEN I have seen by Time's fell hand defac'd
The rich-proud cost of outworn buried age;
When sometime lofty towers I see down-raz'd,
And brass eternal slave to mortal rage;
When I have seen the hungry ocean gain
Advantage on the kingdom of the shore,
And the firm soil win of the watery main,
Increasing store with loss, and loss with store;
When I have seen such interchange of state,
Or state itself confounded to decay;
Ruin hath taught me thus to ruminate—
That Time will come and take my love away.
   This thought is as a death, which cannot choose
   But weep to have that which it fears to lose.

LXV

SINCE brass, nor stone, nor earth, nor boundless sea,
But sad mortality o'ersways their power,
How with this rage shall beauty hold a plea,
Whose action is no stronger than a flower?
O! how shall summer's honey breath hold out
Against the wrackful siege of battering days,
When rocks impregnable are not so stout,
Nor gates of steel so strong, but Time decays?
O fearful meditation! where, alack,
Shall Time's best jewel from Time's chest lie hid?
Or what strong hand can hold his swift foot back?
Or who his spoil of beauty can forbid?
   O! none, unless this miracle have might,
   That in black ink my love may still shine bright.

LXVI

Tir'd with all these, for restful death I cry
As to behold desert a beggar born,
And needy nothing trimm'd in jollity,
And purest faith unhappily forsworn,
And gilded honour shamefully misplac'd,
And maiden virtue rudely strumpeted,
And right perfection wrongfully disgraced,
And strength by limping sway disabled,
And art made tongue-tied by authority,
And folly—doctor-like—controlling skill,
And simple truth miscall'd simplicity,
And captive good attending captain ill:
   Tir'd with all these, from these would I be gone,
   Save that, to die, I leave my love alone.

LXX

That thou art blam'd shall not be thy defect,
For slander's mark was ever yet the fair;
The ornament of beauty is suspect,
A crow that flies in heaven's sweetest air.
So thou be good, slander doth but approve
Thy worth the greater, being woo'd of time;
For canker vice the sweetest buds doth love,
And thou present'st a pure unstained prime.
Thou hast pass'd by the ambush of young days,
Either not assail'd, or victor being charg'd;
Yet this thy praise cannot be so thy praise,
To tie up envy evermore enlarg'd:
   If some suspect of ill mask'd not thy show,
   Then thou alone kingdoms of hearts shouldst owe.

LXXI

No longer mourn for me when I am dead
Than you shall hear the surly sullen bell
Give warning to the world that I am fled
From this vile world, with vilest worms to dwell:
Nay, if you read this line, remember not
The hand that writ it; for I love you so,

WILLIAM SHAKESPEARE

That I in your sweet thoughts would be forgot,
If thinking on me then should make you woe.
O! if,—I say, you look upon this verse,
When I perhaps compounded am with clay,
Do not so much as my poor name rehearse,
But let your love even with my life decay;
    Lest the wise world should look into your moan,
    And mock you with me after I am gone.

LXXII

O! LEST the world should task you to recite
What merit lived in me, that you should love
After my death,—dear love, forget me quite,
For you in me can nothing worthy prove;
Unless you would devise some virtuous lie,
To do more for me than mine own desert,
And hang more praise upon deceased I
Than niggard truth would willingly impart:
O! lest your true love may seem false in this,
That you for love speak well of me untrue,
My name be buried where my body is,
And live no more to shame nor me nor you.
    For I am sham'd by that which I bring forth,
    And so should you, to love things nothing worth.

LXXIII

THAT time of year thou mayst in me behold
When yellow leaves, or none, or few, do hang
Upon those boughs which shake against the cold,
Bare ruin'd choirs, where late the sweet birds sang.
In me thou see'st the twilight of such day
As after sunset fadeth in the west;
Which by and by black night doth take away,
Death's second self, that seals up all in rest.
In me thou see'st the glowing of such fire,
That on the ashes of his youth doth lie,
As the death-bed whereon it must expire
Consum'd with that which it was nourish'd by.
    This thou perceiv'st, which makes thy love more strong,
    To love that well which thou must leave ere long.

LXXIV

But be contented: when that fell arrest
Without all bail shall carry me away,
My life hath in this line some interest,
Which for memorial still with thee shall stay.
When thou reviewest this, thou dost review
The very part was consecrate to thee:
The earth can have but earth, which is his due;
My spirit is thine, the better part of me:
So then thou hast but lost the dregs of life,
The prey of worms, my body being dead;
The coward conquest of a wretch's knife,
Too base of thee to be remembered.
    The worth of that is that which it contains,
    And that is this, and this with thee remains.

LXXVI

Why is my verse so barren of new pride,
So far from variation or quick change?
Why with the time do I not glance aside
To new-found methods and to compounds strange?
Why write I still all one, ever the same,
And keep invention in a noted weed,
That every word doth almost tell my name,
Showing their birth, and where they did proceed?
O! know, sweet love, I always write of you,
And you and love are still my argument;
So all my best is dressing old words new,
Spending again what is already spent:
    For as the sun is daily new and old,
    So is my love still telling what is told.

LXXX

O! how I faint when I of you do write,
Knowing a better spirit doth use your name,
And in the praise thereof spends all his might,
To make me tongue-tied, speaking of your fame!
But since your worth—wide as the ocean is,—
The humble as the proudest sail doth bear,

My saucy bark, inferior far to his,
On your broad main doth wilfully appear.
Your shallowest help will hold me up afloat,
Whilst he upon your soundless deep doth ride;
Or, being wrack'd, I am a worthless boat,
He of tall building and of goodly pride:
    Then if he thrive and I be cast away,
    The worst was this;—my love was my decay.

LXXXI

OR I shall live your epitaph to make,
Or you survive when I in earth am rotten;
From hence your memory death cannot take,
Although in me each part will be forgotten.
Your name from hence immortal life shall have,
Though I, once gone, to all the world must die:
The earth can yield me but a common grave,
When you entombed in men's eyes shall lie.
Your monument shall be my gentle verse,
Which eyes not yet created shall o'er-read;
And tongues to be your being shall rehearse,
When all the breathers of this world are dead;
    You still shall live,—such virtue hath my pen,—
    Where breath most breathes,—even in the mouths of men.

LXXXVI

WAS it the proud full sail of his great verse,
Bound for the prize of all too precious you,
That did my ripe thoughts in my brain inhearse,
Making their tomb the womb wherein they grew?
Was it his spirit, by spirits taught to write
Above a mortal pitch, that struck me dead?
No, neither he, nor his compeers by night
Giving him aid, my verse astonished.
He, nor that affable familiar ghost
Which nightly gulls him with intelligence,
As victors of my silence cannot boast;
I was not sick of any fear from thence:
    But when your countenance fill'd up his line,
    Then lack'd I matter; that enfeebled mine.

LXXXVII

FAREWELL! thou art too dear for my possessing,
And like enough thou know'st thy estimate:
The charter of thy worth gives thee releasing;
My bonds in thee are all determinate.
For how do I hold thee but by thy granting?
And for that riches where is my deserving?
The cause of this fair gift in me is wanting,
And so my patent back again is swerving.
Thyself thou gav'st, thy own worth then not knowing,
Or me, to whom thou gav'st it, else mistaking;
So thy great gift, upon misprision growing,
Comes home again, on better judgment making.
  Thus have I had thee, as a dream doth flatter,
  In sleep a king, but, waking, no such matter.

LXXXVIII

WHEN thou shalt be dispos'd to set me light,
And place my merit in the eye of scorn,
Upon thy side against myself I'll fight,
And prove thee virtuous, though thou art forsworn.
With mine own weakness, being best acquainted,
Upon thy part I can set down a story
Of faults conceal'd, wherein I am attainted;
That thou in losing me shalt win much glory:
And I by this will be a gainer too;
For bending all my loving thoughts on thee,
The injuries that to myself I do,
Doing thee vantage, double-vantage me.
  Such is my love, to thee I so belong,
  That for thy right myself will bear all wrong.

LXXXIX

SAY that thou didst forsake me for some fault,
And I will comment upon that offence:
Speak of my lameness, and I straight will halt,
Against thy reasons making no defence.
Thou canst not, love, disgrace me half so ill,
To set a form upon desired change,

As I'll myself disgrace; knowing thy will,
I will acquaintance strangle, and look strange;
Be absent from thy walks; and in my tongue
Thy sweet beloved name no more shall dwell,
Lest I, too much profane, should do it wrong,
And haply of our old acquaintance tell.
    For thee, against myself I'll vow debate,
    For I must ne'er love him whom thou dost hate.

XC

THEN hate me when thou wilt; if ever, now;
Now, while the world is bent my deeds to cross,
Join with the spite of fortune, make me bow,
And do not drop in for an after-loss:
Ah! do not, when my heart hath 'scap'd this sorrow,
Come in the rearward of a conquer'd woe;
Give not a windy night a rainy morrow,
To linger out a purpos'd overthrow.
If thou wilt leave me, do not leave me last,
When other petty griefs have done their spite,
But in the onset come: so shall I taste
At first the very worst of fortune's might;
    And other strains of woe, which now seem woe,
    Compar'd with loss of thee will not seem so.

XCIV

THEY that have power to hurt and will do none,
That do not do the thing they most do show,
Who, moving others, are themselves as stone,
Unmoved, cold, and to temptation slow;
They rightly do inherit heaven's graces,
And husband nature's riches from expense;
They are the lords and owners of their faces,
Others but stewards of their excellence.
The summer's flower is to the summer sweet,
Though to itself it only live and die,
But if that flower with base infection meet,
The basest weed outbraves his dignity:
    For sweetest things turn sourest by their deeds;
    Lilies that fester smell far worse than weeds.

XCVII

How like a winter hath my absence been
From thee, the pleasure of the fleeting year!
What freezings have I felt, what dark days seen!
What old December's bareness every where!
And yet this time remov'd was summer's time;
The teeming autumn, big with rich increase,
Bearing the wanton burden of the prime,
Like widow'd wombs after their lords' decease:
Yet this abundant issue seem'd to me
But hope of orphans and unfather'd fruit;
For summer and his pleasures wait on thee,
And, thou away, the very birds are mute:
    Or, if they sing, 'tis with so dull a cheer,
    That leaves look pale, dreading the winter's near.

XCVIII

From you have I been absent in the spring,
When proud-pied April, dress'd in all his trim,
Hath put a spirit of youth in every thing,
That heavy Saturn laugh'd and leap'd with him.
Yet nor the lays of birds, nor the sweet smell
Of different flowers in odour and in hue,
Could make me any summer's story tell,
Or from their proud lap pluck them where they grew:
Nor did I wonder at the lily's white,
Nor praise the deep vermilion in the rose;
They were but sweet, but figures of delight,
Drawn after you, you pattern of all those.
    Yet seem'd it winter still, and, you away,
    As with your shadow I with these did play.

XCIX

The forward violet thus did I chide:
Sweet thief, whence didst thou steal thy sweet that smells,
If not from my love's breath? The purple pride
Which on thy soft cheek for complexion dwells
In my love's veins thou hast too grossly dy'd.
The lily I condemned for thy hand,

And buds of marjoram had stol'n thy hair;
The roses fearfully on thorns did stand,
One blushing shame, another white despair,
A third, nor red nor white, had stol'n of both,
And to his robbery had annex'd thy breath;
But, for his theft, in pride of all his growth
A vengeful canker eat him up to death.
    More flowers I noted, yet I none could see
    But sweet or colour it had stol'n from thee.

CIV

To me, fair friend, you never can be old,
For as you were when first your eye I ey'd,
Such seems your beauty still. Three winters cold
Have from the forests shook three summers' pride,
Three beauteous springs to yellow autumn turn'd
In process of the seasons have I seen,
Three April perfumes in three hot Junes burn'd,
Since first I saw you fresh, which yet are green.
Ah! yet doth beauty, like a dial-hand,
Steal from his figure, and no pace perceiv'd;
So your sweet hue, which methinks still doth stand,
Hath motion, and mine eye may be deceiv'd:
    For fear of which, hear this, thou age unbred:
    Ere you were born was beauty's summer dead.

CVI

When in the chronicle of wasted time
I see descriptions of the fairest wights,
And beauty making beautiful old rime,
In praise of ladies dead and lovely knights,
Then, in the blazon of sweet beauty's best,
Of hand, of foot, of lip, of eye, of brow,
I see their antique pen would have express'd
Even such a beauty as you master now.
So all their praises are but prophecies
Of this our time, all you prefiguring;
And, for they look'd but with divining eyes,
They had not skill enough your worth to sing:
    For we, which now behold these present days,
    Have eyes to wonder, but lack tongues to praise.

CVII

Not mine own fears, nor the prophetic soul
Of the wide world dreaming on things to come,
Can yet the lease of my true love control,
Suppos'd as forfeit to a confin'd doom.
The mortal moon hath her eclipse endur'd,
And the sad augurs mock their own presage;
Incertainties now crown themselves assur'd,
And peace proclaims olives of endless age.
Now with the drops of this most balmy time
My love looks fresh, and Death to me subscribes,
Since, spite of him, I'll live in this poor rime,
While he insults o'er dull and speechless tribes:
  And thou in this shalt find thy monument,
   When tyrants' crests and tombs of brass are spent.

CIX

O! never say that I was false of heart,
Though absence seem'd my flame to qualify.
As easy might I from myself depart
As from my soul, which in thy breast doth lie:
That is my home of love: if I have rang'd,
Like him that travels, I return again;
Just to the time, not with the time exchang'd,
So that myself bring water for my stain.
Never believe, though in my nature reign'd
All frailties that besiege all kinds of blood,
That it could so preposterously be stain'd,
To leave for nothing all thy sum of good;
  For nothing this wide universe I call,
   Save thou, my rose; in it thou art my all.

CX

Alas! 'tis true I have gone here and there,
And made myself a motley to the view,
Gor'd mine own thoughts, sold cheap what is most dear,
Made old offences of affections new;
Most true it is that I have look'd on truth
Askance and strangely; but, by all above,

These blenches gave my heart another youth,
And worse essays prov'd thee my best of love.
Now all is done, save what shall have no end:
Mine appetite I never more will grind
On newer proof, to try an older friend,
A god in love, to whom I am confin'd.
  Then give me welcome, next my heaven the best,
  Even to thy pure and most most loving breast.

CXI

O! FOR my sake do you with Fortune chide
The guilty goddess of my harmful deeds,
That did not better for my life provide
Than public means which public manners breeds.
Thence comes it that my name receives a brand,
And almost thence my nature is subdu'd
To what it works in, like the dyer's hand:
Pity me, then, and wish I were renew'd;
Whilst, like a willing patient, I will drink
Potions of eisel 'gainst my strong infection;
No bitterness that I will bitter think,
Nor double penance, to correct correction.
  Pity me, then, dear friend, and I assure ye
  Even that your pity is enough to cure me.

CXVI

LET me not to the marriage of true minds
Admit impediments. Love is not love
Which alters when it alteration finds,
Or bends with the remover to remove:
O, no! it is an ever-fixed mark,
That looks on tempests and is never shaken;
It is the star to every wandering bark,
Whose worth 's unknown, although his height be taken.
Love's not Time's fool, though rosy lips and cheeks
Within his bending sickle's compass come;
Love alters not with his brief hours and weeks,
But bears it out even to the edge of doom.
  If this be error, and upon me prov'd,
  I never writ, nor no man ever lov'd.

CXIX

WHAT potions have I drunk of Siren tears,
Distill'd from limbecks foul as hell within,
Applying fears to hopes, and hopes to fears,
Still losing when I saw myself to win!
What wretched errors hath my heart committed,
Whilst it hath thought itself so blessed never!
How have mine eyes out of their spheres been fitted,
In the distraction of this madding fever!
O benefit of ill! now I find true
That better is by evil still made better;
And ruin'd love, when it is built anew,
Grows fairer than at first, more strong, far greater.
  So I return rebuk'd to my content,
  And gain by ill thrice more than I have spent.

CXX

THAT you were once unkind befriends me now,
And for that sorrow, which I then did feel,
Needs must I under my transgression bow,
Unless my nerves were brass or hammer'd steel.
For if you were by my unkindness shaken,
As I by yours, you 've pass'd a hell of time;
And I, a tyrant, have no leisure taken
To weigh how once I suffer'd in your crime.
O! that our night of woe might have remember'd
My deepest sense, how hard true sorrow hits,
And soon to you, as you to me, then tender'd
The humble salve which wounded bosoms fits!
  But that your trespass now becomes a fee;
  Mine ransoms yours, and yours must ransom me.

CXXI

'TIS better to be vile than vile esteem'd,
When not to be receives reproach of being;
And the just pleasure lost, which is so deem'd
Not by our feeling, but by others' seeing:
For why should others' false adulterate eyes
Give salutation to my sportive blood?

Or on my frailties why are frailer spies,
Which in their wills count bad what I think good?
No, I am that I am, and they that level
At my abuses reckon up their own:
I may be straight though they themselves be bevel;
By their rank thoughts my deeds must not be shown;
  Unless this general evil they maintain,
  All men are bad and in their badness reign.

CXXIII

No, Time, thou shalt not boast that I do change:
Thy pyramids built up with newer might
To me are nothing novel, nothing strange;
They are but dressings of a former sight.
Our dates are brief, and therefore we admire
What thou dost foist upon us that is old;
And rather make them born to our desire
Than think that we before have heard them told.
Thy registers and thee I both defy,
Not wondering at the present nor the past,
For thy records and what we see doth lie,
Made more or less by thy continual haste.
  This I do vow, and this shall ever be;
  I will be true, despite thy scythe and thee.

CXXVII

In the old age black was not counted fair,
Or if it were, it bore not beauty's name;
But now is black beauty's successive heir,
And beauty slander'd with a bastard's shame:
For since each hand hath put on Nature's power,
Fairing the foul with Art's false borrow'd face,
Sweet beauty hath no name, no holy bower,
But is profan'd, if not lives in disgrace.
Therefore my mistress' brows are raven black,
Her eyes so suited, and they mourners seem
At such who, not born fair, no beauty lack,
Sland'ring creation with a false esteem:
  Yet so they mourn, becoming of their woe,
  That every tongue says beauty should look so.

CXXVIII

How oft, when thou, my music, music play'st,
Upon that blessed wood whose motion sounds
With thy sweet fingers, when thou gently sway'st
The wiry concord that mine ear confounds,
Do I envy those jacks that nimble leap
To kiss the tender inward of thy hand,
Whilst my poor lips, which should that harvest reap,
At the wood's boldness by thee blushing stand!
To be so tickl'd, they would change their state
And situation with those dancing chips,
O'er whom thy fingers walk with gentle gait,
Making dead wood more bless'd than living lips.
    Since saucy jacks so happy are in this,
    Give them thy fingers, me thy lips to kiss.

CXXIX

The expense of spirit in a waste of shame
Is lust in action; and till action, lust
Is perjur'd, murderous, bloody, full of blame,
Savage, extreme, rude, cruel, not to trust;
Enjoy'd no sooner but despised straight;
Past reason hunted; and no sooner had,
Past reason hated, as a swallow'd bait,
On purpose laid to make the taker mad:
Mad in pursuit, and in possession so;
Had, having, and in quest to have, extreme;
A bliss in proof,—and prov'd, a very woe;
Before, a joy propos'd; behind, a dream.
    All this the world well knows; yet none knows well
    To shun the heaven that leads men to this hell.

CXXX

My mistress' eyes are nothing like the sun;
Coral is far more red than her lips' red:
If snow be white, why then her breasts are dun;
If hairs be wires, black wires grow on her head.
I have seen roses damask'd, red and white,
But no such roses see I in her cheeks;

And in some perfumes is there more delight
Than in the breath that from my mistress reeks.
I love to hear her speak, yet well I know
That music hath a far more pleasing sound:
I grant I never saw a goddess go,—
My mistress, when she walks, treads on the ground:
   And yet, by heaven, I think my love as rare
   As any she belied with false compare.

CXXXII

THINE eyes I love, and they, as pitying me,
Knowing thy heart torments me with disdain,
Have put on black and loving mourners be,
Looking with pretty ruth upon my pain.
And truly not the morning sun of heaven
Better becomes the grey cheeks of the east,
Nor that full star that ushers in the even,
Doth half that glory to the sober west,
As those two mourning eyes become thy face:
O! let it then as well beseem thy heart
To mourn for me, since mourning doth thee grace,
And suit thy pity like in every part.
   Then will I swear beauty herself is black,
   And all they foul that thy complexion lack.

CXXXIII

BESHREW that heart that makes my heart to groan
For that deep wound it gives my friend and me!
Is 't not enough to torture me alone,
But slave to slavery my sweet'st friend must be?
Me from myself thy cruel eye hath taken,
And my next self thou harder hast engross'd:
Of him, myself, and thee, I am forsaken;
A torment thrice threefold thus to be cross'd.
Prison my heart in thy steel bosom's ward,
But then my friend's heart let my poor heart bail;
Whoe'er keeps me, let my heart be his guard;
Thou canst not then use rigour in my jail:
   And yet thou wilt; for I, being pent in thee,
   Perforce am thine, and all that is in me.

CXXXIV

So, now I have confess'd that he is thine,
And I myself am mortgag'd to thy will,
Myself I'll forfeit, so that other mine
Thou wilt restore, to be my comfort still:
But thou wilt not, nor he will not be free,
For thou art covetous and he is kind;
He learn'd but surety-like to write for me,
Under that bond that him as fast doth bind.
The statute of thy beauty thou wilt take,
Thou usurer, that putt'st forth all to use,
And sue a friend came debtor for my sake;
So him I lose through my unkind abuse.
   Him have I lost; thou hast both him and me:
   He pays the whole, and yet am I not free.

CXXXVIII

When my love swears that she is made of truth,
I do believe her, though I know she lies,
That she might think me some untutor'd youth,
Unlearned in the world's false subtleties.
Thus vainly thinking that she thinks me young,
Although she knows my days are past the best,
Simply I credit her false-speaking tongue:
On both sides thus is simple truth supprest.
But wherefore says she not she is unjust?
And wherefore say not I that I am old?
O! love's best habit is in seeming trust,
And age in love loves not to have years told:
   Therefore I lie with her, and she with me,
   And in our faults by lies we flatter'd be.

CXLI

In faith, I do not love thee with mine eyes,
For they in thee a thousand errors note;
But 'tis my heart that loves what they despise,
Who, in despite of view, is pleas'd to dote.
Nor are mine ears with thy tongue's tune delighted;
Nor tender feeling, to base touches prone.

Nor taste nor smell desire to be invited
To any sensual feast with thee alone:
But my five wits nor my five senses can
Dissuade one foolish heart from serving thee,
Who leaves unsway'd the likeness of a man,
Thy proud heart's slave and vassal wretch to be:
    Only my plague thus far I count my gain,
    That she that makes me sin awards me pain.

CXLVI

POOR soul, the centre of my sinful earth,
Fool'd by these rebel powers that thee array,
Why dost thou pine within and suffer dearth,
Painting thy outward walls so costly gay?
Why so large cost, having so short a lease,
Dost thou upon thy fading mansion spend?
Shall worms, inheritors of this excess,
Eat up thy charge? Is this thy body's end?
Then, soul, live thou upon thy servant's loss,
And let that pine to aggravate thy store;
Buy terms divine in selling hours of dross;
Within be fed, without be rich no more:
    So shalt thou feed on Death, that feeds on men,
    And Death once dead, there 's no more dying then.

CXLVII

MY love is as a fever, longing still
For that which longer nurseth the disease;
Feeding on that which doth preserve the ill,
The uncertain sickly appetite to please.
My reason, the physician to my love,
Angry that his prescriptions are not kept,
Hath left me, and I desperate now approve
Desire is death, which physic did except.
Past cure I am, now Reason is past care,
And frantic-mad with evermore unrest;
My thoughts and my discourse as madmen's are,
At random from the truth vainly express'd;
    For I have sworn thee fair, and thought thee bright,
    Who art as black as hell, as dark as night.

CL

O! FROM what power hast thou this powerful might,
With insufficiency my heart to sway?
To make me give the lie to my true sight,
And swear that brightness doth not grace the day?
Whence hast thou this becoming of things ill,
That in the very refuse of thy deeds
There is such strength and warrantise of skill,
That, in my mind, thy worst all best exceeds?
Who taught thee how to make me love thee more,
The more I hear and see just cause of hate?
O! though I love what others do abhor,
With others thou shouldst not abhor my state:
   If thy unworthiness rais'd love in me,
   More worthy I to be belov'd of thee.

CLI

LOVE is too young to know what conscience is;
Yet who knows not conscience is born of love?
Then, gentle cheater, urge not my amiss,
Lest guilty of my faults thy sweet self prove:
For, thou betraying me, I do betray
My nobler part to my gross body's treason;
My soul doth tell my body that he may
Triumph in love; flesh stays no further reason,
But rising at thy name doth point out thee
As his triumphant prize. Proud of this pride,
He is contented thy poor drudge to be,
To stand in thy affairs, fall by thy side.
   No want of conscience hold it that I call
   Her 'love' for whose dear love I rise and fall.

THOMAS CAMPION
?1567-1619

Follow Your Saint

FOLLOW your saint, follow with accents sweet;
Haste you, sad notes, fall at her flying feet:
There, wrapped in cloud of sorrow pity move,
And tell the ravisher of my soul I perish for her love.
But if she scorns my never-ceasing pain,
Then burst with sighing in her sight and ne'er return again.

All that I sang still to her praise did tend,
Still she was first; still she my songs did end.
Yet she my love and music both doth fly,
The music that her echo is and beauty's sympathy;
Then let my notes pursue her scornful flight:
It shall suffice that they were breathed and died for her delight.

Now Winter Nights Enlarge

Now winter nights enlarge
    The number of their hours;
And clouds their storms discharge
    Upon the airy towers.
Let now the chimneys blaze
    And cups o'erflow with wine,
Let well-tuned words amaze
    With harmony divine.
Now yellow waxen lights
    Shall wait on honey love
While youthful revels, masques, and courtly sights,
    Sleep's leaden spells remove.

    This time doth well dispense
        With lovers' long discourse;
    Much speech hath some defence,
        Though beauty no remorse.
    All do not all things well;
        Some measures comely tread;

Some knotted riddles tell;
    Some poems smoothly read.
The summer hath his joys,
    And winter his delights;
Though Love and all his pleasures are but toys,
    They shorten tedious nights.

from *A Book of Airs*

XX

WHEN thou must home to shades of under ground,
And there arrived, a new admired guest,
The beauteous spirits do engirt thee round,
White Iope, blithe Helen, and the rest,
To hear the stories of thy finished love,
From that smooth tongue whose music hell can move:

Then wilt thou speak of banqueting delights,
Of masks and revels which sweet youth did make,
Of turnies and great challenges of knights,
And all these triumphs for thy beauty's sake:
When thou hast told these honours done to thee,
Then tell, O tell, how thou didst murder me.

XI

NEVER weather-beaten sail more willing bent to shore,
Never tired pilgrim's limbs affected slumber more,
Then my weary spright now longs to fly out of my troubled breast.
    O come quickly, sweetest Lord, and take my soul to rest,

Ever-blooming are the joys of Heaven's high paradise,
Cold age deafs not there our ears, nor vapour dims our eyes;
Glory there the Sun outshines, whose beams the blessed only see:
    O come quickly, glorious Lord, and raise my spright to thee.

XVII

SHALL I come, sweet love, to thee,
    When the evening beams are set?

Shall I not excluded be?
   Will you find no fained let?
      Let me not, for pity, more,
        Tell the long hours at your door.

Who can tell what thief or foe,
   In the cover of the night,
For his prey, will work my woe,
      Or through wicked foul despite:
        So may I die unredressed,
        Ere my long love be possessed.

But, to let such dangers pass,
   Which a lover's thoughts disdain,
'Tis enough in such a place
      To attend love's joys in vain.
        Do not mock me in thy bed,
        While these cold nights freeze me dead.

XVIII

THINK'ST thou to seduce me then with words that have no meaning?
Parrots so can learn to prate, our speech by pieces gleaning:
Nurses teach their children so about the time of weaning.

Learn to speak first, then to woo: to wooing much pertaineth:
He that courts us, wanting art, soon falters when he faineth,
Looks a-squint on his discourse, and smiles when he complaineth.

Skilful anglers hide their hooks, fit baits for every season;
But with crooked pins fish thou, as babes do that want reason;
Gogians only can be caught with such poor tricks of treason.

Ruth forgive me, if I err'd from human heart's compassion
When I laughed sometimes too much to see thy foolish fashion:
But, alas, who less could do that found so good occasion?

JOHN DONNE

1572-1631

The Good-morrow

I WONDER by my troth, what thou and I
Did, till we loved? were we not weaned till then?
But sucked on country pleasures, childishly?
Or snorted we in the seven sleepers' den?
'Twas so; but this, all pleasures fancies be.
If ever any beauty I did see,
Which I desired, and got, 'twas but a dream of thee.

And now good-morrow to our waking souls,
Which watch not one another out of fear;
For love all love of other sights controls,
And makes one little room an everywhere.
Let sea-discoverers to new worlds have gone,
Let maps to other, worlds on worlds have shown,
Let us possess one world, each hath one, and is one.

My face in thine eye, thine in mine appears,
And true plain hearts do in the faces rest;
Where can we find two better hemispheres
Without sharp North, without declining West?
What ever dies, was not mixed equally;
If our two loves be one, or thou and I
Love so alike that none do slacken, none can die.

Song

Go, and catch a falling star,
   Get with child a mandrake root,
Tell me, where all past years are,
   Or who cleft the Devil's foot,
Teach me to hear mermaids singing,
   Or to keep off envy's stinging,
         And find
         What wind
Serves to advance an honest mind.

If thou be'st born to strange sights,
   Things invisible to see,
Ride ten thousand days and nights,
   Till age snow white hairs on thee,
Thou, when thou return'st, wilt tell me
All strange wonders that befell thee,
      And swear
      No where
Lives a woman true, and fair.

If thou find'st one, let me know,
   Such a pilgrimage were sweet;
Yet do not, I would not go,
   Though at next door we might meet,
Though she were true, when you met her,
And last, till you write your letter,
      Yet she
      Will be
False, ere I come, to two, or three.

The Flea

MARK but this flea, and mark in this,
How little that which thou deny'st me is;
It sucked me first, and now sucks thee,
And in this flea, our two bloods mingled be;
Thou know'st that this cannot be said
A sin, nor shame, nor loss of maidenhead,
   Yet this enjoys before it woo,
   And pampered swells with one blood made of two,
   And this, alas, is more than we would do.

Oh stay, three lives in one flea spare,
Where we almost, yea more than married are.
This flea is you and I, and this
Our marriage bed, and marriage temple is;
Though parents grudge, and you, we 're met,
And cloistered in these living walls of jet.
   Though use make you apt to kill me,
   Let not to that, self murder added be,
   And sacrilege, three sins in killing three.

Cruel and sudden, hast thou since
Purpled thy nail, in blood of innocence?
Wherein could this flea guilty be,
Except in that drop which it sucked from thee?
Yet thou triumph'st, and say'st that thou
Find'st not thyself, nor me the weaker now;
    'Tis true, then learn how false, fears be;
    Just so much honour, when thou yield'st to me,
    Will waste, as this flea's death took life from thee.

A Nocturnal upon St. Lucy's Day, being the Shortest Day

'TIS the year's midnight, and it is the day's,
Lucy's, who scarce seven hours herself unmasks;
    The Sun is spent, and now his flasks
    Send forth light squibs, no constant rays;
      The world's whole sap is sunk:
The general balm th' hydroptic earth hath drunk,
Whither, as to the bed's-feet, life is shrunk,
Dead and interred; yet all these seem to laugh,
Compared with me, who am their epitaph.

Study me then, you who shall lovers be
At the next world, that is, at the next Spring:
    For I am every dead thing,
    In whom love wrought new alchemy.
      For his art did express
A quintessence even from nothingness,
From dull privations, and lean emptiness:
He ruined me, and I am re-begot
Of absence, darkness, death; things which are not.

All others, from all things, draw all that 's good,
Life, soul, form, spirit, whence they being have;
    I, by love's limbeck, am the grave
    Of all, that 's nothing. Oft a flood
      Have we two wept, and so
Drowned the whole world, us two; oft did we grow
To be two Chaoses, when we did show
Care to aught else; and often absences
Withdrew our souls, and made us carcases.

JOHN DONNE

But I am by her death (which word wrongs her)
Of the first nothing, the elixir grown;
  Were I a man, that I were one,
  I needs must know; I should prefer,
    If I were any beast,
Some ends, some means; yea plants, yea stones detest,
And love; all, all some properties invest;
If I an ordinary nothing were,
As shadow, a light, and body must be here.

But I am none; nor will my Sun renew.
You lovers, for whose sake, the lesser Sun
  At this time to the Goat is run
  To fetch new lust, and give it you,
    Enjoy your summer all;
Since she enjoys her long night's festival,
Let me prepare towards her, and let me call
This hour her Vigil, and her Eve, since this
Both the year's, and the day's deep midnight is.

Elegy V: His Picture

HERE take my picture; though I bid farewell,
Thine, in my heart, where my soul dwells, shall dwell.
'Tis like me now, but I dead, 'twill be more
When we are shadows both, than 'twas before.
When weather-beaten I come back; my hand,
Perhaps with rude oars torn, or sun-beams tanned,
My face and breast of haircloth, and my head
With care's rash sudden storms being o'erspread,
My body a sack of bones, broken within,
And powder's blue stains scattered on my skin;
If rival fools tax thee to have loved a man,
So foul, and coarse, as Oh, I may seem then,
This shall say what I was: and thou shalt say,
Do his hurts reach me? doth my worth decay?
Or do they reach his judging mind, that he
Should now love less, what he did love to see?
That which in him was fair and delicate,
Was but the milk, which in love's childish state
Did nurse it: who now is grown strong enough
To feed on that, which to disused tastes seems tough.

Elegy VII

NATURE'S lay idiot, I taught thee to love,
And in that sophistry, Oh, thou dost prove
Too subtle: Fool, thou didst not understand
The mystic language of the eye nor hand:
Nor couldst thou judge the difference of the air
Of sighs, and say, this lies, this sounds despair:
Nor by th' eye's water call a malady
Desperately hot, or changing feverously.
I had not taught thee then, the alphabet
Of flowers, how they devisefully being set
And bound up, might with speechless secrecy
Deliver errands mutely, and mutually.
Remember since all thy words used to be
To every suitor; *Ay, if my friends agree*;
Since, household charms, thy husband's name to teach,
Were all the love-tricks, that thy wit could reach;
And since, an hour's discourse could scarce have made
One answer in thee, and that ill array'd
In broken proverbs, and torn sentences.
Thou art not by so many duties his,
That from the world's Common having sever'd thee,
Inlaid thee, neither to be seen, nor see,
As mine: who have with amorous delicacies
Refin'd thee into a blissful Paradise.
Thy graces and good words my creatures be;
I planted knowledge and life's tree in thee,
Which Oh, shall strangers taste? Must I alas
Frame and enamel plate, and drink in glass?
Chafe wax for others' seals? break a colt's force
And leave him then, being made a ready horse?

Elegy XVI: On his Mistress

BY our first strange and fatal interview,
By all desires which thereof did ensue,
By our long starving hopes, by that remorse
Which my words' masculine persuasive force
Begot in thee, and by the memory
Of hurts, which spies and rivals threatened me,
I calmly beg: but by thy father's wrath,
By all pains, which want and divorcement hath,

I conjure thee, and all the oaths which I
And thou have sworn to seal joint constancy,
Here I unswear, and overswear them thus,
Thou shalt not love by ways so dangerous.
Temper, O fair love, love's impetuous rage,
Be my true mistress still, not my feigned page;
I'll go, and, by thy kind leave, leave behind
Thee, only worthy to nurse in my mind
Thirst to come back; O if thou die before,
My soul from other lands to thee shall soar.
Thy (else almighty) beauty cannot move
Rage from the seas, nor thy love teach them love,
Nor tame wild Boreas' harshness; thou hast read
How roughly he in pieces shivered
Fair Orithea, whom he swore he loved.
Fall ill or good, 'tis madness to have proved
Dangers unurged; feed on this flattery,
That absent lovers one in th' other be.
Dissemble nothing, not a boy, nor change
Thy body's habit, nor mind's; be not strange
To thyself only; all will spy in thy face
A blushing womanly discovering grace;
Richly clothed apes, are called apes, and as soon
Eclipsed as bright we call the Moon the Moon.
Men of France, changeable chameleons,
Spitals of diseases, shops of fashions,
Love's fuellers, and the rightest company
Of players, which upon the world's stage be,
Will quickly know thee, and no less, alas!
Th' indifferent Italian, as we pass
His warm land, well content to think thee page,
Will hunt thee with such lust, and hideous rage,
As Lot's fair guests were vexed. But none of these
Nor spongy hydroptic Dutch shall thee displease,
If thou stay here. O stay here, for, for thee
England is only a worthy gallery,
To walk in expectation, till from thence
Our greatest King call thee to his presence.
When I am gone, dream me some happiness,
Nor let thy looks our long-hid love confess,
Nor praise, nor dispraise me, nor bless nor curse
Openly love's force, nor in bed fright thy nurse
With midnight's startings, crying out, oh, oh
Nurse, O my love is slain, I saw him go

O'er the white Alps alone; I saw him, I,
Assailed, fight, taken, stabbed, bleed, fall, and die.
Augur me better chance, except dread Jove
Think it enough for me to have had thy love.

Elegy XIX: To his Mistress going to Bed

COME, Madam, come, all rest my powers defy,
Until I labour, I in labour lie.
The foe oft-times having the foe in sight,
Is tired with standing though he never fight.
Off with that girdle, like heaven's Zone glistering,
But a far fairer world encompassing.
Unpin that spangled breastplate which you wear,
That th' eyes of busy fools may be stopt there.
Unlace yourself, for that harmonious chime
Tells me from you, that now it is bed time.
Off with that happy busk, which I envy,
That still can be, and still can stand so nigh.
Your gown going off, such beauteous state reveals,
As when from flowry meads th' hill's shadow steals.
Off with that wiry Coronet and show
The hairy Diadem which on you doth grow:
Now off with those shoes, and then safely tread
In this love's hallow'd temple, this soft bed.
In such white robes, heaven's Angels used to be
Receiv'd by men; thou Angel bring'st with thee
A heaven like Mahomet's Paradise; and though
Ill spirits walk in white, we easily know,
By this these Angels from an evil sprite,
Those set our hairs, but these our flesh upright.
   Licence my roving hands, and let them go,
Before, behind, between, above, below.
O my America! my new-found-land,
My kingdom, safeliest when with one man mann'd,
My Mine of precious stones, My Empery,
How blest am I in this discovering thee!
To enter in these bonds, is to be free;
Then where my hand is set, my seal shall be.
   Full nakedness! All joys are due to thee,
As souls unbodied, bodies uncloth'd must be,
To taste whole joys. Gems which you women use
Are like Atlanta's balls, cast in men's views,

That when a fool's eye lighteth on a Gem,
His earthly soul may covet theirs, not them.
Like pictures, or like books' gay coverings made
For lay-men, are all women thus array'd;
Themselves are mystic books, which only we
(Whom their imputed grace will dignify)
Must see reveal'd. Then since that I may know,
As liberally, as to a Midwife, show
Thyself: cast all, yea, this white linen hence,
There is no penance due to innocence.

    To teach thee, I am naked first; why then
What needst thou have more covering than a man.

Satire III

KIND pity chokes my spleen; brave scorn forbids
Those tears to issue which swell my eye-lids;
I must not laugh; nor weep sins, and be wise,
Can railing then cure these worn maladies?
Is not our Mistress fair Religion,
As worthy of all our Soul's devotion,
As virtue was to the first blinded age?
Are not heaven's joys as valiant to assuage
Lusts, as earth's honour was to them? Alas,
As we do them in means, shall they surpass
Us in the end, and shall thy father's spirit
Meet blind Philosophers in heaven, whose merit
Of strict life may be imputed faith, and hear
Thee, whom he taught so easy ways and near
To follow, damn'd? O if thou dar'st, fear this;
This fear great courage, and high valour is.
Dar'st thou aid mutinous Dutch, and dar'st thou lay
Thee in ships' wooden sepulchres, a prey
To leaders' rage, to storms, to shot, to dearth?
Dar'st thou dive seas, and dungeons of the earth?
Hast thou courageous fire to thaw the ice
Of frozen North discoveries? and thrice
Colder than Salamanders, like divine
Children in th' oven, fires of Spain, and the line,
Whose countries limbecks to our bodies be,
Canst thou for gain bear? and must every he
Which cries not, Goddess, to thy Mistress, draw,
Or eat thy poisonous words? courage of straw!

O desperate coward, wilt thou seem bold, and
To thy foes and his (who made thee to stand
Sentinel in his world's garrison) thus yield,
And for the forbidden wars, leave th' appointed field?
Know thy foes: the foul Devil (whom thou
Strivest to please,) for hate, not love, would allow
Thee fain, his whole Realm to be quit; and as
The world's all parts wither away and pass,
So the world's self, thy other lov'd foe, is
In her decrepit wane, and thou loving this,
Dost love a withered and worn strumpet; last,
Flesh (itself's death) and joys which flesh can taste,
Thou lovest; and thy fair goodly soul, which doth
Give this flesh power to taste joy, thou dost loathe.
Seek true religion. O where? Mirreus
Thinking her unhous'd here, and fled from us,
Seeks her at Rome; there, because he doth know
That she was there a thousand years ago;
He loves her rags so, as we here obey
The statecloth where the prince sat yesterday.
Crantz to such brave Loves will not be enthrall'd,
But loves her only, who at Geneva is call'd
Religion, plain, simple, sullen, young,
Contemptuous, yet unhandsome; as among
Lecherous humours, there is one that judges
No wenches wholesome, but coarse country drudges.
Graius stays still at home here, and because
Some Preachers, vile ambitious bawds, and laws
Still new like fashions, bid him think that she
Which dwells with us, is only perfect, he
Embraceth her, whom his Godfathers will
Tender to him, being tender, as Wards still
Take such wives as their Guardians offer, or
Pay values. Careless Phrygius doth abhor
All, because all cannot be good, as one
Knowing some women whores, dares marry none.
Gracchus loves all as one, and thinks that so
As women do in divers countries go
In divers habits, yet are still one kind,
So doth, so is Religion; and this blind-
ness too much light breeds; but unmoved thou
Of force must one, and forc'd but one allow;
And the right; ask thy father which is she,
Let him ask his; though truth and falsehood be

Near twins, yet truth a little elder is;
Be busy to seek her, believe me this,
He 's not of none, nor worst, that seeks the best.
To adore, or scorn an image, or protest,
May all be bad; doubt wisely; in strange way
To stand inquiring right, is not to stray;
To sleep, or run wrong is. On a huge hill,
Cragged, and steep, Truth stands, and he that will
Reach her, about must, and about must go;
And what the hill's suddenness resists, win so;
Yet strive so, that before age, death's twilight,
Thy Soul rest, for none can work in that night.
To will, implies delay, therefore now do:
Hard deeds, the body's pains; hard knowledge too
The mind's endeavours reach, and mysteries
Are like the Sun, dazzling, yet plain to all eyes.
Keep the truth which thou hast found; men do not stand
In so ill case here, that God hath with His hand
Sign'd Kings blank-charters to kill whom they hate,
Nor are they Vicars, but hangmen to Fate.
Fool and wretch, wilt thou let thy Soul be tied
To man's laws, by which she shall not be tried
At the last day? Oh, will it then boot thee
To say a Philip, or a Gregory,
A Harry, or a Martin taught thee this?
Is not this excuse for mere contraries,
Equally strong? cannot both sides say so?
That thou mayest rightly obey power, her bounds know;
Those past, her nature, and name is chang'd; to be
Then humble to her is idolatry.
As streams are, Power is; those blest flowers that dwell
At the rough stream's calm head, thrive and do well,
But having left their roots, and themselves given
To the stream's tyrannous rage, alas are driven
Through mills, and rocks, and woods, and at last, almost
Consum'd in going, in the sea are lost:
So perish Souls, which more choose men's unjust
Power from God claimed, than God Himself to trust.

To Sir Henry Wotton

HERE'S no more news, than virtue, I may as well
Tell you *Calais*, or *Saint Michael's* tale for news, as tell
That vice doth here habitually dwell.

Yet, as to get stomachs, we walk up and down,
And toil to sweeten rest, so, may God frown,
If, but to loathe both, I haunt Court, or Town.

For here no one is from th' extremity
Of vice, by any other reason free,
But that the next to him still is worse than he.

In this world's warfare, they whom rugged Fate,
(God's Commissary,) doth so throughly hate,
As in the Court's Squadron to marshal their state:

If they stand arm'd with silly honesty,
With wishing prayers, and neat integrity,
Like Indian 'gainst Spanish hosts they be.

Suspicious boldness to this place belongs,
And to have as many ears as all have tongues;
Tender to know, tough to acknowledge wrongs.

Believe me, Sir, in my youth's giddiest days,
When to be like the Court, was a play's praise,
Plays were not so like Courts, as Courts are like plays.

Then let us at these mimic antics jest,
Whose deepest projects, and egregious gests
Are but dull Morals of a game at Chests.

But now 'tis incongruity to smile,
Therefore I end; and bid farewell a while,
At Court; though *From Court*, were the better style.

Holy Sonnets

I

THOU hast made me, and shall Thy work decay?
Repair me now, for now mine end doth haste,
I run to death, and death meets me as fast,
And all my pleasures are like yesterday;
I dare not move my dim eyes any way,
Despair behind, and death before doth cast

Such terror, and my feeble flesh doth waste
By sin in it, which it towards hell doth weigh;
Only Thou art above, and when towards Thee
By Thy leave I can look, I rise again;
But our old subtle foe so tempteth me,
That not one hour myself I can sustain;
Thy Grace may wing me to prevent his art,
And thou like Adamant draw mine iron heart.

IV

OH my black Soul! now thou art summoned
By sickness, death's herald, and champion;
Thou art like a pilgrim, which abroad hath done
Treason, and durst not turn to whence he is fled,
Or like a thief, which till death's doom be read,
Wisheth himself delivered from prison;
But damn'd and hal'd to execution,
Wisheth that still he might be imprisoned.
Yet grace, if thou repent, thou canst not lack;
But who shall give thee that grace to begin?
Oh make thyself with holy mourning black,
And red with blushing, as thou art with sin;
Or wash thee in Christ's blood, which hath this might
That being red, it dyes red souls to white.

VII

AT the round earth's imagin'd corners, blow
Your trumpets, Angels, and arise, arise
From death, you numberless infinities
Of souls, and to your scatter'd bodies go,
All whom the flood did, and fire shall o'erthrow,
All whom war, dearth, age, agues, tyrannies,
Despair, law, chance, hath slain, and you whose eyes,
Shall behold God, and never taste death's woe.
But let them sleep, Lord, and me mourn a space,
For, if above all these, my sins abound,
'Tis late to ask abundance of Thy grace,
When we are there; here on this lowly ground,
Teach me how to repent; for that 's as good
As if Thou hadst seal'd my pardon, with Thy blood.

JOHN DONNE

IX

IF poisonous minerals, and if that tree,
Whose fruit threw death on else immortal us,
If lecherous goats, if serpents envious
Cannot be damn'd; alas! why should I be?
Why should intent or reason, born in me,
Make sins, else equal, in me more heinous?
And mercy being easy, and glorious
To God; in His stern wrath, why threatens He?
But who am I, that dare dispute with Thee
O God? Oh! of thine only worthy blood,
And my tears, make a heavenly Lethean flood,
And drown in it my sin's black memory;
That Thou remember them, some claim as debt,
I think it mercy, if Thou wilt forget.

X

DEATH be not proud, though some have called thee
Mighty and dreadful, for, thou art not so,
For, those, whom thou think'st, thou dost overthrow,
Die not, poor death, nor yet canst thou kill me.
From rest and sleep, which but thy pictures be,
Much pleasure, then from thee, much more must flow,
And soonest our best men with thee do go,
Rest of their bones, and soul's delivery.
Thou art slave to Fate, Chance, kings, and desperate men,
And dost with poison, war, and sickness dwell,
And poppy, or charms can make us sleep as well,
And better than thy stroke; why swell'st thou then?
One short sleep past, we wake eternally,
And death shall be no more; death, thou shalt die.

XIII

WHAT if this present were the world's last night?
Mark in my heart, O Soul, where thou dost dwell,
The picture of Christ crucified, and tell
Whether that countenance can thee affright,
Tears in His eyes quench the amazing light,
Blood fills His frowns, which from His pierc'd head fell.

And can that tongue adjudge thee unto hell,
Which pray'd forgiveness for His foes' fierce spite?
No, no; but as in my idolatry
I said to all my profane mistresses,
Beauty, of pity, foulness only is
A sign of rigour: so I say to thee,
To wicked spirits are horrid shapes assign'd,
This beauteous form assures a piteous mind.

XIV

BATTER my heart, three-person'd God; for, you
As yet but knock, breathe, shine, and seek to mend;
That I may rise, and stand, o'erthrow me, and bend
Your force, to break, blow, burn and make me new.
I, like an usurp'd town, to another due,
Labour to admit you, but Oh, to no end,
Reason your viceroy in me, me should defend,
But is captiv'd, and proves weak or untrue.
Yet dearly I love you, and would be loved fain,
But am betroth'd unto your enemy:
Divorce me, untie, or break that knot again,
Take me to you, imprison me, for I
Except you enthral me, never shall be free,
Nor ever chaste, except you ravish me.

A Hymn to Christ, at the Author's Last Going into Germany

IN what torn ship soever I embark,
That ship shall be my emblem of Thy Ark;
What sea soever swallow me, that flood
Shall be to me an emblem of Thy blood;
Though Thou with clouds of anger do disguise
Thy face; yet through that mask I know those eyes,
　　Which, though they turn away sometimes,
　　　　They never will despise.

I sacrifice this Island unto Thee,
And all whom I lov'd there, and who lov'd me;
When I have put our seas 'twixt them and me,
Put thou Thy sea betwixt my sins and Thee.

As the tree's sap doth seek the root below
In winter, in my winter now I go,
 Where none but Thee, th' Eternal root
  Of true Love I may know.

Nor Thou nor Thy religion dost control,
The amorousness of an harmonious Soul,
But Thou would'st have that love Thyself: as Thou
Art jealous, Lord, so I am jealous now,
Thou lov'st not, till from loving more, Thou free
My soul: who ever gives, takes liberty:
 O, if Thou car'st not whom I love
  Alas, Thou lov'st not me.

Seal then this bill of my Divorce to All,
On whom those fainter beams of love did fall;
Marry those loves, which in youth scattered be
On Fame, Wit, Hopes (false mistresses) to Thee.
Churches are best for Prayer, that have least light:
To see God only, I go out of sight:
 And to 'scape stormy days, I choose
  An Everlasting night.

Hymn to God my God, in my Sickness

Since I am coming to that Holy room,
 Where, with thy Quire of Saints for evermore,
I shall be made thy Music; as I come
 I tune the Instrument here at the door,
 And what I must do then, think here before.

Whilst my Physicians by their love are grown
 Cosmographers, and I their Map, who lie
Flat on this bed, that by them may be shown
 That this is my South-west discovery
 Per fretum febris, by these straits to die,

I joy, that in these straits, I see my West;
 For, though their currents yield return to none,
What shall my West hurt me? As West and East
 In all flat Maps (and I am one) are one,
 So death doth touch the Resurrection.

Is the Pacific Sea my home? Or are
 The Eastern riches? Is *Jerusalem*?
Anyan, and *Magellan*, and *Gibraltar*,
 All straits, and none but straits, are ways to them,
 Whether where *Japhet* dwelt, or *Cham*, or *Shem*.

We think that *Paradise* and *Calvary*,
 Christ's Cross, and *Adam's* tree, stood in one place;
Look Lord, and find both *Adams* met in me;
 As the first *Adam's* sweat surrounds my face,
 May the last *Adam's* blood my soul embrace.

So, in His purple wrapp'd receive me Lord,
 By these His thorns give me His other Crown;
And as to others' souls I preach'd Thy word,
 Be this my Text, my Sermon to mine own,
 Therefore that He may raise the Lord throws down.

A Hymn to God the Father

I

WILT Thou forgive that sin where I begun,
 Which is my sin, though it were done before?
Wilt Thou forgive that sin, through which I run,
 And do run still: though still I do deplore?
  When Thou hast done, Thou hast not done,
   For, I have more.

II

Wilt Thou forgive that sin by which I have won
 Others to sin? and, made my sin their door?
Wilt Thou forgive that sin which I did shun
 A year, or two: but wallowed in, a score?
  When Thou hast done, Thou hast not done,
   For I have more.

III

I have a sin of fear, that when I have spun
 My last thread, I shall perish on the shore;
Swear by Thyself, that at my death Thy son
 Shall shine as He shines now, and heretofore;
  And, having done that, Thou hast done,
   I fear no more.

BEN JONSON

1573–1637

Song to Celia

DRINK to me only with thine eyes,
    And I will pledge with mine;
Or leave a kiss but in the cup
    And I'll not look for wine.
The thirst that from the soul doth rise
    Doth ask a drink divine;
But might I of Jove's nectar sup,
    I would not change for thine.

I sent thee late a rosy wreath,
    Not so much honouring thee
As giving it a hope that there
    It could not wither'd be;
But thou thereon didst only breathe
    And sent'st it back to me;
Since when it grows, and smells, I swear,
    Not of itself but thee!

An Ode: To Himself

WHERE dost thou careless lie
    Buried in ease and sloth?
Knowledge, that sleeps, doth die;
And this security,
    It is the common moth,
That eats on wits, and arts, and destroys them both.

Are all th' Aonian springs
    Dried up? lies Thespia waste?
Doth Clarius' harp want strings,
That not a nymph now sings!
    Or droop they as disgraced,
To see their seats and bowers by chatt'ring pies defaced?

If hence thy silence be,
　　As 'tis too just a cause;
Let this thought quicken thee—
Minds that are great and free,
　　Should not on fortune pause,
'Tis crown enough to virtue still, her own applause.

What though the greedy fry
　　Be taken with false baits
Of worded balladry,
And think it poësy?
　　They die with their conceits,
And only piteous scorn upon their folly waits.

Then take in hand thy lyre,
　　Strike in thy proper strain,
With Japhet's line, aspire
Sol's chariot for new fire,
　　To give the world again:
Who aided him, will thee, the issue of Jove's brain.

And since our dainty age,
　　Cannot endure reproof,
Make not thyself a page,
To that strumpet the stage,
　　But sing high and aloof,
Safe from the wolf's black jaw, and the dull ass's hoof.

Simplicity and Sweet Neglect

STILL to be neat, still to be drest,
As you were going to a feast;
Still to be powdered, still perfumed:
Lady, it is to be presumed,
Though art's hid causes are not found,
All is not sweet, all is not sound.

Give me a look, give me a face,
That makes simplicity a grace;
Robes loosely flowing, hair as free:
Such sweet neglect more taketh me,
Than all th' adulteries of art.
They strike mine eyes, but not my heart.

BEN JONSON

Echo's Lament for Narcissus

Slow, slow, fresh fount, keep time with my salt tears:
　Yet slower, yet; O faintly, gentle springs:
List to the heavy part the music bears,
　Woe weeps out her division, when she sings.
　　Droop, herbs and flowers,
　　Fall grief in showers,
　　Our beauties are not ours;
　　　O, I could still,
Like melting snow upon some craggy hill,
　　　Drop, drop, drop, drop,
Since Nature's pride is now a withered daffodil.

To Celia

　　Come, my Celia, let us prove,
　　While we can, the sports of love,
　　Time will not be ours for ever,
　　He, at length, our good will sever;
　　Spend not then his gifts in vain;
　　Suns that set may rise again:
　　But if once we lose this light,
　　'Tis with us perpetual night.
　　Why should we defer our joys?
　　Fame and rumour are but toys.

To the Memory of my Beloved, the Author, Mr. William Shakespeare: and what he hath left us

　　To draw no envy, Shakespeare, on thy name,
　　Am I thus ample to thy book and fame;
　　While I confess thy writings to be such,
　　As neither man, nor muse, can praise too much,
　　'Tis true, and all men's suffrage. But these ways
　　Were not the paths I meant unto thy praise;
　　For seeliest ignorance on these may light,
　　Which, when it sounds at best, but echoes right;
　　Or blind affection, which doth ne'er advance
　　The truth, but gropes, and urgeth all by chance;

Or crafty malice might pretend this praise,
And think to ruin, where it seemed to raise.
These are, as some infamous bawd, or whore,
Should praise a matron; what could hurt her more?
But thou art proof against them, and, indeed,
Above the ill fortune of them, or the need.
I therefore will begin: Soul of the age!
The applause, delight, the wonder of our stage,
My Shakespeare, rise! I will not lodge thee by
Chaucer, or Spenser, or bid Beaumont lie
A little further, to make thee a room:
Thou art a monument without a tomb,
And art alive still, while thy book doth live,
And we have wits to read, and praise to give.
That I not mix thee so my brain excuses;
I mean, with great but disproportioned Muses.
For, if I thought my judgement were of years,
I should commit thee, surely, with thy peers.
And tell how far thou didst our Lyly outshine
Or sporting Kyd, or Marlowe's mighty line.
And though thou hadst small Latin and less Greek,
From thence, to honour thee, I will not seek
For names, but call forth thundering Aeschylus,
Euripides, and Sophocles to us,
Pacuvius, Accius, him of Cordova dead
To life again, to hear thy buskin tread,
And shake a stage; or when thy socks were on,
Leave thee alone, for the comparison
Of all that insolent Greece or haughty Rome
Sent forth; or since did from their ashes come.
Triumph, my Britain! Thou hast one to show
To whom all scenes of Europe homage owe.
He was not of an age, but for all time!
And all the Muses still were in their prime,
When, like Apollo, he came forth to warm
Our ears, or, like a Mercury to charm.
Nature herself was proud of his designs,
And joyed to wear the dressing of his lines,
Which were so richly spun, and woven so fit
As, since, she will vouchsafe no other wit.
The merry Greek, tart Aristophanes,
Neat Terence, witty Plautus, now not please;
But antiquated and deserted lie,
As they were not of Nature's family.

Yet must I not give Nature all! Thy art,
My gentle Shakespeare, must enjoy a part.
For though the poet's matter Nature be
His art doth give the fashion. And that he
Who casts to write a living line, must sweat
(Such as thine are), and strike the second heat
Upon the Muses' anvil, turn the same
(And himself with it), that he thinks to frame;
Or for the laurel he may gain a scorn!
For a good poet's made as well as born;
And such wert thou! Look how the father's face
Lives in his issue; even so, the race
Of Shakespeare's mind and manners brightly shines
In his well-turnèd and true-filèd lines;
In each of which he seems to shake a lance
As brandished at the eyes of ignorance.
Sweet Swan of Avon! what a sight it were
To see thee in our waters yet appear,
And make those flights upon the banks of Thames
That so did take Eliza, and our James!
But stay, I see thee in the hemisphere
Advanced, and made a constellation there!
Shine forth, thou star of poets, and with rage,
Or influence, chide or cheer the drooping stage;
Which, since thy flight from hence, hath mourn'd like night,
And despairs day, but for thy volume's light.

A Hymn to God the Father

HEAR me, O God!
    A broken heart
    Is my best part:
Use still thy rod,
    That I may prove
    Therein, thy love.

If thou hadst not
    Been stern to me,
    But left me free,
I had forgot
    Myself and thee.

For sin's so sweet,
   As minds ill bent
   Rarely repent,
Until they meet
   Their punishment:

Who more can crave
   Than thou hast done:
   That gav'st a Son,
To free a slave?
   First made of nought;
   With all since bought.

Sin, Death, and Hell,
   His glorious Name
   Quite overcame;
Yet I rebel,
   And slight the same.

But I'll come in,
   Before my loss,
   Me farther toss,
As sure to win
   Under His Cross.

A Celebration of Charis in Ten Lyric Pieces

1. His Excuse for Loving

LET it not your wonder move,
Less your laughter; that I love.
Though I now write fifty years,
I have had, and have my peers;
Poets, though divine, are men:
Some have loved as old again.
And it is not always face,
Clothes, or fortune gives the grace;
Or the feature, or the youth:
But the language, and the truth,
With the ardour, and the passion,
Gives the lover weight and fashion.
If you then will read the story,
First prepare you to be sorry,

That you never knew till now,
Either whom to love, or how:
But be glad, as soon with me,
When you know, that this is she,
Of whose beauty it was sung,
She shall make the old man young,
Keep the middle age at stay,
And let nothing high decay,
Till she be the reason why,
All the world for love may die.

2. *How He Saw Her*

I BEHELD her, on a day,
When her look outflourished May:
And her dressing did out-brave
All the pride the fields then have:
Far I was from being stupid,
For I ran and called on Cupid:
Love if thou wilt ever see
Mark of glory, come with me;
Where's thy quiver? Bend thy bow:
Here's a shaft, thou art too slow!
And (withal) I did untie
Every cloud about his eye;
But, he had not gained his sight
Sooner, than he lost his might,
Or his courage; for away
Straight he ran, and durst not stay,
Letting bow and arrow fall,
Nor for any threat, or call,
Could be brought once back to look.
I fool-hardy, there uptook
Both the arrow he had quit,
And the bow: with thought to hit
This my object. But she threw
Such a lightning (as I drew)
At my face, that took my sight,
And my motion from me quite;
So that there, I stood a stone,
Mocked of all: and called of one
(Which with grief and wrath I heard)
Cupid's statue with a beard,
Or else one that played his ape,
In a Hercules his shape.

3. *What He Suffered*

AFTER many scorns like these,
Which the prouder beauties please,
She content was to restore
Eyes and limbs, to hurt me more,
And would on conditions, be
Reconciled to love, and me:
First, that I must kneeling yield
Both the bow, and shaft I held
Unto her; which Love might take
At her hand, with oath, to make
Me, the scope of his next draught
Aimèd, with that self-same shaft.
He no sooner heard the law,
But the arrow home did draw
And (to gain her by his art)
Left it sticking in my heart:
Which when she beheld to bleed,
She repented of the deed,
And would fain have changed the fate,
But the pity comes too late.
Loser-like, now, all my wreak
Is, that I have leave to speak,
And in either prose, or song,
To revenge me with my tongue,
Which how dexterously I do
Hear and make example too.

4. *Her Triumph*

SEE the chariot at hand here of Love
    Wherein my lady rideth!
Each that draws, is a swan, or a dove,
    And well the car Love guideth.
As she goes, all hearts do duty
    Unto her beauty;
And enamoured, do wish, so they might
    But enjoy such a sight,
That they still were, to run by her side,
Through swords, through seas, whither she would ride.

Do but look on her eyes, they do light
    All that Love's world compriseth!
Do but look on her hair, it is bright
    As Love's star when it riseth!

Do but mark her forehead's smoother
  Than words that soothe her!
And from her archèd brows, such a grace
  Sheds itself through the face,
As alone there triumphs to the life
All the gain, all the good, of the elements' strife.

Have you seen but a bright lily grow,
  Before rude hands have touched it?
Ha' you marked but the fall o' the snow
  Before the soil hath smutched it?
Ha' you felt the wool o' the beaver,
  Or swansdown ever?
Or have smelt o' the bud o' the briar,
  Or the nard in the fire?
Or have tasted the bag of the bee?
O so white! O so soft! O so sweet is she!

5. *His Discourse with Cupid*

NOBLEST Charis, you that are
Both my fortune, and my star!
And do govern more my blood,
Than the various moon the flood!
Hear, what late discourse of you,
Love, and I have had; and true.
'Mongst my muses finding me,
Where he chanced your name to see
Set, and to this softer strain;
Sure, said he, if I have brain,
This here sung, can be no other
By description, but my mother!
So hath Homer praised her hair;
So, Anacreon drawn the air
Of her face, and made to rise
Just about her sparkling eyes,
Both her brows, bent like my bow.
By her looks I do her know,
Which you call my shafts. And see!
Such my mother's blushes be,
As the bath your verse discloses
In her cheeks, of milk, and roses;
Such as oft I wanton in!
And, above her even chin,
Have you placed the bank of kisses,
Where, you say, men gather blisses,

Ripened with a breath more sweet,
Than when flowers, and west winds meet.
Nay, her white and polished neck,
With the lace that doth it deck,
Is my mother's! Hearts of slain
Lovers, made into a chain!
And between each rising breast,
Lies the valley, called my nest,
Where I sit and proin my wings
After flight; and put new stings
To my shafts! Her very name,
With my mother's is the same.
I confess all, I replied,
And the glass hangs by her side,
And the girdle 'bout her waist,
All is Venus: save unchaste.
But alas, thou see'st the least
Of her good, who is the best
Of her sex; but couldst thou, Love,
Call to mind the forms, that strove
For the apple, and those three
Make in one, the same were she.
For this beauty yet doth hide,
Something more than thou hast spied.
Outward grace weak love beguiles:
She is Venus, when she smiles,
But she's Juno, when she walks,
And Minerva, when she talks.

6. *Claiming a Second Kiss by Desert*

CHARIS, guess, and do not miss,
Since I drew a morning kiss
From your lips, and sucked an air
Thence, as sweet, as you are fair,
What my muse and I have done:
Whether we have lost, or won,
If by us, the odds were laid,
That the bride (allowed a maid)
Looked not half so fresh, and fair,
With the advantage of her hair,
And her jewels, to the view
Of the assembly, as did you!
Or, that did you sit, or walk,
You were more the eye, and talk

Of the court, today, than all
Else that glistered in Whitehall;
So, as those that had your sight,
Wished the bride were changed tonight,
And did think, such rites were due
To no other grace but you!
Or, if you did move tonight
In the dances, with what spite
Of your peers, you were beheld,
That at every motion swelled
So to see a lady tread,
As might all the Graces lead,
And was worthy (being so seen)
To be envied of the queen.
Or if you would yet have stayed,
Whether any would upbraid
To himself his loss of time;
Or have charged his sight of crime,
To have left all sight for you:
Guess of these, which is the true;
And, if such a verse as this,
May not claim another kiss.

7. *Begging Another, on Colour of Mending the Former*

FOR Love's sake, kiss me once again,
    I long, and should not beg in vain,
    Here's none to spy, or see;
        Why do you doubt, or stay?
I'll taste as lightly as the bee,
That doth but touch his flower, and flies away.
Once more, and (faith) I will be gone.
Can he that loves, ask less than one?
    Nay, you may err in this,
        And all your bounty wrong:
This could be called but half a kiss.
What w'are but once to do, we should do long.
I will but mend the last, and tell
Where, how it would have relished well;
    Join lip to lip, and try:
        Each sucks out other's breath.
    And whilst our tongues perplexèd lie,
Let who will think us dead, or wish our death.

8. *Urging Her of a Promise*

CHARIS one day in discourse
Had of Love, and of his force,
Lightly promised, she would tell
What a man she could love well:
And that promise set on fire
All that heard her, with desire.
With the rest, I long expected,
When the work would be effected:
But we find that cold delay,
And excuse spun every day,
As, until she tell her one,
We all fear, she loveth none.
Therefore, Charis, you must do't,
For I will so urge you to't
You shall neither eat, nor sleep,
No, nor forth your window peep,
With your emissary eye,
To fetch in the forms go by:
And pronounce, which band or lace,
Better fits him, than his face;
Nay I will not let you sit
'Fore your idol glass a whit,
To say over every purl
There; or to reform a curl;
Or with secretary Sis
To consult, if fucus this
Be as good, as was the last:
All your sweet of life is past,
Make account unless you can,
(And that quickly) speak your man.

9. *Her Man Described by Her Own Dictamen*

OF your trouble, Ben, to ease me,
I will tell what man would please me.
I would have him if I could,
Noble; or of greater blood:
Titles, I confess, do take me;
And a woman God did make me.
French to boot, at least in fashion,
And his manners of that nation.
Young I'd have him too, and fair,
Yet a man; with crispèd hair

Cast in thousand snares, and rings
For Love's fingers, and his wings:
Chestnut colour, or more slack
Gold, upon a ground of black.
Venus', and Minerva's eyes
For he must look wanton-wise.
Eye-brows bent like Cupid's bow,
Front, an ample field of snow;
Even nose, and cheek (withal)
Smooth as is the billiard ball:
Chin, as woolly as the peach;
And his lip should kissing teach,
Till he cherished too much beard,
And make Love or me afeared.
He would have a hand as soft
As the down, and show it oft;
Skin as smooth as any rush,
And so thin to see a blush
Rising through it ere it came;
All his blood should be a flame
Quickly fired as in beginners
In love's school, and yet no sinners.
'Twere too long to speak of all:
What we harmony do call
In a body should be there.
Well he should his clothes to wear;
Yet no tailor help to make him;
Dressed, you still for man should take him;
And not think he'd eat a stake,
Or were set up in a brake.
Valiant he should be as fire,
Showing danger more than ire;
Bounteous as the clouds to earth;
And as honest as his birth.
All his actions to be such,
As to do no thing too much.
Nor o'er-praise, nor yet condemn;
Nor out-value, nor contemn:
Nor do wrongs, nor wrongs receive;
Nor tie knots, nor knots unweave;
And from baseness to be free,
As he durst love truth and me.
Such a man, with every part,
I could give my very heart;

But of one, if short he came,
I can rest me where I am.

10. Another Lady's Exception, Present at the Hearing

FOR his mind, I do not care,
That's a toy, that I could spare:
Let his title be but great,
His clothes rich, and band sit neat,
Himself young, and face be good,
All I wish is understood.
What you please, you parts may call,
'Tis one good part I'd lie withal.

JOSEPH HALL

1574–1656

The Coxcomb

FIE on all courtesy, and unruly winds,
Two only foes that fair disguisement finds.
   Strange curse! But fit for such a fickle age,
When scalps are subject to such vassalage.
Late travelling along in London way,
Me met, as seemed by his disguised array,
A lusty courtier whose curlèd head,
With abron locks was fairly furnishèd.
I him saluted in our lavish wise:
He answers my untimely courtesies.
His bonnet railed, ere ever he could think,
Th' unruly wind blows off her periwink,
He lights, and runs, and quickly hath him sped,
To overtake his over-running head.
The sportful wind, to mock the headless man,
Tosses apace his pitched Rogerian:
And straight it to a deeper ditch hath blown:
There must my younker fetch his waxen crown.
I looked and laughed, whiles in his raging mind,
He cast all courtesy, and much I marvellèd
To see so large a causeway in his head,

THE COXCOMB: abron] auburn   railed] arranged   Rogerian] false scalp
younker] youngster

And me bethought, that when it first begun,
'Twas some shrewd autumn, that so bared the bone.
Is't not sweet pride, when men their crowns must shade,
With that which irks the hams of every jade,
Or floor-strewed locks off the barber's shears!
But waxen crowns well 'gree with borrowed hairs.

THOMAS DEKKER

1575-1641

A Portrait

My Infelice's face, her brow, her eye,
The dimple on her cheek; and such sweet skill
Hath from the cunning workman's pencil flown,
These lips look fresh and lovely as her own.
False colours last after the true be dead.
Of all the roses grafted on her cheeks,
Of all the graces dancing in her eyes,
Of all the music set upon her tongue,
Of all that was past woman's excellence
In her white bosom; look, a painted board
Circumscribes all.

Golden Slumbers

Golden slumbers kiss your eyes,
Smiles awake you when you rise:
Sleep, pretty wantons, do not cry,
And I will sing a lullaby.
Rock them, rock them, lullaby.

Care is heavy, therefore sleep you.
You are care, and care must keep you:
Sleep, pretty wantons, do not cry,
And I will sing a lullaby.
Rock them, rock them, lullaby.

JOHN FLETCHER

1579–1625

Weep no More

WEEP no more, nor sigh, nor groan,
Sorrow calls no time that's gone:
Violets pluck'd, the sweetest rain
Makes not fresh nor grow again.
Trim thy locks, look cheerfully;
Fate's hid ends eyes cannot see.

The Dead Host's Welcome

'TIS late and cold; stir up the fire;
Sit close, and draw the table nigher;
Be merry, and drink wine that's old,
A hearty medicine 'gainst a cold:
Your beds of wanton down the best,
Where you shall tumble to your rest;
I could wish you wenches too,
But I am dead, and cannot do.
Call for the best the house may ring,
Sack, white, and claret, let them bring,
And drink apace, while breath you have;
You'll find but cold drink in the grave:
Plover, partridge, for your dinner,
And a capon for the sinner,
You shall find ready when you're up,
And your horse shall have his sup:
Welcome, welcome, shall fly round,
And I shall smile, though under ground.

FRANCIS BEAUMONT
1586-1616

On the Tombs in Westminster Abbey

MORTALITY, behold and fear!
What a change of flesh is here!
Think how many royal bones
Sleep within this heap of stones:
Here they lie had realms and lands,
Who now want strength to stir their hands:
Where from their pulpits seal'd with dust
They preach, 'In greatness is no trust.'
Here's an acre sown indeed
With the richest, royal'st seed
That the earth did e'er suck in
Since the first man died for sin:
Here the bones of birth have cried—
'Though gods they were, as men they died.'
Here are sands, ignoble things,
Dropt from the ruin'd sides of kings;
Here's a world of pomp and state,
Buried in dust, once dead by fate.

JOHN WEBSTER
?1580-1625

Call for the robin-redbreast and the wren

CALL for the robin-redbreast and the wren,
Since o'er shady groves they hover,
And with leaves and flowers do cover
The friendless bodies of unburied men.
Call unto his funeral dole
The ant, the field-mouse, and the mole,
To rear him hillocks that shall keep him warm,
And (when gay tombs are robb'd) sustain no harm;
But keep the wolf far thence, that's foe to men,
For with his nails he'll dig them up again.

LORD HERBERT OF CHERBURY

1581-1648

Now that the April of your Youth

Now that the April of your youth adorns
   The garden of your face,
Now that for you each knowing lover mourns,
   And all seek to your grace:
Do not repay affection with scorns.

What though you may a matchless beauty vaunt,
   And that all hearts can move,
By such a power, as seemeth to enchant;
   Yet, without help of love,
Beauty no pleasure to itself can grant.

Then think each minute that you lose a day,
   The longest youth is short,
The shortest age is long; Time flies away,
   And makes us but his sport,
And that which is not Youth's is Age's prey.

See but the bravest horse, that prideth most,
   Though he escape the war,
Either from master to the man is lost,
   Or turned into the car,
Or else must die with being ridden post.

Then lose not beauty, lovers, time and all,
   Too late your fault you see,
When that in vain you would these days recall;
   Nor can you virtuous be,
When without these you have not wherewithall.

Breaking from under that thy Cloudy Veil

BREAKING from under that thy cloudy veil,
   Open and shine yet more, shine out more clear
   Thou glorious golden-beam-darting hair,
Even till my wonder-stricken senses fail.

Shoot out in light, and shine those rays on far,
  Thou much more fair than is the Queen of Love,
  When she doth comb her in her sphere above,
And from a planet turns a blazing-star.

Nay, thou art greater too, more destiny
  Depends on thee, than on her influence,
  No hair thy fatal hand doth now dispense,
But to some one a thread of life must be.

While gracious unto me, thou both dost sunder
  Those glories which, if they united were,
  Might have amazed sense, and shew'st each hair,
Which if alone had been too great a wonder.

And now spread in their goodly length, she appears
  No creature which the earth might call her own,
  But rather one, that in her gliding down,
Heav'n's beams did crown, to show us she was theirs.

And come from thence, how can they fear time's rage
  Which in his power else on earth most strange
  Such golden treasure doth to silver change
By that improper alchemy of Age?

An Ode upon a Question moved, whether Love should continue for ever?

HAVING interr'd her Infant-birth,
  The watry ground that late did mourn,
  Was strew'd with flow'rs for the return
Of the wish'd Bridegroom of the earth.

The well accorded Birds did sing
  Their hymns unto the pleasant time,
  And in a sweet consorted chime
Did welcom in the chearful Spring.

To which, soft whistles of the Wind,
  And warbling murmurs of a Brook,
  And vari'd notes of leaves that shook,
An harmony of parts did bind.

While doubling joy unto each other,
   All in so rare concent was shown,
   No happiness that came alone,
Nor pleasure that was not another.

When with a love none can express,
   That mutually happy pair,
   Melander and *Celinda* fair,
The season with their loves did bless.

Walking thus towards a pleasant Grove,
   What did, it seem'd, in new delight
   The pleasures of the time unite,
To give a triumph to their love,

They stay'd at last, and on the Grass
   Reposed so, as o'r his breast
   She bow'd her gracious head to rest,
Such a weight as no burden was.

While over eithers compassed waste
   Their folded arms were so compos'd,
   As if in straitest bonds inclos'd,
They suffer'd for joys they did taste.

Long their fixt eyes to Heaven bent,
   Unchanged, they did never move,
   As if so great and pure a love
No Glass but it could represent.

When with a sweet, though troubled look,
   She first brake silence, saying, Dear friend,
   O that our love might take no end,
Or never had beginning took!

I speak not this with a false heart,
   (Wherewith his hand she gently strain'd)
   Or that would change a love maintain'd
With so much faith on either part.

Nay, I protest, though Death with his
   Worst Council should divide us here,
   His terrors could not make me fear,
To come where your lov'd presence is.

Only if loves fire with the breath
   Of life be kindled, I doubt,
    With our last air 'twill be breath'd out,
And quenched with the cold of death.

That if affection be a line,
   Which is clos'd up in our last hour;
    Oh how 'twould grieve me, any pow'r
Could force so dear a love as mine.

She scarce had done, when his shut eyes
   An inward joy did represent,
    To hear *Celinda* thus intent
To a love he so much did prize.

Then with a look, it seem'd, deny'd
   All earthly pow'r but hers, yet so,
    As if to her breath he did ow
This borrow'd life, he thus repli'd;

O you, wherein, they say, Souls rest,
   Till they descend pure heavenly fires,
    Shall lustful and corrupt desires
With your immortal seed be blest?

And shall our Love, so far beyond
   That low and dying appetite,
    And which so chast desires unite,
Not hold in an eternal bond?

Is it, because we should decline,
   And wholly from our thoughts exclude
    Objects that may the sense delude,
And study only the Divine?

No sure, for if none can ascend
   Ev'n to the visible degree
    Of things created, how should we
The invisible comprehend?

Or rather since that Pow'r exprest
   His greatness in his works alone,
    B'ing here best in his Creatures known,
Why is he not lov'd in them best?

But is't not true, which you pretend,
   That since our love and knowledge here,
   Only as parts of life appear,
So they with it should take their end.

O no, Belov'd, I am most sure,
   Those vertuous habits we acquire,
   As being with the Soul intire,
Must with it evermore endure.

For if where sins and vice reside,
   We find so foul a guilt remain,
   As never dying in his stain,
Still punish'd in the Soul doth bide.

Much more that true and real joy,
   Which in a vertuous love is found,
   Must be more solid in its ground,
Then Fate or Death can e'r destroy.

Else should our Souls in vain elect,
   And vainer yet were Heavens laws,
   When to an everlasting Cause
They gave a perishing Effect.

Nor here on earth then, nor above,
   Our good affection can impair,
   For where God doth admit the fair,
Think you that he excludeth Love?

These eyes again then, eyes shall see,
   And hands again these hands enfold,
   And all chast pleasures can be told
Shall with us everlasting be.

For if no use of sense remain
   When bodies once this life forsake,
   Or they could no delight partake,
Why should they ever rise again?

And if every imperfect mind
   Make love the end of knowledge here,
   How perfect will our love be, where
All imperfection is refin'd?

Let then no doubt, *Celinda*, touch,
    Much less your fairest mind invade,
    Were not our souls immortal made,
Our equal loves can make them such.

So when one wing can make no way,
    Two joyned can themselves dilate,
    So can two persons propagate,
When singly either would decay.

So when from hence we shall be gone,
    And be no more, nor you, nor I,
    As one anothers mystery,
Each shall be both, yet both but one.

This said, in her up-lifted face,
    Her eyes which did that beauty crown,
    Were like two starrs, that having faln down,
Look up again to find their place:

While such a moveless silent peace
    Did seize on their becalmed sense,
    One would have thought some influence
Their ravish'd spirits did possess.

RICHARD CORBET

1582-1635

Farewell, Rewards and Fairies

FAREWELL, rewards and fairies,
    Good housewives now may say,
For now foul sluts in dairies
    Do fare as well as they.
And though they sweep their hearths no less
    Than maids were wont to do
Yet who of late for cleanliness
    Finds sixpence in her shoe?

Lament, lament, old abbeys,
   The fairies' lost command!
They did but change priests' babies,
   But some have changed your land.
And all your children, sprung from thence,
   Are now grown puritans,
Who live as changelings ever since
   For love of your demesnes.

At morning and at evening both
   You merry were and glad,
So little care of sleep or sloth
   These pretty ladies had;
When Tom came home from labour,
   Or Cis to milking rose,
Then merrily went their tabor,
   And nimbly went their toes.

Witness those rings and roundelays
   Of theirs, which yet remain,
Were footed in Queen Mary's days
   On many a grassy plain;
But since of late Elizabeth,
   And later James came in,
They never danced on any heath
   As when the time hath been.

By which we note the fairies
   Were of the old profession;
Their songs were 'Ave Mary's',
   Their dances were procession.
But now, alas, they all are dead;
   Or gone beyond the seas;
Or farther for religion fled;
   Or else they take their ease.

A tell-tale in their company
   They never could endure!
And whoso kept not secretly
   Their mirth, was punished, sure;
It was a just and christian deed
   To pinch such black and blue.
Oh how the commonwealth doth want
   Such Justices as you!

To his Son Vincent Corbet

WHAT I shall leave thee, none can tell,
But all shall say I wish thee well:
I wish thee, Vin, before all wealth,
Both bodily and ghostly health;
Nor too much wealth nor wit come to thee,
So much of either may undo thee.
I wish thee learning, not for show,
Enough for to instruct and know;
Not such as gentleness require
To prate at table or at fire.
I wish thee all thy mother's graces,
Thy father's fortunes and his places.
I wish thee friends, and one at court,
Not to build on, but support;
To keep thee not in doing many
Oppressions, but from suffering any.
I wish thee peace in all thy ways,
Nor lazy nor contentious days;
And, when thy soul and body part,
As innocent as now thou art.

PHILIP MASSINGER

1583-1640

Song

WHY art thou slow, thou rest of trouble, Death,
  To stop a wretch's breath,
That calls on thee, and offers her sad heart
  A prey unto thy dart?
I am nor young nor fair; be therefore bold:
  Sorrow hath made me old,
Deformed, and wrinkled; all that I can crave
  Is quiet in my grave.
Such as live happy, hold long life a jewel;
  But to me thou art cruel,
If thou end not my tedious misery;
  And I soon cease to be.
Strike, and strike home then; pity unto me,
  In one short hour's delay, is tyranny.

WILLIAM DRUMMOND OF HAWTHORNDEN

1585-1649

Redeem Time Past

MORE oft than once Death whispered in mine ear,
Grave what thou hear'st in diamond and gold,
I am that monarch whom all monarchs fear,
Who hath in dust their far-stretch'd pride uproll'd;

All, all is mine beneath moon's silver sphere,
And nought, save virtue, can my power withhold:
This, not believed, experience true thee told,
By danger late when I to thee came near.

As bugbear then my visage I did show,
That of my horrors thou right use might'st make,
And a more sacred path of living take:—
Now still walk armèd for my ruthless blow:

Trust flattering life no more, redeem time past
And live each day as if it were thy last.

As in a Dusky and Tempestuous Night

As in a dusky and tempestuous night
  A star is wont to spread her locks of gold,
  And while her pleasant rays abroad are roll'd,
Some spiteful cloud doth rob us of her sight,
Fair soul, in this black age so shin'd thou bright,
  And made all eyes with wonder thee behold,
Till ugly Death, depriving us of light,
  In his grim misty arms thee did enfold.

Who more shall vaunt true beauty here to see?
  What hope doth more in any heart remain
  That such perfection shall his reason reign
If Beauty, with thee born, too died with thee?
  World, 'plain no more of Love, nor count his harms;
  With his pale trophies Death hath hung his arms.

Saint John Baptist

THE last and greatest herald of heaven's King,
Girt with rough skins, hies to the deserts wild,
Among that savage brood the woods forth bring,
Which he than man more harmless found and mild:
His food was locusts, and what there doth spring,
With honey that from virgin hives distilled;
Parched body, hollow eyes, some uncouth thing
Made him appear, long since from earth exiled.
Then burst he forth: 'All ye, whose hopes rely
On God, with me amidst these deserts mourn;
Repent, repent, and from old errors turn.'
Who listened to his voice, obeyed his cry?
    Only the echoes, which he made relent,
    Rung from their marble caves, 'Repent, repent!'

WILLIAM BROWNE, OF TAVISTOCK
1588-1643

Praise of Spenser

ALL their pipes were still,
And Colin Clout began to tune his quill
With such deep art, that every one was given
To think Apollo, newly slid from heaven,
Had ta'en a human shape to win his love,
Or with the western swains for glory strove.
He sung th' heroic knights of fairyland
In lines so elegant, of such command,
That had the Thracian played but half so well,
He had not left Eurydice in hell.
But ere he ended his melodious song
An host of angels flew the clouds among,
And rapt this swan from his attentive mates
To make him one of their associates
In heaven's fair choir: where now he sings the praise
Of him that is the first and last of days.
Divinest Spenser, heaven-bred, happy Muse!
Would any power into my brain infuse
Thy worth, or all that poets had before,
I could not praise till thou deserv'st no more.

WILLIAM BROWNE, OF TAVISTOCK

Hail, Thou my Native Soil

HAIL, thou my native soil! thou blessed plot
Whose equal all the world affordeth not!
Show me who can so many crystal rills,
Such sweet-cloth'd valleys or aspiring hills;
Such wood-ground, pastures, quarries, wealthy mines;
Such rocks in whom the diamond fairly shines;
And if the earth can show the like again,
Yet will she fail in her sea-ruling men.
Time never can produce men to o'ertake
The fames of Greenvil, Davies, Gilbert, Drake,
Or worthy Hawkins, or of thousands more
That by their power made the Devonian shore
Mock the proud Tagus; for whose richest spoil
The boasting Spaniard left the Indian soil
Bankrupt of store, knowing it would quit cost
By winning this, though all the rest were lost.

GEORGE WITHER

1588-1667

Shall I, Wasting in Despair

SHALL I, wasting in despair,
Die because a woman's fair?
Or make pale my cheeks with care
'Cause another's rosy are?
Be she fairer than the day
Or the flowery meads in May—
 If she think not well of me,
 What care I how fair she be?

Shall my silly heart be pined
'Cause I see a woman kind;
Or a well disposèd nature
Joinèd with a lovely feature?
Be she meeker, kinder, than
Turtle-dove or pelican,
 If she be not so to me,
 What care I how kind she be?

Shall a woman's virtues move
Me to perish for her love?
Or her well-deservings known
Make me quite forget mine own?
Be she with that goodness blest
Which may merit name of Best;
  If she be not such to me,
  What care I how good she be?

'Cause her fortune seems too high,
Shall I play the fool and die?
She that bears a noble mind,
If not outward helps she find,
Thinks what with them he would do
That without them dares her woo;
  And unless that mind I see,
  What care I how great she be?

Great or good, or kind or fair,
I will ne'er the more despair;
If she love me, this believe,
I will die ere she shall grieve;
If she slight me when I woo,
I can scorn and let her go;
  For if she be not for me,
  What care I for whom she be?

ROBERT HERRICK

1591–1674

A Child's Grace

HERE a little child I stand,
Heaving up my either hand;
Cold as paddocks though they be,
Here I lift them up to Thee,
For a benison to fall
On our meat, and on us all. Amen.

A CHILD'S GRACE: paddocks] toads

Delight in Disorder

A SWEET disorder in the dress
Kindles in clothes a wantonness:
A lawn about the shoulders thrown
Into a fine distraction:
An erring lace, which here and there
Enthrals the crimson stomacher:
A cuff neglectful, and thereby
Ribbands to flow confusedly:
A winning wave, deserving note,
In the tempestuous petticoat:
A careless shoe-string, in whose tie
I see a wild civility:
Do more bewitch me than when art
Is too precise in every part.

To the Virgins, to make much of Time

GATHER ye rosebuds while ye may,
   Old Time is still a-flying:
And this same flower that smiles to-day,
   To-morrow will be dying.

The glorious lamp of heaven, the sun,
   The higher he's a-getting;
The sooner will his race be run,
   And nearer he's to setting.

That age is best, which is the first,
   When youth and blood are warmer;
But being spent, the worse, and worst
   Times still succeed the former.

Then be not coy, but use your time,
   And while ye may, go marry:
For having lost but once your prime,
   You may for ever tarry.

To Daffodils

FAIR daffodils, we weep to see
    You haste away so soon;
As yet the early-rising sun
    Has not attained his noon.
        Stay, stay,
      Until the hasting day
        Has run
      But to the evensong;
And, having prayed together, we
    Will go with you along.

We have short time to stay, as you,
    We have as short a spring;
As quick a growth to meet decay,
    As you, or anything.
        We die,
      As your hours do, and dry
        Away,
      Like to the summer's rain;
Or as the pearls of morning's dew
    Ne'er to be found again.

Upon Julia's Clothes

WHENAS in silks my Julia goes,
Then, then methinks, how sweetly flows
That liquefaction of her clothes!

Next, when I cast mine eyes and see
That brave vibration each way free;
O how that glittering taketh me!

The Hock-cart or Harvest Home

To the Right Honourable Mildmay,
Earl of Westmoreland

COME, sons of summer, by whose toil
We are the lords of wine and oil:
By whose tough labours and rough hands
We rip up first, then reap our lands.

Crown'd with the ears of corn, now come,
And to the pipe sing harvest home.
Come forth, my lord, and see the cart
Dress'd up with all the country art:
See here a maukin, there a sheet,
As spotless pure as it is sweet:
The horses, mares, and frisking fillies,
Clad all in linen white as lilies.
The harvest swains and wenches bound
For joy, to see the hock–cart crown'd.
About the cart, hear how the rout
Of rural younglings raise the shout;
Pressing before, some coming after,
Those with a shout, and these with laughter.
Some bless the cart, some kiss the sheaves,
Some prank them up with oaken leaves:
Some cross the fill-horse, some with great
Devotion stroke the home–borne wheat:
While other rustics, less attent
To prayers than to merriment,
Run after with their breeches rent.
Well, on, brave boys, to your lord's hearth,
Glitt'ring with fire, where, for your mirth,
Ye shall see first the large and chief
Foundation of your feast, fat beef:
With upper stories, mutton, veal
And bacon (which makes full the meal),
With sev'ral dishes standing by,
As here a custard, there a pie,
And here all-tempting frumenty.
And for to make the merry cheer,
If smirking wine be wanting here,
There's that which drowns all care, stout beer;
Which freely drink to your lord's health,
Then to the plough, the commonwealth,
Next to your flails, your fans, your fats,
Then to the maids with wheaten hats:
To the rough sickle, and crook'd scythe,
Drink, frolic boys, till all be blithe.
Feed, and grow fat; and as ye eat
Be mindful that the lab'ring neat,
As you, may have their fill of meat.
And know, besides, ye must revoke
The patient ox unto the yoke,

And all go back unto the plough
And harrow, though they're hang'd up now.
And, you must know, your lord's word's true,
Feed him ye must, whose food fills you;
And that this pleasure is like rain,
Not sent ye for to drown your pain,
But for to make it spring again.

The Argument of His Book

I SING of brooks, of blossoms, birds and bowers,
Of April, May, of June and July-flowers;
I sing of May-poles, hock-carts, wassails, wakes,
Of bridegrooms, brides and of their bridal cakes;
I write of youth, of love, and have access
By these to sing of cleanly wantonness;
I sing of dews, of rains, and piece by piece
Of balm, of oil, of spice and ambergris;
I sing of times trans-shifting, and I write
How roses first came red and lilies white;
I write of groves, of twilights, and I sing
The Court of Mab, and of the Fairy King;
I write of hell; I sing (and ever shall)
Of heaven, and hope to have it after all.

FRANCIS QUARLES
1592-1644

Why dost Thou shade Thy lovely face?

WHY dost Thou shade Thy lovely face? O why
Does that eclipsing hand so long deny
The sunshine of Thy soul-enliv'ning eye?

Without that light, what light remains in me?
Thou art my Life, my Way, my Light; in Thee
I live, I move, and by Thy beams I see.

Thou art my life; If Thou but turn away,
My life's a thousand deaths: Thou art my Way;
Without thee, Lord, I travel not, but stray.

My light Thou art; without Thy glorious sight,
Mine eyes are darkened with perpetual night.
My God, Thou art my Way, my Life, my Light.

Thou art my Way; I wander, if Thou fly:
Thou art my Light; If hid, how blind am I?
Thou art my Life; If Thou withdraw, I die.

Mine eyes are blind and dark; I cannot see;
To whom, or whither should my darkness flee,
But to the Light? and who's that Light but Thee?

My path is lost; my wandering steps do stray;
I cannot safely go, nor safely stay;
Whom should I seek but Thee, my Path, my Way?

O, I am dead: To whom shall I, poor I,
Repair? To whom shall my sad ashes fly
But Life? And where is Life but in Thine eye?

And yet Thou turn'st away Thy face, and fly'st me;
And yet I sue for grace, and Thou deny'st me;
Speak, art Thou angry, Lord, or only try'st me?

Unscreen those heavenly lamps, or tell me why
Thou shadest Thy face; perhaps, Thou think'st no eye
Can view those flames, and not drop down and die.

If that be all, shine forth, and draw Thee nigher;
Let me behold and die; for my desire
Is Phœnix-like to perish in that fire.

Death-conquered Laz'rus was redeemed by Thee;
If I am dead, Lord, set death's prisoner free;
Am I more spent, or stink I worse than he?

If my puffed light be out, give leave to tine
My flameless snuff at that bright Lamp of Thine;
O what's Thy Light the less for lighting mine?

If I have lost my path, great Shepherd, say,
Shall I still wander in a doubtful way?
Lord, shall a lamb of Israel's sheepfold stray?

to tine] to light or kindle

Thou art the pilgrim's path; the blind man's eye;
The dead man's life; on Thee my hopes rely;
If Thou remove, I err; I grope; I die.

Disclose Thy sunbeams; close Thy wings, and stay;
See, see, how I am blind, and dead, and stray,
O Thou, that art my Light, my Life, my Way.

Emblem IV
I Am My Beloved's, and His Desire Is towards Me

LIKE to the arctic needle, that doth guide
  The wandering shade by his magnetic power,
And leaves his silken gnomon to decide
  The question of the controverted hour,
First frantics up and down from side to side,
    And restless beats his crystall'd ivory case
    With vain impatience; jets from place to place,
And seeks the bosom of his frozen bride;
    At length he slacks his motion, and doth rest
His trembling point at his bright pole's beloved breast.

Even so my soul, being hurried here and there,
  By every object that presents delight,
Fain would be settled, but she knows not where;
  She likes at morning what she loathes at night:
She bows to honour, then she lends an ear
    To that sweet swan-like voice of dying pleasure,
    Then tumbles in the scatter'd heaps of treasure;
Now flatter'd with false hope, now foil'd with fear:
    Thus finding all the world's delight to be
But empty toys, good God, she points alone to thee.

But hath the virtued steel a power to move?
  Or can the untouch'd needle point aright?
Or can my wandering thoughts forbear to rove,
  Unguided by the virtue of thy sprite?
Oh hath my laden soul the art to improve
    Her wasted talent, and, unrais'd, aspire
    In this sad moulting time of her desire?
Not first belov'd, have I the power to love?
    I cannot stir but as thou please to move me,
Nor can my heart return thee love until thou love me.

The still commandress of the silent night
  Borrows her beams from her bright brother's eye;
His fair aspéct fills her sharp horns with light,
  If he withdraw, her flames are quench'd and die:
Even so the beams of thy enlightening sprite,
    Infus'd and shot into my dark desire,
    Inflame my thoughts, and fill my soul with fire,
That I am ravish'd with a new delight;
    But if thou shroud thy face, my glory fades,
And I remain a nothing, all compos'd of shades.

Eternal God! O thou that only art,
  The sacred fountain of eternal light,
And blessed loadstone of my better part,
  O thou, my heart's desire, my soul's delight!
Reflect upon my soul, and touch my heart,
    And then my heart shall prize no good above thee;
    And then my soul shall know thee; knowing, love thee;
And then my trembling thoughts shall never start
    From thy commands, or swerve the least degree,
Or once presume to move, but as they move in thee.

GEORGE HERBERT

1593–1632

Discipline

THROW away Thy rod,
Throw away Thy wrath;
    O my God,
Take the gentle path!

For my heart's desire
Unto Thine is bent:
    I aspire
To a full consent.

Not a word or look
I affect to own,
    But by book,
And Thy Book alone.

Though I fail, I weep;
Though I halt in pace,
    Yet I creep
To the throne of grace.

Then let wrath remove;
Love will do the deed:
    For with love
Stony hearts will bleed.

Love is swift of foot;
Love's a man of war,
    And can shoot,
And can hit from far.

Who can 'scape his bow?
That which wrought on Thee,
    Brought Thee low,
Needs must work on me.

Throw away Thy rod;
Though man frailties hath,
    Thou art God:
Throw away Thy wrath!

The Collar

I STRUCK the board, and cried, No more.
    I will abroad.
What? shall I ever sigh and pine?
My lines and life are free; free as the road,
  Loose as the wind, as large as store.
    Shall I be still in suit?
Have I no harvest but a thorn
To let me blood, and not restore
What I have lost with cordial fruit?
    Sure there was wine
Before my sighs did dry it: there was corn
  Before my tears did drown it.
Is the year only lost to me?
  Have I no bays to crown it?
No flowers, no garlands gay? all blasted?
    All wasted?

GEORGE HERBERT

Not so, my heart: but there is fruit,
    And thou hast hands.
Recover all thy sigh-blown age
On double pleasures: leave thy cold dispute
Of what is fit and not; forsake thy cage,
    Thy rope of sands,
Which petty thoughts have made, and made to thee
    Good cable, to enforce and draw,
        And be thy law,
While thou didst wink and would not see.
        Away; take heed:
        I will abroad.
Call in thy death's-head there: tie up thy fears.
        He that forbears
    To suit and serve his need,
        Deserves his load.
But as I rav'd and grew more fierce and wild
        At every word,
    Methought I heard one calling, *Child* ;
        And I replied, *My Lord*.

The Pulley

WHEN God at first made Man,
Having a glass of blessings standing by;
Let us (said He) pour on him all we can:
Let the world's riches, which dispersèd lie,
        Contract into a span.

    So strength first made a way;
Then beauty flow'd, then wisdom, honour, pleasure:
When almost all was out, God made a stay,
Perceiving that alone, of all His treasure,
        Rest in the bottom lay.

    For if I should (said He)
Bestow this jewel also on My creature,
He would adore My gifts instead of Me,
And rest in Nature, not the God of Nature:
        So both should losers be.

Yet let him keep the rest,
But keep them with repining restlessness:
Let him be rich and weary, that at least,
If goodness lead him not, yet weariness
    May toss him to My breast.

Judge not the Preacher for He is thy Judge

JUDGE not the preacher; for He is thy Judge:
If thou mislike him, thou conceiv'st him not.
God calleth preaching folly. Do not grudge
To pick out treasures from an earthen pot.
  The worst speak something good: if all want sense,
  God takes a text, and preacheth patience.

The Quip

THE merry world did on a day
With his train-bands and mates agree
To meet together, where I lay,
And all in sport to jeer at me.

First, Beauty crept into a rose,
Which when I pluck'd not, 'Sir,' said she,
'Tell me, I pray, whose hands are those.'
But thou shalt answer, Lord, for me.

Then Money came, and chinking still,
'What tune is this, poor man?' said he:
'I heard in Music you had skill':
But thou shalt answer, Lord, for me.

Then came brave Glory puffing by
In silks that whistled, who but he!
He scarce allowed me half an eye.
But thou shalt answer, Lord, for me.

Then came quick Wit and Conversation,
And he would needs a comfort be,
And, to be short, make an oration.
But thou shalt answer, Lord, for me.

GEORGE HERBERT

Yet when the hour of thy design
To answer these fine things shall come;
Speak not at large, say, I am Thine:
And then they have their answer home.

Sin

LORD, with what care hast Thou begirt us round!
  Parents first season us; then schoolmasters
Deliver us to laws; they send us bound
  To rules of reason, holy messengers,

Pulpits and Sundays, sorrow dogging sin,
  Afflictions sorted, anguish of all sizes,
Fine nets and stratagems to catch us in,
  Bibles laid open, millions of surprises;

Blessings beforehand, ties of gratefulness,
  The sound of glory ringing in our ears:
Without, our shame; within, our consciences;
  Angels and grace, eternal hopes and fears.

  Yet all these fences and their whole array
  One cunning bosom-sin blows quite away.

Virtue

SWEET day, so cool, so calm, so bright,
The bridal of the earth and sky,
The dew shall weep thy fall to-night;
        For thou must die.

Sweet rose, whose hue angry and brave
Bids the rash gazer wipe his eye,
Thy root is ever in its grave,
        And thou must die.

Sweet spring, full of sweet days and roses,
A box where sweets compacted lie,
My music shows ye have your closes,
        And all must die.

Only a sweet and virtuous soul,
Like season'd timber, never gives;
But though the whole world turn to coal,
      Then chiefly lives.

Love (III)

LOVE bade me welcome: yet my soul drew back,
      Guilty of dust and sin.
But quick-ey'd Love, observing me grow slack
      From my first entrance in,
Drew nearer to me, sweetly questioning,
      If I lack'd any thing.

A guest, I answer'd, worthy to be here:
      Love said, You shall be he.
I the unkind, ungrateful? Ah my dear,
      I cannot look on thee.
Love took my hand, and smiling did reply,
      Who made the eyes but I?

Truth Lord, but I have marr'd them: let my shame
      Go where it doth deserve.
And know you not, says Love, who bore the blame?
      My dear, then I will serve.
You must sit down, says Love, and taste my meat:
      So I did sit and eat.

Prayer (I)

PRAYER the Church's banquet, Angels' age,
God's breath in man returning to his birth,
The soul in paraphrase, heart in pilgrimage,
The Christian plummet sounding heav'n and earth;
Engine against th' Almighty, sinners' tower,
Reversed thunder, Christ-side-piercing spear,
The six-days' world transposing in an hour,
A kind of tune, which all things hear and fear;
Softness, and peace, and joy, and love, and bliss,
Exalted Manna, gladness of the best,
Heaven in ordinary, man well drest,
The milky way, the bird of Paradise,
    Church-bells beyond the stars heard, the souls blood,
    The land of spices; something understood.

THOMAS CAREW

?1595-?1639

A Rapture

I WILL enjoy thee now, my Celia, come,
And fly with me to Love's Elysium.
The giant, Honour, that keeps cowards out,
Is but a masquer, and the servile rout
Of baser subjects only bend in vain
To the vast idol; whilst the nobler train
Of valiant lovers daily sail between
The huge Colossus' legs, and pass unseen
Unto the blissful shore. Be bold and wise,
And we shall enter: the grim Swiss denies
Only to tame fools a passage, that not know
He is but form and only frights in show
The duller eyes that look from far; draw near
And thou shalt scorn what we were wont to fear.
We shall see how the stalking pageant goes
With borrow'd legs, a heavy load to those
That made and bear him; not, as we once thought,
The seed of gods, but a weak model wrought
By greedy men, that seek to enclose the common,
And within private arms empale free woman.
  Come, then, and mounted on the wings of Love
We'll cut the flitting air and soar above
The monster's head, and in the noblest seats
Of those blest shades quench and renew our heats.
There shall the queens of love and innocence,
Beauty and Nature, banish all offence
From our close ivy-twines; there I'll behold
Thy bared snow and thy unbraided gold;
There my enfranchised hand on every side
Shall o'er thy naked polish'd ivory slide.
No curtain there, though of transparent lawn,
Shall be before thy virgin-treasure drawn;
But the rich mine, to the enquiring eye
Exposed, shall ready still for mintage lie,
And we will coin young Cupids. There a bed
Of roses and fresh myrtles shall be spread,

Under the cooler shade of cypress groves;
Our pillows of the down of Venus' doves,
Whereon our panting limbs we'll gently lay,
In the faint respites of our active play:
That so our slumbers may in dreams have leisure
To tell the nimble fancy our past pleasure,
And so our souls, that cannot be embraced,
Shall the embraces of our bodies taste.
Meanwhile the bubbling stream shall court the shore,
Th' enamour'd chirping wood-choir shall adore
In varied tunes the deity of love;
The gentle blasts of western winds shall move
The trembling leaves, and through their close boughs breathe
Still music, whilst we rest ourselves beneath
Their dancing shade; till a soft murmur, sent
From souls entranced in amorous languishment,
Rouse us, and shoot into our veins fresh fire,
Till we in their sweet ecstasy expire.
    Then, as the empty bee that lately bore
Into the common treasure all her store,
Flies 'bout the painted field with nimble wing,
Deflow'ring the fresh virgins of the spring,
So will I rifle all the sweets that dwell
In my delicious paradise, and swell
My bag with honey, drawn forth by the power
Of fervent kisses from each spicy flower.
I'll seize the rose-buds in their perfumed bed,
The violet knots, like curious mazes spread
O'er all the garden, taste the ripen'd cherry,
The warm firm apple, tipp'd with coral berry:
Then will I visit with a wand'ring kiss
The vale of lilies and the bower of bliss;
And where the beauteous region doth divide
Into two milky ways, my lips shall slide
Down those smooth alleys, wearing as they go
A tract for lovers on the printed snow;
Thence climbing o'er the swelling Apennine,
Retire into thy grove of eglantine,
Where I will all those ravish'd sweets distil
Through Love's alembic, and with chemic skill
From the mix'd mass one sovereign balm derive,
Then bring that great elixir to thy hive.
    Now in more subtle wreaths I will entwine
My sinewy thighs, my legs and arms with thine;

Thou like a sea of milk shalt lie display'd,
Whilst I the smooth calm ocean invade
With such a tempest, as when Jove of old
Fell down on Danaë in a storm of gold;
Yet my tall pine shall in the Cyprian strait
Ride safe at anchor and unlade her freight:
My rudder with thy bold hand, like a tried
And skilful pilot, thou shalt steer, and guide
My bark into love's channel, where it shall
Dance, as the bounding waves do rise or fall.
Then shall thy circling arms embrace and clip
My willing body, and thy balmy lip
Bathe me in juice of kisses, whose perfume
Like a religious incense shall consume,
And send up holy vapours to those powers
That bless our loves and crown our sportful hours,
That with such halcyon calmness fix our souls
In steadfast peace, as no affright controls.
There, no rude sounds shake us with sudden starts;
No jealous ears, when we unrip our hearts,
Suck our discourse in; no observing spies
This blush, that glance traduce; no envious eyes
Watch our close meetings; nor are we betray'd
To rivals by the bribed chambermaid.
No wedlock bonds unwreathe our twisted loves,
We seek no midnight arbour, no dark groves
To hide our kisses: there, the hated name
Of husband, wife, lust, modest, chaste or shame,
Are vain and empty words, whose very sound
Was never heard in the Elysian ground.
All things are lawful there, that may delight
Nature or unrestrained appetite;
Like and enjoy, to will and act is one:
We only sin when Love's rites are not done.
  The Roman Lucrece there reads the divine
Lectures of love's great master, Aretine,
And knows as well as Lais how to move
Her pliant body in the act of love;
To quench the burning ravisher she hurls
Her limbs into a thousand winding curls,
And studies artful postures, such as be
Carved on the bark of every neighbouring tree
By learned hands, that so adorn'd the rind
Of those fair plants, which, as they lay entwined,

Have fann'd their glowing fires. The Grecian dame,
That in her endless web toil'd for a name
As fruitless as her work, doth there display
Herself before the youth of Ithaca,
And th' amorous sport of gamesome nights prefer
Before dull dreams of the lost traveller.
Daphne hath broke her bark, and that swift foot
Which th' angry gods had fasten'd with a root
To the fix'd earth, doth now unfetter'd run
To meet th' embraces of the youthful Sun.
She hangs upon him like his Delphic lyre;
Her kisses blow the old, and breathe new fire;
Full of her god, she sings inspired lays,
Sweet odes of love, such as deserve the bays,
Which she herself was. Next her, Laura lies
In Petrarch's learned arms, drying those eyes
That did in such sweet smooth-paced numbers flow,
As made the world enamour'd of his woe.
These, and ten thousand beauties more, that died
Slave to the tyrant, now enlarged deride
His cancell'd laws, and for their time mis-spent
Pay into Love's exchequer double rent.
   Come then, my Celia, we'll no more forbear
To taste our joys, struck with a panic fear,
But will depose from his imperious sway
This proud usurper, and walk free as they,
With necks unyoked; nor is it just that he
Should fetter your soft sex with chastity,
Whom Nature made unapt for abstinence;
When yet this false impostor can dispense
With human justice and with sacred right,
And, maugre both their laws, command me fight
With rivals or with emulous loves that dare
Equal with thine their mistress' eyes or hair.
If thou complain of wrong, and call my sword
To carve out thy revenge, upon that word
He bids me fight and kill; or else he brands
With marks of infamy my coward hands.
And yet religion bids from blood-shed fly,
And damns me for that act. Then tell me why
   This goblin Honour, which the world adores,
   Should make men atheists, and not women whores?

EDMUND WALLER
1606-1687

Song

Go, lovely Rose!
Tell her, that wastes her time and me,
    That now she knows,
When I resemble her to thee,
How sweet and fair she seems to be.

    Tell her that's young
And shuns to have her graces spied,
    That hadst thou sprung
In deserts, where no men abide,
Thou must have uncommended died.

    Small is the worth
Of beauty from the light retired:
    Bid her come forth,
Suffer herself to be desired,
And not blush so to be admired.

    Then die! that she
The common fate of all things rare
    May read in thee:
How small a part of time they share
That are so wondrous sweet and fair!

resemble] liken

JOHN MILTON

1608-1674

On the University Carrier

*who sickened in the time of his vacancy, being forbid to go to
London by reason of the plague*

HERE lies old Hobson, Death hath broke his girt,
And here, alas, hath laid him in the dirt;
Or else, the ways being foul, twenty to one
He's here stuck in a slough, and overthrown.
'Twas such a shifter, that if truth were known,
Death was half glad when he had got him down;
For he had any time this ten years full
Dodged with him betwixt Cambridge and *The Bull*.
And surely Death could never have prevailed,
Had not his weekly course of carriage failed;
But lately finding him so long at home,
And thinking now his journey's end was come,
And that he had ta'en up his latest inn,
In the kind office of a chamberlain
Showed him his room where he must lodge that night,
Pulled off his boots, and took away the light.
If any ask for him, it shall be said,
'Hobson has supped, and's newly gone to bed.'

from *A Mask (Comus)*

Comus. Nay, lady, sit; if I but wave this wand,
Your nerves are all chained up in alabaster,
And you a statue, or as Daphne was
Root-bound, that fled Apollo.
    Lady.   Fool, do not boast;
Thou canst not touch the freedom of my mind
With all thy charms, although this corporal rind
Thou hast immanacled, while Heav'n sees good.
    Comus. Why are you vexed, lady? why do you frown?
Here dwell no frowns, nor anger; from these gates
Sorrow flies far. See, here be all the pleasures

JOHN MILTON

That fancy can beget on youthful thoughts,
When the fresh blood grows lively, and returns
Brisk as the April buds in primrose season.
And first behold this cordial julep here
That flames and dances in his crystal bounds,
With spirits of balm and fragrant syrups mixed.
Not that nepenthes which the wife of Thone
In Egypt gave to Jove-born Helena
Is of such power to stir up joy as this,
To life so friendly, or so cool to thirst.
Why should you be so cruel to yourself,
And to those dainty limbs which Nature lent
For gentle usage and soft delicacy?
But you invert the cov'nants of her trust,
And harshly deal like an ill borrower
With that which you received on other terms,
Scorning the unexempt condition
By which all mortal frailty must subsist,
Refreshment after toil, ease after pain,
That have been tir'd all day without repast,
And timely rest have wanted; but, fair virgin,
This will restore all soon.

   Lady.   'Twill not, false traitor,
'Twill not restore the truth and honesty
That thou hast banished from thy tongue with lies.
Was this the cottage and the safe abode
Thou told'st me of? What grim aspécts are these,
These ugly-headed monsters? Mercy guard me!
Hence with thy brewed enchantments, foul deceiver;
Hast thou betrayed my credulous innocence
With vizored falsehood and base forgery,
And wouldst thou seek again to trap me here
With lickerish baits fit to ensnare a brute?
Were it a draught for Juno when she banquets,
I would not taste thy treasonous offer; none
But such as are good men can give good things,
And that which is not good is not delicious
To a well-governed and wise appetite.

   Comus. O foolishness of men! that lend their ears
To those budge doctors of the Stoic fur,
And fetch their precepts from the Cynic tub,
Praising the lean and sallow Abstinence.
Wherefore did Nature pour her bounties forth
With such a full and unwithdrawing hand,

Covering the earth with odors, fruits, and flocks,
Thronging the seas with spawn innumerable,
But all to please and sate the curious taste?
And set to work millions of spinning worms,
That in their green shops weave the smooth-haired silk
To deck her sons; and that no corner might
Be vacant of her plenty, in her own loins
She hutched th' all-worshiped ore and precious gems
To store her children with. If all the world
Should in a pet of temperance feed on pulse,
Drink the clear stream, and nothing wear but frieze,
Th' All-giver would be unthanked, would be unpraised,
Not half his riches known, and yet despised,
And we should serve him as a grudging master,
As a penurious niggard of his wealth,
And live like Nature's bastards, not her sons,
Who would be quite surcharged with her own weight,
And strangled with her waste fertility;
Th' earth cumbered, and the winged air darked with plumes;
The herds would over-multitude their lords,
The sea o'erfraught would swell, and th' unsought diamonds
Would so emblaze the forehead of the deep,
And so bestud with stars, that they below
Would grow inured to light, and come at last
To gaze upon the sun with shameless brows.
List, lady, be not coy, and be not cozened
With that same vaunted name Virginity;
Beauty is Nature's coin, must not be hoarded,
But must be current, and the good thereof
Consists in mutual and partaken bliss,
Unsavory in th' enjoyment of itself.
If you let slip time, like a neglected rose
It withers on the stalk with languished head.
Beauty is Nature's brag, and must be shown
In courts, at feasts, and high solemnities
Where most may wonder at the workmanship;
It is for homely features to keep home,
They had their name thence; coarse complexïons
And cheeks of sorry grain will serve to ply
The sampler, and to tease the housewife's wool.
What need a vermeil-tinctured lip for that,
Love-darting eyes, or tresses like the morn?
There was another meaning in these gifts,
Think what, and be advised; you are but young yet.

Lady. I had not thought to have unlocked my lips
In this unhallowed air, but that this juggler
Would think to charm my judgment, as mine eyes,
Obtruding false rules pranked in reason's garb.
I hate when vice can bolt her arguments,
And virtue has no tongue to check her pride.
Impostor, do not charge most innocent Nature,
As if she would her children should be riotous
With her abundance; she, good cateress,
Means her provision only to the good,
That live according to her sober laws
And holy dictate of spare Temperance.
If every just man that now pines with want
Had but a moderate and beseeming share
Of that which lewdly pampered luxury
Now heaps upon some few with vast excess,
Nature's full blessings would be well dispensed
In unsuperfluous even proportïon,
And she no whit encumbered with her store;
And then the Giver would be better thanked,
His praise due paid, for swinish gluttony
Ne'er looks to Heav'n amidst his gorgeous feast,
But with besotted base ingratitude
Crams, and blasphemes his Feeder. Shall I go on?
Or have I said enough? To him that dares
Arm his profane tongue with contemptuous words
Against the sun-clad power of Chastity,
Fain would I something say, yet to what end?
Thou hast nor ear nor soul to apprehend
The sublime notion and high mystery
That must be uttered to unfold the sage
And serious doctrine of Virginity,
And thou art worthy that thou shouldst not know
More happiness than this thy present lot.
Enjoy your dear wit and gay rhetoric
That hath so well been taught her dazzling fence;
Thou art not fit to hear thyself convinced.
Yet should I try, the uncontrollèd worth
Of this pure cause would kindle my rapt spirits
To such a flame of sacred vehemence
That dumb things would be moved to sympathize,
And the brute Earth would lend her nerves, and shake,
Till all thy magic structures, reared so high,
Were shattered into heaps o'er thy false head.

Comus. She fables not. I feel that I do fear
Her words set off by some superior power;
And though not mortal, yet a cold shudd'ring dew
Dips me all o'er, as when the wrath of Jove
Speaks thunder and the chains of Erebus
To some of Saturn's crew. I must dissemble,
And try her yet more strongly. Come, no more,
This is mere moral babble, and direct
Against the canon laws of our foundation;
I must not suffer this, yet 'tis but the lees
And settlings of a melancholy blood;
But this will cure all straight; one sip of this
Will bathe the drooping spirits in delight
Beyond the bliss of dreams. Be wise, and taste.

*   *   *

Song

Sabrina fair,
   Listen where thou art sitting
Under the glassy, cool, translucent wave,
   In twisted braids of lilies knitting
The loose train of thy amber-dropping hair;
   Listen for dear honor's sake,
   Goddess of the silver lake,
   Listen and save.
Listen and appear to us
In name of great Oceanus,
By the earth-shaking Neptune's mace,
And Tethys' grave majestic pace,
By hoary Nereus' wrinkled look,
And the Carpathian wizard's hook,
By scaly Triton's winding shell,
And old soothsaying Glaucus' spell,
By Leucothea's lovely hands,
And her son that rules the strands,
By Thetis' tinsel-slippered feet,
And the songs of Sirens sweet,
By dead Parthenope's dear tomb,
And fair Ligea's golden comb,
Wherewith she sits on diamond rocks
Sleeking her soft alluring locks;
By all the nymphs that nightly dance
Upon thy streams with wily glance,

Rise, rise, and heave thy rosy head
From thy coral-paven bed,
And bridle in thy headlong wave,
Till thou our summons answered have.
                                                    Listen and save.

Sabrina rises, attended by water-nymphs, and sings.

  By the rushy-fringèd bank,
Where grows the willow and the osier dank,
   My sliding chariot stays,
Thick set with agate, and the azurn sheen
  Of turkis blue, and emerald green,
    That in the channel strays,
  Whilst from off the waters fleet
  Thus I set my printless feet
  O'er the cowslip's velvet head,
   That bends not as I tread.
Gentle swain, at thy request
  I am here.

   *   *   *

  Spir. To the ocean now I fly,
And those happy climes that lie
Where day never shuts his eye,
Up in the broad fields of the sky.
There I suck the liquid air
All amidst the gardens fair
Of Hesperus, and his daughters three
That sing about the golden tree.
Along the crispèd shades and bow'rs
Revels the spruce and jocund Spring;
The Graces and the rosy-bosomed Hours
Thither all their bounties bring,
That there eternal summer dwells,
And west winds with musky wing
About the cedarn alleys fling
Nard and cassia's balmy smells.
Iris there with humid bow
Waters the odorous banks that blow
Flowers of more mingled hue
Than her purfled scarf can shew,
And drenches with Elysian dew
(List, mortals, if your ears be true)

Beds of hyacinth and roses,
Where young Adonis oft reposes,
Waxing well of his deep wound
In slumber soft, and on the ground
Sadly sits th' Assyrian queen;
But far above in spangled sheen
Celestial Cupid, her famed son, advanced,
Holds his dear Psyche sweet entranced
After her wand'ring labors long,
Till free consent the gods among
Make her his eternal bride,
And from her fair unspotted side
Two blissful twins are to be born,
Youth and Joy; so Jove hath sworn.

   But now my task is smoothly done,
I can fly, or I can run
Quickly to the green earth's end,
Where the bowed welkin slow doth bend,
And from thence can soar as soon
To the corners of the moon.

   Mortals that would follow me,
Love Virtue, she alone is free;
She can teach ye how to climb
Higher than the sphery chime;
Of if Virtue feeble were,
Heav'n itself would stoop to her.

Lycidas

In this monody the author bewails a learned friend, unfortunately drowned in his passage from Chester on the Irish Seas, 1637. And by occasion foretells the ruin of our corrupted clergy, then in their height.

YET once more, O ye laurels, and once more,
Ye myrtles brown, with ivy never sere,
I come to pluck your berries harsh and crude,
And with forced fingers rude
Shatter your leaves before the mellowing year.
Bitter constraint, and sad occasion dear,
Compels me to disturb your season due;
For Lycidas is dead, dead ere his prime,
Young Lycidas, and hath not left his peer.
Who would not sing for Lycidas? He knew
Himself to sing, and build the lofty rhyme.

He must not float upon his wat'ry bier
Unwept, and welter to the parching wind,
Without the meed of some melodious tear.

  Begin then, Sisters of the sacred well
That from beneath the seat of Jove doth spring,
Begin, and somewhat loudly sweep the string.
Hence with denial vain, and coy excuse;
So may some gentle Muse
With lucky words favor my destined urn,
And as he passes turn,
And bid fair peace be to my sable shroud.
For we were nursed upon the self-same hill,
Fed the same flock, by fountain, shade, and rill.

  Together both, ere the high lawns appeared
Under the opening eyelids of the morn,
We drove afield, and both together heard
What time the gray-fly winds her sultry horn,
Batt'ning our flocks with the fresh dews of night,
Oft till the star that rose, at ev'ning, bright
Toward heav'n's descent had sloped his westering wheel.
Meanwhile the rural ditties were not mute,
Tempered to th' oaten flute;
Rough Satyrs danced, and Fauns with clov'n heel
From the glad sound would not be absent long,
And old Damoetas loved to hear our song.

  But O the heavy change, now thou art gone,
Now thou art gone, and never must return!
Thee, Shepherd, thee the woods and desert caves,
With wild thyme and the gadding vine o'ergrown,
And all their echoes mourn.
The willows and the hazel copses green
Shall now no more be seen
Fanning their joyous leaves to thy soft lays.
As killing as the canker to the rose,
Or taint-worm to the weanling herds that graze,
Or frost to flowers, that their gay wardrobe wear,
When first the white-thorn blows;
Such, Lycidas, thy loss to shepherd's ear.

  Where were ye, Nymphs, when the remorseless deep
Closed o'er the head of your loved Lycidas?
For neither were ye playing on the steep
Where your old bards, the famous Druids, lie,
Nor on the shaggy top of Mona high,
Nor yet where Deva spreads her wizard stream.

Ay me, I fondly dream,
Had ye been there!—for what could that have done?
What could the Muse herself that Orpheus bore,
The Muse herself, for her enchanting son
Whom universal nature did lament,
When by the rout that made the hideous roar
His gory visage down the stream was sent,
Down the swift Hebrus to the Lesbian shore?
   Alas! what boots it with uncessant care
To tend the homely slighted shepherd's trade,
And strictly meditate the thankless Muse?
Were it not better done as others use,
To sport with Amaryllis in the shade,
Or with the tangles of Neaera's hair?
Fame is the spur that the clear spirit doth raise
(That last infirmity of noble mind)
To scorn delights, and live laborious days;
But the fair guerdon when we hope to find,
And think to burst out into sudden blaze,
Comes the blind Fury with th' abhorrèd shears,
And slits the thin-spun life. 'But not the praise,'
Phoebus replied, and touched my trembling ears:
'Fame is no plant that grows on mortal soil,
Nor in the glistering foil
Set off to th' world, nor in broad rumor lies,
But lives and spreads aloft by those pure eyes
And perfect witness of all-judging Jove;
As he pronounces lastly on each deed,
Of so much fame in heav'n expect thy meed.'
   O fountain Arethuse, and thou honored flood,
Smooth-sliding Mincius, crowned with vocal reeds,
That strain I heard was of a higher mood.
But now my oat proceeds,
And listens to the herald of the sea
That came in Neptune's plea.
He asked the waves, and asked the felon winds,
What hard mishap hath doomed this gentle swain?
And questioned every gust of rugged wings
That blows from off each beakèd promontory;
They knew not of his story,
And sage Hippotades their answer brings,
That not a blast was from his dungeon strayed;
The air was calm, and on the level brine
Sleek Panope with her all sisters played.

It was that fatal and perfidious bark,
Built in th' eclipse, and rigged with curses dark,
That sunk so low that sacred head of thine.
    Next Camus, reverend sire, went footing slow,
His mantle hairy, and his bonnet sedge,
Inwrought with figures dim, and on the edge
Like to that sanguine flower inscribed with woe.
'Ah, who hath reft,' quoth he, 'my dearest pledge?'
Last came, and last did go,
The Pilot of the Galilean lake;
Two massy keys he bore of metals twain
(The golden opes, the iron shuts amain).
He shook his mitred locks, and stern bespake:
'How well could I have spared for thee, young swain,
Enow of such as for their bellies' sake
Creep and intrude and climb into the fold!
Of other care they little reck'ning make
Than how to scramble at the shearers' feast,
And shove away the worthy bidden guest.
Blind mouths! that scarce themselves know how to hold
A sheep-hook, or have learned aught else the least
That to the faithful herdman's art belongs!
What recks it them? What need they? They are sped;
And when they list, their lean and flashy songs
Grate on their scrannel pipes of wretched straw;
The hungry sheep look up, and are not fed,
But swoln with wind, and the rank mist they draw,
Rot inwardly, and foul contagion spread;
Besides what the grim wolf with privy paw
Daily devours apace, and nothing said;
But that two-handed engine at the door
Stands ready to smite once, and smite no more.'
    Return, Alphéus, the dread voice is past
That shrunk thy streams; return, Sicilian Muse,
And call the vales, and bid them hither cast
Their bells and flow'rets of a thousand hues.
Ye valleys low where the mild whispers use
Of shades and wanton winds and gushing brooks,
On whose fresh lap the swart star sparely looks,
Throw hither all your quaint enameled eyes,
That on the green turf suck the honied show'rs,
And purple all the ground with vernal flow'rs.
Bring the rathe primrose that forsaken dies,
The tufted crowtoe, and pale jessamine,

The white pink, and the pansy freaked with jet,
The glowing violet,
The musk-rose, and the well-attired woodbine,
With cowslips wan that hang the pensive head,
And every flower that sad embroidery wears.
Bid amaranthus all his beauty shed,
And daffadillies fill their cups with tears,
To strew the laureate hearse where Lycid lies.
For so to interpose a little ease,
Let our frail thoughts dally with false surmise;
Ay me! whilst thee the shores and sounding seas
Wash far away, where'er thy bones are hurled,
Whether beyond the stormy Hebrides,
Where thou perhaps under the whelming tide
Visit'st the bottom of the monstrous world;
Or whether thou, to our moist vows denied,
Sleep'st by the fable of Bellerus old,
Where the great Vision of the guarded mount
Looks toward Namancos and Bayona's hold:
Look homeward, Angel, now, and melt with ruth;
And, O ye dolphins, waft the hapless youth.

Weep no more, woeful shepherds, weep no more,
For Lycidas, your sorrow, is not dead,
Sunk though he be beneath the wat'ry floor;
So sinks the day-star in the ocean bed,
And yet anon repairs his drooping head,
And tricks his beams, and with new-spangled ore
Flames in the forehead of the morning sky:
So Lycidas sunk low, but mounted high,
Through the dear might of him that walked the waves,
Where, other groves and other streams along,
With nectar pure his oozy locks he laves,
And hears the unexpressive nuptial song
In the blest kingdoms meek of joy and love.
There entertain him all the saints above,
In solemn troops and sweet societies
That sing, and singing in their glory move,
And wipe the tears for ever from his eyes.
Now, Lycidas, the shepherds weep no more;
Henceforth thou art the Genius of the shore,
In thy large recompense, and shalt be good
To all that wander in that perilous flood.

Thus sang the uncouth swain to th' oaks and rills,
While the still morn went out with sandals gray;

He touched the tender stops of various quills,
With eager thought warbling his Doric lay.
And now the sun had stretched out all the hills,
And now was dropped into the western bay;
At last he rose, and twitched his mantle blue:
To-morrow to fresh woods, and pastures new.

Sonnets

VIII

CAPTAIN or colonel, or knight in arms,
    Whose chance on these defenseless doors may seize,
    If deed of honor did thee ever please,
    Guard them, and him within protect from harms;
He can requite thee, for he knows the charms
    That call fame on such gentle acts as these,
    And he can spread thy name o'er lands and seas,
    Whatever clime the sun's bright circle warms.
Lift not thy spear against the Muses' bow'r:
    The great Emathian conqueror bid spare
    The house of Pindarus, when temple and tow'r
Went to the ground; and the repeated air
    Of sad Electra's poet had the power
    To save th' Athenian walls from ruin bare.

XIV

WHEN Faith and Love, which parted from thee never,
    Had ripened thy just soul to dwell with God,
    Meekly thou didst resign this earthy load
    Of death, called life, which us from life doth sever.
Thy works and alms and all thy good endeavor
    Stayed not behind, nor in the grave were trod;
    But, as Faith pointed with her golden rod,
    Followed thee up to joy and bliss for ever.
Love led them on, and Faith, who knew them best
    Thy handmaids, clad them o'er with purple beams
    And azure wings, that up they flew so dressed,
And spake the truth of thee in glorious themes
    Before the Judge, who thenceforth bid thee rest
    And drink thy fill of pure immortal streams.

XX

LAWRENCE, of virtuous father virtuous son,
　　Now that the fields are dank and ways are mire,
　　Where shall we sometimes meet, and by the fire
　　Help waste a sullen day, what may be won
From the hard season gaining? Time will run
　　On smoother, till Favonius reinspire
　　The frozen earth, and clothe in fresh attire
　　The lily and rose, that neither sowed nor spun.
What neat repast shall feast us, light and choice,
　　Of Attic taste, with wine, whence we may rise
　　To hear the lute well touched, or artful voice
Warble immortal notes and Tuscan air?
　　He who of those delights can judge, and spare
　　To interpose them oft, is not unwise.

XXI

CYRIACK, whose grandsire on the royal bench
　　Of British Themis, with no mean applause
　　Pronounced and in his volumes taught our laws,
　　Which others at their bar so often wrench,
Today deep thoughts resolve with me to drench
　　In mirth that after no repenting draws;
　　Let Euclid rest and Archimedes pause,
　　And what the Swede intends, and what the French.
To measure life learn thou betimes, and know
　　Toward solid good what leads the nearest way;
　　For other things mild Heav'n a time ordains,
And disapproves that care, though wise in show,
　　That with superfluous burden loads the day,
　　And when God sends a cheerful hour, refrains.

XXII

CYRIACK, this three years' day these eyes, though clear
　　To outward view of blemish or of spot,
　　Bereft of light their seeing have forgot;
　　Nor to their idle orbs doth sight appear
Of sun or moon or star throughout the year,
　　Or man or woman. Yet I argue not
　　Against Heav'n's hand or will, nor bate a jot
　　Of heart or hope, but still bear up and steer

Right onward. What supports me, dost thou ask?
    The conscience, friend, to have lost them overplied
    In liberty's defense, my noble task,
Of which all Europe talks from side to side.
    This thought might lead me through the world's vain masque,
    Content though blind, had I no better guide.

from *Paradise Lost*

BOOK I

OF MAN's first disobedience, and the fruit
Of that forbidden tree, whose mortal taste
Brought death into the world, and all our woe,
With loss of Eden, till one greater Man
Restore us, and regain the blissful seat,
Sing, Heav'nly Muse, that on the secret top
Of Oreb, or of Sinai, didst inspire
That shepherd who first taught the chosen seed
In the beginning how the heav'ns and earth
Rose out of Chaos; or if Sion hill
Delight thee more, and Siloa's brook that flowed
Fast by the oracle of God, I thence
Invoke thy aid to my advent'rous song,
That with no middle flight intends to soar
Above th' Aonian mount, while it pursues
Things unattempted yet in prose or rhyme.
And chiefly thou, O Spirit, that dost prefer
Before all temples th' upright heart and pure,
Instruct me, for thou know'st; thou from the first
Wast present, and with mighty wings outspread
Dove-like sat'st brooding on the vast abyss
And mad'st it pregnant: what in me is dark
Illumine, what is low raise and support;
That to the highth of this great argument
I may assert Eternal Providence,
And justify the ways of God to men.
    Say first, for heav'n hides nothing from thy view,
Nor the deep tract of hell, say first what cause
Moved our grand parents in that happy state,
Favored of Heav'n so highly, to fall off
From their Creator, and transgress his will

For one restraint, lords of the world besides?
Who first seduced them to that foul revolt?
Th' infernal Serpent; he it was whose guile,
Stirred up with envy and revenge, deceived
The mother of mankind, what time his pride
Had cast him out from heav'n, with all his host
Of rebel angels, by whose aid aspiring
To set himself in glory above his peers,
He trusted to have equaled the Most High,
If he opposed; and with ambitious aim
Against the throne and monarchy of God
Raised impious war in heav'n and battle proud
With vain attempt. Him the Almighty Power
Hurled headlong flaming from th' ethereal sky
With hideous ruin and combustion down
To bottomless perdition, there to dwell
In adamantine chains and penal fire,
Who durst defy th' Omnipotent to arms.
Nine times the space that measures day and night
To mortal men, he with his horrid crew
Lay vanquished, rolling in the fiery gulf
Confounded though immortal. But his doom
Reserved him to more wrath; for now the thought
Both of lost happiness and lasting pain
Torments him; round he throws his baleful eyes,
That witnessed huge affliction and dismay
Mixed with obdúrate pride and steadfast hate.
At once as far as angels ken he views
The dismal situation waste and wild
A dungeon horrible, on all sides round
As one great furnace flamed, yet from those flames
No light, but rather darkness visible
Served only to discover sights of woe,
Regions of sorrow, doleful shades, where peace
And rest can never dwell, hope never comes
That comes to all; but torture without end
Still urges, and a fiery deluge, fed
With ever-burning sulphur unconsumed:
Such place Eternal Justice had prepared
For those rebellious, here their prison ordained
In utter darkness, and their portion set
As far removed from God and light of heav'n
As from the center thrice to th' utmost pole.
O how unlike the place from whence they fell!

There the companions of his fall, o'erwhelmed
With floods and whirlwinds of tempestuous fire,
He soon discerns, and welt'ring by his side
One next himself in power, and next in crime,
Long after known in Palestine, and named
Beelzebub. To whom th' Arch-Enemy,
And thence in heav'n called Satan, with bold words
Breaking the horrid silence thus began:
    'If thou beest he—but O how fall'n! how changed
From him, who in the happy realms of light
Clothed with transcendent brightness didst outshine
Myriads though bright—if he whom mutual league,
United thoughts and counsels, equal hope
And hazard in the glorious enterprise,
Joined with me once, now misery hath joined
In equal ruin: into what pit thou seest
From what highth fall'n, so much the stronger proved
He with his thunder, and till then who knew
The force of those dire arms? Yet not for those,
Nor what the potent Victor in his rage
Can else inflict, do I repent or change,
Though changed in outward luster, that fixed mind
And high disdain, from sense of injured merit,
That with the mightiest raised me to contend,
And to the fierce contention brought along
Innumerable force of Spirits armed
That durst dislike his reign, and me preferring,
His utmost power with adverse power opposed
In dubious battle on the plains of heav'n,
And shook his throne. What though the field be lost?
All is not lost; the unconquerable will,
And study of revenge, immortal hate,
And courage never to submit or yield:
And what is else not to be overcome?
That glory never shall his wrath or might
Extort from me. To bow and sue for grace
With suppliant knee, and deify his power
Who from the terror of this arm so late
Doubted his empire, that were low indeed,
That were an ignominy and shame beneath
This downfall; since by fate the strength of gods
And this empyreal substance cannot fail,
Since through experience of this great event,
In arms not worse, in foresight much advanced,

We may with more successful hope resolve
To wage by force or guile eternal war
Irreconcilable to our grand Foe,
Who now triumphs, and in th' excess of joy
Sole reigning holds the tyranny of heav'n.'
  So spake th' apostate Angel, though in pain,
Vaunting aloud, but racked with deep despair;
And him thus answered soon his bold compeer:
  'O Prince, O Chief of many thronèd Powers,
That led th' embattled Seraphim to war
Under thy conduct, and in dreadful deeds
Fearless, endangered heav'n's perpetual King,
And put to proof his high supremacy,
Whether upheld by strength, or chance, or fate;
Too well I see and rue the dire event,
That with sad overthrow and foul defeat
Hath lost us heav'n, and all this mighty host
In horrible destruction laid thus low,
As far as gods and heav'nly essences
Can perish: for the mind and spirit remains
Invincible, and vigor soon returns,
Though all our glory extinct, and happy state
Here swallowed up in endless misery.
But what if he our Conqueror (whom I now
Of force believe almighty, since no less
Than such could have o'erpow'red such force as ours)
Have left us this our spirit and strength entire
Strongly to suffer and support our pains,
That we may so suffice his vengeful ire,
Or do him mightier service as his thralls
By right of war, whate'er his business be,
Here in the heart of hell to work in fire,
Or do his errands in the gloomy deep?
What can it then avail though yet we feel
Strength undiminished, or eternal being
To undergo eternal punishment?'
  Whereto with speedy words th' Arch-Fiend replied:
'Fall'n Cherub, to be weak is miserable,
Doing or suffering: but of this be sure,
To do aught good never will be our task,
But ever to do ill our sole delight,
As being the contrary to his high will
Whom we resist. If then his providence
Out of our evil seek to bring forth good,

JOHN MILTON

Our labor must be to pervert that end,
And out of good still to find means of evil;
Which ofttimes may succeed, so as perhaps
Shall grieve him, if I fail not, and disturb
His inmost counsels from their destined aim.
But see the angry Victor hath recalled
His ministers of vengeance and pursuit
Back to the gates of heav'n; the sulphurous hail
Shot after us in storm, o'erblown hath laid
The fiery surge, that from the precipice
Of heav'n received us falling, and the thunder,
Winged with red lightning and impetuous rage,
Perhaps hath spent his shafts, and ceases now
To bellow through the vast and boundless deep.
Let us not slip th' occasion, whether scorn
Or satiate fury yield it from our Foe.
Seest thou yon dreary plain, forlorn and wild,
The seat of desolation, void of light,
Save what the glimmering of these livid flames
Casts pale and dreadful? Thither let us tend
From off the tossing of these fiery waves,
There rest, if any rest can harbor there,
And reassembling our afflicted powers,
Consult how we may henceforth most offend
Our Enemy, our own loss how repair,
How overcome this dire calamity,
What reinforcement we may gain from hope;
If not, what resolution from despair.'
    Thus Satan talking to his nearest mate
With head uplift above the wave, and eyes
That sparkling blazed; his other parts besides
Prone on the flood, extended long and large
Lay floating many a rood, in bulk as huge
As whom the fables name of monstrous size,
Titanian or Earth-born, that warred on Jove,
Briareos or Typhon, whom the den
By ancient Tarsus held, or that sea-beast
Leviathan, which God of all his works
Created hugest that swim th' ocean stream:
Him haply slumb'ring on the Norway foam,
The pilot of some small night-foundered skiff,
Deeming some island, oft, as seamen tell,
With fixèd anchor in his scaly rind
Moors by his side under the lee, while night

JOHN MILTON

Invests the sea, and wishèd morn delays:
So stretched out huge in length the Arch-Fiend lay
Chained on the burning lake; nor ever thence
Had ris'n or heaved his head, but that the will
And high permission of all-ruling Heaven
Left him at large to his own dark designs,
That with reiterated crimes he might
Heap on himself damnation, while he sought
Evil to others, and enraged might see
How all his malice served but to bring forth
Infinite goodness, grace and mercy shown
On man by him seduced, but on himself
Treble confusion, wrath and vengeance poured.

Forthwith upright he rears from off the pool
His mighty stature; on each hand the flames
Driv'n backward slope their pointing spires, and rolled
In billows, leave i' th' midst a horrid vale.
Then with expanded wings he steers his flight
Aloft, incumbent on the dusky air
That felt unusual weight, till on dry land
He lights, if it were land that ever burned
With solid, as the lake with liquid fire,
And such appeared in hue; as when the force
Of subterranean wind transports a hill
Torn from Pelorus, or the shattered side
Of thund'ring Etna, whose combustible
And fueled entrails thence conceiving fire,
Sublimed with mineral fury, aid the winds,
And leave a singèd bottom all involved
With stench and smoke: such resting found the sole
Of unblest feet. Him followed his next mate,
Both glorying to have scaped the Stygian flood
As gods, and by their own recovered strength,
Not by the sufferance of supernal power.

'Is this the region, this the soil, the clime,'
Said then the lost Archangel, 'this the seat
That we must change for heav'n, this mournful gloom
For that celestial light? Be it so, since he
Who now is sovran can dispose and bid
What shall be right: fardest from him is best,
Whom reason hath equaled, force hath made supreme
Above his equals. Farewell, happy fields,
Where joy for ever dwells! Hail, horrors, hail,
Infernal world, and thou, profoundest hell,

269

Receive thy new possessor: one who brings
A mind not to be changed by place or time.
The mind is its own place, and in itself
Can make a heav'n of hell, a hell of heav'n.
What matter where, if I be still the same,
And what I should be, all but less than he
Whom thunder hath made greater? Here at least
We shall be free; th' Almighty hath not built
Here for his envy, will not drive us hence:
Here we may reign secure, and in my choice
To reign is worth ambition, though in hell:
Better to reign in hell than serve in heav'n.
But wherefore let we then our faithful friends,
Th' associates and copartners of our loss,
Lie thus astonished on th' oblivious pool,
And call them not to share with us their part
In this unhappy mansion, or once more
With rallied arms to try what may be yet
Regained in heav'n, or what more lost in hell?'
    So Satan spake, and him Beelzebub
Thus answered: 'Leader of those armies bright,
Which but th' Omnipotent none could have foiled,
If once they hear that voice, their liveliest pledge
Of hope in fears and dangers, heard so oft
In worst extremes, and on the perilous edge
Of battle when it raged, in all assaults
Their surest signal, they will soon resume
New courage and revive, though now they lie
Groveling and prostrate on yon lake of fire,
As we erewhile, astounded and amazed;
No wonder, fall'n such a pernicious highth!'
    He scarce had ceased when the superior Fiend
Was moving toward the shore; his ponderous shield,
Ethereal temper, massy, large, and round,
Behind him cast; the broad circumference
Hung on his shoulders like the moon, whose orb
Through optic glass the Tuscan artist views
At ev'ning from the top of Fesole,
Or in Valdarno, to descry new lands,
Rivers or mountains in her spotty globe.
His spear, to equal which the tallest pine
Hewn on Norwegian hills, to be the mast
Of some great ammiral, were but a wand,
He walked with to support uneasy steps

Over the burning marl, not like those steps
On heaven's azure; and the torrid clime
Smote on him sore besides, vaulted with fire.
Nathless he so endured, till on the beach
Of that inflamèd sea, he stood and called
His legions, angel forms, who lay entranced,
Thick as autumnal leaves that strow the brooks
In Vallombrosa, where th' Etrurian shades
High over-arched embow'r; or scattered sedge
Afloat, when with fierce winds Orion armed
Hath vexed the Red Sea coast, whose waves o'erthrew
Busiris and his Memphian chivalry,
While with perfidious hatred they pursued
The sojourners of Goshen, who beheld
From the safe shore their floating carcasses
And broken chariot wheels; so thick bestrown,
Abject and lost lay these, covering the flood,
Under amazement of their hideous change.
He called so loud that all the hollow deep
Of hell resounded: 'Princes, Potentates,
Warriors, the flow'r of heav'n, once yours, now lost,
If such astonishment as this can seize
Eternal Spirits; or have ye chos'n this place
After the toil of battle to repose
Your wearied virtue, for the ease you find
To slumber here, as in the vales of heav'n?
Or in this abject posture have ye sworn
To adore the Conqueror, who now beholds
Cherub and Seraph rolling in the flood
With scattered arms and ensigns, till anon
His swift pursuers from heav'n gates discern
Th' advantage, and descending tread us down
Thus drooping, or with linkèd thunderbolts
Transfix us to the bottom of this gulf?
Awake, arise, or be for ever fall'n!'
    They heard, and were abashed, and up they sprung
Upon the wing, as when men wont to watch
On duty, sleeping found by whom they dread,
Rouse and bestir themselves ere well awake.
Nor did they not perceive the evil plight
In which they were, or the fierce pains not feel;
Yet to their general's voice they soon obeyed
Innumerable. As when the potent rod
Of Amram's son in Egypt's evil day

Waved round the coast, up called a pitchy cloud
Of locusts, warping on the eastern wind,
That o'er the realm of impious Pharaoh hung
Like night, and darkened all the land of Nile:
So numberless were those bad angels seen
Hovering on wing under the cope of hell
'Twixt upper, nether, and surrounding fires;
Till, as a signal giv'n, th' uplifted spear
Of their great Sultan waving to direct
Their course, in even balance down they light
On the firm brimstone, and fill all the plain;
A multitude, like which the populous North
Poured never from her frozen loins, to pass
Rhene or the Danaw, when her barbarous sons
Came like a deluge on the South, and spread
Beneath Gibraltar to the Libyan sands.
Forthwith from every squadron and each band
The heads and leaders thither haste where stood
Their great commander; godlike shapes and forms
Excelling human, princely dignities,
And powers that erst in heaven sat on thrones;
Though of their names in heav'nly records now
Be no memorial, blotted out and razed
By their rebellion from the Books of Life.
Nor had they yet among the sons of Eve
Got them new names, till wand'ring o'er the earth,
Through God's high sufferance for the trial of man,
By falsities and lies the greatest part
Of mankind they corrupted to forsake
God their Creator, and th' invisible
Glory of him that made them to transform
Oft to the image of a brute, adorned
With gay religions full of pomp and gold,
And devils to adore for deities:
Then were they known to men by various names,
And various idols through the heathen world.
     Say, Muse, their names then known, who first, who last,
Roused from the slumber on that fiery couch,
At their great emperor's call, as next in worth
Came singly where he stood on the bare strand,
While the promiscuous crowd stood yet aloof.
     The chief were those who from the pit of hell,
Roaming to seek their prey on earth, durst fix
Their seats long after next the seat of God,

Their altars by his altar, gods adored
Among the nations round, and durst abide
Jehovah thund'ring out of Sion, throned
Between the Cherubim; yea, often placed
Within his sanctuary itself their shrines,
Abominations; and with cursèd things
His holy rites and solemn feasts profaned,
And with their darkness durst affront his light.
First Moloch, horrid king besmeared with blood
Of human sacrifice, and parents' tears,
Though for the noise of drums and timbrels loud
Their children's cries unheard, that passed through fire
To his grim idol. Him the Ammonite
Worshiped in Rabba and her wat'ry plain,
In Argob and in Basan, to the stream
Of utmost Arnon. Nor content with such
Audacious neighborhood, the wisest heart
Of Solomon he led by fraud to build
His temple right against the temple of God
On that opprobrious hill, and made his grove
The pleasant valley of Hinnom, Tophet thence
And black Gehenna called, the type of hell.
Next Chemos, th' óbscene dread of Moab's sons,
From Aroer to Nebo, and the wild
Of southmost Abarim; in Hesebon
And Horonaim, Seon's realm, beyond
The flow'ry dale of Sibma clad with vines,
And Elealè to th' Asphaltic pool:
Peor his other name, when he enticed
Israel in Sittim on their march from Nile
To do him wanton rites, which cost them woe.
Yet thence his lustful orgies he enlarged
Even to that hill of scandal, by the grove
Of Moloch homicide, lust hard by hate;
Till good Josiah drove them thence to hell.
With these came they who, from the bord'ring flood
Of old Euphrates to the brook that parts
Egypt from Syrian ground, had general names
Of Baalim and Ashtaroth, those male,
These feminine. For Spirits when they please
Can either sex assume, or both; so soft
And uncompounded is their essence pure,
Not tied or manacled with joint or limb,
Nor founded on the brittle strength of bones,

Like cumbrous flesh; but in what shape they choose,
Dilated or condensed, bright or obscure,
Can execute their airy purposes,
And works of love or enmity fulfill.
For those the race of Israel oft forsook
Their living Strength, and unfrequented left
His righteous altar, bowing lowly down
To bestial gods; for which their heads as low
Bowed down in battle, sunk before the spear
Of despicable foes. With these in troop
Came Astoreth, whom the Phoenicians called
Astarte, queen of heav'n, with crescent horns;
To whose bright image nightly by the moon
Sidonian virgins paid their vows and songs;
In Sion also not unsung, where stood
Her temple on th' offensive mountain, built
By that uxorious king, whose heart though large,
Beguiled by fair idolatresses, fell
To idols foul. Thammuz came next behind,
Whose annual wound in Lebanon allured
The Syrian damsels to lament his fate
In amorous ditties all a summer's day,
While smooth Adonis from his native rock
Ran purple to the sea, supposed with blood
Of Thammuz yearly wounded: the love-tale
Infected Sion's daughters with like heat,
Whose wanton passions in the sacred porch
Ezekiel saw, when by the vision led
His eye surveyed the dark idolatries
Of alienated Judah. Next came one
Who mourned in earnest, when the captive ark
Maimed his brute image, head and hands lopped off
In his own temple, on the grunsel edge,
Where he fell flat, and shamed his worshipers:
Dagon his name, sea monster, upward man
And downward fish; yet had his temple high
Reared in Azotus, dreaded through the coast
Of Palestine, in Gath and Ascalon,
And Accaron and Gaza's frontier bounds.
Him followed Rimmon, whose delightful seat
Was fair Damascus, on the fertile banks
Of Abbana and Pharphar, lucid streams.
He also against the house of God was bold:
A leper once he lost and gained a king,

Ahaz his sottish conqueror, whom he drew
God's altar to disparage and displace
For one of Syrian mode, whereon to burn
His odious off'rings, and adore the gods
Whom he had vanquished. After these appeared
A crew who under names of old renown,
Osiris, Isis, Orus, and their train,
With monstrous shapes and sorceries abused
Fanatic Egypt and her priests, to seek
Their wand'ring gods disguised in brutish forms
Rather than human. Nor did Israel scape
Th' infection when their borrowed gold composed
The calf in Oreb; and the rebel king
Doubled that sin in Bethel and in Dan,
Lik'ning his Maker to the grazèd ox—
Jehovah, who in one night when he passed
From Egypt marching, equaled with one stroke
Both her first-born and all her bleating gods.
Belial came last, than whom a Spirit more lewd
Fell not from heaven, or more gross to love
Vice for itself. To him no temple stood
Or altar smoked; yet who more oft than he
In temples and at altars, when the priest
Turns atheist, as did Eli's sons, who filled
With lust and violence the house of God?
In courts and palaces he also reigns
And in luxurious cities, where the noise
Of riot ascends above their loftiest tow'rs,
And injury and outrage; and when night
Darkens the streets, then wander forth the sons
Of Belial, flown with insolence and wine.
Witness the streets of Sodom, and that night
In Gibeah, when the hospitable door
Exposed a matron to avoid worse rape.
These were the prime in order and in might;
The rest were long to tell, though far renowned,
Th' Ionian gods, of Javan's issue held
Gods, yet confessed later than Heav'n and Earth,
Their boasted parents; Titan, Heav'n's first-born,
With his enormous brood, and birthright seized
By younger Saturn; he from mightier Jove,
His own and Rhea's son, like measure found;
So Jove usurping reigned. These, first in Crete
And Ida known, thence on the snowy top

Of cold Olympus ruled the middle air,
Their highest heav'n; or on the Delphian cliff,
Or in Dodona, and through all the bounds
Of Doric land; or who with Saturn old
Fled over Adria to th' Hesperian fields,
And o'er the Celtic roamed the utmost isles.

All these and more came flocking; but with looks
Downcast and damp, yet such wherein appeared
Obscure some glimpse of joy, to have found their Chief
Not in despair, to have found themselves not lost
In loss itself; which on his count'nance cast
Like doubtful hue. But he, his wonted pride
Soon recollecting, with high words, that bore
Semblance of worth, not substance, gently raised
Their fainted courage, and dispelled their fears.
Then straight commands that at the warlike sound
Of trumpets loud and clarions be upreared
His mighty standard; that proud honor claimed
Azazel as his right, a Cherub tall;
Who forthwith from the glittering staff unfurled
Th' imperial ensign, which full high advanced
Shone like a meteor streaming to the wind,
With gems and golden luster rich emblazed,
Seraphic arms and trophies; all the while
Sonorous metal blowing martial sounds;
At which the universal host upsent
A shout that tore hell's concave, and beyond
Frighted the reign of Chaos and old Night.
All in a moment through the gloom were seen
Ten thousand banners rise into the air
With orient colors waving; with them rose
A forest huge of spears; and thronging helms
Appeared, and serried shields in thick array
Of depth immeasurable. Anon they move
In perfect phalanx to the Dorian mood
Of flutes and soft recorders; such as raised
To highth of noblest temper heroes old
Arming to battle, and instead of rage
Deliberate valor breathed, firm and unmoved
With dread of death to flight or foul retreat,
Nor wanting power to mitigate and swage
With solemn touches troubled thoughts, and chase
Anguish and doubt and fear and sorrow and pain
From mortal or immortal minds. Thus they,

Breathing united force with fixèd thought,
Moved on in silence to soft pipes that charmed
Their painful steps o'er the burnt soil; and now
Advanced in view they stand, a horrid front
Of dreadful length and dazzling arms, in guise
Of warriors old with ordered spear and shield,
Awaiting what command their mighty Chief
Had to impose. He through the armèd files
Darts his experienced eye, and soon traverse
The whole battalion views, their order due,
Their visages and stature as of gods;
Their number last he sums. And now his heart
Distends with pride, and hard'ning in his strength
Glories; for never, since created man,
Met such embodied force as named with these
Could merit more than that small infantry
Warred on by cranes: though all the giant brood
Of Phlegra with th' heroic race were joined
That fought at Thebes and Ilium, on each side
Mixed with auxiliar gods; and what resounds
In fable or romance of Uther's son
Begirt with British and Armoric knights;
And all who since, baptized or infidel,
Jousted in Aspramont or Montalban,
Damasco, or Marocco, or Trebisond,
Or whom Biserta sent from Afric shore
When Charlemain with all his peerage fell
By Fontarabbia. Thus far these beyond
Compare of mortal prowess, yet observed
Their dread commander. He above the rest
In shape and gesture proudly eminent
Stood like a tow'r; his form had yet not lost
All her original brightness, nor appeared
Less than Archangel ruined, and th' excess
Of glory obscured: as when the sun new ris'n
Looks through the horizontal misty air
Shorn of his beams, or from behind the moon
In dim eclipse disastrous twilight sheds
On half the nations, and with fear of change
Perplexes monarchs. Darkened so, yet shone
Above them all th' Archangel; but his face
Deep scars of thunder had intrenched, and care
Sat on his faded cheek, but under brows
Of dauntless courage, and considerate pride

Waiting revenge. Cruel his eye, but cast
Signs of remorse and passion to behold
The fellows of his crime, the followers rather
(Far other once beheld in bliss), condemned
For ever now to have their lot in pain,
Millions of Spirits for his fault amerced
Of heav'n, and from eternal splendors flung
For his revolt, yet faithful how they stood,
Their glory withered: as when heaven's fire
Hath scathed the forest oaks or mountain pines,
With singèd top their stately growth though bare
Stands on the blasted heath. He now prepared
To speak; whereat their doubled ranks they bend
From wing to wing, and half enclose him round
With all his peers: attention held them mute.
Thrice he assayed, and thrice in spite of scorn,
Tears such as angels weep burst forth; at last
Words interwove with sighs found out their way:
  'O myriads of immortal Spirits, O Powers
Matchless, but with th' Almighty, and that strife
Was not inglorious, though th' event was dire,
As this place testifies, and this dire change
Hateful to utter. But what power of mind
Foreseeing or presaging, from the depth
Of knowledge past or present, could have feared
How such united force of gods, how such
As stood like these, could ever know repulse?
For who can yet believe, though after loss,
That all these puissant legions, whose exile
Hath emptied heav'n, shall fail to re-ascend
Self-raised, and repossess their native seat?
For me, be witness all the host of heav'n,
If counsels different, or danger shunned
By me, have lost our hopes. But he who reigns
Monarch in heav'n, till then as one secure
Sat on his throne, upheld by old repute,
Consent or custom, and his regal state
Put forth at full, but still his strength concealed,
Which tempted our attempt, and wrought our fall.
Henceforth his might we know, and know our own,
So as not either to provoke, or dread
New war, provoked; our better part remains
To work in close design, by fraud or guile,
What force effected not; that he no less

At length from us may find, who overcomes
By force hath overcome but half his foe.
Space may produce new worlds; whereof so rife
There went a fame in heav'n that he ere long
Intended to create, and therein plant
A generation, whom his choice regard
Should favor equal to the sons of heaven.
Thither, if but to pry, shall be perhaps
Our first eruption, thither or elsewhere;
For this infernal pit shall never hold
Celestial Spirits in bondage, nor th' abyss
Long under darkness cover. But these thoughts
Full counsel must mature. Peace is despaired,
For who can think submission? War then, war
Open or understood must be resolved.'

He spake; and to confirm his words, out flew
Millions of flaming swords, drawn from the thighs
Of mighty Cherubim; the sudden blaze
Far round illumined hell. Highly they raged
Against the Highest, and fierce with graspèd arms
Clashed on their sounding shields the din of war,
Hurling defiance towards the vault of heav'n.

There stood a hill not far whose grisly top
Belched fire and rolling smoke; the rest entire
Shone with a glossy scurf, undoubted sign
That in his womb was hid metallic ore,
The work of sulphur. Thither winged with speed
A numerous brígade hastened: as when bands
Of pioneers with spade and pickaxe armed
Forerun the royal camp, to trench a field
Or cast a rampart. Mammon led them on,
Mammon, the least erected Spirit that fell
From heav'n, for ev'n in heav'n his looks and thoughts
Were always downward bent, admiring more
The riches of heav'n's pavement, trodden gold,
Than aught divine or holy else enjoyed
In vision beatific. By him first
Men also, and by his suggestion taught,
Ransacked the center, and with impious hands
Rifled the bowels of their mother earth
For treasures better hid. Soon had his crew
Opened into the hill a spacious wound
And digged out ribs of gold. Let none admire
That riches grow in hell; that soil may best

Deserve the precious bane. And here let those
Who boast in mortal things, and wond'ring tell
Of Babel, and the works of Memphian kings,
Learn how their greatest monuments of fame,
And strength and art are easily outdone
By Spirits reprobate, and in an hour
What in an age they with incessant toil
And hands innumerable scarce perform.
Nigh on the plain in many cells prepared,
That underneath had veins of liquid fire
Sluiced from the lake, a second multitude
With wondrous art founded the massy ore,
Severing each kind, and scummed the bullion dross.
A third as soon had formed within the ground
A various mold, and from the boiling cells
By strange conveyance filled each hollow nook,
As in an organ from one blast of wind
To many a row of pipes the sound-board breathes.
Anon out of the earth a fabric huge
Rose like an exhalation, with the sound
Of dulcet symphonies and voices sweet,
Built like a temple, where pilasters round
Were set, and Doric pillars overlaid
With golden architrave; nor did there want
Cornice or frieze, with bossy sculptures grav'n;
The roof was fretted gold. Not Babylon,
Nor great Alcairo such magnificence
Equaled in all their glories, to enshrine
Belus or Serapis their gods, or seat
Their kings, when Egypt with Assyria strove
In wealth and luxury. Th' ascending pile
Stood fixed her stately highth, and straight the doors
Op'ning their brazen folds discover wide
Within, her ample spaces, o'er the smooth
And level pavement; from the archèd roof
Pendent by subtle magic many a row
Of starry lamps and blazing cressets fed
With naphtha and asphaltus yielded light
As from a sky. The hasty multitude
Admiring entered, and the work some praise,
And some the architect: his hand was known
In heav'n by many a tow'red structure high,
Where sceptered angels held their residence,
And sat as princes, whom the súpreme King

Exalted to such power, and gave to rule,
Each in his hierarchy, the orders bright.
Nor was his name unheard or unadored
In ancient Greece, and in Ausonian land
Men called him Mulciber; and how he fell
From heav'n, they fabled, thrown by angry Jove
Sheer o'er the crystal battlements: from morn
To noon he fell, from noon to dewy eve,
A summer's day; and with the setting sun
Dropped from the zenith like a falling star,
On Lemnos th' Aégean isle. Thus they relate,
Erring; for he with this rebellious rout
Fell long before; nor aught availed him now
To have built in heav'n high tow'rs; nor did he scape
By all his engines, but was headlong sent
With his industrious crew to build in hell.
    Meanwhile the wingèd heralds by command
Of sovran power, with awful ceremony
And trumpet's sound, throughout the host proclaim
A solemn council forthwith to be held
At Pandemonium, the high capitol
Of Satan and his peers; their summons called
From every band and squarèd regiment
By place or choice the worthiest; they anon
With hundreds and with thousands trooping came
Attended. All access was thronged, the gates
And porches wide, but chief the spacious hall
(Though like a covered field, where champions bold
Wont ride in armed, and at the Soldan's chair
Defied the best of paynim chivalry
To mortal combat or career with lance)
Thick swarmed, both on the ground and in the air,
Brushed with the hiss of rustling wings. As bees
In springtime, when the sun with Taurus rides,
Pour forth their populous youth about the hive
In clusters; they among fresh dews and flowers
Fly to and fro, or on the smoothèd plank,
The suburb of their straw-built citadel,
New rubbed with balm, expatiate and confer
Their state affairs: so thick the airy crowd
Swarmed and were straitened; till the signal giv'n,
Behold a wonder! they but now who seemed
In bigness to surpass Earth's giant sons,
Now less than smallest dwarfs, in narrow room

Throng numberless, like that Pygmean race
Beyond the Indian mount, or fairy elves,
Whose midnight revels by a forest side
Or fountain some belated peasant sees,
Or dreams he sees, while overhead the moon
Sits arbitress, and nearer to the earth
Wheels her pale course; they on their mirth and dance
Intent, with jocund music charm his ear;
At once with joy and fear his heart rebounds.
Thus incorporeal Spirits to smallest forms
Reduced their shapes immense, and were at large,
Though without number still, amidst the hall
Of that infernal court. But far within,
And in their own dimensions like themselves,
The great Seraphic Lords and Cherubim
In close recess and secret conclave sat,
A thousand demi-gods on golden seats,
Frequent and full. After short silence then
And summons read, the great consult began.

BOOK II

HIGH on a throne of royal state, which far
Outshone the wealth of Ormus and of Ind,
Or where the gorgeous East with richest hand
Show'rs on her kings barbaric pearl and gold,
Satan exalted sat, by merit raised
To that bad eminence; and from despair
Thus high uplifted beyond hope, aspires
Beyond thus high, insatiate to pursue
Vain war with Heav'n, and by success untaught,
His proud imaginations thus displayed:
    'Powers and Dominions, Deities of heav'n,
For since no deep within her gulf can hold
Immortal vigor, though oppressed and fall'n,
I give not heav'n for lost. From this descent
Celestial Virtues rising will appear
More glorious and more dread than from no fall,
And trust themselves to fear no second fate.
Me though just right and the fixed laws of heav'n
Did first create your leader, next, free choice,
With what besides, in council or in fight,
Hath been achieved of merit, yet this loss,
Thus far at least recovered, hath much more

Established in a safe unenvied throne
Yielded with full consent. The happier state
In heav'n, which follows dignity, might draw
Envy from each inferior; but who here
Will envy whom the highest place exposes
Foremost to stand against the Thunderer's aim
Your bulwark, and condemns to greatest share
Of endless pain? Where there is then no good
For which to strive, no strife can grow up there
From faction; for none sure will claim in hell
Precedence, none whose portion is so small
Of present pain that with ambitious mind
Will covet more. With this advantage then
To union, and firm faith, and firm accord,
More than can be in heav'n, we now return
To claim our just inheritance of old,
Surer to prosper than prosperity
Could have assured us; and by what best way,
Whether of open war or covert guile,
We now debate; who can advise, may speak.'
    He ceased, and next him Moloch, sceptered king,
Stood up, the strongest and the fiercest Spirit
That fought in heav'n, now fiercer by despair.
His trust was with th' Eternal to be deemed
Equal in strength, and rather than be less
Cared not to be at all; with that care lost
Went all his fear: of God, or hell, or worse
He recked not, and these words thereafter spake:
    'My sentence is for open war. Of wiles,
More unexpert, I boast not: them let those
Contrive who need, or when they need, not now.
For while they sit contriving, shall the rest,
Millions that stand in arms and longing wait
The signal to ascend, sit ling'ring here,
Heav'n's fugitives, and for their dwelling-place
Accept this dark opprobrious den of shame,
The prison of his tyranny who reigns
By our delay? No, let us rather choose,
Armed with hell flames and fury, all at once
O'er heav'n's high tow'rs to force resistless way,
Turning our tortures into horrid arms
Against the Torturer; when to meet the noise
Of his almighty engine he shall hear
Infernal thunder, and for lightning see

Black fire and horror shot with equal rage
Among his angels, and his throne itself
Mixed with Tartarean sulphur and strange fire,
His own invented torments. But perhaps
The way seems difficult and steep to scale
With upright wing against a higher foe?
Let such bethink them, if the sleepy drench
Of that forgetful lake benumb not still,
That in our proper motion we ascend
Up to our native seat; descent and fall
To us is adverse. Who but felt of late,
When the fierce foe hung on our broken rear
Insulting, and pursued us through the deep,
With what compulsion and laborious flight
We sunk thus low? Th' ascent is easy then;
Th' event is feared? Should we again provoke
Our stronger, some worse way his wrath may find
To our destruction, if there be in hell
Fear to be worse destroyed: what can be worse
Than to dwell here, driv'n out from bliss, condemned
In this abhorrèd deep to utter woe;
Where pain of unextinguishable fire
Must exercise us without hope of end
The vassals of his anger, when the scourge
Inexorably, and the torturing hour
Calls us to penance? More destroyed than thus
We should be quite abolished and expire.
What fear we then? What doubt we to incense
His utmost ire? Which to the highth enraged
Will either quite consume us, and reduce
To nothing this essential, happier far
Than miserable to have eternal being;
Or if our substance be indeed divine,
And cannot cease to be, we are at worst
On this side nothing; and by proof we feel
Our power sufficient to disturb his heav'n,
And with perpetual inroads to alarm,
Though inaccessible, his fatal throne;
Which if not victory is yet revenge.'
    He ended frowning, and his look denounced
Desperate revenge, and battle dangerous
To less than gods. On th' other side up rose
Belial, in act more graceful and humane;
A fairer person lost not heav'n; he seemed

For dignity composed and high exploit:
But all was false and hollow, though his tongue
Dropped manna, and could make the worse appear
The better reason, to perplex and dash
Maturest counsels: for his thoughts were low;
To vice industrious, but to nobler deeds
Timorous and slothful: yet he pleased the ear,
And with persuasive accent thus began:
　　'I should be much for open war, O Peers,
As not behind in hate, if what was urged
Main reason to persuade immediate war
Did not dissuade me most, and seem to cast
Ominous conjecture on the whole success:
When he who most excels in fact of arms,
In what he counsels and in what excels
Mistrustful, grounds his courage on despair
And utter dissolution, as the scope
Of all his aim, after some dire revenge.
First, what revenge? The tow'rs of heav'n are filled
With armèd watch, that render all access
Impregnable; oft on the bordering deep
Encamp their legions, or with óbscure wing
Scout far and wide into the realm of Night,
Scorning surprise. Or could we break our way
By force, and at our heels all hell should rise
With blackest insurrection, to confound
Heav'n's purest light, yet our great Enemy
All incorruptible would on his throne
Sit unpolluted, and th' ethereal mold
Incapable of stain would soon expel
Her mischief, and purge off the baser fire,
Victorious. Thus repulsed, our final hope
Is flat despair; we must exasperate
Th' almighty Victor to spend all his rage,
And that must end us, that must be our cure,
To be no more. Sad cure! for who would lose,
Though full of pain, this intellectual being,
Those thoughts that wander through eternity,
To perish rather, swallowed up and lost
In the wide womb of uncreated Night,
Devoid of sense and motion? And who knows,
Let this be good, whether our angry Foe
Can give it, or will ever? How he can
Is doubtful; that he never will is sure.

Will he, so wise, let loose at once his ire,
Belike through impotence, or unaware,
To give his enemies their wish, and end
Them in his anger, whom his anger saves
To punish endless? "Wherefore cease we then?"
Say they who counsel war; "we are decreed,
Reserved, and destined to eternal woe;
Whatever doing, what can we suffer more,
What can we suffer worse?" Is this then worst,
Thus sitting, thus consulting, thus in arms?
What when we fled amain, pursued and strook
With Heav'n's afflicting thunder, and besought
The deep to shelter us? This hell then seemed
A refuge from those wounds. Or when we lay
Chained on the burning lake? That sure was worse.
What if the breath that kindled those grim fires
Awaked should blow them into sevenfold rage
And plunge us in the flames? Or from above
Should intermitted vengeance arm again
His red right hand to plague us? What if all
Her stores were opened and this firmament
Of hell should spout her cataracts of fire,
Impendent horrors, threat'ning hideous fall
One day upon our heads; while we perhaps
Designing or exhorting glorious war,
Caught in a fiery tempest shall be hurled
Each on his rock transfixed, the sport and prey
Of racking whirlwinds, or for ever sunk
Under yon boiling ocean, wrapped in chains;
There to converse with everlasting groans,
Unrespited, unpitied, unreprieved,
Ages of hopeless end? This would be worse.
War therefore, open or concealed, alike
My voice dissuades; for what can force or guile
With him, or who deceive his mind, whose eye
Views all things at one view? He from heav'n's highth
All these our motions vain, sees and derides;
Not more almighty to resist our might
Than wise to frustrate all our plots and wiles.
Shall we then live thus vile, the race of heav'n
Thus trampled, thus expelled to suffer here
Chains and these torments? Better these than worse,
By my advice; since fate inevitable
Subdues us, and omnipotent decree,

The Victor's will. To suffer, as to do,
Our strength is equal, nor the law unjust
That so ordains: this was at first resolved,
If we were wise, against so great a foe
Contending, and so doubtful what might fall.
I laugh when those who at the spear are bold
And vent'rous, if that fail them, shrink and fear
What yet they know must follow, to endure
Exile, or ignominy, or bonds, or pain,
The sentence of their Conqueror. This is now
Our doom; which if we can sustain and bear,
Our súpreme Foe in time may much remit
His anger, and perhaps, thus far removed,
Not mind us not offending, satisfied
With what is punished; whence these raging fires
Will slacken, if his breath stir not their flames.
Our purer essence then will overcome
Their noxious vapor, or inured not feel,
Or changed at length, and to the place conformed
In temper and in nature, will receive
Familiar the fierce heat, and void of pain;
This horror will grow mild, this darkness light,
Besides what hope the never-ending flight
Of future days may bring, what chance, what change
Worth waiting, since our present lot appears
For happy though but ill, for ill not worst,
If we procure not to ourselves more woe.'
    Thus Belial with words clothed in reason's garb,
Counseled ignoble ease, and peaceful sloth,
Not peace; and after him thus Mammon spake:
    'Either to disenthrone the King of heav'n
We war, if war be best, or to regain
Our own right lost. Him to unthrone we then
May hope when everlasting fate shall yield
To fickle chance, and Chaos judge the strife:
The former, vain to hope, argues as vain
The latter; for what place can be for us
Within heav'n's bound, unless heav'n's Lord supreme
We overpower? Suppose he should relent
And publish grace to all, on promise made
Of new subjection; with what eyes could we
Stand in his presence humble, and receive
Strict laws imposed, to celebrate his throne
With warbled hymns, and to his Godhead sing

Forced halleluiahs; while he lordly sits
Our envied Sovran, and his altar breathes
Ambrosial odors and ambrosial flowers,
Our servile offerings? This must be our task
In heav'n, this our delight; how wearisome
Eternity so spent in worship paid
To whom we hate. Let us not then pursue,
By force impossible, by leave obtained
Unácceptáble, though in heav'n, our state
Of splendid vassalage, but rather seek
Our own good from ourselves, and from our own
Live to ourselves, though in this vast recess,
Free, and to none accountable, preferring
Hard liberty before the easy yoke
Of servile pomp. Our greatness will appear
Then most conspicuous, when great things of small,
Useful of hurtful, prosperous of adverse
We can create, and in what place soe'er
Thrive under evil, and work ease out of pain
Through labor and endurance. This deep world
Of darkness do we dread? How oft amidst
Thick clouds and dark doth heav'n's all-ruling Sire
Choose to reside, his glory unobscured,
And with the majesty of darkness round
Covers his throne; from whence deep thunders roar,
Must'ring their rage, and heav'n resembles hell!
As he our darkness, cannot we his light
Imitate when we please? This desert soil
Wants not her hidden luster, gems and gold;
Nor want we skill or art, from whence to raise
Magnificence; and what can heav'n show more?
Our torments also may in length of time
Become our elements, these piercing fires
As soft as now severe, our temper changed
Into their temper; which must needs remove
The sensible of pain. All things invite
To peaceful counsels, and the settled state
Of order, how in safety best we may
Compose our present evils, with regard
Of what we are and where, dismissing quite
All thoughts of war. Ye have what I advise.'

   He scarce had finished, when such murmur filled
Th' assembly as when hollow rocks retain
The sound of blust'ring winds, which all night long

Had roused the sea, now with hoarse cadence lull
Seafaring men o'erwatched, whose bark by chance
Or pinnace anchors in a craggy bay
After the tempest. Such applause was heard
As Mammon ended, and his sentence pleased,
Advising peace; for such another field
They dreaded worse than hell: so much the fear
Of thunder and the sword of Michaël
Wrought still within them; and no less desire
To found this nether empire, which might rise
By policy, and long process of time,
In emulation opposite to heav'n.
Which when Beelzebub perceived, than whom,
Satan except, none higher sat, with grave
Aspect he rose, and in his rising seemed
A pillar of state; deep on his front engraven
Deliberation sat and public care;
And princely counsel in his face yet shone,
Majestic though in ruin: sage he stood,
With Atlantean shoulders fit to bear
The weight of mightiest monarchies; his look
Drew audience and attention still as night
Or summer's noontide air, while thus he spake:
    'Thrones and imperial Powers, offspring of heav'n,
Ethereal Virtues; or these titles now
Must we renounce, and changing style be called
Princes of hell? For so the popular vote
Inclines, here to continue, and build up here
A growing empire; doubtless! while we dream
And know not that the King of heav'n hath doomed
This place our dungeon, not our safe retreat
Beyond his potent arm, to live exempt
From Heav'n's high jurisdiction, in new league
Banded against his throne, but to remain
In strictest bondage, though thus far removed,
Under th' inevitable curb, reserved
His captive multitude. For he, be sure,
In highth or depth, still first and last will reign
Sole king, and of his kingdom lose no part
By our revolt, but over hell extend
His empire, and with iron scepter rule
Us here, as with his golden those in heav'n.
What sit we then projecting peace and war?
War hath determined us, and foiled with loss

Irreparable; terms of peace yet none
Vouchsafed or sought; for what peace will be giv'n
To us enslaved, but custody severe,
And stripes, and arbitrary punishment
Inflicted? And what peace can we return,
But to our power hostility and hate,
Untamed reluctance, and revenge though slow,
Yet ever plotting how the Conqueror least
May reap his conquest, and may least rejoice
In doing what we most in suffering feel?
Nor will occasion want, nor shall we need
With dangerous expedition to invade
Heav'n, whose high walls fear no assault or siege
Or ambush from the deep. What if we find
Some easier enterprise? There is a place
(If ancient and prophetic fame in heav'n
Err not), another world, the happy seat
Of some new race called man, about this time
To be created like to us, though less
In power and excellence, but favored more
Of him who rules above; so was his will
Pronounced among the gods, and by an oath,
That shook heav'n's whole circumference, confirmed.
Thither let us bend all our thoughts, to learn
What creatures there inhabit, of what mold
Or substance, how endued, and what their power,
And where their weakness, how attempted best,
By force or subtlety. Though heav'n be shut,
And heav'n's high Arbitrator sit secure
In his own strength, this place may lie exposed,
The utmost border of his kingdom, left
To their defense who hold it; here perhaps
Some advantageous act may be achieved
By sudden onset, either with hell fire
To waste his whole creation, or possess
All as our own, and drive as we were driven,
The puny habitants; or if not drive,
Seduce them to our party, that their God
May prove their foe, and with repenting hand
Abolish his own works. This would surpass
Common revenge, and interrupt his joy
In our confusion, and our joy upraise
In his disturbance; when his darling sons,
Hurled headlong to partake with us, shall curse

Their frail original, and faded bliss,
Faded so soon. Advise if this be worth
Attempting, or to sit in darkness here
Hatching vain empires.' Thus Beelzebub
Pleaded his devilish counsel, first devised
By Satan, and in part proposed; for whence,
But from the author of all ill, could spring
So deep a malice, to confound the race
Of mankind in one root, and earth with hell
To mingle and involve, done all to spite
The great Creator? But their spite still serves
His glory to augment. The bold design
Pleased highly those infernal States, and joy
Sparkled in all their eyes; with full assent
They vote: whereat his speech he thus renews:
   'Well have ye judged, well ended long debate,
Synod of gods, and like to what ye are,
Great things resolved; which from the lowest deep
Will once more lift us up, in spite of fate,
Nearer our ancient seat; perhaps in view
Of those bright confines, whence with neighboring arms
And opportune excursion we may chance
Re-enter heav'n; or else in some mild zone
Dwell not unvisited of heav'n's fair light
Secure, and at the bright'ning orient beam
Purge off this gloom; the soft delicious air
To heal the scar of these corrosive fires
Shall breathe her balm. But first whom shall we send
In search of this new world, whom shall we find
Sufficient? Who shall tempt with wand'ring feet
The dark unbottomed infinite abyss
And through the palpable obscure find out
His uncouth way, or spread his airy flight
Upborne with indefatigable wings
Over the vast abrupt, ere he arrive
The happy isle; what strength, what art can then
Suffice, or what evasion bear him safe
Through the strict senteries and stations thick
Of angels watching round? Here he had need
All circumspection, and we now no less
Choice in our suffrage; for on whom we send,
The weight of all and our last hope relies.'
   This said, he sat; and expectation held
His look suspense, awaiting who appeared

To second, or oppose, or undertake
The perilous attempt: but all sat mute,
Pondering the danger with deep thoughts; and each
In other's count'nance read his own dismay
Astonished. None among the choice and prime
Of those heav'n-warring champions could be found
So hardy as to proffer or accept
Alone the dreadful voyage; till at last
Satan, whom now transcendent glory raised
Above his fellows, with monarchal pride
Conscious of highest worth, unmoved thus spake;
   'O Progeny of heav'n, empyreal Thrones,
With reason hath deep silence and demur
Seized us, though undismayed. Long is the way
And hard, that out of hell leads up to light;
Our prison strong, this huge convex of fire,
Outrageous to devour, immures us round
Ninefold, and gates of burning adamant
Barred over us prohibit all egress.
These passed, if any pass, the void profound
Of unessential Night receives him next
Wide gaping, and with utter loss of being
Threatens him, plunged in that abortive gulf.
If thence he scape into whatever world,
Or unknown region, what remains him less
Than unknown dangers and as hard escape?
But I should ill become this throne, O Peers,
And this imperial sov'ranty, adorned
With splendor, armed with power, if aught proposed
And judged of public moment, in the shape
Of difficulty or danger could deter
Me from attempting. Wherefore do I assume
These royalties, and not refuse to reign,
Refusing to accept as great a share
Of hazard as of honor, due alike
To him who reigns, and so much to him due
Of hazard more, as he above the rest
High honored sits? Go therefore, mighty Powers,
Terror of heav'n, though fall'n; intend at home,
While here shall be our home, what best may ease
The present misery, and render hell
More tolerable, if there be cure or charm
To respite or deceive, or slack the pain
Of this ill mansion; intermit no watch

Against a wakeful foe, while I abroad
Through all the coasts of dark destruction seek
Deliverance for us all: this enterprise
None shall partake with me.' Thus saying rose
The monarch, and prevented all reply;
Prudent, lest from his resolution raised
Others among the chief might offer now
(Certain to be refused) what erst they feared;
And so refused might in opinion stand
His rivals, winning cheap the high repute
Which he through hazard huge must earn. But they
Dreaded not more th' adventure than his voice
Forbidding, and at once with him they rose;
Their rising all at once was as the sound
Of thunder heard remote. Towards him they bend
With awful reverence prone; and as a god
Extol him equal to the Highest in heav'n.
Nor failed they to express how much they praised,
That for the general safety he despised
His own: for neither do the Spirits damned
Lose all their virtue; lest bad men should boast
Their specious deeds on earth, which glory excites,
Or close ambition varnished o'er with zeal.
    Thus they their doubtful consultations dark
Ended rejoicing in their matchless Chief:
As when from mountain tops the dusky clouds
Ascending, while the north wind sleeps, o'erspread
Heav'n's cheerful face, the louring element
Scowls o'er the darkened landscape snow or show'r;
If chance the radiant sun with farewell sweet
Extend his ev'ning beam, the fields revive,
The birds their notes renew, and bleating herds
Attest their joy, that hill and valley rings.
O shame to men! Devil with devil damned
Firm concord holds, men only disagree
Of creatures rational, though under hope
Of heavenly grace; and God proclaiming peace,
Yet live in hatred, enmity, and strife
Among themselves, and levy cruel wars,
Wasting the earth, each other to destroy:
As if (which might induce us to accord)
Man had not hellish foes enow besides,
That day and night for his destruction wait.
    The Stygian council thus dissolved; and forth

In order came the grand infernal peers;
Midst came their mighty Paramount, and seemed
Alone th' antagonist of Heav'n, nor less
Than hell's dread emperor, with pomp supreme
And god-like imitated state; him round
A globe of fiery Seraphim enclosed
With bright emblazonry and horrent arms.
Then of their session ended they bid cry
With trumpet's regal sound the great result.
Toward the four winds four speedy Cherubim
Put to their mouths the sounding alchemy
By herald's voice explained; the hollow abyss
Heard far and wide, and all the host of hell
With deaf'ning shout returned them loud acclaim.
Thence more at ease their minds and somewhat raised
By false presumptuous hope, the rangèd powers
Disband, and wand'ring each his several way
Pursues, as inclination or sad choice
Leads him perplexed, where he may likeliest find
Truce to his restless thoughts, and entertain
The irksome hours, till his great Chief return.
Part on the plain, or in the air sublime
Upon the wing, or in swift race contend,
As at th' Olympian games or Pythian fields;
Part curb their fiery steeds, or shun the goal
With rapid wheels, or fronted brigades form:
As when to warn proud cities war appears
Waged in the troubled sky, and armies rush
To battle in the clouds; before each van
Prick forth the airy knights, and couch their spears,
Till thickest legions close; with feats of arms
From either end of heav'n the welkin burns.
Others with vast Typhoean rage more fell
Rend up both rocks and hills, and ride the air
In whirlwind; hell scarce holds the wild uproar;
As when Alcides from Oechalia crowned
With conquest, felt th' envenomed robe, and tore
Through pain up by the roots Thessalian pines,
And Lichas from the top of Oeta threw
Into th' Euboic sea. Others more mild,
Retreated in a silent valley, sing
With notes angelical to many a harp
Their own heroic deeds and hapless fall
By doom of battle; and complain that fate

Free virtue should enthrall to force or chance.
Their song was partial, but the harmony
(What could it less when Spirits immortal sing?)
Suspended hell, and took with ravishment
The thronging audience. In discourse more sweet
(For eloquence the soul, song charms the sense)
Others apart sat on a hill retired,
In thoughts more elevate, and reasoned high
Of providence, foreknowledge, will, and fate,
Fixed fate, free will, foreknowledge absolute,
And found no end, in wand'ring mazes lost.
Of good and evil much they argued then,
Of happiness and final misery,
Passion and apathy, and glory and shame,
Vain wisdom all, and false philosophy;
Yet with a pleasing sorcery could charm
Pain for a while or anguish, and excite
Fallacious hope, or arm th' obdurèd breast
With stubborn patience as with triple steel.
Another part, in squadrons and gross bands,
On bold adventure to discover wide
That dismal world, if any clime perhaps
Might yield them easier habitation, bend
Four ways their flying march, along the banks
Of four infernal rivers that disgorge
Into the burning lake their baleful streams:
Abhorrèd Styx, the flood of deadly hate;
Sad Acheron of sorrow, black and deep;
Cocytus, named of lamentation loud
Heard on the rueful stream; fierce Phlegethon,
Whose waves of torrent fire inflame with rage.
Far off from these a slow and silent stream,
Lethe, the river of oblivion, rolls
Her wat'ry labyrinth, whereof who drinks
Forthwith his former state and being forgets,
Forgets both joy and grief, pleasure and pain.
Beyond this flood a frozen continent
Lies dark and wild, beat with perpetual storms
Of whirlwind and dire hail, which on firm land
Thaws not, but gathers heap, and ruin seems
Of ancient pile; all else deep snow and ice,
A gulf profound as that Serbonian bog
Betwixt Damiata and Mount Casius old,
Where armies whole have sunk; the parching air

Burns frore, and cold performs th' effect of fire.
Thither by harpy-footed Furies haled,
At certain revolutions all the damned
Are brought; and feel by turns the bitter change
Of fierce extremes, extremes by change more fierce,
From beds of raging fire to starve in ice
Their soft ethereal warmth, and there to pine
Immovable, infixed, and frozen round,
Periods of time; thence hurried back to fire.
They ferry over this Lethean sound
Both to and fro, their sorrow to augment,
And wish and struggle, as they pass, to reach
The tempting stream, with one small drop to lose
In sweet forgetfulness all pain and woe,
All in one moment, and so near the brink;
But fate withstands, and to oppose th' attempt
Medusa with Gorgonian terror guards
The ford, and of itself the water flies
All taste of living wight, as once it fled
The lip of Tantalus. Thus roving on
In cónfused march forlorn, th' advent'rous bands,
With shudd'ring horror pale, and eyes aghast,
Viewed first their lamentable lot, and found
No rest. Through many a dark and dreary vale
They passed, and many a region dolorous,
O'er many a frozen, many a fiery Alp,
Rocks, caves, lakes, fens, bogs, dens, and shades of death,
A universe of death, which God by curse
Created evil, for evil only good,
Where all life dies, death lives, and Nature breeds,
Perverse, all monstrous, all prodigious things,
Abominable, inutterable, and worse
Than fables yet have feigned, or fear conceived,
Gorgons and Hydras, and Chimeras dire.
　　Meanwhile the Adversary of God and man,
Satan, with thoughts inflamed of highest design,
Puts on swift wings, and toward the gates of hell
Explores his solitary flight; sometimes
He scours the right-hand coast, sometimes the left;
Now shaves with level wing the deep, then soars
Up to the fiery concave tow'ring high:
As when far off at sea a fleet descried
Hangs in the clouds, by equinoctial winds
Close sailing from Bengala, or the isles

Of Ternate and Tidore, whence merchants bring
Their spicy drugs: they on the trading flood
Through the wide Ethiopian to the Cape
Ply stemming nightly toward the pole. So seemed
Far off the flying Fiend. At last appear
Hell bounds high reaching to the horrid roof,
And thrice threefold the gates; three folds were brass,
Three iron, three of adamantine rock,
Impenetrable, impaled with circling fire,
Yet unconsumed. Before the gates there sat
On either side a formidable shape;
The one seemed woman to the waist, and fair,
But ended foul in many a scaly fold
Voluminous and vast, a serpent armed
With mortal sting. About her middle round
A cry of hell-hounds never ceasing barked
With wide Cerberean mouths full loud, and rung
A hideous peal; yet, when they list, would creep,
If aught disturbed their noise, into her womb,
And kennel there, yet there still barked and howled,
Within unseen. Far less abhorred than these
Vexed Scylla bathing in the sea that parts
Calabria from the hoarse Trinacrian shore;
Nor uglier follow the night-hag, when called
In secret, riding through the air she comes,
Lured with the smell of infant blood, to dance
With Lapland witches, while the laboring moon
Eclipses at their charms. The other shape—
If shape it might be called that shape had none
Distinguishable in member, joint, or limb,
Or substance might be called that shadow seemed,
For each seemed either—black it stood as Night,
Fierce as ten Furies, terrible as hell,
And shook a dreadful dart; what seemed his head
The likeness of a kingly crown had on.
Satan was now at hand, and from his seat
The monster moving onward came as fast
With horrid strides; hell trembled as he strode.
Th' undaunted Fiend what this might be admired,
Admired, not feared; God and his Son except,
Created thing naught valued he nor shunned;
And with disdainful look thus first began:
   'Whence and what art thou, execrable Shape,
That dar'st, though grim and terrible, advance

Thy miscreated front athwart my way
To yonder gates? Through them I mean to pass,
That be assured, without leave asked of thee.
Retire, or taste thy folly, and learn by proof,
Hell-born, not to contend with Spirits of heav'n.'
   To whom the goblin full of wrath replied:
'Art thou that traitor angel, art thou he,
Who first broke peace in heav'n and faith, till then
Unbroken, and in proud rebellious arms
Drew after him the third part of heav'n's sons
Conjured against the Highest, for which both thou
And they, outcast from God, are here condemned
To waste eternal days in woe and pain?
And reckon'st thou thyself with Spirits of heav'n,
Hell-doomed, and breath'st defiance here and scorn
Where I reign king, and to enrage thee more,
Thy king and lord? Back to thy punishment,
False fugitive, and to thy speed add wings,
Lest with a whip of scorpions I pursue
Thy ling'ring, or with one stroke of this dart
Strange horror seize thee, and pangs unfelt before.'
   So spake the grisly terror, and in shape,
So speaking and so threat'ning, grew tenfold
More dreadful and deform. On th' other side,
Incensed with indignation Satan stood
Unterrified, and like a comet burned,
That fires the length of Ophiuchus huge
In th' arctic sky, and from his horrid hair
Shakes pestilence and war. Each at the head
Leveled his deadly aim; their fatal hands
No second stroke intend; and such a frown
Each cast at th' other, as when two black clouds
With heav'n's artillery fraught, come rattling on
Over the Caspian, then stand front to front
Hov'ring a space, till winds the signal blow
To join their dark encounter in mid-air:
So frowned the mighty combatants that hell
Grew darker at their frown, so matched they stood;
For never but once more was either like
To meet so great a foe. And now great deeds
Had been achieved, whereof all hell had rung,
Had not the snaky sorceress that sat
Fast by hell gate, and kept the fatal key,
Ris'n, and with hideous outcry rushed between.

'O father, what intends thy hand,' she cried,
'Against thy only son? What fury, O son,
Possesses thee to bend that mortal dart
Against thy father's head? And know'st for whom?
For him who sits above and laughs the while
At thee ordained his drudge, to execute
Whate'er his wrath, which he calls justice, bids,
His wrath which one day will destroy ye both.'
    She spake, and at her words the hellish pest
Forbore; then these to her Satan returned:
    'So strange thy outcry, and thy words so strange
Thou interposest, that my sudden hand
Prevented spares to tell thee yet by deeds
What it intends; till first I know of thee,
What thing thou art, thus double-formed, and why
In this infernal vale first met thou call'st
Me father, and that phantasm call'st my son.
I know thee not, nor ever saw till now
Sight more detestable than him and thee.'
    T' whom thus the portress of hell gate replied:
'Hast thou forgot me then, and do I seem
Now in thine eye so foul? Once deemed so fair
In heav'n, when at th' assembly, and in sight
Of all the Seraphim with thee combined
In bold conspiracy against heav'n's King,
All on a sudden miserable pain
Surprised thee; dim thine eyes, and dizzy swum
In darkness, while thy head flames thick and fast
Threw forth, till on the left side op'ning wide,
Likest to thee in shape and count'nance bright,
Then shining heav'nly fair, a goddess armed
Out of thy head I sprung. Amazement seized
All th' host of heav'n; back they recoiled afraid
At first, and called me *Sin*, and for a sign
Portentous held me; but familiar grown,
I pleased, and with attractive graces won
The most averse, thee chiefly, who full oft
Thyself in me thy perfect image viewing
Becam'st enamored; and such joy thou took'st
With me in secret, that my womb conceived
A growing burden. Meanwhile war arose,
And fields were fought in heav'n; wherein remained
(For what could else?) to our almighty Foe
Clear victory, to our part loss and rout

Through all the empyrean: down they fell
Driv'n headlong from the pitch of heaven, down
Into this deep, and in the general fall
I also; at which time this powerful key
Into my hand was giv'n, with charge to keep
These gates for ever shut, which none can pass
Without my op'ning. Pensive here I sat
Alone, but long I sat not, till my womb,
Pregnant by thee, and now excessive grown,
Prodigious motion felt and rueful throes.
At last this odious offspring whom thou seest,
Thine own begotten, breaking violent way
Tore through my entrails, that with fear and pain
Distorted, all my nether shape thus grew
Transformed; but he my inbred enemy
Forth issued, brandishing his fatal dart
Made to destroy. I fled, and cried out *Death!*
Hell trembled at the hideous name, and sighed
From all her caves, and back resounded *Death!*
I fled, but he pursued (though more, it seems,
Inflamed with lust than rage) and swifter far,
Me overtook, his mother, all dismayed,
And in embraces forcible and foul
Engend'ring with me, of that rape begot
These yelling monsters that with ceaseless cry
Surround me, as thou saw'st, hourly conceived
And hourly born, with sorrow infinite
To me; for when they list, into the womb
That bred them they return, and howl and gnaw
My bowels, their repast; then bursting forth
Afresh, with conscious terrors vex me round,
That rest or intermission none I find.
Before mine eyes in opposition sits
Grim Death my son and foe, who sets them on,
And me his parent would full soon devour
For want of other prey, but that he knows
His end with mine involved; and knows that I
Should prove a bitter morsel, and his bane,
Whenever that shall be; so fate pronounced.
But thou, O father, I forewarn thee, shun
His deadly arrow; neither vainly hope
To be invulnerable in those bright arms,
Though tempered heav'nly, for that mortal dint,
Save he who reigns above, none can resist.'

She finished, and the subtle Fiend his lore
Soon learned, now milder, and thus answered smooth:
'Dear daughter, since thou claim'st me for thy sire,
And my fair son here show'st me, the dear pledge
Of dalliance had with thee in heav'n, and joys
Then sweet, now sad to mention, through dire change
Befall'n us unforeseen, unthought of, know
I come no enemy, but to set free
From out this dark and dismal house of pain
Both him and thee, and all the heav'nly host
Of Spirits that in our just pretenses armed
Fell with us from on high. From them I go
This uncouth errand sole, and one for all
Myself expose, with lonely steps to tread
Th' unfounded deep, and through the void immense
To search with wand'ring quest a place foretold
Should be, and, by concurring signs, ere now
Created vast and round, a place of bliss
In the purlieus of heav'n, and therein placed
A race of upstart creatures, to supply
Perhaps our vacant room, though more removed,
Lest heav'n surcharged with potent multitude
Might hap to move new broils. Be this or aught
Than this more secret now designed, I haste
To know, and this once known, shall soon return,
And bring ye to the place where thou and Death
Shall dwell at ease, and up and down unseen
Wing silently the buxom air, embalmed
With odors; there ye shall be fed and filled
Immeasurably; all things shall be your prey.'
He ceased, for both seemed highly pleased, and Death
Grinned horrible a ghastly smile, to hear
His famine should be filled, and blessed his maw
Destined to that good hour. No less rejoiced
His mother bad, and thus bespake her sire:
  'The key of this infernal pit by due
And by command of heav'n's all-powerful King
I keep, by him forbidden to unlock
These adamantine gates; against all force
Death ready stands to interpose his dart,
Fearless to be o'ermatched by living might.
But what owe I to his commands above
Who hates me, and hath hither thrust me down
Into this gloom of Tartarus profound,

To sit in hateful office here confined,
Inhabitant of heav'n and heav'nly-born,
Here in perpetual agony and pain,
With terrors and with clamors compassed round
Of mine own brood, that on my bowels feed?
Thou art my father, thou my author, thou
My being gav'st me; whom should I obey
But thee, whom follow? Thou wilt bring me soon
To that new world of light and bliss, among
The gods who live at ease, where I shall reign
At thy right hand voluptuous, as beseems
Thy daughter and thy darling, without end.'
    Thus saying, from her side the fatal key,
Sad instrument of all our woe, she took;
And towards the gate rolling her bestial train,
Forthwith the huge portcullis high up drew,
Which but herself not all the Stygian powers
Could once have moved; then in the key-hole turns
Th' intricate wards, and every bolt and bar
Of massy iron or solid rock with ease
Unfastens. On a sudden open fly
With impetuous recoil and jarring sound
Th' infernal doors, and on their hinges grate
Harsh thunder, that the lowest bottom shook
Of Erebus. She opened, but to shut
Excelled her power; the gates wide open stood,
That with extended wings a bannered host
Under spread ensigns marching might pass through
With horse and chariots ranked in loose array;
So wide they stood, and like a furnace mouth
Cast forth redounding smoke and ruddy flame.
Before their eyes in sudden view appear
The secrets of the hoary deep, a dark
Illimitable ocean without bound,
Without dimension; where length, breadth, and highth,
And time and place are lost; where eldest Night
And Chaos, ancestors of Nature, hold
Eternal anarchy, amidst the noise
Of endless wars, and by confusion stand.
For Hot, Cold, Moist, and Dry, four champions fierce,
Strive here for mast'ry, and to battle bring
Their embryon atoms; they around the flag
Of each his faction, in their several clans,
Light-armed or heavy, sharp, smooth, swift or slow,

Swarm populous, unnumbered as the sands
Of Barca or Cyrene's torrid soil,
Levied to side with warring winds, and poise
Their lighter wings. To whom these most adhere,
He rules a moment; Chaos umpire sits,
And by decision more embroils the fray
By which he reigns; next him high arbiter
Chance governs all. Into this wild abyss,
The womb of Nature and perhaps her grave,
Of neither sea, nor shore, nor air, nor fire,
But all these in their pregnant causes mixed
Confus'dly, and which thus must ever fight,
Unless th' Almighty Maker them ordain
His dark materials to create more worlds,
Into this wild abyss the wary Fiend
Stood on the brink of hell and looked a while,
Pondering his voyage; for no narrow frith
He had to cross. Nor was his ear less pealed
With noises loud and ruinous (to compare
Great things with small) than when Bellona storms,
With all her battering engines bent to raze
Some capital city; or less than if this frame
Of heav'n were falling, and these elements
In mutiny had from her axle torn
The steadfast earth. At last his sail-broad vans
He spreads for flight, and in the surging smoke
Uplifted spurns the ground; thence many a league
As in a cloudy chair ascending rides
Audacious, but that seat soon failing, meets
A vast vacuity: all unawares
Flutt'ring his pennons vain plumb down he drops
Ten thousand fadom deep, and to this hour
Down had been falling, had not by ill chance
The strong rebuff of some tumultuous cloud
Instinct with fire and niter hurried him
As many miles aloft. That fury stayed,
Quenched in a boggy Syrtis, neither sea,
Nor good dry land, nigh foundered on he fares,
Treading the crude consistence, half on foot,
Half flying; behoves him now both oar and sail.
As when a gryphon through the wilderness
With wingèd course o'er hill or moory dale,
Pursues the Arimaspian, who by stealth
Had from his wakeful custody purloined

The guarded gold: so eagerly the Fiend
O'er bog or steep, through strait, rough, dense, or rare,
With head, hands, wings, or feet pursues his way,
And swims or sinks, or wades, or creeps, or flies.
At length a universal hubbub wild
Of stunning sounds and voices all confused,
Borne through the hollow dark, assaults his ear
With loudest vehemence; thither he plies,
Undaunted to meet there whatever Power
Or Spirit of the nethermost abyss
Might in that noise reside, of whom to ask
Which way the nearest coast of darkness lies
Bordering on light; when straight behold the throne
Of Chaos, and his dark pavilion spread
Wide on the wasteful deep; with him enthroned
Sat sable-vested Night, eldest of things,
The consort of his reign; and by them stood
Orcus and Ades, and the dreaded name
Of Demogorgon; Rumor next and Chance,
And Tumult and Confusion all embroiled,
And Discord with a thousand various mouths.
    T' whom Satan turning boldly, thus: 'Ye Powers
And Spirits of this nethermost abyss,
Chaos and ancient Night, I come no spy,
With purpose to explore or to disturb
The secrets of your realm, but by constraint
Wand'ring this darksome desert, as my way
Lies through your spacious empire up to light,
Alone, and without guide, half lost, I seek
What readiest path leads where your gloomy bounds
Confine with heav'n; or if some other place
From your dominion won, th' Ethereal King
Possesses lately, thither to arrive
I travel this profound. Direct my course;
Directed, no mean recompense it brings
To your behoof, if I that region lost,
All usurpation thence expelled, reduce
To her original darkness and your sway
(Which is my present journey), and once more
Erect the standard there of ancient Night;
Yours be th' advantage all, mine the revenge.'
    Thus Satan; and him thus the Anarch old
With falt'ring speech and visage incomposed
Answered: 'I know thee, stranger, who thou art,

That mighty leading angel, who of late
Made head against heav'n's King, though overthrown.
I saw and heard, for such a numerous host
Fled not in silence through the frighted deep
With ruin upon ruin, rout on rout,
Confusion worse confounded; and heav'n gates
Poured out by millions her victorious bands
Pursuing. I upon my frontiers here
Keep residence; if all I can will serve
That little which is left so to defend,
Encroached on still through our intestine broils
Weak'ning the scepter of old Night: first hell
Your dungeon stretching far and wide beneath;
Now lately heaven and earth, another world
Hung o'er my realm, linked in a golden chain
To that side heav'n from whence your legions fell.
If that way be your walk, you have not far;
So much the nearer danger; go and speed;
Havoc and spoil and ruin are my gain.'
   He ceased; and Satan stayed not to reply,
But glad that now his sea should find a shore,
With fresh alacrity and force renewed
Springs upward like a pyramid of fire
Into the wild expanse, and through the shock
Of fighting elements, on all sides round
Environed, wins his way; harder beset
And more endangered than when Argo passed
Through Bosporus betwixt the justling rocks,
Or when Ulysses on the larboard shunned
Charybdis, and by th' other whirlpool steered.
So he with difficulty and labor hard
Moved on, with difficulty and labor he;
But he once passed, soon after when man fell,
Strange alteration! Sin and Death amain
Following his track, such was the will of Heav'n,
Paved after him a broad and beaten way
Over the dark abyss, whose boiling gulf
Tamely endured a bridge of wondrous length
From hell continued reaching th' utmost orb
Of this frail world; by which the Spirits perverse
With easy intercourse pass to and fro
To tempt or punish mortals, except whom
God and good angels guard by special grace.

But now at last the sacred influence
Of light appears and from the walls of heav'n
Shoots far into the bosom of dim Night
A glimmering dawn; here Nature first begins
Her fardest verge, and Chaos to retire
As from her outmost works a broken foe,
With tumult less and with less hostile din,
That Satan with less toil and now with ease
Wafts on the calmer wave by dubious light,
And like a weather-beaten vessel holds
Gladly the port, though shrouds and tackle torn;
Or in the emptier waste, resembling air,
Weighs his spread wings, at leisure to behold
Far off th' empyreal heav'n, extended wide
In circuit, undetermined square or round,
With opal tow'rs and battlements adorned
Of living sapphire, once his native seat;
And fast by hanging in a golden chain
This pendent world, in bigness as a star
Of smallest magnitude close by the moon.
Thither full fraught with mischievous revenge,
Accurst, and in a cursèd hour, he hies.

from BOOK IV

O FOR that warning voice, which he who saw
Th' Apocalypse heard cry in heaven aloud,
Then when the Dragon, put to second rout,
Came furious down to be revenged on men,
'Woe to the inhabitants on earth!' that now,
While time was, our first parents had been warned
The coming of their secret foe, and scaped,
Haply so scaped, his mortal snare; for now
Satan, now first inflamed with rage, came down,
The tempter ere th' accuser of mankind,
To wreck on innocent frail man his loss
Of that first battle, and his flight to hell:
Yet not rejoicing in his speed, though bold,
Far off and fearless, nor with cause to boast,
Begins his dire attempt, which nigh the birth
Now rolling, boils in his tumultuous breast,
And like a devilish engine back recoils
Upon himself; horror and doubt distract
His troubled thoughts, and from the bottom stir

The hell within him, for within him hell
He brings, and round about him, nor from hell
One step no more than from himself can fly
By change of place. Now conscience wakes despair
That slumbered, wakes the bitter memory
Of what he was, what is, and what must be
Worse; of worse deeds worse sufferings must ensue.
Sometimes towards Eden which now in his view
Lay pleasant, his grieved look he fixes sad,
Sometimes towards heav'n and the full-blazing sun,
Which now sat high in his meridian tow'r.
Then much revolving, thus in sighs began:
  'O thou that with surpassing glory crowned
Look'st from thy sole dominion like the god
Of this new world; at whose sight all the stars
Hide their diminished heads; to thee I call,
But with no friendly voice, and add thy name,
O sun, to tell thee how I hate thy beams
That bring to my remembrance from what state
I fell, how glorious once above thy sphere;
Till pride and worse ambition threw me down
Warring in heav'n against heav'n's matchless King.
Ah wherefore? He deserved no such return
From me, whom he created what I was
In that bright eminence, and with his good
Upbraided none; nor was his service hard.
What could be less than to afford him praise,
The easiest recompense, and pay him thanks,
How due! Yet all his good proved ill in me,
And wrought but malice; lifted up so high
I sdained subjection, and thought one step higher
Would set me highest, and in a moment quit
The debt immense of endless gratitude,
So burthensome still paying, still to owe;
Forgetful what from him I still received,
And understood not that a grateful mind
By owing owes not, but still pays, at once
Indebted and discharged; what burden then?
O had his powerful destiny ordained
Me some inferior angel, I had stood
Then happy; no unbounded hope had raised
Ambition. Yet why not? Some other Power
As great might have aspired, and me though mean
Drawn to his part; but other Powers as great

Fell not, but stand unshaken, from within
Or from without, to all temptations armed.
Hadst thou the same free will and power to stand?
Thou hadst. Whom hast thou then or what to accuse,
But Heav'n's free love dealt equally to all?
Be then his love accurst, since love or hate,
To me alike, it deals eternal woe.
Nay cursed be thou, since against his thy will
Chose freely what it now so justly rues.
Me miserable! which way shall I fly
Infinite wrath, and infinite despair?
Which way I fly is hell; myself am hell;
And in the lowest deep a lower deep
Still threat'ning to devour me opens wide,
To which the hell I suffer seems a heav'n.
O then at last relent: is there no place
Left for repentance, none for pardon left?
None left but by submission; and that word
Disdain forbids me, and my dread of shame
Among the Spirits beneath, whom I seduced
With other promises and other vaunts
Than to submit, boasting I could subdue
Th' Omnipotent. Ay me, they little know
How dearly I abide that boast so vain,
Under what torments inwardly I groan;
While they adore me on the throne of hell,
With diadem and scepter high advanced,
The lower still I fall, only supreme
In misery; such joy ambition finds.
But say I could repent and could obtain
By act of grace my former state; how soon
Would highth recall high thoughts, how soon unsay
What feigned submission swore: ease would recant
Vows made in pain, as violent and void.
For never can true reconcilement grow
Where wounds of deadly hate have pierced so deep;
Which would but lead me to a worse relapse
And heavier fall: so should I purchase dear
Short intermission bought with double smart.
This knows my Punisher; therefore as far
From granting he, as I from begging peace.
All hope excluded thus, behold instead
Of us outcast, exiled, his new delight,
Mankind created, and for him this world.

So farewell hope, and with hope farewell fear,
Farewell remorse! All good to me is lost;
Evil, be thou my good; by thee at least
Divided empire with heav'n's King I hold
By thee, and more than half perhaps will reign;
As man ere long, and this new world shall know.'
    Thus while he spake, each passion dimmed his face
Thrice changed with pale, ire, envy, and despair,
Which marred his borrowed visage, and betrayed
Him counterfeit, if any eye beheld.
For heav'nly minds from such distempers foul
Are ever clear. Whereof he soon aware,
Each perturbation smoothed with outward calm,
Artificer of fraud; and was the first
That practised falsehood under saintly show,
Deep malice to conceal, couched with revenge:
Yet not enough had practised to deceive
Uriel once warned, whose eye pursued him down
The way he went, and on th' Assyrian mount
Saw him disfigured, more than could befall
Spirit of happy sort: his gestures fierce
He marked and mad demeanor, then alone,
As he supposed, all unobserved, unseen.
So on he fares, and to the border comes
Of Eden, where delicious Paradise,
Now nearer, crowns with her enclosure green
As with a rural mound the champaign head
Of a steep wilderness, whose hairy sides
With thicket overgrown, grotesque and wild,
Access denied; and overhead up grew
Insuperable highth of loftiest shade,
Cedar, and pine, and fir, and branching palm,
A sylvan scene, and as the ranks ascend
Shade above shade, a woody theater
Of stateliest view. Yet higher than their tops
The verdurous wall of Paradise up sprung;
Which to our general sire gave prospect large
Into his nether empire neighboring round.
And higher than that wall a circling row
Of goodliest trees loaden with fairest fruit,
Blossoms and fruits at once of golden hue,
Appeared, with gay enameled colors mixed;
On which the sun more glad impressed his beams
Than in fair evening cloud, or humid bow,

When God hath show'red the earth; so lovely seemed
That landscape. And of pure now purer air
Meets his approach, and to the heart inspires
Vernal delight and joy, able to drive
All sadness but despair; now gentle gales
Fanning their odoriferous wings dispense
Native perfumes, and whisper whence they stole
Those balmy spoils. As when to them who sail
Beyond the Cape of Hope, and now are past
Mozambic, off at sea north-east winds blow
Sabaean odors from the spicy shore
Of Araby the Blest, with such delay
Well pleased they slack their course, and many a league
Cheered with the grateful smell old ocean smiles;
So entertained those odorous sweets the Fiend
Who came their bane, though with them better pleased
Than Asmodëus with the fishy fume,
That drove him, though enamored, from the spouse
Of Tobit's son, and with a vengeance sent
From Media post to Egypt, there fast bound.
   Now to th' ascent of that steep savage hill
Satan had journeyed on, pensive and slow;
But further way found none, so thick entwined,
As one continued brake, the undergrowth
Of shrubs and tangling bushes had perplexed
All path of man or beast that passed that way.
One gate there only was, and that looked east
On th' other side; which when th' Arch-Felon saw,
Due entrance he disdained, and in contempt
At one slight bound high overleaped all bound
Of hill or highest wall, and sheer within
Lights on his feet. As when a prowling wolf,
Whom hunger drives to seek new haunt for prey,
Watching where shepherds pen their flocks at eve
In hurdled cotes amid the field secure,
Leaps o'er the fence with ease into the fold;
Or as a thief bent to unhoard the cash
Of some rich burgher, whose substantial doors,
Cross-barred and bolted fast, fear no assault,
In at the window climbs, or o'er the tiles:
So clomb this first grand thief into God's fold;
So since into his church lewd hirelings climb.
Thence up he flew, and on the Tree of Life,
The middle tree and highest there that grew,

Sat like a cormorant; yet not true life
Thereby regained, but sat devising death
To them who lived; nor on the virtue thought
Of that life-giving plant, but only used
For prospect, what well used had been the pledge
Of immortality. So little knows
Any, but God alone, to value right
The good before him, but perverts best things
To worst abuse, or to their meanest use.
    Beneath him with new wonder now he views
To all delight of human sense exposed
In narrow room Nature's whole wealth, yea more,
A heav'n on earth, for blissful Paradise
Of God the garden was, by him in the east
Of Eden planted; Eden stretched her line
From Auran eastward to the royal tow'rs
Of great Seleucia, built by Grecian kings,
Or where the sons of Eden long before
Dwelt in Telassar. In this pleasant soil
His far more pleasant garden God ordained;
Out of the fertile ground he caused to grow
All trees of noblest kind for sight, smell, taste;
And all amid them stood the Tree of Life,
High eminent, blooming ambrosial fruit
Of vegetable gold; and next to life
Our death, the Tree of Knowledge, grew fast by,
Knowledge of good bought dear by knowing ill.
Southward through Eden went a river large,
Nor changed his course, but through the shaggy hill
Passed underneath ingulfed, for God had thrown
That mountain as his garden mold, high raised
Upon the rapid current, which through veins
Of porous earth with kindly thirst up drawn,
Rose a fresh fountain, and with many a rill
Watered the garden; thence united fell
Down the steep glade, and met the nether flood,
Which from his darksome passage now appears,
And now divided into four main streams
Runs diverse, wand'ring many a famous realm
And country whereof here needs no account;
But rather to tell how, if art could tell,
How from that sapphire fount the crispèd brooks,
Rolling on orient pearl and sands of gold,
With mazy error under pendent shades

Ran nectar, visiting each plant, and fed
Flow'rs worthy of Paradise, which not nice art
In beds and curious knots, but Nature boon
Poured forth profuse on hill and dale and plain,
Both where the morning sun first warmly smote
The open field, and where the unpierced shade
Imbrowned the noontide bow'rs. Thus was this place,
A happy rural seat of various view;
Groves whose rich trees wept odorous gums and balm,
Others whose fruit burnished with golden rind
Hung amiable, Hesperian fables true,
If true, here only, and of delicious taste.
Betwixt them lawns, or level downs, and flocks
Grazing the tender herb, were interposed,
Or palmy hillock, or the flow'ry lap
Of some irriguous valley spread her store,
Flow'rs of all hue, and without thorn the rose.
Another side, umbrageous grots and caves
Of cool recess, o'er which the mantling vine
Lays forth her purple grape, and gently creeps
Luxuriant; meanwhile murmuring waters fall
Down the slope hills, dispersed, or in a lake,
That to the fringèd bank with myrtle crowned
Her crystal mirror holds, unite their streams.
The birds their quire apply; airs, vernal airs,
Breathing the smell of field and grove, attune
The trembling leaves, while universal Pan,
Knit with the Graces and the Hours in dance,
Led on th' eternal spring. Not that fair field
Of Enna, where Prosérpine gathering flow'rs,
Herself a fairer flow'r, by gloomy Dis
Was gathered, which cost Ceres all that pain
To seek her through the world; nor that sweet grove
Of Daphne by Orontes, and th' inspired
Castalian spring, might with this Paradise
Of Eden strive; nor that Nyseian isle
Girt with the river Triton, where old Cham,
Whom Gentiles Ammon call and Libyan Jove,
Hid Amalthea and her florid son
Young Bacchus from his stepdame Rhea's eye;
Nor where Abassin kings their issue guard,
Mount Amara, though this by some supposed
True Paradise, under the Ethiop line
By Nilus' head, enclosed with shining rock,

A whole day's journey high, but wide remote
From this Assyrian garden, where the Fiend
Saw undelighted all delight, all kind
Of living creatures new to sight and strange.
  Two of far nobler shape erect and tall,
God-like erect, with native honor clad
In naked majesty seemed lords of all,
And worthy seemed, for in their looks divine
The image of their glorious Maker shone,
Truth, wisdom, sanctitude severe and pure,
Severe but in true filial freedom placed;
Whence true authority in men; though both
Not equal, as their sex not equal seemed;
For contemplation he and valor formed,
For softness she and sweet attractive grace;
He for God only, she for God in him.
His fair large front and eye sublime declared
Absolute rule; and hyacinthine locks
Round from his parted forelock manly hung
Clust'ring, but not beneath his shoulders broad:
She as a veil down to the slender waist
Her unadornèd golden tresses wore
Disheveled, but in wanton ringlets waved
As the vine curls her tendrils, which implied
Subjection, but required with gentle sway,
And by her yielded, by him best received,
Yielded with coy submission, modest pride,
And sweet reluctant amorous delay.
Nor those mysterious parts were then concealed;
Then was not guilty shame; dishonest shame
Of Nature's works, honor dishonorable,
Sin-bred, how have ye troubled all mankind
With shows instead, mere shows of seeming pure,
And banished from man's life his happiest life,
Simplicity and spotless innocence.
So passed they naked on, nor shunned the sight
Of God or angel, for they thought no ill;
So hand in hand they passed, the loveliest pair
That ever since in love's embraces met,
Adam the goodliest man of men since born
His sons, the fairest of her daughters Eve.
Under a tuft of shade that on a green
Stood whispering soft, by a fresh fountain side
They sat them down; and after no more toil

Of their sweet gard'ning labor than sufficed
To recommend cool Zephyr, and made ease
More easy, wholesome thirst and appetite
More grateful, to their supper fruits they fell,
Nectarine fruits which the compliant boughs
Yielded them, sidelong as they sat recline
On the soft downy bank damasked with flow'rs.
The savory pulp they chew, and in the rind
Still as they thirsted scoop the brimming stream;
Nor gentle purpose, nor endearing smiles
Wanted, nor youthful dalliance, as beseems
Fair couple linked in happy nuptial league,
Alone as they. About them frisking played
All beasts of th' earth, since wild, and of all chase
In wood or wilderness, forest or den;
Sporting the lion ramped, and in his paw
Dandled the kid; bears, tigers, ounces, pards,
Gamboled before them; th' unwieldy elephant
To make them mirth used all his might, and wreathed
His lithe proboscis; close the serpent sly
Insinuating, wove with Gordian twine
His braided train, and of his fatal guile
Gave proof unheeded; others on the grass
Couched, and now filled with pasture gazing sat,
Or bedward ruminating; for the sun
Declined was hasting now with prone career
To th' ocean isles, and in th' ascending scale
Of heav'n the stars that usher evening rose:
When Satan still in gaze, as first he stood,
Scarce thus at length failed speech recovered said:
    'O hell! what do mine eyes with grief behold!
Into our room of bliss thus high advanced
Creatures of other mold, earth-born perhaps,
Not Spirits, yet to heav'nly Spirits bright
Little inferior; whom my thoughts pursue
With wonder, and could love, so lively shines
In them divine resemblance, and such grace
The hand that formed them on their shape hath poured.
Ah gentle pair, ye little think how nigh
Your change approaches, when all these delights
Will vanish and deliver ye to woe,
More woe, the more your taste is now of joy;
Happy, but for so happy ill secured
Long to continue, and this high seat your heav'n

Ill fenced for Heav'n to keep out such a foe
As now is entered; yet no purposed foe
To you whom I could pity thus forlorn,
Though I unpitied. League with you I seek,
And mutual amity so strait, so close,
That I with you must dwell, or you with me
Henceforth; my dwelling haply may not please,
Like this fair Paradise, your sense, yet such
Accept your Maker's work; he gave it me,
Which I as freely give; hell shall unfold,
To entertain you two, her widest gates,
And send forth all her kings; there will be room,
Not like these narrow limits, to receive
Your numerous offspring; if no better place,
Thank him who puts me loth to this revenge
On you who wrong me not, for him who wronged.
And should I at your harmless innocence
Melt, as I do, yet public reason just,
Honor and empire with revenge enlarged
By conquering this new world, compels me now
To do what else though damned I should abhor.'
    So spake the Fiend, and with necessity,
The tyrant's plea, excused his devilish deeds.
Then from his lofty stand on that high tree
Down he alights among the sportful herd
Of those four-footed kinds, himself now one,
Now other, as their shape served best his end
Nearer to view his prey, and unespied
To mark what of their state he more might learn
By word or action marked. About them round
A lion now he stalks with fiery glare;
Then as a tiger, who by chance hath spied
In some purlieu two gentle fawns at play,
Straight couches close, then rising, changes oft
His couchant watch, as one who chose his ground
Whence rushing he might surest seize them both
Gripped in each paw; when Adam first of men
To first of women Eve, thus moving speech
Turned him, all ear to hear new utterance flow:
    'Sole partner and sole part of all these joys,
Dearer thyself than all, needs must the Power
That made us, and for us this ample world,
Be infinitely good, and of his good
As liberal and free as infinite,

That raised us from the dust and placed us here
In all this happiness, who at his hand
Have nothing merited, nor can perform
Aught whereof he hath need; he who requires
From us no other service than to keep
This one, this easy charge, of all the trees
In Paradise that bear delicious fruit
So various, not to taste that only Tree
Of Knowledge, planted by the Tree of Life,
So near grows death to life, whate'er death is,
Some dreadful thing no doubt; for well thou know'st
God hath pronounced it death to taste that Tree,
The only sign of our obedience left
Among so many signs of power and rule
Conferred upon us, and dominion giv'n
Over all other creatures that possess
Earth, air, and sea. Then let us not think hard
One easy prohibition, who enjoy
Free leave so large to all things else, and choice
Unlimited of manifold delights;
But let us ever praise him, and extol
His bounty, following our delightful task
To prune these growing plants, and tend these flow'rs,
Which were it toilsome, yet with thee were sweet.'
    To whom thus Eve replied: 'O thou for whom
And from whom I was formed flesh of thy flesh,
And without whom am to no end, my guide
And head, what thou hast said is just and right.
For we to him indeed all praises owe,
And daily thanks, I chiefly who enjoy
So far the happier lot, enjoying thee
Pre-eminent by so much odds, while thou
Like consort to thyself canst nowhere find.
That day I oft remember, when from sleep
I first awaked, and found myself reposed
Under a shade on flowers, much wond'ring where
And what I was, whence thither brought, and how.
Not distant far from thence a murmuring sound
Of waters issued from a cave and spread
Into a liquid plain, then stood unmoved
Pure as th' expanse of heav'n; I thither went
With unexperienced thought, and laid me down
On the green bank, to look into the clear
Smooth lake, that to me seemed another sky.

As I bent down to look, just opposite
A shape within the wat'ry gleam appeared
Bending to look on me: I started back,
It started back, but pleased I soon returned,
Pleased it returned as soon with answering looks
Of sympathy and love; there I had fixed
Mine eyes till now, and pined with vain desire,
Had not a voice thus warned me: "What thou seest,
What there thou seest, fair creature, is thyself,
With thee it came and goes; but follow me,
And I will bring thee where no shadow stays
Thy coming, and thy soft embraces, he
Whose image thou art, him thou shalt enjoy
Inseparably thine; to him shalt bear
Multitudes like thyself, and thence be called
Mother of human race." What could I do
But follow straight, invisibly thus led?
Till I espied thee, fair indeed and tall,
Under a platane; yet methought less fair,
Less winning soft, less amiably mild,
Than that smooth wat'ry image; back I turned,
Thou following cried'st aloud, "Return, fair Eve,
Whom fli'st thou? Whom thou fli'st, of him thou art,
His flesh, his bone; to give thee being I lent
Out of my side to thee, nearest my heart,
Substantial life, to have thee by my side
Henceforth an individual solace dear.
Part of my soul I seek thee, and thee claim
My other half." With that thy gentle hand
Seized mine, I yielded, and from that time see
How beauty is excelled by manly grace
And wisdom, which alone is truly fair.'
   So spake our general mother, and with eyes
Of conjugal attraction unreproved,
And meek surrender, half embracing leaned
On our first father; half her swelling breast
Naked met his under the flowing gold
Of her loose tresses hid. He in delight
Both of her beauty and submissive charms
Smiled with superior love, as Jupiter
On Juno smiles, when he impregns the clouds
That shed May flowers; and pressed her matron lip
With kisses pure. Aside the Devil turned
For envy, yet with jealous leer malign

Eyed them askance, and to himself thus plained:
   'Sight hateful, sight tormenting! thus these two
Imparadised in one another's arms,
The happier Eden, shall enjoy their fill
Of bliss on bliss, while I to hell am thrust,
Where neither joy nor love, but fierce desire,
Among our other torments not the least,
Still unfulfilled with pain of longing pines;
Yet let me not forget what I have gained
From their own mouths. All is not theirs, it seems;
One fatal tree there stands, of Knowledge called,
Forbidden them to taste. Knowledge forbidden?
Suspicious, reasonless. Why should their Lord
Envy them that? Can it be sin to know,
Can it be death? And do they only stand
By ignorance, is that their happy state,
The proof of their obedience and their faith?
O fair foundation laid whereon to build
Their ruin! Hence I will excite their minds
With more desire to know, and to reject
Envious commands, invented with design
To keep them low whom knowledge might exalt
Equal with gods. Aspiring to be such,
They taste and die; what likelier can ensue?
But first with narrow search I must walk round
This garden, and no corner leave unspied;
A chance but chance may lead where I may meet
Some wand'ring Spirit of heav'n, by fountain side,
Or in thick shade retired, from him to draw
What further would be learnt. Live while ye may,
Yet happy pair; enjoy, till I return,
Short pleasures, for long woes are to succeed.'

from BOOK XII

   To whom thus also th' Angel last replied:
'This having learnt, thou hast attained the sum
Of wisdom; hope no higher, though all the stars
Thou knew'st by name, and all th' ethereal powers,
All secrets of the deep, all Nature's works,
Or works of God in heav'n, air, earth, or sea,
And all the riches of this world enjoy'dst,
And all the rule, one empire; only add

Deeds to thy knowledge answerable, add faith,
Add virtue, patience, temperance, add love,
By name to come called charity, the soul
Of all the rest: then wilt thou not be loth
To leave this Paradise, but shalt possess
A paradise within thee, happier far.
Let us descend now therefore from this top
Of speculation; for the hour precise
Exacts our parting hence; and see the guards,
By me encamped on yonder hill, expect
Their motion, at whose front a flaming sword,
In signal of remove, waves fiercely round;
We may no longer stay: go, waken Eve;
Her also I with gentle dreams have calmed,
Portending good, and all her spirits composed
To meek submission: thou at season fit
Let her with thee partake what thou hast heard,
Chiefly what may concern her faith to know,
The great deliverance by her seed to come
(For by the Woman's Seed) on all mankind:
That ye may live, which will be many days,
Both in one faith unanimous though sad,
With cause for evils past, yet much more cheered
With meditation on the happy end.'
    He ended, and they both descend the hill;
Descended, Adam to the bow'r where Eve
Lay sleeping ran before, but found her waked;
And thus with words not sad she him received:
    'Whence thou return'st, and whither went'st, I know;
For God is also in sleep, and dreams advise,
Which he hath sent propitious, some great good
Presaging, since with sorrow and heart's distress
Wearied I fell asleep. But now lead on;
In me is no delay; with thee to go,
Is to stay here; without thee here to stay,
Is to go hence unwilling; thou to me
Art all things under heav'n, all places thou,
Who for my wilful crime art banished hence.
This further consolation yet secure
I carry hence; though all by me is lost,
Such favor I unworthy am vouchsafed,
By me the Promised Seed shall all restore.'
    So spake our mother Eve, and Adam heard
Well pleased, but answered not; for now too nigh

Th' Archangel stood, and from the other hill
To their fixed station, all in bright array
The Cherubim descended; on the ground
Gliding metéorous, as ev'ning mist
Ris'n from a river o'er the marish glides,
And gathers ground fast at the laborer's heel
Homeward returning. High in front advanced,
The brandished sword of God before them blazed
Fierce as a comet; which with torrid heat,
And vapor as the Libyan air adust,
Began to parch that temperate clime; whereat
In either hand the hast'ning Angel caught
Our ling'ring parents, and to th' eastern gate
Led them direct, and down the cliff as fast
To the subjected plain; then disappeared.
They, looking back, all th' eastern side beheld
Of Paradise, so late their happy seat,
Waved over by that flaming brand, the gate
With dreadful faces thronged and fiery arms.
Some natural tears they dropped, but wiped them soon;
The world was all before them, where to choose
Their place of rest, and Providence their guide:
They hand in hand, with wand'ring steps and slow,
Through Eden took their solitary way.

from *Samson Agonistes*

Samson. A little onward lend thy guiding hand
To these dark steps, a little further on,
For yonder bank hath choice of sun or shade;
There I am wont to sit, when any chance
Relieves me from my task of servile toil,
Daily in the common prison else enjoined me,
Where I, a prisoner chained, scarcely freely draw
The air imprisoned also, close and damp,
Unwholesome draught. But here I feel amends,
The breath of heav'n fresh-blowing, pure and sweet,
With day-spring born; here leave me to respire.
This day a solemn feast the people hold
To Dagon their sea-idol, and forbid
Laborious works; unwillingly this rest
Their superstition yields me; hence will leave
Retiring from the popular noise, I seek

This unfrequented place to find some ease,
Ease to the body some, none to the mind
From restless thoughts, that like a deadly swarm
Of hornets armed, no sooner found alone,
But rush upon me thronging, and present
Times past, what once I was, and what am now.
O wherefore was my birth from Heaven foretold
Twice by an angel, who at last in sight
Of both my parents all in flames ascended
From off the altar, where an off'ring burned,
As in a fiery column charioting
His godlike presence, and from some great act
Or benefit revealed to Abraham's race?
Why was my breeding ordered and prescribed
As of a person separate to God,
Designed for great exploits, if I must die
Betrayed, captived, and both my eyes put out,
Made of my enemies the scorn and gaze;
To grind in brazen fetters under task
With this Heav'n-gifted strength? O glorious strength,
Put to the labor of a beast, debased
Lower than bondslave! Promise was that I
Should Israel from Philistian yoke deliver;
Ask for this great deliverer now, and find him
Eyeless in Gaza at the mill with slaves,
Himself in bonds under Philistian yoke;
Yet stay, let me not rashly call in doubt
Divine prediction; what if all foretold
Had been fulfilled but through mine own default?
Whom have I to complain of but myself?
Who this high gift of strength committed to me,
In what part lodged, how easily bereft me,
Under the seal of silence could not keep,
But weakly to a woman must reveal it,
O'ercome with importunity and tears.
O impotence of mind, in body strong!
But what is strength without a double share
Of wisdom? Vast, unwieldy, burdensome,
Proudly secure, yet liable to fall
By weakest subtleties; not made to rule,
But to subserve where wisdom bears command.
God, when he gave me strength, to show withal
How slight the gift was, hung it in my hair.
But peace! I must not quarrel with the will

Of highest dispensation, which herein
Haply had ends above my reach to know:
Suffices that to me strength is my bane,
And proves the source of all my miseries,
So many, and so huge, that each apart
Would ask a life to wail; but chief of all,
O loss of sight, of thee I most complain!
Blind among enemies, O worse than chains,
Dungeon, or beggary, or decrepit age!
Light, the prime work of God, to me is extinct,
And all her various objects of delight
Annulled, which might in part my grief have eased,
Inferior to the vilest now become
Of man or worm; the vilest here excel me,
They creep, yet see; I, dark in light exposed
To daily fraud, contempt, abuse and wrong,
Within doors, or without, still as a fool,
In power of others, never in my own;
Scarce half I seem to live, dead more than half.
O dark, dark, dark, amid the blaze of noon,
Irrecoverably dark, total eclipse
Without all hope of day!
O first-created beam, and thou great Word,
'Let there be light, and light was over all';
Why am I thus bereaved thy prime decree?
The sun to me is dark
And silent as the moon,
When she deserts the night,
Hid in her vacant interlunar cave.
Since light so necessary is to life,
And almost life itself, if it be true
That light is in the soul,
She all in every part, why was the sight
To such a tender ball as th' eye confined?
So obvious and so easy to be quenched,
And not, as feeling, through all parts diffused,
That she might look at will through every pore?
Then had I not been thus exiled from light,
As in the land of darkness, yet in light,
To live a life half dead, a living death,
And buried; but O yet more miserable!
Myself my sepulchre, a moving grave,
Buried, not yet exempt
By privilege of death and burial

From worst of other evils, pains and wrongs,
But made hereby obnoxious more
To all the miseries of life,
Life in captivity
Among inhuman foes.
But who are these? For with joint pace I hear
The tread of many feet steering this way;
Perhaps my enemies who come to stare
At my affliction, and perhaps to insult,
Their daily practice to afflict me more.
   Chorus. This, this is he; softly a while;
Let us not break in upon him.
O change beyond report, thought, or belief!
See how he lies at random, carelessly diffused,
With languished head unpropped,
As one past hope, abandoned,
And by himself given over;
In slavish habit, ill-fitted weeds
O'erworn and soiled;
Or do my eyes misrepresent? Can this be he,
That heroic, that renowned,
Irresistible Samson? Whom unarmed
No strength of man, or fiercest wild beast could withstand;
Who tore the lion, as the lion tears the kid,
Ran on embattled armies clad in iron,
And, weaponless himself,
Made arms ridiculous, useless the forgery
Of brazen shield and spear, the hammered cuirass,
Chalýbean-tempered steel, and frock of mail
Adamantean proof;
But safe, he who stood aloof,
When insupportably his foot advanced,
In scorn of their proud arms and warlike tools,
Spurned them to death by troops. The bold Ascalonite
Fled from his lion ramp, old warriors turned
Their plated backs under his heel;
Or grov'ling soiled their crested helmets in the dust.
Then with what trivial weapon came to hand,
The jaw of a dead ass, his sword of bone,
A thousand foreskins fell, the flower of Palestine,
In Ramath-lechi, famous to this day;
Then by main force pulled up, and on his shoulders bore
The gates of Azza, post and massy bar,
Up to the hill by Hebron, seat of giants old,

No journey of a Sabbath day, and loaded so;
Like whom the Gentiles feign to bear up heav'n.
Which shall I first bewail,
Thy bondage or lost sight,
Prison within prison
Inseparably dark?
Thou art become (O worst imprisonment!)
The dungeon of thyself; thy soul
(Which men enjoying sight oft without cause complain)
Imprisoned now indeed,
In real darkness of the body dwells,
Shut up from outward light
To incorporate with gloomy night;
For inward light, alas,
Puts forth no visual beam.
O mirror of our fickle state,
Since man on earth unparalleled!
The rarer thy example stands,
By how much from the top of wondrous glory,
Strongest of mortal men,
To lowest pitch of abject fortune thou art fall'n.
For him I reckon not in high estate
Whom long descent of birth
Or the sphere of fortune raises;
But thee whose strength, while virtue was her mate,
Might have subdued the earth,
Universally crowned with highest praises.
    Sam. I hear the sound of words; their sense the air
Dissolves unjointed ere it reach my ear.
    Chor. He speaks; let us draw nigh. Matchless in might,
The glory late of Israel, now the grief!
We come thy friends and neighbors not unknown
From Eshtaol and Zora's fruitful vale
To visit or bewail thee, or if better,
Counsel or consolation we may bring,
Salve to thy sores; apt words have power to swage
The tumors of a troubled mind,
And are as balm to festered wounds.
    Sam. Your coming, friends, revives me, for I learn
Now of my own experience, not by talk,
How counterfeit a coin they are who 'friends'
Bear in their superscription (of the most
I would be understood). In prosperous days
They swarm, but in adverse withdraw their head,

Not to be found, though sought. Ye see, O friends,
How many evils have enclosed me round;
Yet that which was the worst now least afflicts me,
Blindness, for had I sight, confused with shame,
How could I once look up, or heave the head,
Who like a foolish pilot have shipwracked
My vessel trusted to me from above,
Gloriously rigged; and for a word, a tear,
Fool, have divulged the secret gift of God
To a deceitful woman? Tell me, friends,
Am I not sung and proverbed for a fool
In every street, do they not say, 'How well
Are come upon him his deserts'? Yet why?
Immeasurable strength they might behold
In me, of wisdom nothing more than mean;
This with the other should, at least, have paired;
These two proportioned ill drove me transverse.
  Chor. Tax not divine disposal; wisest men
Have erred, and by bad women been deceived;
And shall again, pretend they ne'er so wise.
Deject not then so overmuch thyself,
Who hast of sorrow thy full load besides.
Yet truth to say, I oft have heard men wonder
Why thou shouldst wed Philistian women rather
Than of thine own tribe fairer, or as fair,
At least of thy own nation, and as noble.
  Sam. The first I saw at Timna, and she pleased
Me, not my parents, that I sought to wed,
The daughter of an infidel: they knew not
That what I motioned was of God; I knew
From intimate impulse, and therefore urged
The marriage on; that by occasion hence
I might begin Israel's deliverance,
The work to which I was divinely called.
She proving false, the next I took to wife
(O that I never had! fond wish too late!)
Was in the vale of Sorec, Dálila,
That specious monster, my accomplished snare.
I thought it lawful from my former act,
And the same end, still watching to oppress
Israel's oppressors. Of what now I suffer
She was not the prime cause, but I myself,
Who vanquished with a peal of words (O weakness!)
Gave up my fort of silence to a woman.

JOHN MILTON

Chor. In seeking just occasion to provoke
The Philistine, thy country's enemy,
Thou never wast remiss, I bear thee witness:
Yet Israel still serves with all his sons.

* * *

Chor. Oh how comely it is and how reviving
To the spirits of just men long oppressed,
When God into the hands of their deliverer
Puts invincible might
To quell the mighty of the earth, th' oppressor,
The brute and boist'rous force of violent men,
Hardy and industrious to support
Tyrannic power, but raging to pursue
The righteous and all such as honor truth!
He all their ammunition
And feats of war defeats
With plain heroic magnitude of mind
And celestial vigor armed;
Their armories and magazines contemns,
Renders them useless, while
With winged expedition
Swift as the lightning glance he executes
His errand on the wicked, who surprised
Lose their defense, distracted and amazed.
But patience is more oft the exercise
Of saints, the trial of their fortitude,
Making them each his own deliverer,
And victor over all
That tyranny or fortune can inflict;
Either of these is in thy lot,
Samson, with might endued
Above the sons of men; but sight bereaved
May chance to number thee with those
Whom patience finally must crown.
This Idol's day hath been to thee no day of rest,
Laboring thy mind
More than the working day thy hands;
And yet perhaps more trouble is behind.
For I descry this way
Some other tending; in his hand
A scepter or quaint staff he bears,
Comes on amain, speed in his look.

JOHN MILTON

By his habit I discern him now
A public officer, and now at hand.
His message will be short and voluble.
   Officer. Hebrews, the pris'ner Samson here I seek.
   Chor. His manacles remark him; there he sits.
   Off. Samson, to thee our lords thus bid me say:
This day to Dagon is a solemn feast,
With sacrifices, triumph, pomp, and games;
Thy strength they know surpassing human rate,
And now some public proof thereof require
To honor this great feast, and great assembly;
Rise therefore with all speed and come along,
Where I will see thee heartened and fresh clad
To appear as fits before th' illustrious lords.
   Sam. Thou know'st I am an Hebrew, therefore tell them
Our Law forbids at their religious rites
My presence; for that cause I cannot come.
   Off. This answer, be assured, will not content them.
   Sam. Have they not sword-players, and ev'ry sort
Of gymnic artists, wrestlers, riders, runners,
Jugglers and dancers, antics, mummers, mimics,
But they must pick me out with shackles tired,
And over-labored at their public mill,
To make them sport with blind activity?
Do they not seek occasion of new quarrels,
On my refusal, to distress me more,
Or make a game of my calamities?
Return the way thou cam'st; I will not come.
   Off. Regard thyself; this will offend them highly.
   Sam. Myself? My conscience and internal peace.
Can they think me so broken, so debased
With corporal servitude, that my mind ever
Will condescend to such absurd commands?
Although their drudge, to be their fool or jester,
And in my midst of sorrow and heart-grief
To show them feats and play before their god,
The worst of all indignities, yet on me
Joined with extreme contempt? I will not come.
   Off. My message was imposed on me with speed,
Brooks no delay; is this thy resolution?
   Sam. So take it with what speed thy message needs.
   Off. I am sorry what this stoutness will produce.
   Sam. Perhaps thou shalt have cause to sorrow indeed.

*   *   *

Manoa. I know your friendly minds and—O what noise!
Mercy of Heav'n, what hideous noise was that!
Horribly loud, unlike the former shout.
   Chor. Noise call you it, or universal groan,
As if the whole inhabitation perished?
Blood, death, and dreadful deeds are in that noise,
Ruin, destruction at the utmost point.
   Man. Of ruin indeed methought I heard the noise.
Oh it continues, they have slain my son.
   Chor. Thy son is rather slaying them; that outcry
From slaughter of one foe could not ascend.
   Man. Some dismal accident it needs must be;
What shall we do, stay here or run and see?
   Chor. Best keep together here, lest running thither
We unawares run into danger's mouth.
This evil on the Philistines is fall'n;
From whom could else a general cry be heard?
The sufferers then will scarce molest us here;
From other hands we need not much to fear.
What if his eyesight (for to Israel's God
Nothing is hard) by miracle restored,
He now be dealing dole among his foes,
And over heaps of slaughtered walk his way?
   Man. That were a joy presumptuous to be thought.
   Chor. Yet God hath wrought things as incredible
For his people of old; what hinders now?
   Man. He can, I know, but doubt to think he will;
Yet hope would fain subscribe, and tempts belief.
A little stay will bring some notice hither.
   Chor. Of good or bad so great, of bad the sooner;
For evil news rides post, while good news baits.
And to our wish I see one hither speeding,
An Hebrew, as I guess, and of our tribe.
   Messenger. O whither shall I run, or which way fly
The sight of this so horrid spectacle
Which erst my eyes beheld and yet behold?
For dire imagination still pursues me.
But providence or instinct of nature seems,
Or reason, though disturbed and scarce consulted,
To have guided me aright, I know not how,
To thee first, reverend Manoa, and to these
My countrymen, whom here I knew remaining,
As at some distance from the place of horror,
So in the sad event too much concerned.

Man. The accident was loud, and here before thee
With rueful cry, yet what it was we hear not;
No preface needs, thou seest we long to know.

Mess. It would burst forth; but I recover breath
And sense distract, to know well what I utter.

Man. Tell us the sum, the circumstance defer.

Mess. Gaza yet stands, but all her sons are fall'n,
All in a moment overwhelmed and fall'n.

Man. Sad, but thou know'st to Israelites not saddest
The desolation of a hostile city.

Mess. Feed on that first, there may in grief be surfeit.

Man. Relate by whom.

Mess.   By Samson.

Man.   That still lessens
The sorrow, and converts it nigh to joy.

Mess. Ah, Manoa, I refrain, too suddenly
To utter what will come at last too soon;
Lest evil tidings, with too rude irruption
Hitting thy aged ear, should pierce too deep.

Man. Suspense in news is torture, speak them out.

Mess. Then take the worst in brief: Samson is dead.

Man. The worst indeed! O all my hope's defeated
To free him hence! But Death who sets all free
Hath paid his ransom now and full discharge.
With windy joy this day had I conceived,
Hopeful of his delivery, which now proves
Abortive as the first-born bloom of spring
Nipped with the lagging rear of winter's frost.
Yet ere I give the reins to grief, say first,
How died he? Death to life is crown or shame.
All by him fell, thou say'st; by whom fell he,
What glorious hand gave Samson his death's wound?

Mess. Unwounded of his enemies he fell.

Man. Wearied with slaughter then, or how? Explain.

Mess. By his own hands.

Man.   Self-violence? What cause
Brought him so soon at variance with himself
Among his foes?

Mess.   Inevitable cause
At once both to destroy and be destroyed;
The edifice where all were met to see him,
Upon their heads and on his own he pulled.

Man. O lastly over-strong against thyself!
A dreadful way thou took'st to thy revenge.

More than enough we know; but while things yet
Are in confusion, give us, if thou canst,
Eye-witness of what first or last was done,
Relation more particular and distinct.
   Mess. Occasions drew me early to this city,
And as the gates I entered with sunrise,
The morning trumpets festival proclaimed
Through each high street. Little I had despatched
When all abroad was rumored that this day
Samson should be brought forth to show the people
Proof of his mighty strength in feats and games;
I sorrowed at his captive state, but minded
Not to be absent at that spectacle.
The building was a spacious theater
Half round on two main pillars vaulted high,
With seats where all the lords, and each degree
Of sort, might sit in order to behold;
The other side was open, where the throng
On banks and scaffolds under sky might stand;
I among these aloof obscurely stood.
The feast and noon grew high, and sacrifice
Had filled their hearts with mirth, high cheer, and wine,
When to their sports they turned. Immediately
Was Samson as a public servant brought,
In their state livery clad; before him pipes
And timbrels; on each side went armèd guards,
Both horse and foot before him and behind
Archers, and slingers, cataphracts and spears.
At sight of him the people with a shout
Rifted the air, clamoring their god with praise,
Who had made their dreadful enemy their thrall.
He, patient but undaunted, where they led him,
Came to the place; and what was set before him,
Which without help of eye might be assayed,
To heave, pull, draw, or break, he still performed,
All with incredible, stupendious force,
None daring to appear antagonist.
At length for intermission sake they led him
Between the pillars; he his guide requested
(For so from such as nearer stood we heard),
As over-tired, to let him lean a while
With both his arms on those two massy pillars
That to the archèd roof gave main support.
He unsuspicious led him; which when Samson

Felt in his arms, with head a while inclined,
And eyes fast fixed he stood, as one who prayed,
Or some great matter in his mind revolved.
At last with head erect thus cried aloud:
'Hitherto, Lords, what your commands imposed
I have performed, as reason was, obeying,
Not without wonder or delight beheld.
Now of my own accord such other trial
I mean to show you of my strength, yet greater,
As with amaze shall strike all who behold.'
This uttered, straining all his nerves he bowed;
As with the force of winds and waters pent
When mountains tremble, those two massy pillars
With horrible convulsion to and fro
He tugged, he shook, till down they came and drew
The whole roof after them, with burst of thunder
Upon the heads of all who sat beneath,
Lords, ladies, captains, counselors, or priests,
Their choice nobility and flower, not only
Of this but each Philistian city round,
Met from all parts to solemnize this feast.
Samson, with these inmixed, inevitably
Pulled down the same destruction on himself;
The vulgar only scaped who stood without.

   Chor. O dearly bought revenge, yet glorious!
Living or dying thou hast fulfilled
The work for which thou wast foretold
To Israel, and now li'st victorious
Among thy slain self-killed,
Not willingly, but tangled in the fold
Of dire necessity, whose law in death conjoined
Thee with thy slaughtered foes, in number more
Than all thy life had slain before.

   Semichor. While their hearts were jocund and sublime,
Drunk with idolatry, drunk with wine,
And fat regorged of bulls and goats,
Chanting their idol, and preferring
Before our living Dread who dwells
In Silo, his bright sanctuary,
Among them he a spirit of frenzy sent,
Who hurt their minds,
And urged them on with mad desire
To call in haste for their destroyer;
They only set on sport and play

Unweetingly importuned
Their own destruction to come speedy upon them.
So fond are mortal men
Fall'n into wrath divine,
As their own ruin on themselves to invite,
Insensate left, or to sense reprobate,
And with blindness internal struck.
   Semichor. But he, though blind of sight,
Despised and thought extinguished quite,
With inward eyes illuminated,
His fiery virtue roused
From under ashes into sudden flame,
And as an ev'ning dragon came,
Assailant on the perchèd roosts
And nests in order ranged
Of tame villatic fowl; but as an eagle
His cloudless thunder bolted on their heads.
So virtue, giv'n for lost,
Depressed, and overthrown, as seemed,
Like that self-begotten bird
In the Arabian woods embost,
That no second knows nor third,
And lay erewhile a holocaust,
From out her ashy womb now teemed,
Revives, reflourishes, then vigorous most
When most unactive deemed,
And though her body die, her fame survives,
A secular bird, ages of lives.
   Man. Come, come, no time for lamentation now,
Nor much more cause; Samson hath quit himself
Like Samson, and heroicly hath finished
A life heroic, on his enemies
Fully revenged; hath left them years of mourning,
And lamentation to the sons of Caphtor
Through all Philistian bounds. To Israel
Honor hath left, and freedom—let but them
Find courage to lay hold on this occasion;
To himself and father's house eternal fame;
And, which is best and happiest yet, all this
With God not parted from him, as was feared,
But favoring and assisting to the end.
Nothing is here for tears, nothing to wail
Or knock the breast, no weakness, no contempt,
Dispraise, or blame; nothing but well and fair,

And what may quiet us in a death so noble.
Let us go find the body where it lies
Soaked in his enemies' blood, and from the stream
With lavers pure and cleansing herbs wash off
The clotted gore. I with what speed the while
(Gaza is not in plight to say us nay)
Will send for all my kindred, all my friends,
To fetch him hence and solemnly attend
With silent obsequy and funeral train
Home to his father's house: there will I build him
A monument, and plant it round with shade
Of laurel ever green, and branching palm,
With all his trophies hung, and acts enrolled
In copious legend, or sweet lyric song.
Thither shall all the valiant youth resort,
And from his memory inflame their breasts
To matchless valor and adventures high;
The virgins also shall on feastful days
Visit his tomb with flowers, only bewailing
His lot unfortunate in nuptial choice,
From whence captivity and loss of eyes.
   Chor. All is best, though we oft doubt,
What th' unsearchable dispose
Of Highest Wisdom brings about,
And ever best found in the close.
Oft he seems to hide his face,
But unexpectedly returns
And to his faithful champion hath in place
Bore witness gloriously; whence Gaza mourns,
And all that band them to resist
His uncontrollable intent:
His servants he, with new acquist
Of true experience from this great event,
With peace and consolation hath dismissed,
And calm of mind, all passion spent.

SIR JOHN SUCKLING
1609–1642

Song

WHY so pale and wan, fond lover?
    Prythee, why so pale?
Will, when looking well can't move her,
    Looking ill prevail?
    Prythee, why so pale?

Why so dull and mute, young sinner?
    Prythee, why so mute?
Will, when speaking well can't win her,
    Saying nothing do't?
    Prythee, why so mute?

Quit, quit, for shame! this will not move,
    This cannot take her;
If of herself she will not love,
    Nothing can make her:
    The devil take her!

A Constant Lover

OUT upon it, I have loved
    Three whole days together!
And am like to love three more,
    If it prove fair weather.

Time shall moult away his wings
    Ere he shall discover
In the whole wide world again
    Such a constant lover.

But the spite on 't is, no praise
    Is due at all to me:
Love with me had made no stays,
    Had it any been but she.

Had it any been but she,
And that very face,
There had been at least ere this
A dozen dozen in her place.

from *A Ballad upon a Wedding*

I TELL thee, Dick, where I have been,
Where I the rarest things have seen,
Oh, things beyond compare!
Such sights again cannot be found
In any place on English ground,
Be it at wake or fair.

At Charing Cross, hard by the way
Where we (thou know'st) do sell our hay,
There is a house with stairs;
And there did I see coming down
Such folk as are not in our town,
Forty at least, in pairs.

Amongst the rest, one pestilent fine
(His beard no bigger, though, than thine!)
Walked on before the rest.
Our landlord looks like nothing to him;
The king (God bless him!), 'twould undo him,
Should he go still so dressed.

* * *

But wot you what? The youth was going
To make an end of all his wooing;
The Parson for him stayed.
Yet, by his leave, for all his haste,
He did not so much wish all passed,
Perchance, as did the maid.

The maid (and thereby hangs a tale)
For such a maid no Whitsun ale
Could ever yet produce;
No grape that's kindly ripe could be
So round, so plump, so soft, as she;
Nor half so full of juice!

Her finger was so small, the ring
Would not stay on; which they did bring.
    It was too wide a peck!
And to say truth, for out it must,
It looked like the great collar (just)
    About our young colt's neck.

Her feet, beneath her petticoat,
Like little mice stole in and out,
    As if they feared the light:
But oh! she dances such a way,
No sun, upon an Easter Day,
    Is half so fine a sight!

       *   *   *

Her cheeks so rare a white was on;
No daisy makes comparison,
    Who sees them is undone.
For streaks of red were mingled there,
Such as are on a Katherine pear
    (The side that's next the sun).

Her lips were red, and one was thin
Compared to that was next her chin
    (Some bee had stung it newly).
But, Dick, her eyes so guard her face,
I durst no more upon them gaze,
    Than on the sun in July.

Her mouth so small, when she does speak
Thou'dst swear her teeth her words did break,
    That they might passage get:
But she so handled still the matter,
They came as good as ours or better,
    And are not spent a whit!

       *   *   *

Just in the nick, the cook knocked thrice,
And all the waiters, in a trice,
    His summons did obey.
Each serving-man, with dish in hand,
Marched boldly up like our trained band,
    Presented, and away!

The business of the kitchen's great,
For it is fit that men should eat;
    Nor was it there denied.
Passion o' me! how I run on;
There's that that would be thought upon,
    I trow, besides the bride:

When all the meat was on the table
What man of knife or teeth was able
    To stay to be entreated?
And this the very reason was,
Before the parson could say grace
    The company was seated.

Now hats fly off; and youths carouse:
Healths first go round, and then the house.
    The bride's came thick and thick.
And when 'twas named another's health,
Perhaps he made it hers by stealth.
    (And who could help it, Dick?)

O' th' sudden, up they rise and dance:
Then sit again and sigh and glance,
    Then dance again and kiss.
Thus several ways the time did pass;
Whilst every woman wished her place,
    And every man wished his!

WILLIAM CARTWRIGHT

1611-1643

A New Year's Gift

To Brian Lord Bishop of Sarum upon the author's entering into Holy Orders, 1638

Now that the village reverence doth lie hid,
    As Egypt's Wisdom did,
In birds and beasts, and that the tenant's soul
    Goes with his New Year's fowl;
    So that the cock and hen speak more
    Now than in fables heretofore;

And that the feathered things
Truly make love have wings:
Though we no flying present have to pay,
A quill yet snatch'd from thence may sign the day.

But, being the Canon bars me wit and wine,
Enjoining the true Vine,
Being the bays must yield unto the Cross,
And all be now one loss;
So that my raptures are to steal
And knit themselves in one pure zeal,
And that my each day's breath
Must be a daily death:
Without all strain of fury must I than
Tell you this New Year brings you a new man.

New, not as th' year, to run the same course o'er
Which it hath run before,
Lest in the man himself there be a round,
As in his humour's found,
And that return seem to make good
Circling of actions, as of blood.
Motion as in a mill,
Is busy standing still;
And by such wheeling we but thus prevail,
To make the serpent swallow his own tail.

Nor new by solemnizing looser toys,
And erring with less noise,
Taking the flag and trumpet from the sin,
So to offend within;
As some men silence loud perfumes
And draw them into shorter rooms:
This will be understood
More wary, not more good.
Sins too may be severe, and so, no doubt,
The vice but only sour'd, not rooted out.

But new, by th' using of each part aright,
Changing both step and sight;
That false direction comes not from the eye,
Nor the foot tread awry;

than] then

338

WILLIAM CARTWRIGHT

That neither *that* the way aver
Which doth toward fame, or profit, err,
 Nor *this* tread that path which
 Is not the right, but rich;
That thus the foot being fix'd, thus led the eye,
I pitch my walk low, but my prospect high.

New too, to teach my opinions not t' submit
 To favour, or to wit;
Nor yet to walk on edges, where they may
 Run safe in broader way;
 Nor to search out for new paths, where
 Nor tracks nor footsteps doth appear,
 Knowing that deeps are ways
 Where no impression stays;
Nor servile thus, nor curious, may I then
Approve my faith to heaven, my life to men.

But I who thus present myself as new,
 Am thus made new by you.
Had not your rays dwelt on me, one long night
 Had shut me up from sight.
 Your beams exhale me from among
 Things tumbling in the common throng.
 Who thus with your fire burns,
 Now gives not, but returns.
To others then be this a day of thrift:
They do receive; but you, sir, make the gift.

To Chloe, Who Wished Herself Young Enough For Me

CHLOE, why wish you that your years
 Would backward run, till they meet mine,
That perfect likeness which endears
 Things unto things, might us combine?
Our ages so in date agree
That twins do differ more than we.

There are two births; the one when light
 First strikes the new awaken'd sense;
The other when two souls unite,
 And we must count our life from thence:
When you loved me and I loved you
Then both of us were born anew.

339

Love then to us did new souls give
   And in those souls did plant new powers;
Since when another life we live,
   The breath we breathe is his, not ours:
Love makes those young whom age doth chill,
And whom he finds young keeps young still.

Love, like that angel that shall call
   Our bodies from the silent grave,
Unto one age doth raise us all,
   None too much, none too little have.
Nay, that the difference may be none,
He makes two, not alike, but one.

And now since you and I are such,
   Tell me what's yours, and what is mine?
Our eyes, our ears, our taste, smell, touch,
   Do (like our souls) in one combine—
So by this, I as well may be
Too old for you, as you for me.

SAMUEL BUTLER

1612–1680

Hudibras

WHEN civil fury first grew high,
And men fell out, they knew not why;
When hard words, jealousies, and fears,
Set folks together by the ears,
And made them fight, like mad or drunk,
For Dame Religion as for punk,
Whose honesty they all durst swear for,
Though not a man of them knew wherefore:
When gospel-trumpeter surrounded,
With long-eared rout to battle sounded,
And pulpit, drum ecclesiastic,
Was beat with fist, instead of a stick;
Then did Sir Knight abandon dwelling,
And out he rode a–colonelling.

A wight he was, whose very sight would
Entitle him Mirror of Knighthood;
That never bent his stubborn knee
To any thing but chivalry,
Nor put up blow, but that which laid
Right worshipful on shoulder-blade:
Chief of domestic knights and errant,
Either for cartel or for warrant;
Great on the bench, great in the saddle,
That could as well bind o'er, as swaddle,
Mighty he was at both of these,
And styled of war as well as peace
(So some rats, of amphibious nature,
Are either for the land or water).
But here our authors make a doubt
Whether he were more wise, or stout.
Some hold the one, and some the other;
But howsoe'er they make a pother,
The difference was so small, his brain
Outweighed his rage but half a grain;
Which made some take him for a tool
That knaves do work with, called a fool.
For 't has been held by many, that
As Montaigne, playing with his cat,
Complains she thought him but an ass,
Much more she would Sir Hudibras.
(For that's the name our valiant knight
To all his challenges did write.)
But they're mistaken very much,
'Tis plain enough he was no such;
We grant, although he had much wit,
H' was very shy of using it;
As being loth to wear it out,
And therefore bore it not about,
Unless on holy-days, or so,
As men their best apparel do.
Beside, 'tis known he could speak Greek
As naturally as pigs squeak;
That Latin was no more difficile,
Than to a blackbird 'tis to whistle:
Being rich in both, he never scanted
His bounty unto such as wanted;

swaddle] cudgel

341

But much of either would afford
To many, that had not one word.
For Hebrew roots, although th' are found
To flourish most in barren ground,
He had such plenty, as sufficed
To make some think him circumcised;
And truly so, perhaps, he was,
'Tis many a pious Christian's case.
   He was in logic a great critic,
Profoundly skilled in analytic;
He could distinguish, and divide
A hair 'twixt south and south-west side;
On either which he would dispute,
Confute, change hands, and still confute.
He'd undertake to prove by force
Of argument, a man 's no horse.
He'd prove a buzzard is no fowl,
And that a lord may be an owl,
A calf an alderman, a goose a justice,
And rooks committee-men and trustees.
He'd run in debt by disputation,
And pay with ratiocination.
All this by syllogism, true
In mood and figure, he would do.
   For rhetoric, he could not ope
His mouth, but out there flew a trope;
And when he happened to break off
I' th' middle of his speech, or cough,
H' had hard words, ready to show why,
And tell what rules he did it by;
Else when with greatest art he spoke,
You'd think he talked like other folk.
For all a rhetorician's rules
Teach nothing but to name his tools.
But, when he pleased to show't, his speech
In loftiness of sound was rich;
A Babylonish dialect,
Which learnèd pedants much affect.
It was a parti-coloured dress
Of patched and piebald languages;
'Twas English cut on Greek and Latin,
Like fustian heretofore on satin;
It had an old promiscuous tone,
As if h' had talked three parts in one;

Which made some think, when he did gabble,
Th' had heard three labourers of Babel;
Or Cerberus himself pronounce
A leash of languages at once.
This he as volubly would vent
As if his stock would ne'er be spent:
And truly, to support that charge,
He had supplies as vast and large;
For he could coin, or counterfeit
New words, with little or no wit;
Words so debased and hard, no stone
Was hard enough to touch them on;
And when with hasty noise he spoke 'em;
The ignorant for current took 'em;
That had the orator, who once
Did fill his mouth with pebble stones
When he harangued, but known his phrase,
He would have used no other ways.
    In mathematics he was greater
Than Tycho Brahe, or Erra Pater:
For he, by geometric scale,
Could take the size of pots of ale;
Resolve, by sines and tangents straight,
If bread or butter wanted weight;
And wisely tell what hour o' th' day
The clock doth strike, by Algebra.
    Beside, he was a shrewd philosopher,
And had read ev'ry text and gloss over;
Whate'er the crabbed'st author hath,
He understood b'implicit faith:
Whatever sceptic could inquire for,
For ev'ry why he had a wherefore;
Knew more than forty of them do,
As far as words and terms could go.
All which he understood by rote,
And, as occasion served, would quote;
No matter whether right or wrong:
They might be either said or sung.
His notions fitted things so well,
That which was which he could not tell;
But oftentimes mistook th' one
For th' other, as great clerks have done.
He could reduce all things to acts,
And knew their natures by abstracts;

Where entity and quiddity,
The ghosts of defunct bodies, fly;
Where truth in person does appear
Like words congealed in Northern air.
He knew what 's what, and that 's as high
As metaphysic wit can fly,
In school divinity as able
As he that hight Irrefragable;
Profound in all the nominal
And real ways beyond them all;
And with as delicate a hand,
Could twist as tough a rope of sand.
And weave fine cobwebs, fit for skull
That's empty when the moon is full;
Such as take lodgings in a head
That 's to be let unfurnishèd.
He could raise scruples dark and nice,
And after solve 'em in a trice:
As if divinity had catched
The itch, of purpose to be scratched;
Or, like a mountebank, did wound
And stab herself with doubts profound,
Only to show with how small pain
The sores of faith are cured again;
Although by woful proof we find
They always leave a scar behind.
He knew the seat of paradise,
Could tell in what degree it lies:
And, as he was disposed, could prove it,
Below the moon, or else above it.
What Adam dreamt of when his bride
Came from her closet in his side:
Whether the Devil tempted her
By a High Dutch interpreter:
If either of them had a navel;
Who first made music malleable:
Whether the Serpent at the Fall
Had cloven feet or none at all.
All this without a gloss or comment,
He would unriddle in a moment:
In proper terms, such as men smatter
When they throw out and miss the matter.
   For his Religion, it was fit
To match his learning and his wit;

'Twas Presbyterian true blue;
For he was of that stubborn crew
Of errant saints, whom all men grant
To be the true church militant;
Such as do build their faith upon
The holy text of pike and gun;
Decide all controversies by
Infallible artillery;
And prove their doctrine orthodox
By apostolic blows and knocks;
Call fire and sword and desolation,
A godly-thorough-reformation,
Which always must be carried on,
And still be doing, never done;
As if religion were intended
For nothing else but to be mended.
A sect, whose chief devotion lies
In odd perverse antipathies;
In falling out with that or this,
And finding somewhat still amiss;
More peevish, cross, and splenetic,
Than dog distract or monkey sick;
That with more care keep holy-day
The wrong, than others the right way;
Compound for sins they are inclined to,
By damning those they have no mind to:
Still so perverse and opposite,
As if they worshipped God for spite.
The self-same thing they will abhor
One way, and long another for.
Free will they one way disavow,
Another, nothing else allow.
All piety consists therein
In them, in other men all sin.
Rather than fail, they will defy
That which they love most tenderly,
Quarrel with minced-pies, and disparage
Their best and dearest friend, plum-porridge;
Fat pig and goose itself oppose,
And blaspheme custard through the nose.
Th' apostles of this fierce religion,
Like Mahomet's, were ass and widgeon,

distract] distraught

To whom our knight, by fast instinct
Of wit and temper, was so linked,
As if hypocrisy and nonsense
Had got th' advowson of his conscience.

RICHARD CRASHAW

1613-1649

Wishes to His Supposed Mistress

WHOE'ER she be,
That not impossible she
That shall command my heart and me:

Where'er she lie,
Locked up from mortal eye,
In shady leaves of destiny:

Till that ripe birth
Of studied fate stand forth,
And teach her fair steps to our earth:

Till that divine
Idea take a shrine
Of crystal flesh, through which to shine:

Meet you her, my wishes,
Bespeak her to my blisses,
And be ye called my absent kisses.

I wish her beauty,
That owes not all its duty
To gaudy tire, or glist'ring shoe-tie.

Something more than
Taffata or tissue can,
Or rampant feather, or rich fan.

A face that's best
By its own beauty drest,
And can alone commend the rest.

A face made up
Out of no other shop,
Than what nature's white hand sets ope.

A cheek where youth,
And blood, with pen of truth,
Write, what the reader sweetly ru'th.

A cheek, where grows
More than a morning rose:
Which to no box his being owes.

Lips, where all day
A lover's kiss may play,
Yet carry nothing thence away.

Looks that oppress
Their richest tires, but dress
And clothe their simplest nakedness.

Eyes, that displaces
The neighbour diamond, and outfaces
That sunshine by their own sweet graces.

Tresses that wear
Jewels, but to declare
How much themselves more precious are:

Whose native ray,
Can tame the wanton day
Of gems, that in their bright shades play.

Each ruby there,
Or pearl that dare appear,
Be its own blush, be its own tear.

A well-tamed heart,
For whose more noble smart,
Love may be long choosing a dart.

Eyes, that bestow
Full quivers on love's bow;
Yet pay less arrows than they owe.

Smiles, that can warm
The blood, yet teach a charm,
That chastity shall take no harm.

Blushes, that bin
The burnish of no sin,
Nor flames of aught too hot within.

Joys, that confess
Virtue their mistress,
And have no other head to dress.

Fears, fond and slight,
As the coy bride's, when night
First does the longing lover right.

Days, that need borrow
No part of their good-morrow
From a fore-spent night of sorrow.

Days, that in spite
Of darkness, by the light
Of a clear mind are day all night.

Nights, sweet as they,
Made short by lovers' play,
Yet long by th' absence of the day.

Life, that dares send
A challenge to his end,
And when it comes say 'Welcome, friend!'

Sydneian showers
Of sweet discourse, whose powers
Can crown old winter's head with flowers.

Soft silken hours,
Open suns; shady bowers,
'Bove all; nothing within that lowers.

Whate'er delight
Can make day's forehead bright;
Or give down to the wings of night.

I wish her store
Of worth may leave her poor
Of wishes; and I wish—no more.

Now if time knows
That Her whose radiant brows
Weave them a garland of my vows;

Her whose just bays
My future hopes can raise
A trophy to her present praise;

Her that dares be
What these lines wish to see:
I seek no further, it is she.

'Tis she, and here
Lo I unclothe and clear
My wishes' cloudy character.

May she enjoy it,
Whose merit dare apply it,
But modesty dares still deny it.

Such worth as this is
Shall fix my flying wishes,
And determine them to kisses.

Let her full glory,
My fancies, fly before ye,
Be ye my fictions; but her story.

An Epitaph upon Husband and Wife who Died and were Buried Together

To these, whom death again did wed,
This grave's the second marriage-bed.
For though the hand of Fate could force,
'Twixt soul and body a divorce,
It could not sever man and wife,
Because they both lived but one life.
Peace, good reader, do not weep;
Peace, the lovers are asleep:

They, sweet turtles, folded lie,
In the last knot that love could tie.
Let them sleep, let them sleep on,
Till this stormy night be gone.
And the eternal morrow dawn,
Then the curtains will be drawn,
And they waken with that light,
Whose day shall never sleep in night.

On George Herbert's 'The Temple' Sent to a Gentlewoman

KNOW you, fair, on what you look;
Divinest love lies in this book:
Expecting fire from your eyes,
To kindle this his sacrifice.
When your hands untie these strings,
Think you have an angel by th' wings.
One that gladly will be nigh,
To wait upon each morning sigh.
To flutter in the balmy air
Of your well-perfumèd prayer.

These white plumes of his he'll lend you,
Which every day to heaven will send you:
To take acquaintance of the sphere,
And all the smooth-faced kindred there.
And though Herbert's name do owe
These devotions, fairest, know
That while I lay them on the shrine
Of your white hand, they are mine.

from *The Flaming Heart*

LIVE in these conquering leaves; live all the same;
And walk through all tongues one triumphant flame.
Live here, great Heart: and love and die and kill;
And bleed and wound; and yield and conquer still.
Let this immortal life where'er it comes
Walk in a crowd of loves and martyrdoms.
Let mystic deaths wait on 't; and wise souls be
The love-slain witnesses of this life of thee.

O sweet incendiary! show here thy art,
Upon this carcass of a hard, cold, heart,
Let all thy scattered shafts of light, that play
Among the leaves of thy large books of day,
Combined against this breast at once break in
And take away from me myself and sin,
This gracious robbery shall thy bounty be;
And my best fortunes such fair spoils of me.
O thou undaunted daughter of desires!
By all thy dower of lights and fires;
By all the eagle in thee, all the dove;
By all thy lives and deaths of love;
By thy large draughts of intellectual day,
And by thy thirsts of love more large than they;
By all thy brim-filled bowls of fierce desire,
By thy last morning's draught of liquid fire;
By the full kingdom of that final kiss
That seized thy parting soul, and sealed thee His;
By all the heavens thou hast in Him
Fair sister of the seraphim!
By all of Him we have in thee;
Leave nothing of myself in me.
Let me so read my life, that I
Unto all life of mine may die.

An Ecstacy

LORD, when the sense of Thy sweet grace
   Sends up my soul to seek Thy face.
Thy blessed eyes breed such desire,
I die in love's delicious fire.
     O love, I am Thy sacrifice.
Be still triumphant, blessed eyes.
Still shine on me, fair suns! that I
Still may behold, though still I die.
     Though still I die, I live again;
Still longing so to be still slain,
So gainful is such loss of breath.
I die even in desire of death.
     Still live in me this loving strife
Of living Death and dying Life.
For while Thou sweetly slayest me,
Dead to myself, I live in Thee.

RICHARD LOVELACE

1618–1658

To Lucasta, Going Beyond the Seas

IF to be absent were to be
    Away from thee;
    Or that when I am gone,
    You or I were alone;
Then, my Lucasta, might I crave
Pity from blustering wind, or swallowing wave.

    But I'll not sigh one blast or gale
    To swell my sail,
    Or pay a tear to 'suage
    The foaming blue god's rage;
For whether he will let me pass
Or no, I'm still as happy as I was.

    Though seas and land betwixt us both,
    Our faith and troth,
    Like separated souls,
    All time and space controls:
Above the highest sphere we meet
Unseen, unknown, and greet as angels greet.

    So then we do anticipate
    Our after-fate,
    And are alive i' the skies,
    If thus our lips and eyes
Can speak like spirits unconfined
In Heaven, their earthy bodies left behind.

To Althea from Prison

WHEN Love with unconfinèd wings
    Hovers within my gates;
And my divine Althea brings
    To whisper at the grates:

When I lie tangled in her hair,
　And fettered to her eye;
The birds that wanton in the air,
　Know no such liberty.

When flowing cups run swiftly round
　With no allaying Thames,
Our careless heads with roses bound,
　Our hearts with loyal flames;
When thirsty grief in wine we steep,
　When healths and draughts go free,
Fishes that tipple in the deep,
　Know no such liberty.

When, like committed linnets, I
　With shriller throat shall sing
The sweetness, mercy, majesty,
　And glories of my King;
When I shall voice aloud, how good
　He is, how great should be;
Enlargèd winds that curl the flood,
　Know no such liberty.

Stone walls do not a prison make,
　Nor iron bars a cage;
Minds innocent and quiet take
　That for an hermitage;
If I have freedom in my love,
　And in my soul am free;
Angels alone that soar above,
　Enjoy such liberty.

To Lucasta, Going to the Wars

TELL me not, Sweet, I am unkind,
　That from the nunnery
Of thy chaste breast, and quiet mind,
　To war and arms I fly.

True; a new mistress now I chase,
　The first foe in the field;
And with a stronger faith embrace
　A sword, a horse, a shield.

RICHARD LOVELACE

Yet this inconstancy is such,
　As you too shall adore;
I could not love thee, dear, so much,
　Loved I not honour more.

To the Grasshopper

Oh thou that swingest upon the waving hair
　Of some well-fillèd oaten beard,
Drunk ev'ry night with a delicious tear
　Dropt thee from heaven, where now th' art reared.

The joys of earth and air are thine entire,
　That with thy feet and wings doth hop and fly,
And when thy poppy works thou dost retire
　To thy carved acron-bed to lie.

Up with the day, the sun thou welcomest then,
　Sportest in the gilt plaits of his beams,
And all these merry days makest merry men,
　Thyself, and melancholy streams.

But ah the sickle! golden ears are cropped;
　Ceres and Bacchus bid good night;
Sharp frosty fingers all your flowers have topped
　And what scythes spared, winds shave off quite.

Poor verdant fool! and now green ice! thy joys,
　Large and as lasting as thy perch of grass,
Bid us lay in 'gainst winter, rain, and poise
　Their floods, with an o'erflowing glass.

Thou best of men and friends! we will create
　A genuine summer in each other's breast;
And spite of this cold time and frozen fate
　Thaw us a warm seat to our rest.

Our sacred hearths shall burn eternally
　As vestal flames, the north-wind, he
Shall strike his frost-stretched wings, dissolve and fly
　This Œtna in epitome.

TO THE GRASSHOPPER: acron] acorn

Dropping December shall come weeping in,
    Bewail the usurping of his reign;
But when in showers of old Greek we begin,
    Shall cry, he hath his crown again!

Night as clear Hesper shall our tapers whip
    From the light casements where we play,
And the dark hag from her black mantle strip,
    And stick there everlasting day.

Thus richer than untempted Kings are we,
    That asking nothing, nothing need:
Though Lord of all what seas embrace; yet he
    That wants himself, is poor indeed.

SIR JOHN DENHAM

1615-1669

from *Cooper's Hill*

My eye descending from the hill, surveys
Where Thames amongst the wanton valleys strays.
Thames, the most loved of all the Ocean's sons,
By his old sire, to his embraces runs,
Hasting to pay his tribute to the sea,
Like mortal life to meet eternity;
Though with those streams he no resemblance hold,
Whose foam is amber, and their gravel gold,
His genuine and less guilty wealth t' explore,
Search not his bottom, but survey his shore,
O'er which he kindly spreads his spacious wing,
And hatches plenty for th' ensuing spring;
Nor then destroys it with too fond a stay,
Like mothers which their infants overlay,
Nor, with a sudden and impetuous wave,
Like profuse kings, resumes the wealth he gave.
No unexpected inundations spoil
The mower's hopes, nor mock the ploughman's toil:
But godlike his unwearied bounty flows,
First loves to do, then loves the good he does;
Nor are his blessings to his banks confined,
But free and common, as the sea or wind;

When he to boast, or to disperse his stores,
Full of the tributes of his grateful shores,
Visits the world, and in his flying towers,
Brings home to us, and makes both Indies ours;
Finds wealth where 'tis, bestows it where it wants,
Cities in deserts, woods in cities plants.
So that to us no thing, no place is strange,
While his fair bosom is the world's exchange.
O could I flow like thee, and make thy stream
My great example, as it is my theme!
Though deep, yet clear, though gentle, yet not dull,
Strong without rage, without o'erflowing full.

ABRAHAM COWLEY

1618-1667

In Praise of Hope

HOPE, of all ills that men endure,
    The only cheap and universal cure!
Thou captives' freedom, and thou sick man's health,
Thou loser's victory, and thou beggar's wealth!
    Thou manna, which from Heaven we eat,
    To every taste a several meat!
Thou strong retreat! Thou sure entailed estate,
    Which naught has power to alienate!
Thou pleasant, honest flatterer! for none
Flatter unhappy men, but thou alone!

Hope, thou first-fruits of happiness!
Thou gentle dawning of a bright success!
Thou good preparative, without which our joy
Does work too strong, and whilst it cures, destroy;
    Who out of Fortune's reach dost stand,
    And art a blessing still in hand!
Whilst thee, her earnest-money, we retain,
    We certain are to gain,
Whether she her bargain break, or else fulfil;
Thou only good, not worse, for ending ill!

Brother of Faith, twixt whom and thee
The joys of heaven and earth divided be!

Though faith be heir, and have the fixed estate,
Thy portion yet in moveables is great.
    Happiness itself's all one
    In thee, or in possession!
Only the future's thine, the present his!
    Thine's the more hard and noble bliss;
Best apprehender of our joys, which hast
So long a reach, and yet canst hold so fast.

    Hope, thou sad lovers' only friend!
Thou way that mayest dispute it with the end!
For love I fear's a fruit that does delight
The taste itself less than the smell and sight.
    Fruition more deceitful is
    Than thou canst be, when thou dost miss;
Men leave thee by obtaining, and straight flee
    Some other way again to thee;
And that's a pleasant country, without doubt,
To which all soon return that travel out.

The Chronicle

A Ballad

MARGARITA first possessed,
If I remember well, my breast;
    Margarita first of all!
    But when awhile the wanton maid
    With my restless heart had played,
Martha took the flying ball.

Martha soon did it resign
To the beauteous Catharine,
    Beauteous Catharine gave place
    (Though loth and angry she to part
    With the possession of my heart)
To Eliza's conquering face.

Eliza to this hour might reign,
Had not she evil counsels ta'en.
    Fundamental laws she broke;
    And still new favourites she chose,
    Till up in arms my passions rose,
And cast away her yoke.

Mary then and gentle Anne
Both to reign at once began.
   Alternately they swayed;
     And sometimes Mary was the fair,
     And sometimes Anne the crown did wear;
   And sometimes both I obeyed.

Another Mary then arose
And did rigorous laws impose;
   A mighty tyrant she!
     Long, alas, should I have been
     Under that iron-sceptred Queen,
   Had not Rebecca set me free.

When fair Rebecca set me free,
'Twas then a golden time with me.
   But soon these pleasures fled,
     For the gracious Princess died
     In her youth and beauty's pride,
   And Judith reigned in her stead.

One month, three days, and half an hour
Judith held the sovereign power.
   Wondrous beautiful her face;
     But so weak and small her wit
     That she to govern was unfit,
   And so Susanna took her place.

But when Isabella came,
Armed with a resistless flame
   And the artillery of her eye,
     Whilst she proudly marched about
     Greater conquests to find out,
   She beat out Susan by the by.

But in her place I then obeyed
Black-eyed Bess, her viceroy maid,
   To whom ensued a vacancy.
     Thousand worse passions then possessed
     The interregnum of my breast;
   Bless me from such an anarchy!

Gentle Henrietta then,
And a third Mary next began;

Then Joan and Jane and Audria,
  And then a pretty Thomasine,
  And then another Katharine,
And then a long et cetera.

But should I now to you relate
The strength and riches of their state,
  The powder, patches, and the pins,
    The ribands, jewels, and the rings,
    The lace, the paint and warlike things
That make up all their magazines;

If I should tell the politic arts
To take and keep men's hearts,
  The letters, embassies and spies,
    The frowns, and smiles and flatteries,
    The quarrels, tears, and perjuries
Numberless, nameless, mysteries;

And all the little lime-twigs laid
By Machiavel, the waiting-maid,
  I more voluminous should grow
    (Chiefly if I, like them, should tell
    All change of weathers that befell)
Than Holinshed or Stow.

But I will briefer with them be,
Since few of them were long with me.
  A higher and a nobler strain
    My present Emperess does claim:
    Heleonora first o' th' name,
Whom God grant long to reign.

The Spring

THOUGH you be absent here, I needs must say
The trees as beauteous are, the flowers as gay,
  As ever they were wont to be;
  Nay, the birds' rural music too
  Is as melodious and free,
  As if they sung to pleasure you:
I saw a rose-bud ope this morn; I'll swear
The blushing morning opened not more fair.

How could it be so fair, and you away?
How could the trees be beauteous, flowers so gay?
    Could they remember, but last year,
    How you did them, they you delight,
    The sprouting leaves which saw you here,
    And called their fellows to the sight,
Would, looking round for the same sight in vain,
Creep back into their silent barks again.

Where'er you walked trees were as reverend made,
As when of old gods dwelt in every shade.
    Is't possible they should not know,
    What loss of honour they sustain,
    That thus they smile and flourish now,
    And still their former pride retain?
Dull creatures! 'tis not without cause that she,
Who fled the god of wit, was made a tree.

In ancient times sure they much wiser were,
When they rejoiced the Thracian verse to hear;
    In vain did Nature bid them stay,
    When Orpheus had his song begun,
    They called their wondering roots away,
    And bade them silent to him run.
How would those learned trees have followed you?
You would have drawn them, and their poet too.

But who can blame them now? for, since you're gone,
They're here the only fair, and shine alone.
    You did their natural rights invade;
    Wherever you did walk or sit,
    The thickest boughs could make no shade,
    Although the Sun had granted it:
The fairest flowers could please no more, near you,
Than painted flowers, set next to them, could do.

Whene'er then you come hither, that shall be
The time, which this to others is, to me.
    The little joys which here are now,
    The name of punishments do bear;
    When by their sight they let us know
    How we deprived of greater are.
'Tis you the best of seasons with you bring;
This is for beasts, and that for men, the spring.

Cheer up, my Mates

CHEER up, my mates, the wind does fairly blow;
    Clap on more sail, and never spare;
    Farewell, all lands, for now we are
    In the wide sea of drink, and merrily we go.
Bless me, 'tis hot! another bowl of wine,
    And we shall cut the burning Line:
Hey, boys! she scuds away, and by my head I know
    We round the world are sailing now.
What dull men are those who tarry at home,
When abroad they might wantonly roam,
    And gain such experience, and spy, too,
    Such countries and wonders, as I do!
But pr'ythee, good pilot, take heed what you do,
    And fail not to touch at Peru!
    With gold there the vessel we'll store,
    And never, and never be poor,
    No, never be poor any more.

Anacreontics

(1) Drinking

THE thirsty earth soaks up the rain,
And drinks and gapes for drink again;
The plants suck in the earth, and are
With constant drinking fresh and fair;
The sea itself (which one would think
Should have but little need of drink)
Drinks ten thousand rivers up,
So fill'd that they o'erflow the cup.
The busy Sun (and one would guess
By's drunken fiery face no less)
Drinks up the sea, and when he's done,
The Moon and Stars drink up the Sun.
They drink and dance by their own light,
They drink and revel all the night.
Nothing in Nature's sober found,
But an eternal health goes round.
Fill up the bowl, then, fill it high,
Fill all the glasses there, for why
Should every creature drink but I?
Why, man of morals, tell me why?

(2) *The Epicure*

UNDERNEATH this myrtle shade,
On flowery beds supinely laid,
With odorous oils my head o'erflowing,
And around it roses growing,
What should I do but drink away
The heat and troubles of the day?
In this more than kingly state
Love himself shall on me wait.
Fill to me, Love! nay, fill it up!
And mingled cast into the cup
Wit and mirth and noble fires,
Vigorous health and gay desires.
The wheel of life no less will stay
In a smooth than rugged way:
Since it equally does flee,
Let the motion pleasant be.
Why do we precious ointments shower?—
Nobler wines why do we pour?—
Beauteous flowers why do we spread
Upon the monuments of the dead?
Nothing they but dust can show,
Or bones that hasten to be so.
Crown me with roses whilst I live,
Now your wines and ointments give.
After death I nothing crave,
Let me alive my pleasures have:
All are Stoics in the grave.

(3) *The Swallow*

FOOLISH prater, what dost thou
So early at my window do
With thy tuneless serenade?
Well 't had been had Tereus made
Thee as dumb as Philomel;
There his knife had done but well.
In thy undiscovered nest
Thou dost all the winter rest,
And dreamest o'er thy summer joys
Free from the stormy season's noise:
Free from th' ill thou'st done to me;
Who disturbs or seeks out thee?

Hadst thou all the charming notes
Of the woods' poetic throats,
All thy art could never pay
What thou'st ta'en from me away;
Cruel bird, thou'st ta'en away
A dream out of my arms to-day;
A dream that ne'er must equall'd be
By all that waking eyes may see.
Thou this damage to repair
Nothing half so sweet or fair,
Nothing half so good canst bring,
Tho' men say thou bring'st the Spring.

The Grasshopper

HAPPY insect, what can be
In happiness compared to thee?
Fed with nourishment divine,
The dewy morning's gentle wine!
Nature waits upon thee still,
And thy verdant cup does fill;
'Tis fill'd wherever thou dost tread,
Nature self's thy Ganymede.
Thou dost drink, and dance, and sing;
Happier than the happiest king!
All the fields, which thou dost see,
All the plants belong to thee,
All that summer hours produce,
Fertile made with early juice—
Man for thee doth sow and plough;
Farmer he, and landlord thou!—
Thou dost innocently enjoy;
Nor does thy luxury destroy;
The shepherd gladly heareth thee,
More harmonious than he.
Thee country minds with gladness hear,
Prophet of the ripened year!
Thee Phoebus loves, and does inspire;
Phoebus is himself thy sire.
To thee of all things upon earth,
Life is no longer than thy mirth.
Happy insect, happy thou,
Dost neither age nor winter know.

But when thou'st drunk, and danc'd, and sung
Thy fill, thy flow'ry leaves among,
  (Voluptuous and wise withal,
  Epicurean animal!)
Sated with thy summer feast,
Thou retir'st to endless rest.

To His Mistress

TYRIAN dye why do you wear,
You whose cheeks best scarlet are?
    Why do you fondly pin
    Pure linens o'er your skin,
    Your skin that's whiter far—
Casting a dusky cloud before a star?

Why bears your neck a golden chain?
Did Nature make your hair in vain,
    Of gold most pure and fine?
    With gems why do you shine?
    They, neighbours to your eyes,
Show but like Phosphor when the Sun doth rise.

I would have all my mistress' parts
Owe more to Nature than to arts;
    I would not woo the dress,
    Or one whose nights give less
    Contentment than the day;
She's fair whose beauty only makes her gay.

For 'tis not buildings make a court
Or pomp, but 'tis the King's resort:
    If Jupiter down pour
    Himself, and in a shower
    Hide such bright majesty
Less than a golden one it cannot be.

Music

AWAKE, awake, my Lyre!
And tell thy silent master's humble tale
    In sounds that may prevail;
    Sounds that gentle thoughts inspire:

Though so exalted she
And I so lowly be,
Tell her, such different notes make all thy harmony.

Hark! how the strings awake:
And, though the moving hand approach not near,
Themselves with awful fear
A kind of numerous trembling make.
Now all thy forces try;
Now all thy charms apply;
Revenge upon her ear the conquests of her eye.

Weak Lyre! thy virtue sure
Is useless here, since thou art only found
To cure, but not to wound,
And she to wound, but not to cure.
Too weak too wilt thou prove
My passion to remove;
Physic to other ills, thou'rt nourishment to love.

Sleep, sleep again, my Lyre!
For thou canst never tell my humble tale
In sounds that will prevail,
Nor gentle thoughts in her inspire;
All thy vain mirth lay by,
Bid thy strings silent lie,
Sleep, sleep again, my Lyre, and let thy master die.

Hymn to Light

FIRST born of chaos, who so fair didst come
From the old negro's darksome womb!
Which when it saw the lovely child,
The melancholy mass put on kind looks and smiled.

Thou tide of glory which no rest dost know,
But ever ebb, and ever flow!
Thou golden shower of a true Jove!
Who dost in thee descend, and heaven to earth make love!

Hail, active nature's watchful life and health!
Her joy, her ornament, and wealth!
Hail to thy husband Heat, and thee!
Thou the world's beauteous bride, and lusty bridegroom he!

Say from what golden quivers of the sky
    Do all thy wingèd arrows fly?
    Swiftness and power by birth are thine:
From thy great sire they came, thy sire the word divine.

'Tis, I believe, this archery to show,
    That so much cost in colours thou,
    And skill in painting dost bestow,
Upon thy ancient arms, the gaudy heavenly bow.

Swift as light thoughts their empty carriere run,
    Thy race is finished, when begun,
    Let a post-angel start with thee,
And thou the goal of earth shalt reach as soon as he:

Thou in the moon's bright chariot proud and gay,
    Dost thy bright wood of stars survey;
    And all the year dost with thee bring
Of thousand flowery lights thine own nocturnal spring.

Thou Scythian-like dost round thy lands above
    The sun's gilt tent for ever move,
    And still as thou in pomp dost go
The shining pageants of the world attend thy show.

Nor amidst all these triumphs dost thou scorn
    The humble glow-worms to adorn,
    And with those living spangles gild,
O greatness without pride! the bushes of the field.

Night, and her ugly subjects thou dost fright,
    And sleep, the lazy owl of light;
    Ashamed and fearful to appear
They screen their horrid shapes with the black hemisphere.

With them there hastes, and wildly takes the alarm
    Of painted dreams, a busy swarm,
    At the first opening of thine eye,
The various clusters break, the antic atoms fly.

The guilty serpents, and obscener beasts,
    Creep conscious to their secret rests:
    Nature to thee does reverence pay,
Ill omens, and ill sights removes out of thy way.

carriere] career, course

At thy appearance, grief itself is said
    To shake his wings and rouse his head.
    And cloudy care has often took
A gentle beamy smile reflected from thy look.

At thy appearance, fear itself grows bold;
    Thy sunshine melts away his cold.
    Encouraged at the sight of thee,
To the cheek colour comes, and firmness to the knee.

Even lust, the master of a hardened face,
    Blushes if thou beest in the place,
    To darkness' curtain he retires,
In sympathizing night he rolls his smoky fires.

When goddess, thou liftst up thy wakened head,
    Out of the morning's purple bed,
    Thy choir of birds about thee play,
And all the joyful world salutes the rising day.

The ghosts, and monster spirits, that did presume
    A body's privilege to assume,
    Vanish again invisibly,
And bodies gain again their visibility.

All the world's bravery that delights our eyes
    Is but thy several liveries,
    Thou the rich day on them bestowest,
Thy nimble pencil paints this landscape as thou goest.

A crimson garment in the rose thou wear'st;
    A crown of studded gold thou bear'st,
    The virgin lillies in their white,
Are clad but with the lawns of almost naked light.

The violet, spring's little infant, stands,
    Girt in thy purple swaddling-bands:
    On the fair tulip thou dost dote;
Thou cloth'st it in a gay and parti–coloured coat.

With flame condensed thou dost the jewels fix,
    And solid colours in it mix:
    Flora herself envies to see
Flowers fairer than her own, and durable as she.

Ah, goddess! would thou could'st thy hand with-hold,
    And be less liberal to gold;
    Didst thou less value to it give,
Of how much care, alas, might'st thou poor man relieve!

To me the sun is more delightful far,
    And all fair days much fairer are.
    But few, ah wondrous few there be,
Who do not gold prefer, O goddess, even to thee.

Through the soft way of heaven, and air, and sea,
    Which open all their pores to thee;
    Like a clear river thou dost glide,
And with thy living stream through the close channels slide.

But where firm bodies thy free course oppose,
    Gently thy source the land o'erflows;
    Takes there possession, and does make
Of colours mingled Light, a thick and standing lake.

But the vast ocean of unbounded day
    In the empyræan heaven does stay.
    Thy rivers, lakes, and springs below
From thence took first their rise, thither at last must flow.

The Wish

  WELL then; I now do plainly see
This busy world and I shall ne'er agree.
The very honey of all earthly joy
Does of all meats the soonest cloy;
    And they, methinks, deserve my pity
Who for it can endure the stings,
The crowd and buzz and murmurings,
    Of this great hive, the city.

  Ah yet, ere I descend to th' grave
May I a small house and large garden have;
And a few friends, and many books, both true,
Both wise, and both delightful too!
    And since love ne'er will from me flee,
A mistress moderately fair,
And good as guardian-angels are,
    Only beloved, and loving me.

O fountains! when in you shall I
Myself, eased of unpeaceful thoughts, espy?
O fields! O woods! when, when shall I be made
The happy tenant of your shade?
  Here's the spring-head of pleasure's flood:
Here's wealthy Nature's treasury,
Where all the riches lie that she
  Has coin'd and stamped for good.

Pride and ambition here
Only in far-fetched metaphors appear;
Here nought but winds can hurtful murmurs scatter,
And nought but Echo flatter.
  The gods, when they descended, hither
From heaven did always choose their way:
And therefore we may boldly say
  That 'tis the way too thither.

How happy here should I
And one dear She live, and embracing die!
She who is all the world, and can exclude
In deserts solitude.
  I should have then this only fear:
Lest men, when they my pleasures see,
Should hither throng to live like me,
  And so make a city here.

from *On the Death of Mr. William Harvey*

IT was a dismal and a fearful night:
  Scarce could the Morn drive on th' unwilling light,
When sleep, death's image, left my troubled breast
  By something liker death possessed.
My eyes with tears did uncommanded flow,
  And on my soul hung the dull weight
  Of some intolerable fate.
What bell was that? Ah me! too much I know!

My sweet companion and my gentle peer,
Why hast thou left me thus unkindly here,
Thy end for ever and my life to moan?
  O, thou hast left me all alone!

Thy soul and body, when death's agony
    Besieged around thy noble heart,
    Did not with more reluctance part
Than I, my dearest friend, do part from thee.

My dearest friend, would I had died for thee!
Life and this world henceforth will tedious be:
Nor shall I know hereafter what to do
    If once my griefs prove tedious too.
Silent and sad I walk about all day,
    As sullen ghosts stalk speechless by
    Where their hid treasures lie;
Alas! my treasure's gone, why do I stay?

He was my friend, the truest friend on earth;
A strong and mighty influence joined our birth.
Nor did we envy the most sounding name
    By friendship given of old to fame.
None but his brethren he, and sisters knew
    Whom the kind youth preferred to me;
    And even in that we did agree,
For much above myself I loved them too.

Say, for you saw us, ye immortal lights,
How oft unwearied have we spent the nights,
Till the Ledæan stars, so famed for love,
    Wonder'd at us from above!
We spent them not in toys, in lusts, or wine;
    But search of deep philosophy,
    Wit, eloquence, and poetry—
Arts which I loved, for they, my friend, were thine.

Ye fields of Cambridge, our dear Cambridge, say,
Have ye not seen us walking every day?
Was there a tree about which did not know
    The love betwixt us two?
Henceforth, ye gentle trees, for ever fade;
    Or your sad branches thicker join
    And into darksome shades combine,
Dark as the grave wherein my friend is laid! . . .

Large was his soul: as large a soul as e'er
Submitted to inform a body here;
High as the place 'twas shortly in heaven to have,
    But low and humble as his grave.

So high that all the virtues there did come,
    As to their chiefest seat
    Conspicuous and great;
So low, that for me too it made a room. . . .

Knowledge he only sought, and so soon caught
As if for him knowledge had rather sought;
Nor did more learning ever crowded lie
    In such a short mortality.
Whene'er the skilful youth discoursed or writ,
    Still did the notions throng
    About his eloquent tongue;
Nor could his ink flow faster than his wit.

So strong a wit did nature to him frame
As all things but his judgment overcame;
His judgment like the heavenly moon did show,
    Tempering that mighty sea below.
Oh had he lived in learning's world, what bound
    Would have been able to control
    His over-powering soul?
We have lost in him arts that not yet are found.

His mirth was the pure spirits of various wit,
Yet never did his God or friends forget;
And when deep talk and wisdom came in view,
    Retired, and gave to them their due.
For the rich help of books he always took,
    Though his own searching mind before
    Was so with notions written o'er,
As if wise Nature had made that her book. . . .

With as much zeal, devotion, piety,
He always lived, as other saints do die.
Still with his soul severe account he kept,
    Weeping all debts out ere he slept.
Then down in peace and innocence he lay,
    Like the sun's laborious light,
    Which still in water sets at night,
Unsullied with his journey of the day. . . .

But happy thou, ta'en from this frantic age,
Where ignorance and hypocrisy does rage!
A fitter time for heaven no soul e'er chose—
    The place now only free from those.

There 'mong the blest thou dost forever shine;
  And wheresoe'er thou cast'st thy view
  Upon that white and radiant crew,
See'st not a soul clothed with more light than thine.

On Solitude

HAIL, old patrician trees, so great and good!
  Hail, ye plebeian underwood!
  Where the poetic birds rejoice,
And for their quiet nests and plenteous food,
  Pay with their grateful voice.

Hail, the poor muse's richest manor seat!
  Ye country houses and retreat,
  Which all the happy gods so love,
That for you oft they quit their bright and great
  Metropolis above.

Here nature does a house for me erect,
  Nature the wisest architect,
  Who those fond artists does despise
That can the fair and living trees neglect,
  Yet the dead timber prize.

Here let me careless and unthoughtful lying,
  Hear the soft winds above me flying
  With all their wanton boughs dispute,
And the more tuneful birds to both replying,
  Nor be myself too mute.

A silver stream shall roll his waters near,
  Gilt with the sunbeams here and there,
  On whose enamelled bank I'll walk,
And see how prettily they smile, and hear
  How prettily they talk.

Ah wretched, and too solitary he
  Who loves not his own company!
  He'll feel the weight of 't many a day
Unless he call in sin or vanity
  To help to bear 't away.

O Solitude, first state of human-kind!
  Which blest remain'd till man did find
  Even his own helper's company.
As soon as two (alas!) together joined,
  The serpent made up three.

The god himself, through countless ages thee
  His sole companion chose to be,
  Thee, sacred Solitude alone,
Before the branchy head of number's tree
  Sprang from the trunk of one.

Thou (though men think thine an unactive part)
  Dost break and tame th' unruly heart,
  Which else would know no settled pace,
Making it more well manag'd by thy art
  With swiftness and with grace.

Thou the faint beams of reason's scattered light,
  Dost like a burning-glass unite,
  Dost multiply the feeble heat,
And fortify the strength, till thou dost bright
  And noble fires beget.

Whilst this hard truth I teach, methinks, I see
  The monster London laugh at me,
  I should at thee too, foolish city,
If it were fit to laugh at misery,
  But thy estate I pity.

Let but thy wicked men from out thee go,
  And all the fools that crowd thee so,
  Even thou who dost thy millions boast,
A village less than Islington wilt grow,
  A solitude almost.

Ode to Mr. Hobbes

I

VAST bodies of philosophy
  I oft have seen, and read,
  But all are bodies dead,
Or bodies by art fashioned;

I never yet the living soul could see,
But in thy books and thee.
'Tis only God can know
Whether the fair idea thou dost show
Agree entirely with his own or no.
This I dare boldly tell,
'Tis so like truth 'twill serve our turn as well.
Just, as in nature thy proportions be,
As full of concord their variety,
As firm the parts upon their centre rest,
And all so solid are that they at least
As much as nature, emptiness detest.

2

Long did the mighty Stagirite retain
The universal intellectual reign,
Saw his own country's short-lived leopard slain;
The stronger Roman-eagle did out-fly,
Oftener renewed his age, and saw that die.
Mecha itself, in spite of Mahumet possessed,
And chased by a wild deluge from the East,
His monarchy new planted in the West.
But as in time each great imperial race
Degenerates, and gives some new one place:
So did this noble empire wast,
Sunk by degrees from glories past,
And in the school-men's hands it perished quite at last.
Then nought but words it grew,
And those all barbarous too.
It perished, and it vanished there,
The life and soul breathed out, became but empty air.

3

The fields which answered well the ancients' plow,
Spent and out-worn return no harvest now,
In barren age wild and unglorious lie,
And boast of past fertility,
The poor relief of present poverty.
Food and fruit we now must want
Unless new lands we plant.
We break up tombs with sacrilegious hands;
Old Rubbish we remove;
To walk in ruins, like vain ghosts, we love,
And with fond divining wands

We search among the dead
For treasures buried,
Whilst still the liberal earth does hold
So many virgin mines of undiscovered gold.

4

The Baltic, Euxin, and the Caspian,
And slender-limbed Mediterranean,
Seem narrow creeks to thee, and only fit
For the poor wretched fisher-boats of wit.
Thy nobler vessel the vast ocean tries,
And nothing sees but seas and skies,
Till unknown regions it descries,
Thou great Columbus of the golden lands of new philosophies.
Thy task was harder much than his,
Not only found out first by thee,
And rudely left to future industry,
But thy eloquence and thy wit,
Has planted, peopled, built, and civilized it.

5

I little thought before,
(Nor being my own self so poor
Could comprehend so vast a store)
That all the wardrobe of rich eloquence,
Could have afforded half enough,
Of bright, of new, and lasting stuff,
To clothe the mighty limbs of thy gigantic sense.
Thy solid reason like the shield from heaven
To the Trojan hero given,
Too strong to take a mark from any mortal dart,
Yet shines with gold and gems in every part,
And wonders on it graved by the learn'd hand of art,
A shield that gives delight
Even to the enemy's sight,
Than when they're sure to lose the combat by't.

6

Nor can the snow which now cold age does shed
Upon thy reverend head,
Quench or allay the noble fires within,
But all which thou hast bin,
And all that youth can be thou'rt yet,
So fully still dost thou

Enjoy the manhood, and the bloom of wit,
And all the natural heat, but not the fever too.
So contraries on Ætna's top conspire,
Here hoary frosts, and by them breaks out fire.
A secure peace the faithful neighbors keep,
Th' emboldened snow next to the flame does sleep.
   And if we weigh, like thee,
   Nature, and causes, we shall see
   That thus it needs must be,
To things immortal time can do no wrong,
And that which never is to die, for ever must be young.

Ode to Wit

TELL me, O tell, what kind of thing is Wit,
   Thou who master art of it.
For the first matter loves variety less;
Less women love't, either in love or dress.
   A thousand different shapes it bears,
   Comely in thousand shapes appears.
Yonder we saw it plain; and here 'tis now,
Like spirits in a place, we know not how.

London that vents of false ware so much store,
   In no ware deceives us more.
For men led by the colour, and the shape,
Like Zeuxes' birds fly to the painted grape;
   Some things do through our judgment pass
   As through a multiplying glass.
And sometimes, if the object be too far,
We take a falling meteor for a star.

Hence 'tis a wit that greatest word of fame
   Grows such a common name.
And wits by our creation they become,
Just so, as tit'lar bishops made at Rome.
   'Tis not a tale, 'tis not a jest
   Admir'd with laughter at a feast,
Nor florid talk which can that title gain;
The proofs of wit for ever must remain.

'Tis not to force some lifeless verses meet
    With their five gouty feet.
All ev'ry where, like man's, must be the soul,
And reason the inferior powers control.
    Such were the numbers which could call
    The stones into the Theban wall.
Such miracles are ceased; and now we see
No towns or houses rais'd by poetry.

Yet 'tis not to adorn, and gild each part;
    That shows more cost, than art.
Jewels at nose and lips but ill appear;
Rather than all things wit, let none be there.
    Several lights will not be seen,
    If there be nothing else between.
Men doubt, because they stand so thick i'th' sky,
If those be stars which paint the galaxy.

'Tis not when two like words make up one noise;
    Jests for Dutch men, and English boys.
In which who finds out wit, the same may see
In an'grams and acrostics poetry.
    Much less can that have any place
    At which a virgin hides her face,
Such dross the fire must purge away; 'tis just
The author blush, there where the reader must.

'Tis not such lines as almost crack the stage
    When Bajazet begins to rage.
Nor a tall metaphor in the bombast way,
Nor the dry chips of short lung'd Seneca.
    Nor upon all things to obtrude,
    And force some odd similitude.
What is it then, which like the power divine
We only can by negatives define?

In a true piece of wit all things must be,
    Yet all things there agree.
As in the ark, join'd without force or strife,
All creatures dwelt; all creatures that had life.
    Or as the primitive forms of all
    (If we compare great things with small)
Which without discord or confusion lie,
In that strange mirror of the Deity.

But love that moulds one man up out of two,
  Makes me forget and injure you.
I took you for my self sure when I thought
That you in any thing were to be taught.
    Correct my error with thy pen;
    And if any ask me then,
What thing right wit, and height of genius is,
I'll only shew your lines, and say, 'tis this.

ANDREW MARVELL
1621–1678

Horatian Ode upon Cromwell's Return from Ireland

THE forward youth that would appear
Must now forsake his Muses dear,
    Nor in the shadows sing
    His numbers languishing.
'Tis time to leave the books in dust,
And oil the unuséd armour's rust:
    Removing from the wall
    The corslet of the hall.
So restless Cromwell could not cease
In the inglorious arts of peace,
    But through adventurous war
    Urgéd his active star.
And, like the three-forked lightning, first
Breaking the clouds where it was nurst,
    Did thorough his own side
    His fiery way divide.
For 'tis all one to courage high
The emulous or enemy;
    And with such to enclose
    Is more than to oppose.
Then burning through the air he went
And palaces and temples rent:
    And Caesar's head at last
    Did through his laurels blast.

HORATIAN ODE: thorough] through

'Tis madness to resist or blame
The face of angry heaven's flame:
    And, if we would speak true,
    Much to the man is due,
Who, from his private gardens where
He lived reservèd and austere,
    As if his highest plot
    To plant the bergamot,
Could by industrious valour climb
To ruin the great work of Time,
    And cast the kingdom old
    Into another mould.
Though Justice against Fate complain,
And plead the ancient rights in vain:
    But those do hold or break
    As men are strong or weak.
Nature that hateth emptiness,
Allows of penetration less:
    And therefore must make room
    Where greater spirits come.
What field of all the Civil Wars
Where his were not the deepest scars?
    And Hampton shows what part
    He had of wiser art,
Where, twining subtle fears with hope,
He wove a net of such a scope,
    That Charles himself might chase
    To Carisbrook's narrow case:
That thence the royal actor borne
The tragic scaffold might adorn:
    While round the armèd bands
    Did clap their bloody hands.
He nothing common did or mean
Upon that memorable scene:
    But with his keener eye
    The axe's edge did try.
Nor called the gods with vulgar spite
To vindicate his helpless right,
    But bowed his comely head,
    Down as upon a bed.
This was that memorable hour
Which first assured the forcèd power.
    So when they did design
    The Capitol's first line,

A bleeding head where they begun,
Did fright the architects to run;
    And yet in that the State
    Foresaw its happy fate.
And now the Irish are ashamed
To see themselves in one year tamed:
    So much one man can do,
    That does both act and know.
They can affirm his praises best,
And have, though overcome, confest
    How good he is, how just,
    And fit for highest trust:
Not yet grown stiffer with command,
But still in the Republic's hand:
    How fit he is to sway
    That can so well obey.
He to the Commons' feet presents
A kingdom for his first year's rents;
    And, what he may, forbears
    His fame to make it theirs:
And has his sword and spoils ungirt,
To lay them at the public's skirt.
    So when the falcon high
    Falls heavy from the sky,
She, having killed, no more does search,
But on the next green bough to perch;
    Where, when he first does lure,
    The falconer has her sure.
What may not then our isle presume
While victory his crest does plume!
    What may not others fear
    If thus he crowns each year!
A Caesar he ere long to Gaul,
To Italy an Hannibal,
    And to all states not free
    Shall climacteric be.
The Pict no shelter now shall find
Within his parti-coloured mind;
    But from this valour sad
    Shrink underneath the plaid:
Happy if in the tufted brake
The English hunter him mistake;
    Nor lay his hounds in near
    The Caledonian deer.

ANDREW MARVELL

But thou, the war's and fortune's son,
March indefatigably on;
        And for the last effect
        Still keep the sword erect:
Besides the force it has to fright
The spirits of the shady night,
        The same arts that did gain
        A power must it maintain.

To His Coy Mistress

HAD we but world enough, and time,
This coyness, Lady, were no crime.
We would sit down, and think which way
To walk, and pass our long love's day.
Thou by the Indian Ganges' side
Shouldst rubies find: I by the tide
Of Humber would complain. I would
Love you ten years before the Flood:
And you should, if you please, refuse
Till the conversion of the Jews.
My vegetable love should grow
Vaster than empires, and more slow.
An hundred years should go to praise
Thine eyes, and on thy forehead gaze.
Two hundred to adore each breast:
But thirty thousand to the rest.
An age at least to every part,
And the last age should show your heart.
For, Lady, you deserve this state;
Nor would I love at lower rate.
    But at my back I always hear
Time's wingèd chariot hurrying near:
And yonder all before us lie
Deserts of vast eternity.
Thy beauty shall no more be found;
Nor, in thy marble vault, shall sound
My echoing song: then worms shall try
That long preserved virginity:
And your quaint honour turn to dust;
And into ashes all my lust.
The grave's a fine and private place,
But none I think do there embrace.

Now therefore, while the youthful hue
Sits on thy skin like morning dew,
And while thy willing soul transpires
At every pore with instant fires,
Now let us sport us while we may;
And now, like amorous birds of prey,
Rather at once our time devour,
Than languish in his slow-chapt power.
Let us roll all our strength, and all
Our sweetness, up into one ball:
And tear our pleasures with rough strife,
Thorough the iron gates of life.
Thus, though we cannot make our sun
Stand still, yet we will make him run.

The Picture of Little T. C. in a Prospect of Flowers

SEE with what simplicity
This nymph begins her golden days!
In the green grass she loves to lie,
And there with her fair aspect tames
The wilder flowers, and gives them names:
But only with the roses plays;
And them does tell
What colour best becomes them, and what smell.

Who can foretell for what high cause
This darling of the gods was born?
Yet this is she whose chaster laws
The wanton Love shall one day fear,
And, under her command severe,
See his bow broke and ensigns torn.
Happy who can
Appease this virtuous enemy of man!

O then let me in time compound,
And parley with those conquering eyes;
Ere they have tried their force to wound,
Ere, with their glancing wheels, they drive
In triumph over hearts that strive,
And them that yield but more despise.
Let me be laid,
Where I may see thy glories from some shade.

Meantime, whilst every verdant thing
　Itself does at thy beauty charm,
　　Reform the errors of the Spring;
Make that the tulips may have share
Of sweetness, seeing they are fair;
　And roses of their thorns disarm:
　　　　　　But most procure
That violets may a longer age endure.

But O young beauty of the woods,
　Whom Nature courts with fruits and flowers,
　　Gather the flowers, but spare the buds;
Lest Flora angry at thy crime,
To kill her infants in their prime,
　Do quickly make the example yours;
　　　　　　And, ere we see,
Nip in the blossom all our hopes and thee.

Young Love

COME, little infant, love me now,
　While thine unsuspected years
Clear thine aged father's brow
　From cold jealousy and fears.

Pretty surely 'twere to see
　By young love old time beguiled:
While our sportings are as free
　As the nurses with the child.

Common beauties stay fifteen;
　Such as yours should swifter move;
Whose fair blossoms are too green
　Yet for lust, but not for love.

Love as much the snowy lamb
　Or the wanton kid does prize,
As the lusty bull or ram,
　For his morning sacrifice.

Now then love me: time may take
　Thee before thy time away:
Of this need we'll virtue make,
　And learn love before we may.

So we win of doubtful fate;
   And, if good she to us meant,
We that good shall antedate,
   Or, if ill, that ill prevent.

Thus as kingdoms frustrating
   Other titles to their crown,
In their cradle crown their king,
   So all foreign claims to drown;

So, to make all rivals vain,
   Now I crown thee with my love:
Crown me with thy love again,
   And we both shall monarchs prove.

A Dialogue between the Soul and Body

Soul

O WHO shall, from this dungeon, raise
A soul enslav'd so many ways?
With bolts of bones, that fettered stands
In feet; and manacled in hands.
Here blinded with an eye; and there
Deaf with the drumming of an ear.
A soul hung up, as 'twere, in chains
Of nerves, and arteries, and veins.
Tortured, besides each other part,
In a vain head, and double heart.

Body

O who shall me deliver whole,
From bonds of this tyrannic soul?
Which, stretched upright, impales me so,
That mine own precipice I go;
And warms and moves this needless frame:
(A fever could but do the same.)
And, wanting where its spite to try,
Has made me live to let me die.
A body that could never rest,
Since this ill spirit it possessed.

ANDREW MARVELL

Soul

What magic could me thus confine
Within another's grief to pine?
Where whatsoever it complain,
I feel, that cannot feel, the pain.
And all my care its self employs,
That to preserve, which me destroys:
Constrained not only to endure
Diseases, but, what's worse, the cure:
And ready oft the port to gain,
Am shipwrecked into health again.

Body

But physic yet could never reach
The maladies thou me dost teach;
Whom first the cramp of hope does tear:
And then the palsy shakes of fear.
The pestilence of love does heat:
Or hatred's hidden ulcer eat.
Joy's cheerful madness does perplex:
Or sorrow's other madness vex.
Which knowledge forces me to know;
And memory will not forego.
What but a soul could have the wit
To build me up for sin so fit?
So architects do square and hew,
Green trees that in the forest grew.

The Mower against Gardens

Luxurious man, to bring his vice in use,
    Did after him the world seduce:
And from the fields the flowers and plants allure,
    Where nature was most plain and pure.
He first enclosed within the gardens square
    A dead and standing pool of air:
And a more luscious earth for them did knead,
    Which stupefied them while it fed.
The pink grew then as double as his mind;
    The nutriment did change the kind.
With strange perfumes he did the roses taint,
    And flowers themselves were taught to paint.

385

The tulip, white, did for complexion seek;
  And learned to interline its cheek.
Its onion root they then so high did hold,
  That one was for a meadow sold.
Another world was search'd, through oceans new,
  To find the marvel of Peru.
And yet these rarities might be allow'd,
  To man, that sovereign thing and proud;
Had he not dealt between the bark and tree,
  Forbidden mixtures there to see.
No plant now knew the stock from which it came;
  He grafts upon the wild the tame:
That the uncertain and adulterous fruit
  Might put the palate in dispute.
His green *Seraglio* has its eunuchs too;
  Lest any tyrant him out-do,
And in the cherry he does nature vex,
  To procreate without a sex.
'Tis all enforced; the fountain and the grot;
  While the sweet fields do lie forgot:
Where willing nature does to all dispense
  A wild and fragrant innocence:
And fauns and fairies do the meadows till,
  More by their presence than their skill.
Their statues polished by some ancient hand,
  May to adorn the gardens stand:
But howsoe'er the figures do excel,
  The gods themselves with us do dwell.

HENRY VAUGHAN

1622–1695

The World

I SAW Eternity the other night
Like a great ring of pure and endless light,
  All calm, as it was bright,
And round beneath it, Time, in hours, days, years
    Driven by the spheres
Like a vast shadow moved, in which the world
    And all her train were hurl'd;

The doting Lover in his quaintest strain
                    Did there complain,
Near him, his lute, his fancy, and his flights,
                    Wit's sour delights,
With gloves, and knots the silly snares of pleasure;
                    Yet his dear treasure
All scatter'd lay, while he his eyes did pour
                    Upon a flower.

The darksome Statesman hung with weights and woe
Like a thick midnight-fog moved there so slow
                    He did not stay, nor go;
Condemning thoughts (like sad eclipses) scowl
                    Upon his soul,
And clouds of crying witnesses without
                    Pursued him with one shout.
Yet digg'd the mole, and lest his ways be found,
                    Work'd under ground,
Where he did clutch his prey, but One did see
                    That policy,
Churches and altars fed him, perjuries
                    Were gnats and flies,
It rain'd about him blood and tears, but he
                    Drank them as free.

The fearful Miser on a heap of rust
Sat pining all his life there, did scarce trust
                    His own hands with the dust,
Yet would not place one piece above, but lives
                    In fear of thieves.
Thousands there were as frantic as himself,
                    And hugg'd each one his pelf,
The downright Epicure placed heaven in sense,
                    And scorn'd pretence,
While others, slipped into a wide excess
                    Said little less;
The weaker sort, slight, trivial wares enslave
                    Who think them brave,
And poor, despisèd Truth sat counting by
                    Their victory.

Yet some, who all this while did weep and sing,
And sing, and weep, soar'd up into the ring,
                    But most would use no wing.

O fools (said I) thus to prefer dark night
      Before true light,
To live in grots, and caves, and hate the day
      Because it shows the way,
The way which from this dead and dark abode
      Leads up to GOD,
A way where you might tread the sun, and be
      More bright than he.
But as I did their madness so discuss,
      One whisper'd thus,
This ring the Bridegroom did for none provide
      But for His Bride.

The Night

THROUGH that pure virgin shrine,
  That sacred veil drawn o'er Thy glorious noon,
That men might look and live, as glow-worms shine,
      And face the moon:
  Wise Nicodemus saw such light
As made him know his GOD by night.

  Most blest believer he!
Who in that land of darkness and blind eyes
Thy long expected healing wings could see,
      When Thou didst rise,
  And what can never more be done,
Did at midnight speak with the sun.

  O who will tell me, where
He found Thee at that dead and silent hour!
What hallowed solitary ground did bear
      So rare a flower,
  Within those sacred leaves did lie
The fullness of the Deity.

  No mercy-seat of gold,
No dead and dusty cherub, nor carved stone,
But His own living works did my LORD hold
      And lodge alone;
  Where trees and herbs did watch and peep
And wonder, while the Jews did sleep.

Dear night! this world's defeat;
The stop to busy fools; care's check and curb;
The day of spirits; my soul's calm retreat
    Which none disturb!
  CHRIST'S progress, and His prayer time;
  The hours to which high heaven doth chime.

    GOD'S silent searching flight:
When my LORD'S head is filled with dew, and all
His locks are wet with the clear drops of night;
    His still, soft call;
  His knocking time; the soul's dumb watch,
  When spirits their fair kindred catch.

    Were all my loud, evil days
Calm and unhaunted as in Thy dark tent,
Whose peace but by some angel's wing or voice
    Is seldom rent;
  Then I in Heaven all the long year
  Would keep, and never wander here.

    But living where the sun
Doth all things wake, and where all mix and tire
Themselves and others, I consent and run
    To every mire,
  And by this world's ill-guiding light,
  Err more than I can do by night.

    There is in GOD (some say)
A deep, but dazzling darkness; as men here
Say it is late and dusky, because they
    See not all clear;
  O for that Night! where I in Him
  Might live invisible and dim!

Peace

  MY soul, there is a country
    Far beyond the stars
  Where stands a wingèd sentry
    All skilful in the wars,

There above noise and danger
   Sweet Peace sits crown'd with smiles,
And One born in a manger
   Commands the beauteous files.
He is thy gracious Friend,
   And (O my soul, awake!)
Did in pure love descend
   To die here for thy sake,
If thou canst get but thither,
   There grows the flower of Peace,
The Rose that cannot wither,
   Thy fortress, and thy ease;
Leave then thy foolish ranges;
   For none can thee secure,
But One, who never changes,
   Thy God, thy life, thy cure.

Religion

MY God, when I walk in those groves,
And leaves thy spirit doth still fan,
I see in each shade that there grows
An angel talking with a man.

Under a juniper, some house,
Or the cool myrtle's canopy,
Others beneath an oak's green boughs,
Or at some fountain's bubbling eye;

Here Jacob dreams, and wrestles; there
Elias by a raven is fed,
Another time by th' angel, where
He brings him water with his bread;

In Abr'ham's tent the winged guests
(O how familiar then was heaven!)
Eat, drink, discourse, sit down, and rest
Until the cool, and shady even;

Nay thou thy self, my God, in fire,
Whirl-winds, and clouds, and the soft voice

PEACE: files] hosts

Speak'st there so much, that I admire
We have no conference in these days;

Is the truce broke? or 'cause we have
A mediator now with thee,
Doest thou therefore old treaties waive
And by appeals from him decree?

Or is't so, as some green heads say
That now all miracles must cease?
Though thou hast promis'd they should stay
The tokens of the Church, and peace;

No, no; religion is a spring
That from some secret, golden mine
Derives her birth, and thence doth bring
Cordials in every drop, and wine;

But in her long, and hidden course
Passing through the Earth's dark veins,
Grows still from better unto worse,
And both her taste, and colour stains,

The drilling on, learns to increase
False echoes, and confused sounds,
And unawares doth often seize
On veins of sulphur under ground;

So poison'd, breaks forth in some clime,
And at first sight doth many please,
But drunk, is puddle, or mere slime
And 'stead of physic, a disease;

Just such a tainted sink we have
Like that Samaritan's dead well,
Nor must we for the kernel crave
Because most voices like the shell.

Heal then these waters, Lord; or bring thy flock,
Since these are troubled, to the springing rock,
Look down, great master of the feast; O shine,
And turn once more our water into wine!

The Water-fall

WITH what deep murmurs through time's silent stealth
Doth thy transparent, cool and watery wealth
   Here flowing fall,
   And chide, and call,
As if his liquid, loose retinue stayed
Ling'ring, and were of this steep place afraid,
   The common pass
   Where, clear as glass,
   All must descend
   Not to an end:
But quick'ned by this deep and rocky grave,
Rise to a longer course more bright and brave.

  Dear stream! dear bank, where often I
  Have sat, and pleas'd my pensive eye,
  Why, since each drop of thy quick store
  Runs thither, whence it flow'd before,
  Should poor souls fear a shade or night,
  Who came (sure) from a sea of light?
  Or since those drops are all sent back
  So sure to thee, that none doth lack,
  Why should frail flesh doubt any more
  That what God takes, he'll not restore?
  O useful element and clear!
  My sacred wash and cleanser here,
  My first consigner unto those
  Fountains of life, where the Lamb goes!
  What sublime truths, and wholesome themes,
  Lodge in thy mystical, deep streams!
  Such as dull man can never find
  Unless that Spirit lead his mind,
  Which first upon thy face did move,
  And hatch'd all with his quick'ning love.
  As this loud brook's incessant fall
  In streaming rings restagnates all,
  Which reach by course the bank, and then
  Are no more seen, just so pass men.
  O my invisible estate,
  My glorious liberty, still late!
  Thou art the channel my soul seeks,
  Not this with cataracts and creeks.

Anguish

MY God and King! to thee
    I bow my knee,
I bow my troubled soul, and greet
With my foul heart thy holy feet.
Cast it, or tread it! It shall do
Even what thou wilt, and praise thee too.

My God, could I weep blood,
    Gladly I would;
Or if thou wilt give me that art,
Which through the eyes pours out the heart,
I will exhaust it all, and make
My self all tears, a weeping lake.

O! 'tis an easy thing
    To write and sing;
But to write true, unfeigned verse
Is very hard! O God, disperse
These weights, and give my spirit leave
To act as well as to conceive!

O my God, hear my cry;
    Or let me die!—

ANONYMOUS

BALLADS, SONGS, AND CAROLS

Sir Patrick Spens

THE king sits in Dunfermline toun,
    Drinking the blude-red wine;
'Oh whare will I get gude sailor,
    To sail this ship o' mine?'

Up and spake an eldern knight
    Sat at the king's right knee;
'Sir Patrick Spens is the best sailor,
    That ever sail'd the sea.'

ANONYMOUS

The king has written a braid letter,
  And sign'd it wi' his hand,
And sent it to Sir Patrick Spens,
  Was walking on the strand.

'To Noroway, to Noroway,
  To Noroway o'er the faem;
The king's daughter of Noroway,
  'Tis thou maun bring her hame.'

The first line that Sir Patrick read,
  A loud laugh laughèd he;
The neist line that Sir Patrick read,
  The tear blinded his ee.

'O wha is this has done this deed,
  And tauld the king o' me,
To send us out at this time o' the year,
  To sail upon the sea?

'Be't wind, be it weet, be't hail, be it sleet,
  Our ship must sail the faem,
The king's daughter of Noroway,
  'Tis we must fetch her hame.'

They hoysed their sails on Monenday morn,
  Wi' a' the speed they may;
And they hae landed in Noroway,
  Upon a Wodensday.

They hadna been a week, a week,
  In Noroway, but twae,
When that the lords o' Noroway
  Began aloud to say,

'Ye Scottishmen spend a' our king's goud,
  And a' our queenis fee!'
'Ye lee, ye lee, ye liars loud!
  Fu' loud I hear ye lie!

'For I brought as much white monie,
  As gane my men and me,
And I brought a half-fou o' gude red goud,
  Out o'er the sea wi' me.

gane] would suffice

394

ANONYMOUS

'Make ready, make ready, my merrymen a'!
    Our gude ship sails the morn.'
'Now, ever alake, my master dear,
    I fear a deadly storm!

'I saw the new moon, late yestreen,
    Wi' the auld moon in her arm;
And if we gang to sea, master,
    I fear we'll come to harm!'

They hadna sail'd a league, a league,
    A league but barely three,
When the lift grew dark, and the wind blew loud,
    And gurly grew the sea.

The ankers brak, and the topmasts lap,
    It was sic a deadly storm;
And the waves came o'er the broken ship,
    Till a' her sides were torn.

'O where will I get a gude sailor,
    To take my helm in hand,
Till I get up to the tall topmast,
    To see if I can spy land?'

'O here am I, a sailor gude,
    To take the helm in hand,
Till you go up to the tall topmast,
    But I fear you'll ne'er spy land.'

He hadna gane a step, a step,
    A step but barely ane,
When a bout flew out of our goodly ship,
    And the salt sea it came in.

'Gae, fetch a web o' the silken claith,
    Another o' the twine,
And wap them into our ships' side,
    And let na the sea come in.'

They fetch'd a web o' the silken claith,
    Another o' the twine,

alake] alack   lift] sky   gurly] rough   lap] sprang   bout] bolt
wap] warp

395

And they wapp'd them round the gude ship's side,
　　But still the sea came in.

O laith, laith were our gude Scots lords
　　To weet their cork-heeled shoon!
But lang or a' the play was play'd,
　　They wat their hats aboon.

And mony was the feather-bed
　　That flattered on the faem;
And mony was the gude lord's son
　　That never mair cam hame.

The ladyes wrang their fingers white,
　　The maidens tore their hair,
A' for the sake of their true loves;
　　For them they'll see na mair.

O lang, lang may the ladyes sit,
　　Wi' their fans into their hand,
Before they see Sir Patrick Spens
　　Come sailing to the strand!

And lang, lang may the maidens sit,
　　Wi' the goud kaims in their hair,
A' waiting for their ain dear loves!
　　For them they'll see nae mair.

O forty miles off Aberdeen,
　　'Tis fifty fathom deep,
And there lies gude Sir Patrick Spens
　　Wi' the Scots lords at his feet.

The Wife of Usher's Well

THERE lived a wife at Usher's well,
　　And a wealthy wife was she;
She had three stout and stalwart sons,
　　And sent them o'er the sea.

SIR PATRICK SPENS: flattered] floated　　　　kaims] combs

They hadna been a week from her,
   A week but barely ane,
When word came to the carline wife
   That her three sons were gane.

They hadna been a week from her,
   A week but barely three,
When word came to the carline wife
   That her sons she'd never see.

'I wish the wind may never cease,
   Nor fashes in the flood,
Till my three sons come hame to me,
   In earthly flesh and blood!'

It fell about the Martinmas,
   When nights are lang and mirk,
The carline wife's three sons cam hame,
   And their hats were o' the birk.

It neither grew in syke nor ditch,
   Nor yet in ony sheugh;
But at the gates o' Paradise,
   That birk grew fair eneuch.

'Blow up the fire, my maidens!
   Bring water from the well!
For a' my house shall feast this night,
   Since my three sons are well.'—

And she has made to them a bed,
   She's made it large and wide;
And she's ta'en her mantle her about,
   Sat down at the bedside.

Up then crew the red red cock,
   And up and crew the gray;
The eldest to the youngest said,
   ''Tis time we were away.'

The cock he hadna craw'd but ance
   And clapp'd his wings at a',

---

ane] one   carline] aged   fashes] troubles   mirk] dark   syke] marsh
sheugh] trench, water-furrow

ANONYMOUS

When the youngest to the eldest said,
   'Brother, we must awa'.—

'The cock doth craw, the day doth daw,
   The channerin' worm doth chide;
Gin we be miss'd out o' our place,
   A sair pain we maun bide.'

'Lie still, lie still but a little wee while,
   Lie still but if we may;
Gin my mother should miss us when she wakes,
   She'll go mad ere it be day.'

'Fare ye weel, my mother dear!
   Fareweel to barn and byre!
And fare ye weel, the bonny lass,
   That kindles my mother's fire!'

Robin Hood and Alan a Dale

I

COME listen to me, you gallants so free,
   All you that love mirth for to hear,
And I will you tell of a bold outlàw,
   That lived in Nottinghamshire.

II

As Robin Hood in the forest stood,
   All under the green-wood tree,
There he was ware of a brave young man,
   As fine as fine might be.

III

The youngster was clothed in scarlet red,
   In scarlet fine and gay,
And he did frisk it over the plain,
   And chanted a roundelay.

IV

As Robin Hood next morning stood,
   Amongst the leaves so gay,

THE WIFE OF USHER'S WELL: channerin'] complaining, fretting

398

There did he espy the same young man
   Come drooping along the way.

V

The scarlet he wore the day before,
   It was clean cast away;
And every step he fetcht a sigh,
   'Alack and a well a day!'

VI

Then steppèd forth brave Little John,
   And Much the miller's son,
Which made the young man bend his bow,
   When as he saw them come.

VII

'Stand off, stand off!' the young man said,
   'What is your will with me?' —
'You must come before our master straight,
   Under yon green-wood tree.'

VIII

And when he came bold Robin before,
   Robin asked him courteously,
'O hast thou any money to spare,
   For my merry men and me?'

IX

'I have no money,' the young man said,
   'But five shillings and a ring;
And that I have kept this seven long years,
   To have it at my wedding.

X

'Yesterday I should have married a maid,
   But she from me is tane,
And chosen to be an old knight's delight,
   Whereby my poor heart is slain.'

XI

'What is thy name?' then said Robin Hood,
   'Come tell me, without any fail.' —
'By the faith of my body,' then said the young man,
   'My name it is Alan a Dale.'

399

XII

'What wilt thou give me,' said Robin Hood,
  'In ready gold or fee,
To help thee to thy true-love again,
  And deliver her unto thee?'

XIII

'I have no money,' then quoth the young man,
  'No ready gold nor fee,
But I will swear upon a book
  Thy true servant for to be.'—

XIV

'How many miles is it to thy true-love?
  Come tell me without guile.'—
'By the faith of my body,' then said the young man,
  'It is but five little mile.'

XV

Then Robin he hasted over the plain,
  He did neither stint nor lin,
Until he came unto the church
  Where Alan should keep his weddìng.

XVI

'What hast thou here?' the Bishop then said,
  'I prithee now tell unto me':
'I am a bold harper,' quoth Robin Hood,
  'And the best in the north countrey.'

XVII

'O welcome, O welcome!' the Bishop he said,
  'That musick best pleaseth me.'—
'You shall have no musick,' quoth Robin Hood,
  'Till the bride and the bridegroom I see.'

XVIII

With that came in a wealthy knight,
  Which was both grave and old,
And after him a finikin lass,
  Did shine like the glistering gold.

lin] stop

XIX

'This is no fit match,' quoth bold Robin Hood,
    'That you do seem to make here;
For since we are come into the church,
    The bride she shall choose her own dear.'

XX

Then Robin Hood put his horn to his mouth,
    And blew blasts two or three;
When four and twenty bowmen bold
    Come leaping over the lee.

XXI

And when they came into the churchyard,
    Marching all on a row,
The first man was Alan a Dale,
    To give bold Robin his bow.

XXII

'This is thy true-love,' Robin he said,
    'Young Alan, as I hear say;
And you shall be married at this same time,
    Before we depart away.'

XXIII

'That shall not be,' the Bishop he said,
    'For thy word shall not stand;
They shall be three times asked in the church,
    As the law is of our land.'

XXIV

Robin Hood pull'd off the Bishop's coat,
    And put it upon Little John;
'By the faith of my body,' then Robin said,
    'This cloth doth make thee a man.'

XXV

When Little John went into the quire,
    The people began to laugh;
He asked them seven times in the church,
    Least three times should not be enough.

XXVI

'Who gives me this maid?' said Little John;
  Quoth Robin Hood, 'That do I!
And he that takes her from Alan a Dale
  Full dearly he shall her buy.'

XXVII

And thus having ended this merry wedding,
  The bride looked like a queen,
And so they return'd to the merry green-wood,
  Amongst the leaves so green.

My Lady Greensleeves

ALAS! my love, you do me wrong
  To cast me off discourteously;
And I have lovèd you so long,
  Delighting in your company.

    Greensleeves was all my joy!
    Greensleeves was my delight!
    Greensleeves was my heart of gold!
      And who but my Lady Greensleeves!

I bought thee petticoats of the best,
  The cloth so fine as fine as might be;
I gave thee jewels for thy chest,
  And all this cost I spent on thee.
    Greensleeves, etc.

Thy smock of silk, both fair and white,
  With gold embroidered gorgeously;
Thy petticoat of sendal right:
  And these I bought thee gladly.
    Greensleeves, etc.

Thy gown was of the grassy green,
  The sleeves of satin hanging by;
Which made thee be our harvest queen:
  And yet thou wouldest not love me!
    Greensleeves, etc.

Greensleeves now farewell! adieu!
  God I pray to prosper thee!
For I am still thy lover true:
  Come once again and love me!

    Greensleeves was all my joy!
    Greensleeves was my delight!
    Greensleeves was my heart of gold!
      And who but my Lady Greensleeves!

The Babes in the Wood

I

Now ponder well, you parents dear,
  These words, which I shall write;
A doleful story you shall hear
  In time brought forth to light.
A gentleman of good account
  In Norfolk dwelt of late,
Who did in honour far surmount
  Most men of his estate.

II

Sore sick he was, and like to die,
  No help his life could save;
His wife by him as sick did lie,
  And both possessed one grave.
No love between these two was lost,
  Each was to other kind,
In love they lived, in love they died,
  And left two babes behind:

III

The one a fine and pretty boy,
  Not passing three years old;
The other a girl more young than he,
  And framed in beauty's mould.
The father left his little son,
  As plainly did appear,
When he to perfect age should come,
  Three hundred pounds a year.

IV

And to his little daughter Jane
  Five hundred pounds in gold,
To be paid down on marriage-day,
  Which might not be controlled.
But if the children chanced to die,
  Ere they to age should come,
Their uncle should possess their wealth;
  For so the will did run.

V

'Now, brother,' said the dying man,
  'Look to my children dear;
Be good unto my boy and girl,
  No friends else have they here:
To God and you I recommend
  My children dear this day;
But little while be sure we have
  Within this world to stay.

VI

'You must be father and mother both,
  And uncle all in one;
God knows what will become of them,
  When I am dead and gone.'
With that bespake their mother dear,
  'O brother kind,' quoth she,
'You are the man must bring our babes
  To wealth or misery:

VII

'And if you keep them carefully,
  Then God will you reward;
But if you otherwise should deal,
  God will your deeds regard.'
With lips as cold as any stone,
  They kissed their children small:
'God bless you both, my children dear';
  With that the tears did fall.

VIII

These speeches then their brother spake
  To this sick couple there,

'The keeping of your little ones,
   Sweet sister, do not fear;
God never prosper me nor mine,
   Nor aught else that I have,
If I do wrong your children dear,
   When you are laid in grave.'

IX

The parents being dead and gone,
   The children home he takes,
And brings them straight unto his house,
   Where much of them he makes.
He had not kept these pretty babes
   A twelvemonth and a day,
But, for their wealth, he did devise
   To make them both away.

X

He bargained with two ruffians strong,
   Which were of furious mood,
That they should take these children young,
   And slay them in a wood.
He told his wife an artful tale,
   He would the children send
To be brought up in fair Londòn
   With one that was his friend.

XI

Away then went those pretty babes,
   Rejoicing at that tide,
Rejoicing with a merry mind,
   They should on cock-horse ride.
They prate and prattle pleasantly,
   As they rode on the way,
To those that should their butchers be,
   And work their lives' decay:

XII

So that the pretty speech they had,
   Made Murder's heart relent;
And they that undertook the deed,
   Full sore did now repent.

ANONYMOUS

Yet one of them, more hard of heart,
   Did vow to do his charge,
Because the wretch, that hirèd him,
   Had paid him very large.

XIII

The other won't agree thereto,
   So here they fall to strife;
With one another they did fight,
   About the children's life:
And he that was of mildest mood,
   Did slay the other there,
Within an unfrequented wood;
   The babes did quake for fear!

XIV

He took the children by the hand,
   Tears standing in their eye,
And bade them straightway follow him,
   And look they did not cry;
And two long miles he led them on,
   While they for food complain:
'Stay here,' quoth he; 'I'll bring you bread
   When I come back again.'

XV

These pretty babes, with hand in hand,
   Went wandering up and down;
But never more could see the man
   Approaching from the town;
Their pretty lips with blackberries
   Were all besmeared and dyed,
And when they saw the darksome night,
   They sat them down and cried.

XVI

Thus wandered these poor innocents,
   Till death did end their grief,
In one another's arms they died,
   As wanting due relief:
No burial this pretty pair
   From any man receives,
Till Robin-redbreast piously
   Did cover them with leaves.

ANONYMOUS

XVII

And now the heavy wrath of God
  Upon their uncle fell;
Yea, fearful fiends did haunt his house,
  His conscience felt an hell:
His barns were fired, his goods consumed,
  His lands were barren made;
His cattle died within the field,
  And nothing with him stayed.

XVIII

And in a voyage to Portugal
  Two of his sons did die;
And to conclude, himself was brought
  To want and misery:
He pawned and mortgaged all his land
  Ere seven years came about,
And now at length this wicked act
  Did by this means come out.

XIX

The fellow, that did take in hand
  These children for to kill,
Was for a robbery judged to die,
  Such was God's blessèd will:
Who did confess the very truth
  As here hath been displayed:
The uncle having died in gaol,
  Where he for debt was laid.

XX

You that executors be made,
  And overseërs eke,
Of children that be fatherless,
  And infants mild and meek;
Take you example by this thing,
  And yield to each his right,
Lest God with such like misery
  Your wicked minds requite.

JOHN DRYDEN

1631–1700

A Song for St. Cecilia's Day

November 22, 1687

FROM harmony, from heavenly harmony
    This universal frame began;
  When Nature underneath a heap
    Of jarring atoms lay,
  And could not heave her head,
The tuneful voice was heard from high,
    Arise, ye more than dead.
Then cold and hot and moist and dry
  In order to their stations leap,
    And Music's power obey.
From harmony, from heavenly harmony
    This universal frame began:
    From harmony to harmony
Through all the compass of the notes it ran,
The diapason closing full in Man.
What passion cannot Music raise and quell?
    When Jubal struck the corded shell,
  His listening brethren stood around,
    And, wondering, on their faces fell
  To worship that celestial sound:
Less than a god they thought there could not dwell
    Within the hollow of that shell,
    That spoke so sweetly, and so well.
What passion cannot Music raise and quell?
    The trumpet's loud clangour
      Excites us to arms
    With shrill notes of anger
      And mortal alarms.
    The double double double beat
      Of the thundering drum
      Cries, Hark! the foes come;
Charge, charge, 'tis too late to retreat.
    The soft complaining flute
    In dying notes discovers
    The woes of hopeless lovers,
Whose dirge is whispered by the warbling lute.

Sharp violins proclaim
Their jealous pangs and desperation,
Fury, frantic indignation,
Depth of pains and height of passion,
For the fair, disdainful dame.

But oh! what art can teach
What human voice can reach
The sacred organ's praise?
Notes inspiring holy love,
Notes that wing their heavenly ways
To mend the choirs above.

Orpheus could lead the savage race,
And trees unrooted left their place,
Sequacious of the lyre;
But bright Cecilia raised the wonder higher:
When to her organ vocal breath was given,
An angel heard, and straight appeared
Mistaking earth for heaven.

Grand Chorus

As from the power of sacred lays
The spheres began to move,
And sung the great Creator's praise
To all the Blest above;
So, when the last and dreadful hour
This crumbling pageant shall devour,
The trumpet shall be heard on high,
The dead shall live, the living die,
And Music shall untune the sky.

To the Memory of Mr. Oldham

FAREWELL, too little and too lately known,
Whom I began to think and call my own:
For sure our souls were near allied, and thine
Cast in the same poetic mould with mine.
One common note on either lyre did strike,
And knaves and fools we both abhorred alike.
To the same goal did both our studies drive:
The last set out the soonest did arrive.

Thus Nisus fell upon the slippery place,
Whilst his young friend performed and won the race.
O early ripe! to thy abundant store
What could advancing age have added more?
It might (what nature never gives the young)
Have taught the numbers of thy native tongue.
But satire needs not those, and wit will shine
Through the harsh cadence of a rugged line.
A noble error, and but seldom made,
When poets are by too much force betrayed.
Thy generous fruits, though gathered ere their prime,
Still showed a quickness; and maturing time
But mellows what we write to the dull sweets of rhyme.
Once more, hail, and farewell! farewell, thou young,
But ah! too short, Marcellus of our tongue!
Thy brows with ivy and with laurels bound;
But fate and gloomy night encompass thee around.

Lines Printed under the Engraved Portrait of Milton

In Tonson's folio edition of the 'Paradise Lost', 1688

THREE poets, in three distant ages born,
Greece, Italy, and England did adorn.
The first in loftiness of thought surpassed,
The next in majesty, in both the last:
The force of Nature could no farther go;
To make a third she joined the former two.

Song

I

SYLVIA the fair, in the bloom of fifteen
Felt an innocent warmth, as she lay on the green;
She had heard of a pleasure, and something she guessed
By the towzing and tumbling and touching her breast:
She saw the men eager, but was at a loss,
What they meant by their sighing and kissing so close;
  By their praying and whining,
  And clasping and twining,
  And panting and wishing,
  And sighing and kissing,
  And sighing and kissing so close.

II

Ah she cried, ah for a languishing maid
In a country of Christians to die without aid!
Not a Whig, or a Tory, or trimmer at least,
Or a Protestant parson or Catholic priest,
To instruct a young virgin that is at a loss
What they meant by their sighing and kissing so close;
　　By their praying and whining,
　　And clasping and twining,
　　And panting and wishing,
　　And sighing and kissing,
　　And sighing and kissing so close.

III

Cupid in shape of a swain did appear,
He saw the sad wound, and in pity drew near,
Then show'd her his arrow, and bid her not fear,
For the pain was no more than a maiden may bear;
When the balm was infus'd, she was not at a loss
What they meant by their sighing and kissing so close;
　　By their praying and whining,
　　And clasping and twining,
　　And panting and wishing,
　　And sighing and kissing,
　　And sighing and kissing so close.

The Secular Masque

Enter JANUS.

Janus.　Chronos, Chronos, mend thy pace:
　A hundred times the rolling sun
　Around the radiant belt has run
　　In his revolving race.
　Behold, behold, the goal in sight;
　Spread thy fans, and wing thy flight.

Enter CHRONOS, *with a scythe in his hand and a great globe on his back,
which he sets down at his entrance.*

Chronos.　Weary, weary of my weight,
　Let me, let me drop my freight,

And leave the world behind.
  I could not bear,
  Another year,
The load of human-kind.

Enter MOMUS, *laughing*.

Momus. Ha! ha! ha! Ha! ha! ha! well hast thou done
    To lay down thy pack,
    And lighten thy back.
  The world was a fool, e'er since it begun,
  And since neither Janus, nor Chronos,
      nor I
    Can hinder the crimes
    Or mend the bad times,
  'Tis better to laugh than to cry.

Cho. of all 3. *'Tis better to laugh than to cry.*

Janus. Since Momus comes to laugh below,
    Old Time begin the show,
  That he may see, in every scene,
  What changes in this age have been.

Chronos. Then goddess of the silver bow begin.
[Horns, or Hunting-Music within.

Enter DIANA.

Diana. With horns and with hounds I waken the day,
    And hie to my woodland walks away:
  I tuck up my robe, and am buskined soon,
  And tie to my forehead a waxing Moon.
  I course the fleet stag, unkennel the fox,
  And chase the wild goats o'er summits of
      rocks,
  With shouting and hooting we pierce thro' the sky;
  And Echo turns hunter, and doubles the cry.

Cho. of all. *With shouting and hooting we pierce through the sky,*
  And Echo turns hunter, and doubles the cry.

Janus. Then our age was in its prime:
Chronos. Free from rage.
Diana.   And free from crime.

Momus. A very merry, dancing, drinking,
   Laughing, quaffing, and unthinking time.

Cho. of all. *Then our age was in its prime,*
   Free from rage, and free from crime,
   A very merry, dancing, drinking,
   Laughing, quaffing, and unthinking time.

                        [*Dance of* Diana's *attendants.*

                      Enter MARS.

Mars. Inspire the vocal brass, inspire;
   The world is past its infant age:
      Arms and honour,
      Arms and honour,
   Set the martial mind on fire,
   And kindle manly rage.
     Mars has looked the sky to red;
   And peace, the lazy good, is fled.
    Plenty, peace, and pleasure fly;
      The sprightly green
    In woodland-walks no more is seen;
The sprightly green has drunk the Tyrian
        dye.

Cho. of all. *Plenty, peace,* &c.

Mars. Sound the trumpet, beat the drum;
   Through all the world around,
   Sound a reveille, sound, sound,
   The Warrior God is come.

Cho. of all. *Sound the trumpet,* &c.

Momus. Thy sword within the scabbard keep,
   And let mankind agree;
Better the world were fast asleep,
   Than kept awake by thee.
The fools are only thinner,
   With all our cost and care;
But neither side a winner,
   For things are as they were.

Cho. of all. *The fools are only,* &c.

JOHN DRYDEN

Enter VENUS.

Venus. Calms appear, when storms are past;
  Love will have his hour at last:
  Nature is my kindly care;
  Mars destroys, and I repair;
  Take me, take me, while you may,
  Venus comes not ev'ry day.

Cho. of all. *Take her, take her,* &c.

Chronos. The world was then so light,
    I scarcely felt the weight;
  Joy rul'd the day, and love the night.
  But since the queen of pleasure left the ground,
      I faint, I lag,
      And feebly drag
    The pond'rous orb around.

Momus. All, all of a piece throughout:
    Pointing to Diana. Thy chase had a beast in view;
        to Mars. Thy wars brought nothing about;
        to Venus. Thy lovers were all untrue.

Janus. 'Tis well an old age is out.

Chronos. And time to begin a new.

Cho. of all. *All, all of a piece throughout:*
    Thy chase had a beast in view;
  Thy wars brought nothing about;
    Thy lovers were all untrue.
  'Tis well an old age is out,
    And time to begin a new.
        [*Dance of Huntsmen, Nymphs, Warriors, and Lovers.*

Mac Flecknoe

ALL human things are subject to decay,
And, when Fate summons, monarchs must obey:
This Flecknoe found, who, like Augustus, young
Was call'd to empire and had govern'd long:
In prose and verse was own'd, without dispute
Through all the realms of non-sense, absolute.

This aged Prince now flourishing in peace,
And blest with issue of a large increase,
Worn out with business, did at length debate
To settle the succession of the state;
And pond'ring which of all his sons was fit
To reign, and wage immortal war with wit,
Cried, 'tis resolv'd; for nature pleads that he
Should only rule, who most resembles me:
Sh—— alone my perfect image bears,
Mature in dullness from his tender years;
Sh—— alone of all my sons is he
Who stands confirm'd in full stupidity.
The rest to some faint meaning make pretence,
But Sh—— never deviates into sense.
Some beams of wit on other souls may fall,
Strike through and make a lucid interval;
But Sh——'s genuine night admits no ray,
His rising fogs prevail upon the day:
Besides, his goodly fabric fills the eye
And seems design'd for thoughtless majesty:
Thoughtless as monarch oaks that shade the plain,
And, spread in solemn state, supinely reign.
Heywood and Shirley were but types of thee,
Thou last great prophet of tautology:
Even I, a dunce of more renown than they,
Was sent before but to prepare thy way:
And coarsely clad in Norwich drugget came
To teach the nations in thy greater name.
My warbling lute, the lute I whilom strung,
When to King John of Portugal I sung,
Was but the prelude to that glorious day,
When thou on silver Thames did'st cut thy way,
With well tim'd oars before the royal barge,
Swelled with the pride of thy celestial charge;
And, big with hymn, commander of a host,
The like was ne'er in Epsom blankets tossed.
Methinks I see the new Arion sail,
The lute still trembling underneath thy nail.
At thy well sharpened thumb from shore to shore
The treble squeaks for fear, the basses roar:
Echoes from Pissing-Ally, Sh—— call,
And Sh—— they resound from A—— Hall.
About thy boat the little fishes throng,
As at the morning toast that floats along.

Sometimes, as prince of thy harmonious band,
Thou wield'st thy papers in thy threshing hand.
St. André's feet ne'er kept more equal time,
Not ev'n the feet of thy own Psyche's rhyme:
Though they in number as in sense excel,
So just, so like tautology they fell
That, pale with envy, Singleton forswore ⎫
The lute and sword which he in triumph bore, ⎬
And vow'd he ne'er would act Villerius more. ⎭
Here stopped the good old sire; and wept for joy,
In silent raptures of the hopeful boy.
All arguments, but most his plays, persuade
That for anointed dullness he was made.
   Close to the walls which fair Augusta bind,
(The fair Augusta much to fears inclin'd)
An ancient fabric raised t' inform the sight,
There stood of yore, and Barbican it hight:
A watch tower once, but now, so fate ordains,
Of all the pile an empty name remains.
From its old ruins brothel-houses rise,
Scenes of lewd loves, and of polluted joys,
Where their vast courts the mother-strumpets keep,
And, undisturb'd by watch, in silence sleep.
Near these a nursery erects its head,
Where Queens are formed, and future Heroes bred;
Where unfledged actors learn to laugh and cry, ⎫
Where infant punks their tender voices try, ⎬
And little Maximins the Gods defy. ⎭
Great Fletcher never treads in buskins here,
Nor greater Johnson dares in socks appear.
But gentle Simkin just reception finds
Amidst this monument of vanished minds;
Pure clinches, the suburbian Muse affords;
And Panton waging harmless war with words.
Here Flecknoe, as a place to fame well known,
Ambitiously design'd his Sh——'s throne.
For ancient Dekker prophesi'd long since, ⎫
That in this pile should reign a mighty prince, ⎬
Born for a scourge of wit, and flail of Sense, ⎭
To whom true dullness should some Psyches owe,
But worlds of misers from his pen should flow;
Humorists and hypocrites it should produce,
Whole Raymond families and tribes of Bruce.
   Now Empress Fame had publish'd the renown

Of Sh——'s Coronation through the town.
Rows'd by report of fame, the Nations meet,
From near Bun-Hill and distant Watling-street.
No Persian carpets spread th' imperial way,
But scatter'd limbs of mangled poets lay;
From dusty shops neglected authors come,
Martyrs of Pies and Relics of the bum.
Much Heywood, Shirley, Ogleby there lay,
But loads of Sh—— almost choked the way.
Bilk'd Stationers for Yeomen stood prepar'd
And H—— was Captain of the Guard.
The hoary Prince in majesty appear'd,
High on a throne of his own labours rear'd.
At his right hand our young Ascanius sat
Rome's other hope and pillar of the state.
His brows thick fogs, instead of glories, grace,
And lambent dullness played around his face.
As Hannibal did to the altars come,
Swore by his sire a mortal foe to Rome;
So Sh—— swore, nor should his vow be vain,
That he till death true dullness would maintain;
And, in his father's right, and realm's defence,
Ne'er to have peace with wit, nor truce with sense.
The king himself the sacred unction made,
As king by office, and as priest by trade:
In his sinister hand, instead of ball,
He placed a mighty mug of potent ale;
Love's kingdom to his right he did convey,
At once his sceptre and his rule of sway;
Whose righteous lore the prince had practis'd young
And from whose loins recorded Psyche sprung.
His temples, last, with poppies were o'er-spread,
That nodding seemed to consecrate his head:
Just at that point of time, if Fame not lie,
On his left hand twelve reverend owls did fly.
So Romulus, 'tis sung, by Tiber's brook,
Presage of sway from twice six vultures took.
Th' admiring throng loud acclamations make
And omens of his future Empire take.
The sire then shook the honours of his head,
And from his brows damps of oblivion shed
Full on the filial dullness: long he stood,
Repelling from his breast the raging God:
At length burst out in this prophetic mood:

Heavens bless my son, from Ireland let him reign
To far Barbados on the Western main;
Of his dominion may no end be known,
And greater than his father's be his throne.
Beyond love's kingdom let him stretch his pen;
He paused, and all the people cried Amen.
Then thus continued he, my son, advance
Still in new impudence, new ignorance.
Success let others teach, learn thou from me
Pangs without birth, and fruitless industry.
Let Virtuosos in five years be writ;
Yet not one thought accuse thy toil of wit.
Let gentle George in triumph tread the stage,
Make Dorimant betray, and Loveit rage;
Let Cully, Cockwood, Fopling, charm the pit,
And in their folly show the writer's wit.
Yet still thy fools shall stand in thy defence
And justify their author's want of sense.
Let 'em be all by thy own model made
Of dullness and desire no foreign aid,
That they to future ages may be known,
Not copies drawn, but issue of thy own.
Nay let thy men of wit too be the same,
All full of thee, and differing but in name;
But let no alien S—dl—y interpose
To lard with wit thy hungry Epsom prose.
And when false flowers of Rhetoric thou would'st cull,
Trust Nature, do not labour to be dull;
But write thy best, and top; and in each line
Sir Formal's oratory will be thine.
Sir Formal, though unsought, attends thy quill,
And does thy Northern Dedications fill.
Nor let false friends seduce thy mind to fame,
By arrogating Johnson's hostile name.
Let Father Flecknoe fire thy mind with praise
And Uncle Ogleby thy envy raise.
Thou art my blood, where Johnson has no part:
What share have we in Nature or in Art?
Where did his wit on learning fix a brand
And rail at arts he did not understand?
Where made he love in Prince Nicander's vein,
Or swept the dust in Psyche's humble strain?
Where sold he bargains, whip-stich, kiss my arse,
Promis'd a play and dwindled to a farce?

JOHN DRYDEN

When did his Muse from Fletcher scenes purloin,
As thou whole Eth'ridge dost transfuse to thine?
But so transfused as oils on waters flow,
His always floats above, thine sinks below.
This is thy province, this thy wondrous way,
New humours to invent for each new play:
This is that boasted bias of thy mind,
By which one way, to dullness, 'tis inclined,
Which makes thy writings lean on one side still,
And, in all changes, that way bends thy will.
Nor let thy mountain belly make pretence
Of likeness; thine's a timpany of sense.
A tun of man in thy large bulk is writ,
But sure thou 'rt but a kilderkin of wit.
Like mine thy gentle numbers feebly creep;
Thy Tragic Muse gives smiles, thy Comic sleep.
With whate'er gall thou sett'st thy self to write,
Thy inoffensive Satires never bite.
In thy felonious heart though venom lies,
It does but touch thy Irish pen, and dies.
Thy Genius calls thee not to purchase fame
In keen iambics, but mild anagram:
Leave writing plays, and choose for thy command
Some peaceful province in Acrostic Land.
There thou mayest wings display, and altars raise,
And torture one poor word ten thousand ways;
Or, if thou would'st thy diff'rent talents suit,
Set thy own songs, and sing them to thy lute.
He said, but his last words were scarcely heard,
For Bruce and Longvíl had a trap prepar'd,
And down they sent the yet declaiming bard.
Sinking he left his drugget robe behind,
Borne upwards by a subterranean wind.
The mantle fell to the young prophet's part
With double portion of his father's art.

from *Annus Mirabilis*

202

Now on their coasts our conquering navy rides,
Way-lays their merchants, and their land besets;
Each day new wealth without their care provides;
They lie asleep with prizes in their nets.

419

203

So, close behind some promontory lie
The huge leviathans t' attend their prey;
And give no chase, but swallow in the fry,
Which through their gaping jaws mistake the way.

204

Nor was this all: In ports and roads remote,
Destructive fires among whole
    fleets we send;
Triumphant flames upon the
    water float,
And out-bound ships at home
    their voyage end.

*Burning of
the fleet in
the* Vly *by*
Sir Robert
Holmes.

205

Those various squadrons, variously design'd
Each vessel freighted with a several load,
Each squadron waiting for a several wind,
All find but one, to burn them in the road.

206

Some bound for Guinea, golden sand to find,
Bore all the gauds the simple natives wear:
Some for the pride of Turkish courts design'd,
For folded turbants finest holland bear.

207

Some English wool, vex'd in a Belgian loom,
And into cloth of spungy softness made,
Did into France or colder Denmark doom,
To ruin with worse ware our staple trade.

208

Our greedy sea-men rummage every hold,
Smile on the booty of each wealthier chest;
And, as the priests who with their Gods make bold,
Take what they like, and sacrifice the rest.

209

But, ah! how unsincere are all our joys!
Which, sent from heav'n, like

lightning, make no stay:
Their palling taste the journey's
    length destroys,
Or grief, sent post, o'ertakes them on the way.

*Transit to
the Fire of
London.*

210

Swell'd with our late successes on the foe,
Which France and Holland wanted power to cross,
We urge an unseen fate to lay us low,
And feed their envious eyes with English loss.

211

Each element his dread command obeys,
Who makes or ruins with a smile or frown;
Who as by one he did our nation raise,
So now, he with another pulls us down.

212

Yet London, Empress of the Northern clime,
By an high fate thou greatly didst expire:
Great as the world's, which, at the death of time,
Must fall, and rise a nobler frame by fire.

213

As when some dire usurper Heav'n provides
To scourge his country with a lawless sway:
His birth perhaps some petty village hides,
And sets his cradle out of fortune's way.

214

Till fully ripe his swelling fate breaks out,
And hurries him to mighty mischiefs on:
His prince, surpris'd at first, no ill could doubt,
And wants the pow'r to meet it when 'tis known.

215

Such was the rise of this prodigious fire,
Which in mean buildings first obscurely bred,
From thence did soon to open streets aspire,
And straight to palaces and temples spread.

216

The diligence of trades and noiseful gain,
And luxury, more late, asleep were laid:

All was the night's, and in her silent reign
No sound the rest of nature did invade.

217

In this deep quiet, from what source unknown,
Those seeds of fire their fatal birth disclose;
And first, few scatt'ring sparks about were blown,
Big with the flames that to our ruin rose.

218

Then, in some close-pent room it crept along,
And, smould'ring as it went, in silence fed;
Till th' infant monster, with devouring strong,
Walk'd boldly upright with exalted head.

219

Now like some rich or mighty murderer,
Too great for prison, which he breaks with gold,
Who fresher for new mischiefs does appear
And dares the world to tax him with the old:

220

So scapes th' insulting fire his narrow jail
And makes small out-lets into open air:
There the fierce winds his tender force assail,
And beat him down-ward to his first repair.

221

The winds, like crafty courtesans, with-held
His flames from burning, but to blow them more:
And every fresh attempt he is repell'd
With faint denials, weaker than before.

222

And now, no longer letted of his prey,
He leaps up at it with inrag'd desire:
O'erlooks the neighbours with a wide survey,
And nods at every house his threat'ning fire.

223

The ghosts of traitors from the Bridge descend,
With bold fanatic spectres to rejoice:
About the fire into a dance they bend,
And sing their sabbath notes with feeble voice.

224

Our guardian Angel saw them where he sat
Above the palace of our slumb'ring King;
He sigh'd, abandoning his charge to fate,
And, drooping, oft looked back upon the wing.

225

At length the crackling noise and dreadful blaze
Call'd up some waking lover to the sight;
And long it was ere he the rest could raise,
Whose heavy eye-lids yet were full of night.

226

The next to danger, hot pursu'd by fate,
Half-cloth'd, half-naked, hastily retire:
And frighted mothers strike their breasts, too late,
For helpless infants left amidst the fire.

227

Their cries soon waken all the dwellers near;
Now murmuring noises rise in every street;
The more remote run stumbling with their fear,
And, in the dark, men jostle as they meet.

228

So weary bees in little cells repose;
But if night-robbers lift the well-stor'd hive,
An humming through their waxen city grows,
And out upon each other's wings they drive.

229

Now streets grow throng'd and busy as by day:
Some run for buckets to the hallow'd quire:
Some cut the pipes, and some the engines play;
And some more bold mount ladders to the fire.

230

In vain: For from the east a Belgian wind
His hostile breath through the dry rafters sent;
The Flames impell'd soon left their foes behind
And forward, with a wanton fury went.

231

A key of fire ran all along the shore,
And lighten'd all the river with a blaze:
The waken'd tides began again to roar,
And wond'ring fish in shining waters gaze.

232

Old Father Thames rais'd up his reverend head,
But fear'd the fate of Simoeis would return:
Deep in his ooze he sought his sedgy bed,
And shrunk his waters back into his urn.

233

The fire, mean time walks in a broader gross;
To either hand his wings he opens wide:
He wades the streets, and straight he reaches cross,
And plays his longing flames on th' other side.

234

At first they warm, then scorch, and then they take;
Now with long necks from side to side they feed:
At length, grown strong, their mother-fire forsake,
And a new colony of flames succeed.

235

To every nobler portion of the town
The curling billows roll their restless tide:
In parties now they straggle up and down,
As armies, unoppos'd, for prey divide.

236

One mighty squadron with a side-wind sped,
Through narrow lanes his cumber'd fire does haste:
By pow'rful charms of gold and silver led,
The Lombard bankers and the Change to waste.

237

Another backward to the Tow'r would go,
And slowly eats his way against the wind:
But the main body of the marching foe
Against th' imperial palace is design'd.

238

Now day appears, and with the day the King,
Whose early care had robb'd him of his rest:
Far off the cracks of falling houses ring,
And shrieks of subjects pierce his tender breast.

239

Near as he draws, thick harbingers of smoke
With gloomy pillars cover all the place:
Whose little intervals of night are broke
By sparks, that drive against his sacred face.

240

More than his guards his sorrows made him known,
And pious tears, which down his cheeks did show'r:
The wretched in his grief forgot their own;
(So much the pity of a king has pow'r.)

241

He wept the flames of what he lov'd so well
And what so well had merited his love:
For never prince in grace did more excel,
Or royal city more in duty strove.

242

Nor with an idle care did he behold:
(Subjects may grieve, but monarchs must redress;)
He cheers the fearful and commends the bold,
And makes despairers hope for good success.

243

Himself directs what first is to be done,
And orders all the succours which they bring:
The helpful and the good about him run,
And form an army worthy such a King.

244

He sees the dire contagion spread so fast
That where it seizes, all relief is vain
And therefore must unwillingly lay waste
That country, which would, else, the foe maintain.

245

The powder blows up all before the fire:
Th' amazed flames stand gather'd on a heap;
And from the precipice's-brink retire,
Afraid to venture on so large a leap.

246

Thus fighting fires a while themselves consume,
But straight like Turks, forc'd on to win or die,
They first lay tender bridges of their fume,
And o'er the breach in unctuous vapours fly.

247

Part stays for passage, 'till a gust of wind
Ships o'er their forces in a shining sheet:
Part, creeping under ground, their journey blind,
And, climbing from below, their fellows meet.

248

Thus to some desert plain, or old wood-side,
Dire night-hags come from far to dance their round:
And o'er broad rivers, on their fiends, they ride,
Or sweep in clouds above the blasted ground.

249

No help avails: for, Hydra-like, the fire
Lifts up his hundred heads to aim his way:
And scarce the wealthy can one half retire,
Before he rushes in to share the prey.

250

The rich grow suppliant, and poor grow proud:
Those offer mighty gain, and these ask more;
So void of pity is th' ignoble crowd,
When others' ruin may increase their store.

251

As those who live by shores with joy behold
Some wealthy vessel split or stranded nigh;
And from the rocks leap down for shipwrack'd gold,
And seek the tempest which the others fly:

252

So these but wait the owners' last despair,
And what's permitted to the flames invade:
Ev'n from their jaws they hungry morsels tear,
And, on their backs, the spoils of Vulcan lade.

253

The days were all in this lost labour spent;
And when the weary King gave place to night,
His beams he to his royal brother lent,
And so shone still in his reflective light.

254

Night came, but without darkness or repose,
A dismal picture of the gen'ral doom;
Where souls distracted when the trumpet blows,
And half unready with their bodies come.

255

Those who have homes, when home they do repair,
To a last lodging call their wand'ring friends:
Their short uneasy sleeps are broke with care,
To look how near their own destruction tends.

256

Those who have none, sit round where once it was,
And with full eyes each wonted room require:
Haunting the yet warm ashes of the place,
As murder'd men walk where they did expire.

257

Some stir up coals, and watch the Vestal fire,
Others in vain from sight of ruin run;
And, while through burning lab'rinths they retire,
With loathing eyes repeat what they would shun.

258

The most in fields like herded beasts lie down,
To dews obnoxious on the grassy floor;
And while their babes in sleep their sorrows drown,
Sad parents watch the remnants of their store.

259

While by the motion of the flames they guess
What streets are burning now, and what are near,
An infant waking to the paps would press,
And meets, instead of milk, a falling tear.

260

No thought can ease them but their sovereign's care,
Whose praise th' afflicted as their comfort sing;
Ev'n those, whom want might drive to just despair,
Think life a blessing under such a King.

261

Mean time he sadly suffers in their grief,
Out-weeps a hermit, and out-prays a saint:
All the long night he studies their relief,
How they may be suppli'd, and he may want.

262

O God, said he, thou patron of my days,   *King's*
Guide of my youth in exile and distress!   *Prayer*
Who me unfriended brought'st by wondrous ways,
The kingdom of my fathers to possess:

263

Be thou my judge, with what unwearied care
I since have labour'd for my people's good;
To bind the bruises of a civil war,
And stop the issues of their wasting blood.

264

Thou, who hast taught me to forgive the ill,
And recompense, as friends, the good misled:
If mercy be a precept of thy will,
Return that mercy on thy servant's head.

265

Or, if my heedless youth has stepped astray,
Too soon forgetful of thy gracious hand;
On me alone thy just displeasure lay,
But take thy judgments from this mourning land.

266

We all have sinn'd, and thou has laid us low,
As humble earth from whence at first we came:
Like flying shades before the clouds we show,
And shrink like parchment in consuming flame.

267

O let it be enough what thou hast done;
When spotted deaths ran arm'd thro' every street,
With poison'd darts which not the good could shun,
The speedy could out-fly, or valiant meet.

268

The living few, and frequent funerals then,
Proclaim'd thy wrath on this forsaken place:
And now those few, who are return'd again,
Thy searching judgments to their dwellings trace.

269

O pass not, Lord, an absolute decree,
Or bind thy sentence unconditional:
But in thy sentence our remorse foresee,
And, in that foresight, this thy doom recall.

270

Thy threatings, Lord, as thine thou may'st revoke:
But, if immutable and fix'd they stand,
Continue still thy self to give the stroke,
And let not foreign-foes oppress thy land.

271

Th' Eternal heard, and from the heav'nly quire
Chose out the cherub with the flaming sword:
And bade him swiftly drive th' approaching fire
From where our naval magazines were stor'd.

272

The blessed minister his wings display'd,
And like a shooting star he cleft the night;
He charg'd the flames, and those that disobey'd
He lash'd to duty with his sword of light.

273

The fugitive flames, chastis'd, went forth to prey
On pious structures, by our fathers rear'd;
By which to Heav'n they did affect the way,
Ere faith in Church-men without works was heard.

274

The wanting orphans saw with wat'ry eyes
Their founders' charity in dust laid low,
And sent to God their ever-answer'd cries,
(For he protects the poor, who made them so.)

275

Nor could thy fabric, Paul's, defend thee long,
Though thou wert sacred to thy maker's praise:
Though made immortal by a poet's song,
And poets' songs the Theban walls could raise.

276

The daring flames peep'd in, and saw from far
The awful beauties of the sacred quire:
But, since it was prophan'd by civil war,
Heav'n thought it fit to have it purg'd by fire.

277

Now down the narrow streets it swiftly came,
And, widely opening, did on both sides prey:
This benefit we sadly owe the flame,
If only ruin must enlarge our way.

278

And now four days the Sun had seen our woes;
Four nights the Moon beheld th' incessant fire;
It seem'd as if the stars more sickly rose,
And farther from the fev'rish North retire.

279

In th' Empyrean Heav'n (the bless'd abode,)
The thrones and the dominions prostrate lie.

Not daring to behold their angry God:
And an hush'd silence damps the tuneful sky.

280

At length th' Almighty cast a pitying eye,
And mercy softly touch'd his melting breast:
He saw the town's one half in rubbish lie,
And eager flames drive on to storm the rest.

281

An hollow crystal pyramid he takes,
In firmamental waters dipped above;
Of it a broad extinguisher he makes
And hoods the flames that to their quarry strove.

282

The vanquish'd fires withdraw from every place,
Or, full with feeding, sink into a sleep:
Each household genius shows again his face,
And, from the hearths, the little Lares creep.

283

Our King this more than natural change beholds;
With sober joy his heart and eyes abound:
To the All-good his lifted hands he folds,
And thanks him low on his redeemed ground.

To my Dear Friend, Mr. Congreve
On his Comedy called The Double-dealer

WELL then, the promis'd hour is come at last;
The present age of wit obscures the past:
Strong were our sires, and as they fought they writ,
Conqu'ring with force of arms and dint of wit:
Theirs was the giant race before the Flood;
And thus, when Charles return'd our Empire stood.
Like Janus, he the stubborn soil manur'd,
With rules of husbandry the rankness cur'd:

Tam'd us to manners, when the stage was rude,
And boist'rous English wit with art indu'd.
Our age was cultivated thus at length,
But what we gain'd in skill we lost in strength.
Our builders were with want of genius cursed;
The second temple was not like the first;
Till you, the best Vitruvius, come at length,
Our beauties equal, but excel our strength.
Firm Doric pillars found your solid base,
The fair Corinthian crowns the higher space;
Thus all below is strength, and all above is grace.
In easy dialogue is Fletcher's praise:
He mov'd the mind, but had no pow'r to raise.
Great Johnson did by strength of judgment please,
Yet, doubling Fletcher's force, he wants his ease.
In diff'ring talents both adorn'd their age,
One for the study, t'other for the stage.
But both to Congreve justly shall submit,
One match'd in judgment, both o'er-match'd in wit.
In him all beauties of this age we see,
Etherege his courtship, Southern's purity,
The satire, wit, and strength of manly Wycherly.
All this in blooming youth you have achiev'd;
Nor are your foil'd contemporaries griev'd;
So much the sweetness of your manners move,
We cannot envy you, because we love.
Fabius might joy in Scipio, when he saw
A beardless consul made against the law,
And join his suffrage to the votes of Rome,
Though he with Hannibal was overcome.
Thus old Romano bow'd to Raphael's fame,
And scholar to the youth he taught, became.
 O that your brows my laurel had sustain'd,
Well had I been depos'd, if you had reign'd!
The father had descended for the son,
For only you are lineal to the throne.
Thus, when the state one Edward did depose,
A greater Edward in his room arose:
But now, not I, but poetry is cursed:
For Tom the second reigns like Tom the first.
But let 'em not mistake my patron's part
Nor call his charity their own desert.
Yet this I prophesy: Thou shalt be seen,
(Tho' with some short parenthesis between:)

High on the throne of wit; and, seated there,
Nor mine (that's little) but thy laurel wear,
Thy first attempt an early promise made;
That early promise this has more than paid.
So bold, yet so judiciously you dare,
That your least praise, is to be regular.
Time, place, and action may with pains be wrought,
But genius must be born, and never can be taught.
This is your portion, this your native store:
Heav'n, that but once was prodigal before,
To Shakespeare gave as much; she cou'd not give him more. }

  Maintain your post: that's all the fame you need;
For 'tis impossible you shou'd proceed.
Already I am worn with cares and age,
And just abandoning th' ungrateful stage:
Unprofitably kept at Heav'n's expense,
I live a rent-charge on his providence:
But you, whom ev'ry Muse and Grace adorn,
Whom I foresee to better fortune born,
Be kind to my remains; and oh defend,
Against your judgment, your departed friend!
Let not th' insulting foe my fame pursue;
But shade those laurels which descend to you:
And take for tribute what these lines express;
You merit more, nor cou'd my love do less.

CHARLES SACKVILLE, EARL OF DORSET
1638–1706

Song

Written at Sea, in the First Dutch War (1665), *the night before an Engagement*

To all you ladies now at land
  We men at sea indite;
But first would have you understand
  How hard it is to write:
The Muses now, and Neptune too,
We must implore to write to you—
    With a fa, la, la, la, la.

For though the Muses should prove kind,
  And fill our empty brain,
Yet if rough Neptune rouse the wind
  To wave the azure main,
Our paper, pen, and ink, and we,
Roll up and down our ships at sea—
    With a fa, la, la, la, la.

Then if we write not by each post,
  Think not we are unkind;
Nor yet conclude our ships are lost
  By Dutchmen or by wind:
Our tears we'll send a speedier way,
The tide shall bring them twice a day—
    With a fa, la, la, la, la.

The King with wonder and surprise
  Will swear the seas grow bold,
Because the tides will higher rise
  Than e'er they did of old:
But let him know it is our tears
Bring floods of grief to Whitehall stairs—
    With a fa, la, la, la, la.

Should foggy Opdam chance to know
   Our sad and dismal story,
The Dutch would scorn so weak a foe,
   And quit their fort at Goree:
For what resistance can they find
From men who've left their hearts behind?—
     With a fa, la, la, la, la.

Let wind and weather do its worst,
   Be you to us but kind;
Let Dutchmen vapour, Spaniards curse,
   No sorrow we shall find:
'Tis then no matter how things go,
Or who's our friend, or who's our foe—
     With a fa, la, la, la, la.

To pass our tedious hours away
   We throw a merry main,
Or else at serious ombre play;
   But why should we in vain
Each other's ruin thus pursue?
We were undone when we left you—
     With a fa, la, la, la, la.

But now our fears tempestuous grow
   And cast our hopes away;
Whilst you, regardless of our woe,
   Sit careless at a play:
Perhaps permit some happier man
To kiss your hand, or flirt your fan—
     With a fa, la, la, la, la.

When any mournful tune you hear,
   That dies in every note
As if it sigh'd with each man's care
   For being so remote,
Think then how often love we've made
To you, when all those tunes were play'd—
     With a fa, la, la, la, la.

In justice you cannot refuse
   To think of our distress,
When we for hopes of honour lose
   Our certain happiness:

All those designs are but to prove
Ourselves more worthy of your love—
 With a fa, la, la, la, la.

And now we've told you all our loves,
 And likewise all our fears,
In hopes this declaration moves
 Some pity for our tears:
Let's hear of no inconstancy—
We have too much of that at sea—
 With a fa, la, la, la, la.

SIR CHARLES SEDLEY

1639–1701

Love Still has Something of the Sea

LOVE still has something of the sea
 From whence his mother rose;
No time his slaves from doubt can free,
 Nor give their thoughts repose.

They are becalmed in clearest days,
 And in rough weather tossed;
They wither under cold delays,
 Or are in tempests lost.

One while they seem to touch the port:
 Then straight into the main,
Some angry wind in cruel sport
 Their vessel drives again.

At first disdain and pride they fear,
 Which, if they chance to 'scape,
Rivals and falsehood soon appear
 In a more dreadful shape.

By such degrees to joy they come,
 And are so long withstood,
So slowly they receive the sum,
 It hardly does them good.

'Tis cruel to prolong a pain,
   And to defer a joy,
Believe me, gentle Celemene,
   Offends the wingèd boy.

An hundred thousand oaths your fears
   Perhaps would not remove,
And if I gazed a thousand years
   I could no deeper love.

APHRA BEHN

1640–1689

Song

LOVE in fantastic triumph sate
   Whilst bleeding hearts around him flowed,
For whom fresh pains he did create
   And strange tyrannic power he showed:
From thy bright eyes he took his fires,
   Which round about in sport he hurled;
But 'twas from mine he took desires
   Enough t' undo the amorous world.

From me he took his sighs and tears,
   From thee his pride and cruelty;
From me his languishments and fears,
   And every killing dart from thee.
Thus thou and I the god have armed
   And set him up a deity;
But my poor heart alone is harmed,
   Whilst thine the victor is, and free!

Song

How strongly does my passion flow;
Divided equally 'twixt two?
Damon had ne'er subdued my heart,
Had not Alexis took his part;
Nor could Alexis powerful prove,
Without my Damon's aid, to gain my love.

When my Alexis present is,
Then I for Damon sigh and mourn;
But when Alexis I do miss,
Damon gains nothing but my scorn.
But if it chance they both are by,
For both alike I languish, sigh, and die.

Curse then, thou mighty wingèd god,
This restless fever in my blood;
One golden-pointed dart take back:
But which, O Cupid, wilt thou take?
If Damon's, all my hopes are crost;
Or that of my Alexis, I am lost.

JOHN WILMOT, EARL OF ROCHESTER
1647–1680

The Bowl

VULCAN, contrive me such a cup
    As Nestor used of old;
Show all thy skill to trim it up,
    Damask it round with gold.

Make it so large that, filled with sack
    Up to the swelling brim,
Vast toasts on the delicious lake
    Like ships at sea may swim.

Engrave not battle on his cheek:
    With war I've nought to do.
I'm none of those that took Maestrich,
    Nor Yarmouth leaguer knew.

Let it no name of planets tell,
    Fixed stars or constellations,
For I am no Sir Sidrophel,
    Nor none of his relations.

But carve thereon a spreading vine,
　　Then add two lovely boys;
Their limbs in amorous folds entwine,
　　The type of future joys.

Cupid and Bacchus my saints are;
　　May drink and love still reign!
With wine I wash away my care
　　And then to love again.

Upon Nothing

NOTHING! thou elder brother even to Shade:
Thou hadst a being ere the world was made,
And well fixed, art alone of ending not afraid.

Ere Time and Place were, Time and Place were not,
When primitive Nothing Something straight begot;
Then all proceeded from the great united What.

Something, the general attribute of all,
Severed from thee, its sole original,
Into thy boundless self must undistinguished fall;

Yet Something did thy mighty power command,
And from thy fruitful Emptiness' hand
Snatched men, beasts, birds, fire, water, air, and land.

Matter, the wicked'st offspring of thy race,
By Form assisted, flew from thy embrace,
And rebel Light obscured thy reverend dusky face.

With Form and Matter, Time and Place did join;
Body, thy foe, with these did leagues combine
To spoil thy peaceful realm, and ruin all thy line;

But turncoat Time assists the foe in vain,
And bribed by thee, destroys their short-lived reign,
And to thy hungry womb drives back thy slaves again.

Though mysteries are barred from laic eyes,
And the divine alone with warrant pries
Into thy bosom, where the truth in private lies,

Yet this of thee the wise may truly say:
Thou from the virtuous nothing dost delay,
And to be part of thee the wicked wisely pray.

Great Negative, how vainly would the wise
Inquire, define, distinguish, teach, devise,
Didst thou not stand to point their blind philosophies!

Is or Is Not, the two great ends of Fate,
And True or False, the subject of debate,
That perfect or destroy the vast designs of state—

When they have racked the politican's breast,
Within thy bosom most securely rest,
And when reduced to thee, are least unsafe and best.

But Nothing, why does Something still permit
That sacred monarchs should in council sit
With persons highly thought at best for nothing fit,

While weighty Something modestly abstains
From princes' coffers, and from statesmen's brains,
And Nothing there like stately Nothing reigns?

Nothing! who dwells with fools in grave disguise,
For whom they revered shapes and forms devise,
Lawn sleeves and furs and gowns, when they like thee look wise:

French truth, Dutch prowess, British policy,
Hibernian learning, Scotch civility,
Spaniards' dispatch, Danes wit are mainly seen in thee;

The great man's gratitude to his best friend,
Kings' promises, whores' vows—towards thee they bend,
Flow swiftly into thee, and in thee ever end.

Against Constancy

TELL me no more of constancy,
    The frivolous pretense
Of cold age, narrow jealousy,
    Disease, and want of sense.

UPON NOTHING: Lawn sleeves] part of a bishop's regalia

Let duller fools, on whom kind chance
   Some easy heart has thrown,
Despairing higher to advance,
   Be kind to one alone.

Old men and weak, whose idle flame
   Their own defects discovers,
Since changing can but spread their shame,
   Ought to be constant lovers.

But we, whose hearts do justly swell
   With no vainglorious pride,
Who know how we in love excel,
   Long to be often tried.

Then bring my bath, and strew my bed,
   As each kind night returns;
I'll change a mistress till I'm dead—
   And fate change me to worms.

The Mistress

An age in her embraces passed
   Would seem a winter's day,
Where life and light with envious haste
   Are torn and snatched away.

But oh, how slowly minutes roll
   When absent from her eyes,
That feed my love, which is my soul:
   It languishes and dies.

For then no more a soul, but shade,
   It mournfully does move
And haunts my breast, by absence made
   The living tomb of love.

You wiser men, despise me not
   Whose lovesick fancy raves
On shades of souls, and heaven knows what:
   Short ages live in graves.

Whene'er those wounding eyes, so full
    Of sweetness, you did see,
Had you not been profoundly dull,
    You had gone mad like me.

Nor censure us, you who perceive
    My best beloved and me
Sigh and lament, complain and grieve:
    You think we disagree.

Alas! 'tis sacred jealousy,
    Love raised to an extreme:
The only proof 'twixt her and me
    We love, and do not dream.

Fantastic fancies fondly move
    And in frail joys believe,
Taking false pleasure for true love;
    But pain can ne'er deceive.

Kind jealous doubts, tormenting fears,
    And anxious cares, when past,
Prove our hearts' treasure fixed and dear,
    And make us blest at last.

Impromptu on Charles II

God bless our good and gracious King,
    Whose promise none relies on;
Who never said a foolish thing,
    Nor ever did a wise one.

A Song of a Young Lady to Her Ancient Lover

Ancient person, for whom I
All the flattering youth defy,
Long be it ere thou grow old,
Aching, shaking, crazy, cold;
    But still continue as thou art,
    Ancient person of my heart.

On thy withered lips and dry,
Which like barren furrows lie,
Brooding kisses I will pour
Shall thy youthful [heat] restore
(Such kind showers in autumn fall,
And a second spring recall);
   Nor from thee will ever part,
   Ancient person of my heart.

Thy nobler part, which but to name
In our sex would be counted shame,
By age's frozen grasp possessed,
From [his] ice shall be released,
And soothed by my reviving hand,
In former warmth and vigor stand.
All a lover's wish can reach
For thy joy my love shall teach,
And for thy pleasure shall improve
All that art can add to love.
   Yet still I love thee without art,
   Ancient person of my heart.

ANNE, COUNTESS OF WINCHILSEA

?1660–1720

A Nocturnal Reverie

IN such a night, when every louder wind
Is to its distant cavern safe confined;
And only gentle zephyr fans his wings,
And lonely Philomel, still waking, sings;
Or from some tree, famed for the owl's delight,
She, holloaing clear, directs the wanderers right:
In such a night, when passing clouds give place,
Or thinly veil the heaven's mysterious face;
When in some river, overhung with green,
The waving moon and trembling leaves are seen;
When freshened grass now bears itself upright,
And makes cool banks to pleasing rest invite,
Whence springs the woodbind, and the bramble-rose,
And where the sleepy cowslip sheltered grows;

Whilst now a paler hue the foxglove takes,
Yet chequers still with red the dusky brakes:
When scattered glow-worms, but in twilight fine,
Show trivial beauties watch their hour to shine;
Whilst Salisbury stands the test of every light,
In perfect charms and perfect virtue bright.
When odours, which declined repelling day,
Thro' temperate air uninterrupted stray;
When darkened groves their softest shadows wear
And falling waters we distinctly hear;
When through the gloom more venerable shows
Some ancient fabric, awful in repose,
While sunburnt hills their swarthy looks conceal,
And swelling haycocks thicken up the vale:
When the loosed horse now, as his pasture leads,
Comes slowly grazing through the adjoining meads.
Whose stealing pace, and lengthened shade we fear,
Till torn-up forage in his teeth we hear:
When nibbling sheep at large pursue their food,
And unmolested kine re-chew the cud;
When curlews cry beneath the village walls,
And to her straggling brood the partridge calls;
Their short-lived jubilee the creatures keep,
Which but endures, while tyrant man does sleep:
When a sedate content the spirit feels,
And no fierce light disturbs, whilst it reveals;
But silent musings urge the mind to seek
Something, too high for syllables to speak;
Till the free soul to a composedness charmed,
Finding the elements of rage disarmed,
O'er all below a solemn quiet grown,
Joys in the inferior world, and thinks it like her own:
In such a night let me abroad remain,
Till morning breaks, and all's confused again;
Our cares, our toils, our clamours are renewed,
Our pleasures, seldom reached, again pursued.

MATTHEW PRIOR

1664–1721

A Better Answer

DEAR Chloe, how blubbered is that pretty face!
    Thy cheek all on fire, and thy hair all uncurled:
Prithee quit this caprice; and, as old Falstaff says,
    Let us e'en talk a little like folks of this world.

How canst thou presume, thou hadst leave to destroy
    The beauties which Venus but lent to thy keeping?
Those looks were designed to inspire love and joy:
    More ordinary eyes may serve people for weeping.

To be vexed at a trifle or two that I writ,
    Your judgement at once, and my passion, you wrong:
You take that, for fact, which will scarce be found wit;
    Ods life! must one swear to the truth of a song?

What I speak, my fair Chloe, and what I write, shows
    The difference there is betwixt nature and art:
I court others in verse—but I love thee in prose;
    And they have my whimsies—but thou has my heart.

The god of us verse-men, you known, child, the sun,
    How after his journeys he sets up his rest:
If at morning o'er earth 'tis his fancy to run;
    At night he declines on his Thetis's breast.

So when I am wearied with wandering all day,
    To thee, my delight, in the evening I come:
No matter what beauties I saw in my way,
    They were but my visits, but thou art my home.

Then finish, dear Chloe, this pastoral war;
    And let us like Horace and Lydia agree;
For thou art a girl as much brighter than her,
    As he was a poet sublimer than me.

JONATHAN SWIFT

1667–1745

Stella's Birthday 1720

ALL travellers at first incline
Where'er they see the fairest sign;
And, if they find the chambers neat,
And like the liquor and the meat,
Will call again, and recommend
The Angel Inn to every friend.
What though the painting grows decayed,
The house will never lose its trade:
Nay, though the treacherous tapster, Thomas,
Hangs a new angel two doors from us,
As fine as dauber's hands can make it,
In hopes that strangers may mistake it,
We think it both a shame and sin
To quit the true old Angel Inn.

    Now this is Stella's case in fact;
An angel's face, a little cracked;
(Could poets, or could painters fix
How angels look at thirty-six:)
This drew us in at first to find
In such a form an angel's mind;
And every virtue now supplies
The fainting rays of Stella's eyes.
See at her levee crowding swains,
Whom Stella freely entertains
With breeding, humour, wit, and sense,
And puts them but to small expense;
Their mind so plentifully fills,
And makes such reasonable bills,
So little gets for what she gives,
We really wonder how she lives!
And had her stock been less, no doubt
She must have long ago run out.

    Then who can think we'll quit the place,
When Doll hangs out a newer face;
Or stop and light at Chloe's Head,
With scraps and leavings to be fed?

Then, Chloe, still go on to prate
Of thirty-six, and thirty-eight;
Pursue your trade of scandal-picking,
Your hints, that Stella is no chicken;
Your innuendoes, when you tell us
That Stella loves to talk with fellows:
And let me warn you to believe
A truth, for which your soul should grieve;
That should you live to see the day
When Stella's locks must all be grey,
When age must print a furrowed trace
On every feature of her face;
That you, and all your senseless tribe,
Could art, or time, or nature bribe
To make you look like beauty's queen,
And hold for ever at fifteen;
No bloom of youth can ever blind
The cracks and wrinkles of your mind;
All men of sense will pass your door,
And crowd to Stella's at four score.

On the Death of Dean Swift

THE time is not remote when I
Must by the course of nature die;
When, I foresee, my special friends
Will try to find their private ends:
And tho' 'tis hardly understood
Which way my death can do them good,
Yet thus methinks I hear 'em speak:
  'See how the Dean begins to break!
Poor gentleman, he droops apace!
You plainly find it in his face.
That old vertigo in his head
Will never leave him till he's dead.
Besides, his memory decays:
He recollects not what he says;
He cannot call his friends to mind,
Forgets the place where last he din'd;
Plies you with stories o'er and o'er,
He told them fifty times before.
How does he fancy we can sit
To hear his out-of-fashion wit?

But he takes up with younger folks,
Who for his wine will bear his jokes.
Faith! he must make his stories shorter,
Or change his comrades once a quarter:
In half the time he talks them round,
There must another set be found.

　'For poetry he's past his prime;
He takes an hour to find a rhyme;
His fire is out, his wit decay'd,
His Fancy sunk, his Muse a jade.
I'd have him throw away his pen;—
But there's no talking to some men . . .

　Behold the fatal day arrive!
'How is the Dean?'—'He's just alive.'
Now the departing pray'r is read:
'He hardly breathes.'—'The Dean is dead.'

　Before the passing bell begun,
The news thro' half the town is run.
'O, may we all for death prepare!
What has he left? And who's his heir?'
'I know no more than what the news is;
'Tis all bequeath'd to public uses'—
'To public use! a perfect whim!
What had the public done for him?
Mere envy, avarice, and pride:
He gave it all—but first the died.
And had the Dean, in all the nation,
No worthy friend, no poor relation?
So ready to do strangers good,
Forgetting his own flesh and blood!'

　Now Grub Street wits are all employ'd;
With elegies the town is cloy'd:
Some paragraph in ev'ry paper
To curse the Dean or bless the Drapier.

　The doctors, tender of their fame,
Wisely on me lay all the blame:
'We must confess his case was nice;
But he wou'd never take advice.
Had he been rul'd, for aught appears,
He might have liv'd these twenty years;
For when we open'd him we found
That all his vital parts were sound.

　From Dublin soon to London spread,
'Tis told at Court, 'The Dean is dead.'

Kind Lady Suffolk, in the spleen,
Runs laughing up to tell the Queen.
The Queen, so gracious, mild, and good,
Cries 'Is he gone! 'Tis time he shou'd.
He's dead, you say; why, let him rot.
I'm glad the medals were forgot.
I promis'd him, I own, but when?
I only was a princess then;
But now, as consort of a king,
You know, 'tis quite a diff'rent thing' . . .

   'Perhaps I may allow the Dean
Had too much satire in his vein,
And seem'd determin'd not to starve it,
Because no age cou'd more deserve it.
Yet malice never was his aim;
He lash'd the vice, but spar'd the name;
No individual cou'd resent
Where thousands equally were meant.
His satire points at no defect
But what all mortals may correct;
For he abhorr'd that senseless tribe
Who call it humour when they gibe.
He spar'd a hump or crooked nose,
Whose owners set up not for beaux.
True, genuine dullness mov'd his pity,
Unless it offer'd to be witty.
Those who their ignorance confest
He ne'er offended with a jest;
But laugh'd to hear an idiot quote
A verse from Horace, learn'd by rote.
Vice, if it e'er can be abash'd,
Must be or ridicul'd or lash'd.
If you resent it, who's to blame?
He neither knew you nor your name.
Shou'd vice expect t'escape rebuke
Because its owner is a duke?

   'He knew a hundred pleasant stories,
With all the turns of Whigs and Tories:
Was cheerful to his dying day;
And friends wou'd let him have his way.

   'He gave the little wealth he had
To build a house for fools and mad;
And show'd by one satiric touch,
No nation wanted it so much.

That kingdom he hath left his debtor,
I wish it soon may have a better.'
And since you dread no further lashes,
Methinks you may forgive his ashes.

A Description of the Morning

Now hardly here and there a hackney coach
Appearing, show'd the ruddy morn's approach.
Now Betty from her master's bed had flown,
And softly stole to discompose her own;
The slip-shod 'prentice from his master's door
Had par'd the dirt, and sprinkl'd round the floor.
Now Moll had whirl'd her mop with dext'rous airs,
Prepar'd to scrub the entry and the stairs.
The youth with broomy stumps began to trace
The kennel's edge, where wheels had worn the place.
The small-coal man was heard with cadence deep,
Till drown'd in shriller notes of chimney-sweep:
Duns at his Lordship's gate began to meet;
And brick-dust Moll had scream'd thro' half the street.
The turnkey now his flock returning sees,
Duly let out a-nights to steal for fees:
The watchful bailiffs take their silent stands,
And schoolboys lag with satchels in their hands.

A Description of a City Shower

Careful observers may foretell the hour,
By sure prognostics, when to dread a show'r.
While rain depends, the pensive cat gives o'er
Her frolics, and pursues her tail no more.
Returning home at night, you'll find the sink
Strike your offended sense with double stink.
If you be wise, then go not far to dine:
You'll spend in coach hire more than save in wine.
A coming show'r your shooting corns presage,
Old aches throb, your hollow tooth will rage;
Saunt'ring in coffee-house is Dullman seen;
He damns the climate, and complains of spleen.
Meanwhile the South, rising with dabbled wings,
A sable cloud athwart the welkin flings,

That swill'd more liquor than it cou'd contain,
And, like a drunkard, gives it up again.
Brisk Susan whips her linen from the rope,
While the first drizzling show'r is borne aslope;
Such is that sprinkling which some careless quean
Flirts on you from her mop, not quite so clean;
You fly, invoke the gods; then turning stop
To rail; she, singing, still whirls on her mop.
Nor yet the dust had shunn'd th' unequal strife,
But, aided by the wind, fought still for life,
And wafted with its foe by violent gust,
'Twas doubtful which was rain and which was dust.
Ah, where must needy poet seek for aid,
When dust and rain at once his coat invade?
Sole coats! where dust, cemented by the rain,
Erects the nap, and leaves a cloudy stain!
Now in contiguous drops the flood comes down,
Threat'ning with deluge this devoted town.
To shops in crowds the draggl'd females flie,
Pretend to cheapen goods, but nothing buy.
The Templar spruce, while ev'ry spout's abroach,
Stays till 'tis fair, yet seems to call a coach.
The tuck'd-up sempstress walks with hasty strides,
While streams run down her oil'd umbrella's sides.
Here various kinds, by various fortunes led,
Commence acquaintance underneath a shed.
Triumphant Tories and desponding Whigs
Forget their feuds, and join to save their wigs.
Box'd in a chair the beau impatient sits,
While spouts run clatt'ring o'er the roof by fits,
And ever and anon with frightful din
The leather sounds; he trembles from within.
So when Troy chairmen bore the wooden steed,
Pregnant with Greeks impatient to be freed,
(Those bully Greeks who, as the moderns do,
Instead of paying chairmen, ran them thro',)
Laocoon struck the outside with his spear,
And each imprison'd hero quak'd for fear.
 Now from all parts the swelling kennels flow,
And bear their trophies with them as they go:
Filth of all hues and odour, seem to tell
What street, they sail'd from, by their sight and smell.
They, as each torrent drives with rapid force,
From Smithfield to St. Pulchre's shape their course,

And in huge confluence join'd at Snowhill ridge,
Fall from the Conduit prone to Holborn Bridge.
Sweeping from butchers' stalls, dung, guts and blood,
Drown'd puppies, stinking sprats, all drench'd in mud,
Dead cats and turnip tops come tumbling down the flood.

WILLIAM CONGREVE

1670–1729

from *The Mourning Bride*

Music

MUSIC has charms to soothe a savage breast,
To soften rocks, or bend a knotted oak.
I've read that things inanimate have moved,
And, as with living souls, have been informed,
By magic numbers and persuasive sound.
What then am I? Am I more senseless grown
Than trees, or flint? O force of constant woe!
'Tis not in harmony to calm my griefs. . . .
Why do I live to say you are no more?
Why are all these things thus—Is it of force?
Is there necessity I must be miserable?
Is it of moment to the peace of Heaven
That I should be afflicted thus?—If not,
Why is it thus contrived? Why are things laid
By some unseen hand, so, as of sure consequence
They must to me bring curses, grief of heart,
The last distress of life, and sure despair?

The Aisle of a Temple

'TIS dreadful!
How reverend is the face of this tall pile,
Whose ancient pillars rear their marble heads,
To bear aloft its arched and pond'rous roof,
By its own weight made steadfast and immoveable,
Looking tranquillity! It strikes an awe
And terror on my aching sight: the tombs

And monumental caves of Death look cold,
And shoot a chillness to my trembling heart.
Give me thy hand, and let me hear thy voice;
Nay, quickly speak to me, and let me hear
Thy voice—my own affrights me with its echoes.

AMBROSE PHILIPS (Namby Pamby)

1671–1749

Wit and Wisdom

IN search of wisdom, far from wit I fly;
Wit is a harlot beauteous to the eye,
In whose bewitching arms our early time
We waste, and vigour of our youthful prime.
But when reflection comes with riper years,
And manhood with a thoughtful brow appears;
We cast the mistress off to take a wife,
And, wed to wisdom, lead a happy life.

To Miss Margaret Pulteney

DIMPLY damsel, sweetly smiling,
All caressing, none beguiling,
Bud of beauty, fairly blowing,
Every charm to nature owing,
This and that new thing admiring,
Much of this and that enquiring,
Knowledge by degrees attaining,
Day by day some virtue gaining,
Ten years hence, when I leave chiming,
Beardless poets, fondly rhyming
(Fescu'd now, perhaps, in spelling),
On thy riper beauties dwelling,
Shall accuse each killing feature
Of the cruel, charming creature,
Whom I knew complying, willing,
Tender, and averse to killing.

JOSEPH ADDISON
1672–1719

Hymn

Thanksgiving after Travel

How are Thy servants blest, O Lord!
  How sure is their defence!
Eternal wisdom is their guide,
  Their help Omnipotence.

In foreign realms, and lands remote,
  Supported by Thy care,
Through burning climes I passed unhurt,
  And breathed in tainted air.

Thy mercy sweetened every soil,
  Made every region please;
The hoary Alpine hills it warmed,
  And smoothed the Tyrrhene seas.

Think, O my soul, devoutly think,
  How, with affrighted eyes,
Thou saw'st the wide-extended deep
  In all its horrors rise!

Confusion dwelt in every face,
  And fear in every heart;
When waves on waves, and gulfs on gulfs,
  O'ercame the pilot's art.

Yet then from all my griefs, O Lord,
  Thy mercy set me free;
Whilst, in the confidence of prayer,
  My soul took hold on Thee.

For though in dreadful whirls we hung
  High on the broken wave,
I knew Thou wert not slow to hear,
  Nor impotent to save.

JOSEPH ADDISON

The storm was laid, the winds retired,
    Obedient to Thy will;
The sea that roared at Thy command,
    At Thy command was still.

In midst of dangers, fears, and death,
    Thy goodness I'll adore;
And praise Thee for Thy mercies past,
    And humbly hope for more.

My life, if Thou preserv'st my life,
    Thy sacrifice shall be;
And death, if death must be my doom,
    Shall join my soul to Thee.

ISAAC WATTS

1674–1748

Hymn

WHEN I survey the wondrous Cross
On which the Prince of glory died,
My richest gain I count but loss,
And pour contempt on all my pride.

Forbid it, Lord, that I should boast
Save in the Cross of Christ my God;
All the vain things that charm me most,
I sacrifice them to His Blood.

See from His Head, His Hands, His Feet,
Sorrow and love flow mingling down;
Did e'er such love and sorrow meet,
Or thorns compose so rich a crown!

Were the whole realm of nature mine,
That were an offering far too small;
Love so amazing, so Divine,
Demands my soul, my life, my all.

To Christ, Who won for sinners grace
By bitter grief and anguish sore,
Be praise from all the ransom'd race
For ever and for evermore.

Against Idleness and Mischief

How doth the little busy Bee
  Improve each shining Hour,
And gather Honey all the Day
  From ev'ry op'ning Flow'r!

How skilfully she builds her Cell!
  How neat she spreads the Wax!
And labours hard to store it well
  With the sweet Food she makes.

In Works of Labour or of Skill
  I would be busy too:
For *Satan* finds some Mischief still
  For idle Hands to do.

In Books, or Work, or healthful Play,
  Let my first Years be past,
That I may give for every Day
  Some good Account at last.

JOHN PHILIPS

1676–1709

from *Cyder*

Apple-Culture

WHEN swelling buds their od'rous foliage shed,
And gently harden into fruit, the wise
Spare not the little offsprings, if they grow
Redundant; but the thronging clusters thin
By kind avulsion; else, the starv'ling brood,
Void of sufficient sustenance will yield
A slender Autumn; which the niggard soul
Too late shall weep, and curse his thrify hand
That would not timely ease the pond'rous boughs.

It much conduces all the cares to know
Of gard'ning, how to scare nocturnal thieves,
And how the little race of birds that hop
From spray to spray, scooping the costliest fruit
Insatiate, undisturb'd. Priapus' form
Avails but little; rather guard each row
With the false terrors of a breathless kite.
This done, the tim'rous flock with swiftest wing
Scud through the air; their fancy represents
His mortal talons, and his rav'nous beak
Destructive; glad to shun his hostile gripe,
They quit their thefts, and unfrequent the fields.

Besides, the filthy swine will oft invade
Thy firm inclosure, and with delving snout
The rooted forest undermine; forthwith
Alloo thy furious mastiff, bid him vex
The noxious herd, and print upon their ears
A sad memorial of their past offence.

The flagrant Procyon will not fail to bring
Large shoals of slow, house-bearing snails, that creep
O'er the ripe fruitage, paring slimy tracts
In the sleek rinds, and unprest Cyder drink.
No art averts this pest; on thee it lies,
With morning and with ev'ning hand to rid
The preying reptiles; nor, if wise, wilt thou
Decline this labour, which itself rewards
With pleasing gain, whilst the warm limbec draws
Salubrious water from the nocent brood.

Myriads of wasps now also clustering hang,
And drain a spurious honey from thy groves,
Their winter food; tho' oft repuls'd, again
They rally, undismay'd: but fraud with ease
Ensnares the noisome swarms; let ev'ry bough
Bear frequent vials, pregnant with the dregs
Of moyle, or mum, or treacle's viscous juice;
They, by th' alluring odour drawn, in haste
Fly to the dulcet cates, and crowding sip
Their palatable bane; joyful thou'lt see

The clammy surface all o'erstrewn with tribes
Of greedy insects, that with fruitless toil
Flap filmy pennons oft, to extricate
Their feet, in liquid shackles bound, till death
Bereave them of their worthless souls: such doom
Waits luxury, and lawless love of gain.

THOMAS PARNELL

1679–1718

from *A Night Piece on Death*

How deep yon azure dyes the sky!
Where orbs of gold unnumber'd lie,
While thro' their ranks in silver pride
The nether crescent seems to glide.
The slumb'ring breeze forgets to breathe,
The lake is smooth and clear beneath,
Where once again the spangled show
Descends to meet our eyes below.
The grounds which on the right aspire,
In dimness from the view retire:
The left presents a place of graves,
Whose wall the silent water laves.
That steeple guides thy doubtful sight
Among the livid gleams of night.
There pass with melancholy state,
By all the solemn heaps of fate,
And think, as softly-sad you tread
Above the venerable dead,
'Time was, like thee they life possessed
And time shall be, that thou shalt rest.'
Those graves, with bending osier bound,
That nameless heave the crumbled ground,
Quick to the glancing thought disclose
Where toil and poverty repose.
The flat smooth stones that bear a name,
The chisel's slender help to fame,
(Which ere our set of friends decay
Their frequent steps may wear away)
A middle race of mortals own,

Men, half ambitious, all unknown.
The marble tombs that rise on high,
Whose dead in vaulted arches lie,
Whose pillars swell with sculptur'd stones,
Arms, angels, epitaphs, and bones,
These (all the poor remains of state),
Adorn the rich, or praise the great;
Who while on earth in fame they live,
Are senseless of the fame they give.

Ha! While I gaze, pale Cynthia fades,
The bursting earth unveils the shades!
All slow, and wan, and wrapped with shrouds,
They rise in visionary crowds,
And all with sober accent cry,
'Think, mortal, what it is to die.'

Song

WHEN thy beauty appears
    In its graces and airs
All bright as an angel new dropped from the sky,
At distance I gaze and am awed by my fears:
    So strangely you dazzle my eye!

But when without art
    Your kind thoughts you impart,
When your love runs in blushes through every vein;
When it darts from your eyes, when it pants in your heart,
    Then I know you're a woman again.

There's a passion and pride
    In our sex (she replied),
And thus, might I gratify both, I would do:
Still an angel appear to each lover beside,
    But still be a woman to you.

EDWARD YOUNG

1683–1765

from *Night Thoughts*

Introduction

TIRED Nature's sweet restorer, balmy sleep!
He, like the world, his ready visit pays,
Where fortune smiles; the wretched he forsakes:
Swift on his downy pinion flies from woe,
And lights on lids unsullied with a tear!

　From short, (as usual) and disturbed repose,
I wake: how happy they who wake no more!
Yet that were vain, if dreams infest the grave.
I wake, emerging from a sea of dreams
Tumultuous; where my wrecked, desponding thought
From wave to wave of fancied misery,
At random drove, her helm of reason lost;
Though now restored, 'tis only change of pain,
A bitter change; severer for severe:
The day too short for my distress! and night
Even in the zenith of her dark domain,
Is sunshine, to the colour of my fate.

　Night, sable goddess! from her ebon throne,
In rayless majesty, now stretches forth
Her leaden sceptre o'er a slumbering world:
Silence, how dead! and darkness, how profound!
Nor eye, nor listening ear an object finds;
Creation sleeps. 'Tis, as the general pulse
Of life stood still, and Nature made a pause;
An awful pause! prophetic of her end.

　Silence, and darkness! solemn sisters! twins
From ancient night, who nurse the tender thought
To reason; and on reason built resolve,
(That column of true majesty in man!)
Assist me: I will thank you in the grave;
The grave, your kingdom: there this frame shall fall
A victim sacred to your dreary shrine:
But what are ye? Thou, who didst put to flight
Primaeval silence, when the morning stars
Exulting, shouted, o'er the rising ball;

O thou! whose word from solid darkness struck
That spark; the sun, strike wisdom from my soul;
My soul, which flies to thee, her trust, her treasure;
As misers to their gold, while others rest.
   Through this opaque of nature, and of woe,
This double night, transmit one pitying ray,
To lighten and to cheer: O teach my mind,
(A mind that fain would wander from its woe,)
Lead it through various scenes of life and death,
And from each scene, the noblest truths inspire:
Nor less inspire my conduct, than my song;
Teach my best reason, reason; my best will
Teach rectitude; and fix my firm resolve
Wisdom to wed, and pay her long arrear.
Nor let the vial of thy vengeance poured
On this devoted head, be poured in vain.
   The bell strikes one: we take no note of time,
But from its loss. To give it then a tongue
Is wise in man. As if an angel spoke,
I feel the solemn sound. If heard aright,
It is the knell of my departed hours:
Where are they? With the years beyond the flood:
It is the signal that demands dispatch;
How much is to be done! my hopes and fears
Start up alarmed, and o'er life's narrow verge
Look down—on what? a fathomless abyss;
A dread Eternity! how surely mine!
And can Eternity belong to me,
Poor pensioner on the mercies of an hour?
   How poor, how rich, how abject, how august,
How complicate, how wonderful is man!
How passing wonder He, who made him such!
Who centred in our make such strange extremes!
From different natures, marvellously mixed,
Connexion exquisite of distant worlds!
Distinguished link in being's endless chain!
Midway from nothing to the Deity!
A beam ethereal sullied, and absorbed!
Though sullied, and dishonoured, still divine!
Dim miniature of greatness absolute!
An heir of glory! a frail child of dust!
Helpless immortal! insect infinite!
A worm! A god! I tremble at myself,
And in myself am lost! At home a stranger,

Thought wanders up and down, surprised, amazed,
And wondering at her own: how reason reels!
O what a miracle to man is man,
Triumphantly distressed! what joy, what dread!
Alternately transported, and alarmed!
What can preserve my life? or what destroy?
An angel's arm can't snatch me from the grave;
Legions of angels can't confine me there.
   'Tis past conjecture; all things rise in proof:
While o'er my limbs sleep's soft dominion spread:
What, though my soul fantastic measures trod,
O'er fairy fields; or mourned along the gloom
Of pathless woods; or down the craggy steep
Hurled headlong, swam with pain the mantled pool;
Or scaled the cliff; or danced on hollow winds,
With antic shapes, wild natives of the brain?
Her ceaseless flight, though devious, speaks her nature
Of subtler essence than the trodden clod;
Active, aerial, towering, unconfined,
Unfettered with her gross companion's fall:
Even silent night proclaims my soul immortal:
Even silent night proclaims eternal day:
For human weal, Heaven husbands all events,
Dull sleep instructs, nor sport vain dreams in vain.
   Why then their loss deplore, that are not lost?
Why wanders wretched thought their tombs around
In infidel distress? are angels there?
Slumbers, raked up in dust, ethereal fire?
They live! they greatly live a life on earth
Unkindled, unconceived; and from an eye
Of tenderness, let heavenly pity fall
On me, more justly numbered with the dead:
This is the desert, this the solitude;
How populous, how vital, is the grave!
This is creation's melancholy vault,
The vale funereal, the sad cypress gloom;
The land of apparitions, empty shades:
All, all on earth is shadow, all beyond
Is substance; the reverse is folly's creed;
How solid all, where change shall be no more!

THOMAS TICKELL

1686–1740

To the Earl of Warwick, on the Death of Mr. Addison

IF, dumb too long, the drooping Muse hath stayed,
And left her debt to Addison unpaid,
Blame not her silence, Warwick, but bemoan,
And judge, oh judge, my bosom by your own.
What mourner ever felt poetic fires!
Slow comes the verse, that real woe inspires:
Grief unaffected suits but ill with art,
Or flowing numbers with a bleeding heart.
　　Can I forget the dismal night, that gave
My soul's best part for ever to the grave!
How silent did his old companions tread,
By midnight lamps, the mansions of the dead,
Through breathing statues, then unheeded things,
Through rows of warriors, and through walks of kings!
What awe did the slow solemn knell inspire;
The pealing organ, and the pausing choir;
The duties by the lawn-robed prelate paid;
And the last words, that dust to dust conveyed!
While speechless o'er thy closing grave we bend,
Accept these tears, thou dear departed friend,
Oh gone for ever, take this long adieu;
And sleep in peace, next thy loved Montague!
　　To strew fresh laurels let the task be mine,
A frequent pilgrim, at thy sacred shrine;
Mine with true sighs thy absence to bemoan,
And grave with faithful epitaphs thy stone.
If e'er from me thy loved memorial part,
May shame afflict this alienated heart;
Of thee forgetful if I form a song,
My lyre be broken, and untuned my tongue,
My grief be doubled, from thy image free,
And mirth a torment unchastised by thee.
　　Oft let me range the gloomy isles alone
(Sad luxury! to vulgar minds unknown)
Along the walls where speaking marbles show
What worthies form the hallowed mould below:
Proud names, who once the reins of empire held;

In arms who triumphed; or in arts excelled;
Chiefs, graced with scars, and prodigal of blood;
Stern patriots, who for sacred freedom stood;
Just men, by whom impartial laws were given;
And saints, who taught, and led, the way to heaven
Ne'er to these chambers, where the mighty rest,
Since their foundation, came a nobler guest,
Nor e'er was to the bower of bliss conveyed
A fairer spirit, or more welcome shade.

    In what new region, to the just assigned,
What new employments please th' unbodied mind?
A wingèd Virtue through th' ethereal sky,
From world to world unwearied does he fly?
Or curious trace the long laborious maze
Of heaven's decrees where wondering angels gaze?
Does he delight to hear bold seraphs tell
How Michael battled, and the dragon fell?
Or, mixed with milder cherubim, to glow
In hymns of love, not ill essayed below?
Or dost thou warn poor mortals left behind,
A task well suited to thy gentle mind?
Oh, if sometimes thy spotless form descend,
To me thy aid, thou guardian Genius, lend!
When rage misguides me, or when fear alarms,
When pain distresses, or when pleasure charms,
In silent whisperings purer thoughts impart,
And turn from ill a fray and feeble heart;
Lead through the paths thy virtue trod before,
Till bliss shall join, nor death can part us more.

    That awful form (which, so the heavens decree,
Must still be loved and still deplored by me)
In nightly visions seldom fails to rise,
Or, roused by fancy, meets my waking eyes.
If business calls, or crowded courts inivte,
Th' unblemished statesman seems to strike my sight;
If in the stage I seek to soothe my care,
I meet his soul, which breathes in Cato there;
If pensive to the rural shades I rove,
His shape o'ertakes me in the lonely grove:
'Twas there of Just and Good he reasoned strong,
Cleared some great truth, or raised some serious song;
There patient showed us the wise course to steer,
A candid censor, and a friend severe;
There taught us how to live; and (oh! too high

THOMAS TICKELL

The price for knowledge) taught us how to die.
   Thou hill, whose brow the antique structures grace,
Reared by bold chiefs of Warwick's noble race,
Why, once so loved, whene'er the bower appears,
O'er my dim eyeballs glance the sudden tears!
How sweet were once thy prospects fresh and fair,
Thy sloping walks, and unpolluted air!
How sweet the glooms beneath thy agèd trees,
Thy noontide shadow, and thy evening breeze!
His image thy forsaken bowers restore;
Thy walks and airy prospects charm no more,
No more the summer in the glooms allayed,
Thy evening breezes, and thy noon-day shade.
   From other ills, however fortune frowned,
Some refuge in the muse's art I found:
Reluctant now I touch the trembling string,
Bereft of him, who taught me how to sing,
And these sad accents, murmured o'er his urn,
Betray that absence, they attempt to mourn.
Oh! must I then (now fresh my bosom bleeds,
And Craggs in death to Addison succeeds)
The verse, begun to one lost friend, prolong,
And weep a second in th' unfinished song!
   These works divine, which on his death-bed laid
To thee, O Craggs, th' expiring sage conveyed,
Great, but ill-omened monument of fame,
Nor he survived to give, nor thou to claim.
Swift after him thy social spirit flies,
And close to his, how soon! thy coffin lies.
Blest pair! whose union future bards shall tell
In future tongues: each other's boast! farewell.
Farewell! whom joined in fame, in friendship tried,
No chance could sever, nor the grave divide.

ALLAN RAMSAY

1686–1758

The Lass of Patie's Mill

THE lass of Patie's mill,
  Sae bonny, blithe, and gay,
In spite of all my skill,
  She stole my heart away.
When tedding out the hay,
  Bareheaded on the green,
Love 'midst her locks did play,
  And wantoned in her een.

Her arms white, round, and smooth;
  Breasts rising in their dawn;
To age it would give youth,
  To press them with his hand.
Through all my spirits ran
  An ecstacy of bliss,
When I such sweetness fan'
  Wrapt in a balmy kiss.

Without the help of art,
  Like flowers which grace the wild,
Her sweets she did impart,
  Whene'er she spoke or smiled:
Her looks they were so mild,
  Free from affected pride,
She me to love beguiled;—
  I wished her for my bride.

Oh! had I all the wealth
  Hopetoun's high mountains fill,
Insured long life and health,
  And pleasure at my will;
I'd promise, and fulfil,
  That none but bonnie she,
The lass of Patie's mill,
  Should share the same with me.

ALLAN RAMSAY

An Thou Were My Ain Thing

AN thou were my ain thing,
I would love thee, I would love thee;
An thou were my ain thing
   How dearly I would love thee.

Like bees that suck the morning dew,
Frae flowers of sweetest scent and hue,
Sae wad I dwell upon thy mow
   And gar the gods envý me.

Sae lang 's I had the use of light
I'd on thy beauties feast my sight,
Syne in saft whispers through the night
   I'd tell how much I loved thee.

How fair and ruddy is my Jean!
She moves a goddess o'er the green.
Were I a king thou should be queen—
   Nane but myself aboon thee.

I'd grasp thee to this breast of mine,
Whilst thou like ivy on the vine
Around my stronger limbs should twine,
   Formed handy to defend thee.

Time's on the wing and will not stay,
In shining youth let's make our hay;
Since love admits of no delay,
   O let na scorn undo thee.

While love does at this altar stand
Hae, here's my heart, gie me thy hand,
And with ilk smile thou shalt command
   The will of him who loves thee.

An thou were my ain thing,
I would love thee; I would love thee;
An thou were my ain thing,
   How dearly I would love thee.

mow] mouth

467

JOHN GAY

1685–1732

Fable XXI
The Rat-catcher and Cats

THE rats by night such mischief did,
Betty was every morning chid:
They undermined whole sides of bacon,
Her cheese was sapped, her tarts were taken,
Her pasties, fenced with thickest paste,
Were all demolished and laid waste.
She cursed the cat for want of duty,
Who left her foes a constant booty.

An engineer, of noted skill,
Engaged to stop the growing ill.

From room to room he now surveys
Their haunts, their works, their secret ways,
Finds where they 'scape an ambuscade,
And whence the nightly sally's made.

An envious cat, from place to place,
Unseen, attends his silent pace,
She saw that, if his trade went on.
The purring race must be undone,
So, secretly removes his baits,
And every strategem defeats.

Again he sets the poisoned toils,
And puss again the labour foils.

What foe (to frustrate my designs)
My schemes thus nightly countermines?
Incensed, he cries: this very hour
The wretch shall bleed beneath my power.

So said. A ponderous trap he brought,
And in the fact poor puss was caught.

Smuggler, says he, thou shalt be made
A victim to our loss of trade.

The captive cat with piteous mews
For pardon, life and freedom sues.
A sister of the science spare,
One int'rest is our common care.

What insolence! the man replied,
Shall cats with us the game divide?

468

Were all your interloping band
Extinguished, or expelled the land,
We rat-catchers might raise our fees,
Sole guardians of a nation's cheese!
    A cat, who saw the lifted knife,
Thus spoke, and saved her sister's life.
    In every age and clime we see,
Two of a trade can ne'er agree,
Each hates his neighbour for encroaching;
Squire stigmatizes squire for poaching;
Beauties with beauties are in arms,
And scandal pelts each other's charms;
Kings too their neighbour kings dethrone,
In hope to make the world their own
But let us limit our desires,
Not war like beauties, kings and squires,
For though we both one prey pursue,
There's a game enough for us and you.

Mr. Pope's Welcome from Greece

Upon his having finished his translation of Homer's 'Iliad'

LONG hast thou, friend! been absent from thy soil,
    Like patient Ithacus at siege of Troy;
I have been witness of thy six years' toil,
    Thy daily labours, and thy night's annoy,
Lost to thy native land, with great turmoil,
    On the wide sea, oft threat'ning to destroy:
Methinks with thee I've trod Sigæan ground,
And heard the shores of Hellespont resound.

Did I not see thee when thou first sett'st sail
    To seek adventures fair in Homer's land?
Did I not see thy sinking spirits fail,
    And wish thy bark had never left the strand?
Ev'n in mid ocean often didst thou quail,
    And oft lift up thy holy eye and hand,
Praying the Virgin dear, and saintly choir,
Back to the port to bring thy bark entire.

Cheer up, my friend, thy dangers now are o'er;
   Methinks—nay, sure the rising coasts appear;
Hark how the guns salute from either shore,
   As thy trim vessel cuts the Thames so fair:
Shouts answ'ring shouts, from Kent and Essex roar,
   And bells break loud thro' every gust of air:
Bonfires do blaze, and bones and cleavers ring,
As at the coming of some mighty king.

Now pass we Gravesend with a friendly wind,
   And Tilbury's white fort, and long Blackwall;
Greenwich, where dwells the friend of human kind,
   More visited than or her park or hall,
Withers the good, and (with him ever join'd)
   Facetious Disney, greet thee first of all:
I see his chimney smoke, and hear him say,
Duke! that's the room for Pope, and that for Gay.

Come in, my friends, here shall ye dine and lie,
   And here shall breakfast, and here dine again;
And sup, and breakfast on, (if ye comply)
   For I have still some dozens of champagne:
His voice still lessens as the ship sails by;
   He waves his hand to bring us back in vain;
For now I see, I see proud London's spires;
Greenwich is lost, and Deptford dock retires.

Oh, what a concourse swarms on yonder key!
   The sky re-echoes with new shouts of joy:
By all this show, I ween, 'tis Lord May'r's day,
   I hear the voice of trumpet and hautboy.—
No, now I see them near—oh, these are they
   Who come in crowds to welcome thee from Troy.
Hail to the bard whom long as lost we mourn'd,
From siege, from battle, and from storm return'd!

Of goodly Dames, and courteous Knights, I view
   The silken petticoat and broider'd vest,
Yea peers and mighty Dukes with ribands blue
   (True blue fair emblem of unstained breast.)
Others I see as noble and more true,
   By no court badge distinguish'd from the rest.
First see I Methwen of sincerest mind
As Arthur grave, yet soft as woman kind.

What lady's that to whom he gently bends?
   Who knows not her? ah! those are Wortley's eyes.
How art thou honour'd number'd with her friends?
   For she distinguishes the good and wise.
The sweet tongu'd Murray near her side attends.
   Now to my heart the glance of Howard flies.
Now Harvey fair of face I mark full well,
With thee youth's youngest daughter, sweet Lepell.

I see two lovely sisters hand in hand,
   The fair hair'd Martha and Teresa brown,
Madge Bellenden the tallest of the land
   And smiling Mary soft and fair as down.
Yonder I see the cheerful Duchess stand
   For friendship, zeal and blithsome humour known.
Whence that loud shout in such a hearty strain?
Why, all the Hamiltons are in her train.

See next the decent Scudamore advance,
   With Winchelsea still meditating song.
With her Miss Howe came there by chance,
   Nor knows with whom or why she comes along.
Far off from these see Santlow fam'd for dance,
   And frolic Bicknell and her sister young,
With other names by me not to be nam'd,
Much lov'd in private, not in public fam'd.

But now behold the female band retire,
   And the shrill music of their voice is still'd:
Methinks I see famed Buckingham admire
   That in Troy's ruin thou had'st not been kill'd,
Sheffield who knows to strike the living lyre
   With hand judicious like thy Homer skill'd.
Bathurst impetuous hastens to the coast
Whom you and I strive who shall love the most.

See generous Burlington, with goodly Bruce,
   (But Bruce comes wafted in a soft sedan)
Dan Prior next, belov'd by every muse,
   And friendly Congreve, unreproachful man!
(Oxford by Cunningham hath sent excuse)
   See hearty Watkins comes with cup and can;
And Lewis, who has never friend forsaken;
And Laughton whisp'ring asks—Is Troy town taken?

Earl Warwick comes, of free and honest mind;
  Bold, gen'rous Craggs, whose heart was ne'er disguis'd:
Ah why, sweet St. John, cannot I thee find?
  St. John for ev'ry social virtue priz'd.—
Alas! to foreign climates he's confin'd,
  Or else to see thee here I well surmiz'd:
Thou too, my Swift, dost breathe Boeotian air;
When wilt thou bring back wit and humour here?

Harcourt I see for eloquence renown'd,
  The mouth of justice, oracle of law!
Another Simon is beside him found,
  Another Simon, like as straw to straw.
How Lansdowne smiles, with lasting laurel crown'd!
  What mitred prelate there commands our awe?
See Rochester approving nods his head,
And ranks one modern with the mighty dead.

Carlton and Chandos thy arrival grace;
  Hanmer, whose eloquence th' unbiass'd sways;
Harley, whose goodness opens in his face,
  And shews his heart the seat where virtue stays.
Ned Blount advances next, with busy pace,
  In haste, but saunt'ring, hearty in his ways:
I see the friendly Carylls come by dozens,
Their wives, their uncles, daughters, sons, and cousins.

Arbuthnot there I see, in physic's art,
  As Galen learn'd, or famed Hippocrate;
Whose company drives sorrow from the heart,
  As all disease his medicines dissipate:
Kneller amid the triumph bears his part,
  Who could (were mankind lost) a new create:
What can th' extent of his vast soul confine?
A painter, critic, engineer, divine!

Thee Jervas hails, robust and debonair,
  Now have we conquer'd Homer, friends, he cries:
Dartneuf, grave joker, joyous Ford is there,
  And wond'ring Maine, so fat with laughing eyes:
(Gay, Maine, and Cheney, boon companions dear,
  Gay fat, Maine fatter, Cheney huge of size)
Yea Dennis, Gildon, (hearing thou has riches)
And honest, hatless Cromwell, with red breeches.

O Wanley, whence com'st thou with shorten'd hair,
   And visage from thy shelves with dust besprent?
'Forsooth (quoth he) from placing Homer there,
   For ancients to compyle is myne entente:
Of ancients only hath Lord Harley care;
   But hither me hath my meeke lady sent:—
In manuscript of Greeke rede we thilke same,
But book yprint best plesyth myn gude dame.'

Yonder I see, among th' expecting crowd,
   Evans with laugh jocose, and tragic Young;
High-buskin'd Booth, grave Mawbert, wand'ring Frowd,
   And Titcomb's belly waddles slow along.
See Digby faints at Southern talking loud,
   Yea Steele and Tickell mingle in the throng;
Tickell whose skiff (in partnership they say)
Set forth for Greece, but founder'd in the way.

Lo the two Doncastles in Berkshire known!
   Lo Bickford, Fortescue, of Devon land!
Lo Tooker, Eccleshall, Sykes, Rawlinson:
   See hearty Morley takes thee by the hand.
Ayrs, Grahame, Buckridge joy thy voyage done,
   But who can count the leaves, the stars, the sand.
Lo Stonor, Fenton, Caldwell, Ward, and Broome,
Lo thousands more, but I want rhyme and room.

How lov'd! how honour'd thou! yet be not vain;
   And sure thou art not, for I hear thee say,
All this, my friends, I owe to Homer's strain,
   On whose strong pinions I exalt my lay.
What from contending cities did he gain;
   And what rewards his grateful country pay?
None, none were paid—why then all this for me?
These honours, Homer, had been just to thee.

ALEXANDER POPE

1688–1744

from *An Essay on Criticism*

I

'TIS hard to say, if greater want of skill
Appear in writing or in judging ill;
But, of the two, less dangerous is the offence
To tire our patience, than mislead our sense.
Some few in that, but numbers err in this,
Ten censure wrong for one who writes amiss;
A fool might once himself alone expose,
Now one in verse makes many more in prose.
　　'Tis with our judgments as our watches, none
Go just alike, yet each believes his own.
In poets as true genius is but rare,
True taste as seldom is the critic' share,
Both must alike from Heaven derive their light,
These born to judge, as well as those to write.
Let such teach others who themselves excel,
And censure freely who have written well.
Authors are partial to their wit, 'tis true,
But are not critics to their judgment too?
　　Yet, if we look more closely, we shall find
Most have the seeds of judgment in their mind:
Nature affords at least a glimmering light;
The lines, though touch'd but faintly, are drawn right.
But as the slightest sketch, if justly traced,
Is by ill colouring but the more disgraced,
So by false learning is good sense defaced;
Some are bewilder'd in the maze of schools,
And some made coxcombs Nature meant but fools.
In search of wit these lose their common sense,
And then turn critics in their own defence:
Each burns alike, who can, or cannot write,
Or with a rival's, or an eunuch's spite.
All fools have still an itching to deride,
And fain would be upon the laughing side.
If Mævius scribble in Apollo's spite,
There are who judge still worse than he can write.

Some have at first for wits, than poets pass'd,
Turn'd critics next, and proved plain fools at last.
Some neither can for wits nor critics pass,
As heavy mules are neither horse nor ass.
Those half-learn'd witlings, numerous in our isle,
As half-form'd insects on the banks of Nile;
Unfinish'd things, one knows not what to call,
Their generation's so equivocal:
To tell them would a hundred tongues require,
Or one vain wit's, that might a hundred tire.

But you who seek to give and merit fame,
And justly bear a critic's noble name,
Be sure yourself and your own reach to know,
How far your genius, taste, and learning go;
Launch not beyond your depth, but be discreet,
And mark that point where sense and dulness meet.

Nature to all things fix'd the limits fit,
And wisely curb'd proud man's pretending wit.
As on the land while here the ocean gains,
In other parts it leaves wide sandy plains;
Thus in the soul while memory prevails,
The solid power of understanding fails;
Where beams of warm imagination play,
The memory's soft figures melt away.
One science only will one genius fit:
So vast is art, so narrow human wit:
Not only bounded to peculiar arts,
But oft in those confined to single parts.
Like kings we lose the conquests gain'd before,
By vain ambition still to make them more:
Each might his servile province well command,
Would all but stoop to what they understand.

First follow Nature, and your judgment frame
By her just standard, which is still the same:
Unerring Nature, still divinely bright,
One clear, unchanged, and universal light,
Life, force, and beauty, must to all impart,
At once the source, and end, and test of Art.
Art from that fund each just supply provides;
Works without show, and without pomp presides:
In some fair body thus th' informing soul
With spirits feeds, with vigour fills the whole,
Each motion guides, and every nerve sustains;
Itself unseen, but in th' effects remains.

Some, to whom Heaven in wit has been profuse,
Want as much more to turn it to its use;
For wit and judgment often are at strife,
Though meant each other's aid, like man and wife.
'Tis more to guide, than spur the Muse's steed;
Restrain his fury, than provoke his speed:
The winged courser, like a generous horse,
Shows most true mettle when you check his course.

　　Those rules of old discover'd, not devised,
Are Nature still, but Nature methodised:
Nature, like liberty, is but restrain'd
By the same laws which first herself ordain'd.

　　Hear how learn'd Greece her useful rules indites,
When to repress, and when indulge our flights:
High on Parnassus' top her sons she show'd,
And pointed out those arduous paths they trod;
Held from afar, aloft, the immortal prize,
And urged the rest by equal steps to rise.
Just precepts thus from great examples given,
She drew from them what they derive from Heaven.
The generous critic fann'd the poet's fire,
And taught the world with reason to admire.
Then criticism the Muse's handmaid proved,
To dress her charms, and make her more beloved:
But following wits from that intention stray'd,
Who could not win the mistress, woo'd the maid;
Against the poets their own arms they turn'd,
Sure to hate most the men from whom they learn'd.
So modern 'pothecaries, taught the art
By doctor's bills to play the doctor's part,
Bold in the practice of mistaken rules,
Prescribe, apply, and call their masters fools.
Some on the leaves of ancient authors prey,
Nor time nor moths e'er spoil'd so much as they:
Some drily plain, without invention's aid,
Write dull receipts how poems may be made.
These leave the sense, their learning to display,
And those explain the meaning quite away.

　　You then whose judgment the right course would steer,
Know well each Ancient's proper character:
His fable, subject, scope in every page;
Religion, country, genius of his age:
Without all these at once before your eyes,
Cavil you may, but never criticise.

Be Homer's works your study and delight,
Read them by day, and meditate by night;
Thence form your judgment, thence your maxims bring,
And trace the Muses upward to their spring.
Still with itself compared, his text peruse;
And let your comment be the Mantuan Muse.
　　When first young Maro in his boundless mind
A work to outlast immortal Rome design'd,
Perhaps he seem'd above the critic's law,
And but from Nature's fountains scorn'd to draw:
But when to examine every part he came,
Nature and Homer were, he found, the same.
Convinced, amazed, he checks the bold design;
And rules as strict his labour'd work confine,
As if the Stagyrite o'erlook'd each line.
Learn hence for ancient rules a just esteem;
To copy Nature is to copy them.
　　Some beauties yet no precepts can declare,
For there's a happiness as well as care.
Music resembles poetry, in each
Are nameless graces which no methods teach,
And which a master-hand alone can reach.
If, where the rules not far enough extend,
(Since rules were made but to promote their end)
Some lucky licence answer to the full
The intent proposed, that licence is a rule.
Thus Pegasus, a nearer way to take,
May boldly deviate from the common track.
Great wits sometimes may gloriously offend,
And rise to faults true critics dare not mend;
From vulgar bounds with brave disorder part,
And snatch a grace beyond the reach of art,
Which, without passing through the judgment, gains
The heart, and all its end at once attains.

* * *

II

　　Of all the causes which conspire to blind
Man's erring judgment, and misguide the mind,
What the weak head with strongest bias rules,
Is PRIDE, the never-failing vice of fools.
Whatever Nature has in worth denied,
She gives in large recruits of needless pride;

For as in bodies, thus in souls we find
What wants in blood and spirits, swell'd with wind:
Pride, where wit fails, steps in to our defence,
And fills up all the mighty void of sense.
If once right reason drives that cloud away,
Truth breaks upon us with resistless day.
Trust not yourself; but your defects to know,
Make use of every friend—and every foe.
A little learning is a dangerous thing;
Drink deep, or taste not the Pierian spring:
There shallow draughts intoxicate the brain,
And drinking largely sobers us again.
Fired at first sight with what the Muse imparts,
In fearless youth we tempt the height of arts,
While from the bounded level of our mind,
Short views we take, nor see the lengths behind;
But more advanced, behold with strange surprise
New distant scenes of endless science rise!
So pleased at first the towering Alps we try,
Mount o'er the vales, and seem to tread the sky,
The eternal snows appear already passed,
And the first clouds and mountains seem the last:
But, those attain'd, we tremble to survey
The growing labours of the lengthen'd way,
The increasing prospect tires our wandering eyes,
Hills peep o'er hills, and Alps on Alps arise!
    A perfect judge will read each work of wit
With the same spirit that its author writ:
Survey the WHOLE, nor seeks slight faults to find
Where Nature moves, and rapture warms the mind,
Nor lose, for that malignant dull delight,
The generous pleasure to be charm'd with wit.
But in such lays as neither ebb nor flow,
Correctly cold, and regularly low,
That shunning faults, one quiet tenor keep;
We cannot blame indeed—but we may sleep.
In wit, as Nature, what affects our hearts
Is not th' exactness of peculiar parts;
'Tis not a lip, or eye, we beauty call,
But the joint force and full result of all.
Thus when we view some well-proportion'd dome,
(The world's just wonder, and ev'n thine, O Rome!)
No single parts unequally surprise,
All comes united to th' admiring eyes;

No monstrous height, or breadth or length appear;
The whole at once is bold and regular.
   Whoever thinks a faultless piece to see,
Thinks what ne'er was, nor is, nor e'er shall be,
In every work regard the writer's end,
Since none can compass more than they intend;
And if the means be just, the conduct true,
Applause, in spite of trivial faults, is due.
As men of breeding, sometimes men of wit,
To avoid great errors, must the less commit:
Neglect the rules each verbal critic lays,
For not to know some trifles, is a praise.
Most critics, fond of some subservient art,
Still make the whole depend upon a part:
They talk of principles, but notions prize,
And all to one loved folly sacrifice.

*   *   *

   Some to Conceit alone their taste confine,
And glittering thoughts struck out at every line;
Pleased with a work where nothing's just or fit;
One glaring chaos and wild heap of wit.
Poets, like painters, thus, unskill'd to trace
The naked Nature and the living grace,
With gold and jewels cover every part,
And hide with ornaments their want of art.
True wit is Nature to advantage dress'd;
What oft was thought, but ne'er so well express'd;
Something, whose truth convinced at sight we find,
That gives us back the image of our mind.
As shades more sweetly recommend the light,
So modest plainness sets off sprightly wit.
For works may have more wit than does 'em good,
As bodies perish through excess of blood.
   Others for Language all their care express,
And value books, as women men, for dress:
Their praise is still,—The style is excellent;
The sense, they humbly take upon content.
Words are like leaves; and where they most abound,
Much fruit of sense beneath is rarely found.
False eloquence, like the prismatic glass,
Its gaudy colours spreads on every place;
The face of Nature we no more survey,
All glares alike, without distinction gay:

But true expression, like th' unchanging sun,
Clears and improves whate'er it shines upon,
It gilds all objects, but it alters none.
Expression is the dress of thought, and still
Appears more decent, as more suitable;
A vile conceit in pompous words express'd
Is like a clown in regal purple dress'd:
For different styles with different subjects sort,
As several garbs, with country, town, and court.
Some by old words to fame have made pretence,
Ancients in phrase, mere moderns in their sense;
Such labour'd nothings, in so strange a style,
Amaze the unlearn'd, and make the learned smile.
Unlucky as Fungoso in the play,
These sparks with awkward vanity display
What the fine gentleman wore yesterday;
And but so mimic ancient wits at best,
As apes our grandsires, in their doublets dress'd.
In words, as fashions, the same rule will hold;
Alike fantastic, if too new, or old:
Be not the first by whom the new are tried,
Nor yet the last to lay the old aside.
    But most by numbers judge a poet's song:
And smooth or rough, with them, is right or wrong:
In the bright muse, though thousand charms conspire,
Her voice is all these tuneful fools admire;
Who haunt Parnassus but to please their ear,
Not mend their minds; as some to church repair,
Not for the doctrine, but the music there.
These equal syllables alone require,
Though oft the ear the open vowels tire;
While expletives their feeble aid do join;
And ten low words oft creep in one dull line:
While they ring round the same unvaried chimes,
With sure returns of still expected rhymes;
Where'er you find 'the cooling western breeze,'
In the next line, it 'whispers through the trees':
If crystal streams 'with pleasing murmurs creep':
The reader's threaten'd (not in vain) with 'sleep.'
Then, at the last and only couplet fraught
With some unmeaning thing they call a thought,
A needless Alexandrine ends the song,
That, like a wounded snake, drags its slow length along.
Leave such to tune their own dull rhymes, and know

What's roundly smooth, or languishingly slow;
And praise the easy vigour of a line,
Where Denham's strength, and Waller's sweetness join.
True ease in writing comes from art, not chance,
As those move easiest who have learn'd to dance.
'Tis not enough no harshness gives offence,
The sound must seem an echo to the sense:
Soft is the strain when Zephyr gently blows,
And the smooth stream in smoother numbers flows;
But when loud billows lash the sounding shore,
The hoarse, rough verse should like the torrent roar.
When Ajax strives some rock's vast weight to throw,
The line too labours, and the words move slow:
Not so, when swift Camilla scours the plain,
Flies o'er the unbending corn, and skims along the main.
Hear how Timotheus' varied lays surprise,
And bid alternate passions fall and rise!
While, at each change, the son of Libyan Jove
Now burns with glory, and then melts with love;
Now his fierce eyes with sparkling fury glow,
Now sighs steal out, and tears begin to flow:
Persians and Greeks like turns of Nature found,
And the world's victor stood subdued by sound!
The power of music all our hearts allow,
And what Timotheus was, is DRYDEN now.

　　Avoid extremes; and shun the fault of such,
Who still are pleased too little or too much.
At every trifle scorn to take offence,
That always shows great pride, or little sense;
Those heads, as stomachs, are not sure the best,
Which nauseate all, and nothing can digest.
Yet let not each gay turn thy rapture move;
For fools admire, but men of sense approve:
As things seem large which we through mists descry,
Dulness is ever apt to magnify.

*　　*　　*

　　But where's the man who counsel can bestow,
Still pleased to teach, and yet not proud to know?
Unbiass'd, or by favour, or by spite;
Not dully prepossess'd, nor blindly right;
Though learn'd, well-bred; and though well-bred, sincere;
Modestly bold, and humanly severe:

Who to a friend his faults can freely show,
And gladly praise the merit of a foe?
Bless'd with a taste exact, yet unconfined;
A knowledge both of books and human kind;
Generous converse; a soul exempt from pride;
And love to praise, with reason on his side?

   Such once were critics; such the happy few,
Athens and Rome in better ages knew.
The mighty Stagyrite first left the shore,
Spread all his sails, and durst the deeps explore;
He steer'd securely, and discover'd far,
Led by the light of the Mæonian star.
Poets, a race long unconfined, and free,
Still fond and proud of savage liberty,
Received his laws; and stood convinced 'twas fit,
Who conquer'd Nature, should preside o'er Wit.

   Horace still charms with graceful negligence,
And without method talks us into sense,
Will, like a friend, familiarly convey
The truest notions in the easiest way.
He, who supreme in judgment, as in wit,
Might boldly censure, as he boldly writ,
Yet judged with coolness, though he sung with fire;
His precepts teach but what his works inspire.
Our critics take a contrary extreme,
They judge with fury, but they write with phlegm:
Nor suffers Horace more in wrong translations
By wits, than critics in as wrong quotations.

   See Dionysius Homer's thoughts refine,
And call new beauties forth from every line!

   Fancy and art in gay Petronius please,
The scholar's learning with the courtier's ease.

   In grave Quintilian's copious work, we find
The justest rules and clearest method join'd:
Thus useful arms in magazines we place,
All ranged in order, and disposed with grace,
But less to please the eye, than arm the hand,
Still fit for use, and ready at command.

   Thee, bold Longinus! all the Nine inspire,
And bless their critic with a poet's fire.
An ardent judge, who, zealous in his trust,
With warmth gives sentence, yet is always just:
Whose own example strengthens all his laws:
And is himself that great sublime he draws.

Thus long succeeding critics justly reign'd,
Licence repress'd, and useful laws ordain'd.
Learning and Rome alike in empire grew;
And arts still follow'd where her eagles flew;
From the same foes, at last, both felt their doom,
And the same age saw Learning fall, and Rome.
With Tyranny, then Superstition join'd,
As that the body, this enslaved the mind;
Much was believed, but little understood,
And to be dull was construed to be good;
A second deluge learning thus o'errun,
And the monks finish'd what the Goths begun.

At length Erasmus, that great injured name,
(The glory of the priesthood, and the shame!)
Stemm'd the wild torrent of a barbarous age,
And drove those holy Vandals off the stage.

But see! each Muse, in Leo's golden days,
Starts from her trance, and trims her wither'd bays;
Rome's ancient Genius, o'er its ruins spread,
Shakes off the dust, and rears his reverend head.
Then Sculpture and her sister-arts revive;
Stones leaped to form, and rocks began to live;
With sweeter notes each rising temple rung;
A Raphael painted, and a Vida sung.
Immortal Vida: on whose honour'd brow
The poet's bays and critic's ivy grow:
Cremona now shall ever boast thy name,
As next in place to Mantua, next in fame!

But soon by impious arms from Latium chased,
Their ancient bounds the banish'd Muses pass'd;
Thence Arts o'er all the northern world advance,
But critic-learning flourish'd most in France;
The rules a nation, born to serve, obeys;
And Boileau still in right of Horace sways.
But we, brave Britons, foreign laws despised,
And kept unconquer'd, and uncivilised;
Fierce for the liberties of wit and bold,
We still defied the Romans, as of old.
Yet some there were, among the sounder few
Of those who less presumed, and better knew,
Who durst assert the juster ancient cause,
And here restored Wit's fundamental laws.
Such was the Muse, whose rules and practice tell,
'Nature's chief Masterpiece is writing well,'

Such was Roscommon, not more learn'd than good,
With manners generous as his noble blood;
To him the wit of Greece and Rome was known,
And every author's merit, but his own.
Such late was Walsh—the Muse's judge and friend,
Who justly knew to blame or to commend:
To failings mild, but zealous for desert;
The clearest head, and the sincerest heart.
This humble praise, lamented shade! receive,
This praise at least a grateful Muse may give:
The Muse, whose early voice you taught to sing,
Prescribed her heights, and pruned her tender wing,
(Her guide now lost) no more attempts to rise,
But in low numbers short excursions tries:
Content, if hence the unlearn'd their wants may view,
The learn'd reflect on what before they knew;
Careless of censure, nor too fond of fame;
Still pleased to praise, yet not afraid to blame;
Averse alike to flatter, or offend;
Not free from faults, not yet too vain to mend.

from *Windsor Forest*

To the Right Honourable George Lord Lansdowne

Non injussa cano: Te nostræ, Vare, myricæ,
Te Nemus omne canet; nec Phœbo gratior ulla est,
Quam sibi quæ Vari præscripsit pagina nomen.—VIRG.

[My pastoral Muse her humble tribute brings;
And yet not wholly uninspir'd she sings:
For all who read, and reading, not disdain
These rural poems, and their lowly strain,
The name of Varus oft inscribed shall see
In every grove and every vocal tree,
And all the sylvan reign shall sing of thee:
Thy name, to Phœbus and the Muses known,
Shall in the front of every page be shown;
For he who sings thy praise secures his own.—DRYDEN.]

THY forest, Windsor! and thy green retreats,
At once the Monarch's and the Muse's seats,
Invite my lays. Be present, sylvan maids!
Unlock your springs, and open all your shades.
GRANVILLE commands; your aid, O Muses, bring!
What Muse for GRANVILLE can refuse to sing?

The groves of Eden, vanish'd now so long,
Live in description, and look green in song:
These, were my breast inspired with equal flame,
Like them in beauty, should be like in fame.
Here hills and vales, the woodland and the plain,
Here earth and water seem to strive again;
Not chaos-like together crush'd and bruised,
But, as the world harmoniously confused:
Where order in variety we see,
And where, though all things differ, all agree.
Here waving groves a chequer'd scene display,
And part admit, and part exclude the day;
As some coy nymph her lover's warm address
Not quite indulges, nor can quite repress.
There, interspersed in lawns and opening glades,
Thin trees arise that shun each other's shades.
Here in full light the russet plains extend:
There, wrapt in clouds the bluish hills ascend.
Even the wild heath displays her purple dyes,
And 'midst the desert, fruitful fields arise,
That crown'd with tufted trees and springing corn,
Like verdant isles the sable waste adorn.
Let India boast her plants, nor envy we
The weeping amber, or the balmy tree,
While by our oaks the precious loads are borne,
And realms commanded which those trees adorn.
Not proud Olympus yields a nobler sight,
Though gods assembled grace his towering height,
Than what more humble mountains offer here,
Where, in their blessings, all those gods appear.
See Pan with flocks, with fruits Pomona crown'd,
Here blushing Flora paints th' enamell'd ground,
Here Ceres' gifts in waving prospect stand,
And nodding tempt the joyful reaper's hand;
Rich Industry sits smiling on the plains,
And peace and plenty tell, a STUART reigns.
  Not thus the land appear'd in ages past,
A dreary desert, and a gloomy waste,
To savage beasts and savage laws a prey,
And kings more furious and severe than they;
Who claim'd the skies, dispeopled air and floods,
The lonely lords of empty wilds and woods:
Cities laid waste, they storm'd the dens and caves
(For wiser brutes were backward to be slaves).

What could be free, when lawless beasts obey'd,
And even the elements a tyrant sway'd?
In vain kind seasons swell'd the teeming grain,
Soft showers distill'd and suns grew warm in vain;
The swain with tears his frustrate labour yields,
And famish'd dies amidst his ripen'd fields.
What wonder then, a beast or subject slain
Were equal crimes in a despotic reign?
Both doom'd alike for sportive tyrants bled,
But while the subject starv'd, the beast was fed.
Proud Nimrod first the bloody chase began,
A mighty hunter, and his prey was man;
Our haughty Norman boasts that barbarous name,
And makes his trembling slaves the royal game.
The fields are ravish'd from th' industrious swains,
From men their cities, and from gods their fanes:
The levell'd towns with weeds lie cover'd o'er;
The hollow winds through naked temples roar;
Round broken columns clasping ivy twined;
O'er heaps of ruin stalk'd the stately hind;
The fox obscene to gaping tombs retires,
And savage howlings fill the sacred quires.
Awed by his Nobles, by his Commons cursed,
Th' oppressor ruled tyrannic where he durst,
Stretch'd o'er the poor and Church his iron rod,
And served alike his vassals and his God.
Whom even the Saxon spared, and bloody Dane,
The wanton victims of his sport remain.
But see, the man who spacious regions gave
A waste for beasts, himself denied a grave!
Stretch'd on the lawn his second hope survey,
At once the chaser, and at once the prey:
Lo Rufus, tugging at the deadly dart,
Bleeds in the forest like a wounded hart.
Succeeding monarchs heard the subjects' cries,
Nor saw displeased the peaceful cottage rise.
Then gathering flocks on unknown mountains fed,
O'er sandy wilds were yellow harvests spread.
The forests wonder'd at th' unusual grain,
And sacred transport touch'd the conscious swain.
Fair Liberty, Britannia's goddess, rears
Her cheerful head, and leads the golden years.

*   *   *

Here too, 'tis sung, of old Diana stray'd,
And Cynthus' top forsook for Windsor shade!
Here was she seen o'er airy wastes to rove,
Seek the clear spring, or haunt the pathless grove;
Here arm'd with silver bows, in early dawn,
Her buskin'd virgins traced the dewy lawn.

    Above the rest a rural nymph was famed,
Thy offspring, Thames! the fair Lodona named:
(Lodona's fate, in long oblivion cast,
The Muse shall sing, and what she sings shall last.)
Scarce could the goddess from her nymph be known,
But by the crescent, and the golden zone.
She scorn'd the praise of beauty, and the care;
A belt her waist, a fillet binds her hair;
A painted quiver on her shoulder sounds,
And with her dart the flying deer she wounds.
It chanced, as eager of the chase, the maid
Beyond the forest's verdant limits stray'd,
Pan saw and loved, and, burning with desire,
Pursued her flight, her flight increased his fire.
Not half so swift the trembling doves can fly,
When the fierce eagle cleaves the liquid sky;
Not half so swiftly the fierce eagle moves,
When through the clouds he drives the trembling doves;
As from the god she flew with furious pace,
Or as the god, more furious, urged the chase.
Now fainting, sinking, pale, the nymph appears;
Now close behind, his sounding steps she hears;
And now his shadow reach'd her as she run,
His shadow lengthen'd by the setting sun;
And now his shorter breath, with sultry air,
Pants on her neck, and fans her parting hair.
In vain on Father Thames she calls for aid,
Nor could Diana help her injured maid.
Faint, breathless, thus she pray'd, nor pray'd in vain:
'Ah, Cynthia! ah—though banish'd from thy train,
Let me, O let me, to the shades repair,
My native shades—there weep, and murmur there.'
She said, and melting as in tears she lay,
In a soft silver stream dissolved away.
The silver stream her virgin coldness keeps,
For ever murmurs, and for ever weeps;
Still bears the name the hapless virgin bore,
And bathes the forest where she ranged before.

In her chaste current oft the goddess laves,
And with celestial tears augments the waves.
Oft in her glass the musing shepherd spies
The headlong mountains and the downward skies,
The watery landskip of the pendant woods,
And absent trees that tremble in the floods;
In the clear azure gleam the flocks are seen,
And floating forests paint the waves with green,
Through the fair scene roll slow the ling'ring streams,
Then foaming pour along, and rush into the Thames.
    Thou, too, great father of the British floods!
With joyful pride survey'st our lofty woods;
Where towering oaks their growing honours rear
And future navies on thy shores appear.
Not Neptune's self from all her streams receives
A wealthier tribute, than to thine he gives.
No seas so rich, so gay no banks appear.
No lake so gentle, and no spring so clear.
Nor Po so swells the fabling poet's lays,
While led along the skies his current strays,
As thine, which visits Windsor's famed abodes,
To grace the mansion of our earthly gods:
Nor all his stars above a lustre show,
Like the bright beauties on thy banks below;
Where Jove, subdued by mortal passion still,
Might change Olympus for a nobler hill.

from *The Rape of the Lock*

CANTO I

AND now, unveil'd, the toilet stands display'd,
Each silver vase in mystic order laid.
First, robed in white, the nymph intent adores,
With head uncover'd, the cosmetic powers.
A heavn'nly image in the glass appears,
To that she bends, to that her eye she rears;
Th' inferior priestess, at her altar's side,
Trembling, begins the sacred rites of pride.
Unnumber'd treasures ope at once, and here
The various offerings of the world appear;
From each she nicely culls with curious toil,
And decks the goddess with the glitt'ring spoil.

This casket India's glowing gems unlocks,
And all Arabia breathes from yonder box.
The tortoise here and elephant unite,
Transform'd to combs, the speckled and the white.
Here files of pins extend their shining rows,
Puffs, powders, patches, Bibles, billet-doux.
Now awful beauty puts on all its arms;
The fair each moment rises in her charms,
Repairs her smiles, awakens every grace,
And calls forth all the wonders of her face:
Sees by degrees a purer blush arise,
And keener lightnings quicken in her eyes.
The busy sylphs surround their darling care,
These set the head, and those divide the hair,
Some fold the sleeve, while others plait the gown;
And Betty's praised for labours not her own.

CANTO II

Not with more glories, in th' ethereal plain,
The sun first rises o'er the purpled main,
Than, issuing forth, the rival of his beams
Launch'd on the bosom of the silver Thames.
Fair nymphs and well-dress'd youths around her shone,
But every eye was fix'd on her alone.
On her white breast a sparkling cross she wore,
Which Jews might kiss, and infidels adore.
Her lively looks a sprightly mind disclose,
Quick as her eyes, and as unfix'd as those:
Favours to none, to all she smiles extends;
Oft she rejects, but never once offends.
Bright as the sun, her eyes the gazers strike,
And, like the sun, they shine on all alike.
Yet graceful ease, and sweetness void of pride,
Might hide her faults, if belles had faults to hide:
If to her share some female errors fall,
Look on her face, and you'll forget them all.
  This nymph, to the destruction of mankind,
Nourish'd two locks, which graceful hung behind
In equal curls, and well conspired to deck
With shining ringlets the smooth ivory neck.
Love in these labyrinths his slaves detains,
And mighty hearts are held in slender chains.
With hairy springes we the birds betray,
Slight lines of hair surprise the finny prey,

Fair tresses man's imperial race insnare,
And beauty draws us with a single hair.

    Th' adventurous baron the bright locks admired;
He saw, he wish'd, and to the prize aspired.
Resolved to win, he meditates the way,
By force to ravish, or by fraud betray;
For when success a lover's toils attends,
Few ask, if fraud or force attain'd his ends.

    For this, ere Phœbus rose, he had implored
Propitious Heaven, and every power adored:
But chiefly Love—to Love an altar built,
Of twelve vast French romances, neatly gilt.
There lay three garters, half a pair of gloves;
And all the trophies of his former loves:
With tender billet-doux he lights the pyre,
And breathes three amorous sighs to raise the fire.
Then prostrate falls, and begs with ardent eyes
Soon to obtain, and long possess the prize:
The powers gave ear, and granted half his prayer,
The rest, the winds dispersed in empty air.

    But now secure the painted vessel glides,
The sun-beams trembling on the floating tides;
While melting music steals upon the sky,
And soften'd sounds along the waters die;
Smooth flow the waves, the zephyrs gently play,
Belinda smiled, and all the world was gay.
All but the sylph—with careful thoughts oppress'd,
Th' impending woe sat heavy on his breast.
He summons straight his denizens of air;
The lucid squadrons round the sails repair:
Soft o'er the shrouds aërial whispers breathe,
That seem'd but zephyrs to the train beneath.
Some to the sun their insect-wings unfold,
Waft on the breeze, or sink in clouds of gold;
Transparent forms, too fine for mortal sight,
Their fluid bodies half dissolved in light.
Loose to the wind their airy garments flew,
Thin glittering textures of the filmy dew,
Dipp'd in the richest tincture of the skies,
Where light disports in ever-mingling dyes;
While ev'ry beam new transient colours flings,
Colours that change whene'er they wave their wings.
Amid the circle on the gilded mast,
Superior by the head, was Ariel placed;

His purple pinions op'ning to the sun,
He raised his azure wand, and thus begun:
  'Ye sylphs and sylphids to your chief give ear;
Fays, fairies, genii, elves, and dæmons, hear:
Ye know the spheres, and various tasks assign'd
By laws eternal to the aërial kind.
Some in the fields of purest ether play,
And bask and whiten in the blaze of day.
Some guide the course of wand'ring orbs on high,
Or roll the planets through the boundless sky.
Some less refined beneath the moon's pale light
Pursue the stars that shoot athwart the night,
Or suck the mists in grosser air below,
Or dip their pinions in the painted bow,
Or brew fierce tempests on the wintry main,
Or o'er the glebe distil the kindly rain.
Others on earth o'er human race preside,
Watch all their ways, and all their actions guide:
Of these the chief the care of nations own,
And guard with arms divine the British throne.
  'Our humbler province is to tend the fair,
Not a less pleasing, though less glorious care;
To save the powder from too rude a gale,
Nor let the imprison'd essences exhale;
To draw fresh colours from the vernal flowers;
To steal the rainbows, ere they drop in showers,
A brighter wash; to curl their waving hairs,
Assist their blushes and inspire their airs;
Nay, oft, in dreams, invention we bestow,
To change a flounce, or add a furbelow.
  'This day, black omens threat the brightest fair
That e'er deserved a watchful spirit's care;
Some dire disaster, or by force, or flight;
But what, or where, the Fates have wrapp'd in night.
Whether the nymph shall break Diana's law,
Or some frail china-jar receive a flaw,
Or stain her honour or her new brocade;
Forget her prayers, or miss a masquerade;
Or lose her heart, or necklace, at a ball;
Or whether Heaven has doom'd that Shock must fall.
Haste, then, ye spirits! to your charge repair:
The flutt'ring fan be Zephyretta's care;
The drops to thee, Brillante, we consign;
And, Momentilla, let the watch be thine;

Do thou, Crispissa, tend her fav'rite lock;
Ariel himself shall be the guard of Shock.
  'To fifty chosen sylphs, of special note,
We trust th' important charge, the petticoat:
Oft have we known that seven-fold fence to fail,
Though stiff with hoops, and arm'd with ribs of whale;
Form a strong line about the silver bound,
And guard the wide circumference around.
  'Whatever spirit, careless of his charge,
His post neglects, or leaves the fair at large,
Shall feel sharp vengeance soon o'ertake his sins,
Be stopp'd in vials, or transfix'd with pins;
Or plunged in lakes of bitter washes lie,
Or wedged whole ages in a bodkin's eye:
Gums and pomatums shall his flight restrain,
While clogg'd he beats his silken wings in vain:
Or alum styptics with contracting power
Shrink his thin essence like a rivell'd flower:
Or, as Ixion fix'd, the wretch shall feel
The giddy motion of the whirling wheel,
In fumes of burning chocolate shall glow,
And tremble at the sea that froths below!'
  He spoke; the spirits from the sails descend;
Some, orb in orb, around the nymph extend;
Some thrid the mazy ringlets of her hair;
Some hang upon the pendants of her ear:
With beating hearts the dire event they wait,
Anxious and trembling for the birth of Fate.

*　　*　　*

CANTO III

BUT when to mischief mortals bend their will,
How soon they find fit instruments of ill!
Just then, Clarissa drew with tempting grace
A two-edged weapon from her shining case:
So ladies, in romance, assist their knight,
Present the spear, and arm him for the fight.
He takes the gift with reverence and extends
The little engine on his fingers' ends;
This just behind Belinda's neck he spread,
As o'er the fragrant steams she bends her head.
Swift to the lock a thousand sprites repair,
A thousand wings, by turns, blow back the hair;

And thrice they twitch'd the diamond in her ear;
Thrice she look'd back, and thrice the foe drew near.
Just in that instant, anxious Ariel sought
The close recesses of the virgin's thought:
As on the nosegay in her breast reclin'd,
He watch'd th' ideas rising in her mind,
Sudden he view'd, in spite of all her art,
An earthly lover lurking at her heart.
Amazed, confused, he found his power expired,
Resign'd to fate, and with a sigh retired.
The peer now spreads the glitt'ring forfex wide,
T' inclose the lock; now joins it, to divide.
Ev'n then, before the fatal engine closed,
A wretched sylph too fondly interposed;
Fate urged the shears, and cut the sylph in twain,
(But airy substance soon unites again)
The meeting points the sacred hair dissever
From the fair head, for ever, and for ever!

*   *   *

CANTO IV

BUT anxious cares the pensive nymph oppress'd,
And secret passions labour'd in her breast.
Not youthful kings in battle seized alive,
Not scornful virgins who their charms survive,
Not ardent lovers robb'd of all their bliss,
Not ancient ladies when refused a kiss,
Not tyrants fierce that unrepenting die,
Not Cynthia when her manteau's pinn'd awry,
E'er felt such rage, resentment, and despair,
As thou, sad virgin! for thy ravish'd hair.

   For, that sad moment, when the sylphs withdrew,
And Ariel weeping from Belinda flew,
Umbriel, a dusky, melancholy sprite,
As ever sullied the fair face of light,
Down to the central earth, his proper scene,
Repair'd to search the gloomy Cave of Spleen.

   Swift on his sooty pinions flits the gnome,
And in a vapour reach'd the dismal dome.
No cheerful breeze this sullen region knows,
The dreaded east is all the wind that blows.
Here in a grotto, shelter'd close from air,
And screen'd in shades from day's detested glare,

She sighs for ever on her pensive bed,
Pain at her side, and Megrim at her head.
Two handmaids wait the throne: alike in place,
But diff'ring far in figure and in face.
Here stood Ill-nature like an ancient maid,
Her wrinkled form in black and white array'd;
With store of prayers, for mornings, nights, and noons,
Her hand is fill'd; her bosom with lampoons.
   There Affectation, with sickly mien,
Shows in her cheek the roses of eighteen,
Practised to lisp, and hang the head aside,
Faints into airs, and languishes with pride,
On the rich quilt sinks with becoming woe,
Wrapp'd in a gown, for sickness, and for show.
The fair ones feel such maladies as these,
When each new night-dress gives a new disease.
   A constant vapour o'er the palace flies;
Strange phantoms rising as the mists arise;
Dreadful, as hermits' dreams in haunted shades,
Or bright, as visions of expiring maids.
Now glaring fiends, and snakes on rolling spires,
Pale spectres, gaping tombs, and purple fires:
Now lakes of liquid gold, Elysian scenes,
And crystal domes, and angels in machines.
   Unnumber'd throngs on every side are seen
Of bodies changed to various forms by Spleen.
Here living tea-pots stand, one arm held out,
One bent; the handle this, and that the spout:
A pipkin there, like Homer's tripod walks;
Here sighs a jar, and there a goose-pie talks:
Men prove with child, as powerful fancy works,
And maids turn'd bottles call aloud for corks.
   Safe pass'd the gnome through this fantastic band,
A branch of healing spleen-wort in his hand.
Then thus address'd the power: 'Hail, wayward Queen!
Who rule the sex to fifty from fifteen;
Parent of vapours, and of female wit,
Who give th' hysteric or poetic fit;
On various tempers act by various ways,
Make some take physic, others scribble plays;
Who cause the proud their visits to delay,
And send the godly in a pet to pray;
A nymph there is, that all thy power disdains,
And thousands more in equal mirth maintains.

But oh! if e'er thy gnome could spoil a grace,
Or raise a pimple on a beauteous face,
Like citron waters matrons' cheeks inflame,
Or change complexions at a losing game;
If e'er with airy horns I planted heads,
Or rumpled petticoats, or tumbled beds,
Or caused suspicion when no soul was rude,
Or discomposed the head-dress of a prude,
Or e'er to costive lap-dog gave disease,
Which not the tears of brightest eyes could ease;
Hear me, and touch Belinda with chagrin,
That single act gives half the world the spleen.'
   The Goddess with a discontented air
Seems to reject him, though she grants his prayer.
A wonderous bag with both her hands she binds,
Like that where once Ulysses held the winds;
There she collects the force of female lungs,
Sighs, sobs, and passions, and the war of tongues.
A vial next she fills with fainting fears,
Soft sorrows, melting griefs, and flowing tears.
The gnome rejoicing bears her gifts away,
Spreads his black wings, and slowly mounts to day.
   Sunk in Thalestris' arms the nymph he found,
Her eyes dejected, and her hair unbound.
Full o'er their heads the swelling bag he rent,
And all the furies issued at the vent.
Belinda burns with more than mortal ire,
And fierce Thalestris fans the rising fire;
'O wretched maid!' she spread her hands, and cried,
(While Hampton's echoes, 'Wretched maid!' replied)
'Was it for this you took such constant care
The bodkin, comb, and essence to prepare?
For this your locks in paper durance bound?
For this with torturing irons wreathed around?
For this with fillets strain'd your tender head,
And bravely bore the double loads of lead?
Gods! shall the ravisher display your hair,
While the fops envy and the ladies stare?
Honour forbid! at whose unrivall'd shrine
Ease, pleasure, virtue, all our sex resign.
Methinks already I your tears survey,
Already hear the horrid things they say,
Already see you a degraded toast,
And all your honour in a whisper lost!

How shall I then your helpless fame defend?
'Twill then be infamy to seem your friend!
And shall this prize, th' inestimable prize,
Exposed through crystal to the gazing eyes,
And heighten'd by the diamond's circling rays,
On that rapacious hand for ever blaze?
Sooner shall grass in Hyde Park Circus grow,
And wits take lodgings in the sound of Bow;
Sooner let earth, air, sea, to Chaos fall,
Men, monkeys, lap–dogs, parrots, perish all!'

*   *   *

'Restore the lock!' she cries; and all around
'Restore the lock!' the vaulted roofs rebound.
Not fierce Othello in so loud a strain
Roar'd for the handkerchief that caused his pain.
But see how oft ambitious aims are cross'd,
And chiefs contend till all the prize is lost!
The lock, obtain'd with guilt, and kept with pain,
In every place is sought, but sought in vain:
With such a prize no mortal must be blest,
So Heaven decrees! with Heaven who can contest?
   Some thought it mounted to the lunar sphere,
Since all things lost on earth are treasured there.
There heroes' wits are kept in pond'rous vases,
And beaux' in snuff-boxes and tweezer-cases.
There broken vows, and death-bed alms are found,
And lovers' hearts with ends of riband bound,
The courtier's promises, and sick man's prayers,
The smiles of harlots, and the tears of heirs,
Cages for gnats, and chains to yoke a flea,
Dried butterflies, and tomes of casuistry.
   But trust the Muse—she saw it upward rise,
Though mark'd by none but quick, poetic eyes:
(So Rome's great founder to the heavens withdrew,
To Proculus alone confess'd in view)
A sudden star it shot through liquid air,
And drew behind a radiant trail of hair.
Not Berenice's lock first rose so bright,
The heavens bespangling with dishevell'd light.
The sylphs behold it kindling as it flies,
And pleased pursue its progress through the skies.
   This the beau-monde shall from the Mall survey,
And hail with music its propitious ray.

This the blest lover shall for Venus take,
And send up vows from Rosamonda's lake.
This Partridge soon shall view in cloudless skies,
When next he looks through Galileo's eyes;
And hence th' egregious wizard shall foredoom
The fate of Louis, and the fall of Rome.

    Then cease, bright nymph! to mourn thy ravish'd hair,
Which adds new glory to the shining sphere!
Not all the tresses that fair head can boast
Shall draw such envy as the lock you lost.
For, after all the murders of your eye,
When, after millions slain, yourself shall die;
When those fair suns shall set, as set they must,
And all those tresses shall be laid in dust;
This lock, the Muse shall consecrate to fame,
And 'midst the stars inscribe Belinda's name.

from *The Dunciad*

To Dr. Jonathan Swift

Book I

ARGUMENT

    The proposition, the invocation, and the inscription. Then the original of the great empire of Dulness, and cause of the continuance thereof. The college of the goddess in the city, with her private academy for poets in particular; the governors of it, and the four cardinal virtues. Then the poem hastes into the midst of things, presenting her on the evening of a Lord Mayor's day, revolving the long succession of her sons, and the glories past and to come. She fixes her eyes on Bays to be the instrument of that great event which is the subject of the poem. He is described pensive among his books, giving up the cause, and apprehending the period of her empire: after debating whether to betake himself to the church, or to gaming, or to party-writing, he raises an altar of proper books, and (making first his solemn prayer and declaration) purposes thereon to sacrifice all his unsuccessful writings. As the pile is kindled, the goddess, beholding the flame from her seat, flies and puts it out by casting upon it the poem of Thulé. She forthwith reveals herself to him, transports him to her temple, unfolds her arts, and initiates him into her mysteries; then announcing the death of Eusden, the Poet Laureate, anoints him, carries him to court, and proclaims him successor.

      THE mighty mother, and her son, who brings
      The Smithfield muses to the ear of kings,
      I sing. Say you, her instruments, the great!
      Call'd to this work by Dulness, Jove, and Fate;

You by whose care, in vain decried, and curst,
Still Dunce the second reigns like Dunce the first;
Say, how the goddess bade Britannia sleep,
And pour'd her spirit o'er the land and deep.

   In eldest time, ere mortals writ or read,
Ere Pallas issued from the Thunderer's head,
Dulness o'er all possess'd her ancient right,
Daughter of Chaos and eternal Night:
Fate in their dotage this fair idiot gave,
Gross as her sire, and as her mother grave,
Laborious, heavy, busy, bold, and blind,
She ruled, in native anarchy, the mind.

   Still her old empire to restore she tries,
For, born a goddess, Dulness never dies.

   O thou! whatever title please thine ear,
Dean, Drapier, Bickerstaff, or Gulliver!
Whether thou choose Cervantes' serious air,
Or laugh and shake in Rabelais' easy chair,
Or praise the court, or magnify mankind,
Or thy grieved country's copper chains unbind;
From thy Bœotia though her pow'r retires,
Mourn not, my Swift, at aught our realm acquires.
Here pleased behold her mighty wings outspread
To hatch a new Saturnian age of lead.

   Close to those walls where Folly holds her throne,
And laughs to think Monro would take her down,
Where o'er the gates, by his famed father's hand,
Great Cibber's brazen, brainless brothers stand;
One cell there is, conceal'd from vulgar eye,
The cave of Poverty and Poetry.
Keen, hollow winds howl through the bleak recess,
Emblem of music caused by emptiness.
Hence bards, like Proteus long in vain tied down,
Escape in monsters, and amaze the town.
Hence miscellanies spring, the weekly boast
Of Curll's chaste press, and Lintot's rubric post:
Hence hymning Tyburn's elgiac lines,
Hence journals, medleys, merc'ries, magazines:
Sepulchral lies, our holy walls to grace,
And new-year odes, and all the Grub Street race.

   In clouded majesty here Dulness shone;
Four guardian virtues, round, support her throne:
Fierce champion Fortitude, that knows no fears
Of hisses, blows, or want, or loss of ears:

Calm Temperance, whose blessings those partake
Who hunger and who thirst for scribbling sake:
Prudence, whose glass presents th' approaching jail:
Poetic justice, with her lifted scale,
Where, in nice balance, truth with gold she weighs,
And solid pudding against empty praise.
   Here she beholds the chaos dark and deep,
Where nameless somethings in their causes sleep,
Till Genial Jacob, or a warm third day,
Call forth each mass, a poem, or a play:
How hints, like spawn, scarce quick in embryo lie,
How new-born nonsense first is taught to cry,
Maggots half-form'd in rhyme exactly meet,
And learn to crawl upon poetic feet.
Here one poor word an hundred clenches makes,
And ductile Dulness new meanders takes;
There motley images her fancy strike,
Figures ill-pair'd, and similes unlike.
She sees a mob of metaphors advance,
Pleased with the madness of the mazy dance!
How tragedy and comedy embrace;
How farce and epic get a jumbled race;
How Time himself stands still at her command,
Realms shift their place, and ocean turns to land.
Here gay Description Egypt glads with show'rs,
Or gives to Zembla fruits, to Barca flow'rs;
Glitt'ring with ice here hoary hills are seen,
There painted valleys of eternal green.
In cold December fragrant chaplets blow,
And heavy harvests nod beneath the snow.
   All these, and more, the cloud-compelling queen
Beholds through fogs, that magnify the scene.
She, tinsell'd o'er in robes of varying hues,
With self-applause her wild creation views;
Sees momentary monsters rise and fall,
And with her own fool's-colours gilds them all.
   'Twas on the day, when Thorold rich and grave,
Like Cimon, triumph'd both on land and wave:
(Pomps without guilt, of bloodless swords and maces,
Glad chains, warm furs, broad banners, and broad faces)
Now night descending, the proud scene was o'er,
But lived, in Settle's numbers, one day more.
Now mayors and shrieves all hush'd and satiate lay,
Yet eat, in dreams, the custard of the day;

While pensive poets painful vigils keep,
Sleepless themselves to give their readers sleep.
Much to the mindful queen the feast recalls
What city swans once sung within the walls;
Much she revolves their arts, their ancient praise,
And sure succession down from Heywood's days.
She saw, with joy, the line immortal run,
Each sire impress'd and glaring in his son:
So watchful Bruin forms, with plastic care,
Each growing lump, and brings it to a bear.
She saw old Pryn in restless Daniel shine,
And Eusden eke out Blackmore's endless line;
She saw slow Philips creep like Tate's poor page,
And all the mighty mad in Dennis rage.
   In each she marks her image full express'd,
But chief in Bays's monster-breeding breast;
Bays, form'd by Nature stage and town to bless,
And act, and be, a coxcomb with success.
Dulness with transport eyes the lively dunce,
Rememb'ring she herself was Pertness once.
Now (shame to Fortune!) an ill run at play
Blank'd his bold visage, and a thin third day:
Swearing and supperless the hero sate,
Blasphemed his gods, the dice, and damn'd his fate.
Then gnaw'd his pen, then dash'd it on the ground,
Sinking from thought to thought, a vast profound!
Plunged for his sense, but found no bottom there,
Yet wrote and founder'd on, in mere despair.
Round him much embryo, much abortion lay,
Much future ode, and abdicated play;
Nonsense precipitate, like running lead,
That slipp'd through cracks and zig-zags of the head;
All that on Folly Frenzy could beget,
Fruits of dull heat, and sooterkins of wit.
Next, o'er his books his eyes began to roll,
In pleasing memory of all he stole,
How here he sipped, how there he plundered snug,
And sucked all o'er, like an industrious bug.
Here lay poor Fletcher's half-eat scenes, and here
The frippery of crucified Molière;
There hapless Shakespeare, yet of Tibbald sore,
Wished he had blotted for himself before.
The rest on outside merit but presume,
Or serve (like other fools) to fill a room;

Such with their shelves as due proportion hold,
Or their fond parents dressed in red and gold;
Or where the pictures for the page atone,
And Quarles is saved by beauties not his own.
Here swells the shelf with Ogilby the great;
There, stamped with arms, Newcastle shines complete:
Here all his suff'ring brotherhood retire,
And 'scape the martyrdom of jakes and fire:
A Gothic library! of Greece and Rome
Well purged, and worthy Settle, Banks, and Broome.
    But, high above, more solid learning shone,
The classics of an age that heard of none;
There Caxton slept, with Wynkyn at his side,
One clasped in wood, and one in strong cow-hide.
There saved by spice, like mummies, many a year,
Dry bodies of divinity appear;
De Lyra there a dreadful front extends,
And here the groaning shelves Philemon bends.
    Of these, twelve volumes, twelve of amplest size,
Redeemed from tapers and defrauded pies,
Inspired he seizes; these are altar raise;
An hecatomb of pure unsullied lays
That altar crowns; a folio common-place
Founds the whole pile, of all his works the base;
Quartos, octavos, shape the less'ning pyre;
A twisted birthday ode completes the spire.
    Then he: 'Great tamer of all human art!
First in my care, and ever at my heart;
Dulness! whose good old cause I yet defend,
With whom my muse began, with whom shall end,
E'er since Sir Fopling's periwig was praise,
To the last honours of the Butt and Bays;
O thou! of bus'ness the directing soul!
To this our head like bias to the bowl,
Which, as more pond'rous, made its aim more true,
Obliquely waddling to the mark in view:
O! ever gracious to perplexed mankind,
Still spread a healing mist before the mind;
And, lest we err by wit's wild dancing light,
Secure us kindly in our native night.
Or, if to wit a coxcomb make pretence,
Guard the sure barrier between that and sense;
Or quite unravel all the reas'ning thread,
And hang some curious cobweb in its stead!

As, forced from wind-guns, lead itself can fly,
And pond'rous slugs cut swiftly through the sky;
As clocks to weight their nimble motion owe,
The wheels above urged by the load below:
Me emptiness and dulness could inspire,
And were my elasticity and fire.
Some demon stole my pen (forgive the offence)
And once betrayed me into common sense:
Else all my prose and verse were much the same;
This prose on stilts, that poetry fall'n lame.
Did on the stage my fops appear confined?
My life gave ampler lessons to mankind.
Did the dead letter unsuccessful prove?
The brisk example never failed to move.
Yet sure had Heav'n decreed to save the state,
Heav'n had decreed these works a longer date.
Could Troy be saved by any single hand,
This grey-goose weapon must have made her stand.
What can I now? my Fletcher cast aside,
Take up the Bible, once my better guide?
Or tread the path by vent'rous heroes trod,
This box my thunder, this right hand my God?
Or chaired at White's amidst the doctors sit,
Teach oaths to gamesters, and to nobles wit?
Or bidst thou rather party to embrace?
(A friend to party thou, and all her race;
'Tis the same rope at different ends they twist;
To dulness Ridpath is as dear as Mist.)
Shall I, like Curtius, desp'rate in my zeal,
O'er head and ears plunge for the commonweal?
Or rob Rome's ancient geese of all their glories,
And cackling save the monarchy of Tories?
Hold—to the minister I more incline;
To serve his cause, O queen! is serving thine.
And see! thy very gazetteers give o'er,
Even Ralph repents, and Henley writes no more.
What then remains? Ourself. Still, still remain
Cibberian forehead, and Cibberian brain.
This brazen brightness, to the squire so dear;
This polished hardness, that reflects the peer:
This arch absurd, that wit and fool delights;
This mess, tossed up of Hockley-hole and White's;
Where dukes and butchers join to wreathe my crown,
At once the bear and fiddle of the town.

'O born in sin, and forth in folly brought!
Works damned, or to be damned! (your father's fault)
Go, purified by flames ascend the sky,
My better and more Christian progeny!
Unstained, untouched, and yet in maiden sheets;
While all your smutty sisters walk the streets.
Ye shall not beg, like gratis-given Bland,
Sent with a pass, and vagrant through the land;
Not sail with Ward, to ape-and-monkey climes,
Where vile Mundungus trucks for viler rhymes:
Not sulphur-tipt, emblaze an ale-house fire;
Not wrap up oranges, to pelt your sire!
O! pass more innocent, in infant state,
To the mild limbo of our father Tate:
Or peaceably forgot, at one be blest
In Shadwell's bosom with eternal rest!
Soon to that mass of nonsense to return,
Where things destroyed are swept to things unborn.'
    With that, a tear (portentous sign of grace!)
Stole from the master of the seven-fold face;
And thrice he lifted high the birthday brand,
And thrice he dropt it from his quiv'ring hand;
Then lights the structure, with averted eyes:
The rolling smokes involve the sacrifice.
The opening clouds disclose each work by turns;
Now flames the Cid, and now Perolla burns;
Great Cæsar roars, and hisses in the fires;
King John in silence modestly expires;
No merit now the dear Nonjuror claims,
Molière's old stubble in a moment flames.
Tears gushed again, as from pale Priam's eyes
When the last blaze sent Ilion to the skies.
    Roused by the light, old Dulness heaved the head,
Then snatched a sheet of Thulé from her bed;
Sudden she flies, and whelms it o'er the pyre;
Down sink the flames, and with a hiss expire.
    Her ample presence fills up all the place;
A veil of fogs dilates her awful face:
Great in her charms! as when on shrieves and may'rs
She looks, and breathes herself into their airs.
She bids him wait her to her sacred dome:
Well pleased he entered, and confessed his home.
So spirits ending their terrestrial race
Ascend, and recognise their native place.

This the great mother dearer held than all
The clubs of Quidnuncs, or her own Guildhall:
Here stood her opium, here she nursed her owls,
And here she planned th' imperial seat of fools.

Here to her chosen all her works she shows;
Prose swelled to verse, verse loit'ring into prose:
How random thoughts now meaning chance to find,
Now leave all memory of sense behind;
How prologues into prefaces decay,
And these to notes are frittered quite away.
How index-learning turns no student pale,
Yet holds the eel of science by the tail:
How, with less reading than makes felons scape,
Less human genius than God gives an ape,
Small thanks to France, and none to Rome or Greece,
A past, vamped, future, old, revived, new piece,
'Twixt Plautus, Fletcher, Shakespeare and Corneille,
Can make a Cibber, Tibbald, or Ozell.

The Goddess then, o'er his annointed head,
With mystic words, the sacred opium shed.
And lo! her bird (a monster of a fowl,
Something betwixt a Heideggre and owl)
Perched on his crown. 'All hail! and hail again,
My son: the promised land expect thy reign.
Know, Eusden thirsts no more for sack or praise;
He sleeps among the dull of ancient days;
Safe, where no critics damn, no duns molest,
Where wretched Withers, Ward, and Gildon rest,
And high-born Howard, more majestic sire,
With 'Fool of Quality' completes the quire.
Thou, Cibber! thou, his laurel shalt support,
Folly, my son, has still a friend at court.
Lift up your gates, ye princes, see him come!
Sound, sound, ye viols; be the cat-call dumb!
Bring, bring the madding bay, the drunken vine;
The creeping, dirty, courtly ivy join.
And thou! his aide-de-camp, lead on my sons,
Light-armed with points, antitheses, and puns.
Let Bawdry, Billingsgate, my daughters dear,
Support his front, and oaths bring up the rear:
And under his, and under Archer's wing,
Gaming and Grub Street skulk behind the king.

'O! when shall rise a monarch all our own,
And I, a nursing-mother, rock the throne;

'Twixt prince and people close the curtain draw,
Shade him from light, and cover him from law;
Fatten the courtier, starve the learned band,
And suckle armies, and dry-nurse the land:
Till senates nod to lullabies divine,
And all be sleep, as at an ode of thine.'
  She ceased. Then swells the chapel-royal throat:
'God save King Cibber!' mounts in every note.
Familiar White's, 'God save King Colley!' cries;
'God save King Colley!' Drury Lane replies:
To Needham's quick the voice triumphal rode,
But pious Needham dropt the name of God:
Back to the Devil the last echoes roll,
And 'Coll!' each butcher roars at Hockley Hole.
  So when Jove's block descended from on high
(As sings thy great forefather Ogilby)
Loud thunder to its bottom shook the bog,
And the hoarse nation croaked, 'God save King Log!'

Book II

ARGUMENT

The king being proclaimed, the solemnity is graced with public games and sports of various kinds; not instituted by the hero, as by Æneas in Virgil, but for greater honour by the goddess in person (in like manner as the games Pythia, Isthmia, etc., were anciently said to be ordained by the gods, and as Thetis herself appearing, according to Homer, *Odyss.* xxiv., proposed the prizes in honour of her son Achilles). Hither flock the poets and critics, attended, as is but just, with their patrons and booksellers. The goddess is first pleased, for her disport, to propose games to the booksellers, and setteth up the phantom of a poet, which they contend to overtake. The races described, with their divers accidents. Next, the game for a poetess. Then follow the exercises for the poets, of tickling, vociferating, diving: The first holds forth the arts and practices of dedicators, the second of disputants and fustian poets, the third of profound, dark, and dirty party-writers. Lastly, for the critics, the goddess proposes (with great propriety) an exercise, not of their parts, but their patience, in hearing the works of two voluminous authors, one in verse and the other in prose, deliberately read without sleeping. The various effects of which, with the several degrees and manners of their operation, are here set forth; till the whole number, not of critics only, but of spectators, actors, and all present, fall asleep; which naturally and necessarily ends the games.

This labour passed, by Bridewell all descend,
(As morning pray'r and flagellation end)
To where Fleet-ditch with disemboguing streams
Rolls the large tribute of dead dogs to Thames,
The king of dykes! than whom no sluice of mud
With deeper sable blots the silver flood.
'Here strip, my children! here at once leap in,
Here prove who best can dash through thick and thin,
And who the most in love of dirt excel,
Or dark dexterity of groping well.
Who flings most filth, and wide pollutes around
The stream, be his the weekly journals bound;
A pig of lead to him who dives the best;
A peck of coals a-piece shall glad the rest.'
    In naked majesty Oldmixon stands,
And Milo-like surveys his arms and hands;
Then, sighing, thus, 'And am I now three-score?
Ah why, ye gods, should two and two make four?'
He said, and climbed a stranded lighter's height,
Shot to the black abyss, and plunged downright.
The senior's judgment all the crowd admire,
Who but to sink the deeper, rose the higher.
    Next Smedley dived, slow circles dimpled o'er
The quaking mud, that closed, and oped no more.
All look, all sigh, and call on Smedley lost;
'Smedley' in vain resounds through all the coast.
    Then essayed; scarce vanished out of sight,
He buoys up instant, and returns to light:
He bears no token of the sabler streams,
And mounts far off among the swans of Thames.
    True to the bottom see Concanen creep,
A cold, long-winded native of the deep;
If perseverance gain the diver's prize,
Not everlasting Blackmore this denies;
No noise, no stir, no motion canst thou make,
Th' unconscious stream sleep o'er thee like a lake.
    Next plunged a feeble, but a desp'rate pack,
With each a sickly brother at his back:
Sons of a day! just buoyant on the flood,
Then numbered with the puppies in the mud.
Ask ye their names? I could as soon disclose
The names of these blind puppies as of those.
Fast by, like Niobe, (her children gone)
Sits mother Osborne, stupefied to stone!

And monumental brass this record bears,
'These are,—ah no! these were, the gazetteers!'
  Not so bold Arnall; with a weight of skull,
Furious he dives, precipitately dull.
Whirlpools and storms his circling arm invest.
With all the might of gravitation blest.
No crab more active in the dirty dance,
Downward to climb, and backward to advance.
He brings up half the bottom on his head,
And loudly claims the journals and the lead.
  The plunging prelate, and his pond'rous grace,
With holy envy gave one layman place.
When lo! a burst of thunder shook the flood;
Slow rose a form, in majesty of mud;
Shaking the horrors of his sable brows,
And each ferocious feature grim with ooze.
Greater he looks, and more than mortal stares;
Then thus the wonders of the deep declares.
  First he relates, how sinking to the chin,
Smit with his mien the mud-nymphs sucked him in:
How young Lutetia, softer than the down,
Nigrina black, and Merdamante brown,
Vied for his love in jetty bowers below,
As Hylas fair was ravished long ago.
Then sung, how shown him by the nut-brown maids
A branch of Styx here rises from the shades,
That tinctured as it runs with Lethe's streams,
And wafting vapours from the land of dreams,
(As under seas Alpheus' secret sluice
Bears Pisa's off'rings to his Arethuse)
Pours into Thames: and hence the mingled wave
Intoxicates the pert, and lulls the grave:
Here brisker vapours o'er the temple creep,
There, all from Paul's to Aldgate drink and sleep.
  Thence to the banks where rev'rend bards repose,
They led him soft; each rev'rend bard arose;
And Milbourn chief, deputed by the rest,
Gave him the cassock, surcingle, and vest.
'Receive' (he said) 'these robes which once were mine,
Dulness is sacred in a sound divine.'
  'Proceed, great days! till learning fly the shore,
Till birch shall blush with noble blood no more,
Till Thames see Eton's sons for ever play,
Till Westminster's whole year be holiday,

Till Isis' elders reel, their pupils' sport,
And Alma Mater lie dissolved in port!'
  'Enough! enough!' the raptured monarch cries;
And through the iv'ry gate the vision flies.

Epistle to Dr. Arbuthnot

Neque sermonibus vulgi dederis te, nec in præmiis humanis spem posueris rerum tuarum; suis te oportet illecebris ipsa virtus trahat ad verum decus. Quid de te alii loquantur, ipsi videant, sed loquentur tamen.—CICERO.

[And do not yield yourself up to the speeches of the vulgar, nor in your affairs place hope in human rewards: virtue ought to draw you to true glory by its own allurements. Why should others speak of you? Let them study themselves—yet they will speak.]

ADVERTISEMENT

  This paper is a sort of bill of complaint, begun many years since, and drawn up by snatches, as the several occasions offered. I had no thoughts of publishing it, till it pleased some persons of rank and fortune (the authors of *Verses to the Imitator of Horace*, and of an *Epistle to a Doctor of Divinity from a Nobleman at Hampton Court*) to attack, in a very extraordinary manner, not only my writings (of which, being public, the public is judge), but my person, morals, and family, whereof, to those who know me not, a truer information may be requisite. Being divided between the necessity to say something of myself and my own laziness to undertake so awkward a task, I thought it the shortest way to put the last hand to this Epistle. If it have anything pleasing, it will be that by which I am most desirous to please, the truth and the sentiment; and if anything offensive, it will be only to those I am least sorry to offend, the vicious or the ungenerous.

  Many will know their own pictures in it, there being not a circumstance but what is true; but I have for the most part spared their names, and they may escape being laughed at if they please.

  I would have some of them know it was owing to the request of the learned and candid friend to whom it is inscribed that I make not as free use of theirs as they have done of mine. However, I shall have this advantage and honour on my side, that whereas, by their proceeding, any abuse may be directed at any man, no injury can possibly be done by mine, since a nameless character can never be found out but by its truth and likeness.

    P. SHUT, shut the door, good John! fatigued, I said;
    Tie up the knocker, say I'm sick, I'm dead.
    The Dog-star rages! nay 'tis past a doubt,
    All Bedlam, or Parnassus, is let out:
    Fire in each eye, and papers in each hand,
    They rave, recite, and madden round the land.

What walls can guard me, or what shades can hide?
They pierce my thickets, through my grot they glide,
By land, by water, they renew the charge,
They stop the chariot, and they board the barge.
No place is sacred, not the church is free,
Ev'n Sunday shines no Sabbath-day to me:
Then from the Mint walks forth the man of rhyme,
Happy! to catch me, just at dinner-time.

Is there a parson, much bemused in beer,
A maudlin poetess, a rhyming peer,
A clerk, foredoom'd his father's soul to cross,
Who pens a stanza, when he should engross?
Is there, who, lock'd from ink and paper, scrawls
With desperate charcoal round his darken'd walls?
All fly to Twit'nam, and in humble strain
Apply to me, to keep them made or vain.
Arthur, whose giddy son neglects the laws,
Imputes to me and my damn'd works the cause:
Poor Cornus sees his frantic wife elope,
And curses wit, and poetry, and Pope.

Friend to my life! (which did not you prolong,
The world had wanted many an idle song)
What drop or nostrum can this plague remove?
Or which must end me, a fool's wrath or love?
A dire dilemma! either way I'm sped,
If foes, they write, if friends, they read me dead.
Seized and tied down to judge, how wretched I!
Who can't be silent, and who will not lie:
To laugh, were want of goodness and of grace,
And to be grave, exceeds all power of face.
I sit with sad civility, I read
With honest anguish, and an aching head;
And drop at last, but in unwilling ears,
This saving counsel,—'Keep your piece nine years.'

'Nine years!' cries he, who, high in Drury Lane,
Lull'd by soft zephyrs through the broken pane,
Rhymes ere he wakes, and prints before Term ends,
Obliged by hunger, and request of friends:
'The piece, you think, is incorrect? why take it,
I'm all submission; what you'd have it, make it.'

Three things another's modest wishes bound,
My friendship, and a prologue, and ten pound.

Pitholeon sends to me: 'You know his grace,
I want a patron; ask him for a place.'

Pitholeon libell'd me—'But here's a letter
Informs you, Sir, 'twas when he knew no better.
Dare you refuse him? Curll invites to dine,
He'll write a journal, or he'll turn divine.'
Bless me! a packet. ''Tis a strange sues,
A virgin tragedy, an orphan Muse.'
If I dislike it, 'Furies, death and rage!'
If I approve, 'Commend it to the stage.'
There (thank my stars) my whole commission ends,
The players and I are, luckily, no friends;
Fired that the house reject him, ''Sdeath! I'll print it,
And shame the fools—Your interest, Sir, with Lintot.'
Lintot, dull rogue! will think your price too much:
'Not, Sir, if you revise it, and retouch.'
All my demurs but double his attacks:
And last he whispers, 'Do; and we go snacks.'
Glad of a quarrel, straight I clap the door:
Sir, let me see your works and you no more.
    'Tis sung, when Midas' ears began to spring
(Midas, a sacred person and a king),
His very minister who spied them first
(Some say his queen) was forced to speak or burst:
And is not mine, my friend, a sorer case,
When every coxcomb perks them in my face!
    A. Good friend, forbear! you deal in dangerous things,
I'd never name queens, ministers, or kings:
Keep close to ears, and those let asses prick,
'Tis nothing——*P.* Nothing? if they bite and kick?
Out with it, DUNCIAD! let the secret pass,
That secret to each fool, that he's an ass:
The truth once told (and wherefore should we lie?)
The Queen of Midas slept, and so may I.
    You think this cruel? Take it for a rule,
No creature smarts so little as a fool.
Let peals of laughter, Codrus! round thee break,
Thou unconcerned canst hear the mighty crack:
Pit, box, and gallery in convulsions hurl'd,
Thou stand'st unshook amidst a bursting world.
Who shames a scribbler? break one cobweb through,
He spins the slight, self-pleasing thread anew:
Destroy his fib or sophistry, in vain,
The creature's at his dirty work again,
Throned in the centre of his thin designs,
Proud of a vast extent of flimsy lines!

Whom have I hurt? has poet yet, or peer,
Lost the arch'd eyebrow, or Parnassian sneer?
And has not Colley still his lord, and whore?
His butchers Henley, his Freemasons Moore?
Does not one table Bavius still admit?
Still to one bishop Philips seem a wit?
Still Sappho——*A*. Hold! for God's sake—you'll offend:
No names—be calm—learn prudence of a friend.
I too could write, and I am twice as tall;
But foes like these——*P*. One flatterer's worse than all.
Of all mad creatures, if the learn'd are right,
It is the slaver kills, and not the bite.
A fool quite angry is quite innocent:
Alas! 'tis ten times worse when they repent.

One dedicates in high heroic prose,
And ridicules beyond a hundred foes:
One from all Grub Street will my fame defend,
And, more abusive, calls himself my friend.
This prints my letters, that expects a bribe,
And others roar aloud, 'Subscribe, subscribe!'

There are, who to my person pay their court:
I cough like Horace, and, though lean, am short.
Ammon's great son one shoulder had too high—
Such Ovid's nose,—and, 'Sir! you have an eye.'
Go on, obliging creatures, make me see
All that disgraced my betters met in me.
Say, for my comfort, languishing in bed,
'Just so immortal Maro held his head';
And, when I die, be sure you let me know
Great Homer died three thousand years ago.
Why did I write? what sin to me unknown
Dipp'd me in ink, my parents', or my own?
As yet a child, nor yet a fool to fame,
I lisp'd in numbers, for the numbers came.
I left no calling for this idle trade,
No duty broke, no father disobey'd:
The Muse but served to ease some friend, not wife,
To help me through this long disease, my life;
To second, ARBUTHNOT! thy art and care,
And teach the being you preserved to bear.

But why then publish? Granville the polite,
And knowing Walsh, would tell me I could write;
Well-natured Garth inflamed with early praise,
And Congreve loved, and Swift endured my lays;

The courtly Talbot, Somers, Sheffield read,
Even mitred Rochester would nod the head,
And St. John's self (great Dryden's friend before)
With open arms received one poet more.
Happy my studies, when by these approved!
Happier their author, when by these beloved!
From these the world will judge of men and books,
Not from the Burnets, Oldmixons, and Cookes.

   Soft were my numbers; who could take offence
While pure description held the place of sense?
Like gentle Fanny's was my flowery theme,
A painted mistress, or a purling stream.
Yet then did Gildon draw his venal quill;
I wish'd the man a dinner, and sate still.
Yet then did Dennis rave in furious fret;
I never answer'd—I was not in debt.
If want provoked, or madness made them print,
I waged no war with Bedlam or the Mint.

   Did some more sober critic come abroad—
If wrong, I smiled; if right, I kiss'd the rod.
Pains, reading, study, are their just pretence,
And all they want is spirit, taste, and sense.
Commas and points they set exactly right,
And 'twere a sin to rob them of their mite;
Yet ne'er one sprig of laurel graced these ribalds,
From slashing Bentley down to piddling Tibbalds:
Each wight, who reads not, and but scans and spells,
Each word-catcher, that lives on syllables,
Even such small critics, some regard may claim,
Preserved in Milton's or in Shakespeare's name.
Pretty! in amber to observe the forms
Of hairs, or straws, or dirt, or grubs, or worms!
The things, we know, are neither rich nor rare,
But wonder how the devil they got there.

   Were others angry—I excused them too;
Well might they rage, I gave them but their due.
A man's true merit 'tis not hard to find;
But each man's secret standard in his mind,
That casting-weight pride adds to emptiness,
This, who can gratify, for who can guess?
The bard whom pilfer'd Pastorals renown,
Who turns a Persian tale for half-a-crown,
Just writes to make his barrenness appear,
And strains from hard-bound brains, eight lines a-year;

He, who still wanting, though he lives on theft,
Steals much, spends little, yet has nothing left:
And he, who now to sense, now nonsense leaning,
Means not, but blunders round about a meaning:
And he, whose fustians' so sublimely bad,
It is not poetry, but prose run mad:
All these, my modest satire bade translate,
And own'd that nine such poets made a Tate.
How did they fume, and stamp, and roar, and chafe!
And swear, not Addison himself was safe.

   Peace to all such! but were there one whose fires
True genius kindles, and fair fame inspires;
Blest with each talent, and each art to please,
And born to write, converse, and live with ease;
Should such a man, too fond to rule alone,
Bear, like the Turk, no brother near the throne,
View him with scornful, yet with jealous eyes,
And hate for arts that caused himself to rise;
Damn with faint praise, assent with civil leer,
And, without sneering, teach the rest to sneer;
Willing to wound, and yet afraid to strike,
Just hint a fault, and hesitate dislike;
Alike reserved to blame, or to commend,
A timorous foe, and a suspicious friend;
Dreading e'en fools, by flatterers besieged,
And so obliging, that he ne'er obliged;
Like Cato, give his little senate laws,
And sit attentive to his own applause;
While wits and Templars every sentence raise,
And wonder with a foolish face of praise—
Who but must laugh, if such a man there be?
Who would not weep, if Atticus were he?

   What though my name stood rubric on the walls,
Or plaster'd posts, with claps, in capitals?
Or smoking forth, a hundred hawkers load,
On wings of winds came flying all abroad?
I sought no homage from the race that write;
I kept, like Asian monarchs, from their sight:
Poems I heeded (now be rhym'd so long)
No more than thou, great George! a birthday song.
I ne'er with wits or witlings pass'd my days,
To spread about the itch of verse and praise;
Nor like a puppy, daggled through the town,
To fetch and carry, sing-song up and down;

Nor at rehearsals sweat, and mouth'd, and cried,
With handkerchief and orange at my side;
But sick of fops, and poetry, and prate,
To Bufo left the whole Castalian state.

Proud as Apollo on his forked hill,
Sate full-blown Bufo, puff'd by every quill;
Fed with soft dedication all day long,
Horace and he went hand in hand in song.
His library (where busts of poets dead
And a true Pindar stood without a head)
Received of wits an undistinguish'd race,
Who first his judgment asked, and then a place:
Much they extoll'd his pictures, much his seat,
And flatter'd every day, and some days eat:
Till grown more frugal in his riper days,
He paid some bards with port, and some with praise,
To some a dry rehearsal was assign'd,
And others (harder still) he paid in kind.
Dryden alone (what wonder?) came not nigh,
Dryden alone escaped this judging eye:
But still the great have kindness in reserve,
He help'd to bury whom he help'd to starve.

May some choice patron bless each grey goose quill!
May every Bavius have his Bufo still!
So when a statesman wants a day's defence,
Or Envy holds a whole week's war with Sense,
Or simple pride for flattery makes demands,
May dunce by dunce be whistled off my hands!
Bless'd be the great! for those they take away,
And those they left me—for they left me GAY;
Left me to see neglected Genius bloom,
Neglected die, and tell it on his tomb:
Of all thy blameless life the sole return
My verse, and QUEENSBERRY weeping o'er thy urn!

Oh let me live my own, and die so too!
(To live and die is all I have to do:)
Maintain a poet's dignity and ease,
And see what friends, and read what books I please:
Above a patron, though I condescend
Sometimes to call a minister my friend.
I was not born for courts or great affairs:
I pay my debts, believe, and say my prayers;
Can sleep without a poem in my head,
Nor know if Dennis be alive or dead.

Why am I ask'd what next shall see the light?
Heavens! was I born for nothing but to write?
Has life no joys for me? or (to be grave)
Have I no friend to serve, no soul to save?
'I found him close with Swift—Indeed? no doubt
(Cries prating Balbus) something will come out.'
'Tis all in vain, deny it as I will:
'No, such a genius never can lie still';
And then for mine obligingly mistakes
The first lampoon Sir Will or Bubo makes.
Poor guiltless I! and can I choose but smile,
When every coxcomb knows me by my style?
    Cursed be the verse, how well soe'er it flow,
That tends to make one worthy man my foe,
Give Virtue scandal, Innocence a fear,
Or from the soft-eyed virgin steal a tear!
But he who hurts a harmless neighbour's peace,
Insults fall'n worth, or beauty in distress,
Who loves a lie, lame slander helps about,
Who writes a libel, or who copies out;
That fop, whose pride affects a patron's name,
Yet absent, wounds an author's honest fame;
Who can your merit selfishly approve,
And show the sense of it without the love;
Who has the vanity to call you friend,
Yet wants the honour, injured, to defend;
Who tells whate'er you think, whate'er you say,
And if he lie not, must at least betray;
Who to the dean and silver bell can swear,
And sees at Canons what was never there;
Who reads, but with a lust to misapply,
Makes satire a lampoon, and fiction lie;
A lash like mine no honest man shall dread,
But all such babbling blockheads in his stead.
    Let Sporus tremble——A. What? that thing of silk,
Sporus, that mere white curd of ass's milk?
Satire or sense, alas! can Sporus feel,
Who breaks a butterfly upon a wheel?
    P. Yet let me flap this bug with gilded wings,
This painted child of dirt, that stinks and stings;
Whose buzz the witty and the fair annoys,
Yet wit ne'er tastes, and beauty ne'er enjoys:
So well-bred spaniels civilly delight
In mumbling of the game they dare not bite.

Eternal smiles his emptiness betray,
As shallow streams run dimpling all the way,
Whether in florid impotence he speaks,
And, as the prompter breathes, the puppet squeaks;
Or at the ear of Eve, familiar toad!
Half froth, half venom, spits himself abroad,
In puns, or politics, or tales, or lies,
Or spite, or smut, or rhymes, or blasphemies.
His wit all see-saw, between that and this,
Now high, now low, now master up, now miss,
And he himself one vile antithesis.
Amphibious thing! that acting either part,
The trifling head, or the corrupted heart;
Fop at the toilet, flatterer at the board,
Now trips a lady, and now struts a lord.
Eve's tempter thus the Rabbins have express'd,
A cherub's face, a reptile all the rest.
Beauty that shocks you, parts that none will trust,
Wit that can creep, and pride that licks the dust.

   Not Fortune's worshipper, nor Fashion's fool,
Not Lucre's madman, nor Ambition's tool,
Not proud, nor servile; be one poet's praise,
That, if he pleased, he pleased by manly ways:
That flattery, even to kings, he held a shame,
And thought a lie in verse or prose the same;
That not in Fancy's maze he wander'd long,
But stoop'd to Truth, and moralised his song:
That not for Fame, but Virtue's better end,
He stood the furious foe, the timid friend,
The damning critic, half-approving wit,
The coxcomb hit, or fearing to be hit;
Laughed at the loss of friends he never had,
The dull, the proud, the wicked, and the mad;
The distant threats of vengeance on his head,
The blow unfelt, the tear he never shed;
The tale revived, the lie so oft o'erthrown,
Th' imputed trash, and dulness not his own;
The morals blacken'd when the writings 'scape,
The libell'd person, and the pictured shape;
Abuse, on all he loved, or loved him, spread,
A friend in exile, or a father dead;
The whisper, that to greatness still too near,
Perhaps yet vibrates on his sovereign's ear—
Welcome for thee, fair Virtue! all the past:

For thee, fair Virtue! welcome even the last!
   A. But why insult the poor, affront the great?
   P. A knave's a knave, to me, in every state;
Alike my scorn, if he succeed or fail,
Sporus at court, or Japhet in a jail,
A hireling scribbler, or a hireling peer,
Knight of the post corrupt, or of the shire;
If on a pillory, or near a throne,
He gain his prince's ear, or lose his own.
   Yet soft by nature, more a dupe than wit,
Sappho can tell you how this man was bit:
This dreaded satirist Dennis will confess
Foe to his pride, but friend to his distress:
So humble, he has knocked at Tibbald's door,
Has drunk with Cibber, nay has rhymed for Moore.
Full ten years slander'd, did he once reply?
Three thousand suns went down on Welsted's lie;
To please a mistress one aspersed his life;
He lash'd him not, but let her be his wife:
Let Budgell charge low Grub Street on his quill,
And write whate'er he pleased, except his will;
Let the two Curlls of town and court abuse
His father, mother, body, soul, and Muse.
Yet why? that father held it for a rule,
It was a sin to call our neighbour fool:
That harmless mother thought no wife a whore:
Hear this, and spare his family, James Moore!
Unspotted names, and memorable long!
If there be force in virtue, or in song.
   Of gentle blood (part shed in honour's cause,
While yet in Britain honour had applause)
Each parent sprung—*A.* What fortune, pray?—*P.* Their own,
And better got, than Bestia's from the throne.
Born to no pride, inheriting no strife,
Nor marrying discord in a noble wife,
Stranger to civil and religious rage,
The good man walk'd innoxious through his age.
No courts he saw, no suits would ever try,
Nor dared an oath, nor hazarded a lie.
Unlearn'd, he knew no schoolman's subtle art,
No language, but the language of the heart.
By nature honest, by experience wise,
Healthy by temperance, and by exercise,
His life, though long, to sickness pass'd unknown,

His death was instant, and without a groan.
O grant me thus to live, and thus to die!
Who sprung from kings shall know less joy than I.
　O friend! may each domestic bliss be thine!
Be no unpleasing melancholy mine:
Me, let the tender office long engage,
To rock the cradle of reposing age,
With lenient arts extend a mother' breath,
Make languour smile, and smooth the bed of death.
Explore the thought, explain the asking eye,
And keep awhile one parent from the sky!
On cares like these if length of days attend,
May Heaven, to bless those days, preserve my friend,
Preserve him social, cheerful, and serene,
And just as rich as when he served a queen.
　A. Whether that blessing be denied or given,
Thus far was right, the rest belongs to Heaven.

JOHN BYROM

1692–1763

The Nimmers

Two foot-companions once in deep discourse—
'Tom,' says the one, 'Let's go and steal a horse.'
'Steal!' says the other, in a huge surprise,
'He that says I'm a thief, I say he lies.'
'Well, well,' replied his friend, 'No such affront;
I did but ask ye: if you won't, you won't.'
So they jogged on, till, in another strain,
The querist moved to honest Tom again.
'Suppose,' says he; 'for supposition's sake—
'Tis but a supposition that I make!—
Suppose that we should filch a horse, I say?'
'Filch? filch?' quoth Tom, demurring by the way;
'That's not so bad as downright theft, I own;
But—yet—methinks—'twere better let alone.
It soundeth something pitiful, and low;
Shall we go filch a horse, you say? why, no;
I'll filch no filching; and I'll tell no lie;
Honesty's the best policy, say I!'

Struck with such vast integrity quite dumb,
His comrade paused; at last, says he, 'Come, come!
Thou art an honest fellow, I agree—
Honest and poor; alas! that should not be,
And dry into the bargain, and no drink!
Shall we go nim a horse, Tom?—What dost think?'

How clear are things when liquor's in the case!
Tom answers quick, with casuistic grace:
'Nim? Yes, yes, yes, let's nim with all my heart;
I see no harm in nimming, for my part.
Hard is the case, now I look sharp into 't,
That honesty should trudge i' th' dirt afoot;
So many empty horses round about,
That honesty should wear its bottoms out!
Besides, shall honesty be choked with thirst?
Were it my Lord Mayor's horse, I'd nim it first!
And, by the by, my lad, no scrubby tit!
There is the best that ever wore a bit
Not far from hence.' 'I take ye,' quoth his friend,
'Is not yon stable, Tom, our journey's end?'

Good wits will jump; both meant the very steed,
The top o' th' country, both for shape and speed.
So to 't they went, and with a halter round
His feathered neck, they nimmed him off the ground.

And now, good people, we should next relate
Of these adventurers the luckless fate.
Poor Tom!—but here the sequel is to seek,
Not being yet translated from the Greek.
Some say, that Tom would honestly have peached,
But by his blabbing friend was over-reached;
Others insist upon 't that both the elves
Were, in like manner, halter-nimmed themselves.

It matters not:—the Moral is the thing,
For which our purpose, neighbours, was to sing.
If it should hit some few amongst the throng,
Let 'em not lay the fault upon the song!
Fair warning, all: He that has got a cap
Now put it on, or else beware a rap!
'Tis but a short one, it is true, but yet
Has a long reach with it, *videlicet*:
'Twixt right and wrong, how many gentle trimmers
Will neither steal nor filch, but will be plaguy nimmers.

Desiderium

MY spirit longeth for Thee,
  Within my troubled breast;
Although I be unworthy
  Of so divine a Guest.

Of so divine a Guest,
  Unworthy though I be;
Yet has my heart no rest,
  Unless it come from Thee.

Unless it come from Thee,
  In vain I look around;
In all that I can see,
  No rest is to be found.

No rest is to be found,
  But in Thy blessèd love;
O! let my wish be crowned,
  And send it from above!

HENRY CAREY

?1693–1743

Sally in Our Alley

OF all the girls that are so smart
  There's none like pretty Sally;
She is the darling of my heart,
  And she lives in our alley.
There is no lady in the land
  Is half so sweet as Sally;
She is the darling of my heart,
  And she lives in our alley.

Her father he makes cabbage-nets,
  And through the streets does cry 'em;
Her mother she sells laces long
  To such as please to buy 'em:

But sure such folks could ne'er beget
   So sweet a girl as Sally!
She is the darling of my heart,
   And she lives in our alley.

When she is by, I leave my work,
   I love her so sincerely;
My master comes like any Turk,
   And bangs me most severely:
But let him bang his bellyful,
   I'll bear it all for Sally;
She is the darling of my heart,
   And she lives in our alley.

Of all the days that's in the week
   I dearly love but one day—
And that's the day that comes betwixt
   A Saturday and Monday;
For then I'm dressed all in my best
   To walk abroad with Sally;
She is the darling of my heart,
   And she lives in our alley.

My master carries me to church,
   And often am I blamèd
Because I leave him in the lurch
   As soon as text is namèd;
I leave the church in sermon-time
   And slink away to Sally;
She is the darling of my heart,
   And she lives in our alley.

When Christmas comes about again,
   O, then I shall have money;
I'll hoard it up, and box it all,
   I'll give it to my honey:
I would it were ten thousand pound,
   I'd give it all to Sally;
She is the darling of my heart,
   And she lives in our alley.

My master and the neighbours all
   Make game of me and Sally,
And, but for her, I'd better be
   A slave and row a galley;
But when my seven long years are out,
   O, then I'll marry Sally;
Oh, then we'll wed, and then we'll bed—
   But not in our alley!

MATTHEW GREEN

1696–1737

from *The Spleen*

WHEN by its magic lantern Spleen
With frightful figures spread life's scene,
And threat'ning prospects urg'd my fears,
A stranger to the luck of heirs;
Reason, some quiet to restore,
Show'd part was substance, shadow more;
With Spleen's dead weight tho' heavy grown
In life's rough tide I sunk not down,
But swam, 'till Fortune threw a rope,
Buoyant on bladders fill'd with hope.

I always choose the plainest food
To mend viscidity of blood.
Hail! water-gruel, healing pow'r,
Of easy access to the poor;
Thy help love's confessors implore,
And doctors secretly adore;
To thee I fly, by thee dilute—
Through veins my blood does quicker shoot,
And by swift currents throws off clean
Prolific particles of Spleen.

I never sick by drinking grow,
Nor keep myself a cup too low,
And seldom Chloe's lodgings haunt,
Thirsty of spirits which I want.

Hunting I reckon very good
To brace the nerves, and stir the blood:
But after no field-honours itch,
Achiev'd by leaping hedge and ditch.
While Spleen lies soft relax'd in bed,
Or o'er coal-fire inclines the head,
Hygeia's sons with hound and horn,
And jovial cry, awake the morn.
These see her from the dusky plight,
Smear'd by th' embraces of the night,
With roral wash redeem her face,
And prove herself of Titan's race,
And, mounting in loose robes the skies,
Shed light and fragrance as she flies.
Then horse and hound fierce joy display,
Exulting at the hark-away,
And in pursuit o'er tainted ground
From lungs robust field-notes resound.
Then, as St. George the dragon slew,
Spleen pierced, trod down, and dying view;
While all their spirits are on wing;
And woods, and hills, and valleys ring . . .
  In rainy days keep double guard,
Or Spleen will surely be too hard;
Which, like those fish by sailors met,
Fly highest while their wings are wet.
In such dull weather, so unfit
To enterprise a work of wit,
When clouds one yard of azure sky,
That's fit for simile, deny,
I dress my face with studious looks,
And shorten tedious hours with books.
But if dull fogs invade the head,
That mem'ry minds not what is read,
I sit in window dry as ark,
And on the drowning world remark;
Or at some coffee house I stray
For news, the manna of the day,
And from the hipp'd discourses gather
That politics go by the weather!
Then seek good-humour'd tavern chums,
And play at cards, but for small sums;
Or with the merry fellows quaff,
And laugh aloud with them that laugh;

Or drink a joco-serious cup
With souls who've took their freedom up,
And let my mind, beguil'd by talk,
In Epicurus' garden walk,
Who thought it Heav'n to be serene;
Pain, hell and purgatory, Spleen . . .
  Me never did ambition seize,
Strange fever most inflam'd by ease!
The active lunacy of pride,
That courts jilt Fortune for a bride,
This par'dise tree, so fair and high,
I view with no aspiring eye:
Like aspen shake the restless leaves,
And Sodom-fruit our pains deceives,
Whence frequent falls give no surprise
But fits of Spleen call'd growing wise.
Greatness in glittering forms display'd
Affects weak eyes much us'd to shade,
And by its falsely envied scene
Gives self-debasing fits of Spleen.
We shou'd be pleas'd that things are so,
Who do for nothing see the show,
And, middle-siz'd, can pass between
Life's hubbub safe, because unseen;
And midst the glare of greatness trace
A watery sunshine in the face,
And pleasures fled to, to redress
The sad fatigue of idleness.
  Contentment, parent of delight,
So much a stranger to our sight,
Say, goddess, in what happy place
Mortals behold thy blooming face;
Thy gracious auspices impart,
And for thy temple, choose my heart.
They, whom thou deignest to inspire,
Thy science learn, to bound desire;
By happy alchemy of mind
They turn to pleasure all they find;
They both disdain in outward mien
The grave and solemn garb of Spleen,
And meretricious arts of dress,
To feign a joy, and hide distress;
Unmov'd when the rude tempest blows,
Without an opiate they repose;

And cover'd by your shield, defy
The whizzing shafts that round them fly;
Nor, meddling with the gods' affairs,
Concern themselves with distant cares;
But place their bliss in mental rest,
And feast upon the good possess'd.

WILLIAM OLDYS

1696–1761

On a Fly Drinking Out of His Cup

BUSY, curious, thirsty fly!
Drink with me and drink as I:
Freely welcome to my cup,
Couldst thou sip and sip it up:
Make the most of life you may,
Life is short and wears away.

Both alike are mine and thine
Hastening quick to their decline:
Thine's a summer, mine's no more,
Though repeated to threescore.
Threescore summers, when they're gone,
Will appear as short as one!

JOHN DYER

?1698–1758

Grongar Hill

SILENT Nymph, with curious eye!
Who the purple ev'ning lie
On the mountain's lonely van,
Beyond the noise of busy man,
Painting fair the form of things,
While the yellow linnet sings;

Or the tuneful nightingale
Charms the forest with her tale;
Come with all thy various hues,
Come, and aid thy sister Muse;
Now while Phœbus riding high
Gives lustre to the land and sky!
Grongar Hill invites my song,
Draw the landskip bright and strong;
Grongar, in whose mossy cells
Sweetly musing Quiet dwells:
Grongar, in whose silent shade
For the modest Muses made,
So oft I have, the even still,
At the fountain of a rill,
Sate upon a flow'ry bed,
With my hands beneath my head;
And stray'd my eyes o'er Towy's flood,
Over mead and over wood,
From house to house, from hill to hill,
Till Contemplation had her fill.

About her chequer'd sides I wind,
And leave his brooks and meads behind,
And groves and grottos where I lay,
And vistas shooting beams of day:
Wider and wider spreads the vale,
As circles on a smooth canal:
The mountains round, unhappy fate,
Sooner or later, of all height!
Withdraw their summits from the skies,
And lessen as the others rise:
Still the prospect wider spreads,
Adds a thousand woods and meads,
Still it widens, widens still,
And sinks the newly risen hill.

Now I gain the mountain's brow,
What a landskip lies below!
No clouds, no vapours intervene,
But the gay, the open scene
Does the face of Nature show,
In the hues of Heav'n's bow!
And swelling to embrace the light,
Spreads around beyond the sight.

Old castles on the cliffs arise,
Proudly tow'ring in the skies!

Rushing from the woods, the spires
Seem from hence ascending fires!
Half his beams Apollo sheds
On the yellow mountain heads!
Gilds the fleeces of the flocks;
And glitters on the broken rocks!
   Below me trees unnumber'd rise,
Beautiful in various dyes:
The gloomy pine, the poplar blue,
The yellow beech, the sable yew,
The slender fir that taper grows,
The sturdy oak, with broad-spread boughs.
And beyond the purple grove,
Haunt of Phyllis, queen of love!
Gaudy as the op'ning dawn,
Lies a long and level lawn,
On which a dark hill, steep and high,
Holds and charms the wand'ring eye!
Deep are his feet in Towy's flood,
His sides are cloth'd with waving wood,
And ancient towers crown his brow,
That cast an awful look below;
Whose ragged walls the ivy creeps,
And with her arms from falling keeps.
So both a safety from the wind
On mutual dependence find.
   'Tis now the raven's bleak abode;
'Tis now th' apartment of the toad;
And there the fox securely feeds,
And there the pois'nous adder breeds,
Conceal'd in ruins, moss and weeds:
While ever and anon there falls
Huge heaps of hoary, moulder'd walls.
Yet time has seen, that lifts the low,
And level lays the lofty brow,
Has seen this broken pile complete,
Big with the vanity of state:
But transient is the smile of Fate!
A little rule, a little sway,
A sunbeam in a winter's day,
Is all the proud and mighty have
Between the cradle and the grave.
   And see the rivers how they run,
Thro' woods and meads, in shade and sun,

Sometimes swift and sometimes slow,
Wave succeeding wave they go
A various journey to the deep,
Like human life to endless sleep!
Thus is nature's vesture wrought
To instruct our wand'ring thought;
Thus she dresses green and gay,
To disperse our cares away.

    Ever changing, ever new,
When will the landskip tire the view!
The fountain's fall, the river's flow,
The woody valleys, warm and low;
The windy summit, wild and high,
Roughly rushing on the sky!
The pleasant seat, the ruin'd tow'r,
The naked rock, the shady bow'r;
The town and village, dome and farm,
Each give each a double charm,
As pearls upon an Ethiop's arm.

    See on the mountain's southern side,
Where the prospect opens wide,
Where the evening gilds the tide,
How close and small the hedges lie!
What streaks of meadows cross the eye!
A step, methinks, may pass the stream,
So little distant dangers seem;
So we mistake the future's face,
Ey'd through hope's deluding glass;
As yon summits soft and fair,
Clad in colours of the air,
Which, to those who journey near,
Barren, brown, and rough appear.
Still we tread, tir'd, the same coarse way,
The present's still a cloudy day.

    Oh, may I with myself agree,
And never covet what I see:
Content me with an humble shade
My passions tam'd, my wishes laid;
For while our wishes wildly roll,
We banish quiet from the soul:
'Tis thus the busy beat the air;
And misers gather wealth and care.

    Now, ev'n now my joy runs high,
As on the mountain turf I lie;

While the wanton Zephyr sings
And in the vale perfumes his wings;
While the waters murmur deep,
While the shepherd charms his sheep;
While the birds unbounded fly,
And with music fill the sky.
Now, ev'n now my joys run high.

   Be full, ye courts, be great who will;
Search for Peace with all your skill:
Open wide the lofty door,
Seek her on the marble floor,
In vain ye search, she is not there,
In vain ye search the domes of care!
Grass and flowers Quiet treads,
On the meads and mountain heads,
Along with Pleasure close ally'd,
Ever by each other's side:
And often, by the murm'ring rill,
Hears the thrush while all is still,
Within the groves of Grongar Hill.

ROBERT BLAIR

1699–1746

from *The Grave*

Peace the End of the Good Man

              SURE the last end
Of the good man is peace! How calm his exit!
Night-dews fall not more gently to the ground,
Nor weary worn-out winds expire so soft.
Behold him! in the evening tide of life,
A life well spent, whose early care it was
His riper years should not upbraid his green:
By unperceived degrees he wears away;
Yet, like the sun, seems larger at his setting!
High in his faith and hopes, look how he reaches
After the prize in view! and, like a bird
That's hampered, struggles hard to get away!
Whilst the glad gates of sight are wide expanded
To let new glories in, the first fair fruits
Of the fast-coming harvest.

All impelled onward alike

On this side, and on that, men see their friends
Drop off, like leaves in autumn; yet launch out
Into fantastic schemes, which the long livers,
In the world's hale and undegenerate days,
Could scarce have leisure for! Fools that we are!
Never to think of death, and of ourselves
At the same time! As if to learn to die
Were no concern of ours. Oh! more than sottish!
For creatures of a day, in gamesome mood
To frolic on Eternity's dread brink,
Unapprehensive; when for aught we know
The very first swol'n surge shall sweep us in.
Think we, or think we not, time hurries on
With a resistless unremitting stream,
Yet treads more soft than e'er did midnight thief,
That slides his hand under the miser's pillow,
And carries off his prize. What is this world?
What but a spacious burial-field unwalled,
Strewed with death's spoils, the spoils of animals
Savage and tame, and full of dead men's bones?
The very turf on which we tread, once lived:
And we that live must lend our carcases
To cover our own offspring; in their turns
They too must cover theirs. 'Tis here all meet!
The shivering Icelander, and sunburnt Moor;
Men of all climes who never met before,
And of all creeds, the Jew, the Turk, and Christian.
Here the proud prince, and favourite yet prouder,
His sovereign's keeper, and the people's scourge,
Are huddled out of sight. Here lie abashed
The great negotiators of the earth,
And celebrated masters of the balance,
Deep read in stratagems, and wiles of courts:
Now vain their treaty-skill! Death scorns to treat.
Here the o'erloaded slave flings down his burthen
From his galled shoulders; and when the cruel tyrant,
With all his guards and tools of power about him,
Is mediating new unheard of hardships,
Mocks his short arm, and quick as thought escapes
When tyrants vex not, and the weary rest.

ROBERT BLAIR

The Grave-yard on a Stormy Night

SEE yonder hallow'd fane, the pious work
Of names once fam'd, now dubious or forgot,
And buried midst the wreck of things which were:
There lie interr'd the more illustrious dead.
The wind is up: hark how it howls! Methinks
Till now I never heard a sound so dreary.
Doors creak, and windows clap, and night's foul bird,
Rook'd in the spire, screams loud! The gloomy aisles,
Black-plaister'd, and hung round with shreds of 'scutcheons
And tatter'd coats of arms, send back the sound,
Laden with heavier airs, from the low vaults,
The mansions of the dead! Rous'd from their slumbers,
In grim array the grizly spectres rise,
Grin horrible, and obstinately sullen
Pass and repass, hush'd as the foot of night!
Again the screech owl shrieks—ungracious sound!
I'll hear no more; it makes one's blood run chill.

Quite round the pile, a row of rev'rend elms,
Co-eval near with that, all ragged show,
Long lash'd by the rude winds; some rift half down
Their branchless trunks, others so thin atop
That scarce two crows cou'd lodge in the same tree.
Strange things, the neighbours say, have happen'd here.
Wild shrieks have issu'd from the hollow tombs;
Dead men have come again, and walk'd about;
And the great bell has toll'd unrung, untouch'd!
Such tales their cheer, at wake or gossiping,
When it draws near the witching time of night.

Oft in the lone churchyard at night I've seen,
By glimpse of moon-shine, chequ'ring through the trees,
The schoolboy, with his satchel in his hand,
Whistling aloud to bear his courage up,
And lightly tripping o'er the long, flat stones,
(With nettles skirted, and with moss o'ergrown)
That tell in homely phrase who lie below.
Sudden he starts! and hears, or thinks he hears,
The sound of something purring at his heels.
Full fast he flies, and dares not look behind him,
Till, out of breath, he overtakes his fellows;
Who gather round, and wonder at the tale

ROBERT BLAIR

Of horrid apparition, tall and ghastly,
That walks at dead of night, or takes his stand
O'er some new-open'd grave; and, strange to tell,
Evanishes at crowing of the cock!

JAMES THOMSON

1700–1748

from *The Seasons*

FLUSHED by the spirit of the genial year,
Now from the virgin's cheek a fresher bloom
Shoots less and less the live carnation round;
Her lips blush deeper sweets; she breathes of youth;
The shining moisture swells into her eyes
In brighter flow; her wishing bosom heaves
With palpitations wild; kind tumults seize
Her veins, and all her yielding soul is love.
From the keen gaze her lover turns away,
Full of the dear ecstatic power, and sick
With sighing languishment. Ah then, ye fair!
Be greatly cautious of your sliding hearts:
Dare not the infectious sigh; the pleading look,
Downcast and low, in meek submission dressed,
But full of guile. Let not the fervent tongue,
Prompt to deceive with adulation smooth,
Gain on your purposed will. Nor in the bower
Where woodbines flaunt and roses shed a couch,
While evening draws her crimson curtains round,
Trust your soft minutes with betraying man.
    And let the aspiring youth beware of love,
Of the smooth glance beware; for 'tis too late,
When on his heart the torrent-softness pours.
Then wisdom prostrate lies, and fading fame
Dissolves in air away; while the fond soul,
Wrapt in gay visions of unreal bliss,
Still paints the illusive form, the kindling grace,
The enticing smile, the modest-seeming eye,
Beneath whose beauteous beams, belying Heaven,
Lurk searchless cunning, cruelty, and death:
And still, false-warbling in his cheated ear,

Her siren voice enchanting draws him on
To guileful shores and meads of fatal joy.
   Even present, in the very lap of love
Inglorious laid—while music flows around,
Perfumes, and oils, and wine, and wanton hours—
Amid the roses fierce repentance rears
Her snaky crest: a quick-returning pang
Shoots through the conscious heart, where honour still
And great design, against the oppressive load
Of luxury, by fits, impatient heave.
   But absent, what fantastic woes, aroused,
Rage in each thought, by restless musing fed,
Chill the warm cheek, and blast the bloom of life!
Neglected fortune flies; and, sliding swift,
Prone into ruin fall his scorned affairs.
'Tis nought but gloom around: the darkened sun
Loses his light. The rosy-bosomed Spring
To weeping fancy pines; and yon bright arch,
Contracted, bends into a dusky vault.
All Nature fades extinct; and she alone
Heard, felt, and seen, possesses every thought,
Fills every sense, and pants in every vein.
Books are but formal dulness, tedious friends;
And sad amid the social band he sits,
Lonely and unattentive. From the tongue
The unfinish'd period falls: while, borne away
On swelling thought, his wafted spirit flies
To the vain bosom of his distant fair;
And leaves the semblance of a lover, fixed
In melancholy site, with head declined,
And love-dejected eyes.

                    *   *   *

   'Tis done! Dread Winter spreads his latest glooms,
And reigns tremendous o'er the conquered year.
How dead the vegetable kingdom lies!
How dumb the tuneful! Horror wide extends
His desolate domain. Behold, fond man!
See here thy pictured life; pass some few years,
Thy flowering Spring, thy Summer's ardent strength,
Thy sober Autumn fading into age,
And pale concluding Winter comes at last
And shuts the scene. Ah! whither now are fled
Those dreams of greatness? those unsolid hopes

Of happiness? those longings after fame?
Those restless cares? those busy bustling days?
Those gay-spent festive nights? those veering thoughts,
Lost between good and ill, that shared thy life?
All now are vanished! Virtue sole survives—
Immortal, never-failing friend of man,
His guide to happiness on high. And see!
'Tis come, the glorious morn! the second birth
Of heaven and earth! awakening nature hears
The new-creating word, and starts to life
In every heightened form, from pain and death
For ever free. The great eternal scheme,
Involving all, and in a perfect whole
Uniting, as the prospect wider spreads,
To reason's eye refined clears up apace.
Ye vainly wise! ye blind presumptuous! now,
Confounded in the dust, adore that Power
And Wisdom—oft arraigned: see now the cause
Why unassuming worth in secret lived
And died neglected: why the good man's share
In life was gall and bitterness of soul:
Why the lone widow and her orphans pined
In starving solitude; while luxury
In palaces lay straining her low thought
To form unreal wants: why heaven-born truth
And moderation fair wore the red marks
Of superstition's scourge; why licensed pain,
That cruel spoiler, that embosomed foe,
Embittered all our bliss. Ye good distressed!
Ye noble few! who here unbending stand
Beneath life's pressure, yet bear up a while,
And what your bounded view, which only saw
A little part, deemed evil is no more:
The storms of wintry time will quickly pass,
And one unbounded Spring encircle all.

DAVID MALLET

1705–1765

William and Margaret

'TWAS at the silent solemn hour,
  When night and morning meet;
In glided Margaret's grimly ghost,
  And stood at William's feet.

Her face was like an April morn,
  Clad in a wintry cloud;
And clay-cold was her lily hand
  That held her sable shroud.

So shall the fairest face appear,
  When youth and years are flown:
Such is the robe that kings must wear,
  When death has reft their crown.

Her bloom was like the springing flower,
  That sips the silver dew;
The rose was budded in her cheek,
  Just opening to the view.

But love had, like the canker-worm,
  Consumed her early prime;
The rose grew pale, and left her cheek;
  She died before her time.

'Awake!' she cried, 'thy true love calls,
  Come from her midnight grave:
Now let thy pity hear the maid,
  Thy love refused to save.

'This is the dark and dreary hour
  When injured ghosts complain;
When yawning graves give up their dead
  To haunt the faithless swain.

'Bethink thee, William, of the fault,
    Thy pledge and broken oath:
And give me back my maiden vow,
    And give me back my troth.

'Why did you promise love to me,
    And not that promise keep?
Why did you swear mine eyes were bright,
    Yet leave those eyes to weep?

'How could you say my face was fair,
    And yet that face forsake?
How could you win my virgin heart,
    Yet leave that heart to break?

'Why did you say, my lip was sweet,
    And made the scarlet pale?
And why did I, young, witless maid!
    Believe the flattering tale?

'That face, alas! no more is fair;
    Those lips no longer red:
Dark are my eyes, now closed in death,
    And every charm is fled.

'The hungry worm my sister is;
    This winding-sheet I wear:
And cold and weary lasts our night,
    Till that last morn appear.

'But hark!—the cock has warned me hence;
    A long and late adieu!
Come, see, false man, how low she lies,
    Who died for love of you.'

The lark sung loud; the morning smiled,
    With beams of rosy red:
Pale William quaked in every limb,
    And raving left his bed.

He hied him to the fatal place
    Where Margaret's body lay;
And stretched him on the grass-green turf,
    That wrapped her breathless clay.

536

And thrice he called on Margaret's name,
    And thrice he wept full sore;
Then laid his cheek to her cold grave,
    And word spake never more.

CHARLES WESLEY

1707–1788

Wrestling Jacob

COME, O Thou Traveller unknown,
    Whom still I hold, but cannot see,
My Company before is gone,
    And I am left alone with Thee,
With Thee all Night I mean to stay,
And wrestle till the Break of Day.

I need not tell Thee who I am,
    My Misery, or Sin declare,
Thyself hast call'd me by my Name,
    Look on thy Hands, and read it there,
But who, I ask Thee, who art Thou,
Tell me thy Name, and tell me now?

In vain Thou strugglest to get free,
    I never will unloose my Hold:
Art Thou the Man that died for me?
    The Secret of thy Love unfold;
Wrestling I will not let Thee go,
Till I thy Name, thy Nature know.

Wilt Thou not yet to me reveal
    Thy new, unutterable Name?
Tell me, I still beseech Thee, tell,
    To know it Now resolv'd I am;
Wrestling I will not let Thee go,
Till I thy Name, thy Nature know.

'Tis all in vain to hold thy Tongue,
  Or touch the Hollow of my Thigh:
Though every Sinew be unstrung,
  Out of my Arms Thou shalt not fly;
Wrestling I will not let Thee go,
Till I thy Name, thy Nature know.

What tho' my shrinking Flesh complain,
  And murmur to contend so long,
I rise superior to my Pain,
  When I am weak then I am strong,
And when my All of Strength shall fail,
I shall with the GOD-man prevail.

My Strength is gone, my Nature dies,
  I sink beneath thy weighty Hand,
Faint to revive, and fall to rise;
  I fall, and yet by Faith I stand,
I stand, and will not let Thee go,
Till I thy Name, thy Nature know.

Yield to me Now——for I am weak;
  But confident in Self-despair:
Speak to my Heart, in Blessings speak,
  Be conquer'd by my Instant Prayer,
Speak, or Thou never hence shalt move,
And tell me, if thy Name is LOVE.

'Tis Love, 'tis Love! Thou diedst for Me,
  I hear thy Whisper in my Heart.
The Morning breaks, the Shadows flee:
  Pure UNIVERSAL LOVE Thou art,
To me, to All thy Bowels move,
Thy Nature, and thy Name is LOVE.

My Prayer hath Power with GOD; the Grace
  Unspeakable I now receive,
Thro' Faith I see Thee Face to Face,
  I see Thee Face to Face, and live:
In vain I have not wept, and strove,
Thy Nature, and thy Name is LOVE.

I know Thee, Saviour, who Thou art,
   Jesus the feeble Sinner's Friend;
Nor wilt Thou with the Night depart,
   But stay, and love me to the End;
Thy Mercies never shall remove,
Thy Nature, and thy Name is LOVE.

The Sun of Righteousness on Me
   Hath rose with Healing in his Wings,
Wither'd my Nature's Strength; from Thee
   My Soul its Life and Succour brings,
My Help is all laid up above;
Thy Nature, and thy Name is LOVE.

Contented now upon my Thigh
   I halt, till Life's short Journey end;
All Helplessness, all Weakness I,
   On Thee alone for Strength depend,
Nor have I Power, from Thee, to move;
Thy Nature, and thy Name is LOVE.

Lame as I am, I take the Prey,
   Hell, Earth, and Sin with Ease o'ercome;
I leap for Joy, pursue my Way,
   And as a bounding Hart fly home,
Thro' all Eternity to prove
Thy Nature, and thy Name is LOVE.

SAMUEL JOHNSON

1709–1784

from *London*

By numbers here from shame or censure free,
All crimes are safe, but hated poverty.
This, only this, the rigid law pursues,
This, only this, provokes the snarling muse.
The sober trader at a tatter'd cloak,
Wakes from his dream, and labours for a joke;
With brisker air the silken courtiers gaze,
And turn the varied taunt a thousand ways.

Of all the griefs that harrass the distress'd,
Sure the most bitter is a scornful jest;
Fate never wounds more deep the gen'rous heart,
Than when a blockhead's insult points the dart.

   Has heaven reserv'd, in pity to the poor,
No pathless waste, or undiscover'd shore;
No secret island in the boundless main?
No peaceful desert yet unclaim'd by SPAIN?
Quick let us rise, the happy seats explore,
And bear oppression's insolence no more.
This mournful truth is ev'ry where confess'd,
SLOW RISES WORTH, BY POVERTY DEPRESS'D:
But here more slow, where all are slaves to gold,
Where looks are merchandise, and smiles are sold;
Where won by bribes, by flatteries implor'd,
The groom retails the favours of his lord.

   But hark! th' affrighted crowd's tumultuous cries
Roll thro' the streets, and thunder to the skies;
Rais'd from some pleasing dream of wealth and pow'r,
Some pompous palace, or some blissful bower,
Aghast you start, and scarce with aching sight
Sustain th' approaching fire's tremendous light;
Swift from pursuing horrors take your way,
And leave your little ALL to flames a prey;
Then thro' the world a wretched vagrant roam,
For where can starving merit find a home?
In vain your mournful narrative disclose,
While all neglect, and most insult your woes.

   Should heaven's just bolts Orgilio's wealth confound,
And spread his flaming palace on the ground,
Swift o'er the land the dismal rumour flies,
And public mournings pacify the skies;
And laureat tribe in servile verse relate,
How virtue wars with persecuting fate;
With well-feign'd gratitude the pension'd band
Refund the plunder of the beggar'd land.
See! while he builds, the gaudy vassals come,
And crowd with sudden wealth the rising dome;
The price of boroughs and of souls restore,
And raise his treasures higher than before.
Now bless'd with all the baubles of the great,
The polish'd marble, and the shining plate,
Orgilio sees the golden pile aspire,
And hopes from angry heav'n another fire.

Could'st thou resign the park and play content,
For the fair banks of Severn or of Trent;
There might'st thou find some elegant retreat,
Some hireling senator's deserted seat;
And stretch thy prospects o'er the smiling land,
For less than rent the dungeons of the Strand;
There prune thy walks, support thy drooping flow'rs,
Direct thy rivulets, and twine thy bow'rs;
And, while thy grounds a cheap repast afford,
Despise the dainties of a venal lord:
There ev'ry bush with nature's musick rings,
There ev'ry breeze bears health upon its wings;
On all thy hours security shall smile,
And bless thine evening walk and morning toil.

Prepare for death, if here at night you roam,
And sign your will before you sup from home.
Some fiery fop, with new commission vain,
Who sleeps on brambles till he kills his man;
Some frolic drunkard, reeling from a feast,
Provokes a broil, and stabs you for a jest.
Yet ev'n these heroes, mischievously gay,
Lords of the street, and terrors of the way;
Flush'd as they are with folly, youth and wine,
Their prudent insults to the poor confine;
Afar they mark the flambeau's bright approach,
And shun the shining train, and golden coach.

In vain, these dangers past, your doors you close,
And hope the balmy blessings of repose:
Cruel with guilt, and daring with despair,
The midnight murd'rer bursts the faithless bar;
Invades the sacred hour of silent rest,
And leaves, unseen, a dagger in your breast.

The Vanity of Human Wishes

The Tenth Satire of Juvenal Imitated

LET observation with extensive view,
Survey mankind, from China to Peru;
Remark each anxious toil, each eager strife,
And watch the busy scenes of crowded life;
Then say how hope and fear, desire and hate,
O'erspread with snares the clouded maze of fate,

Where wav'ring man, betray'd by vent'rous pride,
To tread the dreary paths without a guide,
As treach'rous phantoms in the mist delude,
Shuns fancied ills, or chases airy good;
How rarely reason guides the stubborn choice.
Rules the bold hand, or prompts the suppliant voice;
How nations sink, by darling schemes oppress'd,
When vengeance listens to the fool's request.
Fate wings with ev'ry wish th' afflictive dart,
Each gift of nature, and each grace of art,
With fatal heat impetuous courage glows,
With fatal sweetness elocution flows,
Impeachment stops the speaker's pow'rful breath,
And restless fire precipitates on death.

But scarce observ'd, the knowing and the bold
Fall in the gen'ral massacre of gold;
Wide-wasting pest! that rages unconfin'd,
And crouds with crimes the records of mankind;
For gold his sword the hireling ruffian draws,
For gold the hireling judge distorts the laws;
Wealth heap'd on wealth, nor truth nor safety buys,
The dangers gather as the treasures rise.

Let hist'ry tell where rival kings command,
And dubious title shakes the madded land,
When statutes glean the refuse of the sword,
How much more safe the vassal than the lord;
Low skulks the hind beneath the rage of pow'r,
And leaves the wealthy traitor in the Tow'r,
Untouch'd his cottage, and his slumbers sound,
Tho' confiscation's vulturs hover round.

The needy traveller, serene and gay,
Walks the wild heath, and sings his toil away.
Does envy seize thee? crush th' upbraiding joy,
Increase his riches and his peace destroy;
Now fears in dire vicissitude invade,
The rustling brake alarms, and quiv'ring shade,
Nor light nor darkness bring his pain relief,
One shews the plunder, and one hides the thief.

Yet still one gen'ral cry the skies assails,
And gain and grandeur load the tainted gales;
Few know the toiling statesman's fear or care,
Th' insidious rival and the gaping heir.

Once more, Democritus, arise on earth,
With cheerful wisdom and instructive mirth,

See motley life in modern trappings dress'd,
And feed with varied fools th' eternal jest:
Thou who couldst laugh where want enchain'd caprice,
Toil crush'd conceit, and man was of a piece;
Where wealth unlov'd without a mourner died
And scarce a sycophant was fed by pride;
Where ne'er was known the form of mock debate,
Or seen a new-made mayor's unwieldy state;
Where change of fav'rites made no change of laws,
And senates heard before they judg'd a cause;
How wouldst thou shake at Britain's modish tribe,
Dart the quick taunt, and edge the piercing gibe?
Attentive truth and nature to descry,
And pierce each scene with philosophic eye.
To thee were solemn toys or empty show,
The robes of pleasure and the veils of woe:
All aid the farce, and all thy mirth maintain,
Whose joys are causeless, or whose griefs are vain.

Such was the scorn that fill'd the sage's mind,
Renew'd at ev'ry glance on humankind;
How just that scorn ere yet thy voice declare,
Search every state, and canvass ev'ry pray'r.

Unnumber'd suppliants crowd Preferment's gate,
Athirst for wealth, and burning to be great;
Delusive Fortune hears th' incessant call,
They mount, they shine, evaporate, and fall.
On ev'ry stage the foes of peace attend,
Hate dogs their flight, and insult mocks their end.
Love ends with hope, the sinking statesman's door
Pours in the morning worshiper no more;
For growing names the weekly scribbler lies,
To growing wealth the dedicator flies,
From every room descends the painted face,
That hung the bright Palladium of the place,
And smok'd in kitchens, or in auctions sold,
To better features yields the frame of gold;
For now no more we trace in ev'ry line
Heroic worth, benevolence divine:
The form distorted justifies the fall,
And detestation rids th' indignant wall.

But will not Britain hear the last appeal,
Sign her foes doom, or guard her fav'rites zeal?
Through Freedom's sons no more remonstrance rings,
Degrading nobles and controuling kings;

SAMUEL JOHNSON

Our supple tribes repress their patriot throats,
And ask no questions but the price of votes;
With weekly libels and septennial ale,
Their wish is full to riot and to rail.

In full-blown dignity, see Wolsey stand,
Law in his voice, and fortune in his hand:
To him the church, the realm, their pow'rs consign,
Thro' him the rays of regal bounty shine,
Turn'd by his nod the stream of honour flows,
His smile alone security bestows:
Still to new heights his restless wishes tow'r,
Claim leads to claim, and pow'r advances pow'r;
Till conquest unresisted ceas'd to please,
And rights submitted, left him none to seize.
At length his sov'reign frowns—the train of state
Mark the keen glance, and watch the sign to hate.
Where-e'er he turns he meets a stranger's eye,
His suppliants scorn him, and his followers fly;
At once is lost the pride of aweful state,
The golden canopy, the glitt'ring plate,
The regal palace, the luxurious board,
The liv'ried army, and the menial lord.
With age, with cares, with maladies oppress'd,
He seeks the refuge of monastic rest.
Grief aids disease, remember'd folly stings,
And his last sighs reproach the faith of kings.

Speak thou, those thoughts at humble peace repine,
Shall Wolsey's wealth, with Wolsey's end be thine?
Or liv'st thou now, with safer pride content,
The wisest justice on the banks of Trent?
For why did Wolsey near the steeps of fate,
On weak foundations raise th' enormous weight?
Why but to sink beneath misfortune's blow,
With louder ruin to the gulfs below?

What gave great Villiers to th' assassin's knife,
And fixed disease on Harley's closing life?
What murder'd Wentworth, and what exil'd Hyde,
By kings protected, and to kings ally'd?
What but their wish indulg'd in courts to shine,
And pow'r too great to keep, or to resign?

When first the college rolls receive his name,
The young enthusiast quits his ease for fame;
Through all his veins the fever of renown
Burns from the strong contagion of the gown;

O'er Bodley's dome his future labours spread,
And Bacon's mansion trembles o'er his head.
Are these thy views? proceed, illustrious youth,
And virtue guard thee to the throne of Truth!
Yet should thy soul indulge the gen'rous heat,
Till captive Science yields her last retreat;
Should Reason guide thee with her brightest ray,
And pour on misty Doubt resistless day;
Should no false Kindness lure to loose delight,
Nor Praise relax, nor Difficulty fright;
Should tempting Novelty thy cell refrain,
And Sloth effuse her opiate fumes in vain;
Should Beauty blunt on fops her fatal dart,
Nor claim the triumph of a letter'd heart;
Should no Disease thy torpid veins invade,
Nor Melancholy's phantoms haunt thy shade;
Yet hope not life from grief or danger free,
Nor think the doom of man revers'd for thee:
Deign on the passing world to turn thine eyes,
And pause awhile from letters, to be wise;
There mark what ills the scholar's life assail,
Toil, envy, want, the patron, and the jail.
See nations slowly wise, and meanly just,
To buried merit raise the tardy bust.
If dreams yet flatter, once again attend,
Hear Lydiat's life, and Galileo's end.
  Nor deem, when learning her last prize bestows,
The glitt'ring eminence exempt from foes;
See when the vulgar 'scape, despis'd or aw'd,
Rebellion's vengeful talons seize on Laud.
From meaner minds, tho' smaller fines content,
The plunder'd palace or sequester'd rent;
Mark'd out by dangerous parts he meets the shock,
And fatal Learning leads him to the block:
Around his tomb let Art and Genius weep,
But hear his death, ye blockheads, hear and sleep.
  The festal blazes, the triumphal show,
The ravish'd standard, and the captive foe,
The senate's thanks, the gazette's pompous tale,
With force resistless o'er the brave prevail.
Such bribes the rapid Greek o'er Asia whirl'd,
For such the steady Romans shook the world;
For such in distant lands the Britons shine,
And stain with blood the Danube or the Rhine;

This pow'r has praise, that virtue scarce can warm,
Till fame supplies the universal charm.
Yet Reason frowns on War's unequal game,
Where wasted nations raise a single name,
And mortgag'd states their grandsires wreaths regret,
From age to age in everlasting debt;
Wreaths which at last the dear-bought right convey
To rust on medals, or on stones decay.
  On what foundation stands the warrior's pride,
How just his hopes let Swedish Charles decide;
A frame of adamant, a soul of fire,
No dangers fright him, and no labours tire;
O'er love, o'er fear, extends his wide domain,
Unconquer'd lord of pleasure and of pain;
No joys to him pacific scepters yield,
War sounds the trump, he rushes to the field;
Behold surrounding kings their power combine,
And one capitulate, and one resign;
Peace courts his hand, but spreads her charms in vain;
'Think nothing gain'd, he cries, till nought remain,
'On Moscow's walls till Gothic standards fly,
'And all be mine beneath the polar sky.'
The march begins in military state,
And nations on his eye suspended wait;
Stern Famine guards the solitary coast,
And Winter barricades the realms of Frost;
He comes, not want and cold his course delay;—
Hide, blushing Glory, hide Pultowa's day:
The vanquish'd hero leaves his broken bands,
And shows his miseries in distant lands;
Condemn'd a needy supplicant to wait,
While ladies interpose, and slaves debate.
But did not Chance at length her error mend?
Did no subverted empire mark his end?
Did rival monarchs give the fatal wound?
Or hostile millions press him to the ground?
His fall was destin'd to a barren strand,
A petty fortress, and a dubious hand;
He left the name, at which the world grew pale,
To point a moral, or adorn a tale.
  All times their scenes of pompous woes afford,
From Persia's tyrant to Bavaria's lord.
In gay hostility, and barb'rous pride,
With half mankind embattled at his side,

Great Xerxes comes to seize the certain prey,
And starves exhausted regions in his way;
Attendant Flattery counts his myriads o'er,
Till counted myriads sooth his pride no more;
Fresh praise is try'd till madness fires his mind,
The waves he lashes, and enchains the wind;
New pow'rs are claim'd, new pow'rs are still bestow'd,
Till rude resistance lops the spreading god;
The daring Greeks deride the martial show,
And heap their valleys with the gaudy foe;
Th' insulted sea with humbler thoughts he gains,
A single skiff to speed his flight remains;
Th' incumber'd oar scarce leaves the dreaded coast
Through purple billows and a floating host.
    The bold Bavarian, in a luckless hour,
Tries the dread summits of Cesarean pow'r,
With unexpected legions bursts away,
And sees defenceless realms receive his sway;
Short sway! fair Austria spreads her mournful charms,
The queen, the beauty, sets the world in arms;
From hill to hill the beacons rousing blaze
Spreads wide the hope of plunder and of praise;
The fierce Croatian, and the wild Hussar,
And all the sons of ravage crowd the war;
The baffled prince in honour's flatt'ring bloom
Of hasty greatness finds the fatal doom,
His foes derision, and his subjects blame,
And steals to death from anguish and from shame.
    Enlarge my life with multitude of days,
In health, in sickness, thus the suppliant prays;
Hides from himself his state, and shuns to know,
That life protracted is protracted woe.
Time hovers o'er, impatient to destroy,
And shuts up all the passages of joy:
In vain their gifts the bounteous seasons pour,
The fruit autumnal, and the vernal flow'r,
With listless eyes the dotard views the store,
He views, and wonders that they please no more;
Now pall the tasteless meats, and joyless wines,
And Luxury with sighs her slave resigns.
Approach, ye minstrels, try the soothing strain,
Diffuse the tuneful lenitives of pain:
No sounds alas would touch th' impervious ear,
Though dancing mountains witness'd Orpheus near;

Nor lute nor lyre his feeble pow'rs attend,
Nor sweeter music of a virtuous friend,
But everlasting dictates crowd his tongue,
Perversely grave, or positively wrong.
The still returning tale, and ling'ring jest,
Perplex the fawning niece and pamper'd guest,
While growing hopes scarce awe the gath'ring sneer,
And scarce a legacy can bribe to hear;
The watchful guests still hint the last offence,
The daughter's petulance, the son's expense,
Improve his heady rage with treach'rous skill,
And mould his passions till they make his will.

Unnumber'd maladies his joints invade,
Lay seige to life and press the dire blockade;
But unextinguish'd Avarice still remains,
And dreaded losses aggravate his pains;
He turns, with anxious heart and crippled hands,
His bonds of debt, and mortgages of lands;
Or views his coffers with suspicious eyes,
Unlocks his gold, and counts it till he dies.

But grant, the virtues of a temp'rate prime
Bless with an age exempt from scorn or crime;
An age that melts with unperceiv'd decay,
And glides in modest Innocence away;
Whose peaceful day Benevolence endears,
Whose night congratulating Conscience cheers;
The gen'ral fav'rite as the gen'ral friend:
Such age there is, and who shall wish its end?

Yet ev'n on this her load Misfortune flings,
To press the weary minutes flagging wings:
New sorrow rises as the day returns,
A sister sickens, or a daughter mourns.
Now kindred Merit fills the sable bier,
Now lacerated Friendship claims a tear.
Year chases year, decay pursues decay,
Still drops some joy from with'ring life away;
New forms arise, and diff'rent views engage,
Superfluous lags the vet'ran on the stage,
Till pitying Nature signs the last release,
And bids afflicted worth retire to peace.

But few there are whom hours like these await,
Who set unclouded in the gulfs of fate.
From Lydia's monarch should the search descend,
By Solon caution'd to regard his end,

In life's last scene what prodigies surprise,
Fears of the brave, and follies of the wise?
From Marlb'rough's eyes the streams of dotage flow,
And Swift expires a driveller and a show.
   The teeming mother, anxious for her race,
Begs for each birth the fortune of a face:
Yet Vane could tell what ills from beauty spring;
And Sedley curs'd the form that pleas'd a king.
Ye nymphs of rosy lips and radiant eyes,
Whom Pleasure keeps too busy to be wise,
Whom Joys with soft varieties invite,
By day the frolick, and the dance by night,
Who frown with vanity, who smile with art,
And ask the latest fashion of the heart,
What care, what rules your heedless charms shall save,
Each nymph your rival, and each youth your slave?
Against your fame with fondness hate combines,
The rival batters, and the lover mines.
With distant voice neglected Virtue calls,
Less heard and less, the faint remonstrance falls;
Tir'd with contempt, she quits the slipp'ry reign,
And Pride and Prudence take her seat in vain.
In crowd at once, where none the pass defend,
The harmless Freedom, and the private Friend.
The guardians yield, by force superior ply'd;
By Int'rest, Prudence; and by Flatt'ry, Pride.
Now beauty falls betray'd, despis'd, distress'd,
And hissing Infamy proclaims the rest.
   Where then shall Hope and Fear their objects find?
Must dull Suspense corrupt the stagnant mind?
Must helpless man, in ignorance sedate,
Roll darkling down the torrent of his fate?
Must no dislike alarm, no wishes rise,
No cries attempt the mercies of the skies?
Enquirer, cease, petitions yet remain,
Which heav'n may hear, nor deem religion vain.
Still raise for good the supplicating voice,
But leave to heav'n the measure and the choice,
Safe in his pow'r, whose eyes discern afar
The secret ambush of a specious pray'r.
Implore his aid, in his decisions rest,
Secure whate'er he gives, he gives the best.
Yet when the sense of sacred presence fires,
And strong devotion to the skies aspires,

Pour forth thy fervours for a healthful mind,
Obedient passions, and a will resign'd;
For love, which scarce collective man can fill;
For patience sov'reign o'er transmuted ill;
For faith, that panting for a happier seat,
Counts death kind Nature's signal of retreat:
These goods for man the laws of heav'n ordain,
These goods he grants, who grants the pow'r to gain;
With these celestial wisdom calms the mind,
And makes the happiness she does not find.

Prologue at the Opening of the Theatre in Drury-Lane 1747

WHEN Learning's Triumph o'er her barb'rous Foes
First rear'd the Stage, immortal Shakespeare rose;
Each Change of many-colour'd Life he drew,
Exhausted Worlds, and then imagin'd new:
Existence saw him spurn her bounded Reign,
And panting Time toil'd after him in vain:
His pow'rful Strokes presiding Truth impress'd,
And unresisted Passion storm'd the Breast.

   Then Johnson came, instructed from the School,
To please in Method, and invent by Rule;
His studious Patience, and laborious Art,
By regular Approach essay'd the Heart;
Cold Approbation gave the ling'ring Bays,
For those who durst not censure, scarce cou'd praise.
A Mortal born he met the general Doom,
But left, like Egypt's Kings, a lasting Tomb.

   The Wits of Charles found easier Ways to Fame,
Nor wish'd for Johnson's Art, or Shakespeare's Flame;
Themselves they studied, as they felt, they writ,
Intrigue was Plot, Obscenity was Wit.
Vice always found a sympathetic friend;
They pleas'd their Age, and did not aim to mend.
Yet Bards like these aspir'd to lasting Praise,
And proudly hop'd to pimp in future days.
Their cause was gen'ral, their supports were strong,
Their slaves were willing, and their Reign was long;
Till Shame regain'd the Post that Sense betray'd,
And Virtue call'd Oblivion to her Aid.

   Then crush'd by Rules, and weaken'd as refin'd,

For Years the Pow'r of Tragedy declin'd;
From Bard, to Bard, the frigid Caution crept,
Till Declamation roar'd, while Passion slept.
Yet still did Virtue deign the Stage to tread,
Philosophy remain'd, though Nature fled.
But forc'd at length her antient Reign to quit,
She saw great Faustus lay the Ghost of Wit:
Exulting Folly hail'd the joyful Day,
And Pantomine, and Song, confirm'd her Sway.

　　But who the coming Changes can presage,
And mark the future Periods of the Stage?—
Perhaps if Skill could distant Times explore,
New Behns, new Durfeys, yet remain in Store.
Perhaps, where Lear has rav'd, and Hamlet died,
On flying Cars new Sorcerers may ride.
Perhaps, for who can guess th' Effects of Chance?
Here Hunt may box, or Mahomet may dance.

　　Hard is his lot, that here by Fortune plac'd,
Must watch the wild Vicissitudes of Taste;
With ev'ry Meteor of Caprice must play,
And chase the new-blown Bubbles of the Day.
Ah! let not Censure term our Fate our Choice,
The Stage but echoes back the publick Voice.
The Drama's Laws the Drama's Patrons give,
For we that live to please, must please to live.

　　Then prompt no more the Follies you decry,
As Tyrants doom their Tools of Guilt to die;
'Tis yours this Night to bid the Reign commence
Of rescu'd Nature, and reviving Sense;
To chase the Charms of Sound, the Pomp of Show,
For useful Mirth, and salutary Woe;
Bid scenic Virtue form the rising Age,
And Truth diffuse her Radiance from the Stage.

Prologue to
'A Word to the Wise'

THIS night presents a play, which public rage,
Or right, or wrong, once hooted from the stage;
From zeal or malice now no more we dread,
For English vengeance *wars not with the dead*.
A generous foe regards, with pitying eye,
The man whom fate has laid, where all must lye.

To wit, reviving from its author's dust,
Be kind, ye judges, or at least be just:
Let no resentful petulance invade
Th' oblivious grave's inviolable shade.
Let one great payment every claim appease,
And him who cannot hurt, allow to please;
To please by scenes unconscious of offence,
By harmless merriment, or useful sense.
Where aught of bright, or fair, the piece displays,
Approve it only—'tis too late to praise.
If want of skill, or want of care appear,
Forbear to hiss—the Poet cannot hear.
By all, like him, must praise and blame be found;
At best, a fleeting gleam, or empty sound.
Yet then shall calm reflection bless the night,
When liberal pity dignify'd delight;
When pleasure fired her torch at Virtue's flame,
And mirth was bounty with a humbler name.

An Epitaph on Claudy Phillips, a Musician

PHILLIPS! whose touch harmonious could remove
The pangs of guilty pow'r, and hapless love,
Rest here distrest by poverty no more,
Find here that calm thou gav'st so oft before;
Sleep undisturb'd within this peaceful shrine,
Till angels wake thee with a note like thine.

Verses in Baretti's Commonplace Book

AT sight of sparkling bowls or beauteous dames,
When fondness melts me, or when wine inflames,
I too can feel the rapture, fierce and strong;
I too can pour the extemporary song:
But though the numbers for a moment please,
Though music thrills, or sudden sallies seize,
Yet, lay the sonnet for an hour aside,
Its charms are fled and all its powers destroyed.
What soon is perfect, soon alike is past;
That slowly grows, which must for ever last.

SAMUEL JOHNSON

Epitaph on Hogarth

THE Hand of Art here torpid lies
  That wav'd th' essential form of Grace,
Here death has clos'd the curious eyes
  That saw the manners in the Face.

If Genius warm thee, Reader, stay,
  If Merit touch thee, shed a tear,
Be Vice and Dulness far away
  Great Hogarth's honour'd Dust is here.

Parodies in the Ballad Style

I

THE tender infant, meek and mild,
  Fell down upon the stone;
The nurse took up the squealing child,
  But still the child squeal'd on.

II

I PUT my hat upon my head
  And walk'd into the Strand,
And there I met another man
  Who's hat was in his hand.

III

I THEREFORE pray thee, Renny dear,
  That thou wilt give to me,
With cream and sugar soften'd well,
  Another dish of tea.

IV

IF the man who turnips cries,
Cry not when his father dies,
'Tis a proof that he had rather
Have a turnip than his father.

SAMUEL JOHNSON

A Short Song of Congratulation

LONG-EXPECTED one and twenty
Ling'ring year at last is flown,
Pomp and Pleasure, Pride and Plenty
Great Sir John, are all your own.

Loosen'd from the Minor's tether,
Free to mortgage or to sell,
Wild as wind, and light as feather
Bid the slaves of thrift farewell.

Call the Bettys, Kates, and Jennys
Ev'ry name that laughs at Care,
Lavish of your Grandsire's guineas,
Show the Spirit of an heir.

All that prey on vice and folly
Joy to see their quarry fly,
Here the Gamester light and jolly
There the Lender grave and sly.

Wealth, Sir John, was made to wander,
Let it wander as it will;
See the Jocky, see the Pander,
Bid them come, and take their fill.

When the bonny Blade carouses,
Pockets full, and Spirits high,
What are acres? What are houses?
Only dirt, or wet or dry.

If the Guardian or the Mother
Tell the woes of wilful waste,
Scorn their counsel and their pother,
You can hang or drown at last.

On the Death of Dr. Robert Levet

CONDEMN'D to hope's delusive mine,
    As on we toil from day to day,
By sudden blasts, or slow decline,
    Our social comforts drop away.

Well tried through many a varying year,
  See Levet to the grave descend;
Officious, innocent, sincere,
  Of ev'ry friendless name the friend.

Yet still he fills affection's eye,
  Obscurely wise, and coarsely kind;
Nor, letter'd arrogance, deny
  Thy praise to merit unrefin'd.

When fainting nature call'd for aid,
  And hovering death prepar'd the blow,
His vig'rous remedy display'd
  The power of art without the show.

In misery's darkest caverns known,
  His useful care was ever nigh,
Where hopeless anguish pour'd his groan,
  And lonely want retir'd to die.

No summons mock'd by chill delay,
  No petty gain disdain'd by pride,
The modest wants of ev'ry day
  The toil of ev'ry day supplied.

His virtues walk'd their narrow round,
  Nor made a pause, nor left a void;
And sure th' Eternal Master found
  The single talent well employ'd.

The busy day, the peaceful night,
  Unfelt, uncounted, glided by;
His frame was firm, his powers were bright,
  Tho' now his eightieth year was nigh.

Then with no throbbing fiery pain,
  No cold gradations of decay,
Death broke at once the vital chain,
  And free'd his soul the nearest way.

WILLIAM SHENSTONE

1714—1763

Written at an Inn at Henley

To thee, fair freedom! I retire
  From flattery, cards, and dice, and din;
Nor art thou found in mansions higher
  Than the low cot, or humble inn.

'Tis here with boundless power I reign;
  And every health which I begin,
Converts dull port to bright champagne;
  Such freedom crowns it, at an inn.

I fly from pomp, I fly from plate!
  I fly from falsehood's specious grin;
Freedom I love, and form I hate,
  And choose my lodgings at an inn.

Here, waiter! take my sordid ore,
  Which lackeys else might hope to win;
It buys, what courts have not in store;
  It buys me freedom at an inn.

Whoe'er has travelled life's dull round,
  Where'er his stages may have been,
May sigh to think he still has found
  The warmest welcome at an inn.

THOMAS GRAY

1716–1771

Ode on a Distant Prospect of Eton College

YE distant spires, ye antique towers
  That crown the watery glade,
Where grateful Science still adores
  Her Henry's holy shade;

And ye, that from the stately brow
Of Windsor's heights th' expanse below
  Of grove, of lawn, of mead survey,
Whose turf, whose shade, whose flowers among
Wanders the hoary Thames along
  His silver-winding way:

Ah happy hills! ah pleasing shade!
  Ah fields beloved in vain!
Where once my careless childhood strayed,
  A stranger yet to pain!
I feel the gales that from ye blow
A momentary bliss bestow,
  As waving fresh their gladsome wing
My weary soul they seem to soothe,
And, redolent of joy and youth,
  To breathe a second spring.

Say, Father Thames, for thou hast seen
  Full many a sprightly race
Disporting on thy margent green
  The paths of pleasure trace;
Who foremost now delight to cleave
With pliant arm, thy glassy wave?
  The captive linnet which enthral?
What idle progeny succeed
To chase the rolling circle's speed
  Or urge the flying ball?

While some on earnest business bent
  Their murmuring labours ply
'Gainst graver hours, that bring constraint
  To sweeten liberty:
Some bold adventurers disdain
The limits of their little reign
  And unknown regions dare descry:
Still as they run they look behind,
They hear a voice in every wind,
  And snatch a fearful joy.

Gay hope is theirs by fancy fed,
  Less pleasing when possest;
The tear forgot as soon as shed,
  The sunshine of the breast:

Theirs buxom health, of rosy hue,
Wild wit, invention ever new,
   And lively cheer, of vigour born;
The thoughtless day, the easy night,
The spirits pure, the slumbers light
   That fly th' approach of morn.

Alas! regardless of their doom
   The little victims play!
No sense have they of ills to come
   Nor care beyond to-day:
Yet see how all around then wait
The Ministers of human fate
   And black Misfortune's baleful train!
Ah show them where in ambush stand
To seize their prey, the murderous band!
   Ah, tell them they are men!

These shall the fury Passions tear,
   The vultures of the mind,
Disdainful Anger, pallid Fear,
   And Shame that skulks behind,
Or pining Love shall waste their youth;
Or Jealousy with rankling tooth
   That inly gnaws the secret heart,
And Envy wan, and faded Care,
Grim-visaged comfortless Despair,
   And Sorrow's piercing dart.

Ambition this shall tempt to rise,
   Then whirl the wretch from high,
To bitter Scorn a sacrifice
   And grinning Infamy.
The stings of Falsehood those shall try,
And hard Unkindness' altered eye,
   That mocks the tear it forced to flow;
And keen Remorse with blood defiled,
And moody Madness laughing wild
   Amid severest woe.

Lo, in the vale of years beneath
   A griesly troop are seen,
The painful family of Death,
   More hideous than their Queen:

griesly] horrible

558

This racks the joints, this fires the veins,
That every labouring sinew strains,
   Those in the deeper vitals rage:
Lo, Poverty, to fill the band,
That numbs the soul with icy hand,
   And slow-consuming Age.

To each his sufferings: all are men,
   Condemned alike to groan;
The tender for another's pain,
   Th' unfeeling for his own.
Yet, ah! why should they know their fate,
Since sorrow never comes too late,
   And happiness too swiftly flies?
Thought would destroy their paradise.
No more;—where ignorance is bliss,
   'Tis folly to be wise.

Elegy Written in a Country Churchyard

THE curfew tolls the knell of parting day,
   The lowing herd wind slowly o'er the lea,
The plowman homeward plods his weary way,
   And leaves the world to darkness and to me.

Now fades the glimmering landscape on the sight,
   And all the air a solemn stillness holds,
Save where the beetle wheels his droning flight,
   And drowsy tinklings lull the distant folds;

Save that from yonder ivy-mantled tower
   The moping owl does to the moon complain
Of such as, wand'ring near her secret bower,
   Molest her ancient solitary reign.

Beneath those rugged elms, that yew-tree's shade,
   Where heaves the turf in many a mould'ring heap,
Each in his narrow cell for ever laid,
   The rude forefathers of the hamlet sleep.

The breezy call of incense-breathing morn,
   The swallow twitt'ring from the straw-built shed,
The cock's shrill clarion, or the echoing horn,
   No more shall rouse them from their lowly bed.

For them no more the blazing hearth shall burn,
  Or busy housewife ply her evening care:
No children run to lisp their sire's return,
  Or climb his knees the envied kiss to share.

Oft did the harvest to their sickle yield,
  Their furrow oft the stubborn glebe has broke:
How jocund did they drive their team afield!
  How bowed the woods beneath their sturdy stroke!

Let not Ambition mock their useful toil,
  Their homely joys, and destiny obscure;
Nor Grandeur hear with a disdainful smile
  The short and simple annals of the poor.

The boast of heraldry, the pomp of power,
  And all that beauty, all that wealth e'er gave,
Awaits alike th' inevitable hour:
  The paths of glory lead but to the grave.

Nor you, ye proud, impute to These the fault,
  If Memory o'er their tomb no trophies raise,
Where through the long-drawn aisle and fretted vault
  The pealing anthem swells the note of praise.

Can storied urn or animated bust
  Back to its mansion call the fleeting breath?
Can Honour's voice provoke the silent dust,
  Or Flatt'ry soothe the dull cold ear of death?

Perhaps in this neglected spot is laid
  Some heart once pregnant with celestial fire;
Hands, that the rod of empire might have swayed,
  Or waked to ecstasy the living lyre.

But Knowledge to their eyes her ample page
  Rich with the spoils of time did ne'er unroll;
Chill Penury repressed their noble rage,
  And froze the genial current of the soul.

Full many a gem of purest ray serene
  The dark unfathomed caves of ocean bear:
Full many a flower is born to blush unseen,
  And waste its sweetness on the desert air.

Some village Hampden that with dauntless breast
  The little tyrant of his fields withstood,
Some mute inglorious Milton here may rest,
  Some Cromwell guiltless of his country's blood.

Th' applause of list'ning senates to command,
  The threats of pain and ruin to despise,
To scatter plenty o'er a smiling land,
  And read their history in a nation's eyes,

Their lot forbade: nor circumscribed alone
  Their growing virtues, but their crimes confined;
Forbade to wade through slaughter to a throne.
  And shut the gates of mercy on mankind,

The struggling pangs of conscious truth to hide,
  To quench the blushes of ingenuous shame,
Or heap the shrine of Luxury and Pride
  With incense kindled at the Muse's flame.

Far from the madding crowd's ignoble strife
  Their sober wishes never learned to stray;
Along the cool sequestered vale of life
  They kept the noiseless tenor of their way.

Yet ev'n these bones from insult to protect
  Some frail memorial still erected nigh,
With uncouth rhymes and shapeless sculpture decked,
  Implores the passing tribute of a sigh.

Their name, their years, spelt by th' unlettered Muse,
  The place of fame and elegy supply:
And many a holy text around she strews,
  That teach the rustic moralist to die.

For who, to dumb Forgetfulness a prey,
  This pleasing anxious being e'er resigned,
Left the warm precincts of the cheerful day,
  Nor cast one longing ling'ring look behind?

On some fond breast the parting soul relies,
  Some pious drops the closing eye requires;
E'en from the tomb the voice of Nature cries,
  E'en in our Ashes live their wonted fires.

For thee, who, mindful of th' unhonoured dead,
  Dost in these lines their artless tale relate;
If chance, by lonely contemplation led,
  Some kindred spirit shall inquire thy fate,

Haply some hoary-headed Swain may say,
  'Oft have we seen him at the peep of dawn
Brushing with hasty steps the dews away
  To meet the sun upon the upland lawn.

'There at the foot of yonder nodding beech
  That wreathes its old fantastic roots so high,
His listless length at noontide would he stretch,
  And pore upon the brook that babbles by.

'Hard by yon wood, now smiling as in scorn,
  Mutt'ring his wayward fancies he would rove,
Now drooping, woeful wan, like one forlorn,
  Or crazed with care, or crossed in hopeless love.

'One morn I missed him on the customed hill,
  Along the heath and near his fav'rite tree;
Another came; nor yet beside the rill,
  Nor up the lawn, nor at the wood was he;

'The next with dirges due in sad array
  Slow through the church-way path we saw him borne.
Approach and read (for thou canst read) the lay
  Graved on the stone beneath yon aged thorn:'

THE EPITAPH

Here rests his head upon the lap of Earth
  A Youth to Fortune and to Fame unknown.
Fair Science frowned not on his humble birth,
  And Melancholy marked him for her own.

Large was his bounty, and his soul sincere,
  Heaven did a recompense as largely send:
He gave to Mis'ry all he had, a tear,
  He gained from Heaven ('twas all he wished) a friend.

No further seek his merits to disclose,
  Or draw his frailties from their dread abode,
(There they alike in trembling hope repose,)
  The bosom of his Father and his God.

THOMAS GRAY

On a Favourite Cat, Drowned in a Tub of Goldfishes

'TWAS on a lofty vase's side,
Where China's gayest art had dyed
   The azure flowers that blow;
Demurest of the tabby kind,
The pensive Selima reclined,
   Gazed on the lake below.

Her conscious tail her joy declared;
The fair round face, the snowy beard,
   The velvet of her paws,
Her coat, that with the tortoise vies,
Her ears of jet, and emerald eyes.
   She saw; and purred applause.

Still had she gazed; but 'midst the tide
Two angel forms were seen to glide,
   The Genii of the stream:
Their scaly armour's Tyrian hue
Through richest purple to the view
   Betrayed a golden gleam.

The hapless Nymph with wonder saw:
A whisker first and then a claw,
   With many an ardent wish,
She stretched in vain to reach the prize.
What female heart can gold despise?
   What Cat's adverse to fish?

Presumptuous Maid! with looks intent
Again she stretched, again she bent,
   Nor knew the gulf between.
(Malignant Fate sat by, and smiled.)
The slipp'ry verge her feet beguiled,
   She tumbled headlong in.

Eight times emerging from the flood
She mewed to every watery god,
   Some speedy aid to send.
No Dolphin came, no Nereid stirred:
Nor cruel *Tom*, nor *Susan* heard.
   A Fav'rite has no friend!

THOMAS GRAY

From hence, ye Beauties, undeceived,
Know, one false step is ne'er retrieved,
  And be with caution bold.
Not all that tempts your wand'ring eyes
And heedless hearts, is lawful prize;
  Nor all that glisters, gold.

from *The Progress of Poesy*

IN climes beyond the solar road,
Where shaggy forms o'er ice-built mountains roam,
The Muse haes broke the twilight gloom
  To cheer the shiv'ring native's dull abode.
And oft, beneath the odorous shade
Of Chili's boundless forests laid,
She deigns to hear the savage youth repeat
In loose numbers wildly sweet
Their feather-cinctured chiefs, and dusky loves.
Her track, where'er the Goddess roves,
Glory pursue and generous Shame,
Th' unconquerable Mind, and Freedom's holy flame.

Woods, that wave o'er Delphi's steep,
Isles, that crown th' Ægean deep,
  Fields, that cool Ilissus laves,
  Or where Maeander's amber waves
In lingering lab'rinths creep,
  How do your tuneful echoes languish,
  Mute, but to the voice of anguish?
Where each old poetic mountain
  Inspiration breathed around:
Every shade and hallowed fountain
  Murmured deep a solemn sound:
Till the sad Nine, in Greece's evil hour,
  Left their Parnassus for the Latian plains.
Alike they scorn the pomp of tyrant Power,
  And coward Vice, that revels in her chains.
When Latium had her lofty spirit lost,
They sought, O Albion! next thy sea-encircled coast.

The Bard

A Pindaric Ode

'RUIN seize thee, ruthless King!
  Confusion on thy banners wait!
Though fanned by Conquest's crimson wing
  They mock the air with idle state.
Helm, nor hauberk's twisted mail,
Nor e'en thy virtues, tyrant, shall avail
To save thy secret soul from nightly fears,
From Cambria's curse, from Cambria's tears!'
—Such were the sounds that o'er the crested pride
  Of the first Edward scattered wild dismay,
As down the steep of Snowdon's shaggy side
  He wound with toilsome march his long array:—
Stout Glo'ster stood aghast in speechless trance;
'To arms!' cried Mortimer, and couched his quivering lance.

  On a rock, whose haughty brow
Frowns o'er old Conway's foaming flood,
  Robed in the sable garb of woe,
With haggard eyes the poet stood;
(Loose his beard and hoary hair
Streamed like a meteor to the troubled air;)
And with a master's hand and prophet's fire
Struck the deep sorrows of his lyre:
'Hark, how each giant oak and desert cave
  Sighs to the torrent's awful voice beneath!
O'er thee, O King! their hundred arms they wave
  Revenge on thee in hoarser murmurs breathe;
Vocal no more, since Cambria's fatal day,
To high-born Hoel's harp, or soft Llewellyn's lay.

'Cold is Cadwallo's tongue,
  That hushed the stormy main:
Brave Urien sleeps upon his craggy bed:
  Mountains, ye mourn in vain
  Modred, whose magic song
Made huge Plinlimmon bow his cloud-topt head.
  On dreary Arvon's shore they lie
Smeared with gore and ghastly pale:

Far, far aloof the affrighted ravens sail;
   The famished eagle screams, and passes by.
Dear lost companions of my tuneful art,
   Dear as the light that visits these sad eyes,
Dear as the ruddy drops that warm my heart,
   Ye died amidst your dying country's cries—
No more I weep. They do not sleep;
   On yonder cliffs, a griesly band,
I see them sit; they linger yet,
   Avengers of their native land:
With me in dreadful harmony they join;
And weave with bloody hands the tissue of thy line.

' "Weave the warp and weave the woof,
   The winding-sheet of Edward's race:
Give ample room and verge enough
   The characters of hell to trace.
Mark the year and mark the night
When Severn shall re-echo with affright
The shrieks of death through Berkley's roof that ring,
Shrieks of an agonizing king!
   She-wolf of France, with unrelenting fangs
That tear'st the bowels of thy mangled mate,
   From thee be born, who o'er thy country hangs
The scourge of heaven! What terrors round him wait!
Amazement in his van, with flight combined,
And sorrow's faded form, and solitude behind.

' "Mighty victor, mighty lord,
   Low on his funeral couch he lies!
No pitying heart, no eye, afford
   A tear to grace his obsequies.
Is the sable warrior fled?
Thy son is gone. He rests among the dead.
The swarm that in thy noon-tide beam were born?
—Gone to salute the rising morn.
Fair laughs the morn, and soft the zephyr blows,
   While proudly riding o'er the azure realm
In gallant trim the gilded vessel goes:
   Youth on the prow, and Pleasure at the helm:
Regardless of the sweeping whirlwind's sway,
That, hushed in grim repose, expected his evening prey.

'"Fill high the sparkling bowl,
The rich repast prepare;
   Reft of a crown, he yet may share the feast:
Close by the regal chair
   Fell Thirst and Famine scowl
   A baleful smile upon their baffled guest.
Heard ye the din of battle bray,
   Lance to lance, and horse to horse?
   Long years of havoc urge their destined course.
And through the kindred squadrons mow their way.
   Ye towers of Julius, London's lasting shame,
With many a foul and midnight murder fed,
   Revere his consort's faith, his father's fame,
And spare the meek usurper's holy head!
Above, below, the rose of snow,
   Twined with her blushing foe, we spread:
The bristled boar in infant-gore
   Wallows beneath the thorny shade.
Now, brothers, bending o'er the accursèd loom,
Stamp we our vengeance deep, and ratify his doom.

'"Edward, lo! to sudden fate
   (Weave we the woof; The thread is spun;)
Half of thy heart we consecrate.
   (The web is wove; The work is done.)"
Stay, O stay! nor thus forlorn
Leave me unblessed, unpitied, here to mourn:
In yon bright track that fires the western skies
They melt, they vanish from my eyes.
But O! what solemn scenes on Snowdon's height
   Descending slow their glittering skirts unroll?
Visions of glory, spare my aching sight,
   Ye unborn ages, crowd not on my soul!
No more our long-lost Arthur we bewail:—
All hail, ye genuine kings! Britannia's issue, hail!

'Girt with many a baron bold
Sublime their starry fronts they rear;
   And gorgeous dames, and statesmen old
In bearded majesty, appear.
In the midst a form divine!
Her eye proclaims her of the Briton-line:
Her lion-port, her awe-commanding face
Attempered sweet to virgin-grace.

What strings symphonious tremble in the air,
  What strains of vocal transport round her play!
Hear from the grave, great Taliessin, hear;
  They breathe a soul to animate thy clay.
Bright Rapture calls, and soaring as she sings,
Waves in the eye of heaven her many-coloured wings.

   'The verse adorn again
   Fierce war, and faithful love,
And Truth severe, by fairy Fiction drest.
   In buskined measures move
Pale grief, and pleasing pain,
With horror, tyrant of the throbbing breast.
A voice as of the cherub-choir
   Gales from blooming Eden bear,
   And distant warblings lesson on my ear,
That lost in long futurity expire.
Fond impious man, think'st thou yon sanguine cloud
   Raised by thy breath, has quenched the orb of day?
To-morrow he repairs the golden flood
   And warms the nations with redoubled ray.
Enough for me: with joy I see
   The different doom our fates assign:
Be thine despair and sceptred care;
   To triumph and to die are mine.'
—He spoke, and headlong from the mountain's height
Deep in the roaring tide he plunged to endless night.

The Descent of Odin

   UPROSE the King of Men with speed,
   And saddled strait his coal-black steed:
   Down the yawning steep he rode
   That leads to Hela's drear abode.
   Him the Dog of darkness spied:
   His shaggy throat he open'd wide,
   While from his jaws with carnage fill'd
   Foam & human gore distill'd:
   Hoarse he bays with hideous din,
   Eyes, that glow, & fangs, that grin,
   And long pursues with fruitless yell
   The Father of the powerful spell.

Onward still his way he takes,
(The groaning earth beneath him shakes)
Till full before his fearless eyes
The portals nine of hell arise.
 Right against the eastern gate
By the moss-grown pile he sate,
Where long of yore to sleep was laid
The dust of the prophetic Maid.
Facing to the northern clime
Thrice he traced the runic rhyme,
Thrice pronounc'd in accents dread
The thrilling verse, that wakes the Dead,
Till from out the hollow ground
Slowly breath'd a sullen sound.
 Pr: What call unknown, what charms presume
To break the quiet of the tomb?
Who thus afflicts my troubled sprite,
And drags me from the realms of night?
Long on these mould'ring bones have beat
The winter's snow, the summer's heat
The drenching dews, & driving rain!
Let me, let me sleep again.
Who is he with voice unblest,
That calls me from the bed of rest?
 O: A Traveller to thee unknown
Is he, that calls, a Warriour's Son.
Thou the deeds of light shalt know,
Tell me what is done below,
For whom yon glitt'ring board is spread,
Drest for whom yon golden bed.
 Pr: Mantling in the goblet see
The pure bev'rage of the bee,
O'er it hangs the shield of gold;
'Tis the drink of *Balder* bold:
Balder's head to death is giv'n.
Pain can reach the Sons of heav'n!
Unwilling I my lips unclose,
Leave me, leave me to repose.
 O: Once again my call obey.
Prophetess, arise & say,
What dangers *Odin*'s Child await,
Who the Author of his fate.
 Pr: In *Hoder*'s hand the Heroe's doom:
His Brother sends him to the tomb.

Now my weary lips I close.
Leave me, leave me to repose.
   O: Prophetess, my spell obey,
Once again arise & say,
Who th' Avenger of his guilt,
By whom shall *Hoder*'s blood be spilt.
   Pr: In the caverns of the west
By *Odin*'s fierce embrace comprest
A wond'rous Boy shall *Rinda* bear,
Who ne'er shall comb his raven-hair,
Nor wash his visage in the stream,
Nor see the sun's departing beam:
Till he on *Hoder*'s coarse shall smile
Flaming on the fun'ral pile.
Now my weary lips I close;
Leave me, leave me to repose.
   O: Yet a while my call obey.
Prophetess, awake & say,
What Virgins these in speechless woe,
That bend to earth their solemn brow,
That their flaxen tresses tear,
And snowy veils, that float in air.
Tell me, whence their sorrows rose:
Then I leave thee to repose.
   Pr: Ha! no Traveller art thou,
King of Men, I know thee now,
Mightiest of a mighty line—
   O: No boding Maid of skill divine
Art thou, nor Prophetess of good;
But Mother of the giant-brood!
   Pr: Hie thee hence & boast at home,
That never shall Enquirer come
To break my iron-sleep again:
Till *Lok* has burst his tenfold chain.
Never, till substantial Night
Has reassum'd her ancient right;
Till wrap'd in flames, in ruin hurl'd,
Sinks the fabrick of the world.

WILLIAM COLLINS

1721–1759

Ode to Evening

IF aught of oaten stop, or pastoral song,
May hope, chaste eve, to soothe thy modest ear,
    Like thy own solemn springs,
    Thy springs and dying gales;

O nymph reserved, while now the bright-haired sun
Sits in yon western tent, whose cloudy skirts,
    With brede ethereal wove,
    O'er hang his wavy bed:

Now air is hushed, save where the weak-eyed bat
With short shrill shriek flits by on leathern wing,
    Or where the beetle winds
    His small but sullen horn,

As oft he rises, 'midst the twilight path
Against the pilgrim borne in heedless hum:
    Now teach me, maid composed
    To breathe some softened strain,

Whose numbers, stealing through thy darkening vale,
May not unseemly with its stillness suit,
    As, musing slow, I hail
    Thy genial loved return!

For when thy folding-star arising shows
His paly circlet, at his warning lamp
    The fragrant hours, and elves
    Who slept in buds the day,

And many a nymph who wreathes her brows with sedge,
And sheds the freshening dew, and lovelier still,
    The pensive pleasures sweet,
    Prepare thy shadowy car:

brede] braid, embroidery

Then lead, calm votaress, where some sheety lake
Cheers the lone heath, or some time-hallowed pile
    Or upland fallows grey
    Reflect its last cool gleam.

Or if chill blustering winds, or driving rain,
Prevent my willing feet, be mine the hut
    That from the mountain's side
    Views wilds and swelling floods,

And hamlets brown, and dim-discovered spires,
And hears their simple bell, and marks o'er all
    Thy dewy fingers draw
    The gradual dusky veil.

While spring shall pour his show'rs, as oft he wont,
And bathe thy breathing tresses, meekest eve!
    While summer loves to sport
    Beneath thy lingering light;

While sallow autumn fills thy lap with leaves,
Or winter, yelling through the troublous air,
    Affrights thy shrinking train,
    And rudely rends thy robes:

So long, regardful of thy quiet rule,
Shall fancy, friendship, science, rose-lipped health
    Thy gentlest influence own,
    And hymn thy favourite name!

An Ode on the Popular Superstitions of the Highlands of Scotland, Considered as the Subject of Poetry

HOME, thou return'st from Thames, whose naiads long
    Have seen thee ling'ring, with a fond delay,
Mid those soft friends, whose hearts, some future day,
    Shall melt, perhaps, to hear thy tragic song.
Go, not unmindful of that cordial youth,
    Whom, long endeared, thou leav'st by Lavant's side;
Together let us wish him lasting truth,
    And joy untainted with his destined bride.
Go! nor regardless, while these numbers boast
    My short-lived bliss, forget my social name;

But think far off how, on the southern coast,
   I met thy friendship with an equal flame!
Fresh to that soil thou turn'st, whose every vale
   Shall prompt the poet, and his song demand:
To thee thy copious subjects ne'er shall fail;
   Thou need'st but take the pencil to thy hand,
And paint what all believe who own thy genial land.

II

There must thou wake perforce thy Doric quill,
   'Tis Fancy's land to which thou sett'st thy feet,
Where still, 'tis said, the fairy people meet
   Beneath each birken shade or mead or hill.
There each trim lass that skims the milky store
   To the swart tribes their creamy bowl allots;
By night they sip it round the cottage-door,
   While airy minstrels warble jocund notes.
There every herd, by sad experience, knows
   How, winged with fate, their elf-shot arrows fly.
When the sick ewe her summer food foregoes,
   Or, stretched on earth, the heart-smit heifers lie.
Such airy beings awe th' untutored swain:
   Nor thou, though learned, his homelier thoughts neglect;
Let thy sweet muse the rural faith sustain:
   These are the themes of simple, sure effect,
That add new conquests to her boundless reign,
And fill, with double force, her heart-commanding strain.

III

Ev'n yet preserved, how often may'st thou hear,
   Where to the pole the Boreal mountains run,
Taught by the father to his list'ning son
   Strange lays, whose power had charmed a Spenser's ear.
At every pause, before thy mind possessed,
   Old Runic bards shall seem to rise around,
With uncouth lyres, in many-coloured vest,
   Their matted hair with boughs fantastic crowned:
Whether thou bid'st the well-taught hind repeat
   The choral dirge that mourns some chieftain brave,
When every shrieking maid her bosom beat,
   And strewed with choicest herbs his scented grave;

Or whether, sitting in the shepherd's shiel,
  Thou hear'st some sounding tale of war's alarms;
When, at the bugle's call, with fire and steel,
  The sturdy clans poured forth their bony swarms,
And hostile brothers met to prove each other's arms.

IV

'Tis thine to sing, how framing hideous spells
  In Sky's lone isle the gifted wizard seer,
Lodged in the wintry cave with ——,
  Or in the depth of Uist's dark forests dwells:
How they, whose sight such dreary dreams engross,
  With their own visions oft astonished droop,
When o'er the wat'ry strath or quaggy moss
  They see the gliding ghosts unbodied troop.
Or if in sports, or on the festive green,
  Their —— glance some fated youth descry,
Who, now perhaps in lusty vigour seen
  And rosy health, shall soon lamented die.
For them the viewless forms of air obey,
  Their bidding heed, and at their beck repair.
They know what spirit brews the stormful day,
  And heartless, oft like moody madness stare
To see the phantom train their secret work prepare.

[25 lines lost.]

VI

What though far off, from some dark dell espied
  His glimm'ring mazes cheer th' excursive sight,
Yet turn, ye wand'rers, turn your steps aside,
  Nor trust the guidance of that faithless light;
For watchful, lurking 'mid th' unrustling reed,
  At those mirk hours the wily monster lies,
And listens oft to hear the passing steed,
  And frequent round him rolls his sullen eyes,
If chance his savage wrath may some weak wretch surprise.

VII

Ah, luckless swain, o'er all unblest indeed!
  Whom late bewildered in the dank, dark fen,
Far from his flocks and smoking hamlet then!
  To that sad spot ————:

shiel] hut

574

On him enraged, the fiend, in angry mood,
Shall never look with pity's kind concern,
But instant, furious, raise the whelming flood
  O'er its drowned bank, forbidding all return.
Or, if he meditate his wished escape
  To some dim hill that seems uprising near,
To his faint eye the grim and grisly shape,
  In all its terrors clad, shall wild appear.
Meantime, the wat'ry surge shall around him rise,
  Poured sudden forth from every swelling source.
What now remains but tears and hopeless sighs!
  His fear-shook limbs have lost their youthly force,
And down the waves he floats, a pale and breathless corse.

VIII

For him, in vain, his anxious wife shall wait,
  Or wander forth to meet him on his way;
For him, in vain, at to-fall of the day,
  His babes shall linger at th' unclosing gate!
Ah, ne'er shall he return! Alone, if night
  Her travelled limbs in broken slumbers steep,
With dropping willows dressed, his mournful sprite
  Shall visit sad, perchance, her silent sleep:
Then he, perhaps, with moist and wat'ry hand,
  Shall fondly seem to press her shudd'ring cheek
And with his blue swoln face before her stand,
  And shiv'ring cold, these piteous accents speak:
'Pursue, dear wife, thy daily toils pursue
  At dawn or dusk, industrious as before;
Nor e'er of me one hapless thought renew,
  While I lie welt'ring on the oziered shore,
Drowned by the kelpie's wrath, nor e'er shall aid thee more!'

IX

Unbounded is thy range; with varied style
  Thy muse may, like those feath'ry tribes which spring
From their rude rocks, extend her skirting wing
  Round the moist marge of each cold Hebrid isle,
To that hoar pile which still its ruin shows:
  In whose small vaults a pigmy-folk is found,
Whose bones the delver with his spade upthrows,
  And culls them, wond'ring from the hallowed ground!

kelpie] a malignant water sprite

Or thither where beneath the show'ry west
   The mighty kings of three fair realms are laid;
Once foes, perhaps, together now they rest.
   No slaves revere them, and no wars invade:
Yet frequent now, at midnight's solemn hour,
   The rifted mounds their yawning cells unfold,
And forth the monarchs stalk with sov'reign power
   In pageant robes, and wreathed with sheeny gold,
And on their twilight tombs aerial council hold.

X

But O! o'er all, forget not Kilda's race,
   On whose bleak rocks, which brave the wasting tides,
Fair nature's daughter, virtue, yet abides.
   Go, just, as they, their blameless manners traced
Then to my ear transmit some gentle song
   Of those whose lives are yet sincere and plain,
Their bounded walks the rugged cliffs along,
   And all their prospect but the wintry main.
With sparing temp'rance, at the needful time,
   They drain the sainted spring, or, hunger-prest,
Along th' Atlantic rock undreading climb,
   And of its eggs despoil the solan's nest.
Thus blest in primal innocence they live,
   Sufficed and happy with that frugal fare
Which tasteful toil and hourly danger give.
   Hard is their shallow soil, and bleak and bare;
Nor ever vernal bee was heard to murmur there!

XI

Nor need'st thou blush, that such false themes engage
   Thy gentle mind, of fairer stores possessed;
For not alone they touch the village breast,
   But filled in elder time th' historic page,
There Shakespeare's self, with every garland crowned,

   . . . .

   In musing hour, his wayward sisters found,
And with their terrors dressed the magic scene.
   From them he sung, when mid his bold design,
Before the Scot afflicted and aghast,
   The shadowy kings of Banquo's fated line,
Through the dark cave in gleamy pageant past.
   Proceed, nor quit the tales which, simply told,

Could once so well my answ'ring bosom pierce;
  Proceed, in forceful sounds and colours bold
The native legends of thy land rehearse;
To such adapt thy lyre and suit thy powerful verse.

XII

In scenes like these, which, daring to depart
  From sober truth, are still to nature true,
And call forth fresh delight to fancy's view,
  Th' heroic muse employed her Tasso's art!
How have I trembled, when at Tancred's stroke,
  Its gushing blood the gaping cypress poured;
When each live plant with mortal accents spoke,
  And the wild blast up-heaved the vanished sword!
How have I sat, when piped the pensive wind,
  To hear his harp, by British Fairfax strung.
Prevailing poet, whose undoubting mind
  Believed the magic wonders which he sung!
Hence at each sound imagination glows;

  . . . .

  Hence his warm lay with softest sweetness flows;
Melting it flows, pure, num'rous, strong and clear,
And fills th' impassioned heart, and wins th' harmonious ear.

XIII

All hail, ye scenes that o'er my soul prevail,
  Ye ———— friths and lakes which, far away,
Are by smooth Annan filled, or past'ral Tay,
  Or Don's romantic springs, at distance, hail!
The time shall come when I, perhaps, may tread
  Your lowly glens, o'erhung with spreading broom,
Or o'er your stretching heaths by fancy led:

  . . . .

Then will I dress once more the faded bower,
  Where Jonson sat in Drummond's [classic] shade,
Or crop from Tiviots dale each [lyric flower],
  And mourn on Yarrow's banks [where Willy's laid].
Meantime, ye pow'rs, that on the plains which bore,
  The cordial youth, on Lothian's plains attend,
Where'er he dwell, on hill, or lowly muir,
  To him I lose, your kind protection lend,
And, touched with love like mine, preserve my absent friend.

How Sleep the Brave

How sleep the brave, who sink to rest
By all their country's wishes blest!
When Spring, with dewy fingers cold,
Returns to deck their hallowed mould,
She there shall dress a sweeter sod
Than Fancy's feet have ever trod.
By fairy hands their knell is rung;
By forms unseen their dirge is sung;
There Honour comes, a pilgrim grey,
To bless the turf that wraps their clay;
And Freedom shall awhile repair
To dwell, a weeping hermit, there!

Ode to Simplicity

O THOU, by Nature taught
To breathe her genuine thought
In numbers warmly pure and sweetly strong:
Who first on mountains wild,
In fancy, loveliest child,
Thy babe and pleasure's, nursed the pow'rs of song.

Thou, who with hermit heart
Disdain'st the wealth of art,
And gauds, and pageant weeds, and trailing pall:
But com'st a decent maid,
In Attic robe arrayed,
O chaste, unboastful nymph, to thee I call!

By all the honeyed store
On Hybla's thymy shore,
By all her blooms and mingled murmurs dear,
By her whose love-lorn woe,
In evening musings slow,
Soothed sweetly sad Electra's poet's ear:

By old Cephisus deep,
Who spread his wavy sweep
In warbled wand'rings round thy green retreat;
On whose enamelled side,
When holy Freedom died,
No equal haunt allured thy future feet!

O sister meek of truth,
  To my admiring youth
Thy sober aid and native charms infuse!
  The flow'rs that sweetest breathe,
  Though beauty culled the wreath,
Still ask thy hand to range their ordered hues.

  While Rome could none esteem,
  But virtue's patriot theme,
You loved her hills, and led her laureate band;
  But stayed to sing alone
  To one distinguished throne,
And turned thy face, and fled her altered land.

  No more, in hall or bower,
  The passions own thy power.
Love, only Love her forceless numbers mean;
  For thou hast left her shrine,
  Nor olive more, nor vine,
Shall gain thy feet to bless the servile scene.

  Though taste, though genius bless
  To some divine excess,
Faint's the cold work till thou inspire the whole;
  What each, what all supply,
  May court, may charm our eye,
Thou, only thou, canst raise the meeting soul!

  Of these let others ask,
  To aid some mighty task,
I only seek to find thy temperate vale;
  Where oft my reed might sound
  To maids and shepherds round,
And all thy sons, O Nature, learn my tale.

CHRISTOPHER SMART

1722–1771

from *The Song to David*

O THOU, that sit'st upon a throne,
With harp of high majestic tone,
  To praise the King of Kings;
And voice of heaven-ascending swell,
Which, while its deeper notes excel,
  Clear, as a clarion, rings:

To bless each valley, grove, and coast,
And charm the cherubs to the post
  Of gratitude in throngs;
To keep the days on Zion's mount,
And send the year to his account,
  With dances and with songs:

O Servant of God's holiest charge,
The minister of praise at large,
  Which thou may'st now receive;
From thy blest mansion hail and hear,
From topmost eminence appear
  To this the wreath I weave.

He sang of God—the mighty source
Of all things—the stupendous force
  On which all strength depends;
From whose right arm, beneath whose eyes,
All period, power, and enterprise
  Commences, reigns, and ends.

Angels—their ministry and meed,
Which to and fro with blessings speed,
  Or with their citterns wait;
Where Michael with his millions bows,
Where dwells the seraph and his spouse,
  The cherub and her mate.

Of man—the semblance and effect
Of God and Love—the Saint elect
   For infinite applause—
To rule the land, and briny broad,
To be laborious in his laud,
   And heroes in his cause.

The world, the clustering spheres, He made;
The glorious light, the soothing shade,
   Dale, champaign, grove, and hill;
The multitudinous abyss,
Where Secrecy remains in bliss,
   And Wisdom hides her skill.

Trees, plants, and flowers—of virtuous root;
Gem yielding blossom, yielding fruit,
   Choice gums and precious balm;
Bless ye the nosegay in the vale,
And with the sweetness of the gale
   Enrich the thankful psalm.

Of fowl—e'en every beak and wing
Which cheer the winter, hail the spring,
   That live in peace or prey;
They that make music, or that mock,
The quail, the brave domestic cock,
   The raven, swan, and jay.

Of fishes—every size and shape,
Which nature frames of light escape,
   Devouring man to shun:
The shells are in the wealthy deep,
The shoals upon the surface leap,
   And love the glancing sun.

Of beasts—the beaver plods his task;
While the sleek tigers roll and bask,
   Nor yet the shades arouse:
Her cave the mining coney scoops;
Where o'er the mead the mountain stoops,
   The kids exult and browse.

Of gems—their virtue and their price,
Which hid in earth from man's device,
    Their darts of lustre sheathe;
The jasper of the master's stamp,
The topaz blazing like a lamp
    Among the mines beneath.

Blest was the tenderness he felt
When to his graceful harp he knelt,
    And did for audience call;
When Satan with his hand he quelled,
And in serene suspense he held
    The frantic throes of Saul.

His furious foes no more maligned
As he such melody divined,
    And sense and soul detained;
Now striking strong, now soothing soft,
He sent the godly sounds aloft,
    Or in delight refrained.

When up to heaven his thoughts he piled,
From fervent lips fair Michal smiled,
    As blush to blush she stood;
And chose herself the queen, and gave
Her utmost from her heart, 'so brave,
    And plays his hymns so good.'

The pillars of the Lord are seven,
Which stand from earth to topmost heaven;
    His wisdom drew the plan;
His Word accomplished the design,
From brightest gem to deepest mine,
    From Christ enthroned to man.

Thou art—to give and to confirm,
For each his talent and his term;
    All flesh thy bounties share:
Thou shalt not call thy brother fool;
The porches of the Christian school
    Are meekness, peace, and prayer.

Open, and naked of offence,
Man's made of mercy, soul, and sense;
   God armed the snail and wilk;
Be good to him who pulls thy plough;
Due food and care, due rest, allow
   For her that yields thee milk.

Rise up before the hoary head,
And God's benign commandment dread,
   Which says thou shalt not die:
'Not as I will, but as thou wilt,'
Prayed He whose conscience knew no guilt;
   With whose blessed pattern vie.

Use all thy passions!—love is thine,
And joy, and jealousy divine;
   Thine hope's eternal fort,
And care thy leisure to disturb,
With fear concupiscence to curb,
   And rapture to transport.

Act simply, as occasion asks;
Put mellow wine in seasoned casks;
   Till not with ass and bull:
Remember thy baptismal bond;
Keep from commixtures foul and fond,
   Nor work thy flax with wool.

Distribute: pay the Lord his tithe,
And make the widow's heart-strings blithe;
   Resort with those that weep:
As you from all and each expect,
For all and each thy love direct,
   And render as you reap.

The slander and its bearer spurn,
And propagating praise sojourn
   To make thy welcome last;
Turn from old Adam to the New;
By hope futurity pursue;
   Look upwards to the past.

Control thine eye, salute success,
Honour the wiser, happier bless,
   And for thy neighbour feel;
Grudge not of mammon and his leaven,
Work emulation up to heaven
   By knowledge and by zeal.

O David, highest in the list
   Of worthies, on God's ways insist,
   The genuine word repeat:
Vain are the documents of men,
And vain the flourish of the pen
   That keeps the fool's conceit.

from *Jubilate Agno*

For I will consider my Cat Jeoffry.

For he is the servant of the Living God duly and daily serving him.

For at the first glance of the glory of God in the East he worships in his way.

For is this done by wreathing his body seven times round with elegant quickness.

For then he leaps up to catch the musk, which is the blessing of God upon his prayer.

For he rolls upon prank to work it in.

For having done duty and received blessing he begins to consider himself.

For this he performs in ten degrees.

For first he looks upon his fore-paws to see if they are clean.

For secondly he kicks up behind to clear away there.

For thirdly he works it upon stretch with the fore paws extended.

For fourthly he sharpens his paws by wood.

For fifthly he washes himself.

For Sixthly he rolls upon wash.

For Seventhly he fleas himself, that he may not be interrupted upon the beat.

For Eighthly he rubs himself against a post.

For ninthly he rubs himself against a post.

For tenthly he goes in quest of food.

For having consider'd God and himself he will consider his neighbour.

For if he meets another cat he will kiss her in kindness.

For when he takes his prey he plays with it to give it a chance.

For one mouse in seven escapes by his dallying.

For when his day's work is done his business more properly begins.

For he keeps the Lord's watch in the night against the adversary.

For he counteracts the powers of darkness by his electrical skin & glaring eyes.

For he counteracts the Devil, who is death, by brisking about the life.

For in his morning orisons he loves the sun and the sun loves him.

For he is of the tribe of Tiger.

For the Cherub Cat is a term of the Angel Tiger.

For he has the subtlety and hissing of a serpent, which in goodness he suppresses.

For he will not do destruction if he is well-fed, neither will he spit without provocation.

For he purrs in thankfulness, when God tells him he's a good Cat.

For he is an instrument for the children to learn benevolence upon.

For every house is incompleat without him & a blessing is lacking in the spirit.

For the Lord commanded Moses concerning the cats at the departure of the Children of Israel from Egypt.

For every family had one cat at least in the bag.

For the English Cats are the best in Europe.

For he is the cleanest in the use of his fore-paws of any quadrupede.

For the dexterity of his defence is an instance of the love of God to him exceedingly.

For he is the quickest to his mark of any creature.

For he is tenacious of his point.

For he is a mixture of gravity and waggery.

For he knows that God is his Saviour.

For there is nothing sweeter than his peace when at rest.

For there is nothing brisker than his life when in motion.

For he is of the Lord's poor and so indeed is he called by benevolence perpetually—Poor Jeoffry! poor Jeoffry! the rat has bit thy throat.

For I bless the name of the Lord Jesus that Jeoffry is better.

For the divine spirit comes about his body to sustain it in compleat cat.

For his tongue is exceeding pure so that it has in purity what it wants in musick.

For he is docile and can learn certain things.

For he can set up with gravity which is patience upon approbation.

For he can fetch and carry, which is patience in employment.

For he can jump over a stick which is patience upon proof positive.

For he can spraggle upon waggle at the word of command.

For he can jump from an eminence into his master's bosom.

For he can catch the cork and toss it again.

For he is hated by the hypocrite and miser.

For the former is afraid of detection.

For the latter refuses the charge.
For he camels his back to bear the first notion of business.
For he is good to think on, if a man would express himself neatly.
For he made a great figure in Egypt for his signal services.
For he killed the Icneumon-rat very pernicious by land.
For his ears are so acute that they sting again.
For from this proceeds the passing quickness of his attention.
For by stroaking of him I have found out electricity.
For I have perceived God's light about him both wax and fire.
For the Electrical fire is the spiritual substance, which God sends from
    heaven to sustain the bodies both of man and beast.
For God has blessed him in the variety of his movements.
For, tho he cannot fly, he is an excellent clamberer.
For his motions upon the face of the earth are more than any other
    quadrupede.
For he can tread to all the measures upon the musick.
For he can swim for life.
For he can creep.

JOSEPH WARTON

1722–1800

The Dying Indian

THE dart of Izdabel prevails! 'twas dipt
In double poison—I shall soon arrive
At the blest island, where no tigers spring
On heedless hunters; where ananas bloom
Thrice in each moon; where rivers smoothly glide,
Nor thund'ring torrents whirl the light canoe
Down to the sea; where my forefathers feast
Daily on hearts of Spaniards! O my son,
I feel the venom busy in my breast;
Approach and bring my crown, deck'd with the teeth
Of that bold Christian who first dar'd deflow'r
The virgins of the Sun; and, dire to tell!
Robb'd Pachacamac's altar of its gems!
I mark'd the spot where they interr'd this traitor,
And once at midnight stole I to his tomb,
And tore his carcass from the earth, and left it
A prey to poisonous flies. Preserve this crown

JOSEPH WARTON

With sacred secrecy; if e'er returns
Thy much lov'd mother from the desert woods,
Where, as I hunted late, I hapless lost her,
Cherish her age. Tell her, I ne'er have worshipp'd
With those that eat their God. And when disease
Preys on her languid limbs, then kindly stab her
With thine own hands, nor suffer her to linger,
Like Christian cowards, in a life of pain.
I go! great Copac beckons me! Farewell!

Ode to Evening

HAIL, meek-eyed maiden, clad in sober grey,
Whose soft approach the weary woodman loves,
As, homeward bent to kiss his prattling babes,
He jocund whistles through the twilight groves.

When Phœbus sinks beneath the gilded hills,
You lightly o'er the misty meadows walk,
The drooping daisies bathe in dulcet dews,
And nurse the nodding violet's slender stalk.

The panting Dryads, that in day's fierce heat
To inmost bow'rs and cooling caverns ran,
Return to trip in wanton evening dance,
Old Sylvan, too, returns, and laughing Pan.

To the deep wood the clam'rous rooks repair,
Light skims the swallow o'er the watery scene,
And from the sheep-cotes and fresh furrow'd field,
Stout ploughmen meet to wrestle on the green.

The swain that artless sings on yonder rock,
His nibbling sheep and length'ning shadow spies,
Pleas'd with the cool, the calm, refreshful hour,
And with hoarse hummings of unnumber'd flies.

Now ev'ry passion sleeps; desponding Love,
And pining Envy, ever-restless Pride;
An holy calm creeps o'er my peaceful soul,
Anger and mad ambition's storms subside.

O modest Evening, oft let me appear
A wand'ring votary in thy pensive train,
List'ning to ev'ry wildly warbling throat
That fills with farewell notes the darkening plain.

OLIVER GOLDSMITH

1728–1774

The Deserted Village

SWEET Auburn! loveliest village of the plain,
Where health and plenty cheered the labouring swain,
Where smiling spring its earliest visit paid,
And parting summer's lingering blooms delayed:
Dear lovely bowers of innocence and ease,
Seats of my youth, when every sport could please,
How often have I loitered o'er thy green,
Where humble happiness endeared each scene;
How often have I paused on every charm,
The sheltered cot, the cultivated farm,
The never-failing brook, the busy mill,
The decent church that topped the neighbouring hill,
The hawthorn bush, with seats beneath the shade,
For talking age and whisp'ring lovers made;
How often have I blessed the coming day,
When toil remitting lent its turn to play,
And all the village train, from labour free,
Led up their sports beneath the spreading tree;
While many a pastime circled in the shade,
The young contending as the old surveyed;
And many a gambol frolicked o'er the ground,
And sleights of art and feats of strength went round;
And still as each repeated pleasure tired,
Succeeding sports the mirthful band inspired;
The dancing pair that simply sought renown,
By holding out to tire each other down;
The swain mistrustless of his smutted face,
While secret laughter tittered round the place;
The bashful virgin's side-long looks of love,
The matron's glance that would those looks reprove,
These were thy charms, sweet village; sports like these,
With sweet succession, taught e'en toil to please;
These round thy bowers their cheerful influence shed,
These were thy charms—But all these charms are fled.

Sweet smiling village, loveliest of the lawn,
Thy sports are fled, and all thy charms withdrawn;

Amidst thy bowers the tyrant's hand is seen,
And desolation saddens all thy green:
One only master grasps the whole domain,
And half a tillage stints thy smiling plain:
No more thy glassy brook reflects the day,
But choked with sedges, works its weedy way.
Along thy glades, a solitary guest,
The hollow-sounding bittern guards its nest;
Amidst thy desert walks the lapwing flies,
And tires their echoes with unvaried cries.
Sunk are thy bowers in shapeless ruin all,
And the long grass o'ertops the mould'ring wall;
And trembling, shrinking from the spoiler's hand,
Far, far away, thy children leave the land.

Ill fares the land, to hast'ning ills a prey,
Where wealth accumulates, and men decay:
Princes and lords may flourish, or may fade;
A breath can make them, as a breath has made;
But a bold peasantry, their country's pride,
When once destroyed, can never be supplied.

A time there was, ere England's griefs began,
When every rood of ground maintained its man;
For him light labour spread her wholesome store,
Just gave what life required, but gave no more:
His best companions, innocence and health;
And his best riches, ignorance of wealth.

But times are altered; trade's unfeeling train,
Usurp the land and dispossess the swain;
Along the lawn, where scattered hamlets rose,
Unwieldy wealth and cumbrous pomp repose;
And every want to opulence allied,
And every pang that folly pays to pride.
Those gentle hours that plenty bade to bloom,
Those calm desires that asked but little room,
Those healthful sports that graced the peaceful scene,
Lived in each look, and brightened all the green;
These, far departing, seek a kinder shore,
And rural mirth and manners are no more.

Sweet Auburn! parent of the blissful hour,
Thy glades forlorn confess the tyrant's power.

Here as I take my solitary rounds,
Amidst thy tangling walks and ruined grounds,
And, many a year elapsed, return to view
Where once the cottage stood, the hawthorn grew,
Remembrance wakes with all her busy train,
Swells at my breast, and turns the past to pain.

In all my wand'rings round this world of care,
In all my griefs—and God has given my share—
I still had hopes my latest hours to crown,
Amidst these humble bowers to lay me down;
To husband out life's taper at the close,
And keep the flame from wasting by repose.
I still had hopes, for pride attends us still,
Amidst the swains to show my book-learned skill,
Around my fire an evening group to draw,
And tell of all I felt, and all I saw;
And, as a hare, whom hounds and horns pursue,
Pants to the place from whence at first she flew,
I still had hopes, my long vexations passed,
Here to return—and die at home at last.

O blest retirement, friend to life's decline,
Retreats from care, that never must be mine,
How happy he who crowns in shades like these,
A youth of labour with an age of ease;
Who quits a world where strong temptations try
And, since 'tis hard to combat, learns to fly!
For him no wretches, born to work and weep,
Explore the mine, or tempt the dangerous deep;
No surly porter stands in guilty state
To spurn imploring famine from the gate;
But on he moves to meet his latter end,
Angels around befriending Virtue's friend;
Bends to the grave with unperceived decay,
While resignation gently slopes the way;
And, all his prospects bright'ning to the last,
His Heaven commences ere the world be passed!

Sweet was the sound, when oft at evening's close
Up yonder hill the village murmur rose;
There, as I passed with careless steps and slow,
The mingling notes came softened from below;

The swain responsive as the milk-maid sung,
The sober herd that lowed to meet their young;
The noisy geese that gabbled o'er the pool,
The playful children just let loose from school;
The watchdog's voice that bayed the whisp'ring wind,
And the loud laugh that spoke the vacant mind;
These all in sweet confusion sought the shade,
And filled each pause the nightingale had made.
But now the sounds of population fail,
No cheerful murmurs fluctuate in the gale,
No busy steps the grass-grown foot-way tread,
For all the bloomy flush of life is fled.
All but yon widowed, solitary thing
That feebly bends beside the plashy spring;
She, wretched matron, forced, in age, for bread,
To strip the brook with mantling cresses spread,
To pick her wintry faggot from the thorn,
To seek her nightly shed, and weep till morn;
She only left of all the harmless train,
The sad historian of the pensive plain.

Near yonder copse, where once the garden smiled,
And still where many a garden flower grows wild:
There, where a few torn shrubs the place disclose,
The village preacher's modest mansion rose.
A man he was to all the country dear,
And passing rich with forty pounds a year;
Remote from towns he ran his godly race,
Nor e'er had changed, nor wished to change his place;
Unpractised he to fawn, or seek for power,
By doctrines fashioned to the varying hour;
For other aims his heart had learned to prize,
More skilled to raise the wretched than to rise.
His house was known to all the vagrant train,
He chid their wand'rings, but relieved their pain;
The long-remembered beggar was his guest,
Whose beard descending swept his aged breast;
The ruined spendthrift, now no longer proud,
Claimed kindred there, and had his claims allowed;
The broken soldier, kindly bade to stay,
Sat by his fire, and talked the night away;
Wept o'er his wounds, or tales of sorrow done,
Shouldered his crutch, and showed how fields were won.

Pleased with his guests, the good man learned to glow,
And quite forgot their vices in their woe;
Careless their merits, or their faults to scan,
His pity gave ere charity began.

Thus to relieve the wretched was his pride,
And e'en his failings leaned to virtue's side;
But in his duty prompt at every call,
He watched and wept, he prayed and felt, for all.
And, as a bird each fond endearment tries
To tempt its new-fledged offspring to the skies,
He tried each art, reproved each dull delay,
Allured to brighter worlds, and led the way.

Beside the bed where parting life was laid,
And sorrow, guilt, and pain, by turns dismayed,
The reverend champion stood. At his control,
Despair and anguish fled the struggling soul;
Comfort came down the trembling wretch to raise,
And his last falt'ring accents whispered praise.

At church, with meek and unaffected grace,
His looks adorned the venerable place;
Truth from his lips prevailed with double sway,
And fools, who came to scoff, remained to pray.
The service passed, around the pious man,
With steady zeal, each honest rustic ran;
E'en children followed with endearing wile,
And plucked his gown, to share the good man's smile.
His ready smile a parent's warmth expressed,
Their welfare pleased him, and their cares distressed;
To them his heart, his love, his griefs were given,
But all his serious thoughts had rest in Heaven.
As some tall cliff, that lifts its awful form,
Swells from the vale, and midway leaves the storm,
Though round its breast the rolling clouds are spread,
Eternal sunshine settles on its head.

Beside yon straggling fence that skirts the way,
With blossomed furze unprofitably gay,
There, in his noisy mansion, skilled to rule,
The village master taught his little school;

A man severe he was, and stern to view;
I knew him well, and every truant knew;
Well had the boding tremblers learned to trace
The day's disasters in his morning face;
Full well they laughed, with counterfeited glee,
At all his jokes, for many a joke had he;
Full well the busy whisper, circling round,
Conveyed the dismal tidings when he frowned;
Yet he was kind; or if severe in aught
The love he bore to learning was in fault;
The village all declared how much he knew;
'Twas certain he could write, and cypher too;
Lands he could measure, terms and tides presage,
And e'en the story ran that he could gauge.
In arguing too, the parson owned his skill,
For e'en though vanquished, he could argue still;
While words of learned length and thund'ring sound
Amazed the gazing rustics ranged around,
And still they gazed, and still the wonder grew,
That one small head could carry all he knew.

But past is all his fame. The very spot
Where many a time he triumphed, is forgot.
Near yonder thorn, that lifts its head on high,
Where once the sign-post caught the passing eye,
Low lies that house where nut-brown draughts inspired,
Where grey-beard mirth and smiling toil retired,
Where village statesmen talked with looks profound,
And news much older than their ale went round.
Imagination fondly stoops to trace
The parlour splendours of that festive place;
The white-washed wall, the nicely sanded floor,
The varnished clock that clicked behind the door;
The chest contrived a double debt to pay,
A bed by night, a chest of drawers by day;
The pictures placed for ornament and use,
The twelve good rules, the royal game of goose;
The hearth, except when winter chilled the day,
With aspen boughs, and flowers, and fennel gay;
While broken tea-cups, wisely kept for show,
Ranged o'er the chimney, glistened in a row.

Vain, transitory splendours! Could not all
Reprieve the tottering mansion from its fall!

Obscure it sinks, nor shall it more impart
An hour's importance to the poor man's heart;
Thither no more the peasant shall repair
To sweet oblivion of his daily care;
No more the farmer's news, the barber's tale,
No more the wood-man's ballad shall prevail;
No more the smith his dusky brow shall clear,
Relax his pond'rous strength, and lean to hear;
The host himself no longer shall be found
Careful to see the mantling bliss go round;
Nor the coy maid, half willing to be pressed,
Shall kiss the cup to pass it to the rest.

    Yes! let the rich deride, the proud disdain,
These simple blessings of the lowly train;
To me more dear, congenial to my heart,
One native charm, than all the gloss of art;
Spontaneous joys, where Nature has its play,
The soul adopts, and owns their first-born sway;
Lightly they frolic o'er the vacant mind,
Unenvied, unmolested, unconfined:
But the long pomp, the midnight masquerade,
With all the freaks of wanton wealth arrayed,
In these, ere triflers half their wish obtain,
The toiling pleasure sickens into pain;
And, e'en while fashion's brightest arts decoy,
The heart distrusting asks, if this be joy.

    Ye friends to truth, ye statesmen, who survey
The rich man's joys increase, the poor's decay,
'Tis yours to judge, how wide the limits stand
Between a splendid and a happy land.
Proud swells the tide with loads of freighted ore,
And shouting Folly hails them from her shore;
Hoards, e'en beyond the miser's wish abound,
And rich men flock from all the world around.
Yet count our gains. This wealth is but a name
That leaves our useful products still the same.
Not so the loss. The man of wealth and pride
Takes up a space that many poor supplied;
Space for his lake, his park's extended bounds,
Space for his horses, equipage, and hounds;
The robe that wraps his limbs in silken sloth

Has robbed the neighbouring fields of half their growth,
His seat, where solitary sports are seen,
Indignant spurns the cottage from the green;
Around the world each needful product flies,
For all the luxuries the world supplies:
While thus the land adorned for pleasure, all
In barren splendour feebly waits the fall.

As some fair female unadorned and plain,
Secure to please while youth confirms her reign,
Slights every borrowed charm that dress supplies,
Nor shares with art the triumph of her eyes:
But when those charms are passed, for charms are frail,
When time advances, and when lovers fail,
She then shines forth, solicitous to bless,
In all the glaring impotence of dress.
Thus fares the land, by luxury betrayed,
In nature's simplest charms at first arrayed;
But verging to decline, its splendours rise,
Its vistas strike, its palaces surprise;
While scourged by famine from the smiling land,
The mournful peasant leads his humble band;
And while he sinks, without one arm to save,
The country blooms—a garden, and a grave.

Where then, ah! where, shall poverty reside,
To 'scape the pressure of contiguous pride?
If to some common's fenceless limits strayed,
He drives his flock to pick the scanty blade,
Those fenceless fields the sons of wealth divide,
And e'en the bare-worn common is denied.

If to the city sped—What waits him there?
To see profusion that he must not share;
To see ten thousand baneful arts combined
To pamper luxury, and thin mankind;
To see those joys the sons of pleasure know
Extorted from his fellow creature's woe.
Here, while the courtier glitters in brocade,
There the pale artist plies the sickly trade;
Here, while the proud their long-drawn pomps display,
There the black gibbet glooms beside the way.
The dome where Pleasure holds her midnight reign
Here, richly decked, admits the gorgeous train;

Tumultuous grandeur crowds the blazing square,
The rattling chariots clash, the torches glare.
Sure scenes like these no troubles e'er annoy!
Sure these denote one universal joy!
Are these thy serious thoughts?—Ah, turn thine eyes
Where the poor houseless shiv'ring female lies.
She once, perhaps, in village plenty bless'd,
Has wept at tales of innocence distress'd;
Her modest looks the cottage might adorn,
Sweet as the primrose peeps beneath the thorn;
Now lost to all; her friends, her virtue fled,
Near her betrayer's door she lays her head,
And, pinched with cold, and shrinking from the shower.
With heavy heart deplores that luckless hour,
When idly first, ambitious of the town,
She left her wheel and robes of country brown.

    Do thine, sweet Auburn, thine, the loveliest train,
Do thy fair tribes participate her pain?
E'en now, perhaps, by cold and hunger led,
At proud men's doors they ask a little bread!

    Ah, no. To distant climes, a dreary scene,
Where half the convex world intrudes between,
Through torrid tracts with fainting steps they go,
Where wild Altama murmurs to their woe.
Far different there from all that charmed before,
The various terrors of that horrid shore;
Those blazing suns that dart a downward ray,
And fiercely shed intolerable day;
Those matted woods where birds forget to sing,
But silent bats in drowsy clusters cling;
Those pois'nous fields with rank luxuriance crowned,
Where the dark scorpion gathers death around;
Where at each step the stranger fears to wake
The rattling terrors of the vengeful snake;
Where crouching tigers wait their hapless prey,
And savage men more murd'rous still than they;
While oft in whirls the mad tornado flies,
Mingling the ravaged landscape with the skies.
Far different these from every former scene,
The cooling brook, the grassy-vested green,
The breezy covert of the warbling grove,
That only sheltered thefts of harmless love.

Good heaven! what sorrows gloomed that parting day,
That called them from their native walks away;
When the poor exiles, every pleasure passed,
Hung round their bowers, and fondly looked their last,
And took a long farewell, and wished in vain
For seats like these beyond the western main;
And shudd'ring still to face the distant deep,
Returned and wept, and still returned to weep.
The good old sire, the first prepared to go
To new-found worlds, and wept for others' woe;
But for himself, in conscious virtue brave,
He only wished for worlds beyond the grave.
His lovely daughter, lovelier in her tears,
The fond companion of his helpless years,
Silent went next, neglectful of her charms,
And left a lover's for a father's arms.
With louder plaints the mother spoke her woes,
And bless'd the cot where every pleasure rose
And kissed her thoughtless babes with many a tear,
And clasped them close, in sorrow doubly dear;
Whilst her fond husband strove to lend relief
In all the silent manliness of grief.

O Luxury! thou curs'd by Heaven's decree,
How ill exchange are things like these for thee!
How do thy potions, with insidious joy
Diffuse their pleasures only to destroy!
Kingdoms, by thee, to sickly greatness grown,
Boast of a florid vigour not their own;
At every draught more large and large they grow,
A bloated mass of rank unwieldy woe;
Till sapped their strength, and every part unsound,
Down, down they sink, and spread a ruin round.

E'en now the devastation is begun,
And half the business of destruction done;
E'en now, methinks, as pond'ring here I stand,
I see the rural virtues leave the land:
Down where yon anchoring vessel spreads the sail,
That idly waiting flaps with every gale,
Downward they move, a melancholy band,
Pass from the shore, and darken all the strand.
Contented toil, and hospitable care,
And kind connubial tenderness, are there;

And piety, with wishes placed above,
And steady loyalty, and faithful love.
And thou, sweet Poetry, thou loveliest maid.
Still first to fly where sensual joys invade;
Unfit in these degenerate times of shame,
To catch the heart, or strike for honest fame;
Dear charming nymph, neglected and decried,
My shame in crowds, my solitary pride;
Thou source of all my bliss, and all my woe,
That found'st me poor at first, and keep'st me so;
Thou guide by which the nobler arts excel,
Thou nurse of every virtue, fare thee well!
Farewell, and Oh! where'er thy voice be tried,
On Torno's cliffs, or Pambamarca's side,
Whether where equinoctial fervours glow,
Or winter wraps the polar world in snow,
Still let thy voice, prevailing over time,
Redress the rigours of th' inclement clime;
Aid slighted truth; with thy persuasive strain
Teach erring man to spurn the rage of gain;
Teach him, that states of native strength possess'd,
Though very poor, may still be very bless'd;
That trade's proud empire hastes to swift decay,
As ocean sweeps the laboured mole away;
While self-dependent power can time defy,
As rocks resist the billows and the sky.

Elegy on the Death of a Mad Dog

GOOD people all, of every sort,
    Give ear unto my song;
And if you find it wond'rous short,
    It cannot hold you long.

In Islington there was a man,
    Of whom the world might say,
That still a godly race he ran,
    Whene'er he went to pray.

A kind and gentle heart he had,
    To comfort friends and foes;
The naked every day he clad,
    When he put on his clothes.

And in that town a dog was found,
   As many dogs there be,
Both mongrel, puppy, whelp, and hound,
   And curs of low degree.

This dog and man at first were friends;
   But when a pique began,
The dog, to gain some private ends,
   Went mad and bit the man.

Around from all the neighbouring streets
   The wond'ring neighbours ran,
And swore the dog had lost his wits,
   To bite so good a man.

The wound it seemed both sore and sad
   To every Christian eye;
And while they swore the dog was mad,
   They swore the man would die.

But soon a wonder came to light,
   That showed the rogues they lied:
The man recovered of the bite,
   The dog it was that died.

from *The Vicar of Wakefield*

Song

WHEN lovely woman stoops to folly,
   And finds too late that men betray,
What charm can soothe her melancholy,
   What art can wash her guilt away?

The only art her guilt to cover,
   To hide her shame from every eye,
To give repentance to her lover,
   And wring his bosom, is—to die.

JOHN SCOTT OF AMWELL

1730–1783

Ode XIII

    I HATE that drum's discordant sound,
Parading round, and round, and round:
To thoughtless youth it pleasure yields,
And lures from cities and from fields,
    To sell their liberty for charms
    Of tawdry lace, and glittering arms;
    And when Ambition's voice commands,
To march and fight, and fall, in foreign lands.

    I hate that drum's discordant sound,
Parading round, and round, and round:
To me it talks of ravaged plains,
And burning towns, and ruined swains,
And mangled limbs, and dying groans,
And widows' tears, and orphans' moans;
    And all that Misery's hand bestows
To fill the catalogue of human woes.

THOMAS WARTON THE YOUNGER

1728–1790

from *The Pleasures of Melancholy*

BENEATH yon ruin'd abbey's moss-grown piles
Oft let me sit, at twilight hour of eve,
Where through some western window the pale moon
Pours her long-levell'd rule of streaming light;
While sullen sacred silence reigns around,
Save the lone screech-owl's note, who builds his bow'r
Amid the mould'ring caverns dark and damp,
Or the calm breeze, that rustles in the leaves
Of flaunting ivy, that with mantle green
Invests some wasted tow'r. Or let me tread
Its neighbouring walk of pines, where mus'd of old
The cloister'd brothers: through the gloomy void
That far extends beneath their ample arch,
As on I pace, religious horror wraps

My soul in dread repose. But when the world
Is clad in midnight's raven-colour'd robe,
'Mid hollow charnel let me watch the flame
Of taper dim, shedding a livid glare
O'er the wan heaps; while airy voices talk
Along the glimm'ring walls; or ghostly shape
At distance seen, invites with beck'ning hand
My lonesome steps, through the far-winding vaults.
Nor undelightful is the solemn noon
Of night, when haply wakeful from my couch
I start: Lo, all is motionless around!
Roars not the rushing wind; the sons of men
And ev'ry beast in mute oblivion lie;
All nature's husht in silence and in sleep.
O, then how fearful is it to reflect
That through the still globe's awful solitude,
No being wakes but me! till stealing sleep
My drooping temples bathes in opiate dews.
Nor then let dreams, of wanton folly born,
My senses lead through flow'ry paths of joy;
But let the sacred Genius of the night
Such mystic visions send, as Spenser saw,
When thro' bewilder'd Fancy's magic maze,
To the fell house of Busyrane he led
Th' unshaken Britomart; or Milton knew,
When in abstracted thought he first conceived
All heav'n in tumult, and the Seraphim
Came tow'ring, arm'd in adamant and gold ...

    Few know that elegance of soul refin'd,
Whose soft sensation feels a quicker joy
From Melancholy's scenes, than the dull pride
Of tasteless splendour and magnificence
Can e'er afford. Thus Elöise, whose mind
Had languished to the pangs of melting love,
More genuine transport found, as on some tomb
Reclin'd, she watch'd the tapers of the dead;
Or through the pillar'd aisles, and pale shrines
Of imaged saints and intermingled graves,
Mus'd a veil'd votaress; than Flavia feels,
As thro' the mazes of the festive ball,
Proud of her conquering charms, and beauty's blaze,
She floats amid the silken sons of dress,
And shines the fairest of th' assembled fair.
    When azure noontide cheers the dædal globe,
And the blest regent of the golden day

Rejoices in his bright meridian tower,
How oft my wishes ask the night's return
That best befriends the melancholy mind!
Hail, sacred Night! Thou too shalt share my song!
Sister of ebon-sceptred Hecate, hail!
Whether in congregated clouds thou wrap'st
Thy viewless chariot, or with silver crown
Thy beaming head encirclest, ever hail!
What tho' beneath thy gloom the sorceress-train,
Far in obscured haunt of Lapland moors,
With rhymes uncouth the bloody cauldron bless;
Tho' Murder wan beneath thy shrouding shade
Summons her slow-ey'd vot'ries to devise
Of secret slaughter, while by one blue lamp
In hideous conference sits the list'ning band,
And starts at each low wind or wakeful sound;
What tho' thy stay the pilgrim curseth oft,
As all benighted in Arabian wastes
He hears the wilderness around him howl
With roaming monsters, while on his hoar head
The black-descending tempest ceaseless beats;
Yet more delightful to my pensive mind
Is thy return, than blooming morn's approach,
Ev'n then, in youthful pride of op'ning May,
When from the portals of the saffron east
She sheds fresh roses, and ambrosial dews. . . .
Yet not ungrateful is the morn's approach,
When dropping wet she comes, and clad in clouds,
While thro' the damp air scowls the louring south,
Black'ning the landscape's face, that grove and hill
In formless vapours undistinguish'd swim:
Th' afflicted songsters of the sadden'd groves
Hail not the sullen gloom; the waning elms
That, hoar thro' time, and rang'd in thick array,
Enclose with stately row some rural hall,
Are mute, nor echo with the clamours hoarse
Of rooks, rejoicing in their airy boughs;
While to the shed the dripping poultry crowd,
A mournful train; secure the village hind
Hangs o'er the crackling blaze, nor tempts the storm;
Fix'd in the unfinish'd furrow rests the plough:
Rings not the high wood with enliven'd shouts
Of early hunter; all is silence drear;
And deepest sadness wraps the face of things.

WILLIAM COWPER

1731–1800

Loss of the 'Royal George'

TOLL for the brave—
The brave! that are no more:
  All sunk beneath the wave,
Fast by their native shore.

  Eight hundred of the brave,
Whose courage well was tried,
  Had made the vessel heel
And laid her on her side;

  A land-breeze shook the shrouds,
And she was overset;
  Down went the *Royal George*
With all her crew complete.

  Toll for the brave—
Brave Kempenfelt is gone,
  His last sea-fight is fought,
His work of glory done.

  It was not in the battle,
No tempest gave the shock,
  She sprang no fatal leak,
She ran upon no rock;

  His sword was in the sheath,
His fingers held the pen,
  When Kempenfelt went down
With twice four hundred men.

  Weigh the vessel up,
Once dreaded by our foes,
  And mingle with your cup
The tears that England owes;

  Her timbers yet are sound,
And she may float again,
  Full charged with England's thunder,
And plough the distant main;

  But Kempenfelt is gone,
His victories are o'er;
  And he and his eight hundred
Must plough the wave no more.

On the Receipt of My Mother's Picture out of Norfolk, the gift of my cousin Ann Bodham

OH that those lips had language! Life has passed
With me but roughly since I heard thee last.
Those lips are thine—thy own sweet smiles I see,
The same that oft in childhood solaced me;
Voice only fails, else, how distinct they say,
'Grieve not, my child, chase all thy fears away!'
The meek intelligence of those dear eyes
(Blest be the art that can immortalize,
The art that baffles time's tyrannic claim
To quench it) here shines on me still the same.

   Faithful remembrancer of one so dear,
Oh welcome guest, though unexpected, here!
Who bidd'st me honour with an artless song,
Affectionate, a mother lost so long,
I will obey, not willingly alone,
But gladly, as the precept were her own;
And, while that face renews my filial grief,
Fancy shall weave a charm for my relief—
Shall steep me in Elysian reverie,
A momentary dream, that thou art she.

   My mother! when I learned that thou wast dead,
Say, wast thou conscious of the tears I shed?
Hovered thy spirit o'er thy sorrowing son,
Wretch even then, life's journey just begun?
Perhaps thou gav'st me, though unseen, a kiss;
Perhaps a tear, if souls can weep in bliss—
Ah that maternal smile! it answers—Yes.
I heard the bell tolled on thy burial day,
I saw the hearse that bore thee slow away,
And, turning from my nurs'ry window, drew
A long, long sigh, and wept a last adieu!
But was it such?—It was.—Where thou art gone
Adieus and farewells are a sound unknown.
May I but meet thee on that peaceful shore,
The parting sound shall pass my lips no more!
Thy maidens grieved themselves at my concern,
Oft gave me promise of a quick return.
What ardently I wished, I long believed,
And, disappointed still, was still deceived;

By disappointment every day beguiled,
Dupe of *to-morrow* even from a child.
Thus many a sad to-morrow came and went,
Till, all my stock of infant sorrow spent,
I learned at last submission to my lot;
But, though I less deplored thee, ne'er forgot.
    Where once we dwelt our name is heard no more,
Children not thine have trod my nurs'ry floor;
And where the gard'ner Robin, day by day,
Drew me to school along the public way,
Delighted with my bauble coach, and wrapped
In scarlet mantle warm, and velvet capped,
'Tis now become a history little known,
That once we called the past'ral house our own.
Short-lived possession! but the record fair
That mem'ry keeps of all thy kindness there,
Still outlives many a storm that has effaced
A thousand other themes less deeply traced.
Thy nightly visits to my chamber made,
That thou might'st know me safe and warmly laid.
Thy morning bounties ere I left my home,
The biscuit, or confectionary plum;
The fragrant waters on my cheeks bestowed
By thy own hand, till fresh they shone and glowed.
All this, and more endearing still than all,
Thy constant flow of love, that knew no fall,
Ne'er roughened by those cataracts and brakes
That humour interposed too often makes;
All this still legible in mem'ry's page,
And still to be so, to my latest age,
Adds joy to duty, makes me glad to pay
Such honours to thee as my numbers may;
Perhaps a frail memorial, but sincere,
Not scorned in heaven, though little noticed here.
    Could time, his flight reversed, restore the hours,
When, playing with thy vesture's tissued flowers,
The violet, the pink, and jessamine,
I pricked them into paper with a pin,
(And thou wast happier than myself the while,
Would'st softly speak, and stroke my head and smile)
Could those few pleasant hours again appear,
Might one wish bring them, would I wish them here?
I would not trust my heart—the dear delight
Seems so to be desired, perhaps I might.—

But no—what here we call our life is such,
So little to be loved, and thou so much,
That I should ill requite thee to constrain
Thy unbound spirit into bonds again.
    Thou, as a gallant bark from Albion's coast
(The storms all weathered and the ocean crossed)
Shoots into port at some well-havened isle,
Where spices breathe and brighter seasons smile,
There sits quiescent on the floods that show
Her beauteous form reflected clear below,
While airs impregnated with incense play
Around her, fanning light her streamers gay;
So thou, with sails how swift! hast reached the shore
'Where tempests never beat nor billows roar,'
And thy loved consort on the dang'rous tide
Of life, long since, has anchored at thy side.
But me, scarce hoping to attain that rest,
Always from port withheld, always distressed—
Me howling winds drive devious, tempest tossed,
Sails ripped, seams op'ning wide, and compass lost,
And day by day some current's thwarting force
Sets me more distant from a prosp'rous course.
But oh the thought, that thou art safe, and he!
That thought is joy, arrive what may to me.
My boast is not that I deduce my birth
From loins enthroned, and rulers of the earth;
But higher far my proud pretensions rise—
The son of parents passed into the skies.
And now, farewell—time, unrevoked, has run
His wonted course, yet what I wished is done.
By contemplation's help, not sought in vain,
I seem t' have lived my childhood o'er again;
To have renewed the joys that once were mine,
Without the sin of violating thine:
And, while the wings of fancy still are free,
And I can view this mimic show of thee,
Time has but half succeeded in his theft—
Thyself removed, thy power to soothe me left.

from *The Winter Morning Walk*

ACQUAINT thyself with God, if thou wouldst taste
His works. Admitted once to his embrace,
Thou shalt perceive that thou wast blind before:
Thine eye shall be instructed; and thine heart
Made pure shall relish, with divine delight,
Till then unfelt, what hands divine have wrought.
Brutes graze the mountain-top, with faces prone,
And eyes intent upon the scanty herb
It yields them; or, recumbent on its brow,
Ruminate heedless of the scene outspread
Beneath, beyond, and stretching far away
From inland regions to the distant main.
Man views it, and admires; but rests content
With what he views. The landscape has his praise,
But not its Author. Unconcerned who formed
The paradise he sees, he finds it such,
And, such well pleased to find it, asks no more.
Not so the mind that has been touched from Heaven,
And in the school of sacred wisdom taught
To read his wonders, in whose thought the world,
Fair as it is, existed ere it was.
Not for its own sake merely, but for His
Much more who fashioned it, he gives it praise,
Praise that, from earth resulting, as it ought,
To earth's acknowledged Sovereign, finds at once
Its only just proprietor in Him.
The soul that sees him or receives sublimed
New faculties, or learns at least to employ
More worthily the powers she owned before;
Discerns in all things what, with stupid gaze
Of ignorance, till then she overlooked,
A ray of heavenly light, gilding all forms
Terrestrial in the vast and the minute—
The unambiguous footsteps of the God
Who gives its lustre to an insect's wing,
And wheels his throne upon the rolling worlds.

WILLIAM FALCONER

1732–1769

from *The Shipwreck*

The ship sets out

THE sun's bright orb, declining all serene,
Now glanc'd obliquely o'er the woodland scene.
Creation smiles around; on every spray
The warbling birds exalt their evening lay.
Blithe skipping o'er yon hill, the fleecy train
Join the deep chorus of the lowing plain:
The golden lime and orange there were seen,
On fragrant branches of perpetual green.
The crystal streams that velvet meadows lave,
To the green ocean roll with chiding wave.
The glassy ocean hush'd forgets to roar,
But trembling murmurs on the sandy shore:
And lo! his surface, lovely to behold!
Glows in the west a sea of living gold!
While, all above, a thousand liveries gay
The skies with pomp ineffable array.
Arabian sweets perfume the happy plains;
Above, beneath, around enchantment reigns!
While yet the shades on Time's eternal scale,
With long vibration deepen o'er the vale;
While yet the songsters of the vocal grove,
With dying numbers tune the soul to love;
With joyful eyes th' attentive master sees
Th' auspicious omens of an eastern breeze—
Now radiant Vesper leads the starry train,
And Night slow draws her veil o'er land and main;
Round the charg'd bowl the sailors form a ring;
By turns recount the wondrous tale, or sing;
As love or battle, hardships of the main,
Or genial wine, awake the homely strain:
Then some the watch of night alternate keep,
The rest lie buried in oblivious sleep.
    Deep midnght now involves the livid skies,
While infant breezes from the shore arise.
The waning moon, behind a watery shroud,

Pale glimmer'd o'er the long protracted cloud.
A mighty ring around her silver throne,
With parting meteors cross'd, portentous shone.
This in the troubled sky full oft prevails;
Oft deem'd a signal of tempestuous gales.—
While young ARION sleeps, before his sight
Tumultuous swim the visions of the night.
Now blooming ANNA with her happy swain
Approach'd the sacred Hymeneal fane:
Anon tremendous lightnings flash between;
And funeral pomp, and weeping loves are seen!
Now with PALEMON up a rocky steep,
Whose summit trembles o'er the roaring deep,
With painful step he climb'd; while far above
Sweet ANNA charm'd them with the voice of love.
Then sudden from the slippery height they fell,
While dreadful yawn'd beneath the jaws of Hell.—
Amid this fearful trance a thundering sound
He hears—and thrice the hollow decks rebound.
Upstarting from his couch, on deck he sprung;
Thrice with shrill note the boatswain's whistle rung.
All hands unmoor! proclaims a boisterous cry:
All hands unmoor! the cavern'd rocks reply.
Rous'd from repose, aloft the sailors swarm,
And with their levers soon the windlass arm.
The order given, up springing with a bound,
They lodge the bars, and wheel their engine round; }
At every turn the clanging pauls resound.
Up-torn reluctant from its oozy cave,
The ponderous anchor rises o'er the wave.
Along their slippery masts the yards ascend,
And high in air the canvass wings extend:
Redoubling cords the lofty canvass guide,
And thro' inextricable mazes glide.
The lunar rays with long reflection gleam,
To light the vessel o'er the silver stream:
Along the glassy plain serene she glides,
While azure radiance trembles on her sides.
From east to north the transient breezes play,
And in the Egyptian quarter soon decay.
A calm ensues; they dread the adjacent shore;
The boats with rowers arm'd are sent before:
With cordage fasten'd to the lofty prow,
Aloof to sea the stately ship they tow.

The nervous crew their sweeping oars extend,
And pealing shouts the shore of Candia rend.
Success attends their skill; the danger's o'er;
The port is doubled and beheld no more.

  Now Morn, her lamp pale glimmering on the sight,
Scatter'd before her van reluctant Night.
She comes not in refulgent pomp array'd,
But sternly frowning, wrapt in sullen shade.
Above incumbent vapours, Ida's height,
Tremendous rock! emerges on the sight.
North-east the guardian isle of Standia lies,
And westward Freschin's woody capes arise.

  With whining postures now the wanton sails
Spread all their snares to charm th' inconstant gales.
The swelling stud-sails now their wings extend,
Then stay-sails sidelong to the breeze ascend:[1]
While all to court the wandering breeze are plac'd;
With yards now thwarting, now obliquely brac'd.

  The dim horizon lowering vapours shroud,
And blot the sun yet struggling in the cloud:
Thro' the wide atmosphere, condens'd with haze,
His glaring orb emits a sanguine blaze.
The pilots now their rules of art apply,
The mystic needle's devious aim to try.
The compass plac'd to catch the rising ray,[2]
The quadrant's shadows studious they survey!
Along the arch the gradual index slides.
While Phœbus down the vertic-circle glides.
Now seen on ocean's utmost verge to swim,
He sweeps it vibrant with his nether limb.
Their sage experience thus explores the height,
And polar distance of the source of light:
Then thro' the chiliad's triple maze they trace
Th' analogy that proves the magnet's place,
The wayward steel, to truth thus reconcil'd,
No more th' attentive pilot's eye beguil'd.

    The natives, while the ship departs the land,
Ashore with admiration gazing stand.

---

[1] Studding-sails are long narrow sails, which are only used in fine weather and fair winds, on the outside of the larger square-sails. Stay-sails are three-cornered sails, which are hoisted up on the stays, when the wind crosses the ship's course, either directly or obliquely. (*Author*)

[2] The operation of taking the sun's azimuth, in order to discover the eastern or western variation of the magnetic needle. (*Author*).

Majestically slow, before the breeze,
In silent pomp she marches on the seas.
Her milk-white bottom casts a softer gleam,
While trembling thro' the green translucent stream.
The wales, that close above in contrast shone,
Clasp the long fabric with a jetty zone.
BRITANNIA, riding awful on the prow,
Gaz'd o'er the vassal waves that roll'd below;
Where'er she mov'd, the vassal waves were seen
To yield obsequious and confess their queen.
Th' imperial trident grac'd her dexter hand,
Of power to rule the surge like Moses' wand,
Th' eternal empire of the main to keep,
And guide her squadrons o'er the trembling deep.

The ship is lost

And now, lash'd on by destiny severe,
With horror fraught, the dreadful scene drew near!
The ship hangs hovering on the verge of death,
Hell yawns, rocks rise, and breakers roar beneath! —
In vain, alas! the sacred shades of yore
Would arm the mind with philosophic lore;
In vain they'd teach us, at the latest breath,
To smile serene amid the pangs of death.
Even Zeno's self, and Epictetus old,
This fell abyss had shudder'd to behold.
Had Socrates, for godlike virtue fam'd,
And wisest of the sons of men proclaim'd,
Beheld this scene of phrenzy and distress,
His soul had trembled to its last recess! —
O yet confirm my heart, ye Powers above,
This last tremendous shock of Fate to prove.
The tottering frame of reason yet sustain!
Nor let this total ruin whirl my brain!

In vain the cords and axes were prepar'd,
For now th' audacious seas insult the yard;
High o'er the ship they throw a horrid shade,
And o'er her burst in terrible cascade.
Uplifted on the surge, to heaven she flies,
Her shatter'd top half-buried in the skies,
Then headlong plunging thunders on the ground,
Earth groans! air trembles! and the deeps resound!

Her giant bulk the dread concussion feels,
And quivering with the wound in torment reels.
So reels, convuls'd with agonizing throes,
The bleeding bull beneath the murd'rer's blows—
Again she plunges! hark! a second shock
Tears her strong bottom on the marble rock:
Down on the vale of Death, with dismal cries,
The fated victims shuddering roll their eyes
In wild despair; while yet another stroke,
With deep convulsion, rends the solid oak:
Till like the mine, in whose infernal cell
The lurking demons of destruction dwell,
At length asunder torn, her frame divides;
And crashing spreads in ruin o'er the tides.

   Oh were it mine with tuneful Maro's art
To wake to sympathy the feeling heart;
Like him the smooth and mournful verse to dress
In all the pomp of exquisite distress!
Then too, severely taught by cruel Fate,
To share in all the perils I relate,
Then might I, with unrivall'd strains deplore
Th' impervious horrors of a leeward shore.—

   As o'er the surge the stooping main-mast hung,
Still on the rigging thirty seamen clung;
Some, struggling, on a broken crag were cast,
And there by oozy tangles grappled fast,
Awhile they bore th' o'erwhelming billows' rage,
Unequal combat with their fate to wage;
Till all benumb'd and feeble they forego
Their slippery hold, and sink to shades below.
Some, from the main-yard-arm impetuous thrown
On marble ridges, die without a groan.
Three with PALEMON on their skill depend,
And from the wreck on oars and rafts descend.
Now on the mountain-wave on high they ride,
Then downward plunge beneath th' involving tide;
Till one, who seems in agony to strive,
The whirling breakers heave on shore alive;
The rest a speedier end of anguish knew,
And prest the stony beach, a lifeless crew!

WILLIAM JULIUS MICKLE

1735–1788

There's Nae Luck About The House[1]

AND are ye sure the news is true?
  And are ye sure he's weel?
Is this a time to think o' wark?
  Ye jades, lay by your wheel;
Is this the time to spin a thread,
  When Colin's at the door?
Reach down my cloak, I'll to the quay,
  And see him come ashore.
For there's nae luck about the house,
  There's nae luck at a';
There's little pleasure in the house
  When our gudeman's awa'.

And gie to me my bigonet,
  My bishop's satin gown;
For I maun tell the baillie's wife
  That Colin's in the town.
My Turkey slippers maun gae on,
  My stockins pearly blue;
It's a' to pleasure our gudeman,
  For he's baith leal and true.

Rise, lass, and mak a clean fireside,
  Put on the muckle pot;
Gie little Kate her button gown
  And Jock his Sunday coat;
And mak their shoon as black as slaes,
  Their hose as white as snaw;
It's a' to please my ain gudeman,
  For he's been long awa'.

bigonet] head-dress

---

[1] The above song is sometimes attributed to Jean Adam, who died in 1765, but the evidence points almost conclusively to Mickle's authorship.

There's twa fat hens upo' the coop
  Been fed this month and mair;
Mak haste and thraw their necks about
  That Colin weel may fare;
And spread the table neat and clean,
  Gar ilka thing look braw,
For wha can tell how Colin fared
  When he was far awa'?

Sae true his heart, sae smooth his speech,
  His breath like caller air;
His very foot has music in 't
  As he comes up the stair—
And will I see his face again?
  And will I hear him speak?
I'm downright dizzy wi' the thought,
  In troth I'm like to greet!

If Colin's weel, and weel content,
  I hae nae mair to crave:
And gin I live to keep him sae,
  I'm blest aboon the lave:
And will I see his face again,
  And will I hear him speak?
I'm downright dizzy wi' the thought,
  In troth I'm like to greet.
For there's nae luck about the house,
  There's nae luck at a';
There's little pleasure in the house
  When our gudeman's awa'.

thraw] twist   caller] fresh, cool   lave] remainder

JAMES BEATTIE

1735–1803

Edwin, The Minstrel

THERE lived in Gothic days, as legends tell,
A shepherd-swain, a man of low degree;
Whose sires, perchance, in Fairyland might dwell,
Sicilian groves, or vales of Arcady;
But he, I ween, was of the north countrie;
A nation famed for song, and beauty's charms;
Zealous, yet modest; innocent, though free;
Patient of toil; serene amidst alarms;
Inflexible in faith; invincible in arms.

The shepherd-swain of whom I mention made,
On Scotia's mountains fed his little flock;
The sickle, scythe, or plough he never swayed;
An honest heart was almost all his stock;
His drink the living water from the rock:
The milky dams supplied his board, and lent
Their kindly fleece to baffle winter's shock;
And he, though oft with dust and sweat besprent,
Did guide and guard their wanderings, wheresoe'er they went. . . .

And yet poor Edwin was no vulgar boy;
Deep thought oft seemed to fix his infant eye,
Dainties he heeded not, nor gaud, nor toy,
Save one short pipe of rudest minstrelsy;
Silent when glad; affectionate, though shy;
And now his look was most demurely sad,
And now he laughed aloud, yet none knew why.
The neighbours stared and sighed, yet blessed the lad;
Some deemed him wonderous wise, and some believed him mad.

But why should I his childish feats display?
Concourse, and noise, and toil he ever fled;
Nor cared to mingle in the clamorous fray
Of squabbling imps; but to the forest sped,
Or roamed at large the lonely mountain's head,
Or where the maze of some bewildered stream
To deep untrodden groves his footsteps led,

There would he wander wild, till Phoebus' beam,
Shot from the western cliff, released the weary team.

Th' exploit of strength, dexterity, or speed,
To him nor vanity nor joy could bring.
His heart, from cruel sport estranged, would bleed
To work the woe of any living thing,
By trap, or net, by arrow, or by sling;
These he detested; those he scorned to wield:
He wished to be the guardian, not the king,
Tyrant far less, or traitor of the field.
And sure the sylvan reign unbloody joy might yield.

Lo! where the stripling wrapt in wonder, roves
Beneath the precipice o'erhung with pine;
And sees on high, amidst th' encircling groves,
From cliff to cliff the foaming torrents shine;
While waters, woods, and winds in concert join,
And echo swells the chorus to the skies.
Would Edwin this majestic scene resign
For aught the huntsman's puny craft supplies?
Ah! no: he better knows great Nature's charms to prize.

And oft he traced the uplands, to survey,
When o'er the sky advanced the kindling dawn,
The crimson cloud, blue main, and mountain gray,
And lake, dim-gleaming on the smoky lawn:
Far to the west the long, long vale withdrawn,
Where twilight loves to linger for a while,
And now he faintly kens the bounding fawn,
And villager abroad at early toil.
But, lo! the sun appears! and heaven, earth, ocean, smile.

And oft the craggy cliff he loved to climb,
When all in mist the world below was lost.
What dreadful pleasure! there to stand sublime,
Like shipwrecked mariner on desert coast,
And view th' enormous waste of vapour, tost
In billows, lengthening to th' horizon round,
Now scooped in gulfs, with mountains now embossed!
And hear the voice of mirth and song rebound,
Flocks, herds, and waterfalls, along the hoar profound!

In truth he was a strange and wayward wight,
Fond of each gentle and each dreadful scene.
In darkness, and in storm, he found delight;
Nor less, than when on ocean-wave serene,
The southern sun diffused his dazzling sheen.
Even sad vicissitude amused his soul:
And if a sigh would sometimes intervene,
And down his cheek a tear of pity roll,
A sigh, a tear, so sweet, he wished not to control.

ISOBEL PAGAN

1740–1821

Ca' the Yowes to the Knowes

Ca' the yowes to the knowes,
Ca' them where the heather grows,
Ca' them where the burnie rows,
   My bonnie dearie.

As I gaed down the water side,
There I met my shepherd lad;
He rowed me sweetly in his plaid,
   And he ca'd me his dearie.

'Will ye gang down the water side,
And see the waves sae sweetly glide
Beneath the hazels spreading wide?
   The moon it shines fu' clearly.'

'I was bred up at nae sic school,
My shepherd lad, to play the fool,
And a' the day to sit in dool,
   And naebody to see me.'

'Ye sall get gowns and ribbons meet,
Cauf-leather shoon upon your feet,
And in my arms ye'se lie and sleep,
   And ye sall be my dearie.'

vowes] ewes   knowes] hillocks   rows] rolls   rowed] wrapped
dool] sorrow   lift] sky

'If ye'll but stand to what ye've said,
I'se gang wi' you, my shepherd lad,
And ye may row me in your plaid,
    And I sall be your dearie.'

'While waters wimple to the sea,
While day blinks in the lift sae hie,
Till clay-cauld death sall blin' my e'e,
    Ye aye sall be my dearie!'

ANNA LETITIA BARBAULD

1743–1825

Life

LIFE! I know not what thou art,
But know that thou and I must part;
And when, or how, or where we met,
I own to me 's a secret yet.
But this I know, when thou art fled,
Where'er they lay these limbs, this head,
No clod so valueless shall be
As all that then remains of me.

O whither, whither dost thou fly?
Where bend unseen thy trackless course?
    And in this strange divorce,
Ah, tell where I must seek this compound I?
To the vast ocean of empyreal flame
    From whence thy essence came
Dost thou thy flight pursue, when freed
From matter's base encumbering weed?
    Or dost thou, hid from sight,
    Wait, like some spell-bound knight,
Through blank oblivious years th' appointed hour
To break thy trance and reassume thy power?
Yet canst thou without thought or feeling be?
O say, what art thou, when no more thou'rt thee?

Life! we've been long together,
Through pleasant and through cloudy weather;

'Tis hard to part when friends are dear;
Perhaps 'twill cost a sigh, a tear;—
Then steal away, give little warning,
    Choose thine own time;
Say not Good-night, but in some brighter clime
    Bid me Good-morning!

Ode to Spring

SWEET daughter of a rough and stormy sire,
Hoar Winter's blooming child, delightful Spring!
    Whose unshorn locks with leaves
    And swelling buds are crowned;

From the green islands of eternal youth
(Crowned with fresh blooms, and ever-springing shade)
    Turn, hither turn thy step,
    O thou, whose powerful voice,

More sweet than softest touch of Doric reed,
Or Lydian flute, can soothe the madding winds,
    And through the stormy deep
    Breathe thine own tender calm.

Thee, best beloved! the virgin train await
With songs and festal rites, and joy to rove
    Thy blooming wilds among,
    And vales and dewy lawns,

With untired feet; and cull thy earliest sweet,
To weave fresh garlands for the glowing brow
    Of him, the favoured youth
    That prompts their whispered sigh.

Unlock thy copious stores,—those tender showers
That drop their sweetness on the infant buds;
    And silent dews that swell
    The milky ear's green stem,

And feed the flowering osier's early shoots;
And call those winds which through the whispering boughs
    With warm and pleasant breath
    Salute the bowing flowers.

Now let me sit beneath the whitening thorn
And mark thy spreading tints steal o'er the dale,
   And watch with patient eye
   Thy fair unfolding charms.

O nymph, approach! while yet the temperate sun
With bashful forehead through the cool moist air
   Throws his young maiden beams,
   And with chaste kisses woos

The earth's fair bosom; while the streaming veil
Of lucid clouds with wind and frequent shade
   Protects thy modest blooms
   From his severer blaze.

Sweet is thy reign, but short: the red dog-star
Shall scorch thy tresses, and the mower's scythe
   Thy greens, thy flowerets all,
   Remorseless shall destroy.

Reluctant shall I bid thee then farewell;
For O! not all that Autumn's lap contains,
   Nor Summer's ruddiest fruits,
   Can aught for thee atone,

Fair Spring! whose simplest promise more delights,
Then all their largest wealth, and through the heart
   Each joy and new-born hope
   With softest influence breathes.

THOMAS HOLCROFT

1745–1809

Gaffer Gray

Ho, why dost thou shiver and shake,
   Gaffer Gray?
And why does thy nose look so blue?
   ''Tis the weather that's cold,
   'Tis I'm grown very old,
And my doublet is not very new,
   Well-a–day!'

Then line thy worn doublet with ale;
   Gaffer Gray;
And warm thy old heart with a glass.
   'Nay, but credit I've none,
   And my money's all gone;
Then say how may that come to pass?
   Well-a-day!'

Hie away to the house on the brow,
   Gaffer Gray;
And knock at the jolly priest's door.
   'The priest often preaches
   Against worldly riches,
But ne'er gives a mite to the poor,
   Well-a-day!'

The lawyer lives under the hill,
   Gaffer Gray;
Warmly fenced both in back and in front.
   'He will fasten his locks,
   And will threaten the stocks,
Should he ever more find me in want,
   Well-a-day!'

The squire has fat beeves and brown ale,
   Gaffer Gray;
And the season will welcome you there.
   'His fat beeves and his beer,
   And his merry new year,
Are all for the flush and the fair,
   Well-a-day!'

My keg is but low, I confess,
   Gaffer Gray;
What then? While it lasts, man, we'll live.
   'The poor man alone,
   When he hears the poor moan,
Of his morsel a morsel will give,
   Well-a-day!'

CHARLES DIBDIN

1745–1814

Tom Bowling

HERE, a sheer hulk, lies poor Tom Bowling,
The darling of our crew;
No more he'll hear the tempest howling,
For death has broached him to.
His form was of the manliest beauty,
His heart was kind and soft;
Faithful below Tom did his duty,
And now he's gone aloft. (*twice*)

Tom never from his word departed,
His virtues were so rare;
His friends were many, and true hearted,
His Poll was kind and fair.
And then he'd sing so blithe and jolly,
Ah! many's the time and oft;
But mirth is turned to melancholy,
For Tom is gone aloft.

Yet shall poor Tom find pleasant weather,
When He, Who all commands,
Shall give, to call life's crew together,
The word to pipe all hands.
Thus Death, who kings and tars dispatches,
In vain Tom's life has doffed;
For though his body's under hatches,
His soul is gone aloft.

The Jolly Young Waterman

AND did you not hear of a jolly young waterman,
  Who at Blackfriars Bridge used for to ply;
And he feathered his oars with such skill and dexterity,
  Winning each heart and delighting each eye:
He looked so neat and rowed so steadily,
The maidens all flocked to his boat so readily,
And he eyed the young rogues with so charming an air,
That this waterman ne'er was in want of a fare.

What sights of fine folks he oft rowed in his wherry,
   'Twas cleaned out so nice, and so painted withal,
He was always first oars when the fine city ladies
   In a party to Ranelagh went, or Vauxhall.
And oftentimes would they be giggling and leering,
But 'twas all one to Tom, their jibing and jeering.
For loving, or liking, he little did care,
For this waterman ne'er was in want of a fare.

And yet, but to see how strangely things happen;
   As he rowed along, thinking of nothing at all,
He was plied by a damsel so lovely and charming,
   That she smiled and so straightway in love he did fall.
And would this young damsel but banish his sorrow,
He'd wed her to-night before even to-morrow,
And how should this waterman ever know care,
When he's married and never in want of a fare?

ROBERT FERGUSSON

1750–1774

The Daft Days

Now mirk December's dowie face
Glowrs owr the rigs wi' sour grimace,
While, thro' his *minimum* o' space,
      The bleer-ey'd sun,
Wi' blinkin' light and stealin' pace,
      His race doth run.

Frae naked groves nae birdie sings;
To shepherd's pipe nae hillock rings;
The breeze nae od'rous flavour brings
      Frae Borean cave;
And dwynin' Nature, droops her wings,
      Wi' visage grave.

Mankind but scanty pleasure glean
Frae snawy hill or barren plain,
Whan Winter, 'midst his nipping train,
      Wi' frozen spear,
Sends drift owr a' his bleak domain,
      And guides the weir.

daft] mad   mirk] dark   dowie] sad   glowrs] stares
dwynin'] decaying

ROBERT FERGUSSON

Auld Reikie! thou'rt the canty hole,
A bield for mony a cauldrife soul,
Wha snugly at thine ingle loll,
              Baith warm and couth;
While round they gar the bicker roll
              To weet their mouth.

When merry Yule-day comes I trow,
You'll scantlins find a hungry mou;
Sma' are our cares, our stamacks fou
              O' gusty gear,
And kickshaws, strangers to our view.
              Sin' fairn-year.

Ye browster wives! now busk ye bra,
And fling your sorrows far awa';
Then, come and gie's the tither blaw
              Of reaming ale,
Mair precious than the Well of Spa,
              Our hearts to heal.

Then, tho' at odds wi' a' the warl',
Amang oursells we'll never quarrel;
Tho' Discord gie a cankered snarl
              To spoil our glee,
As lang's there's pith into the barrel
              We'll drink and 'gree.

Fiddlers! your pins in temper fix,
And roset weel your fiddlesticks,
But banish vile Italian tricks
              From out your quorum,
Nor *fortes* wi' *pianos* mix—
              Gie's *Tullochgorum*.

For nought can cheer the heart sae weel
As can a canty Highland reel;
It even vivifies the heel
              To skip and dance:
Lifeless is he wha canna feel
              Its influence.

canty] jolly   bield] shelter   cauldrife] cold   couth] comfortable
gar] make   bicker] bowl, goblet   gusty] windy   fairn-year] last year
browster] brewer   busk] deck   bra] finely   blaw] draught
reaming] foaming   pins] pegs   roset] rosin

Let mirth abound; let social cheer
Invest the dawning of the year;
Let blithesome innocence appear
            To crown our joy;
Nor envy, wi' sarcastic sneer,
            Our bliss destroy.

And thou, great god of *aqua vitæ*!
Wha sways the empire of this city—
When fou we're sometimes capernoity—
            Be thou prepared
To hedge us frae that black banditti,
            The City Guard.

Drinking Song

Tune: 'Lumps of Pudding'

HOLLO! keep it up, boys—and push around the glass,
Let each seize his bumper, and drink to his lass:
Away with dull thinking—'tis madness to think—
And let those be sober who've nothing to drink.
            Tal de ral, &c.

Silence that vile clock, with its iron tongu'd bell,
Of the hour that's departed still ringing the knell:
But what is't to us that the hours flie away;
'Tis only a signal to moisten the clay.

Huzza, boys! let each take a bumper in hand,
And stand—if there's any one able to stand.
How all things dance round me!—'tis life, tho' my boys:
Of drinking and spewing how great are the joys?

My head! oh my head!—but no matter, 'tis life;
Far better than mopping [*sic*] at home with one's wife.
The pleasures of drinking you're sure must be grand,
When I'm neither able to think, speak, nor stand.

THE DAFT DAYS: capernoity] peevish

JOHN PHILPOT CURRAN

1750–1817

The Deserter

IF sadly thinking,
With spirits sinking,
Could more than drinking
   My cares compose,
A cure for sorrow
From sighs I'd borrow,
And hope to-morrow
   Would end my woes.
But as in wailing
There's nought availing,
And Death unfailing
   Will strike the blow,
Then for that reason,
And for a season,
Let us be merry
   Before we go.
To joy a stranger,
A way-worn ranger,
In every danger
   My course I've run;
Now hope all ending,
And Death befriending,
His last aid lending,
   My cares are done:
No more a rover,
Or hapless lover,
My griefs are over,
   My glass runs low;
Then for that reason,
And for a season,
Let us be merry
   Before we go!

RICHARD BRINSLEY SHERIDAN
1751–1816

Song from *The Duenna*
Oh, the days when I was young

OH, the days when I was young,
 When I laughed in fortune's spite;
Talked of love the whole day long,
 And with nectar crowned the night!
Then it was, old Father Care,
 Little recked I of thy frown;
Half thy malice youth could bear,
 And the rest a bumper drown.

Truth, they say, lies in a well,
 Why, I vow I ne'er could see;
Let the water-drinkers tell,
 There it always lay for me;
For when sparkling wine went round,
 Never saw I falsehood's mask;
But still honest truth I found
 In the bottom of each flask.

True, at length my vigour's flown,
 I have years to bring decay;
Few the locks that now I own,
 And the few I have are grey.
Yet, old Jerome, thou mayst boast
 While thy spirits do not tire,
Still beneath thy age's frost
 Glows a spark of youthful fire.

Song from *The School for Scandal*
Here's to the Maiden of Bashful Fifteen

HERE'S to the maiden of bashful fifteen;
 Here's to the widow of fifty;
Here's to the flaunting extravagant quean,
 And here's to the housewife that's thrifty.

RICHARD BRINSLEY SHERIDAN

Chorus

Let the toast pass,—
Drink to the lass,
I'll warrant she'll prove an excuse for the glass.

Here's to the charmer whose dimples we prize;
　Now to the maid who has none, sir:
Here's to the girl with a pair of blue eyes,
　And here's to the nymph with but *one*, sir.
　　Chorus. Let the toast pass, &c.

Here's to the maid with a bosom of snow;
　Now to her that's as brown as a berry:
Here's to the wife with a face full of woe,
　And now to the girl that is merry.
　　Chorus. Let the toast pass, &c.

For let 'em be clumsy, or let 'em be slim,
　Young or ancient, I care not a feather;
So fill a pint bumper quite up to the brim,
　And let us e'en toast them together.
　　Chorus. Let the toast pass, &c.

THOMAS CHATTERTON

1752–1770

Mynstrelles Songe

O! SYNGE untoe mie roundelaie,
O! droppe the brynie teare wythe mee,
Daunce ne moe atte hallie daie,
Lycke a reynynge[1] ryver bee;
　Mie love ys dedde,
　Gon to hys death-bedde,
　Al under the wyllowe tree.

Blacke hys cryne[2] as the wyntere nyghte,
Whyte hys rode[3] as the sommer snowe,
Rodde hys face as the mornynge lyghte,
Cale he lyes ynne the grave belowe;

[1] running　[2] hair　[3] complexion. [Chatterton's notes.]　cale] cold.

628

Mie love ys dedde,
Gon to hys deathe-bedde,
Al under the wyllowe tree.
Swote hys tyngue as the throstles note,
Quycke ynn daunce as thoughte canne bee,
Defte hys taboure, codgelle stote,
O! hee lyes bie the wyllowe tree:
  Mie love ys dedde,
  Gonne to hys deathe-bedde,
  Alle underre the wyllowe tree.

Harke! the ravenne flappes hys wynge,
In the briered delle belowe;
Harke! the dethe-owle loude dothe synge,
To the nyghte-mares as heie goe;
  Mie love ys dedde,
  Gonne to hys deathe-bedde,
  Al under the wyllowe tree.

See! the whyte moone sheenes onne hie;
Whyterre ys mie true loves shroude;
Whyterre yanne the mornynge skie,
Whyterre yanne the evenynge cloude;
  Mie love ys dedde,
  Gon to hys deathe-bedde,
  Al under the wyllowe tree.

Heere, uponne mie true loves grave,
Schalle the baren fleurs be layde,
Nee one hallie Seyncte to save
Al the celness of a mayde.
  Mie love ys dedde,
  Gonne to hys death-bedde,
  Alle under the wyllowe tree.

Wythe mie hondes I'lle dente the brieres
Rounde his hallie corse to gre,
Ouphante fairie, lyghte youre fyres,
Heere mie boddie stylle schalle bee.
  Mie love ys dedde,
  Gon to hys death-bedde,
  Al under the wyllowe tree.

heie] they   celness] coldness   Ouphante] elfin

Comme, wythe acorne-coppe & thorne,
Drayne mie hartys blodde awaie;
Lyfe and all yttes goode I scorne,
Daunce bie nete, or feaste by daie.
    Mie love ys dedde,
    Gon to hys death-bedde,
    Al under the wyllowe tree.

Waterre wytches, crownede wythe reytes,[1]
Bere mee to yer leathalle tyde.
I die; I comme; mie true love waytes.
Thos the damselle spake, and dyed.

An Excelente Balade of Charitie

*A wroten bie the gode prieste
Thomas Rowley[2], 1464*

IN Virgyne the sweltrie sun gan sheene,
And hotte upon the mees[3] did caste his raie;
The apple rodded[4] from its palie greene,
And the mole[5] peare did bende the leafy spraie;
The peede chelandri[6] sunge the livelong daie;
'Twas nowe the pride, the manhode of the yeare,
And eke the grounde was dighte[7] in its mose defte[8] aumere[9]

The sun was glemeing in the midde of daie,
Deadde still the aire, and eke the welken[10] blue,
When from the sea arist[11] in drear arraie
A hepe of cloudes of sable sullen hue,
The which full fast unto the woodlande drewe,
Hiltring[12] attenes[13] the sunnis fetive[14] face,
And the blacke tempeste swolne and gatherd up apace.

---

[1] Water-flags [C.'s note]

AN EXCELENTE BALADE OF CHARITIE: [2] Thomas Rowley, the author, was born at Norton Malreward in Somersetshire, educated at the Convent of St. Kenna at Keyneham, and died at Westbury in Gloucestershire. [3] meads [4] reddened, ripened [5] soft [6] pied goldfinch [7] drest, arrayed [8] neat, ornamental [9] a loose robe or mantle [10] the sky, the atmosphere [11] arose [12] hiding, shrouding [13] at once [14] beauteous [C.'s notes.]

Beneathe an holme, faste by a pathwaie side,
Which dide unto Seyncte Godwine's covent[1] lede,
A hapless pilgrim moneynge did abide,
Pore in his viewe, ungentle[2] in his weede,
Longe bretful[3] of the miseries of neede,
Where from the hail-stone coulde the almer[4] flie?
He had no housen theere, ne anie covent nie.

Look in his glommed[5] face, his sprighte there scanne;
Howe woe-be-gone, how withered, forwynd[6], deade!
Haste to thie church-glebe-house[7], asshrewed[8] manne!
Haste to thie kiste[9], thie onlie dortoure[10] bedde.
Cale, as the claie whiche will gre on thie hedde,
Is Charitie and Love aminge highe elves;
Knightis and Barons live for pleasure and themselves.

The gatherd storme is rype; the bigge drops falle;
The forswat[11] meadowes smethe[12], and drenche[13] the raine;
The comyng ghastness do the cattle pall[14],
And the full flockes are drivynge ore the plaine;
Dashde from the cloudes the waters flott[15] againe;
The welkin opes; the yellow levynne[16] flies;
And the hot fierie smothe[17] in the wide lowings[18] dies.

Liste! now the thunder's rattling clymmynge[19] sound
Cheves[20] slowlie on, and then embollen[21] clangs,
Shakes the hie spyre, and losst, dispended, drown'd,
Still on the gallard[22] eare of terroure hanges;
The windes are up; the lofty elmen swanges;
Again the levynne and the thunder poures,
And the full cloudes are braste[23] attenes in stonen showers.

---

[1] It would have been *charitable*, if the author had not pointed at personal characters in this Ballad of Charity. The Abbot of St. Godwin's at the time of the writing of this was Ralph dc Bellomont, a great stickler for the Lancastrian family. Rowley was a Yorkist [2] beggarly [3] filled with [4] beggar [5] clouded, dejected. A person of some note in the literary world is of opinion that *glum* and *glom* are modern cast words; and from this circumstance doubts the authenticity of Rowley's Manuscripts. Glum-mong in the Saxon signifies twilight, a dark or dubious light; and the modern word *gloomy* is derived from the Saxon *glum* [6] dry, sapless [7] the grave [8] accursed, unfortunate [9] coffin [10] a sleeping room [11] sun-burnt [12] smoke [13] drink [14] *pall*, a contraction from *apall*, to fright [15] fly [16] lightning [17] steam, or vapours [18] flames [19] noisy [20] moves [21] swelled, strengthened [22] frighted [23] burst [C.'s notes.]

Spurreynge his palfrie oere the watrie plaine,
The Abbote of Seyncte Godwynes convente came;
His chapournette[1] was drented with the reine,
And his pencte[2] gyrdle met with mickle shame;
He aynewarde tolde his bederoll[3] at the same;
The storme encreasen, and he drew aside,
With the mist[4] almes craver neere to the holme to bide.

His cope[5] was all of Lyncolne clothe so fyne,
With a gold button fasten'd neere his chynne;
His autremete[6] was edged with golden twynne,
And his shoone pyke a loverds[7] mighte have binne;
Full well is shewn he thoughten coste no sinne:
The trammels of the palfrye pleasde his sighte,
For the horse-millanare[8] his head with roses dighte.

An almes, sir prieste! the droppynge pilgrim saide,
O! let me waite within your covente dore,
Till the sunne sheneth hie above our heade,
And the loude tempeste of the aire is oer;
Helpless and ould am I alas! and poor;
No house, ne friend, ne moneie in my pouche;
All yatte I call my owne is this my silver crouche.

Varlet, replyd the Abbatte, cease your dinne;
This is no season almes and prayers to give;
Mie porter never lets a faitour[9] in;
None touch mie rynge who not in honour live.
And now the sonne with the blacke cloudes did stryve,
And shettynge on the grounde his glairie raie,
The Abbatte spurrde his steede, and eftsoones roadde awaie.

Once moe the skie was blacke, the thounder rolde;
Faste reyneynge oer the plaine a prieste was seen;
Ne dighte full proude, ne buttoned up in golde;
His cope and jape[10] were graie, and eke were clene;
A Limitoure he was of order seene;
And from the pathwaie side then turned hee,
Where the pore almer laie binethe the holmen tree.

---

[1] a small round hat, not unlike the shapournette in heraldry, formerly worn by Ecclesiastics and Lawyers   [2] painted   [3] He told his beads backwards; a figurative expression to signify cursing   [4] poor, needy   [5] a cloke   [6] a loose white robe, worn by Priests   [7] a lord's   [8] I believe this trade is still in being, though but seldom employed   [9] a beggar, or vagabond   [10] a short surplice, worn by Friars of an inferior class, and secular priests [C.'s notes.]

An almes, sir priest! the droppynge pilgrim sayde,
For sweet Seyncte Marie and your order sake.
The Limitoure then loosen'd his pouche threade,
And did thereoute a groate of silver take;
The mister pilgrim dyd for halline[1] shake.
Here take this silver, it maie eathe[2] thie care;
We are Goddes stewards all, nete[3] of oure owne we bare.

But ah! unhailie[4] pilgrim, lerne of me,
Scathe anie give a rentrolle to their Lorde.
Here take my semecope[5], thou arte bare I see;
Tis thyne; the Seynctes will give me mie rewarde.
He left the pilgrim, and his waie aborde.
Virgynne and hallie Seyncte, who sitte yn gloure[6],
Or give the mittee[7] will, or give the gode man power.

There Lackethe Somethynge Stylle

THE boddynge flourettes bloshes atte the lyghte;
The mees be sprenged wyth the yellowe hue;
Yn daiseyd mantels ys the mountayne dyghte
The nesh[8] yonge cowslepe bendethe wyth the dewe;
The trees enlesed, yntoe Heavenne straughte,
Whenn gentle wyndes doe blowe, to whestling dynne ys
broughte.

The evenynge commes, and brynges the dewe alonge;
The roddie welkynne sheeneth to the eyne;
Arounde the alestake Mynstrells synge the songe;
Yonge ivie rounde the doore poste do entwyne;
I laie mee onn the grasse; yette, to mie wylle,
Albeytte all ys fayre, there lackethe somethynge stylle.

So Adam thoughtenne, whan, ynn Paradyse,
All Heavenn and Erthe dyd hommage to hys mynde;
Ynn Womman alleyne mannes pleasaunce lyes;
As Instrumentes joie were made the kynde.
Go, take a wyfe untoe thie armes, and see
Wynter, and brownie hylles, wyll have a charme for thee.

---

[1] joy   [2] ease   [3] nought   [4] unhappy   [5] a short under-cloke
[6] glory   [7] mighty, rich   [8] tender   [C.'s notes.]   Limitoure] A
licensed begging friar   aborde] went on   Albeytte] Albeit
THERE LACKETHE SOMETHYNGE STYLLE: bloshes] blushes   sprenged] sprinkled
enlesed] enleafed

Whanne Autumpne blake[1] and sonne-brente doe appere,
With hys goulde honde guylteynge the falleynge lefe,
Bryngeynge oppe Wynterr to folfylle the yere,
Beerynge uponne hys backe the riped shefe;
Whan al the hyls wythe woddie sede ys whyte;
Whanne levynne-fyres and lemes do mete from far the syghte;

Angelles bee wrogte to bee of neidher kynde;
Angelles alleyne fromme chafe[2] desyre bee free;
Dheere ys a somwhatte evere yn the mynde,
Yatte, wythout wommanne, cannot stylled bee;
Ne seyncte yn celles, botte, havynge blodde and tere,[3]
Do fynde the spryte to joie on syghte of womanne fayre.

GEORGE CRABBE

1754–1832

The Village

BOOK II

No longer truth, though shown in verse, disdain,
But own the Village Life a life of pain.
I too must yield, that oft amid these woes
Are gleams of transient mirth and hours of sweet repose,
Such as you find on yonder sportive Green,
The 'squire's tall gate and churchway-walk between;
Where loitering stray a little tribe of friends,
On a fair Sunday when the sermon ends.
Then rural beaux their best attire put on,
To win their nymphs, as other nymphs are won;
While those long wed go plain, and, by degrees,
Like other husbands, quit their care to please.
Some of the sermon talk, a sober crowd,
And loudly praise, if it were preach'd aloud;
Some on the labours of the week look round,
Feel their own worth, and think their toil renown'd;
While some, whose hopes to no renown extend,
Are only pleased to find their labours end.

[1] naked   [2] hot.   [3] health.   [C.'s notes.]

Thus, as their hours glide on, with pleasure fraught,
Their careful masters brood the painful thought;
Much in their mind they murmur and lament,
That one fair day should be so idly spent;
And think that Heaven deals hard, to tithe their store
And tax their time for preachers and the poor.

Yet still, ye humbler friends, enjoy your hour,
This is your portion, yet unclaim'd of power;
This is Heaven's gift to weary men oppress'd,
And seems the type of their expected rest.
But yours, alas! are joys that soon decay;
Frail joys, begun and ended with the day;
Or yet, while day permits those joys to reign,
The village vices drive them from the plain.

See the stout churl, in drunken fury great,
Strike the bare bosom of his teeming mate!
His naked vices, rude and unrefined,
Exert their open empire o'er the mind;
But can we less the senseless rage despise,
Because the savage acts without disguise?

Yet here disguise, the city's vice, is seen,
And Slander steals along and taints the Green:
At her approach domestic peace is gone,
Domestic broils at her approach come on;
She to the wife the husband's crime conveys,
She tells the husband when his consort strays,
Her busy tongue through all the little state
Diffuses doubt, suspicion, and debate;
Peace, tim'rous goddess! quits her old domain,
In sentiment and song content to reign.

Nor are the nymphs that breathe the rural air
So fair as Cynthia's, nor so chaste as fair:
These to the town afford each fresher face,
And the clown's trull receives the peer's embrace;
From whom, should chance again convey her down,
The peer's disease in turn attacks the clown.

Here too the 'squire, or 'squire-like farmer, talk,
How round their regions nightly pilferers walk;
How from their ponds the fish are borne, and all
The rip'ning treasures from their lofty wall;
How meaner rivals in their sports delight,
Just rich enough to claim a doubtful right;
Who take a licence round their fields to stray,
A mongrel race! the poachers of the day.

And hark! the riots of the Green begin,
That sprang at first from yonder noisy inn;
What time the weekly pay was vanish'd all,
And the slow hostess scored the threat'ning wall;
What time they ask'd their friendly feast to close,
A final cup, and that will make them foes;
When blows ensue that break the arm of toil,
And rustic battle ends the boobies' broil.

Save when to yonder Hall they bend their way,
Where the grave justice ends the grievous fray;
He who recites, to keep the poor in awe,
The law's vast volume—for he knows the law:—
To him with anger or with shame repair
The injured peasant and deluded fair.

Lo! at his throne the silent nymph appears,
Frail by her shape, but modest in her tears;
And while she stands abash'd, with conscious eye,
Some favourite female of her judge glides by,
Who views with scornful glance the strumpet's fate,
And thanks the stars that made her keeper great;
Near her the swain, about to bear for life
One certain evil, doubts 'twixt war and wife;
But, while the falt'ring damsel takes her oath,
Consents to wed, and so secures them both.

Yet, why, you ask, these humble crimes relate,
Why make the poor as guilty as the great?
To show the great, those mightier sons of pride,
How near is vice the lowest are allied;
Such are their natures and their passions such,
But these disguise too little, those too much:
So shall the man of power and pleasure see
In his own slave as vile a wretch as he;
In his luxurious lord the servant find
His own low pleasures and degenerate mind:
And each in all the kindred vices trace
Of a poor, blind, bewilder'd, erring race;
Who, a short time in varied fortune past,
Die, and are equal in the dust at last.

And you, ye poor, who still lament your fate,
Forbear to envy those you call the great;
And know, amid those blessings they possess,
They are, like you, the victims of distress;
While sloth with many a pang torments her slave,
Fear waits on guilt, and danger shakes the brave.

Oh! if in life one noble chief appears,
Great in his name, while blooming in his years;
Born to enjoy whate'er delights mankind,
And yet to all you feel or fear resign'd;
Who gave up joys and hopes, to you unknown,
For pains and dangers greater than your own:
If such there be, then let your murmurs cease,
Think, think of him, and take your lot in peace.

And such there was:—Oh! grief, that checks our pride!
Weeping we say, there was—for Manners died:
Beloved of Heaven, these humble lines forgive,
That sing of Thee, and thus aspire to live.

As the tall oak, whose vigorous branches form
An ample shade and brave the wildest storm,
High o'er the subject wood is seen to grow,
The guard and glory of the trees below;
Till on its head the fiery bolt descends,
And o'er the plain the shatter'd trunk extends;
Yet then it lies, all wond'rous as before,
And still the glory, though the guard no more:

So THOU, when every virtue, every grace,
Rose in thy soul, or shone within thy face;
When, though the son of Granby, thou wert known
Less by thy father's glory than thy own;
When Honour loved and gave thee every charm,
Fire to thy eye and vigour to thy arm;
Then from our lofty hopes and longing eyes,
Fate and thy virtues call'd thee to the skies;
Yet still we wonder at thy tow'ring fame,
And, losing thee, still dwell upon thy name.

Oh! ever honour'd, ever valued! say,
What verse can praise thee, or what work repay?
Yet verse (in all we can) thy worth repays,
Nor trusts the tardy zeal of future days;—
Honours for thee thy country shall prepare,
Thee in their hearts, the good, the brave shall bear;
To deeds like thine shall noblest chiefs aspire,
The Muse shall mourn thee, and the world admire.

In future times, when, smit with Glory's charms,
The untried youth first quits a father's arms;—
'Oh! be like him,' the weeping sire shall say;
'Like Manners walk, who walk'd in Honour's way;
'In danger foremost, yet in death sedate,
'Oh! be like him in all things, but his fate!'

637

If for that fate such public tears be shed,
That Victory seems to die now THOU art dead;
How shall a friend his nearer hope resign,
That friend a brother, and whose soul was thine?
By what bold lines shall we his grief express,
Or by what soothing numbers make it less?
    'Tis not, I know, the chiming of a song,
Nor all the powers that to the Muse belong,
Words aptly cull'd and meanings well express'd,
Can calm the sorrows of a wounded breast;
But Virtue, soother of the fiercest pains,
Shall heal that bosom, Rutland, where she reigns.
    Yet hard the task to heal the bleeding heart,
To bid the still-recurring thoughts depart,
Tame the fierce grief and stem the rising sigh,
And curb rebellious passion with reply;
Calmly to dwell on all that pleased before,
And yet to know that all shall please no more—
Oh! glorious labour of the soul, to save
Her captive powers, and bravely mourn the brave.
    To such these thoughts will lasting comfort give—
Life is not measured by the time we live:
'Tis not an even course of threescore years,
A life of narrow views and paltry fears,
Gray hairs and wrinkles and the cares they bring,
That take from death the terrors or the sting;
But 'tis the gen'rous spirit, mounting high
Above the world, that native of the sky;
The noble spirit, that, in dangers brave,
Calmly looks on, or looks beyond the grave:—
Such Manners was, so he resign'd his breath,
If in a glorious, then a timely death.
    Cease then that grief, and let those tears subside;
If Passion rule us, be that passion pride;
If Reason, Reason bids us strive to raise
Our fallen hearts, and be like him we praise;
Or, if Affection still the soul subdue,
Bring all his virtues, all his worth in view,
And let Affection find its comfort too:
For how can Grief so deeply wound the heart,
When Admiration claims so large a part?
    Grief is a foe; expel him, then, thy soul;
Let nobler thoughts the nearer views control!
Oh! make the age to come thy better care;

See other Rutlands, other Granbys there!
And, as thy thoughts through streaming ages glide,
See other heroes die as Manners died:
And, from their fate, thy race shall nobler grow,
As trees shoot upwards that are pruned below;
Or as old Thames, borne down with decent pride,
Sees his young streams run warbling at his side;
Though some, by art cut off, no longer run,
And some are lost beneath the summer's sun—
Yet the pure stream moves on, and, as it moves,
Its power increases and its use improves;
While plenty round its spacious waves bestow,
Still it flows on, and shall for ever flow.

from *The Lover's Journey*

The sun is in the heavens, and the proud day,
Attended with the pleasures of the world,
Is all too wanton.   *King John*, Act III, Scene 3

The lunatic, the lover, and the poet,
Are of imagination all compact.
    Midsummer Night's Dream, Act V, Scene 2

Oh! how the spring of love resembleth
  Th' uncertain glory of an April day,
Which now shows all her beauty to the sun,
  And by and by a cloud bears all away.

And happily I have arrived at last
Unto the wished haven of my bliss.
    Taming of the Shrew, Act V, Scene 1

IT is the soul that sees; the outward eyes
Present the object, but the mind descries;
And thence delight, disgust, or cool indiff'rence rise:
When minds are joyful, then we look around,
And what is seen is all on fairy ground;
Again they sicken, and on every view
Cast their own dull and melancholy hue;
Or, if absorb'd by their peculiar cares,
The vacant eye on viewless matter glares,
Our feelings still upon our views attend,
And their own natures to the objects lend;

Sorrow and joy are in their influence sure,
Long as the passion reigns th' effects endure;
But love in minds his various changes makes,
And clothes each object with the change he takes;
His light and shade on every view he throws,
And on each object, what he feels, bestows.

Fair was the morning, and the month was June,
When rose a lover; love awakens soon;
Brief his repose, yet much he dreamt the while
Of that day's meeting, and his Laura's smile;
Fancy and love that name assign'd to her,
Call'd Susan in the parish-register;
And he no more was John—his Laura gave
The name Orlando to her faithful slave.

Bright shone the glory of the rising day,
When the fond traveller took his favourite way;
He mounted gaily, felt his bosom light,
And all he saw was pleasing in his sight.

'Ye hours of expectation, quickly fly,
And bring on hours of blest reality;
When I shall Laura see, beside her stand,
Hear her sweet voice, and press her yielded hand.'

First o'er a barren heath beside the coast
Orlando rode, and joy began to boast.

'This neat low gorse,' said he, 'with golden bloom,
Delights each sense, is beauty, is perfume;
And this gay ling, with all its purple flowers,
A man at leisure might admire for hours;
This green-fringed cup-moss has a scarlet tip,
That yields to nothing but my Laura's lip;
And then how fine this herbage! men may say
A heath is barren; nothing is so gay:
Barren or bare to call such charming scene
Argues a mind possess'd by care and spleen.'

Onward he went, and fiercer grew the heat,
Dust rose in clouds before the horse's feet;
For now he pass'd through lanes of burning sand,
Bounds to thin crops or yet uncultured land;
Where the dark poppy flourish'd on the dry
And sterile soil, and mock'd the thin-set rye.

'How lovely this!' the rapt Orlando said;
With what delight is labouring man repaid!
The very lane has sweets that all admire,
The rambling suckling and the vigorous brier;

See! wholesome wormwood grows beside the way,
Where dew-press'd yet the dog-rose bends the spray;
Fresh herbs the fields, fair shrubs the banks adorn,
And snow-white bloom falls flaky from the thorn;
No fostering hand they need, no sheltering wall,
They spring uncultured and they bloom for all.'
    The lover rode as hasty lovers ride,
And reach'd a common pasture wild and wide;
Small black-legg'd sheep devour with hunger keen
The meagre herbage, fleshless, lank, and lean;
Such o'er thy level turf, Newmarket! stray,
And there, with other *black-legs* find their prey:
He saw some scatter'd hovels; turf was piled
In square brown stacks; a prospect bleak and wild!
A mill, indeed, was in the centre found,
With short sear herbage withering all around;
A smith's black shed opposed a wright's long shop,
And join'd an inn where humble travellers stop.
    'Ay, this is Nature,' said the gentle 'squire;
'This ease, peace, pleasure—who would not admire?
With what delight these sturdy children play,
And joyful rustics at the close of day;
Sport follows labour, on this even space
Will soon commence the wrestling and the race;
Then will the village-maidens leave their home,
And to the dance with buoyant spirits come;
No affectation in their looks is seen,
Nor know they what disguise or flattery mean;
Nor aught to move an envious pang they see,
Easy their service, and their love is free;
Hence early springs that love, it long endures,
And life's first comfort, while they live, ensures:
They the low roof and rustic comforts prize,
Nor cast on prouder mansions envying eyes:
Sometimes the news at yonder town they hear,
And learn what busier mortals feel and fear;
Secure themselves, although by tales amazed,
Of towns bombarded and of cities razed;
As if they doubted, in their still retreat,
The very news that makes their quiet sweet,
And their days happy—happier only knows
He on whom Laura her regard bestows.'
    On rode Orlando, counting all the while
The miles he pass'd and every coming mile;

Like all attracted things, he quicker flies,
The place approaching where th' attraction lies;
When next appear'd a *dam*—so call the place—
Where lies a road confined in narrow space;
A work of labour, for on either side
Is level fen, a prospect wild and wide,
With dikes on either hand by ocean's self supplied:
Far on the right the distant sea is seen,
And salt the springs that feed the marsh between;
Beneath an ancient bridge, the straiten'd flood
Rolls through its sloping banks of slimy mud;
Near it a sunken boat resists the tide,
That frets and hurries to th' opposing side;
The rushes sharp, that on the borders grow,
Bend their brown flow'rets to the stream below,
Impure in all its course, in all its progress slow:
Here a grave *Flora scarcely deigns to bloom,
Nor wears a rosy blush, nor sheds perfume;
The few dull flowers that o'er the place are spread
Partake the nature of their fenny bed;
Here on its wiry stem, in rigid bloom,
Grows the salt lavender that lacks perfume;
Here the dwarf sallows creep, the septfoil harsh,
And the soft slimy mallow of the marsh;
Low on the ear the distant billows sound,
And just in view appears their stony bound;
No hedge nor tree conceals the glowing sun,
Birds, save a wat'ry tribe, the district shun,
Nor chirp among the reeds where bitter waters run.
  'Various as beauteous, Nature, is thy face,'
Exclaim'd Orlando: 'all that grows has grace;
All are appropriate—bog, and marsh, and fen,

* The ditches of a fen so near the ocean are lined with irregular patches of a coarse and stained lava; a muddy sediment rests on the horse-tail and other perennial herbs, which in part conceal the shallowness of the stream; a fat-leaved pale-flowering scurvy-grass appears early in the year, and the razor-edged bull-rush in the summer and autumn. The fen itself has a dark and saline herbage; there are rushes and *arrow-head*, and in a few patches the flakes of the cotton-grass are seen, but more commonly the *sea-aster*, the dullest of that numerous and hardy genus; a *thrift*, blue in flower, but withering and remaining withered till the winter scatters it; the *saltwort*, both simple and shrubby; a few kinds of grass changed by their soil and atmosphere, and low plants of two or three denominations undistinguished in a general view of the scenery;—such is the vegetation of the fen when it is at a small distance from the ocean; and in this case there arise from it effluvia strong and peculiar, half-saline, half-putrid, which would be considered by most people as offensive, and by some as dangerous; but there are others to whom singularity of taste or association of ideas has rendered it agreeable and pleasant.

Are only poor to undiscerning men;
Here may the nice and curious eye explore
How Nature's hand adorns the rushy moor;
Here the rare moss in secret shade is found,
Here the sweet myrtle of the shaking ground;
Beauties are these that from the view retire,
But well repay th' attention they require;
For these my Laura will her home forsake,
And all the pleasures they afford partake.'
   Again the country was enclosed, a wide
And sandy road has banks on either side;
Where, lo! a hollow on the left appear'd,
And there a gipsy-tribe their tent had rear'd;
'Twas open spread, to catch the morning sun,
And they had now their early meal begun,
When two brown boys just left their grassy seat,
The early trav'ller with their pray'rs to greet:
While yet Orlando held his pence in his hand,
He saw their sister on her duty stand;
Some twelve years old, demure, affected, sly,
Prepared the force of early powers to try;
Sudden a look of languor he descries,
And well-feign'd apprehension in her eyes;
Train'd but yet savage, in her speaking face
He mark'd the features of her vagrant race;
When a light laugh and roguish leer express'd
The vice implanted in her youthful breast:
Forth from the tent her elder brother came,
Who seem'd offended, yet forbore to blame
The young designer, but could only trace
The looks of pity in the trav'ller's face:
Within, the father, who from fences nigh
Had brought the fuel for the fire's supply,
Watch'd now the feeble blaze, and stood dejected by:
On ragged rug, just borrow'd from the bed,
And by the hand of coarse indulgence fed,
In dirty patchwork negligently dress'd,
Reclined the wife, an infant at her breast;
In her wild face some touch of grace remain'd,
Of vigour palsied and of beauty stain'd;
Her bloodshot eyes on her unheeding mate
Were wrathful turn'd, and seem'd her wants to state,
Cursing his tardy aid—her mother there
With gipsy-state engrass'd the only chair;

Solemn and dull her look; with such she stands,
And reads the milk-maid's fortune in her hands,
Tracing the lines of life; assumed through years,
Each feature now the steady falsehood wears;
With hard and savage eye she views the food,
And grudging pinches their intruding brood;
Last in the group, the worn-out grandsire sits
Neglected, lost, and living but by fits;
Useless, despised, his worthless labours done,
And half protected by the vicious son,
Who half supports him; he with heavy glance
Views the young ruffians who around him dance;
And, by the sadness in his face, appears
To trace the progress of their future years
Through what strange course of misery, vice, deceit,
Must wildly wander each unpractised cheat!
What shame and grief, what punishment and pain,
Sport of fierce passions, must each child sustain—
Ere they like him approach their latter end,
Without a hope, a comfort, or a friend!
    But this Orlando felt not; 'Rogues,' said he,
'Doubtless they are, but merry rogues they be;
They wander round the land, and be it true,
They break the laws—then let the laws pursue
The wanton idlers; for the life they live,
Acquit I cannot, but I can forgive.'
This said, a portion from his purse was thrown,
And every heart seem'd happy like his own.
    He hurried forth, for now the town was nigh—
'The happiest man of mortal men am I.'
Thou art! but change in every state is near,
(So while the wretched hope, the blest may fear);
'Say, where is Laura?'—'That her words must show,'
A lass replied; 'read this, and thou shalt know!'
    'What, gone!'—her friend insisted—forced to go:—
'Is vex'd, was teased, could not refuse her!—No?'
'But you can follow:' 'Yes:' 'The miles are few,
The way is pleasant; will you come?—Adieu!
Thy Laura!' 'No! I feel I must resign
The pleasing hope, thou hadst been here, if mine:
A lady was it?—Was no brother there?
But why should I afflict me if there were?'
'The way is pleasant:' 'What to me the way?
I cannot reach her till the close of day.

My dumb companion! is it thus we speed?
Not I from grief nor thou from toil art freed;
Still art thou doom'd to travel and to pine,
For my vexation—What a fate is mine!
    'Gone to a friend, she tells me; I commend
Her purpose; means she to a female freind?
By Heaven, I wish she suffer'd half the pain
Of hope protracted through the day in vain:
Shall I persist to see th' ungrateful maid?
Yes, I will see her, slight her, and upbraid:
What! in the very hour? She knew the time,
And doubtless chose it to increase her crime.'
    Forth rode Orlando by a river's side,
Inland and winding, smooth, and full and wide,
That roll'd majestic on, in one soft-flowing tide;
The bottom gravel, flow'ry were the banks,
Tall willows, waving in their broken ranks;
The road, now near, now distant, winding led
By lovely meadows which the waters fed;
He pass'd the way-side inn, the village spire,
Nor stopp'd to gaze, to question, or admire;
On either side the rural mansions stood,
With hedge-row trees, and hills high-crown'd with wood,
And many a devious stream that reach'd the nobler flood.
    'I hate these scenes,' Orlando angry cried,
'And these proud farmers! yes, I hate their pride:
See! that sleek fellow, how he strides along,
Strong as an ox, and ignorant as strong;
Can yon close crops a single eye detain
But his who counts the profits of the grain?
And these vile beans with deleterious smell,
Where is their beauty? can a mortal tell?
These deep fat meadows I detest; it shocks
One's feelings there to see the grazing ox;—
For slaughter fatted, as a lady's smile
Rejoices man, and means his death the while.
Lo! now the sons of labour! every day
Employ'd in toil, and vex'ed in every way;
Theirs is but mirth assumed, and they conceal,
In their affected joys, the ills they feel:
I hate these long green lanes; there's nothing seen
In this vile country but eternal green;
Woods! waters! meadows! Will they never end?
'Tis a vile prospect:—Gone to see a friend!'—

GEORGE CRABBE

[The lovers clear up their misunderstanding; but, when 'Orlando' rides back the same way, his mind is engrossed in thoughts and the landscape has no effect on him, thus illustrating the third proposition set out in the opening lines. (J.W.)]

INDEX OF POETS

INDEX OF FIRST LINES